The Eurail Guide to Train Travel
in the
New Europe

Houghton Mifflin Company
Boston • New York 1996

For information about this and other Houghton Mifflin trade and reference
books and multimedia products, visit The Bookstore at Houghton Mifflin
on the World Wide Web at http://www.hmco.com/trade/.

ISBN: 0-395-75658-8
ISSN: 0085-0330

KPT 10 9 8 7 6 5 4 3 2 1
Printed in the United States of America

Using the Eurail Guide

For twenty-six years, the *Eurail Guide* has offered comprehensive coverage of train travel throughout the world. 1996 marks the first year that the Editors of the *Eurail Guide* can offer consumers the choice of two indispensable books: *The Eurail Guide to World Train Travel,* which covers rail trips in 120 countries worldwide, and this guide, *The Eurail Guide to Train Travel in the New Europe*, whose pages are devoted solely to rail travel in the "new" Europe (the European Union, the much-changed and increasingly visited Central and Eastern European countries, and Great Britain). *The Eurail Guide to Train Travel in the New Europe* has been carefully designed to help train travelers move swiftly from city to city and capture both the pleasures and efficiency of rail travel in Europe. But, to make the most of this guide, there are **ten** key features of this book, and train travel in general, that you should always keep in mind.

• **Check and double-check departure and arrival times** The *Eurail Guide* offers you hundreds of precise timetables and schedules — in fact, the most complete, compact selection of schedules available to individuals. Train schedules have been selected to serve as model itineraries. Although all times listed here are accurate according to the published Thomas Cook schedules (the number appearing at the front of each schedule refers to the Thomas Cook Timetable number), precise times in all countries are subject to change and modification without notice. In addition to this, new trains and supplementary and seasonal trains are added and deleted all the time. This is normal and standard. In fact, train schedules undergo minor changes in Europe every three months. Thus it will always be necessary to check and double-check the departure and arrival times listed here and in all timetables. Most likely, changes will be slight and have little or no effect on the excursions described in this guide. However, a few minutes here and there might make the difference between a swift connection and a wasted afternoon.

• **Prices** Although the prices for train tickets and passes listed here were verified and accurate at printing, don't take them for gospel — all prices are subject to change. There are usually increases of 2%–5% in a given year, and certain trains require supplementary fares which, too, are subject to change. Note: Prices in this book are in U.S. dollars and British pounds based on December 1995 exchange rates. To calculate prices in other currencies, consult current exchange rates. Remember, the rate listed in the daily newspaper is the rate between banks. The rate you will get is usually at least 5% lower.

• **The 24-hour clock** International train schedules are almost always quoted according to the 24-hour clock, and thus the *Eurail Guide* maintains this practice. You might not be used to seeing 6 P.M. written as 18:00 or midnight as 24:00. Between midnight and 1:00 A.M. time is depicted as 00:01 to 00:59. This might seem like the military, but it's standard fare around the world and good to get used to.

• **Travel days and dates** Unless designated otherwise, all schedules shown in this guide indicate daily departures. Likewise, schedules featured here are based on the prime travel season of late May to late September. That is when the majority of *Eurail Guide* users plan to travel. It's true that schedules tend to change slightly during the off-season and thus, as with the timetables, checking and rechecking schedules is highly recommended.

A note on certain schedules: British timetables differ from the Continental pattern. Summer timetables for British rail service begin on the first Monday of May. Changes occur on various dates—first in October and then again in January. Unless designated otherwise, the departure and arrival times given in this book are for the summer tourist season and apply to trips that will be made from late May to late September. In most cases these schedules change only slightly during September-May.

In most European countries, a summer timetable goes into effect on the last Sunday of May or the first Sunday of June, and remains in effect until and including the last Saturday in September. Winter schedules usually start on the Sunday following the last Saturday of September and run until and including the Saturday preceding the last Sunday of May of the following year.

• **Frequency** Highly traveled routes and lines between major cities are served by frequent train service. It is therefore not necessary in these cases to list all times of all trains. Train options from Paris to Lyon or London to Manchester are just too numerous to list. When the word "frequent" has been noted, you can count on a minimum of one train every hour in the period indicated.

• **Order of excursions listed** In the *Eurail Guide* you will find numerous suggestions of preselected roundtrip excursions or circle trips originating from key locations or base cities. The order in which these roundtrip excursions are listed is as follows:

(1) One-day excursions from a base city to an interesting destination, including practical travel information and information on what to see and do there. The schedules for one-day, roundtrip excursions, however, do not always reflect all the departure times from either the base city or the destination city. Only those departure times involved in making a one-day roundtrip are shown. On particular

routes, there are frequently later departure times from the base city and earlier departure times from the destination city than those shown, although these clearly would not be applicable to the one-day, roundtrip excursions.

(2) Scenic train rides, many of which can be made as a one-day roundtrip or circle trip.

(3) International rail service (trips to adjoining countries).

• **Stations**   It is important to remember that many cities have more than one train station. In such cases, the name of the applicable train station is indicated (in parentheses) after the name of the city. In Austria, Germany, and Switzerland, train stations often do not have names, in which case the station is always indicated by the generic "Hauptbahnhof."

• **Before Leaving**   Never plan to travel without finding out if the countries you are going to tour offer low-price train passes. And when those countries do provide train passes, make sure to inquire before you leave home if these passes need to be purchased in your country of origin or if they need to be bought in the country you will be visiting. There's nothing worse than a great deal you can't cash in on.

• **Reader Response**   Information concerning international travel is constantly changing. The editors of the *Eurail Guide* wholeheartedly welcome correspondence from readers who have suggestions, tips, and pertinent information that can be verified and incorporated into the next annually revised edition. Thank you in advance for helping fellow rail travelers. Address all your letters to: Houghton Mifflin *Eurail Guide*, c/o Marnie Patterson, 222 Berkeley Street, Boston, MA 02116.

Acknowledgments

Since that first slim (96 page) edition of *The Eurail Guide* appeared in 1971, train travel, especially in Europe, has continually improved and flourished. So has *The Eurail Guide*. For this, the first edition devoted solely to train travel in European destinations, there are many to thank.

This book could not have been made possible were it not for its parents, Marvin and Barbara Saltzman and Katharyn Ashe. They conceived of the idea and their creativity and love for the project will remain in its pages for many editions to come. Many thanks are also due David Applefield whose writing and research have brought new depth to the Eastern and Central European chapters and to all of the book's introductory material, and Catharyn Tivy, who gave this edition of *The Eurail Guide* its new and improved look.

We are also grateful to the many railways and tourist commissions for providing us information, including extraordinary assistance from Cecile Campeau and Andrew Lazarus of Rail Europe; Michael Fox, Britrail Travel International; and Stephen Forsyth, Forsyth Travel Library.

The other important members of *The Eurail Guide* family are the scores of readers who have written to us over the years telling of their train travel experiences. Comments about your train journeys are welcome and appreciated.

- Marnie Patterson,
Editorial Director

Contents

Chapter 1

11 • Appreciating the Pleasures of Train Travel

Chapter 2

15 • Deciding How to Travel: Choosing a Eurailpass
     Eurailpass Rules and Pointers
17 • Eurail Guide Route Chart
18 • Eurailpass Prices
     The Passes
22 • Eurailpass Bonuses
27 • Where to Purchase Eurailpasses
28 • Other Passes and Discounts
33 • Student Discount Cards

Chapter 3

35 • How to Plan a Rail Itinerary
36 • Reservations: Train and Hotel
42 • Preparing for an Autumn Tour
42 • Documenting Yourself
44 • Other Useful Sources

Chapter 4

45 • Don't Miss the Train!
     Cities with More than One Train Station
46 • Finding Your Train Car: Train Splitting
48 • Train Changing: The Connection Time
50 • Car-Sleeper Express Service

Chapter 5

51 • Valuable Train and Travel Tips
52 • Customs Procedures and Duty-Free Shopping
53 • Overcoming Jet Lag

54 • Traveling By Night
55 • Baggage
57 • Eating on Trains
58 • Airport-City Rail Connections
58 • Lost Money and Passports
59 • Day Rooms
59 • Last-Minute Checklist
59 • Signs - The International Language

Chapter 6 - Train Travel with a Eurailpass in Western Europe

62 • Austria
93 • Belgium
93 • Luxembourg
93 • Netherlands (Holland)
134 • France
190 • Germany
252 • Greece
263 • Iberian Peninsula: Spain & Portugal
308 • Republic of Ireland
315 • Italy
378 • Denmark
391 • Finland
399 • Norway
417 • Sweden
427 • Switzerland

Chapter 7 - Train Travel in Britain (England, Wales, and Scotland)

507 • British Train Passes, Prices, and Conditions
512 • London's Rail Stations
513 • Days of the Week Variances
515 • Connections with the Continent
519 • One-Day Train Excursions from London
543 • A Day Through Wales
544 • Rail Connection with Ireland
544 • Rail Connections with Scotland
545 • Scotland

Chapter 8 - Train Travel in Non-Eurailpass Europe

552 • Central and Eastern Europe
554 • Albania
557 • Bulgaria
564 • Commonwealth of Independent States
565 • Armenia
566 • Azerbaijan
566 • Belarus
566 • Georgia
567 • Kazakhstan
567 • Kyrgyzstan
568 • Moldova
568 • Russia
575 • The Trans-Siberian Timetable
586 • Tajikistan
587 • Turkmenistan
587 • Ukraine
588 • Uzbekistan
589 • Baltic States
593 • Czech Republic
604 • Slovak Republic
607 • Hungary
614 • Poland
624 • Romania
633 • Yugoslavia (Serbia, Montenegro and Kosova)
634 • Kosova
634 • Bosnia-Herzegovina
634 • Slovenia
635 • Croatia

Chapter 9 - Accessing Useful Resources

639 • *Eurail Guide* Route Chart
      • 1996 European Train Ticket Prices
665 • Index of cities, resorts, and places of interest

Appreciating the Pleasures of Train Travel

Since that first slim edition (96 pages) of the *Eurail Guide* appeared in 1971, train travel, especially in Europe, has continually improved and flourished. The 36 Trans Europ Express trains that were in service in 1980 have since been replaced by a fleet of more than 90 much faster and more frequent EuroCity trains. Dozens of those futuristic, high-profile, ultra-speed TGV trains (up to 238 miles per hour) now grace many European tracks.

In 1995 more than 60,000,000 passengers crossed the English Channel via the conventional train-plus-ferry. Today, the downtown-to-downtown London-Paris (or the opposite) journey has been reduced from the present seven hours to a mere three hours, and the London-Brussels trip from five hours to only three and a quarter hours. Time and distances are shrinking while the comfort and pleasure are increasing.

All EuroCity trains, in compliance with strict standards of speed, punctuality, safety, comfort, air-conditioning, and food and beverage services, have steadily improved train travel as an excellent means of touring. This tendency is not letting up as more inter-European TGV (train de grande vitesse) lines and services are opening up each year, and the visionary EuroStar high-speed service between London, Paris, and Brussels via the EuroTunnel which is revolutionizing train travel. As dry as statistics can be, those of the thirty-eight new trains - costing $40,000,000 a piece; each carrying six first-class cars, ten second-class cars, and two bar cars; a capacity of up to 800 passengers; and speeds close to 200 miles per hour - are undeniably impressive. It's a long way from the clunky way backpackers roughed it in the late sixties and early seventies! Train travel in much of Europe today challenges - and in some cases, surpasses - air travel in terms of speed, comfort, price, and certainly scenery.

For more than a quarter of a century the editors of the *Eurail Guide* have claimed that the most economical, safest, most convenient, interesting, and pleasant way to travel and really see the world is by train. Although it's doubtful you need convincing, consider the following:

• When traveling by train, departures are almost never delayed by weather, as is often the case with air or automobile travel.

• When traveling by train, departures and arrivals are in the center of cities, not in far-off suburbs, saving travelers lots of time, effort and expense. In fact, in Europe and Japan, many high-speed trains actually get you from a hotel in one city to a

hotel in another city faster than by airplane when the distance is 250-350 miles.
• The cost of the least expensive, non-airconditioned compact car in Europe, for 350 miles-per-day travel, can easily come to more than $80 per day - with value-added taxes on rentals being wildly expensive (over 20% in Denmark, Hungary, Sweden, Norway, Austria, and Finland, and approaching that in Italy, France, and Britain). 1995 weekly rates for B-category automobiles with standard transmission and drop-off in the same country averaged $569 in Finland, $449 in Ireland, $389 in Sweden, $319 in Austria, and $299 in France. For an automatic transmission Mercedes Benz, typical prices in 1994 were: $1,429 in Britain, $1,279 in Ireland, $1,239 in Denmark, $1,099 in Austria and $1,059 in Norway. When you count the cost of insurance, servicing, overnight parking fees ($10-$20 per night at most hotels), substantial drop-off charges, and astronomical gasoline prices - sample prices-per-gallon for regular unleaded in 1994 were: $3.77 in Holland, $3.70 in Italy, $3.47 in France, and $3.34 in Germany - the case for train travel becomes increasingly clear. To add insult to injury, autoroute tolls can provoke cardiac arrest in travelers used to the New Jersey Turnpike or the Sunshine State Parkway. In 1992, motorists had to pay $43 in tolls for the 183-mile drive from Bilbao to Zaragoza. The 86-mile trip from Milan to Turin was $13. It was $14 to go 104 miles from Nice to Aix-en-Provence. *The Consumer Reports Travel Letter* stated in 1992 that extensive driving in France or Italy "will add $5-$15 to your daily cost."

Then, of course, there is the fatigue of driving, the exasperation of congested traffic, insane holiday patterns in many European countries, and the increasing nuisance and health risk of intense diesel fumes on major European roadways.

Now consider the train.

One can travel on high-speed, air-conditioned trains with any of more than 80 bargain European train passes for $10-$30 per day. The first-class, 15-day Eurailpass, the first-class Eurail Saverpass, and the first-class Eurail Flexipass all represent fantastic bargains in comparison to car rental or air travel, as do also the many European national and regional train passes listed throughout chapters 6 and 7.

By train travel you reach thousands of interesting destinations not accessible by air. Let's not talk about the worries, frustrations, and delays of socked-in airports, check-in requirements, baggage waits; or, by car, unexpected flat tires, the trauma of unfamiliar and congested arteries of foreign cities, strange traffic laws, and the many other problems, expenses, and inconveniences connected with airplane and auto travel. Let's focus on trains.

Whether in London or Tokyo, you will find food, information on local tours, assistance in obtaining lodging, money exchange, waiting rooms where you can relax, shoe repair, etc. at the principal rail stations. There is also the local flavor.

If you plan your itineraries well, you will see an array of visual delights that airplane passengers never see: indescribable seashores, vineyards tinted with afternoon sunlight, castles that have been straddling hilltops for centuries, raging rivers, breathtaking waterfalls, Alpine summits, remote villages founded before Christ, fjords, forests, lovely orchards and pastures - a feast of colorful scenes to enjoy long after the trip ends. You can take pictures or shoot video footage without having to pull over or take your eye from the road. You can meet strangers native to the country you're in or passengers also on their way somewhere new to you. You're free to read, to write, to drink, to flirt (this depends on your situation), to sleep, to daydream, to take a walk.

On a train you experience the sublime sensation of freedom, never losing your connection to the landscape around you, yet are detached from the trappings of daily life outside. You're a spectator and a participant all at once, and even at high speeds you come to understand another country through its changing terrain, land formations and distances between places. Traveling by train can elevate the act of travel from the banality of transportation to the poetic experience - all without sacrificing practicality!

As you approach your destination, you can feel the charge of excitement as people around you prepare their belongings and the train begins to brake. The new cityscape comes into focus and you feel energized, maybe even rested and refreshed. Perhaps you've even had time to shave or put on your makeup. A cup of local espresso or a glass of beer may await you at the end of the platform.

You say good-bye, maybe exchange addresses with those Amsterdam businessmen, students from Oslo or that Greek army officer, Croatian geologist, Uruguayan cardiologist, North Dakota farmer and his Chinese-Canadian wife, Emily, who gave you a bunch of Italian grapes, the family from Brazil with the twins, a Russian woman living in Frankfurt, the professor of French from Boston who knows your dentist. You get the picture. Your sense of the world and its people has grown overnight and you're glad to be alive. Welcome to train travel!

A Eurailpass must be validated at the
ticket office of your first departure. The
clerk will write on your pass the first
and last day it can be used, your
passport number, and he will stamp it
with his railroad office stamp.

You must start to use
your Eurailpass within
six months after the date
of purchase.

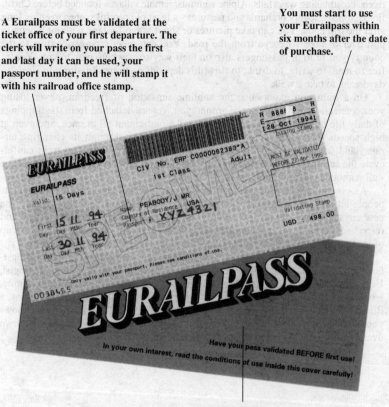

Your Eurailpass must be
kept in its cover at all times.
Without the cover, the pass
is invalid.

Note: If you fail to have your pass validated before your first departure, the train conductor can do this for you. However, there is a $3 fee for this kind of post-departure validation. Always be ready to present your passport. When a conductor checks or validates your pass, he will ask to see your passport too.

Deciding How to Travel: Choosing a Eurailpass

Since 1959, that famous train travel bargain called the Eurailpass has been offered by Western European rail companies throughout the world, revolutionizing the scope of low-budget travel. This particularly came into mode during the sixties and seventies, when Europe instantly became accessible to young North Americans traveling by backpack and by train.

Currently there are twelve different Eurailpasses and options entitling one to unlimited first, or second-class train travel plus free or reduced fares on many bus and boat lines in the following 17 countries: Austria, Belgium, Denmark, Finland, France, Germany, Greece, Holland, Hungary, The Irish Republic, Italy, Luxembourg, Norway, Portugal, Spain, Sweden, and Switzerland. In addition, Eurailpasses are honored on those trains running to and from the airports of the following cities: Amsterdam, Barcelona, Bilbao, Brussels, Dusseldorf, Geneva, Frankfurt, Malaga, Paris, Pisa, Vienna, and Zurich.

Over 100,000 miles of European train travel is available to those in possession of a pass. Rest assured that despite the four main options open to train travelers over the age of twenty-six - first-class tickets, Eurailpasses, national passes, and second-class tickets - train travel with one or more of the Eurailpasses is the most economical and interesting way of experiencing international travel. But there are lots of distinctions, nuances, and tips you need to know in order to maximize the impact and enjoyment of your journey.

Eurailpass Rules and Pointers

• **Refunds** All Eurailpasses are non-refundable if lost or stolen. So be careful. It is forbidden to lend or borrow a Eurailpass. Treat your card like a passport. If you present an unused Eurailpass to a Eurailpass office before its validity begins, you are entitled to a refund of 85% of the purchase price. Otherwise, do not expect refunds for unused cards. Lost or stolen passes, though, can be replaced if the user can successfully produce the "proof-of-purchase" stub from the two-part pass issued at purchase.

• **Validity** All Eurailpasses become valid on the first day they are used, after first having been recorded at the ticket office of the station from where the first journey began. You must start to use your Eurailpass within six months after the date of purchase. Thus, a purchase on February 1 necessitates a first use prior to August 1. Longer delays invalidate the pass. It's a good idea to protect yourself from having your pass rendered partially or wholly invalid because the validity dates were entered incorrectly. The Eurailpass must be validated at the station ticket office at your first departure before you depart. At that time, the clerk writes on the pass both the first and last day it can be used. Before he does this, write a note with what you believe are the validity dates, show it to him, and ask him if he agrees with those dates. Only when he says your dates are correct, or explains why they are not, should you hand your pass to him for the dates to be entered on it. Once the clerk has written validity dates on the face of your Eurailpass, those dates cannot be changed, because any alteration of the dates invalidates the pass. If one fails to have the Eurailpass validated before boarding the first train ride, the train conductor can do so. However, there is a $3 fee for a post-departure validation. After your Eurailpass has been validated, remove the "proof-of-purchase" stub from the two-part pass. From then on, as you would do with traveler's checks, keep that stub separate from the pass. It is this stub that is required for a replacement in case the pass itself is lost or stolen.

• **Savings** Eurailpasses offer users unlimited travel, meaning precisely that: You can literally travel 24 hours a day for the entire period of validity. Countless travelers have used three and four times the price of their pass in train travel, saving hundreds of dollars from what their itinerary would have cost had they used ordinary tickets. The bargain does not end there. Tickets for the high-speed (EC), Inter-City (IC), and super-speed "TGV" trains cost more than an ordinary, slower train on the same route, with supplementary charges ranging from around $5 to over $18. Happily Eurailpasses include unlimited use of EC, IC, and TGV trains without having to pay anything extra.

On the other hand, not all Eurailpasses are wholly economical. Some European itineraries are less expensive using regular train tickets or using one or a combination of the many national and regional rail passes described elsewhere in this guide (see France Railpass, German Flexipass, Benelux Tourrail, etc.). The only way to find out if a Eurailpass or one of the numerous other passes will save you money is to compare their price with the total prices of tickets for particular itineraries.

• **Classes** Most train systems have first and second-class cars. If you have hesitations about second-class space in Europe, don't. Seats are completely acceptable, especially on trains in Austria, Belgium, Denmark, Finland, France, Germany, Holland, the Irish Republic, Luxembourg, Norway, Sweden, and Switzerland.

Although first-class is more comfortable and less crowded, it is of course more expensive. If you are considering traveling in the often crowded second-class, compute second-class fares at two-thirds of the first-class fares shown. This will give you the approximate price of a second-class ticket. While second-class is usually more crowded than first-class, often the disadvantage of having to stand because all the seats are occupied can be simply overcome by arriving early at the rail station. In Europe, first-class cars (and the first-class portion of mixed-class cars) are often marked by a yellow line running above the windows on the outside of the train. Note: Even though second-class tickets cost 66% of the first-class tickets, the cost of a typical itinerary using second-class tickets is often more expensive than when traveling first-class with a Eurailpass!

• **Reservations** Many of the EC, IC, and TGV trains require reservations, the price of which is often included in the supplement and the cost of the supplement is covered by the pass. However, Eurailpass travelers must still pay the small fee of usually $3 for each seat reservation.

• **Time savings** Eurailpasses add precious time to a travel schedule, in that travelers no longer need to stand in a ticket-selling line when in possession of a Eurailpass or Eurail Youthpass. Delays in line of up to 30 minutes are not uncommon.

   With or without a pass, if reserved seats are required or desired, it is necessary to allocate time for the separate seat reservation line when you have not made reservations before starting your trip. For more information about reservations see Chapter 3.

• **Itineraries** In addition to the 100,000 available miles of track, there are more than 700 train trips in and between the 17 Eurailpass countries listed in this guide for Eurailpass holders. See the Route Chart in Chapter 9. The first step in using the Route Chart is to make a list of your itinerary destinations. It is advisable to schedule any part of your trip that is not in the 17 Eurailpass countries (such as England, Yugoslavia, etc.) either before or after the days you are touring the countries in which your Eurailpass is valid, so as to avoid consuming Eurailpass days and thus be able to buy the shortest and least expensive Eurailpass necessary. Next, consult the Route Chart and note the first-class fare for each leg of your trip that can be covered by Eurailpass.

Eurail Guide Route Chart

Thanks to the unique and essential Route Chart found in Chapter 9, scheduling your train travel, matching your trips with validity periods of the available train passes, computing all ticket prices, and, perhaps most importantly, determining the most advantageous Eurailpass, national pass, or series of ordinary tickets to purchase has been made easy and accurate. The Route Chart is accurate enough to help you decide whether you want to make a particular trip in one day or break it up into two or more shorter trips. With the Route Chart you can quickly discover the least expensive way to complete your itinerary, and, if using one of the passes, how to coordinate timetables. Essentially you become your own, personalized travel agent!

How to Use the Route Chart

Travel time figures between two cities represent the longest or shortest possible time for each trip. The time stated for many routes when using a night train, can obviously be reduced significantly on a day train. Many night trains in Europe deliberately slow down or stop mid-journey so as not to arrive at major cities at an impractical, early time. Additionally there may be two or more trains running during the day, one of which is a fast express that makes the trip in less time than what is indicated on the Route Chart. So, take into consideration that the guide deliberately errs only on the long side. Despite this, the time shown in the *Eurail Guide* Route Chart, as a rule, is rarely more than 10% greater than the fastest time between two cities.

Eurailpass Prices

Prices quoted in this guide are based on current exchange rates and information and thus are subject to modification. Individual country pass (sold only in issuing countries) prices are shown in their respective currencies and are also subject to modification.

Most sources for Eurailpasses and ordinary tickets sold by individual European countries charge a non-refundable $10 handling fee per order (not "per pass"). Some travel agencies may also charge a handling fee. Be aware.

The Passes

····· Eurailpass

Commentary: Depending on your itinerary, the least expensive formula can be buying a combination of Eurailpass and ordinary train tickets. For example, when traveling by train in excess of the 21-day period with the $90 Geneva-Zurich ride scheduled for the last day, you'll save $60 by buying a 21-day Eurailpass plus an ordinary ticket for the twenty-second day ($648 + $90 = $738) instead of buying a $798 one-month Eurailpass. On the other hand, if the trip on the twenty-second day is $151 or more, (Frankfurt-Copenhagen was $217 in 1994), you'll save money buying a one-month Eurailpass even though it is being used only 22 days. Calculate carefully before purchasing.

1996 Prices Per Person
• First-class, consecutive days:
     $522 for 15 days
     $678 for 21 days

$838 for 1 month
$1,148 for 2 months
$1,468 for 3 months
-There is a 50% discount for children between the ages of four and eleven.
-Note that children also count toward the minimum group number.
-Children under four travel free.

••••• Eurail Flexipass

This pass is the same as Eurailpass, but non-consecutive travel days within a 2-month period.

1995 Prices Per Person
$616 for any 10 days within a 2-month period
$812 for any 15 days within a 2-month period
-There is a 50% discount for children between the ages of four and eleven.
-Note that children also count toward the minimum group number.

••••• Eurail Saverpass

This pass for unlimited first-class travel allows three or more people to travel together between April 1 and September 30 with the same privileges as the consecutive-days Eurailpass described above, but with several (precise) advantages. Between October 1 and March 31, only two persons need to travel together.

1995 Prices Per Person
$452 for 15 days
$578 for 21 days
$712 for 1-month
-There is a 50% discount for children between the ages of four and eleven.
-Note that children also count toward the minimum group number.

••••• EurailDrive Pass

-Same privileges as the Eurailpass. Features four days of unlimited first-class train travel plus three days of a Hertz rental car with unlimited mileage, tax, basic liability insurance, and drop-off (providing that drop-off is within the same country as that in which the car is rented).
-There is also an option to buy up to five additional days of either train travel and/or car rental.
-This pass (up to 17 days of travel) must be used within two months.
Commentary: The 1996 per-person price for two or more persons when using the category of smallest car is $339. An option for single travelers is available at $419. Up to five additional rail days (at $55 per day) and up to five additional car days (at $55 per day for smallest car) are available.

····· Europass

-A flexible pass for unlimited first-class train travel in five of the 17 Eurailpass countries: France, Germany, Italy, Spain, and Switzerland.

-Sold worldwide outside Europe by travel agencies and Rail Europe (U.S. and Canadian offices listed under France).

-If only three or four countries are selected, they must border each other. For example, one cannot select Germany, Switzerland, and Spain.

1996 Prices Per Person

For three countries:	$316 for any five days
	$358 for any six days
	$400 for any seven days

For four countries:	$442 for any eight days
	$484 for any nine days
	$526 for any ten days

For five countries:	$568 for any eleven days
	$610 for any twelve days
	$652 for any thirteen days
	$694 for any fourteen days
	$736 for any fifteen days

Rail travel in any or all of four other countries can be added.
1995 Adult First-Class Prices:

	$45 for Austria
	$42 for Belgium
	$90 for Greece
	$29 for Portugal

-Half fare for children between the ages of four and eleven. Under four, free.

····· Europass for Couples

New: two people traveling together for five-seven days can take advantage of a new first-class Europass for four countries with costs only half for the second passenger

1996 Prices Per Couple

For three countries:	$474 for any five days
	$537 for any six days
	$600 for any seven days

- No discounts for children.

Europass Bonuses In addition to the regular rail routes, the following European transportation routes and services are included in the Europass:

France: the scenic Digne-Nice-Digne train route.

Germany: steamers operated by KD German Rhine Line (Cologne-Mainz-Cologne), and on the Mosel and Cochem Rivers. Also on the Mannheim-Nuremberg "Castle Road" and the Frankfurt/M-Fussen "Romantic Road" guided bus tours.

Switzerland: regular steamer service on the Rhine River (Schaffhausen-Kreuzliner-Schaffhausen), Aere River (Biel-Solothurn-Biel), and on the lakes of Biel, Brienz, Geneva, Lucerne, Murten, Neuchatel, Thun, and Zurich.

•••••Euro Youthpass

This is a particularly advantageous pass limited to those under age twenty-six, offering unlimited second-class train travel with the same conditions as the Europass.

1995 Prices Per Person

For four countries:	$210 for any five days
	$239 for any six days
	$268 for any seven days
	$297 for any eight days
	$326 for any nine days
	$355 for any ten days

For five countries:	$384 for any eleven days
	$413 for any twelve days
	$442 for any thirteen days
	$471 for any fourteen days
	$500 for any fifteen days

•••••Europass Drive

This pass lets you alternate the train - for longer distances, with the rental car for side trips. Car rental through Avis or Hertz in three categories of manual transmission. Train travel available for first-class travel only. This pass is good for any 8 days (5 rail, 3 car) within a two-month period plus 5 additional car days in the bordering Europass countries you choose.

1996 Prices for first-class trains, economy cars:

$610 for two adults, $55 for additional car day

$465 for one adult, $75 for additional car day

$31.50 for each additional rail day for two-adult package; $42 for additional rail day for one-adult package.

••••• Eurail Youthpass

This pass is for unlimited second-class train travel in the same 17 countries which honor the first-class Eurailpass. It is often more advantageous for youths under twenty-six than the first-class Eurailpass. Compare and chose carefully. Note: the buyer of a Eurail Youthpass must prove that he or she is under twenty-six years of age on the first day of using the pass.

1996 Prices Per Person
    $418 for fifteen days
    ($100+ less than the 15-day, first-class Eurailpass.)
    $598 for one month
    ($240 less than the one-month, first-class Eurailpass.)
    $798 for two months
    ($350 less than the two-month, first-class Eurailpass.)

••••• Eurail Youth Flexipass

This pass allows for unlimited second-class train travel within a two-month period.

1996 Prices Per Person
    $438 for any ten days
    $588 for any fifteen days

Eurostar Channel Tunnel Tickets

In late 1994, the French, British and Belgian Railways received approval from the Intergovernmental Safety Commission to begin operation of trains through the Channel Tunnel. This service linked Paris to London in 3 hours and Brussels to London in 3 hours and 15 minutes. Since the innaugural trip, over two million passengers have used Eurostar between London-Paris and London-Brussels. Service between Paris-Brussels will begin in June 1996.

    Eurostar links the three capitals with service almost every hour. Prices change frequently. At the time this book was printed, prices were as follows: London-Paris and London-Brussels (roundtrip, refundable): first class (with complimentary meal at you r seat for first class, buffet car for standard class) $344, standard class $242. There are also special fares for 26 and younger, Eurail passholders, and group rates.

Tickets are available in Britain, Belgium or France or from Rail Europe in the U.S. and Canada (call 1-800-EUROSTAR).

Eurailpass Bonuses

In addition to unlimited train travel, the Eurailpasses include numerous free bonuses or reduced prices for boat trips, buses and private railways. Many of these bonuses are not listed in the Eurailpass brochure, such as discounts on several Norwegian fjord boats and Swiss cable cars. It is always a good idea to show your Eurailpass before purchasing any bus, boat, cable car or train ticket in Europe. You have nothing to lose, and sometimes you'll be pleased to profit by an unexpected perk. In many cases, rides that are not covered completely with a Eurailpass will, however, include a discount. There is no reason to miss out on these. Here are the readily known discounts available to Eurailpass holders:

Austria
• Two track railways: (1) Puchberg am Schneeberg-Hochschneeberg and (2) St. Wolfgang-Schafbergspitze.
• Danube cruise between Passau and Vienna.
• Steamers on Lake Wolfgang.
• 50% Reduction on Lake Constance, Linz-Passau-Linz, and Vienna-Budapest ships.

Belgium
• 35% reduction on the Ostend-Dover ferry operated by Regie belgie des Transports Maritimes.

Denmark
• Ferry crossings: Aarhus-Kalundborg, Knudshoved-Halskov, Nyborg-Korsor, Fynshav-Bojden, Rodby Faerge-Puttgarden (Germany), Gedser-Warnemunde (Germany), Helsingor-Helsingborg (Sweden), and Frederikshavn-Goteborg (Sweden).
• 50% reduction on the Flyvebadene Company hydrofoil between Copenhagen and Malmo (25% for Eurail Youthpass).
• 20% reduction on the Steamship Company DFDS between Esbjerg and Harwich, New Castle and Faeroe Islands, and Copenhagen and Oslo.
• 30% reduction on the Color Line for the ship between Hirtshals and Kristiansand (Norway).

Finland
• Free passage on day sailings in both directions of the Silja Line Helsinki-Stockholm ferry. On night sailings, a bed in at least a four-bed cabin ($12) must be used. It can be upgraded to a higher cabin class at extra charge.
• 50% reduction on the Helsinki-Travemunde (Germany) ferry.
• Free rides on buses which operate on occasion as train substitutes.

France
• Irish Ferries ships between LeHavre-Rosslare, Cherbourg-Rosslare, and (late June to late August) LeHavre-Cork. (Port taxes are extra, payable in Irish Pounds. Reservations are required at all times for cabins, and during July and August for seats (Irish £5.20 including the port tax).
• Digne-Nice-Digne rail trip.

Germany
• Free sightseeing cruises on the Rhine, between Cologne and Mainz, and on the Mosel, between Koblenz and Cochem. (Eurail Youthpass holders pay an extra

charge on express-steamers. Everyone pays an extra charge on hydrofoils.)
• Three ferry crossings: Puttgarden-Rodby Faerge (Denmark), Warnemunde-Gedser (Denmark), and Sassnitz-Trelleborg (Sweden). Sassnitz is the most direct gateway from Berlin to Stockholm or Oslo, with both day and night trains operating on these routes.
• Two free bus rides: "Romantic Road" (Frankfurt-Munich-Frankfurt) and "Castle Road" (Mannheim-Nuremberg-Mannheim).
• Bus lines of Regionale Omnibus Verkehrsgesellschaften der Deutschen Bundesbahn.
• 50% reduction on three boat lines: Travemunde-Trelleborg (Sweden), Rostock-Trelleborg, and Travemunde-Helsinki ferries. Lake Constance cruises between Romanshorn and Rorschach and Lindau. Day trips by steamer: Passau-Linz-Passau.
• 25% reduction on two mountain railroads: Garmisch-Zugspitze (Schneeferner-haus) mountain railroad and selected cable cars in the summit area. Freiburg (Breisgau)-Schauinsland mountain railroad.

Greece
• The ferry crossing from Patras to Brindisi (see note under "Italy" Chapter 6).
• 30% reduction on Adriatica di Navagazione Line for ships Piraeus-Venice-Piraeus and Piraeus-Alexandria-Piraeus.

Italy
• The ferry crossing from Brindisi to Patras (see notes under "Italy" Chapter 6).
• 30% reduction on Adriatica di Navagazione's cruises Venice-Piraeus-Venice and Venice-Alexandria-Venice.
Warning: It's imperative to read notes under the Italy section before planning your itinerary! Don't let yourself be diverted to other ships at the Patras or Brindisi rail stations away from the Hellenic Mediterranean Line or Adriatica di Navagazione Line (the only ferries that honor Eurailpasses). Others make the voyage but charge large fees. Numerous cases have been cited of passengers deceived into believing these ships accept Eurailpasses. Steep charges were extorted after it was too late for passengers to leave departed ferries and return to the correct docks. The two proper lines charge pass holders $14 between June 10 and September 30. Reservations ($3 each) are advisable when using Eurailpass.

Hungary
• 50% reduction on Budapest-Vienna ships.

Ireland
• Irish Ferries ships: Rosslare-LeHavre, Rosslare-Cherbourg and (late June to late August) Cork-Le Havre. Port taxes are extra, payable in Irish pounds. Reservations are required at all times for cabins, and during July and August for seats (Irish £5.20 including the port tax).

Norway
• 30% reduction on the boat trip between Kristians and Hirtshals (Denmark) on Color Line steamships.

Sweden
• Five free boat trips: Stockholm-Helsinki. Note that passage is covered by Eurailpass only for those who reserve and pay for a bed on Silja Line. Stockholm-Aland Islands-Turku. Note that Eurailpass covers only a seat; payment is charged for a cabin. Helsingborg-Helsingor (Denmark). Goteborg-Frederikshavn (Denmark). Trelleborg-Sassnitz (Germany).
• 50% reduction (25% for Eurail Youthpass) on the Flyvebadene Company hydrofoil Malmo-Copenhagen.
• 50% reduction on the Trelleborg-Travemunde (Germany) and Trelleborg-Rostock ferries.

Switzerland
• Lake boats on the Biel, Brienz, Geneva, Lucerne, Murten, Neuchatel, Thun, and Zurich lakes.
• River boats on the Rhine (Schaffhausen-Kreuzlingen) and Aare (Biel-Solothurn) rivers.
• 50% reduction on Lake Constance boats between Romanshorn-Friedrichshafen and Rorschach-Lindau.
• 35% reduction on the Alpnachstad-Mt. Pilatus funicular and the Kriens-Mt. Pilatus cable car.
• 35% reduction on the entrance fee to Lucerne's Transport Museum, the largest of its kind in Europe.

••••• Rail Europ Senior (Senior Citizen Pass)
This senior-citizen pass offers senior citizens (age sixty and older) a 30% discount on first or second-class train tickets. Purchasers must buy a national senior pass from one of the issuing countries. That pass becomes a Rail Europ Senior Card. The pass is only sold to persons who can prove that they are permanent residents of one of the participating countries: Austria, Belgium, Croatia Serbie Slovenia, the Czech Republic, Denmark, Finland, France, Germany, Great Britain, Greece, Holland, Hungary, the Irish Republic, Italy, Luxembourg, Norway, Portugal, Slovakia, Spain, Sweden, and Switzerland. Valid for one year, these passes are sold at main rail stations of the issuing countries.

Use of Rail Europ Senior is limited by each of the participating countries. In France this pass is called the Carte Vermeil Plein Temps, which costs 265 FF and allows as much as a 50% discount on French trains (for "Blue Period" travel). A traveler using the Carte Vermeil Plein Temps or a Rail Europ Senior card issued by any other country cannot start a train ride between noon Friday and noon Saturday, from 15:00 Sunday to noon Monday, on certain holidays, or during various periods of heavy traffic. Few seats are allocated to holders of Carte Vermeil on some TGV trains, other high-speed trains, and EuroCity trains. Remember, the limitations on use of Rail Europ Senior can be significantly different in each of the participating countries.

••••• Inter Rail Cards

The famous Inter Rail Card offers unlimited, second-class train travel, but can be purchased only in Europe and Morocco, and is valid only for persons under twenty-six years old who can prove that they have resided at least six months in the issuing country. The bearer can travel half fare in the issuing country and free on the railways of the other countries purchased. This is very advantageous to young travelers already residing or studying in Europe.

The validity period begins on the first day the card is used, and that day must be within two months after the card is purchased. The card also allows discounts on ship services (Irish Sea, Spain-Morocco, France-Corsica, Italy-Greece), as well as on selected Swiss private railways.

The Inter Rail Card is sold at most rail stations in the following 28 countries and must be paid for in the currency of the country that issues it.

The price is more or less the same in the 28 participating countries, but does experience some fluctuation according to exchange rates. In France, the price is 2,142 FF. The 28 countries are divided into seven zones, and the pass is sold in four versions.

One-zone pass	Two weeks of unlimited travel	$210
Two-zone pass	One month of unlimited travel	$250
Three-zone pass	One month of unlimited travel	$280
Global seven-zone pass	One month of unlimited travel	$315

The Zones

Zone 1:	Great Britain, Northern Ireland, the Irish Republic
Zone 2:	Finland, Norway, Sweden
Zone 3:	Austria, Denmark, Germany, Switzerland
Zone 4:	Bulgaria, Croatia, the Czech Republic, Hungary, Poland, Romania, Slovakia
Zone 5:	Belgium, France, The Netherlands, Luxembourg
Zone 6:	Morocco, Portugal, Spain
Zone 7:	Greece, Italy, Slovenia, the European part of Turkey, and the Brindisi-Patras-Brindisi ferry

•••••EuroTrain Tickets

These tickets are discounted up to 40% on train and ship passage to over 2,000 destinations in all of Eastern and Western Europe (22 countries), including Turkey and Morocco, for anyone under twenty-six years old on the first day of travel, regardless of residence. A ticket is valid for two months and allows as many stop-overs as desired.

Available in the U.K. from Eurotrain, Dept. E-93, 52 Grosvenor Gardens, London SW1W 0AG. In France, an equivalent discount service is called B.I.G.E.

Where to Purchase Eurailpasses

Many travel agents are equipped to sell most Eurailpasses, however, the following sources specialize in train passes and offer them directly to the public:

U.S.A. and CANADA

German Rail Inc.
3400 Peachtree Rd., NE
Atlanta, GA   30326

GermanRail Inc.
20 Park Plaza
Boston, MA 02116

Rail Europe
2100 Central Ave.
Boulder, CO 80301

CIT (Italian State Railways)
756 Route 83
Bennsenville, IL 60106

GermanRail Inc.
9501 W. Devon Ave.
Rosemont, IL 60018

CIT (Italian State Railways)
342 Madison Ave., #207
New York, NY 10173

German Rail Inc.
122 42nd St. 10168
New York, NY

Rail Europe
2087 Dundas East
Mississauga, Ont. Canada
L4X 1M2

GermanRail Inc.
222 W. Las Colinas
Irving, TX 75039

CIT (Italian State Railways)
6033 W. Century Blvd.,
Los Angeles, CA 90045

German Rail Inc.
11933 Wilshire Blvd.
Los Angeles, CA 90045

CIT (Italian State Railways)
1450 Cousillors
Montreal, P.Q., Canada (H3A 2E6)

CIT Tours, Inc.
80 Tiverton Court, #401
Marktown, Ont. Canada L3R OG4

German Rail Inc.
904 The East Mall
Etobicoke, Ont., L3R OG4 Canada

German Rail Inc.
240 Stockton St.
San Francisco, CA 94108

Rail Europe
226-230 Westchester Ave.
White Plains, NY 10604

Elsewhere in the World

AUSTRALIA: CIT-Australia Pty. Ltd.; Concorde International Travel; Thomas Cook Pty. Ltd.; Rail Plus
EGYPT: Thomas Cook Overseas Ltd.
HONG KONG: Hong Kong Student Travel Ltd.; Schenker Travel, Thomas Cook Overseas Ltd.
INDIA: Travel Corporation India Ltd.
INDONESIA: Pantravel Travel & Tourism Service
ISRAEL : European World Representatives
JAPAN: Japan Travel Bureau; Ohshu Express Ltd.; Recruit From A Inc.; Travel Plaza International Inc.
KOREA: Seoul Travel Service, Ltd.
MALAYSIA: Boustead Travel Services Sdn. Bhd.
NEW ZEALAND: Atlantic and Pacific Travel International, Ltd.; Thomas Cook Holidays
PAKISTAN: American Express International Banking Corp.
PHILIPPINES: PCI Travel Corporation; Thomas Cook Inc.
SAUDI ARABIA: Alrajhi Wings for Travel and Tourism; Orient Travel & Tours
SINGAPORE: American Express Travel Service; Thomas Cook Travel Services
SOUTH AFRICA: World Travel Agency Ltd.
SRI LANKA: Aitken Spence Travels Ltd.
TAIWAN: American Express International Ltd.; Federal Transportation Ltd.
THAILAND: DITS Travel (Diethelm International Transport Services, Ltd.)
UNITED ARAB EMIRATES: Thomas Cook A.L. Rostamani (Pvt) Ltd.

Other Passes and Discounts

Aside from the Eurailpass and Eurail Youthpass, there are alternative ways of saving money when traveling in Europe by train: special discount tickets, coupons, and special passes issued independently by various countries. Although details on all of them appear in this guide under the respective country listings, and most must be purchased in the respective country, the following is a listing of European train company offices and agents outside of Europe, other than the U.S. and Canadian offices listed on the previous pages, which handle special discount tickets.

Since regulations on discount tickets change frequently, it is suggested that you contact the office nearest you for information before leaving for Europe.

Austria

Austrian National Tourist Office
P.O. Box 491938
Los Angeles, CA 90049

1010 Ouest Rue Sherbrooke, Suite #1410
Montreal, Quebec, Canada H3A 2R7

P.O. Box 1142
New York, NY 10108-1142

2 Bloor Street East, Suite #3330
Toronto, Ontario, Canada M4W 1A8

Belgium
Reservations and tickets for Belgian trains are provided by the offices of Rail Europe, addresses for which appear under France.

780 Third Ave., Suite #1501
New York, NY 10017

Denmark
Scandinavian Tourist Boards
655 Third Ave.
New York, NY 10017

Finland
Finnish Tourist Board
1900 Avenue of the Stars, Suite #1070
Los Angeles, CA 90067

655 Third Ave.
New York, NY 10017

P.O. Box 246, Station "Q"
Toronto, Ontario, Canada M4T 2M1

France
Rail Europe
2100 Central Ave.
Boulder, CO 80301

11 East Adams St.
Chicago, IL 60603

800 Corporate Dr
Fort Lauderdale, FL 33334

2087 Dundas East
Mississauga, Ontario, Canada L4X 1M2

643 Notre Dame Ouest
Montreal, Canada H3C 1H8

360 Post St.
San Francisco, CA 94108

100 Wilshire Blvd.,
Santa Monica, CA 90401

409 Granville St.,
Vancouver, B.C., V6C 1T2, Canada

226–230 Westchester Ave.,
White Plains, NY 10604

Germany
German Rail Inc.
222 W. Las Colinas, Suite #1050
Irving, TX 75039

11933 Wilshire Blvd.
Los Angeles, CA 90025

9501 W. Devon Ave.
Rosemont, IL 60018-4832

904 The East Mall
Etobicoke, Ontario, Canada M9B 6K2

Great Britain
BritRail Travel International
1500 Broadway
New York, NY 10036-4015

Greece
Greek National Tourist Organization
168 No. Michigan Ave.
Chicago, IL 60601

611 W. 6th St.
Los Angeles, CA 90017

1233 Rue De la Montagne
Montreal, Canada H3G 1Z2

645 Fifth Ave.
New York, NY 10022

1300 Bay St.
Toronto, Ontario, Canada M5R 3K8

Holland
Netherlands Board of Tourism
225 No. Michigan Ave., Suite #326
Chicago, IL 60601

25 Adelaide St. East, Suite #710
Toronto, Ontario, Canada M5C 1Y2

Ireland
Irish Tourist Board
345 Park Ave.
New York, NY 10154

160 East Bloor St., Suite #1150
Toronto, Ontario, Canada M4W 1B9

Italy
Italian State Railways
6033 W. Century Blvd., Suite #980
Los Angeles, CA 90045

1450 Councillors St., Suite #750
Montreal, P.Q. Canada H3A 2E6

342 Madison Ave., #207
New York, NY 10173

80 Tiverton Court, #401
Markham, Ontario, Canada L3R 0G4

Luxembourg
Luxembourg National Tourist Office
17 Beekman Place
New York, NY 10022

Norway
Scandinavian Tourist Boards
655 Third Ave.
New York, NY 10017

Poland
Polish National Tourist Office
333 No. Michigan Ave.
Chicago, IL 60601

275 Madison Ave., Suite #1171
New York, NY 10016

Orbis Polish Travel Bureau, Inc. 3
42 Madison Ave.
New York, NY 10173

Portugal
Portuguese National Tourist Office
590 Fifth Ave.
New York, NY 10036

60 Bloor St. West, Suite #1005
Toronto, Ontario, Canada M4W 3B8

Spain
Tourist Office of Spain
8383 Wilshire Blvd., Suite #960
Beverly Hills, CA 90211

845 N. Michigan Ave., Suite #915E
Chicago, IL 60611

1221 Brickell Ave. , Suite #1850
Miami, FL 33131

665 Fifth Ave.
New York, NY 10022

102 Bloor St. West, Suite 1400
Toronto, Ontario, Canada M5S 1M8

Sweden
Scandinavian Tourist Boards
655 Third Ave.
New York, NY 10017

Switzerland
Swiss National Tourist Office
150 No. Michigan Ave., Suite 2930
Chicago, IL 60601

222 No. Sepulveda Blvd., Suite #1570
El Segundo, CA 90245

608 Fifth Ave.
New York, NY 10020

925 The East Mall
Etobicoke, Ontario, Canada M9B 6K1

Student Discount Cards

• International Student Identity Card (ISIC)
This well-recognized card (more than a million issued every year) is an international passport to low-cost travel for students over the age of twelve. Bearers of the ISI card are entitled to discounts on rail, air, bus, and ferry travel, as well as entrance fees to museums, theaters, cinemas, and other places of interest in approximately 60 countries.

Cards issued in the U.S. carry basic accident/sickness insurance, which includes emergency evacuation insurance coverage up to $10,000 and features a 24-hour, toll-free ISIC Help Line. The toll-free number helps students replace lost traveler's checks or passports, or locate English-speaking doctors and lawyers.

Although there is no maximum age limit for the card itself, some transportation companies (airlines, steamships, etc.) and other vendors have imposed their own age restrictions for the use of this card. If you're over thirty, some companies, movie houses, etc. don't like the idea of your profiting from student status. Try to insist.

Upon buying the card, students also receive the International Student Identity Handbook, which lists worldwide discounts and benefits. Even if a student discount is not posted, holders of the card should always ask about a discount before paying the full price.

Developed and regulated by the International Student Travel Confederation, the card carries the owner's full name, birth date, citizenship, school name, and photo. The official U.S. sponsor of the card is CIEE (Council on International Educational Exchange). The card is available from CIEE's Council Travel offices nationwide as well as from hundreds of university and college campus offices.

The 1996 card is valid September 1, 1995 through December 31, 1996 and costs $16. Applications must also include a passport-size photo (with name printed on back) and proof of current student status (copy of transcript, letter from registrar, or copy of bill showing payment of enrollment fees). For insurance purposes, applicants must provide the name, address, and telephone number of beneficiaries.

Student Travels, a free magazine that covers traveling, studying, and working abroad, and describes CIEE's products and services, is available by calling (212) 661-1414, extension 1108.

• Go 25: International Youth Travel Card

This card is not limited to students and is available to anyone regardless of nationality who is at least twelve but not over twenty-five at the time of purchase. Proof of age may be a passport (or photocopy of the data page from a passport), copy of a driver's license, or copy of a birth certificate. The benefits include significantly reduced fares on regularly scheduled airlines between the U.S. and Europe, Asia and Latin America, and also from Europe to Africa, Asia, and the Middle East.

The Go-25 Card also offers holders advantages concerning in-hospital health care and accident insurance while traveling outside the U.S. The card affords users access to the aid provided by the Traveler's Assistance Centers in case of medical, legal, and financial emergencies while abroad. Lastly, it provides certain discounts on transportation, tours, accommodations, restaurants, museums, theaters, cultural attractions, and historic sites.

The card is valid for one year and costs $16.

To Apply for Both Cards

For an application and the location of an issuing office nearest you in the U.S. or Canada, call (800) GET-AN-ID (438-2643) between 09:00 and 17:00 ET.

CHAPTER 3

How to Plan a Rail Itinerary

Every successful train trip contains three essential dimensions: the amount of time you have, the interesting destinations you choose, and the scenic routes you decide to take.

Amount of Time

When time and budget permit, it is recommended that the minimum length of a train trip through Europe should be 23 days, including your arrival and departure days. Of the 21 remaining days, when arriving in Europe from a great distance such as North America - especially the West Coast - you should not plan on much for your first day, other than getting settled into your hotel and recovering from the fatigue of the journey and, more importantly, the change of time zones. Very few people are immune to the temporary handicap of jet lag, and most travelers are well advised to go to bed and postpone any appreciable activity until the second day after the flight. That leaves only 20 active days for sightseeing, which is not really that much time if you plan on visiting numerous European countries.

Most travel writers recommend staying a minimum of two or three nights in most cities you visit, with only occasional one-nighters mixed in the itinerary. This, of course, depends a lot on you. You may opt for five nights in Paris and only two in Munich, or three in Vienna but one in Budapest. Even the sturdiest traveler, though, develops a psychosis when spending too many consecutive nights in different hotel rooms. Besides, if you travel mostly by day, as is suggested in order to see the countryside and meet and converse with fellow passengers, you will arrive in a city late in the day. And if you leave the next morning, you are certainly not going to see much in that city.

But on a two-night basis you can cover 10-11 different cities during your 21 full days in Europe. Reducing a trip to 14 days means reducing the number of cities to five or six. If 14 days is your limit, the 15-day Eurailpass and some fast footwork will still let you have a happy tour while covering a great deal of the continent. All this depends on your time restrictions.

Choosing Destinations

After deciding on the length of time one has to tour, the next step in itinerary planning is to pick the places to be visited, and most people usually have more cities in mind than time, energy and distance will allow. Unless you are indifferent to 15-hour journeys that bring you into a destination late at night, knowing the travel time between each point on your itinerary is essential. The timetables in this book give you that information on more than 9,000 different rail trips.

The common sense approach is to consult a map with a mileage scale and visualize what is practical and what is not while composing a list of places to see. Part of this narrowing-down process depends on what interests you the most. List destinations in order of your priority. Could you really spend three weeks in Europe and not visit the Sistine Chapel? Would your Aunt Olga forgive you if you passed up that invitation at her cousin's farm in Bergen? You decide. Obviously, if, for example, seeing the great art masterpieces is a priority, you'd want to select Paris and Florence over Avignon and Naples. If your interest is Alpine scenery, you are going to concentrate on Bern and Salzburg, not Barcelona and Copenhagen.

Selecting Routes

At this point, you have determined how many days you will be in Europe, where you want to go, and what's feasible in that time. You should now consider the most rewarding routes and the use of special trains.

The journey from Paris to Marseilles, for example, can be made on any one of a dozen ordinary, slower, and often more scenic trains instead of the high-speed TGV. If you'd like to stop for lunch in Dijon, don't take the TGV. However, if you'd like to get to Marseilles by noon and be on the beach by 2 P.M., you better opt for the faster train. A traveler has the same sort of choices of railway routes all over the world; the fastest train is not necessarily the most interesting, and yet the commonplace, slow train may be a real waste of time - or be an extraordinary experience. Be aware that there are choices, and then evaluate them.

Reservations—Train and Hotel

Train Reservations

Since 1989, it has become increasingly easy to make train reservations before arriving in Europe. Most travel agencies now can sell you all of your tickets and/or make all of both your seat and sleeper reservations. This does not mean that you must have seat reservations: they are required only on selected trains. However, anyone traveling on main routes during peak tourist months without reserved space will probably make the trip standing in the aisle and being brushed up against every 30 seconds by passengers ambling along the corridor. Keep in mind that Europeans can, and do, reserve train seats up to two months in advance. Don't be alarmed to see a very ordinary train from Bordeaux to Tours on an October Monday morning completely sold-out.

Reservation clerks in many European cities speak little or no English, although most train stations have multilingual information stands staffed with friendly workers. Writing out your request in clear and simple terms can save you much time in communicating and help insure against getting a less than perfect reservation. You should note on paper your destination, time and day of departure, and any other preferences. Be sure to follow the European custom of showing the day of the month first, followed by the number of the month. July 8 is "8/7." And use the 24-hour clock! If you wanted to take a train to Milan, leaving at 1:50 P.M. on July 8, your note should read "Milan -13:50- 8/7."

Eating and Seating

If you decide to dine at your seat or in your train compartment rather than in the restaurant car, you might want to request a window seat when making your train reservations. On most European trains - other than the TGVs - these are the only seats that have a full, fold out table. In some compartments, the seats next to the sliding door also have a fold out table. Other seats have airplane-style meal trays. Moreover, window seats, especially in train cars with six-seat compartments, afford you a better view of the scenery.

Smoking or non-smoking?

Another variation in seat reservations is that on nearly all European trains you can reserve seats in compartments where smoking is either prohibited or permitted. Depending on your preference, this can make a great deal of difference in either enjoying or detesting your trip. In Europe, smokers can be vehement about their habit and don't always understand or care about the arguments for not smoking. Carefully selecting your reserved seat is thus your guarantee to comfort.

Picking Sides

And still another reservation option to keep in mind is the side of the train you prefer to be seated on. Often there is a decided sightseeing advantage on one side and a corresponding disadvantage on the alternate side. Think of the Alps or the Mediterranean or Lake Como. Obviously if you are traveling along the Riviera, the view of the Mediterranean is possible only on the left side if you are traveling west, and on the right side when going east. After logic tells you which side of the train offers the best view, inquire while making your seat reservation if there is seating on that side.

Train Reservations: Pros and Cons

When reservations are made in Europe, the reservation charge ranges from $2 to $8 per ride. Reservations for seats on Europe's greatest trains can be made as much as two months in advance, and many Europeans grab spaces on them soon after they become available to be reserved. Casual tourists may discover a few days before they want to travel on a special train that it is completely sold-out.

While most European trains do not require reservations, many do: French TGVs, some of the Eurocity trains that go between countries, overnight trains, and the new ultramodern Euro Star. Such trains accept reservations two months in advance of your travel date. That is why it is wise to reserve seats even before you arrive in the countries you plan to travel in.

Reserving Before You Leave

For holders of Eurailpasses, French train tickets, French national passes, or the national passes for most other European countries, note that if you purchased your tickets or passes from a North American office of Rail Europe, train reservations (required and optional) for most European countries can be made for you by that same issuing office. This can be very helpful. Rail Europe charges $10 per person, per train reservation (including cable fee), plus a single $10 service charge for shipping and handling. Thus, two people reserving seats on three trains means six reservations or $60 plus $10, making a total of $70.

The North American offices of Italian State Railways listed in this guide also make reservations for train trips in Italy and most (but not all) other European countries, but only when a Eurailpass has been purchased from them. Note, though, that they do not make reservations in connection with Italian passes or ordinary train tickets. The maximum number of reservations they will make is three trips per pass. Their fee is $10 per train seat, which includes all communication fees. The cost for two people reserving seats on three trains, therefore, is $60. However, two people traveling together are not permitted to reserve six trains.

Holders of a Eurailpass who make seat reservations after arriving in Europe are exempt from the reservation fee. This does not apply to Italy's special "Pendolino" trains though for which a hefty supplement ranging from $6 to $28 is charged. Those supplements, however, include both a reservation fee and a meal!

If you have purchased your Eurailpass, German national pass, or tickets for German trains from one of the North American offices of German Rail (U.S. and Canadian offices listed in this guide), these offices will reserve any number of trains up to 10 days prior to each train's departure at a charge of $10 per person, per train, plus $7.50 per order for Federal Express charges.

It is always advisable to have the office that issues you the Eurailpass to telex or fax your reservation requests to Europe. This can result in your obtaining seats which might otherwise have been sold to someone else if your request had been slowed down by the mail.

Reserving on the Spot: Avoiding the Lines

If, on the other hand, you wait to reserve train space just before each departure, keep in mind that at most European stations you must get in one line for a ticket and in a different line for a seat reservation. Of course, if you have a Eurailpass you eliminate having to wait in the ticket line for a long time.

As a matter of fact, you can face long waits in as many as five different lines - and part of the trick of making the most of your limited time is to avoid standing in any. The lines include: information, ticket purchases, seat reservation, hotel accommodations, and baggage checkroom. There are tricks to eliminating line waiting for general information discussed in Chapter 4. Having a Eurailpass solves the ticket line wait. The solution to the hotel accommodation line, of course, is to make reservations before you leave home. The baggage check room problem is discussed in Chapter 5.

There is another way to reduce the amount of time spent in either the ticket or seat reservation lines. These lines are far shorter Monday to Thursday than they are on the weekend. Midmorning tends to be a better time to buy tickets or make reservations than during the lunch hours or in the early evening when it is the height of the commuter rush hours. During the mid-June to mid-September tourist season, it is often advantageous to have a hotel concierge or *pensione* owner obtain your reservations for you.

In any case, be sure to make reservations in the country you will be touring as much in advance as possible, preferably upon your arrival in the city you will be continuing your tour from. Requirements for reservations vary from country to country and, within a country, from city to city. In some Italian cities, for example, reservations cannot be made less than two hours before a departure. Milan requires three hours notice. Rome requires five hours notice! Let's say that your trip consisted of a New York-Paris flight, followed by a train trip to Geneva, and a second one from Geneva-Rome. Make the Paris-Geneva reservation on your first day in Paris, and make the Geneva-Rome reservation upon arriving at the Geneva station.

Five Simple Train Reservation Tips

1. When you leave your compartment to go to the W.C. (toilet), dining car, or merely to stretch your legs, leave some object on your seat — newspaper, hat, something to inhibit unreserved seat-grabbers from settling down in your space during your absence. While it is true that the conductor will aid you in removing an interloper, finding the conductor, explaining the problem and using his intervention is somewhat more bothersome than simply preventing the event.

2. Do not waste time trying to make a seat reservation for a train trip within Belgium, Holland, Luxembourg, or Switzerland. These countries sell seat reservations only for rides going into another country. However, finding a seat on trains of these countries is not a problem except on peak travel days.

3. On a normal working day, even though the reservation clerk claims all seats on a certain train are already reserved, you can often hop aboard and find an empty seat. Many European business people, when undecided as to which train they will be taking, make several advance reservations so as to cover all possibilities - and then forfeit the fee on unused reservations. This practice accounts for some unused seats being marked "reserved." If traveling without seat reservations, be careful not to waste time taking a reserved seat while the unreserved ones are being filled up. Check the seat chart outside each compartment or on each seat before you sit down. If you're ousted by the legitimate reservation holder, you may have to stand during the rest of the ride.

4. If the required advance time for making a seat reservation has run out, seek the conductor and, in your most charming manner, tell him (or her, although there are very few women conductors) your destination and seek his assistance in finding you a seat. As a brand of their own, train conductors are for the most part remarkably courteous, good humored, and cooperative and many, you will observe, welcome the opportunity of using their authority constructively.

5. Never, never discard a train ticket until after your trip has been fully completed and you have left the arrival station. You will frequently ride a train for hours without being asked to show a ticket or pass. Then, after you get off the train, you could discover that you are required to show your ticket or pass at the station exit, as is true in many London subway stations. If you have thrown your ticket away, you will undoubtedly end up having to buy a second one. Your best bet is to always hold onto your ticket, whether or not a conductor checks it.

Hotel Reservations

Once you have decided on the main elements, namely the amount of days, the specific cities, the trains and the routes, and train reservations you are ready to consider whether you want to reserve hotels in advance. There are pros and cons to both. In any case, all *Eurail Guide* recommendations are based on information recently verified by first-hand experience. The qualification "recently" is noteworthy, because quality of hotel and restaurant services are subject to periodic fluctuations. Management changes (and quality with it) faster than annually revised editions of any guide can wholly keep up with. When possible, consult competent travel agents, travel publications, and travel information sources that have current input from recent travelers. The best information comes from people who have just been there. To maximize your chances of landing great information, ask lots of questions.

In this guide, when faced with options, the preferences expressed tend to be oriented toward choices that maximize comfort and security. In most cases, this guide recommends its readers to reserve hotel accommodations well in advance, and, when possible, to reserve train seats whenever you are sure you want to be on a particular train on a certain date.

Some travelers object vehemently to such pre-planning tactics such as advanced reservations, claiming that you cannot be as footloose or carefree as you would like, linger where you have discovered unexpected attractions, or make impetuous detours or departures. There is no question that for those travelers forced to lead ordered routines, there are few activities that offer as much freedom as does train travel. The spontaneous choices you can make are vast. The feature that many people find irresistible about European trains is how easily one can, an hour after starting a ride going in one direction, abort at an approaching station and head elsewhere. Depending on how strongly this flexibility motivates you, and to what degree you are willing to endure the consequences of venturing into the unknown, advance hotel reservations may not be important to you.

On the other hand, if you ever have played an entire night of poker without holding one winning hand; or arrived in Copenhagen on the opening day of a World Bank Conference (no rooms within 20 miles); or traveled to Paris where the International Air Show opened on the day of your arrival, the most popular horse race on the Continent was being run the next day (no room within 30 miles), and your next stop was Dijon, where your first six choices of hotels were *complet*, even though nothing special was happening that week, you might want to re-think the advantages of advanced bookings.

From May through early October, European and non-European tourists pack all classes of hotels in leading European cities. Trade shows and business conventions pick up the slack instantly in September, October, March, and April. A hotel in Bordeaux (not Paris or Rome, mind you) responded to a request for reservations on July 13 that it was booked for the two nights needed in early October! Sometimes the difficulty of finding a room stems from a local holiday, a long weekend, a special event, or a large party that has booked all the rooms in a small region.

If you travel Europe without advance room reservations from March through October, it is wise to arrive in your destination city early in the day. Rooms available because of no-shows or last-minute cancellations frequently are taken before mid-afternoon. Otherwise you can spend a lot of time room hunting.

Upon arriving without a hotel reservation, go at once to the tourist accommodations desk in the train station. For a fee of $1 to $2, a host or hostess will telephone hotels, pensions, or bed and breakfasts to find you a room that comes close to your specifications. In certain cities (Amsterdam, Bergen, Brussels, etc.), this convenient service is not offered at the station but can be found at the city tourist office, often only across the road from the rail station, but sometimes quite a distance from it.

In the peak summer touring months you will find long lines and if, as is usually the case, your stay is brief, you will have to devote precious visiting time to obtain a room. When traveling in groups of two or more, it is effective for one person to remain at the station guarding the luggage while the other or others canvass the area near the station to find a room. All over Europe you will find many hotels within a radius of two or three blocks from the rail station. Many non-Europeans are unaware that stations even in the smallest cities have comfortable waiting rooms with upholstered chairs. If you follow this technique, be sure to use the shelter of these waiting rooms. Do not leave luggage unattended for even a few minutes. Aside from the risk of theft, Europeans are very sensitive to all potential risks of terrorism. In Paris and London train stations, the police tend to collect and blow-up all unattended bags.

Another housing solution used successfully by many is: get out of town immediately and stay in the suburbs, don't even attempt to battle the hustle and hassle of finding a hotel room downtown in a major city. This is possible, provided that the suburb is linked by train with the city you want to tour. Just pick a town of moderate size about 30–45 minutes train travel time away from a major metropolis and head there. On the plus side, you're more likely to find an affordable room. On the down side though, the town may be less interesting or downright dull and ugly and train service may be limited at night, forcing you to forego those theater tickets or late-night bar-hopping.

Preparing for an Autumn Tour

One thing that is nearly always overlooked in European, off-season itinerary planning is that after early September - and Fall is outstanding for touring Europe - English-language city sightseeing tours are often discontinued as the volume of tourists decline, particularly in important but smaller cities such as Avignon, Verona, Rouen, Tours, etc. If this poses a problem for you, in that you were counting on taking these city tours, there's no reason to despair. Nearly every city in Europe, even hamlets such as the charming port of Honfleur in Normandy, has a tourist office that supplies comprehensive folders in English. These folders include fine city maps, interesting descriptions of principal attractions and suggested walking tours which allow visitors to find on their own, and at their own pace, the most worthwhile historic sites, museums, churches, palaces, and other local high spots usually available in a motor coach sightseeing tour.

By early September, though, many city tourist offices run out of the current brochures. To insure against this disappointment there is a precaution you can take. Early in the year, write to the cities you plan to visit and request copies of literature and tourist maps in English. This can also help you decide what to visit and how long to spend at a destination.

Simply address your request to "Tourist Office" in each respective city or village. You'll be surprised how much this easy preparation will add to your travel enjoyment.

Documenting Yourself

It is more than useful, it is necessary, to arm yourself with a varied collection of up-to-date and informative guides, maps, and books if you want to be an informed and intelligent traveler. There are literally hundreds of sources of published information, ranging from great collections of general travel guides covering entire continents to highly specialized and thematic guides covering everything from restaurants and hotels to churches, cemeteries, wines, boutiques and even Paris *arrondissements*. You neither want to load yourself down, nor spend your whole trip with your nose in a book, but a carefully chosen selection of documentation is essential. As Alvin Toffler so poignantly documented in Powershift, it is information, even more so than cash, that opens doors in our contemporary world. This is equally true in the realm of individual travel, especially when it comes to destinations that are experiencing rapid change. Here are a few helpful suggestions on how to "document" yourself before venturing off.

Consumer Reports Travel Letter   Consumers Union produces a highly useful 24-page monthly newsletter on travel called the Consumer Reports Travel Letter (CRTL), in which worldwide travel services, money saving opportunities on major travel purchases, and astute tips on avoiding travel scams and overcharges are discussed. Throughout the year, CRTL presents annual country-by-country evaluations of train passes, company-by-company comparisons of rental car rates, ratings of major airline and hotel services, and a wide variety of strategies for finding the best travel values and keeping travel costs to a minimum. CRTL was one of the first consumer travel publications to highlight discount airline tickets from consolidators and to describe and compare half-price hotel programs. Like other Consumers Union publications, CRTL remains wholly unbiased and is careful about not accepting advertising or free travel services. For its $39 annual subscription, write to: CRTL, Dept. 'E', 101 Truman Avenue, Yonkers, NY 10703, or telephone (800) 234-1970.

Thomas Cook European Timetable   The venerable *Thomas Cook European Timetable* has been published in England consistently (under seven other titles) since 1873 with the sole interruption occurring during the war years. Its younger sibling, the *Overseas Timetable*, founded in 1981, was prompted by the increased interest in train travel outside of Europe. These publications have become the bibles of reliable and comprehensive train schedules for much of the world. The *European Timetable* (covering Britain and the Continent), scheduled for monthly publication on the first day of each month, comes out with great regularity although sometimes with slight delays. The *Overseas Timetable*, which covers the rest of the world, is issued every other month, beginning in January. Summer European train schedules appear in the June, July, August and September *European Timetable* issues. The latter contains an advance Winter Supplement. Similarly, the February through May issues contain advance Summer Service Supplements.

    In addition to train, boat, and bus schedules, these publications, codified with an extensive array of symbols for services and other data, which are translated into ordinary language at the start of each edition, also provide information on available food services and sleeping accommodations.

    The Thomas Cook publications are condensations of much more extensive national timetables published by all major countries. Inexpensive and complete national timetables can be purchased at rail stations in many countries.

    Because some countries do not offer their own timetables, or run short of them, Thomas Cook's is valuable for carrying along on a trip as well as for studying at home while planning an itinerary. Numerous readers have reported that having a copy while touring allows them to make impromptu changes in travel plans. One flaw in Thomas Cook's system consists of its reliance at times on individuals of varying competence in underdeveloped countries where governments have not responded to pleas for "official information."

Caution: As Thomas Cook states in each edition, the services shown are subject to alteration, and travelers should recheck departure times upon arriving in each station.

Both publications can be obtained in North America from Forsyth Travel Library, P.O. Box 2975, Shawnee Mission, KS 66201, or by telephoning at 800-FORSYTH, Monday-Saturday, 09:00-16:30 Central Standard Time. Visa and Master-Card are accepted. Both cost $24.95, plus $4 for shipping. A combined purchase of the *European Timetable* and the Rail Map of Europe costs $33.95 plus shipping.

Eurail Timetable/Horaire Eurail/Eurail Fahrplan   The Eurail Timetable/ Horaire Eurail/Eurail Fahrplan contains most connections between important cities in Western Europe. It is sold at major European rail stations and is highly useful.

Horaires Lignes Affaires   There is another timetable, specialized and far more condensed than Thomas Cook's, that is free. Offered by the French National Rail-roads (see North American addresses), the very useful 32-page mini-folder is called *Horaires Lignes Affaires* (Business Route Timetable). Containing May-September schedules, it has timetables for many trains that connect French cities with each other and with foreign countries.

Other Useful Sources

Insight Guides   In total, there are over 200 titles in the *Insight Guide* series covering destinations large and small all around the globe. *Insight Guides* introduce a traveler to a destination with history, culture, and color photography. Read them before you go for "insight" in to the culture you're about to experience or peruse after you return from your trip to remind you of the sights you've just seen.

Insight Pocket Guides   Unlike most travel guides, Insight Pocket Guides are designed for those on a limited schedule, who need essential information in a format that is clear, concise and easy to access. In each Insight Pocket Guide, travelers will find practical and specific advice on what to do and where to go without the clutter and unnecessary detail found in many planning guides. As with the Insight Guides, Pocket Guides cover destinations all over the world and have brilliant color photography.

Insight Guides and Insight Pocket Guides are available in most travel and trade bookstores. To order by phone in the U.S.: 800-225-3362 or Canada: (416) 475-9126.

CHAPTER 4

Don't Miss The Train!

Cities with More than One Train Station

After arriving three days ago from London's Victoria Station at Paris's Gare du Nord station, you've spent a few absolutely lovely days in the French City of Lights, and now it's time to say au revoir and move on. Your train for Marseilles leaves in an hour and you've properly taken the *Métro* across town, blew kisses to the Eiffel Tower, and have returned in blissful innocence to the same station where you first arrived. You look up at the board of departures and gasp; there are no trains to Marseilles! "Impossible," you whelp, you've paid for secure reservations. You rush to the information window ready to scream or sue somebody. There is a line - a woman with lots of gold jewelry, a French poodle in each arm, and a cigarette dangling from her lips, is inquiring about the car-train to Bezier over the Toussaint long-weekend. There are now only ten minutes before your supposed departure time and you are jumping out of your skin. Finally you reach the front of the line only to learn from a SNCF clerk who keeps saying in his accented English, "Too bad, too bad," that Paris has six major train stations, and you needed to be at the Gare de Lyon, not the Gare du Nord, and now there's no time to make the departure. "Too bad." You'll lose the TGV reservation fee and, worse, the next TGV gets you to Marseilles too late to attend the Prince concert you reserved tickets for on your Amex card, and that cute hotel that you'd reserved four months earlier promised to hold the room only until 6 P.M. And tomorrow you need time to visit the museum before catching the train to Genoa. Everything is going wrong. Panic. Sniffle.

This cruel dramatization is just a friendly reminder that major cities have more than one major train station. Determine beforehand whether your departure or transfer city has more than one station, and if so, make sure you know from which one the train on which you are planning to continue your trip departs. Inquire at the information booth upon arrival or simply consult the Thomas Cook European Timetable. Do not rely on getting that information an hour or so before your departure from someone such as your hotel clerk or a taxi or bus driver. If you are making a transfer, be certain that there is adequate time to get from one station to the other.

Here is a handy reference chart listing the 70 European cities with more than one rail station.

Antwerp	Dublin	Lodz	Prague
Athens	Dunkerque	London	Ramsgate

Barcelona	Essen	Lyon	Rome
Basel	Exeter	Madrid	Rotterdam
Belfast	Folkestone	Malmo	San Sebastian
Belgrade	Geneva	Manchester	Seville
Berlin	Genoa	Marseilles	Southampton
Bilbao	Glasgow	Milan	Stockholm
Boulogne	Halsingborg	Moscow	Tilbury
Brussels	Hamburg	Munich	Tours
Bucharest	Harwich	Naples	Turin
Budapest	Hendaye	Newhaven	Venice
Calais	Irun	Oporto	Vienna
Casablanca	Le Havre	Orleans	Warsaw
Cologne	Leningrad	Oslo	Weymouth
Como	Liege	Paris	Wiesbaden
Copenhagen	Lisbon	Portsmouth	Zurich
Dover	Liverpool		

A Handy Vocabulary Chart for the Word "Train Station"

estacion	(Spain)
statione	(Italy)
Bahnhof	(Austria, Germany, and Switzerland)
la gare	(France)
Train station	(U.K. and Ireland)
Gare	(Belgium and Luxembourg)
Järnvägstation	(Sweden)
togstation (s-tog)	(Danish)

Finding Your Train Car: Train Splitting

How can one fail to admire the superhuman efficiency of Europe's vast international rail systems? Thousands of trains daily transport millions of people while achieving a dependability factor that is nearly perfect. An important part of this remarkable capacity is the technique of avoiding unnecessary duplication of personnel and equipment by switching cars, splitting trains, and calibrating transfer times between connections to a bare minimum.

There are a few simple things to remember when boarding your train. Before you leave the central hall of the station, ask if the car in which you will be starting your journey is going all the way to your destination. Often it is scheduled to be switched to another train or will at a particular city break from the rest of the train and join a piece of another train heading to a completely different destination. If this is the case, you must know at what point you must transfer from this train to another train en route to your destination or switch to another car on the initial train you've boarded. It's easier than it sounds.

If your car is to be switched to another train, note the name of the city where the switching will occur, the time it will take place, and the name of the stop just prior to the switching point. When you are on the correct track, and you are ready to board your train, your last step is to mount the correct car. Where a train originally consists of cars that are eventually going to different destinations, each car is clearly marked with the name of the city where it originated and the name of the city where it will terminate. Frequently, the sign will also designate some of the key cities where it makes stops. For example,

VENEZIA

Bologna — Firenze

ROMA

This sign shows that this train car originated in Venezia, makes stops at Bologna and Firenze, and terminates in Roma. If you're not versed in one or more foreign languages, you might find the names of certain cities to be less than obvious to you. Your mind will quickly learn to make the simple deduction that Venezia is Venice, Firenze is Florence, and Roma, of course, is Rome. It's a little trickier when, for example, you're boarding a French train headed for Prague via Germany. Or an Italian train heading to France. Did you know that Paris in Italian is Parigi or that Antwerp is the Flemish name for Anvers? Or that the German city of Aachen is Aix-la-Chapelle in French?

Next to the foldout steps that lead up into the train car you'll always see either the number "1" or "2" written on the side of the car or flashed on a digital panel, designating first-class or second-class seats. You may find a first-class car coupled to a second-class car, both marked with the same origin-destination sign. Or, a single car may be marked "1" at one end and "2" at the other end, indicating that one half is first-class and the other half is second-class. Although train cars are numbered, the order often gets shuffled. Generally, the first-class cars are found closest to the station hall and thus require less of a walk for the higher paying customers.

If you decide to sit in another car that will not be going all the way to your destination, what you must be careful about is that a car change or splitting doesn't occur while you are several cars away from your seat (and from your baggage, which usually is stowed either in your compartment or at the end of your car). You don't want to end up going in a direction that is not in your plans, and you certainly don't want to chug off to Luxembourg while your suitcases are heading to Munich or Vienna!

One U.S. Army colonel traveling with his family reported such an experience: while off to grab a sandwich in the bar car, the train split. "I got about as far as what had been the middle of the train…and there was no more train! I was heading off towards an unknown direction, without my family, at approximately 80 mph. with all of our money but without my passport or train ticket." The brave soldier who'd gone involuntarily AWOL finally circled back and met up with his worried wife and kids in Metz, "practically in a pool of tears."

Moral: Don't stray from your car while the train is stopped in a station. When traveling as a family or small group, each person should carry his or her own money, passport, and ticket or train pass.

Train Changing: The Connection Time

Frequently you will find that you cannot take a train directly to some point, and will need to change trains at a designated city. In many cases the connections are very convenient, so that you change from one train to another with only a short waiting period at the transfer station. For example, there is no direct train from Zurich to the popular location of Locarno, but the Zurich-Milan train arrives in Bellinzona at 12:33, and a train for Locarno departs Bellinzona just three minutes later at 12:36. This is completely normal and should not create too much stress. The track for the Bellinzona-Locarno train is next to the track on which you arrive from Zurich, making this change effortless. Even if the Zurich-Milan train is running a few minutes late - and you will be amazed how rarely trains in Western Europe are even slightly off schedule - your walk from one train to the other on this connection is about ten feet, and in the case of short delays the second train, or local train, will wait for the first train, or principal train.

On the other hand, international trains from Eastern countries (Turkey, Greece, etc.) usually arrive late due to delays at border-crossings. In these cases, and in the case of short transfer time in large city stations, the problem is the distance between tracks. Be ready to step off the first train as soon as it pulls into the transfer station. You may find you are arriving on Track #2 and departing from Track #21, a considerable distance and invariably involving first descending into the underground walkway that connects all tracks, and then climbing up the steps leading to your departure track. This transfer problem is compounded if your first train arrives late and the second train is an express train which cannot detain its scheduled departure time.

Normally your first train will arrive on schedule and you have more than enough time to make the change. However, it is best to inquire on board the first train with the conductor for the number of the track on which you are arriving and the number of the track from which your departing train leaves. You might have to make a mad dash for it. Sometimes you'll have to jump on the closest car of a train that is just about to pull out and then weave your way through the corridors a half a mile until you finally make it to your reserved seat or at least to a car that is heading to your destination. Such intense situations make for exciting stories, but do tend to be rather stressful.

One American expatriate from Boston writes about a harrowing experience worth sharing with other train travelers. Several years ago, he dropped off his wife and four-year-old son one Sunday in front of the Frankfurt main station, 30 minutes in advance of their train departure to Berlin, and then went off to return their car rental only to find that the Sunday drop-off point was two kilometers away. Unable to find a ride back or hail a taxi, he was forced to frantically hitchhike back to the station, and finally ran searching madly for the right track, noticing on the large clock overhead that it was exactly the time of departure! The right track eluded him and he rushed over to the train board and gleaned the schedule. Track 17. Off he dashed to the far end of the station only to spot that the Berlin train was already pulling out of *Gleis* 17! Warning bells were cautioning to keep away from the moving train. Sprinting behind and then alongside the last car in a scene reminiscent of the war film "Von Ryan's Express," he began slapping wildly at the glass panel of the already shut train door and screaming out of desperation in his broken German, "Mein Kind, mein Kind ist im Zug," (My child is on the train!). Adrenaline pumped, and, miraculously, the massive Bundesbahn locomotive - already half-way out of the station screeched to a halt. It was the first time in history that a tourist had ever stopped a passenger train in Germany; and the conductor, red with anger and ready to slap the obstructive traveler with a stiff fine, collared the man demanding that he quickly board the train and "produce the child." That is what he did, saving himself from prosecution and finally joining his family on the trip to Berlin.

Know your track number!

A Handy Vocabulary Chart for the Word "Track"

Anden	(Spain)
Binario	(Italy)
Gleis	(Austria, Germany, and Switzerland)
Perron	(Denmark)
Quai	(France)
Spår	(Sweden)
Spor	(Holland and Belgium)
Spor	(Norway)
Track	(U.K. and Ireland)
Voie	(Belgium and Luxembourg)

Most train stops in Europe are efficiently very brief: two or three minutes. Where a stop is fairly generous, say 20 minutes or more, it is often because some car on the train is being switched to another train and possibly also to another track in that station. You may be seated facing forward when you pull into a station and depart riding backwards!

Unwary passengers are apt to get out of the train at a stop and wander away, discovering too late that their train has left without them! When you have the urge to stretch your legs, get some fresh air, and check out the trackside attractions, try not to venture away more than a few feet away from the door of the train car. That way, if your car is being switched or the stop is shorter than you anticipated, you can jump back aboard.

Car-Sleeper Express Service

Europe's "Car-Sleeper Express Service" is one of the fastest growing train services in Europe today. Essentially you can sleep in a *couchette* or sleeping compartment on the same train that carries your auto. You can also ship your car ahead on an "Auto Express" while you ride on another train, and find your car waiting for you at your destination. Started by French Rail in 1957, this service is now offered in Austria, Belgium, Britain, Holland, Italy, Spain, and Germany, and links cities in those countries as well as in Portugal and Switzerland. The system annually moves more than 500,000 people and more than 160,000 cars. Inquire with the national rail offices or agents in your country. If you are buying a car in Europe with the idea of using it overseas and then shipping it home, this service might be very useful.

CHAPTER 5

Valuable Train and Travel Tips

Before Leaving Home: A Few Precautions

• It is always wise to make photocopies of your airline ticket, the identification page of your passport, your driver's license, and the credit cards you take with you. Leave one set of photocopies at home and take another set with you, storing it in a separate place from the originals.

• Leave a list of the serial numbers of your traveler's checks at home. Take a copy of that list on your trip, but keep separate from the checks. As you cash each check, tally the ones that remain unredeemed. This way you can spot if there is anything missing.

• If you wear glasses or contact lenses, pack an extra set. If there are any particular medicines you need, bring along an ample supply as well as a copy of prescriptions and generic names of those drugs. Keep these in your carry-on luggage. Leave medicines in their original labeled containers so as not to complicate customs processing. If any medications contain narcotics, carry a letter from your physician attesting to your need to take them. Leave a copy of your medical and dental records with a relative or friend.

• Include a tag or label with your name and address inside each piece of luggage, and lock your bags.

• Leave a copy of your itinerary with a relative or friend should it be necessary to contact you in case of an emergency. Some people contact their consulate when traveling in a foreign country. This can be particularly helpful when traveling in dangerous or unstable regions, but is otherwise unnecessary.

• Find out if your insurance policies cover you for theft, loss, accident, and illness while you are in another country. If yes, write down the procedures to follow in case an incident occurs.

What Weather to Expect

These general descriptions of seasonal weather patterns may be at least moderately helpful in your planning of where to go and when.

• North America and Europe
Spring: April-June, Summer: July-September, Fall: October-December. Winter: January-March.

• Mexico and Central America
Very rainy May-October.

• South America, Australia and New Zealand
Spring: October-December, Summer: January-March, Fall: April-June, Winter: July-September.

• Asia
Year-round tropical heat in Hong Kong, India, Indonesia, Malaysia, the Philippines, Singapore, Thailand, and the South Pacific islands. Typhoon season is June-September in Japan, August to mid-October in Taiwan. The monsoon months in India are June-August. The rainy season in most of Asia is May-September but is June-November in the Philippines.

• North Africa
Extremely hot, except December-February in Egypt.

• Middle East
Israel has mild Mediterranean temperatures year round. Iran, Iraq, Jordan, Lebanon, and Syria have four seasons similar to those in North America and Europe.

Customs Procedures and Duty-Free Shopping

It is good to know a few things about customs regulations before you begin your journey. Foreign-made articles taken abroad from the U.S. are subject to duty each time they are brought back into the U.S., unless you have acceptable proof of prior possession such as a bill of sale, insurance policy, jeweler's appraisal, or receipt of purchase. Watches, cameras, tape recorders, or articles identified by serial number or permanently affixed markings may be taken to the U.S. Customs office nearest you and registered before departure. The certificate of registration is valid for all future trips. This may be a slight hassle obtaining, but it is an effective way of being reassured if you travel with highly valuable or duty-susceptible items.

As for duty-free shopping, items in "duty-free" shops in major airports are not always the bargains they are played up to be. Only by comparison shopping can you be sure whether it is worthwhile buying that Hermés scarf, Mont Blanc pen, or Sony Walkman at the duty-free shop. Cigarettes and alcohol do tend to be well-priced. Remember that duty within EU countries has been erased. There is complete free trade. Furthermore, upon returning to your home country (non-EU) you may sometimes find that you must pay duty on your "duty-free" purchases. Duty-free means only that the airport store from which you made a purchase did not have to pay a duty when it bought the article.

To know what you can and cannot bring back to the country of your residence and what the duty tax (if any) will be when returning with articles purchased abroad, request a copy of the helpful booklet "Know Before You Go" published by the U.S. Customs Service, Custom Information Section, 6 World Trade Center, New York, N.Y. 10048.

Only a fool tries to smuggle through customs an article on which there is an embargo or outright ban or attempts to avoid paying duty for something that is subject to import tax. If caught, the penalty when entering the United States can be a combination of having the article seized, paying a fine on the amount of the U.S. value, and being subject to criminal prosecution. For example, if you buy a $1,000 piece of jade in Hong Kong and don't declare it, you'd be in violation of the 1993 law that stipulates that there is an exemption only on the first $400 of goods entering the U.S. which were purchased anywhere outside the U.S. other than the U.S. Virgin Islands, American Samoa, and Guam. After that first $400, the flat duty for the next $1,000 is 10%. Technically you would owe a duty of $60. In trying to avoid this $60 tax, you could lose the jade, be forced to pay a fine of $1,000, and face a jail sentence.

Another point: Do not try to bring home fruits, vegetables, plants, animal or fish products, or any perishable foods that cannot be cleared by your country's agriculture department. Without such clearance, it is a certainty such items will be confiscated and you may be subject to a fine. One traveler from Portland recently returned from Paris to the U.S. carrying the uneaten apple from his airline meal. He did not declare this food item and was fined $50 in Newark Airport. At Boston's Logan Airport, Agriculture Department officials use beagle dogs to sniff out smuggled foods and plants.

Overcoming Jet Lag

When your trip involves between a five- and nine-hour time change, those first few days of your overseas trip can be sluggish. There are ways, though, that you can greatly reduce the fatigue of jet lag and be more energetic sooner on your journey.

First, when traveling in a closed compartment such as airplanes or train compartments, drink as much water as you can to overcome dehydration resulting from lack of fresh air or from airconditioning. Remember that the more alcoholic beverages you absorb, the faster your body dehydrates. It's wiser to eat lightly or at least refrain from overeating if you want to feel better upon arriving. Dress comfortably by wearing loose clothing. Exercise as much as possible in flight or when in a closed compartment for a long time.

At one time SAS and Lufthansa published concise booklets describing exercises that can be performed by passengers while seated. Northwest Airlines shows an inflight aerobics video on its overseas flights. If you don't mind seeming ridiculous, mimic the motions involved in rowing a boat and picking apples from an over-head branch. Rise up and sit down repeatedly. Alternately, raise your knees to your elbows. Nod your head and turn it vigorously from side to side. Turn your hands at the wrist while spreading and closing your fingers. Lift your heels up and then place them down firmly, while placing pressure on your toes. With toes up, rotate your feet in large circles. European travelers of course will think you've lost your marbles, but as the French are so fond of saying while shrugging shoulders and pursing lips, "Tant-pis" (What the heck!). You'll feel fine tomorrow.

Traveling by Night

There are some advantages to traveling by night train. You can hop from one place to another without sacrificing daytime activities in either the departure city or the arrival city. Also, by traveling at night in a regular sitting compartment, not in an extra-fare couchette or sleeping compartment, the holder of a Eurailpass can make a substantial contribution to a budget by dispensing with room rent. Attention: Even on comfortable trains, a night in a seat is not going to leave you in the best of moods in the morning. And, although you can wash in train bathrooms, the water is cold and not drinkable, the hygienic state of things is not always up to snuff, especially at the end of a long journey, and the movement of the speeding train makes it a bit tough to shave or put on or take off makeup.

On some trains the seats in the regular sitting compartments can be adjusted so that your seat and the one facing you to either come together or nearly meet, and many who are fortunate enough to be in a compartment that is not full are able to stretch out. This is one technique for eliminating hotel bills, which many students and other economy prone tourists have used successfully. However, if the seat opposite you is occupied, both you and the other passenger are going to spend the night sitting up. On a packed night train from Cairo to Luxor, a student from Philadelphia bragged of actually sleeping in the luggage rack above the seats. In the summer, be prepared to see everything.

The offsetting drawbacks of night trains are considerable. The pleasant act of meeting and conversing with Europeans and tourists from other parts of the world is reduced when you travel at night. And, of course, the scenery is se-verely dulled. If you are a light sleeper by nature, it's probable that you won't sleep well on trains, and certainly not while curled up in a seat.

Train sleeping accommodations vary from one European country to another, but generally they consist of *couchette* compartments (berths) or sleeping car compartments (beds). A blanket and a pillow are provided for each berth in a couchette compartment. There is no way to tuck the blanket in. It just slides around during the night. The sheet is often a fitted pouch which functions as top sheet and bottom sheet - you slip in between the halves. Some people undress fully or partially for bed, but a lot of this depends on your own sense of comfort in that each couchette in second class consists of six bunks, three on each side with a bottom, middle, and upper berth each. Privacy is thus minimal, yet dignity is never sacrificed.

The first-class *couchette* is a berth with four instead of six bunks (consisting of two rows of two bunks each). The 1995 price for each first-class bunk runs around $15 for holders of a first-class ticket or train pass. With either a first- or second-class ticket or with a train pass, the 1995 price per berth is around $23 in a four-berth compartment, $15 in a six-berth compartment.

Sleeping car compartments, called *wagon-lits* in French, and *schlafwagen* in German, are available in either a "small" or a "large" format. All are equipped with a power plug and a wash basin. The newer and faster trains have both 220- and 110- volt current, whereas the older trains only have the local 220. The small compartments convert to one, two, or three beds.

European rail authorities have stated repeatedly that specific prices for these sleeping car compartments (which vary in different areas of Europe) will not be available until the moment the reservation is confirmed. It is fair to estimate using the 1994 prices. For example, the Paris-Zurich night trip, with one bed in a small compartment, would cost about $105 plus the price of a first-class ticket ($117), thus a total of $222. For a large compartment with two beds, requiring two first-class tickets at $117, add about $70 per person for the compartment, thus $187 per person.

At those prices it might be better to sleep in a first-class hotel!

Note that neither *couchettes* nor compartments are included in the Eurailpass or any national train passes.

Don't worry about oversleeping or missing your early morning destination. You can always rely on being awakened, and not so gently, by the voice of a stationmaster bellowing over the public address system at stops along the way. Twenty minutes or so before you arrive at your destination, the train conductor will rap his knuckles on the door of your compartment and yell something like, "Leipzig, twenty minutes." When the train crosses international borders during the night, it is completely normal for the train conductor to collect passports before everyone goes to sleep. He will present the documents to the border police and return them to you in the morning. This avoids unnecessary disturbances. With the easing of internal European borders with the EU (European Union), border crossings have become extremely lax, although some routes in the summer are watched more closely for potential drug and terrorist movements.

Baggage

Karl Baedeker wrote in 1891, in the fourteenth edition of his Switzerland Handbook For Travelers: "The traveler will save both time and money by planning his tour carefully before leaving home. A super abundance of luggage infallibly increases the delays, annoyances, and expenses of travel. To be provided with enough luggage, and no more, may be considered the second golden rule for the traveler."

Criticism you will hear most about rail travel in Europe concerns the problems of storing and handling luggage. Don't count on being able to get a porter - many small cities don't have them. Nearly all the large cities with porters have too few. Some stations provide self-service carts, but the stations which do so often don't have enough of them at peak times.

An effective procedure if you travel in pairs is for one of you to guard your luggage while the other hurries toward the station to find a cart and returns to the track with it.

When boarding a train, you want to avoid the difficulty of hauling your luggage down the narrow corridors of several cars. Before your train arrives, examine the train diagram on the platform. The sequence of cars and the platform location for each car are indicated for all long-distance trains. Try to place yourself and your luggage at the correct site for boarding your car. This little procedure will simplify your life.

On many trains there is a storage area for luggage at one or at both ends of the car. On most trains you have to store your baggage on a rack above your seat, which tends to be very high. Lifting a 30-pound (or heavier) weight above one's head can be a physical strain for the elderly or those who have a physical disability.

On the whole, it is much better to travel with two small, relatively light-weight suitcases or duffel bags per person than with one monstrous case. The small ones are easier to lift, and there's a better chance of being able to store them under the seat or in station lockers.

Some trains have a baggage car, although the newer and faster trains have baggage services in which the luggage, bikes, etc. don't necessarily travel on the same train with you. Using the traditional baggage car is almost always inconvenient, and although the charge is reasonable - about $6 per piece, with a limit of 66 pounds each - it is more expensive than having your cases with you in your own car or in your compartment. Also, unless you verify that your luggage is to travel on the same train as you, it may go on another train - possibly arriving a day after your arrival. If you want luggage to arrive at your destination prior to your arrival, you can arrange to send it in advance and it will be held in the "checked luggage" room at your destination. Usually, no charge is made for the first two or three days of storage, however, after that, a small daily fee must be paid when claiming the bags.

Additionally when your bags are in the baggage car, you don't have access to them, and you may have to wait up to 30 minutes for your cases to be unloaded. In some countries, a well placed tip can help convince the porter to unload your gear surprisingly fast. Waiting for cases to be unloaded, in turn, delays you in getting to the room reservation desk at the tourist accommodation office inside the station - a delay that can cost you getting a decent room that night. Every minute counts in obtaining an available room during peak travel days in the high season. Waiting at the baggage car also delays you in getting into what can often be a very long line for taxis.

When you arrive in a city with more luggage than you need for that destination, savvy travelers opt to store excess stuff in a station locker. Others wisely return to the station the night before their departure so as to store luggage in a locker and facilitate the haul to the station the following morning.

Although there are baggage checkrooms at nearly all major rail stations, using a checkroom instead of a rental locker eats up precious time you could have used more pleasantly and productively. There are frequently long lines both when you leave your luggage and again when you are claiming it. If you use checkrooms instead of rental lockers, be sure to leave yourself adequate time prior to your train's departure to retrieve your suitcases. And, although these check-rooms are secure, it isn't all that reassuring leaving any valuables in unlocked luggage.

The most convenient and safest method of storing luggage is to place it in a 24-hour rental locker. Unfortunately the lockers present their own set of problems. Several European stations have too few lockers, have strict time limitations, and are too small for large bags. Again, small suitcases make better sense.

Another wise maneuver is to have small change on hand for each country you visit. It goes without saying, the lockers in each country work only with the local coins. You cannot use a *kroner* in France, or a *franc* in Denmark!

Eating on Trains

Food in the dining cars tends to be expensive, and the choice can be limited, although in the last few years the quality of food services has radically improved. In restaurant cars of *de luxe* trains, the lunch is a fixed menu, very tasty, and highly caloric. On ordinary trains, the restaurant car food is adequate…but still a bit pricey. On the French TGV, the bar cars are very comfortable and the choice and quality of the sandwiches is surprisingly good. Not only can you buy sandwiches and drinks, you can purchase newspapers and magazines, telephone cards for the phones onboard, cognac, and some gift items.

Dining in the restaurant car of a train speeding across Europe has to be one of the most graceful and elegant experiences in life. If you can manage to relax about the prices and not see the linen table cloth and heavy silverware as pretensions but as remnants of an old European style, you should have a jolly good time.

Here are a few examples of meals (with prices) on major European train routes. Amsterdam-Paris "Etoile du Nord" serves crayfish, duck or lamb chops, potatoes *Lyonnaise*, steamed vegetables, cheeses and rolls, and pastry for a cool $55. Dinner on the Oslo-Bergen trip may include salad, poached salmon with boiled potatoes, and beer for $42. Dinner on the Paris-Lisbon run of the "Sud Express" can be $36 for vegetable soup, wild turkey with rice, fava beans, flan and fruit, and coffee. Tuck in your napkin and enjoy. You can't do this between Albany and Buffalo! Note that on many trains, you must reserve a seat in the restaurant car for the entire trip if you want lunch or dinner.

Both budget travelers and many of those who can't afford the meals served on trains buy their food at a market or delicatessen or one of those great French charcuteries before they board a train. A hunk of cheese and some bread, salads, meats, patés, fruits, and wine can make for a copious and sensuous, yet informal eating experience.

Before making the 12-hour ride from Copenhagen to Amsterdam, try buying a dozen, delicious smorre-brod sandwiches in a shop just a block from the Copenhagen station. The variety includes shrimp, salmon, ham, chicken, and beef, all garnished with tasty cucumbers, asparagus, and tomatoes. For four meals for two people you can eat well at a total of $36. If you find the idea of "picnicking" attractive, you can ask your hotel or *pensione* to pack a lunch for you, or you can purchase food either at a store near the station, in a restaurant at the station, from a food market inside the station, or, along the way, from vendors that push carts up and down the platforms at many station stops.

You will find restaurants and food stores located in many principal rail stations. Food stores in the Copenhagen, Stuttgart, Vienna, and Zurich rail stations offer meat, cheeses, salads, breads, pastries, etc. that are excellent. In Germany, it is only in the main train station of a city that you can buy food after the traditional closing times of most shops: 6:30 P.M.

Remember in any case that it's always a good idea to bring along some food and a bottle of water on a long journey.

Airport-City Rail Connections
Here is a handy list of fast train travel times in minutes between major cities and their airports.
Amsterdam (18 minutes)
Barcelona (18)
Brussels (20)
Frankfurt (14)
London (50 minutes from Heathrow, 30 minutes from Gatwick)
Malaga (12)
Paris (37 minutes from De Gaulle, 35 minutes from Orly)
Rome (24)
Vienna (25)
Zurich (11)
(For a complete listing see Table #5 in Thomas Cook's *European Timetable*.)

Lost Money and Passports
Losing or having your money or passport stolen is a certain way to spoil at least a part of your trip. The best precaution is to carry a minimal amount of cash at one time. Traveler's checks and major credit cards are safer. Remember to record the numbers in a safe place. Also guard your return airplane ticket as closely as your cash, traveler's checks, and passport. Each year, approximately 3,000 U.S. pass-

ports are stolen and another 11,000 are lost. There is an increasingly aggressive market for American and European passports in Latin America and Asia. So take precautions.

If, despite all your precautions, you discover that your passport has been taken or is simply missing, don't panic. Here's what you do. First, notify the local police and obtain a signed copy of the police report. Take this document to the local office of your country's consulate. It is not necessary to go to your embassy: It is your consulate, not your embassy, that will assist you by issuing a replacement passport. Obtaining a replacement is expedited if you can provide the passport number. Otherwise, you might have a few days to wait. If, in addition to the passport number, you have a certified copy of your birth certificate or certificate of citizenship, the consulate usually can issue a new passport the same day without telexing or wiring the State Department back home. In order to issue a new passport, two ID photos are required. Note that U.S. passport requirements include very specific dimensions for photos, which are obtainable at only certain photographers or photo stores. Consulates always have a list of places that can make these photos in each foreign city.

Obviously, it's best not to lose your papers. The delay of missed connections, additional hotel bills, and taxis (to police, consulate, photographer, airline office, etc.) can amount to a terrible expense.

Day Rooms

Many non-Europeans are unfamiliar with an extremely convenient service called "day rooms" available at some rail stations. With this accommodation, the tenant has privacy, a place to change clothes, and sometimes even bathing facilities. Some day rooms have beds. The advantages of a rail station day room over a conventional hotel room are that it is usually cheaper and it is located at the station.

Last-Minute Checklist

Here are several important tips that can greatly increase the pleasure (or reduce the struggle) of your international travel.

• Carry as little luggage as possible. You will arrive at many rail stations where it is a long walk from the train to the taxis (often requiring walking up and down stairs) and will find that there are neither porters nor carts. If the luggage you take is a burden, bring along a lightweight folding luggage rack.

• Bring a bottle of mineral water on any long trip. Most trains only provide drinking water in the bar car.

• Pack soft-ply toilet paper, wash-and-dry packets, and plastic bags. The bags are useful for storing leftover food items, wet soap and damp or dirty laundry.

Signs—The International Language

What follows is a sampling of helpful signs you'll find in train stations all over the world.

Language. Don't worry. Europeans like to practice their conversational English, especially on trains. For detailed information, consult the English-speaking staff at tourist offices, information bureaus, and hotels. At the railroad stations, pictograms lead you not only to the information desk but to any other facility you may be looking for. There are also the highly visible and efficient timetables posted inside the railroad station for get-it-yourself train information. Once you acquire the knack of reading them (and we shall tell you how, later on), they will get you on the right train at the right time on the right track.

Information

Temporary Luggage Storage. At almost every large station you'll find coin-operated lockers. Else, use the special baggage storage indicated by a pictogram and/or the legend: CONSIGNE DES BAGGAGES . . . GEPAECKAUFBEWAHRUNG . . . CONSIGNA DE EQUIPAJES . . . DEPOSITO BAGAGLIO. You'll get a claim check which you have to present when you pick your luggage up again.

Baggage
check room

Locker

Checking Your Luggage Through. Time and circumstances permitting, take your bulky luggage or bicycle along on your train, but not with you. Wherever international border crossings and train regulations don't stand in your way, avoid the hassle by checking your extra pieces through to your destination, to ride in the luggage-car. The right counter for this service is indicated by a pictogram.

Luggage registration
office

Door-to-Door Luggage Service. If you really want to travel light in France or Germany—with a claim check instead of luggage—find out whether your train station in the city you're in is one of those which pick up your luggage where you're staying and deliver it at your next stay. If that's the case, the small service fee is worth every penny of it.

Baggage Claim

Border and Customs Control. Be in your seat. Immigration officials will inspect your passport and whatever visa or other required documents right in your compartment, while the train moves across border points. You will be asked whether you have anything to declare, but as a foreign tourist in transit, especially with a EURAILPASS or STUDENT-RAIL-PASS, you will be given the appropriate considerations.

Customs

Your Helpful Porter. You'll recognize him by his uniform or official badge. You can usually find one as your cab pulls up to the station. If not, look for him inside. Consult the proper pictogram to find the porters' room. You can rely on your porter to get you to the right track, train, and car. He will put you in a smoker or non-smoker, as you wish. will try his best to find a vacant window-seat, and will place your luggage into the overhead rack.

Call for porter

Washroom Facilities. You can freshen up in a "W.C." (Water Closet) at either end of your car. In most long distance trains next to the "WC" are separate Washrooms. And remember not to drink the tap water; it is not potable.

WC

Rest rooms

A Seat Reservation. Even though you can travel on a European train in most cases without a seat reservation, it's always nice to have a reserved seat—at a window, if possible, or where you want your lunch or dinner served (yes, advance reservations can be made on some TEE trains for meals to be served in your seat). EURAILPASS and STUDENT-RAILPASS holders must pay for seat reservations, but it's very little for a lot of convenience.

Reservation

Changing Money. A railroad station is a good place to exchange the bills and coins of one currency for another. Look for the sign where the action is: BUREAU DE CHANGE... GELDWECHSEL... WECHSELSTUBE... OFICINA DE CAMBIO... OFFICIO CAMBEIO... UFFICIO CAMBIO ...or just follow the pertinent pictogram.

Currency exchange

Which Ticket Window for What. At larger stations tickets for domestic and international travel are purchased at different windows. But as a EURAILPASS or STUDENT-RAILPASS holder, you have your ticket already. So all you'll really want is either the information or reservation window or desk—except in Spain, where you must get a boarding pass at the station before you can board a train.

Tickets

Services for Businessmen. If you are combining pleasure with business, there are a number of TEE and Intercity trains on which you can hire a secretary, send telegrams or make telephone calls, make car-rental reservations ahead of arrival, or reserve a taxi to pick you up at your destination.

Rent-a-car

Taxi stand

AUSTRIA

CHAPTER 6

EURAILPASS EUROPE

AUSTRIA

Overview

Trail travel in Austria promises to be not only an aesthetically exciting experience but an informative one as Austria has recently become a jumping off point for travel and trade with the rapidly evolving central and eastern European countries. When heading north, east, and south from Vienna, western travelers are destined to meet up with Hungarians, Czechs, Slovaks, Bulgarians, Romanians, and Russians, Europe's new travelers.

The Austrian Federal Railway, called the OBB (Osterreichische Bundesbahnen) is well-known for being on time and for providing clean and efficient service, although in the summer months the most popular routes can be overflowing with travelers attracted by the captivating Alps and enchanting music festivals. While travel between the major cities is swift and regular, the local mountain trains can be painfully slow although blissfully scenic. Train travel in Austria on the whole is a pleasant experience although in the words of one Viennese publisher, Austria can be tiring in that the Austrians tend to look inward as if the whole world were Austrian.

General Information

• Children under six travel free. Half-fare for children between the ages six and 14. Travelers over 15 must pay full fare.

• Special "through tickets" are required for "privileged trains," which cross German or Italian borders from one part of Austria to another without border formalities (customs, passport and currency control). These trains do not allow passengers to board or leave the train in Germany or Italy.

• The second-class couchette cars on most Austrian internal routes and on some international services have four berths per compartment instead of six. A supplement of 33% over the price of a couchette in a six-berth compartment is charged for them. Inquire about this when reserving a couchette.

The signs you will see at railstations in Austria are:

ABFAHRT	DEPARTURE
ANKUNFT	ARRIVAL
AUSGANG	EXIT
AUSKUNFT	INFORMATION
BAHNHOF	STATION
BAHNSTEIG	PLATFORM

DAMEN	WOMEN
EINGANG	ENTRANCE
FAHRKARTEN-SCHALTER	TICKET OFFICE
FAHRPLAN	TIMETABLE
GEPACKAUFBEWAHRUNG	BAGGAGE CHECKROOM
GLEIS	TRACK
HERREN	MEN
PLATZ RESERVIERUNG	SEAT RESERVATION
RAUCHER	SMOKING COMPARTMENT
SCHLAFWAGEN	SLEEPING CAR
SPEISEWAGEN	RESTAURANT CAR

Summer Time

Austria changes to Summer Time on the last Sunday of March and converts back to Standard Time on the last Sunday of September.

Austrian Holidays

Here is a list of Austrian holidays:

January 1: New Year's Day; **January 6:** Epiphany, Easter, Easter Monday; **May 1:** Labor Day, Ascension Day, Whit Monday, Corpus Christi Day; **August 15:** Assumption Day; October 26: National holiday; November 1: All Saints Day; **December 8:** Immaculate Conception; December 25: Christmas Day; **December 26**: St. Stephen's Day.

AUSTRIA'S TRAIN PASSES

European East Pass See Eastern Europe

Austrian Railpass Sold worldwide by travel agencies, by Rail Europe, and by DER Tours/GermanRail.

Also sold in Austria at travel agencies and railstations. Vouchers for this pass are sold at many major railstations near the Austrian border (such as Munich and Zurich), to be exchanged for Rabbit Card after entering Austria.

This pass is valid for unlimited travel on all Austrian Federal Railway lines and on state and private rail lines in Austria any 4 days within 10 days.

The 1996 prices for passengers 26 and older are: $165 for *first*-class, $111 for *second*-class. Children under 7 travel free.

Junior Railpass Same privileges as above. The 1996 prices for persons who are under 26 years old on the first day of travel: $95 for *first*-class, $64 for *second*-class.

Senior Citizen Half-Fare In 1996, women 60 and over and men who are 65 and older can buy train and bus tickets at half-price after purchasing a Senior Citizen's Identification for 240 Austrian schillings, available at all railstations and major post offices in Austria, and also at the Hauptbahnhof stations in Frankfurt, Munich and Zurich.

The ID (valid for one calendar year) can also be obtained by mail by sending a travelers check in the amount of $25 or equivalent, a photostat of the passport page which has a picture and states the holder's age, plus one passport-size photo to: OeBB Verkehrsein-nahmen-und Reklamationsstelle, Mariannengasse 20, A-1090 Wien, Austria.

This discount is *not* valid on municipal transit lines (subway, trolley, bus).

Bundesnetzkarte (National Network Pass) Sold only in Austria. Unlimited train travel in all of Austria. The 1996 *first*-class prices are: 5,400 Austrian schillings for one month, AS-43,100 for one year. *Second*-class: AS-3,600 and AS-28,700.

Regional-Netzkarten (Regional Network Pass) Sold only in Austria. Unlimited train travel in any one of the country's 18 provinces for any 4 days within 10 days. The 1996 prices are: 630 Austrian schillings for *first*-class, AS-470 for *second*-class.

Kilometer Bank Sold only in Austria. Valid for *both* first and second-class seats. May be used by 1–6 persons traveling together on trips of over 70 km one way. Can be used in first or second-class. The conductor deducts trip distance for each passenger age 16 or older. Only half the distance is charged for each child age 6–15. No charge for children under age 6.

The 1996 prices are: 1,900 Austrian schillings for 2,000 km, AS-2,850 for 3,000 km, AS-3,800 for 4,000 km, and AS-4,750 for 5,000 km.

The maximum kilometers charged against this pass for any one trip are 600. Any number of kilometers above that are free.

For *first-class* use, one kilometer is counted as 1.5 kilometers.

EURAILPASS BONUSES IN AUSTRIA

Two track railways: (1) Puchberg am Schneeberg–Hochschneeberg and (2) St. Wolfgang–Schafbergspitze. The Danube cruise between Passau and Vienna. Steamers on Lake Wolfgang. Reduction of 50% on Lake Constance, Linz–Passau (and v.v), and Vienna–Budapest ships.

ONE-DAY EXCURSIONS AND CITY-SIGHTSEEING

Here are 31 one-day rail trips that can be made comfortably from Innsbruck, Linz, Salzburg and Vienna, returning to them in most cases before dinnertime. Notes are provided on what to see and do at each destination. The number after the name of each route is the Cook's timetable.

Innsbruck

Marvelous Winter resort. Gateway to many cable railway trips (Hungerburg, Hafelekar, Igls, Patscherkofel). See the 28 bronze statues around the enormous and magnificent tomb of Maximilian I in the 16th century Court Church and the effigy of King Arthur there. The silver altar at the Silver Chapel.

The roof (2,657 gold plated tiles) on Goldenes Dachl, built in 1500. The Museum of Tyrolean Folk Art, considered the most important collection of costumes and rustic furniture in Austria. The 18th century Roman-style Triumphal Arch. Reisenrundgemalde, a huge circular fresco depicting the Battle of Bergisel. The splendid views of the city and surrounding mountains from Bergisel Kaiserjager, containing the museum of the Tyrolean Imperial Light Infantry.

The excellent art collection of Archduke Ferdinand II at Schloss Ambras, open daily except Tuesday in Summer. The Alpen Zoo. The 18th century Imperial Palace. The paintings and furniture at the Tyrolean Regional Museum in the Arsenal of Emperor Maxmillian I.

Linz

Visit the schloss (castle) where Emperor Fredrich III lived, with its Upper Austrian Regional Museum collections of prehistoric and Roman antiquities, medieval armor and weapons, musical instruments and regional arts and crafts, open Tuesday-Saturday 10:00–18:00, Sunday 10:00–16:00.

Martinskirche, one of Austria's oldest churches. The medieval, Renaissance and Baroque exhibits in the City Museum at 7 Bethlehemstrasse, open Monday-Friday 09:00–18:00, Saturday and Sunday 15:00–17:00.

Take the 20-minute tram ride from the Urfahr section to Postlingberg, a hill on the south side of the Danube, to visit the Town Hall and see the view from there.

Kremsmunster, an enchanting small town established in 777, is a 30-minute drive south of Linz. Visit it in order to see the treasures in the monastery. It houses a fabulous library as well as an exceptional museum of natural history and early scientific instruments, a picture gallery, an art gallery, a fine collection of stained glass, and an armory.

Among its more than 100,000 rare books, 886 incunabula (books produced before movable type was invented in the 16th century), and 910 old manuscripts are the 2 famous "jewels" of the 230-foot-long library: the 8th and 9th century splendidly illuminated parchments called Codex Millenarius Major and Codex Minor. All 4 large rooms of the library are furnished with beautiful baroque bookcases.

Salzburg

Do not miss seeing the most amusing place in Europe, the 17th century Hellbrunn Palace. The 16th century 200-pipe barrel organ (played 3 times every day) in the 12th century fortress, 500 feet above the town (Festung Hohensalzburg) where 40-minute guided tours start every 15 minutes 09:00–17:30 daily in July and August. The traditional Music Festival (last week of July until the end of August).

Guided tours of the incredibly opulent rooms in The Residenz, the 17th century city palace of Salzburg's archbishops, start at 10:00, 10:30, 11:00, 11:30, 13:00, 13:30, 14:00, 14:30 and 15:00, Monday-Friday. The gallery of paintings in The Residenz (including Titian and Rembrandt) is open daily 10:00–17:00.

The painted ceilings in the 17th century Festspeilhaus. The collection of Mozart musical instruments and family memorabilia in the Mozart Museum, his birthplace (9 Getreidegasse), open daily 09:00–19:00. The vast musical library at Bibliotheca Mozartiana. St. Sebastian's Cemetery (Linzergasse 41). The 17th century Cathedral. The Universitatskirche. The Gothic cloister in the 9th century Benedictine Abbey of St. Peter.

The Glockenspiel Tower particularly at 07:00, 11:00 and 18:00 for the carillon concerts. The ancient marketplace, Alter Markt. The marble Angel Staircase and the Salzburger Barock-Museum in the 17th century Schloss Mirabell, and the marvelous gardens there. The superb collection of prehistoric objects, fossils and meteorites at the Natural History Museum.

Take the cable car to the top (5,800 feet) of Untersberg for a breathtaking view of Salzburg and the Alps. There are other good views of the city and river from Hettwer Bastion and also from the top of Monchsberg, Kapuzinerberg and Gaisberg.

Vienna (Wien)

The main tourist office (38 Kartnerstrasse) is open daily 09:00–19:00.

There is 30-minute train service [Table 835] from *Vienna (Nord) to the city's Schwechat Airport (Flughafen)* daily at 05:09, 05:47, 06:23 and hourly from 07:30 to 20:30, plus 10:07, 18:07 and 21:45. Also, daily except Sundays and holidays: at 06:47, 16:07 and 17:07.

Rail service *from the Airport to Vienna (Nord)* departs the Airport daily at 06:11, 06:34, 07:27 and hourly from 08:05 to 21:05, plus 11:26, 18:46 and 22:20. Also daily except Sundays and holidays: at 05:31, 07:05, 07:12 and 08:26.

For a glimpse at the world's most beautiful horses and extraordinary riding skill, see the Spanish Riding School. The view from the top of the south steeple of the 13th century Saint Stephen's Cathedral, reached by climbing 365 steps. That steeple is open daily 09:00–16:30.

Another great view is from the top of the Donauturm (Danube Tower). or from the hills in the Vienna Woods. Vienna's most elegant shopping streets are 2 pedestrian malls that run south and east from St. Stephen's: Karntnerstrasse and Graben. Three-hour boat trips on the Danube Canal operate daily except Monday at 10:00, 13:00 and 16:30 from Schwedenbrucke, a bridge that is a 15-minute walk from St. Stephen's.

See the Opera House. The Art Gallery. The Burgtheater. The Rathaus (City Hall). The gigantic Ferris Wheel and the miniature railway in the Prater amusement park.

Guided tours of some of the 1,400 rooms in Schonbrunn Castle, Vienna's Versailles, are offered daily 09:00–12:00 and 13:00–16:00. It is a 20-minute ride from Burgring on streetcar # 58.

Visit Tierpark, the zoo, in the Schonbrunner Schlosspark. The 2 museums of modern art, one in Palais Liechtensten, the other in Schweizer Garten. See the crown jewels of the Holy Roman Empire and the Austrian Empire, in the Imperial Apartments at the Hofburg (Imperial Palace), open Monday–Saturday 08:30–16:00 and Sunday 08:30–12:30.

The collection of great paintings (Titian, Rubens, Rembrandt) and Egyptian, Greek, Etruscan and Roman antiquities at the Museum of Art History on Ringstrasse, open Tuesday and

Friday 10:00–21:00, Wednesday and Thursday 09:00–18:00, Saturday and Sunday 09:00–18:00.

The many art museums in Belvedere Palace (medieval, baroque and modern art), open Tuesday-Saturday from 10:00 to varying afternoon hours, Sunday 09:00–12:00. The 20 centuries of memorabilia in the Historical Museum in the Karlsplatz, open Tuesday–Friday 10:00–16:00, Saturday 14:00–18:00, Sunday 09:00–17:00.

The Sigmund Freud Museum at 19 Berggasse, where the founder of psychoanalysis lived and practiced for many years, open Monday-Friday 09:00–13:00, Saturday and Sunday 09:00–15:00.

The many art museums in Belvedere Palace, open Tuesday–Sunday 10:00–16:00. The beautiful Austrian National Library at 1 Josefplatz. The great churches: Peterskirche and Karlskirche.

The finest collection of Durer paintings in the world and one of the world's largest graphics collections (1,000,000 prints from 5 centuries and 45,000 drawings) at the Albertina, 1 Augustinerstrasse, open Monday, Tuesday and Thursday 10:00–16:00, Wednesday 10:00–18:00, Friday 10:00–14:00, Saturday and Sunday 10:00–13:00.

The paintings of Kandinsky and other moderns at the Museum of the 20th Century in Schweizer Garten (near the Southeast Railroad Terminal), open daily except Wednesday 10:00–18:00. Works by Austrian painters and sculptors since World War II at the Museum of Modern Art in the Liechtenstein Palace, 1 Furstengasse, open daily except Tuesday 10:00–18:00.

The great paintings (Hieronymus, Bosch, Rubens, Titian, Van Dyck) at the Academy of Fine Arts, 3 Schillerplatz, open Tuesday, Thursday and Friday 10:00–14:00, Wednesday 10:00–13:00, Saturday and Sunday 09:00–13:00.

The treasures of the Holy Roman Empire, including the 10th century crown, at the Imperial Treasury, open Monday, Wednesday, Thursday and Friday 10:00–16:00, Saturday and Sunday 09:00–16:00 (November–March) or 09:00–18:00 (April–October).

Treasures collected by the Hapsburgs (including paintings by Pieter Bruegel the Elder and Rubens) at the Museum of Fine Arts on Maria-Theresien-Platz, open Tuesday–Friday 10:00–18:00, Saturday and Sunday 09:00–16:00 (November–March) or 09:00–18:00 (April–October).

The Austrian Baroque Museum and the Museum of Austrian Medieval art are located in the Lower Belvedere.

Vienna's largest outdoor food market (Naschmarkt) runs between Rechte Wienzeile and Linke Wienzeile.

Sightseeing flights over Vienna operate from the Schwechat Airport.

Take trolley car # 38 from Schottentor (in central Vienna) to **Grinzing**, the wine-tasting village. Continue from there on bus # 38A to the small Church of St. Joseph on the top of the 1,585-feet high **Kahlenberg**, from where Hungary and Czechoslovakia can be seen on clear days.

In the following timetables, where a city has more than one railstation we have designated the particular station after the name of the city (in parentheses). **Where no station is designated for cities in Austria, Switzerland and West Germany, the station is "Hauptbahnhof."**

Innsbruck - Bregenz - Innsbruck   800

Dep. Innsbruck	07:02 (1)	09:02 (1)	Dep. Bregenz	12:17 (1)	14:17 (1+2)
Arr. Bregenz	09:44	11:44	Arr. Innsbruck	14:58	16:58

(1) Restaurant car. (2) Plus other departures from Bregenz at 16:17 (1), 17:18 (1), 18:17 (1), 20:17 (1) and 21:38, arriving Innsbruck 18:58, 19:51, 20:58, 22:58 and 00:34.

Sights in **Bregenz**: Divided into 2 sections, features of the lower town include the lakeshore, the shopping district and the Voralberg Museum. The upper town has churches. Situated on the shore of the Bodensee (Lake Constance), easy day trips can be made from here to Innsbruck, Munich, Salzburg and Zurich.

The annual Music Festival (light opera and ballet on an unusual water stage in the lake) runs mid-July to mid-August. Take the funicular to the top (3,200 feet) of Pfander Mountain for a spectacular view of Bodensee, the Rhine River and the town of Lindau (see notes about Lindau under "Munich-Lindau"). The funicular runs 08:30–20:00 (until 22:00 in mid-Summer). Steamboats are operated on the lake from early April to early October.

Innsbruck - Igls - Innsbruck

Four miles from Innsbruck by suburban railway is the great ski resort of Igls.

Innsbruck - Kitzbuhel - Innsbruck   810

Dep. Innsbruck	07:20 (1)	09:20 (1)	11:20 (1)
Arr. Kitzbuhel	60 minutes later		

Sights in **Kitzbuhel**: This is one of the major winter resorts in the Alps. Cable cars take you from Kitzbuhel to many mountaintops. The city has one museum, some old churches.

Dep. Kitzbuhel	11:33	12:31 (2)	13:34 (1)	14:31 (2)	15:39 (1) 16:31 (2+3)
Arr. Innsbruck	60 minutes later				

(1) Light refreshments. (2) Restaurant car. (3) Plus other departures from Kitzbuhel at 17:26 (1), 18:23 (3), 19:33 (1), 20:32 (3) and 21:33 (1).

Innsbruck - Mayrhofen - Innsbruck 800

All of the Jenbach–Mayrhofen and v.v trains are second class only.

Dep. Innsbruck	09:02	13:02	15:02
Arr. Jenbach	09:20	13:20	15:20

Change from a standard-gauge train to a narrow-gauge train. Table 805

Dep. Jenbach	09:50	13:50	15:50
Arr. Mayrhofen	10:47	14:47	16:47

Sights in **Mayrhofen**: This is a popular Winter resort, with horse sleighs.

Dep. Mayrhofen	13:20	15:20	17:20	18:20
Arr. Jenbach	14:13	16:13	18:13	19:13

Change from a narrow-gauge train to a standard-gauge train. Table 800

Dep. Jenbach	14:38	16:38	18:38	20:38
Arr. Innsbruck	20 minutes later			

Innsbruck - Munich - Innsbruck 785

Dep. Innsbruck	07:07	09:07	09:43
Arr. Munich	09:52	11:52	12:39

Dep. Munich	14:00	15:00 (1)	17:00 (1)	18:00 (2)
Arr. Innsbruck	16:39	18:04	20:54	20:54

(1) Change trains in Mittenwald. (2) Change trains in Garmisch.

Innsbruck - St. Anton - Innsbruck 800

Dep. Innsbruck	07:02 (1)	09:02 (1)	11:02 (1)	11:53	12:44 (1)
Arr. St. Anton	08:20	10:20	12:20	13:33	13:54

Sights in **St. Anton:** A popular ski center since 1907, located at the eastern end of the 6-mile-long Arlberg Tunnel. The enormous number of ski lifts here offer a great variety of slopes.

Dep. St. Anton	11:37 (1)	12:03 (1)	13:37 (1)	14:00 (1)	15:37 (1)	16:03 (1+2)
Arr. Innsbruck	12:58	13:16	14:58	15:13	16:58	17:16

(1) Restaurant car. (2) Plus other departures from St. Anton at 17:37 (1), 18:39 (1), 19:37 (1), 21:37 (1) and 23:13.

Innsbruck - Salzburg - Innsbruck (via Zell am See)   800 + 810

The route via Zell-am-See is one of the most scenic rides in Austria, as well as a trip to an interesting destination. Exceptionally beautiful views of gorges, lakes, mountains and rivers.

All of these trains have a restaurant car.

Dep. Innsbruck	07:02 (3)	08:17 (1)	09:02 (3)	09:51 (1+4)
Dep. Zell-am-See	-0-	10:20	-0-	12:20
Arr. Salzburg	09:00	11:51	11:00	13:51

Sights in **Zell-am-See:** Minutes by bus from year-around glacier skiing.

Dep. Salzburg	13:00 (3)	14:08 (1+2)	15:00 (3)	16:08 (1+2)	17:00 (3+5)
Dep. Zell-am-See	-0-	15:41	-0-	17:41	-0-
Arr. Innsbruck	14:58	17:35	16:58	19:35	18:58

(1) Of the 2 routes between Innsbruck and Salzburg, this train takes the more interesting one (via Zell-am-See), one of the most scenic rail trips in Austria. (2) Operates late September to late May. (3) Via Kufstein. (4) Plus other departures from Innsbruck at 11:07 (3) and 13:02 (3), arriving Salzburg 13:00 and 15:00. (5) Plus other Salzburg departures at 18:14 (1+2), 19:00 (3) and 21:20 (3), arriving Innsbruck 21:35, 20:58 and 23:12.

Linz - Munich - Linz   67

All of these trains charge a supplement for first-class which includes seat reservation fee and have a restaurant car.

Dep. Linz	07:48	10:46		Dep. Munich	16:25	18:25
Arr. Munich	10:35	13:36		Arr. Linz	19:12	21:12

Linz - Salzburg - Linz   800

All of these trains have a restaurant car.

Dep. Linz	Frequent times from 05:34 to 23:30
Arr. Salzburg	1 to 2 hours later
Dep. Salzburg	Frequent times from 04:53 to 22:05
Arr. Linz	1 to 2 hours later

Linz - Vienna - Linz   800

Most of these trains have a restaurant car.

Dep. Linz	Frequent times from 04:30 to 23:15
Arr. Vienna (Westbf.)	1½ to 2 hours later
Dep. Vienna (Westbf.)	Frequent times from 04:40 to 23:30
Arr. Linz	1½ to 2 hours later

Salzburg - Zell am See - Innsbruck - Salzburg   800 + 810

The route via Zell-am-See is one of the most scenic rides in Austria, as well as a trip to an interesting destination. Exceptionally beautiful views of gorges, lakes, mountains and rivers.

These trains have a restaurant car, unless designated otherwise.

Dep. Salzburg	07:00 (1)	08:08 (2+3)	09:00 (1)	10:08 (2+3)	10:38 (1)
Dep. Zell-am-See	-0-	09:41	-0-	11:41	-0-
Arr. Innsbruck	08:58	12:12	10:58	14:09	12:36

Sights in **Zell-am-See**: Minutes by bus from year-around glacier skiing.

Dep. Innsbruck	11:51 (2+3)	13:02 (1)	13:20 (2+4)	13:51 (2+3)	15:02 (1+5)
Dep. Zell-am-See	14:20	-0-	15:16	16:20	-0-
Arr. Salzburg	15:51	15:00	16:53	17:51	17:00

(1) Via Kufstein. (2) Of the 2 routes between Salzburg and Innsbruck, this train takes the most interesting one (via Zell-am-See), one of the most scenic rail trips in Austria. (3) Operates late September to late May. (4) Change trains in Bischofshofen. Light refreshments on both trains. (5) Plus other departures from Innsbruck at frequent times from 15:20 to 21:14.

Salzburg - Kitzbuhel - Salzburg 810

All of these trains have a restaurant car.

Dep. Salzburg	06:11	08:08	10:08	12:08
Arr. Kitzbuhel	09:12	10:24	12:24	14:24

Sights in **Kitzbuhel**: See notes about Kitzbuhel under "Innsbruck–Kitzbuhe."

Dep. Kitzbuhel	13:29	15:29	17:29	02:22
Arr. Salzburg	15:51	17:51	19:51	02:40

Salzburg - Linz - Salzburg 800

Most of these trains have a restaurant car.

Dep. Salzburg	Frequent times from 04:53 to 22:05
Arr. Linz	80 minutes later

Dep. Linz	Frequent times from 05:34 to 23:30
Arr. Salzburg	80 minutes later

Salzburg - Munich - Salzburg 790

All of these trains charge a supplement for first-class which includes a reservtion fee and have a restaurant car, unless designated otherwise.

Dep. Salzburg	04:08 (1)	04:35 (2)	10:18	12:09	
Arr. Munich	06:03	06:13	12:07	13:36	
Dep. Munich	12:25 (3)	13:25	15:25	16:25	17:51 (2+4)
Arr. Salzburg	13:55	14:53	16:55	17:53	19:40

(1) No supplement charged. No restaurant car. (2) No supplement charged. Light refreshments. (3) Light refreshments. (4) Plus other Munich departures at 18:25, 19:51 (2), 20:50 (1), 21:51 (2) and 23:19 (1), arriving Salzburg 19:55, 21:40, 22:24, 23:40 and 01:01.

Salzburg - Schafbergspitze - Salzburg

A very scenic one-day trip that includes views of the 8-mile-long **Wolfgangsee (Lake Wolfgang)**, the warmest lake in Austria (79 degrees in Summer). The narrow gauge steam rack railway climbs 5,682 feet to the top of the **Schafberg**, from where there are glorious views of 13 lakes and many mountains. The ride from Schafbergspitze back to St. Wolfgang must be booked immediately on arrival at the summit. This railway operates May to October.

Bus. 812

Dep. Salzburg	06:45 (1)	08:15	09:15	11:25	12:15	13:15 (1)
Arr. Strobl	07:59	09:19	10:29	12:39	12:29	14:29

Change buses. 813

Dep. Strobl	08:15 (1)	09:40 (1)	10:40 (1)	12:40	13:40	14:40
Arr. St. Wolfgang	08:30	09:55	10:55	12:55	13:55	14:55

Change to steam rack railway. 813

Dep. St. Wolfgang	Train operates when it has at least 20 passengers.
Arr. Schafbergspitze	39 minutes after departing St. Wolfgang

• • •

Dep. Schafbergspitze	At random times
Arr. St. Wolfgang	39 minutes after departing Shafbergspitze

Change to bus. 813

Dep.St. Wolfgang	10:05 (6)	12:10	13:15	15:05	16:15 (5)
Arr. Strobl	10:18	12:23	13:28	15:18	16:30

Change buses. 812

Dep. Strobl	10:41 (2)	12:41	13:41 (3)	15:41	16:41
Arr. Salzburg	11:55	13:55	14:55	16:55	17:55

(1) Runs daily, except Sundays and holidays. (2) Runs Monday-Friday, except holidays. (3) Operates mid-July to mid-September. (4) Mid-July to late September: runs daily. Late September to mid-July: runs daily, except Sundays and holidays. (5) Plus other St. Wolfgang departures at 17:15 (4), 18:15 and 20:00 (3), arriving Salzburg 18:55, 19:55 and 21:40.(6) Sundays only.

Salzburg - Vienna - Salzburg   800

Marvelous views of the Alps and pretty farmland on this ride.

All of these trains have a restaurant car.

Dep. Salzburg	06:05	07:00 (1)	08:05	09:05 (1)	10:05	11:05 (1)
Arr. Vienna (Westbf.)	09:25	09:45	11:25	12:25	13:25	14:25

Dep. Vienna (Westbf.)	13:35 (1)	14:40	15:40	16:00 (1)	17:00 (1)
Arr. Salzburg	3 hours later				

(1) Supplement charged for first-class includes reservation fee. (2) Plus other Vienna departures at 18:40, 19:40, 20:40 and 21:25, arriving Salzburg 21:55, 22:55, 00:12 and 00:43.

Vienna - Baden - Vienna

A local tram runs at frequent time from the center of Vienna to Baden and v.v.

Sights in **Baden**: Only 16 miles from Vienna, Baden is an alternative to staying in Vienna.

Famous since the 1st century for the curative powers of its hot sulphur springs. Many of the rooms in hotels here have a faucet in the bathroom that carries mineral water. See the Baroque Trinity Column. Try your luck in the Casino in Kurpark.

Visit the house where Beethoven lived, at 10 Rathausgasse, open daily except Thursdays, May–September, 09:00–11:00 and 15:00–17:00.

Vienna - Budapest - Vienna 890

Dep. Vienna (Sud.)	07:14 (1)	08:03 (3)	Dep Budapest (Kel.)	17:25	18:30 (3+5)
Arr Budapest (Kel.)	10:03 (2)	11:08	Arr. Vienna (Sud.)	20:50 (4)	21:45

(1) Restaurant car. (2) Departs/arrives Budapest's Deli railstation. (3) Reservation required. Restaurant car. (4) Arrives Vienna's Westbahnhof railstation. (5) Plus other Budapest departures at 19:05(1+2) and 21:20, arriving Vienna 21:58 (Sud.) and 00:44 (Sud.).

Vienna - Graz - Vienna 830

All of these trains have light refreshments.

Dep. Vienna (Sudbf.)	06:22	07:22 (1)	08:22	09:22 (1)	10:22	12:22
Dep. Bruck a.d. Mur	08:20	09:36 (1)	10:20	11:36	12:20	14:20
Arr. Graz	08:55	10:10	10:55	12:10	12:55	14:55

•   •   •

Dep. Graz	13:05	13:50 (1)	15:05	15:50(1)	17:05	17:50 (1+2)
Dep. Bruck a.d. Mur	13:43	14:36 (1)	15:43	16:36	17:43	18:36 (1)
Arr. Vienna (Sudbf.)	15:33	16:33	17:33	18:33	19:33	20:33

(1) Change trains in Bruck an der Mur. (2) Plus other departures from Graz at 19:05 and 21:05 (1), arriving Vienna 21:33, and 23:33 .

Sights in **Graz**: A 2½-hour motorcoach sightseeing tour of Graz starts from in front of the Opera House weekdays at 10:00, June through September

From the main square (Hauptplatz) with its many markets of vegetables, fruits and flowers, go to the arcades with shops in the 17th century Luegghaus. Then to the City Hall (Rathaus) to see the city's symbol, a carved white panther.

Follow Neutorgasse to the Joanneum (state Museum of Styria), one of the world's oldest museums, to see its archaeological collection, library, paintings and exhibits of Styrian crafts (09:00–12:00 daily, 14:30–17:00 Monday, Wednesday and Friday).

Continue on Landhausgasse and Herrengasse to the splendid Renaissance Landhaus. Next door, in the 4-story, 17th century Styrian Armory (Zeughaus) is an exhibit of 17th century armor (for both men and horses) said to be the best and largest collection in Europe (same hours as the Joanneum). Its 32,000 weapons include complete suits of armor, guns, helmets, swords, lances, shields and breastplates.

Walk on Opernring to the outstanding Opera House and then through marvelous Stadtpark with its fantastic double-spiral Gothic staircase and cross the Glacis to visit the city's oldest church, 13th century Leekirche, the Church of the Teutonic Order.

Pass the castle and see the Diocesan Museum and Treasury in the 15th century Cathedral. Across a narrow street is the 17th century Mausoleum of Emperor Ferdinand II and his mother (Maria of Bavaria), open 11:00–12:00 and 14:00–15:00 from May to September, only 11:00–12:00 the rest of the year.

Don't miss the folk dance by carved wood figures performing at 11:00 and 18:00 on the 400-year-old clock in Glockenspielplatz. Nearby is the 116-foot-high belfry which has a 4-ton bell that the people here call "Liesl." See the exhibits of regional costumes, tools, folk art, etc. in the Volkskundemuseum (Folk Art Museum of Styria) open Monday, Wednesday and Friday 14:30–17:00.

Cable cars leave every 15 minutes from 38 Kaiser Franz Josef Kai for the 350 foot ascent to the top of Schlossberg (Castle Hill), from where there is a great view of Graz, its suburbs, the Mur Valley and the Alps.

Drink Schilcher (the local rose wine) and Steiermark beer. Local food specialties to sample are: Steierische Wurzelfleisch (pork shoulder), Sulmtaler Krainer (smoked pork sausage) and Steierische Brettljause (a dish of bacon, sausage, cheese, peppers and tomatoes served on a wooden platter).

Take the tram to **Eggenberg** to see the hunting museum in the 17th century castle there. Go to the top of Castle Hill (Schlossberg) by foot or funicular for a great view of Graz and tour the Bell Tower and Clock Tower, where the big hands show the hour and the small hands the minutes.

Take a local bus to nearby **Stubing**, which has the largest open-air museum in Austria (ancient wood churches, peasants' homes). Another tour goes to **Koflach**, where a stud farm that is an auxiliary of Vienna's Spanish Riding School has been breeding thoroughbred horses since 1798.

Vienna - Linz - Vienna 800

Most of these trains have a restaurant car.

Dep. Vienna (Westbf.)	Frequent times from 04:40 to 23:30.
Arr. Linz	2 hours later.
Dep. Linz	Frequent times from 04:30 to 23:15.
Arr. Vienna (Westbf.)	2 hours later.

Vienna - Melk - Vienna   Train Ride + Danube Boat Trip

The Melk-Vienna boat is covered by Eurailpass.

Train 800			*Danube Steamship 843*	
Dep. Vienna (Westbf.)	08:44 (1)	12:26	Dep. Melk	14:55 (2)
Arr. Melk	09:45	13:38	Arr. Vienna	20:15 (3)

(1) Light refreshments. (2) Operates from mid-May to late September (3) Arrives at Vienna's Reichs-brucke.

Sights in **Melk**: Walk from the railstation up the hill to the Abbey, built in 1133 but completely reconstructed 1702 to 1736. English-language guided tours are offered sometimes. There is a splendid view of the Danube from the terrace.

At the top of the stone Emperor's Stairway is the 644-foot-long Emperor's Corridor, off which are several rooms whose doors are made of highly decorated rare wood and in which many treasures are displayed. Also on this floor are the magnificently decorated Marble Hall (actually faux marble stucco), the gilded bookcases of inlaid wood in the Library (over 85,000 books and 1,200 manuscripts from the 9th to the 15th centuries), and the Abbey church with a pulpit made entirely of gold.

A restaurant at the Abbey serves a hearty lunch. For the return trip to Vienna by boat, go to the main river dock, not to the dock below the abbey.

Vienna - Salzburg - Vienna 800

All of these trains have a restaurant car.

Dep. Vienna (Westbf.)	06:00 (1)	06:40	07:35 (1)	07:40	08:40	09:00 (1+2)
Arr. Salzburg	09:00	09:55	10:35	10:55	11:52	11:58
Dep. Salzburg	14:05	15:05	15:25 (1)	16:05	17:05	18:00 (1+3)
Arr. Vienna (Westbf.)	17:25	18:25	18:30	19:25	20:25	21:05

(1) Supplement charged for first-class includes reservation fee. (2) Plus other departures from Vienna at 09:35 (1), 09:40 and 10:40, arriving Salzburg 12:35, 12:55 and 13:55. (3) Plus other Salzburg departures at 18:05, 19:05, 19:25 (1), 20:00 (1), 20:05, 21:05 and 21:57 (1), arriving Vienna 21:25, 22:25, 22:30, 23:05, 23:25, 00:25 and 00:58.

Vienna - Sopron - Vienna   830 + 833

A day-trip into Hungary.

Change trains in Wiener Neustadt.

Dep. Vienna (Sud)	07:52	10:52	Dep. Sopron	13:39	16:55 (1)
Arr. Sopron	09:11	12:11	Arr. Vienna (Sud)	15:05	18:33(2)

(1) Plus another Sopron departure at 19:39, arriving Vienna 21:05. (2) Monday -Friday except holidays.

Sights in **Sopron**: A 900-year-old architectural treasure, with 240 perfectly preserved historic buildings. The Castle has a Roman foundation and a Norman basement. Visit the 13th century Goat Church and Church of St. Michael. The 15th century synagogue. St. George Church. Holy Ghost Church. The 16th century Lyceum. The 18th century Trinity Statue. The rococo Erdody Palace. Many museums: Liszt, Stonework, Pharmacy, Guild History, and Fabricius House.

SCENIC RAIL TRIPS

Innsbruck - Brennero   380

The beautiful mountain scenery here can be seen either on an easy one-day roundtrip from Innsbruck or as a portion of the Innsbruck–Verona–Milan route.

Dep. Innsbruck	06:37 (1)	10:26 (2)	12:48	14:04 (3)	15:22 (4)
Arr. Brennero	07:38	11:08	13:20	14:45	16:12

• • •

Dep. Brennero	07:29	12:04 (4)	15:14 (5)	16:04	16:23
Arr. Innsbruck	08:10	12:27	15:55	16:37	16:59

(1) Second-class only. Light refreshments. (2) Light refreshments. (3) Runs daily, except Sundays and holidays. (4) Supplement charged for first-class includes reservation fee. Restaurant car. (5) Runs daily, except Sundays and holidays.

Innsbruck - Buchs   800

The excellent mountain scenery here can be seen either on an easy one-day roundtrip from Innsbruck or as a portion of the Innsbruck–Zurich route.

All of these trains have a restaurant car, unless designated otherwise.

Dep. Innsbruck	07:02	09:02 (2)	11:02 (2)	12:44 (3)	14:44(3)
Arr. Buchs	09:47(2)	11:50	13:51	15:08	17:08

• • •

Dep. Buchs	10:52 (3)	12:44 (3)	14:52 (3)	16:03 (2)	17:18 (2+4)
Arr. Innsbruck	13:16	15:13	17:16	18:58	19:51

(1) No restaurant car. (2) Change trains in Feldkirch. (3) Supplement charged for first-class includes resrvation fee. (4) Plus other Buchs departures at 18:19 (2), 20:18 (2) and 22:53, arriving Innsbruck 20:58, 22:58 and 01:37.

Innsbruck - Bruck an der Mur - Vienna

This indirect route from Innsbruck to Vienna, traveling south of the main line (via Linz), offers excellent mountain scenery. As the schedules below indicate, a stopover of up to 7 hours in Bruck an der Mur is possible.

All of the trains have light refreshments unless designated otherwise.

810				
Dep. Innsbruck	05:20	07:20	09:20	11:20
Arr. Selzthal	09:28	11:28	13:28	15:28
Change trains. 825				
Dep. Selzthal	09:32	11:32	13:32	15:32
Arr. Leoben	10:29	12:29	14:29	16:29
Change trains.				
830				
Dep. Leoben	10:25	12:25	15:20	17:20
Arr. Bruck an der Mur	10:36	12:36	15:33 (2)	17:33 (2)
Arr. Vienna (Sudbf.)	12:40	14:40 (1)	17:40	19:40

(1) Arrives at the Ost platforms. (2) Change trains in Bruck an der Mur.

Sights in **Bruck an der Mur**: Located in the Styrian Alps, at the meeting of the Mur and Murz rivers, on the main route between Vienna and Graz. See the 17th century Wrought Iron Well, the outstanding example of Styrian ironwork. The 15th and 16th century houses. The Parish Church.

Innsbruck - Feldkirch - Innsbruck   800

Very good mountain scenery. As the schedules shown below indicate, a stopover of 2-8 hours in Feldkirch is possible.

All of these trains have a restaurant car, unless designated otherwise.

Dep. Innsbruck	07:02	09:02	11:02	13:02	15:02	17:02
Arr. Feldkirch	09:14	11:15	13:14	15:14	17:14	19:14

Sights in **Feldkirch**: A medieval town, next to the Swiss border. See the Old Town and Marketplace. The 12-foot-thich walls at the 16th century Schattenburg Castle. The local museum, open daily except Wednesday afternoon.

Dep. Feldkirch	10:44	12:44	14:44	16:44	17:44 (1)	20:44
Arr. Innsbruck	12:58	14:58	16:58	18:58	19:51	22:50

(1) Supplement charged for first-class includes reservation fee.

Innsbruck - Garmisch - Zugspitze   785

The outstanding mountain scenery here can be seen either on an easy one-day roundtrip from Innsbruck or as a portion of the Innsbruck–Munich route.

For the first way:

Dep. Innsbruck	07:07	07:59	09:07 (1)	09:43 (2)	11:07	12:00
Arr. Garmisch	08:24	09:24	10:24	11:09 (3)	12:24 (3)	13:24
Change trains.						

The following schedule allows one to ride one cable route to the summit of Zugspitze and ride a different cable route back to Garmisch.

783

Dep. Garmisch	08:35	09:35	10:35	11:35	12:35	14:35
Arr. Eibsee	09:15	10:15	11:15	12:15	13:15	15:15

Change to cable railway.

Dep. Eibsee	Every 30 minutes from 08:00 to 17:30
Arr. Zugspitze	10 minutes later

(1) Change trains in Mittenwald. (2) Supplement charged. Restaurant car. (3) As the Garmisch departures show, there is time to lunch in Garmisch and take a later train to Eibsee and Zugspitze. See departures above.

Use a different cable railway in returning to Garmisch.

In 1994, all of the times Zugspitze-Schneefernerhaus and Schneefernerhaus-Garmisch were estimated.

787
Dep. Zugspitze   Every 30 minutes from 08:15 to 16:45
Arr. Schneefernerhaus   4 minutes later

                            •   •   •

787 Train

Dep. Schneefernerhaus	10:00	11:00	13:00	14:00	15:00	17:00
Arr. Garmisch	11:20 (1)	12:20 (1)	14:20	15:20	16:20	18:20
Change trains. 785						
Dep. Garmisch	11:26 (2)	12:26	14:26	16:05 (3)	16:26 (2)	
Arr. Innsbruck	12:41	13:48	15:47	17:40	18:04	

(1) As the Garmisch departures show, there is time to lunch in Garmisch and take a later train to Innsbruck or Munich. (2) Change trains in Mittenwald. (3) Supplement charged. Restaurant car.

Here is the schedule for continuing on from Garmisch to Munich.

785

Dep. Garmisch	11:34	12:27	13:34	14:27	15:34	16:27 (1)
Arr. Munich	12:51	13:51	14:51	15:51	16:51	17:53

(1) Plus other departures from Garmisch at 17:34, 18:31, 19:34, 20:27 and 21:31.

Innsbruck - Salzburg - Innsbruck

The good canyon, lake, river and mountain scenery on this route can be seen either on an easy one-day roundtrip from Innsbruck (see details under "Innsbruck–Zell am See–Salzburg – Innsbruck"), or as a portion of the Innsbruck–Vienna route (see below).

Innsbruck - Vienna   800

Here are the schedules for going across Austria.

All of these trains have a restaurant car, unless designated otherwise.

Dep. Innsbruck	07:02	09:02	11:07	13:02	15:02	17:02 (1)
Arr. Vienna (Westbf.)	12:25	14:25	16:25	18:25	20:25	22:25

(1) Plus another departure from Innsbruck at 19:02, arriving Vienna 00:25.

Linz - Selzthal - Amstetten - Linz

The Selzthal–Amstetten portion of this easy one-day circle trip affords fine river, canyon and mountain scenery. There are good views of the colorful **Enns Valley**.

All of the Linz–Selzthal and v.v. trains have light refreshments. All of the Selzthal–Amstetten and v.v. trains are second-class only. All of the Amstetten–Linz and v.v. trains have a restaurant car.

825				
Dep. Linz	08:40	10:40	12:40	14:40
Arr. Selzthal	10:16	12:16	14:16	16:16

Change trains.

826				
Dep. Selzthal	10:19	12:19	14:19	16:19
Arr. Amstetten	12:50	14:50	16:50	18:50

Change trains.

800				
Dep. Amstetten	12:54	14:54	16:54	18:54
Arr. Linz	13:32	15:32	17:32	19:32

The same trip can be made in reverse, using this schedule:

800				
Dep. Linz	08:27	10:27	12:27	14:27
Arr. Amstetten	09:02	11:02	13:02	15:02

Change trains.

826				
Dep. Amstetten	09:10	11:10	13:10	15:10
Arr. Selzthal	11:41	13:41	15:41	17:41

Change trains.

825				
Dep. Selzthal	11:44	13:44	15:44	17:44
Arr. Linz	13:20	15:20	17:20	19:20

Salzburg - Zell am See - Innsbruck

There are exceptionally beautiful views of canyon, lakes, mountains and rivers on one of the most scenic rides in Austria. Schedules for this trip appear earlier in this section under both "Innsbruck–Salzburg" and "Salzburg–Innsbruck."

Salzburg - Gmunden - Stainach - Salzburg

There is fine mountain and lake scenery on the Gmunden–Stainach portion of this circle trip.

800

Dep. Salzburg	06:05 (1)	12:05 (1)
Arr. Attnang	06:50	12:50

Change trains.

815

Dep. Attnang	07:25 (2)	13:25 (2)
Dep. Gmunden	07:44	13:44
Dep. Bad Ischl	08:22	14:22
Dep. Hallstatt	08:46	14:46
Dep. Bad Aussee	09:06	15:06
Arr. Stainach	09:42	15:42

Change trains.

32

Dep. Stainach	09:55 (3)	20:49 (4)
Arr. Salzburg	12:04	22:48

(1) Restaurant car. (2) Second-class only. (3) Supplement charged for first-class includes seat reservation fee. Light refreshments. (4) Light refreshments.

Sights in **Gmunden**: A colorful little town. Artistic pottery has been made here since the 15th century. See the porcelain-tiled clocktower of the Renaissance Town Hall in the main square (Rathausplatz). Stroll from there along the beautiful flowerbeds and chestnut trees of the Esplanade to the yacht harbor and lakeshore beach. Walk on the breakwater to the Ort Chateau, built on a small island.

Sights in **Bad Ischl**: A popular mineral water spa since 1822. This is the center of the Salzkammergut resort region. Visit the home of composer Franz Lehar, now a museum. The Imperial Villa.

Sights in **Hallstaat**: One of Europe's oldest permanent settlements, it dates back to the 5th century B.C. The local museum traces the prehistoric stages of this region's culture.

See the colorful houses (blue, red, yellow or beige), every balcony and window festooned with flowers. It is a short walk to several waterfalls. Close to one that rushes through the town is a 16th century church that has a splendidly carved late Gothic altar.

You can see a unique collection of neatly piled, gaily decorated skulls of generations of villagers in the charnel house. There has never been enough land here for a cemetery.

Sights in **Bad Aussee**: This was the center of the salt region in the 15th century. Still popular for health-inducing brine baths. Both a Summer resort and Winter sports area. There are many picturesque lakes here.

Salzburg - Vienna

Marvelous views of the Alps and pretty farmland. See schedules for Vienna–Salzburg.

Salzburg - Villach - Salzburg   820

The excellent canyon and mountain scenery on this ride can be seen either on an easy one-day roundtrip from Salzburg or as a portion of the Salzburg–Venice route.

For the first way:

Dep. Salzburg	07:08 (1)	09:08 (1)	11:08 (1)	13:08 (1)	15:08 (2)
Arr. Villach	09:43	11:43	13:43	15:43	17:44

•   •   •

Dep. Villach	10:19 (2)	12:18 (2)	14:19 (1)	16:19 (1)	18:19 (1)
Arr. Salzburg	12:53	14:53	16:53	18:53	20:53

(1) Light refreshments. (2) Supplement charged for first-class includes reservation fee. Restaurant car

Here is the schedule for going from Salzburg to Italy:

88		*390*	
Dep. Salzburg	09:08 (1)	Dep. Venice (Mestre)	15:31
Arr. Venice (Mestre)	15:18	Arr. Venice (S.L.)	15:40
Change trains.			

(1) Supplement charged. Restaurant car.

The very scenic Klagenfurt–Udine–Trieste portion of the Vienna–Trieste route is described under "Vienna–Trieste." A departure from Salzburg can connect with that trip at Villach.

Vienna - Puchberg am Schneeberg - Hochschneeberg - Vienna

The ride from Hoshschneeberg back to Puchberg must be booked immediately on arrival at the summit.

These schedules are Monday-Friday.

(Unsere Bahn)

Dep. Vienna (Sud)	06:52	07:52	09:52	10:52	11:52	13:52
Arr. Wiener Neustadt	07:30	08:30	10:30	11:30	12:30	14:30
Change trains.						
Dep. Wiener Neustadt	07:36	08:36	10:36	11:36	12:36	14:36
Arr. Puchberg	08:26	09:26	11:26	12:26	13:26	15:26

Change to steam rack railway.
Dep. Puchberg   (Puchberg-Hochschneeberg services run May-October subject to demand.)
Arr. Hochschneeberg

Sights in **Puchberg**: Located at the foot of the mountain called Schneeberg, the eastern edge of the Alps. A Summer and Winter resort. Popular for water cures and weight-loss treatment.

Sights in **Hochschneeberg**: At 5,900 feet, there are good views and a restaurant at the peak.

Dep. Hochschneeberg
Arr. Puchberg   (Hochschneeberg-Puchberg services run May-October subject to demand.)

Change trains.						
Dep. Puchberg	15:37	16:37	17:37	18:37	-0-	19:37
Arr. Wiener Neustadt	16:23	17:23	18:23	19:23	-0-	20:23
Change trains.						
Dep. Wiener Neustadt	16:30	17:30	18:30	19:05	-0-	20:30
Arr. Vienna (Sud)	17:00	18:05	19:05	19:40	-0-	21:05

(1) Return journey to Puchberg must be booked *on arrival.*

Vienna - Bruck an der Mur - Innsbruck

This indirect route from Vienna to Innsbruck, traveling south of the main line (via Linz), offers excellent mountain scenery. The schedules allow a stopover in Bruck an der Mur.

820 + 830

Dep. Vienna (Sud)	09:22 (1)	11:22 (1)
Dep. Bruck an der Mur	11:24	13:24
Dep. Villach	14:19	16:10
Arr. Bischofshofen	16:09	18:09
Change trains. 810		
Dep. Bischofshofen	16:53 (2)	18:58 (2)
Arr. Innsbruck	19:35	22:09

(1) Light refreshments. (2) Restaurant car.

Sight in **Bruck an der Mur**: See "Innsbruck–Bruck an der Mur."

Vienna - Klagenfurt - Udine - Trieste

The marvelous farm and lake scenery on this route includes seeing **Worthersee**, a lake fed by warm springs that is very popular for swimming and boating, and the beautiful coastline from Udine to Trieste.

The great Worthersee resort area is open June through mid-September. The region around **Klagenfurt** has attractive lakes, rolling hills and wildlife parks.

Even if you don't stay there, at least watch for that area a few minutes before the stop at Klagenfurt. An early departure from Vienna is recommended in order to be able to see the Adriatic shore approaching Trieste in the afternoon sunlight, as we have done.

The comfortable local train from Udine hurtles downhill too fast to permit picture-taking, but you will have a memory of that truly beautiful scene forever. Have a seat on the right-hand side of the train for the best possible view.

Not only is Trieste a worthwhile one-day stopover, it is also ideal as a base for several short rail trips into Yugoslavia such as Villa Opicina, Sezana, Pivka, Postojna and Ljubljana. While staying in Trieste, it is also easy to make a one-day rail excursion to see the sights in Udine.

88			*378*		
Dep. Vienna (Sud.)	07:18 (1)	13:22 (2)	Dep. Udine	14:30 (3)	20:47
Dep. Klagenfurt	11:21	17:46	Arr. Trieste	15:36	21:56
Arr. Udine	13:58	20:40			
Change trains.					

(1) Supplement charged for first-class includes reservation fee. Restaurant car. (2) Restaurant car. (3) Second-class only. Runs Monday-Saturday.

Sights in **Trieste**: City buses go to Miramare Castle, Maximilian and Charlotte's lovely sea-side palace. Constructed in 1856, it has been restored. The fine library and much of the original furniture are exhibited. Charlotte returned here after their tragic brief time as rulers of Mexico, made insane by Maximillan's death. The Piazza deli'Unita is reminiscent of Piazza San Marco in Venice. The 15th century Castello di San Giusto. The 14th century Cathedral of San Giusto. The ruins of a Roman amphitheater. The Civic Museum of History and Art. Take a taxi or bus from the railstation up to the 15th century Castello di San Giusto for views of the city and to see the collection of weapons and armor there. It is a scenic 30-minute bus trip (#45, from Piazza G. Oberdan) to visit **Grotta Gigante**, a cave large enough to contain St. Peter's Cathedral.

If you are starting from Salzburg, this is the schedule:

88		378	
Dep. Salzburg	09:08 (1)	Dep. Udine	14:30 (2)
Arr. Udine	13:58	Arr. Trieste	15:36
Change trains.			

(1) Supplement charged. Restaurant car. (2) Second-class only.

Now for the one-day excursion to Udine:

Trieste - Udine - Trieste 378

Dep. Trieste	07:00	07:42	08:35 (1)	09:05 (2)	10:55	12:27 (3)
Arr. Udine	08:17	08:53	10:03	10:33	12:12	13:37

Sights in **Udine**: The collection of paintings in the Civic Museum and Gallery, a 20-minute walk from the railstation.

Tiepolo's paintings are featured in both the Bishop's Palace and the Cathedral. Visit Piazza della Liberta,

Dep. Udine	12:35	13:03 (1)	13:42 (3)	14:30 (3)	15:35 (1)	16:56 (3+4)
Arr. Trieste	13:45	14:34	15:06	15:36	16:43	18:10

(1) Runs daily, except Sundays and holidays. (2) Runs Sunday only. (3) Second-class only. (4) Plus other departures from Udine at 17:35 (1), 18:02 (1), 18:32 (3), 19:35 (3) and 20:45, arriving Trieste 19:00, 19:12, 19:39, 20:54 and 21:53.

Danube Cruise

This service operates daily from mid-May to late September.

845

Dep. Vienna (Reich.)	08:00	Dep. Linz	09:15
Arr. Durnstein	13:35	Arr. Durnstein	16:10
Arr. Linz	22:55	Arr. Vienna (Schif.)	20:15

Sights in **Durnstein**: This small, fortified town is at the foot of a ridge surrounded by vineyards. Richard the Lion Hearted was held for for an enormous ransom in the Castle, from which there is a wonderful view of Durnstein and the valley below it.

The town's Parish Church and its main street are interesting.

INTERNATIONAL ROUTES
FROM AUSTRIA

The Austrian gateways for travel to Germany (and on to Copenhagen) are Innsbruck, Salzburg and Vienna. Vienna is also the access point for travel to Poland and Czechoslovakia (and on to Russia), Hungary, Romania and Yugoslavia (and on to Bulgaria, Greece and Turkey). Innsbruck, Salzburg and Vienna are also starting points for trips to Italy. Innsbruck is also the gateway to Switzerland (and on to Belgium, France, Holland and Luxembourg).

Innsbruck - Munich   785

Dep. Innsbruck	07:59	09:07	09:43 (3)	11:07 (4)	14:00	15:07 (5)
Arr. Mittenwald	08:39	09:43	10:37	11:54	14:44	15:59
Dep. Mittenwald	09:03	10:03 (2)	10:48	12:03	15:03	16:02
Arr. Garmisch	09:24	10:24	11:09	12:24	15:24	16:23 (1)
Dep. Garmisch	09:34	10:27	11:18	12:27	15:34	16:27
Arr. Munich	10:51	11:52	12:38	13:51	16:51	17:53

(1) All direct trains. (2) Restaurant car. (3) Direct train to Munich. No train changes. Supplement charged. Restaurant car. (4) Direct train to Munich. No train changes. (5) Plus other departures from Innsbruck at 16:00, 17:05 (5), 19:07 and 21:05, arriving Munich 18:53, 19:56, 21:52 and 23:52.

Vienna - Salzburg - Munich 67

If you are starting this trip in Salzburg, arrive at the Salzburg railstation sufficiently in advance of departure time to complete the German Customs clearance that takes place before boarding the train. There are departures fom Salzburg in addition to those shown here, at frequent times from 06:18 to 23:58 (Table 790).

Dep. Vienna (West)	06:00 (1)	09:00 (1)	09:40 (2)	10:40 (3)	11:40 (2+5)
Arr. Salzburg	09:00	12:04	12:55 (2)	13:55 (3)	14:55 (2)
Dep. Salzburg	09:05	12:09	13:05	14:18	15:05
Arr. Munich (Hbf.)	10:35	13:36	14:35	16:07	16:34

(1) Supplement charged for first-class includes reservation fee. Restaurant car. (2) Change trains in Salzburg. Restaurant car on both trains. Salzburg-Munich: supplement charged. (3) Change trains in Salzburg. Vienna-Salzburg: restaurant car. Salzburg-Munich: light refreshments. (4) Has first-class coach and second-class couchettes. (5) Plus other departures from Vienna at 16:00 (1), 18:40 (3) and 23:30 (4) and departing Salzburg at 19:05 (1), 20:18 (3), 21:55 (1), 22:15 (3) and 04:08 (4), arriving Munich 20:36, 22:00, 24:00 and 06:03.

Vienna - Prague - Berlin 60 + 96a

Dep. Vienna (Sud.)	07:39 (1)	11:39 (1)	20:25 (2)
Arr. Prague (Hole)	12:32	16:37	01:48
Arr. Berlin (Licht.)	-0-	21:26	07:14 (3)

(1) Supplement charged for first-class includes reservation fee. Restaurant car. (2) Carries a sleeping car. Also has second-class couchettes. Coach is second-class only. (3) Arrives at Berlin's Hauptbahnhof railstation.

Vienna - Warsaw (or Kiev) - Minsk - Moscow

Both of these trains carry only sleeping cars.

94 a

Dep. Vienna (Sudbahnhof)	21:50
Arr. Warsaw (Centralna)	10:22
Dep. Warsaw (Wschodnia)	11:11
Arr. Kiev	- 0 - (1)
Arr. Minsk	22:27
Arr. Moscow (Smolenskaya)	12:06

(1) Day 3.

Vienna - Budapest - Bucharest   61 + 890

Dep. Vienna (Westbf.)	10:05 (7)	13:20	08:30
Arr. Budapest (Keleti)	13:28	16:43	11:53
Arr. Bucharest (Nord)	-0-	-0-	-0-

Dep. Vienna (Westbf.)	18:20 (3+9)
Dep. Vienna (Sudbf.)	-0-
Arr. Budapest (Keleti)	21:38
Arr. Bucharest (Nord)	-0-

(1) Departs from Vienna's Hutteldorf railstation. Carries a sleeping car. Also has couchettes. (2) Arrives at Budapest's Ferencvaros railstation. (3) Supplement charged for first-class includes reservation fee. Restaurant car. (4) Arrives Budapest's Deli railstation. (5) Restaurant car. (6) Second-class only. (7) Restaurant car. Second-class only. (8) Carries a sleeping car. Also has couchettes. (9) Plus another Vienna (West.) departure at 19:08 (8), arriving Budapest (Keleti) 22:33 and Bucharest (Nord) 14:40 on Day 2.

Vienna - Belgrade and Athens

61

Dep. Vienna (Westbf.)	08:03 (1)	19:05 (2)	23:00 (4)
Arr. Belgrade	16:45	07:11 (2+3)	08:49 (3)
Change trains. 945			
Dep. Belgrade	22:00 (5)	07:40 (5)	18:00 (7)
Dep. Thessaloniki	-0-	21:38	07:41
Arr. Athens	-0-	06:33 (6)	-0- (6)

(1) Departs from Vienna's Sudbahnhof railstation. Restaurant car. (2) Direct train to Athens. No train change in Belgrade. Has couchettes. (3) Day 3 from Vienna. (4) Carries a sleeping car. Also has couchettes. Coaches are second-class only. (5) Carries a sleeping car. Also has couchettes. (6) Day 4 from Vienna. (7) Departs from Belgrade's Centar railstation. Carries a sleeping car. Also has couchettes.

Vienna - Belgrade - Istanbul   61 + 97 b

This train carries a sleeping car and has couchettes to Belgrade. The Vienna-Istanbul portion has couchettes and second-class coaches.

Dep. Vienna (West.)	23:00		Dep. Belgrade	22:00
During Summer Time,			*All year,*	
set your watch back one hour.			*set your watch forward 2 hours.*	
Arr. Belgrade	09:07 (1)		Arr. Istanbul	19:59 (2)

(1) Day 2 from Vienna. (2) Day 2 from Belgrade.

Innsbruck - Verona and Milan or Venice   76

Dep. Innsbruck	01:38 (1)	08:39 (2)	10:26 (3)	11:22 (3)
Arr. Verona (P.N.)	05:40 (1)	12:10 (2)	14:40	15:04(4+7)
Change trains.				
Dep. Verona (P.N.)	05:45 (1)	-0-	14:27 (4)	15:00 (3)
Arr. Milan (Cen.)	-0-	14:05	-0-	16:45
Arrive Venice (S.L.)	08:45	-0-	15:52	-0-

(1) Direct train to Venice. No train change in Verona. Has couchettes. Coach is second-class. (2) Direct train to Milan. No train change in Verona. Supplement charged for first-class includes reservation fee. Restaurant car. (3) Light refreshments. (4) Supplement charged for first-class includes reservation fee. Restaurant car or light refreshments. (5) Direct train to Venice. No train change in Verona. Supplement charged for first-class includes reservation fee. Restaurant car. (6) Direct train to Milan. No train change in Verona. Carries a sleeping car. Also has couchettes. Coach is second-class. (7) Plus other Innsbruck departures at 11:22 (4), 15:22 (5) and 17:22 (4), arriving *Venice* 17:15, 20:42 and 23:16. Also other Innsbruck departures at 15:22 (4) (terminates Venice SL at 20:35) 17:22 (2) (terminates in Milan 22:55) and 23:45 (6) (terminates in Verona at 03:35.)

Innsbruck - Verona - Bologna - Florence - Rome   76

Dep. Innsbruck	01:38 (1)	10:26 (2)	11:22 (3)	22:22 (1)	23:45 (4)
Arr. Verona (P.N.)	05:40	14:40	15:04	02:14	03:35
Arr. Bologna	07:47	16:14	17:16	04:08	05:32
Arr. Florence (S.M.N.)	09:06	-0-	18:23	-0-	-0-
Arr. Rome (Ter.)	-0-	-0-	20:30	08:15	-0-

(1) Carries a sleeping car. Also has couchettes. (2) Light refreshments. (3) Supplement charged for first-class includes reservation fee. Restaurant car. (4) Has couchettes. Coaches are second-class.

Vienna - Nurnberg - Frankfurt - Cologne   66

All of these trains charge a supplement and have a restaurant car, unless designated otherwise.

Dep. Vienna (Westbf.)	08:00	10:00	12:00	14:00	22:18 (1)
Arr. Nurnberg	13:14	15:14	17:14	19:14	03:54
Arr. Frankfurt	15:35	17:35	19:35	21:35	06:43
Arr. Cologne	18:05	20:05	22:05	00:07	09:21

(1) Carries a sleeping car. Also has couchettes. Light refreshments.

Vienna - Salzburg - Munich - Paris   32

Dep. Vienna (West.)	09:00 (1)	16:00 (2)	19:40 (3)	23:30 (4)
Dep. Salzburg	12:09	19:05	23:07	03:45
Arr. Munich (Hbf.)	13:38 (1)	20:36	-0- (3)	05:54
Change trains.				
Dep. Munich	13:48	21:06 (3)	-0-	07:48 (2)
Arr. Paris (Est.)	22:18	07:04	09:30	16:20

(1) Direct train to Paris. No train change in Munich. Restaurant car. (2) Supplement charged for first-class includes reservation fee. Restaurant car. (3) Direct train to Paris. Does not call on Munich. Carries a sleeping car. Also has couchettes. Coach is second-class. Light refreshments. (4) Has couchettes.

Vienna - Venice   88 + 391

Dep. Vienna (Sud.)	13:22 (1)	19:45 (1+2)	20:15 (2+3)	22:22 (4)
Arr. Venice (S.L.)	22:28	04:10 (5)	04:42	08:32

(1) Restaurant car. (2) Carries a sleeping car. Also has couchettes. (3) Late May to mid-June: runs daily. Mid-June to late Septermber: runs Friday, Saturday and Sunday. (4) Carries a sleeping car. Also has couchettes. Coach is second-class. (5) Runs Monday-Thursday.

Innsbruck - Zurich   86

There is marvelous Alpine scenery on this route. About 2½ hours before reaching Zurich, the train passes through one of Europe's longest rail tunnels, the 6.3-mile-long Arlberg.

Dep. Innsbruck	04:15 (1)	09:02 (2) 12:44 (3)	14:44 (4+5)
Arr. Zurich	08:26	13:26 16:26	18:26

(1) Carries a sleeping car. Also has couchettes. (2) Restaurant car Innsbruck to Feldkirch. Change trains in Feldkirch at 11:17. (3) Supplement charged for first-class includes reservation fee. Restaurant car. (4) Supplement charged for first-class includes reservation fee. Has a first-class Observation Car. Restaurant car. (5) Plus other departures from Innsbruck at 16:53 (4) and 18:44 (3), arriving Zurich 20:41 and 22:26.

BENELUX

BELGIUM, NETHERLANDS AND LUXEMBOURG

Overview

Although the term Benelux is still widely used to signify Belgium, The Netherlands, and Luxembourg, these three little nations cannot really be spoken about as one entity. It is true that in Flemish Belgium and The Netherlands the people speak more or less the same language and that the currency in Belgium and Luxembourg is interchangeable, but, nonetheless, train travel in these three countries and tourism in general are distinct. The Dutch Railways (Nederlandse Spoorwegen, NS) are highly dependable and although not as fancy or high-tech as the French or German trains, wholly efficient and pleasant. The Belgian National Railways, which like everything else in Belgium has a Flemish (Nationale Maatschappij der Belgishche Spoorwegen, NMBS) and French name (Société Nationale des Chemins de fer Belges, SNCB), runs mostly without incident, although has been known to halt services at times of national labor strikes.

GENERAL INFORMATION

Belgium

• Children under six travel free on Belgian trains, children ages 6 to 11 pay half-fare, children 12 and over must pay full fare.
• There is frequent 19-minute train service 05:39 to 23:14 from Brussels' (Central) and 15-minute train service between 05:43 and 23:18 from Brussels (Nord) to the National Airport [table 201] and from the Airport to Brussels: 05:24 to 23:46.

Holland

• Children under four travel free on Dutch trains, children ages 4 to 9 pay half-fare, children 10 and over must pay full fare.
• An 18-minute train ride between Amsterdam's Central rail station and Schipol Airport [table 238]runs frequently between 00:14 and 23:38.

Luxembourg

• Children under four travel free on Luxembourgois trains, children ages four to 11 pay

BENELUX

half-fare, children 12 and over must pay full fare.

• Between Luxembourg's Gare Centrale and Findel Airport [table 5] there are frequent buses.

The signs you will see at railstations in Belgium, Holland and Luxembourg are:

	BELGIUM and LUXEMBOURG	HOLLAND
Arrival	Arrivee	Aankomst
Departure	Depart	Vertrek
Exit	Sortie	Uitgang
Information	Renseignements	Inlichtingen
Luggage Check-Room	Consigne	Hetbagagedepot
Men	Messieurs	Heren
Restaurant Car	Wagon-Restaurant	Restauratie-Wagen
Sleeping Car	Wagon-Lit	Slaapcoupe
Smoking Compartment	Fumeurs	Rokers
Station	Gare	Station
Timetable	Horaire	Spoorboekje
Track	Quai	Spoor
Women	Dames	Dames

Summer Time

Belgium, Holland and Luxembourg change to Summer Time on the last Sunday of March and convert back to Standard Time on the last Sunday of September.

A list of holidays is helpful because some trains will be noted later in this section as not running on holidays. Also, those trains which operate on holidays are filled, and it is necessary to make reservations for them long in advance.

Belgium's Holidays

NOTE: When any holiday falls on Sunday, the following day is also a holiday.

January 1	New Year's Day	July 21	Independence Day
	Easter	August 15	Assumption Day
	Easter Monday	November 1	All Saints Day
May 1	Labor Day	November 11	Armistice Day
	Ascension Day		(World War I)
	Whit Sunday	December 25	Christmas Day
	Whit Monday		

Holland's Holidays

January 1	New Year's Day	May 1	Labor Day
	Good Friday		Ascension Day
	Easter		Whit Monday
	Easter Monday	December 25	Christmas Day
April 30	Queen's Birthday	December 26	Boxing Day

Luxembourg's Holidays

January 1	New Year's Day		Whit Monday
	Shrove Monday	June 23	National Holiday
	Easter	August 15	Assumption Day
	Easter Monday	December 25	Christmas Day
May 1	Labor Day	December 26	Boxing Day
	Ascension Day		

EURAILPASS BONUSES

A 35% reduction on the normal fare for the Ostend–Dover ferry operated by Regie belge des Transports Maritimes. Reduced fare tickets are available only in Ostend and Dover. There are no Eurailpass bonuses in Holland or Luxembourg.

BENELUX TOURRAIL PASS

This pass is for any 5 days of unlimited travel out of a one month period on all the rail lines of Belgium, Holland and Luxembourg, plus railway buses in Luxembourg. Sold at the railstations of all 3 countries and also by the U.S. and Canadian offices of the Netherlands Board of Tourism (800-598-8501) and Rail Europe (see "Holland" and "France"). The 1996 adult prices are: $217 for *first*-class, $155 for *second*-class. Junior Benelux, for persons under 26 on first day of travel, is for *second*-class seats and costs $104. Children under 4 travel free when not occupying a separate seat.

BELGIUM'S TRAIN PASSES

Tourrail Pass Sold at Belgian railstations. Unlimited train travel in Belgium for any 5 days out of a 17-day period.

The 1996 *first*-class price is 2,825 Belgian francs. *Second*-class: Bf-2,020.

Children under 6 travel free.

Half-Fare Card Sold at Belgian railstations. Entitles the traveler to unlimited first-class and second-class train travel at half-fare for one month. The 1996 price is 560 Belgian francs. Validity period starts on the day chosen by the holder of the card.

The Go Pass Provides 10 *second*-class trips for persons 6 to under 26 years old. The 1996 price is 1,316 Belgian francs.

HOLLAND'S TRAIN PASSES

The 7-Day Rail Pass, Public Transport Link and Domino passes are sold by U.S.A. and Canadian travel agencies and the office of Netherlands Board of Tourism at 225 No. Michigan Ave., Suite #326, Chicago, IL 60601.

7-Day Rail Pass Seven consecutive days of unlimited train travel. The 1996 prices: $134 for *first*-class, $90 for *second*-class.

Public Transport Link Available only in combination with the 7-Day Rail Pass (above). Provides unlimited use of city buses and streetcars throughout Holland. Price for children is the same as for adults: $14.

Domino Sold in the U.S.A. Canada by travel agencies and the offices of Netherlands Board of Tourism listed under "Holland." *Both versions of Domino (below) are valid for one month and cover unlimited train travel.*

Adult Domino The 1996 *first*-class prices are: $84 for 3 days, $135 for 5 days, and $250 for 10 days. For *second*-class: $64, $100 and $178.

Junior Domino For persons age 12 to 25. Available for *second*-class only. The 1996 prices are: $46 for 3 days, $71 for 5 days, and $124 for 10 days.

PASSES SOLD ONLY IN HOLLAND

These passes are sold at railstations and accredited travel agencies. A "Public Transport Link" that provides unlimited use of all city transit services throughout Holland (buses and streetcars) is available only in combination with all of the following passes, except "Multi Rover." Prices are the same for both adults and children.

One-Day Holland Tours Netherlands Railways offers during the Spring and Summer months 72 one-day excursions from Amsterdam to interesting destinations. Eurailpass holders pay only for the non-rail portions of these trips and for admission fees.

An example is the day that starts with a train ride from Amsterdam to Koog-Zaandijk to first see 17th and 18th century wood houses brought there from many parts of Holland and then a variety of windmills, some of which still operate. After you visit the Zaandam Clockwork Museum, where Dutch clocks from 1500 to 1850 are displayed, you take a 45-minute boat ride along other old houses and windmills. Coffee or a soft drink and a pancake at a restaurant are included in the price.

One-Day Rail Pass One day of unlimited train travel. The 1996 prices: 67 Dutch florins for first-class, Dfl-58 for second-class.

One Month Rail Pass Unlimited train travel for one month (expample: June 3–July 2). The 1996 prices: 765 Dutch florins for first-class, Dfl-510 for second-class.

Rail Rover One day of unlimited train travel. During June, July and August, it is valid all day, any day. From September through May: valid only after 09:00 on Monday–Friday, all day on Saturday and Sunday. Priced for 2–6 persons.

The 1996 first-class prices: 132 Dutch florins for 2 persons, Dfl-159 for 3, Dfl-180 for 4, Dfl-205 for 5, and Dfl-228 for 6. Second-class: Dfl-88, Dfl-105, Dfl-120, Dfl-135, and Dfl-150.

Teenage Rover For people under age 18. Four days of unlimited second-class train travel. Sold only in June, July and August plus the Easter, fall and Christmas holidays. Proof of age (passport) and a passport photo are required. The 1996 price: 56 Dutch florins.

Summer Tour Unlimited train travel for any 3 days within 10 days during July and August. The 1996 first-class prices: 104 Dutch florins for one person, Dfl-149 for 2 persons. Second-class: Dfl-79 and Dfl-109.

LUXEMBOURG'S SPECIAL TICKETS

Valid on both trains and all public buses, including Luxembourg-City buses. Not valid for journeys departing from or arriving at border stations. Children under age 6 travel free.

All of the prices shown below are second-class. A supplement of 70 Luxemburg francs is charged for first-class.

Short-Distance Ticket Valid for a trip of up to one hour. The 1996 price is 35 Luxembourg francs. For a one-month ticket: 1996 price is 650 Luxembourg francs.

Book of 10 Short-Distance Tickets The 1996 price is 270 Luxembourg francs.

One-Day Network Ticket Valid for unlimited travel throughout the country from the time first used on one day until 08:00 the next morning. The 1996 price is 140 Luxembourg francs.

Book of 5 One-Day Network Tickets The 1996 price is 540 Luxembourg francs.

One-Month Network Ticket The 1996 price is 1,300 Luxembourg francs.

Group Pass For groups of 10 or more persons. If a roundtrip is in one day, the 1996 price is 70 Luxembourg francs per person. It is 140 Luxembourg francs per person if return takes place on the following day.

Senior Citizen Half-Fare A 50% reduction on both first and second-class train tickets for people over age 65. Presentation of identity card or passport required as proof of age. Not valid for journeys departing from or arriving at border stations.

ONE-DAY EXCURSIONS AND CITY-SIGHTSEEING

Here are 59 one-day rail trips that can be made comfortably from 3 major Benelux cities (Amsterdam, Brussels and Luxembourg City), returning to them in most cases before dinner time. (Five of these trips offer, in addition to interesting destinations, scenic fields of flowers in bloom mid-March through May.) Notes are provided on what to see and do at each destination. The number after the name of each route is the Cook's timetable. Three other one-day trips are recommended for exceptional scenery.

Schedules for international connections conclude this section.

Amsterdam

Trains depart Amsterdam's Central, RAI and Zuid railstations for Schipol (the airport) and from Schipol to Amsterdam at frequent times during all 24 hours. The journey takes 18 minutes.

The Tourist Office in the Central railstation is open daily 08:45–23:00 from Easter to September 30.

Your city sightseeing in Amsterdam should include the Rijkmuseum (State Museum) collection of Rembrandt, Rubens, Goya and El Greco paintings (42 Stadhouderskade). Also exhibited there are Dresden china, delftware, tapestries, prints, furniture, dollhouses and sculpture.

See the works of Chagall, Cezanne, Picasso, Calder, Pollack, Rodin, Braque and Warhol at the Stedelijkmuseum (Municipal Museum), 13 Paulus Potterstraat. A complete spectrum of Van Gogh paintings plus several by Gauguin and Toulouse-Lautrec at the Museum Vincent van Gogh (7–11 Paulus Potterstraat). The display of Indonesian and Far Eastern art and anthropology at the Tropical Museum.

The exhibit of 300 ship models, many atlases and charts, and 5,000 books in the National Shipping Museum (1–7 Kattenburgplein). Rembrandt's house (4–6 Jodenbreestraat). The Flea Market, near Rembrandt's house. Exhibits depicting the city's history since its founding in 1270, at the Amsterdam Historical Museum (92 Kalversraat).

The history of Jews in Holland since 1590, at the Jewish Historical Museum (4

Nieumarkt). The altar and organ at the attic church of the 17th century Amstelkring Museum (40 Oudezijds Voorburgwal), the last of the "hidden" Catholic churches in Holland, with interesting 17th and 18th century furniture.

All 9 museums are open Tuesday-Saturday 10:00–17:00 and on Sundays and holidays 13:00–17:00.

Visit the Anne Frank House (263 Prinsengracht), open Monday-Saturday 9:00–17:00 and on Sundays and holidays 10:00–17:00. Take a 75-minute ride in a glass-roofed canal boat, starting at the piers in front of Central railstation or at Stadhouderskade, near the Rijksmuseum.

Royal Palace. The Tower of Tears. Nieuwe Kerk on the Dam, open Monday-Saturday 10:00–17:00, Sunday 12:00–15:00. Mint Tower. Free samples when ending the tour of Heineken Brewery, Monday–Friday starting at 09:30. The Flower Market (Bloemenmarkt), open Monday–Friday. Several diamond-cutting factories.

The Theater Museum (168 Herengracht), open Tuesday–Friday 10:00–17:00, Sundays and holidays 11:00–17:00. See Willet Holthuyen Museum (5 Herengracht), a classical 17th century canal house, elegantly furnished in the style of Holland's Golden Age. Open Monday-Saturday 09:30–17:00, Sundays and holidays 13:00–17:00.

Take an inexpensive half-day bus tour to the heart of the tulip district. It is near Aalsmeer, less than 45 minutes from Amsterdam. Visit the daily Aalsmeer Flower Auction, close to Amsterdam's Schipol Airport. The peak time at the auction is 08:00–10:00.

Brussels

Sightseeing starts in Grand Place, the ornate town square with many gilded buildings. Inside Hotel de Ville (Town Hall), there is a tapestry museum open daily in Summer, Monday–Friday in Winter. Next to it is a reproduction of a 17th century brewery. See the 15th century Notre Dame des Victoires church and the 17th century Flemish houses in nearby Place du Grand Sablon.

The marvelous Place Parc de Bruxeles gardens and lakes. The Royal Palace, at one end of this park, is open daily except Monday 09:30–16:00 for about 6 weeks during Summer. The Belgian Parliament is located at the other end of the park.

One of the world's best collections of 15th and 16th century Flemish and Dutch paintings (Rubens, Brueghel, Bosch) is exhibited at the Museum of Ancient Art & Modern Art on Rue de la Regence, open daily except Monday 10:00–17:00.

Nearby, the collection of rare musical instruments in the Royal Conservatory of Music at the Petit Sablon (also on Rue de la Regence), open Tuesday, Thursday and Saturday 14:30–16:30, Sunday 10:30-22:00, Wednesday 20:00–22:00.

The collection of paintings by both medieval masters (one section devoted entirely to Bruegel) and also those of later centuries through the 19th, in the Beaux Arts Museum at 3 Rue de la Regence. Then go through a short passageway to the new (1984) Modern Art Museum (Henry Moore, Dali, Magritte, Delvaux). Both museums are open daily except Monday 10:00–17:00.

See the impressive array of African art in The Royal Museum of Central Africa, 12km east, in Tervuren Park & Arboretum. The view from the Palais de Justice. The Law Courts.

The tapestries in the 13th century Cathedral of St. Michael.

The Brussels City Museum. The Museum of Arms and Armor. The museum of sculptures by Constantin Meunier, whose work depicts the dignity of laborers. The Postal Museum. The Royal Greenhouses. The Brueghel Museum, in the house where the painter lived his last 6 years.

The Railway Museum, on the mezzanine of Brussels' Nord railstation. The Art Nouveau pieces in the Horta Museum at 25 Rue Americaine, open daily except Mondays and holidays 14:00–17:30.

The most famous gourmet food emporium here is the Rob store at Boulevard de la Woluwe 28. (Take the subway from the center of town to the Tomberg stop and then bus #42, which stops in front of Rob.) Fruits from all over the world, an assortment of 25 ordinary and exotic pates (baby boar!), eel cooked in green sauce, snails marinated in wine sauce, numerous fish (live trout, Scotch salmon, Norwegian lobsters), 600 different wines, 35 types of mustard, chocolates galore.

A bus can be taken 10 miles to **Waterloo.**

Luxembourg City

The Citadel, with its 53 forts connected by 16 miles of tunnels. Fish Market, site of the city's oldest buildings. The State Museum, open daily except Monday 10:00–12:00 and 14:00–18:00. The Palais Grand-Ducal. The splendid view from the bridge that crosses the River Alzette. The Palais Municipal, on the Place d'Armes. The Municipal Art Gallery, open daily except Monday during Summer, only on Saturday and Sunday the rest of the year. City Hall. The old quarter, Pfaffenthal, with its medieval buildings. The Fort of Three Acorns. Malakoff Tower. The Church of St. Michael.

The Three Towers, marking the outer limits of the town in 1050. Notre Dame Cathedral. The 4th century Chapel of St. Quirinus, one of the oldest shrines in Christendom. The Museum of History and Art. General Patton's grave in the U.S. Military Cemetery, 3 miles away, at **Hamm.**

In the following timetables, where a city has more than one railstation we have designated the particular station after the name of the city (in parentheses).

On day trips from Amsterdam that we have designated "H-L," you will see in the area between Haarlem and Leiden, from mid-March through May, fields of tulips, narcissus, crocus and other bulb flowers in bloom. The region is known as the "Champs de Fleurs" (Fields of Flowers).

Amsterdam - Alkmaar - Amsterdam   225

| Dep. Amsterdam | every 30 minutes from 07:22 to 23:22 |
| Arr. Alkmaar | 30 minutes later |

Sights in **Alkmaar**: The Friday Cheese Market, from the end of April until the end of September, 10:00–12:00. The organ at St. Lawrence Church.

Dep. Alkmaar	every 30 minutes from 08:08 to 23:38
Arr. Amsterdam	30 minutes later

Amsterdam - Alkmaar - Haarlem - Amsterdam   225 + 224

It is easy to visit both Alkmaar and Haarlem in a single day-trip.

Dep Amsterdam	twice each hour		Dep. Haarlem	twice each hour.
Arr. Alkmaar	30 minutes later.		Arrive Amsterdam	19 minutes later.
Change trains.				
Dep. Alkmaar	twice each hour.			
Arr. Haarlem	28 minutes later.			

Amsterdam - Amersfoort - Amsterdam   230

Dep. Amsterdam	Frequent times from 06:32 to 23:32
Arr. Amersfoort	34 minutes later

Sights in **Amersfoort**: A beautiful citadel town with many canals and ancient streets. Popular among antique collectors and for taking side trips to **Spakenburg** (a quaint fishing village on the old Zuider Zee), **Laren** (to visit the Singer Museum), **Zeist** (to see the beautifully-furnished castle there), **Baarn** (to visit Palace Soestdijk, the residence of the former Queen Juliana, **Muiden** (to see the 15th century moated castle, Muiderslot).

Dep. Amersfoort	Frequent times from 07:24 to 23:23
Arr. Amsterdam	34 minutes later

Amsterdam - Antwerp - Amsterdam   18

Dep. Amsterdam	Frequent times from 06:23 to 21:25
Arr. Antwerp (Cen.)	2 hours and 20 minutes later

Sights in **Antwerp:** To the right of the railstation is one of the best zoos in the world, set in a beautiful garden. It is open daily 08:30–17:00. Walk through the maze of streets called Grote Markt (art galleries, bakeries, fruit stalls, antique shops).

You can watch diamonds being cut and polished at Diamond Land, 33 Appelmanstraat, open daily except Sunday 09:00–18:00. There is a good exhibit of the history of diamonds at the Provincial Museum of Safety, 28–30 Jezusstraat, open Wednesday-Saturday 10:00–17:00, with demonstrations on Saturday 14:00–17:00.

Visit the Cathedral, open April through mid-October: Monday-Friday 12:00–17:00, Saturday 12:00–15:00, Sunday 13:00–17:00. The rest of the year: Monday 14:00–17:00, Saturday 12:00–15:00, Sunday 13:00–17:00.

Flemish, Italian, French, Dutch and German masterpieces in the Gallery of Fine Arts, open daily except Monday 10:00–17:00. Rubens House, with many of his paintings, at 9–11 Wapper, open daily 10:00–17:00. The 16th century printing shop in the Plantin-Moretus Museum. The Marine Museum.

The Mayer van den Bergh Museum. The Folklore Museum. Town Hall. Guild Houses. Vieille Bourse (the Old Stock Exchange). The Rockox Mansion. The view of Antwerp from the 24th floor of Torengebouw.

Now a classy suburb of Antwerp, **Middelheim** was first settled in the 14th century. See there the more than 300 statues (by Henry Moore, Vic Gentil, Charles Leplae and many other great sculptors) in the 30-acre Middelheim Open-Air Museum of Sculpture, founded in 1950. It is 30 minutes by bus #17, #27 or #32, from Antwerp's Central railstation. The bus driver will tell you where to get off, and the walk to the sculpture park is 15 minutes from there, passing many splendid mansions.

One can begin circling the park-museum by starting either toward the left of the entrance (in the direction of the statue of Balzac) or to the right, along a tree-shaded stream and through a lawn that has many statues.

The park (admission free) is open daily 10:00 to sunset about 17:00 in Winter, 21:00 in Summer.

Dep. Antwerp (Cen.)	Frequent times from 07:54 to 22:00
Arr. Amsterdam	2 hours and 20 minutes later

Amsterdam - Apeldoorn 231

Dep. Amsterdam (Cen.)	2 minutes after every hour from 07:02 to 22:02
Arr. Apeldoorn	1 hour and 4 minutes later

Sights in **Apeldoorn:** From the railstation, take buses #102, #104 and #106 to the Het Loo Palace. Set in a 27,000-acre Royal Forest, the palace was a private residence for the Dutch royal family until it became a state museum in 1971.

Both the lavish, enormous palace and the geometric patterns of its extraordinary gardens are well worth visiting. Seventeenth century tapestries, magnificent furniture, exceptional Delft pottery and fine paintings (Rembrandt, Vermeer, van Ruisdael) are exhibited in the palace.

Dep. Apeldoorn	26 minutes after every hour from 07:26 to 23:26
Arr. Amsterdam (Cen.)	1 hour and 4 minutes later

Amsterdam - Arnhem - Amsterdam   240

Dep. Amsterdam (Cent.)	Frequent times from 06:06 to 23:49
Arr. Arnhem	60–70 minutes later

Sights in **Arnhem:** The nearly 3-square-mile Netherlands Open-Air Museum, a col- lection of several farm villages, depicting rural lifestyles from the 18th to early 20th centuries. Colored arrows direct visitors to one, 2 and 4-hour tours. Open April–October, Monday-Friday 09:00–17:00, Sunday 10:00–17:00. At the craft exhibits, wood shoes are chiseled, bread is baked, baskets and paper are made. See a blacksmith at his forge. Don't fail to try the little pancake balls called "poffertjes," and then eat some pannekoeken (traditional Dutch pancakes) and wafelen (waffles).

Also visit the 16th century Grootekerk (Ptotestant Church) and the extensively-restored Eusebiuskerk, a Gothic church. See the Duivelshuis (devil's house). The best collection of Van Gogh is at the Kroller-Muller Museum in the nearby National Park. Special buses go the several miles from the railstation to the museum and surrounding 13,300-acre national park during June, July and August. The museum is open Tuesday–Saturday 10:00–17:00, Sunday 11:00–17:00.

Dep. Arnhem	Frequent times from 06:37 to 23:40
Arr. Amsterdam (Cent.)	60–70 minutes later

Amsterdam - Bonn

All of the Amsterdam–Cologne and v.v trains charge a supplement.

28

Dep. Amsterdam (Cen.)	06:02 (1)	07:06 (1)	08:00 (3)	09:00 (3)	11:06 (1)
Arr. Cologne	08:42	09:42	10:57	11:57	13:42
Change trains.					
710 + 711					
Dep. Cologne	09:19	10:19	11:19	12:19	14:19
Arr. Bonn	09:51	10:51	11:51	12:51	14:51

Sights in **Bonn**: See notes about Bonn under "Cologne–Bonn"

Dep. Bonn	12:12	14:12	16:12	18:12	20:12
Arr. Cologne	12:38	14:38	16:38	18:38	20:38
Change trains.					
28					
Dep. Cologne	13:17 (1)	15:17 (1)	17:17 (1)	19:02 (3)	21:17 (1)
Arr. Amsterdam	15:51	17:51	19:51	21:51	23:51

(1) Light refreshments. (3) Restaurant car.

Amsterdam - Brussels - Amsterdam   205

Dep. Amsterdam	06:23	07:25	08:25	09:25	10:25	11:25
Arr. Brussels (Nord)	09:21	10:21	11:21	12:21	13:21	14:21
Arr. Brussels (Cen.)	09:26	10:26	11:26	12:26	13:26	14:26
Arr. Brussels (Midi)	09:30	10:30	11:30	12:30	13:30	14:30
Dep. Brussels (Midi)	13:10	14:10	15:10	16:10	17:10	18:10 (1)
Dep. Brussels (Cen.)	13:14	14:14	15:14	16:14	17:14	18:14
Dep. Brussels (Nord)	13:19	14:19	15:19	16:19	17:19	18:19
Arr. Amsterdam	16:08	17:08	18:08	19:08	20:08	21:08

(1) Plus other departures from Brussels (Midi) at 19:10, 20:10 and 21:10, arriving Amsterdam 22:08, 23:08 and 00:10.

Amsterdam - Cologne   28

All of these trains charge a supplement.

Amsterdam	06:02 (1)	07:06 (1)	08:00 (2)	09:00 (2)	11:06 (1)
Arr. Cologne	08:42	09:42	10:57	11:57	13:42
Dep. Cologne	13:17 (1)	15:17 (1)	17:17 (1)	18:02 (2)	19:02 (2)
Arr. Amsterdam	15:51	17:51	19:51	20:51	21:51

(1) Light refreshments. (2) Restaurant car.

Amsterdam - Delft - Amsterdam (H-L)   220

Dep. Amsterdam (Cen.)	Frequent times from 00:18 to 23:43
Arr. Delft	60 minutes later

Sights in **Delft**: The tourist information office (on the main square) provides a brochure that describes a walking tour which includes all of the city's principal sights.

See the 14th century New Church, where members of the Dutch royal family are buried. The Mausoleum of William the Silent at the 15th century New Church. The 17th century Prinsenhof (Princes Court), housing the Municipal Museum. Tetar van Elven Museum, containing the works of Vermeer and Pieter de Hoogh. Old Church. The Grain Market. Town Hall. The Old Delft Canal.

The Delft Pottery Factory ("De Porceleyne Fles") at 196 Rotterdamsweg is open May–September 09:00–17:00 Monday-Saturday and 13:00–18:00 on Sunday. It is open 09:00–17:00 Monday–Saturday from October through April. Its tour includes visiting a showroom, a shop and exhibits of antique tiles and mural ceramics.

| Dep. Delft | Frequent times from 00:25 to 23:58 |
| Arr. Amsterdam (Cen.) | 60 minutes later |

Amsterdam - Den Haag - Amsterdam (H-L)   220

| Dep. Amsterdam | 2–3 times each hour from 05:31 to 23:43 |
| Arr. Den Haag (H.S.) | 45–50 minutes later |

Sights in **Den Haag**: Binnenhof, a complex of palaces and courtyards, including the 13th century Hall of Knights (an 118-by-56-foot banquet hall where Holland's Parliament meets every September), and Gevangenpoort, Holland's 14th century prison.

Mauritshuis, a great art gallery (Rembrandt, Vermeers, Rubens) The finest collection in the world of 19th century Dutch art, at the Gemeente Museum. The collection of Rembrandts at the Bredius Museum. The Peace Palace. The Hidden Church, at 38 Molenstraat. The Mesdag Museum. The Costume Museum. Municipal Museum. The miniature city of Madurodam, with everything on a scale of 1/25th life size.

The marvelous paintings in the Johan de Witt Huis at Kneuterdijk 6, open Monday-Saturday 10:00–17:00, and on Sundays and holidays 11:00–17:00. The more than 1,000 puppets and marionettes at the Puppet Museum. The 5 miles of wide, beautiful beach.

| Dep. Den Haag (H.S.) | 2–3 times each hour from 05:39 to 00:38 |
| Arr. Amsterdam | 45–50 minutes later |

Amsterdam - Den Haag + Utrecht - Amsterdam (H-L)

It is possible to visit both Den Haag (see sightseeing notes above) and Utrecht in one day.

220
| Dep. Amsterdam | Frequent departures from 05:31 to 23:43 |
| Arr. Den Haag (**H.S.**) | 45–50 minutes later |

Change trains and railstations.
230
| Dep. Den Haag (**Cen.**) | Frequent times from 07:36 to 22:36 |
| Arr. Utrecht | 40 minutes later |

Change trains
240
| Dep. Utrecht | Frequent times from 07:15 to 00:20 |
| Arr. Amsterdam | 30 minutes later |

For those who prefer the direct trip to Utrecht and to have more time there, refer to notes under "Amsterdam–Utrecht"

Sights in **Utrecht**: The 13th century Dom Cathedral, and the view from the top of its 465 steps (300 feet high). In fall, winter and spring the tower is open only on weekends. Nearby is the Music Box and Street Organ Museum on Achter de Dom, open Tuesday-Saturday 11:00-16:00. Next door is the Museum of Contemporary Art at 14 Achter de Dom.

The museum of mechanical instruments, at 38 Lange Nieuwstraat. The Netherlands Railway Museum, at 6 Van Oldenberneveltlaan, open Tuesday–Saturday 10:00–17:00, Sundays 13:00–17:00. The 11th century St. Peter's Church. The paintings and Viking ship in the Centraal Museum at 1 Agnietenstraat, open Tuesday-Saturday 10:00–17:00, Sundays and holidays 14:00–17:00.

The ancient fish market, Vis Markt, an institution at the same location since the 12th century. The largest medieval art collection in Holland, at the Museum of Religious Art in Het Catherijneconvent (St. Catherine's Church and Convent).

The collection of 180 musical instruments ("from music box to barrel organ") displayed at the van Speeldos tot Pierement Museum. The Gold, Silver and Clock Museum. The Museum of Contemporary Art. The Museum of the Insurance Business.

Nearby interesting villages: **Breukelen**, for which New York's Brooklyn was named (castles, 17th century mansions), **Oudewater** (famous for its stork colony and 3-aisle church), and **Loenen** (known for its 18th century houses and their lovely gardens).

Amsterdam - Dusseldorf - Amsterdam   28

All of these trains charge a supplement.

Dep. Amsterdam (Cen.)	06:02 (1)	07:06 (1)	08:00 (2)	09:00 (2)	11:06 (1)
Arr. Dusseldorf	08:19	09:19	10:32	11:32	13:19

Sights in **Dusseldorf**: See notes about Dusseldorf under "Cologne–Dusseldorf"

Dep. Dusseldorf	13:39 (1)	15:39 (1)	17:39 (1)	18:26 (2)	19:26 (2+3)
Arr. Amsterdam (Cen.)	15:51	17:51	19:51	20:51	21:51

(1) Light refreshments. (2) Restaurant car. (3) Plus another Dusseldorf departure at 21:39 (1).

Amsterdam - Enkhuizen - Amsterdam   225

Local trains run every 30 minutes 07:19–23:19 for the 62-minute trip north from Amsterdam's Central railstation. Trains depart Enkhuizen every 30 minutes 08:09–23:09 for the 64-minute trip back to Amsterdam.

It is a 4-minute walk from the Enkhuizen railstation to its ferry dock. Boats depart every 15 minutes to the 700-acre Zuider Zee Open Air Museum, open summer months 10:00–17:00.

This museum consists of 130 houses, portraying life and work from 1880 to 1932. Allow at least 2 hours to tour it. Then take a 10-minute walk to the Binnenmuseum, an indoor complex of 15 exhibition halls displaying fine examples of furniture, fishing boats, toys and other items. It is open mid-February to December 31: Monday–Saturday 10:00-17:00, Sunday 12:00–17:00.

Amsterdam - Gouda - Amsterdam   239

Dep. Amsterdam	22 minutes after each hour, from 07:22 to 22:22
Arr. Gouda	50 minutes later

Sights in **Gouda**: Stained-glass in Sint Janskerk. The 15th century Town Hall. The famous Thursday cheese market.

Dep. Gouda	18 minutes after each hour, from 06:18 to 23:18
Arr. Amsterdam	50 minutes later

Amsterdam - Haarlem - Amsterdam   220

Dep. Amsterdam (Cen.)	Twice each hour, from 07:09 to 00:46
Arr. Haarlem	14 minutes later

Sights in **Haarlem**: It is only a few minutes' walk from the railstation to town center, Grote Markt, where jousting tournaments took place in the Middle Ages. Nearby is the 14th century Town Hall and many cafes.

Works by Franz Hals and many other great painters plus Delft tiles, Flemish wallpaper made of gilded and painted panels of leather, silver tankards and candlestands, pikes and swords, and stained and painted glass windows at the Frans Hals Museum at 62 Groot Heiligland (Note the address. That is the only mark outside the building!). This museum is only a 20-minute walk from the railstation, or take buses 1, 2, 3, 5, 6, 70 or 71.

In St. Bavo's, Holland's most beautiful church, hear the massive 5,000-pipe Baroque organ (ivory and tortoise shell keyboard) built in 1738 by Christiaan Muller. Mozart played it when he was 10 years old. It can be heard Sundays at 10:00 and 19:00, also at free concerts Tuesday at 20:15.

The World Clock at 88 Wagenweg. Teyler's Museum at 16 Spaarme (open Tuesday-Saturday 10:00–17:00), to see 16th to 20th century Dutch, Italian and French paintings as well as antique musical instruments, telescopes and globes.

Dep. Haarlem	Twice each hour, from 07:36 to 01:16
Arr. Amsterdam (Cen.)	14 minutes later

Amsterdam - Hoorn - Amsterdam 225

| Dep. Amsterdam | Freq. times 07:19-00:31 | Dep. Hoorn | Freq. times 06:33-23:35 |
| Arr. Hoorn | 40 minutes later | Arr. Amsterdam | 40 minutes later |

Sights in **Hoorn**: The full-scale enactment of 17th century trades and crafts in Hoorn's "Old Dutch Market" takes place in the Rodesteen Square on Wednesdays mid-June to mid-August: folk dances and stalls with basket weaving, net mending and the making of wood shoes. Daily from mid-June to mid-August (plus Saturdays and Sundays from mid-August through mid-September), a steam train with antique coaches operates between Hoorn and · **Medemblik**.

See Hoorn's 17th century mansions and warehouses. The collection of paintings and antiques in the West Friesian Museum. The 17th century Weighhouse. The 16th century Hospital of St. John. The 2 medieval churches: Noorderkerk and Oosterkerk. The 16th century St. Mary Tower and East Gate, remains of the original fortification. The 17th century almshouse, St. Pietershof.

Amsterdam - Leiden - Amsterdam (H-L) 220

| Dep. Amsterdam | Frequent times during all 24 hours |
| Arr. Leiden | 33 minutes later |

Sights in **Leiden**: Pieterskerk, the church where the Pilgrim fathers worshipped for 10 years before setting sail for America in 1620. The University. The Royal Arms Museum. The National Museum of Antiquities. The Municipal Museum. The National Ethnological Museum. The nearby flower center, called **Keukenhof**.

| Dep. Leiden | Frequent times during all 24 hours |
| Arr. Amsterdam | 33 minutes later |

Amsterdam - Maastricht - Amsterdam 245

All of these trains have light refreshments.

| Dep. Amsterdam | 06:32 (1) Plus frequent times daily 07:32-22:02 |
| Arr. Maastricht | 2½ hours after departing Amsterdam |

Sights in **Maastricht**: The 6th century St. Servatius Church, oldest church in Holland, where Charlemagne occasionally attended mass. There is a large statue of him in the rear of the church. Shoppers from not only nearby Dutch cities but even from Belgium, France and Germany come to the Market Day (produce and pastries) at Town Hall Square, Fridays 08:00–13:00.

See the carved wood columns of the choir in the 10th century Basilica of Our Gracious Lady. The many 17th and 18th century houses on the Stokstraat Quarter, each having a plaque that shows the construction date, the owner's name and his trade. Some of the old houses are now antique shops, art galleries and boutiques. Try the local Limburger cheese and gingerbread in one of the sidewalk cafes on famous Vrijthof Square.

A bus departs from the railstation for the short trip to the Mount St. Peter caves, consisting of 200 miles of labyrinths where people hid during a Spanish invasion in 1570. It was originally a sandstone quarry, worked from Roman times until the end of the 19th century. Since 1584, famous visitors (Napoleon, Archduke Ferdinand of Spain, Voltaire, Sir Walter Scott) have scratched their signatures on the walls of the very cold and very damp caves.

Dep. Maastricht	Frequent times from 07:31 to 21:31
Arr. Amsterdam	2½ hours later

(1) Runs Monday–Friday, except holidays.

Amsterdam - Paris - Amsterdam   18

Both of these trains charge a supplement.

Dep. Amsterdam (Cen.)	06:57 (1)	Dep. Paris (Nord)	18:38 (2)
Arr. Paris (Nord)	12:59	Arr. Amsterdam (Cen.)	23:59

(1) Runs daily. Light refreshments. (2) Reservation required. Runs daily, except Saturday. Restaurant car.

Amsterdam - Rotterdam - Amsterdam (H-L)   220 + 239

Dep. Amsterdam	Frequent times during all 24 hours
Arr. Rotterdam (Cent.)	60–70 minutes later

Sights in **Rotterdam**: The Netherlands Tourist Information Bureau has offices all over Holland. Look for its "VVV" sign.

Don't miss the view of the city and port from the top of the 340-foot high Euromast, open daily 09:00–22:00 March 15–October 14, and 09:00–18:00 October 15–March 14. Nearby, Heineken's Brewery (Crookswijksesingel 50).

The fantastic collection of 15th to 19th century Flemish and Dutch paintings and a wing of modern sculpture and art (Van Gogh and Kandinsky to the present day) as well as objects of glass, pewter, silver, lace, furniture and tiles in the Boymans-van Beuningen Museum (Mathenesserlaan 18–20).

Devices used by smugglers to defraud customs, at the Profesor van der Poel Tax Museum (Parklaan 14). The collection of globes, ships and atlases in the Maritime Museum (Leuvehaven 1). Many old vessels there can be visited.

The 75-minute boat trip in the harbor, one of the world's largest ports, departing every

45 minutes from Willemsplein Landing.

Stroll through the noteworthy Lijnbaan shopping center. Hear a free lunchtime concert every day at De Doelen, an enormous complex of music and congress halls, just across from Central railstation.

Unwind in the 10,000-acre Zuiderpark, Plaswijck Park, Zuiderparkgordel, Het Park, and the Kralingse Bos (woods). See the wide variety of trees in Arboretum Trompenburg.

Visit the collection of elephants, orangutans, tigers (Sumatran, Siberian and Bengal), great apes, reptiles and seals in the Blijdorp Zoo (open 09:00–17:00).

Enjoy many statues located throughout the city, particularly Mastroianni's "Kiss," at the Central Railroad Station. Visit "De Ster," a working windmill (spice and snuff grinding) near Kralingse Lake.

The collection of folk art of primitive cultures from the non-Western world at the Museum of Ethnology (Willemskade 25). Complete 17th, 18th and 19th-century interiors at the Rotterdam Historical Museum in the Schielands Huis (Korte Hoogstraat 31). Many art galleries, including Lijnbaan Centrum (Linjbaan 165) and Kunstzaal (Zuidplein 120). The Henrik Chabot Museum. The 14th century church, St. Laurenskerk.

Nearby **Delfshaven** is the port from which the Puritans started their voyage to the New World, sailing from there on July 22, 1620, before boarding the Mayflower off the English coast. That group spent its last night praying in Delfshaven's Reformed Church, now called Pelgrimvaderskerk (Pilgrim Fathers' Church). A stained-glass window and a plaque there commemorate the Pilgrims' sailing. Visit the "De Dubbelde Palmboom" Museum (with everyday objects used centuries ago in Rotterdam) and a pewter workshop in the Sack Carriers guildhouse.

The enormous hydraulic project of the Haringvliet sluices can be seen in nearby **Stellendam**.

Dep. Rotterdam (Cent.)	Frequent times during all 24 hours
Arr. Amsterdam	60–70 minutes later

Amsterdam - Rotterdam + Den Haag - Amsterdam (H-L)   220

This circle trip allows seeing only a few of the sights in Rotterdam (see notes in preceding listing) and in Den Haag (see notes earlier in this section), but one can see something of both Rotterdam and Den Haag in this one-day trip.

Dep. Amsterdam (Cen.)	Frequent times during all 24 hours
Arr. Rotterdam (Cen.)	65 minutes later
Dep. Rotterdam (Cen.)	Frequent times from 05:15 to 01:02
Arr. Den Haag (Hbf.)	16–24 minutes later
Dep. Den Haag	Frequent times from 05:39 to 00:38
Arr. Amsterdam (Cen.)	35–55 minutes later

Amsterdam - Utrecht - Amsterdam (H-L)   240 + 245

Dep. Amsterdam   Frequent times from 06:06 to 23:49
Arr. Utrecht   36–44 minutes later

Sights in **Utrecht**: see notes about sightseeing in Utrecht under "Amsterdam–Den Haag +
Utrecht–Amsterdam"

Dep. Utrecht   3–4 times each hour from 06:37 until 00:20
Arr. Amsterdam   36–44 minutes later

Amsterdam - Zwolle - Amsterdam   230

All of these trains have light refreshments.

Dep. Amsterdam   Hourly, from 06:32 to 23:32
Arr. Zwolle   80 minutes later

Sights in **Zwolle**: Hear the famous Schnitger Organ in the magnificent St. Michael's
Church. There are many beautiful buildings in this more than 700-year old town on the
Ijssel River. This is a popular base for taking side trips to **Hattem** (great for local arts and
crafts) and **Giethoorn** (the Venice of Holland, where everything moves on water).

Dep. Zwolle   Hourly, from 07:48 to 22:48
Arr. Amsterdam   80 minutes later

Brussels - Aachen - Brussels   200

All of these trains have light refreshments.

Dep. Brussels (Midi)	06:47	07:47	09:47 (1)	10:47	11:47 (1)
Dep. Brussels (Cen.)	06:52	07:52	09:52	10:47	11:52
Dep. Brussels (Nord)	06:57	07:57	09:57	10:52	11:57
Arr. Aachen	08:43	09:43	11:53	12:43	13:51

Sights in **Aachen**: Charlemagne's 8th century treasury at the Cathedral contains an extraordinary collection of German medieval ecclesiastical gold and silver, including the Shrine of
the Virgin Mary, completed in 1236. The Grand Coronation Chamber in Town Hall.

Dep. Aachen	13:05	14:10 (1)	15:05	16:07 (1)	17:05	19:05 (2)
Arr. Brussels (Nord)	14:47	15:48	16:47	17:49	18:47	20:47
Arr. Brussels (Cen.)	14:52	-0-	16:52	-0-	18:52	20:52
Arr. Brussels (Midi)	14:55	15:56	16:56	18:01	18:56	20:56

(1) Restaurant car. (2) Plus another Aachen departure at 21:05, arriving Brussels (Nord) 22:47.

Brussels - Amsterdam - Brussels   18

Dep. Brussels (Midi)	Frequent times from 06:10 to 21:10
Dep. Brussels (Cen.)	4 minutes after departing Midi station
Dep. Brussels (Nord)	4 minutes after departing Central station
Arr. Amsterdam	3 hours after departing Brussels (Midi)

Sights in **Amsterdam**: See notes about sightseeing in Amsterdam.

Dep. Amsterdam	Frequent times from 06:23 to 20:25
Arr. Brussels (Nord)	3 hours later
Arr. Brussels (Cen.)	4 minutes after arriving Nord station
Arr. Brussels (Midi)	4 minutes after arriving Central station

Brussels - Antwerp - Brussels   205

Dep. Brussels (Midi)	Frequent times from 06:10 to 23:30
Dep. Brussels (Cen.)	4 minutes later
Dep. Brussels (Nord)	4 minutes after departing Central station
Arr. Antwerp (Cen.)	45 minutes after departing Brussels (Midi)

Sights in **Antwerp**: See notes about sightseeing in Antwerp under "Amsterdam–Antwerp–Amsterdam"

Dep. Antwerp (Cen.)	Frequent times from 06:19 to 23:19
Arr. Brussels (Nord)	40 minutes later
Arr. Brussels (Cen.)	4 minutes after arriving Nord station
Arr. Brussels (Midi)	4 minutes after departing Central station

Brussels - Brugge - Brussels   200

Dep. Brussels (Nord)	Frequent times from 05:47 to 22:47
Dep. Brussels (Cen.)	4 minutes after departing Nord station
Dep. Brussels (Midi)	7 minutes after departing Central station
Arr. Brugge	60 minutes after departing Brussels (Midi)

Sights in **Brugge**: The splendid view from the top of the 255-foot-high 13th century Belfry (365 steps), with its famous 47-bell carillon, in the city's main square, Markt. The Belfry's tower is closed 12:00–14:00. The interesting 15th century Town Hall and 15th century Recorders' House are on this square. The Tourist office is in the nearby Government Palace. (Many cafes are located in this area.)

At the 12th century Basilica of the Holy Blood, a phial said to contain a few drops of Christ's blood is displayed on Fridays. It was brought to Brugge in 1150 from the Second Crusade. Also there: a fine display of gold, silver and copper artwork. Open daily, except 12:00–14:30.

See the lace, pottery, gold pieces, musical instruments and weapons in the 15th century mansion that houses the Gruuthuse Museum. The small museum in the 13th century Saint Saviour's Cathedral. The black slate and gilded brass 16th century effigies and Michelangelo's white carrara marble Madonna with Child statue in the Church of Our Lady. Behind the Church, the Dutch masterpieces at the Groeninge Museum (open daily 09:30–12:00 and 14:00–17:00).

The collection of Old Flemish School paintings at the Hans Memling Museum, in a section of the 13th century Hospital of St. John (open 09:00–12:30 and 14:00–18:00 in Summer, 09:00–12:00 and 14:00–16:00 the rest of the year). Paintings and silverwork at the Archer's Guild of St. Sebastian. Ter Buerze, the world's first stock exchange, now a bank, on the corner of Acadamiesstraat and Vlamingstraat.

St. John's, the most beautiful of Belgium's 140 functioning windmills, built in 1770. Nearby is the beach resort **Knokke-Heist** (many hotels, shops and nightclubs).

Canal boats leave from several docks for half-hour cruises with English-language guides.

Dep. Brugge	Frequent times from 05:48 to 22:50
Arr. Brussles (Midi)	One hour later
Arr. Brussels (Cen.)	10 minutes after arriving Midi station
Arr. Brussels (Nord)	3 minutes after arriving Central station

Brussels - Cologne (Koln) - Brussels   200

Dep. Brussels (Midi)	06:47	07:47	09:47	10:47	12:03 (1)
Dep. Brussels (Cen.)	4 minutes after departing Midi station				
Dep. Brussels (Nord)	5 minutes after departing Central station				
Arr. Cologne	09:42	10:42	12:42	13:42	14:42
Dep. Cologne	13:14 (1)	14:14	15:14 (1)	16:14	18:14 (2)
Arr. Brussels (Nord)	15:46	16:45	17:45	18:45	20:45
Arr. Brussels (Cen.)	-0-	16:50	-0-	18:50	20:50
Arr. Brussels (Midi)	15:56	16:56	18:01	18:56	20:56

(1) Supplement charged. Restaurant car. (2) Plus another Cologne departure at 20:14, arriving Brussels (Nord) 22:45.

Brussels - Gent - Brussels 200

Dep. Brussels (Nord)	Frequent times from 05:47 to 23:17
Dep. Brussels (Cen.)	4 minutes after departing Nord station
Dep. Brussels (Midi)	5 minutes after departing Central station
Arr. Gent (St. Pieters)	40–50 minutes after departing Nord station

Sights in **Gent**: Located at the confluence of the Lys and Scheldt rivers. Flanked by many canals lined with 15th century gabled buildings.

The Tourist Office, located in the 14th century Town Hall, is near the 14th century Belfry and the 15th century Cloth Hall, where a 20-minute sound and light program commemorates ancient Gent. Two-hour walking tours start at the Tourist Office. A 30-minute boat tour on the canals gives a fine perspective of Gent's past.

See the superior collection of paintings at the Fine Arts Museum. The collection of furniture at the Museum of Decorative Arts. The reproductions of medieval Gent homes, ironwork, costumes and weapons at the Byloke Museum.

The fantastic altarpiece in St. Bavo's Cathedral. West from it is Graseli, the city's oldest port, lined by famous guild houses. Gent's other medieval harbor, Koornlei, is on the opposite bank from Graseli. Many of the old houses there were restored and reconstructed at the beginning of the 20th century.

See the foreboding dungeons and torture chambers in the 12th century Gravensteen (Castle of the Counts), modeled 8 centuries ago on forts visited by Philip of Alsace when he led Crusaders in Syria. Sint Jorishof, built in 1228 and operated as a hotel since the 15th century. It is believed to be the oldest hotel in Europe, with 70 rooms in the original building.

The largest indoor plant and flower show (nearly 7 acres) is held in Gent in April, every 5 years. The 31st show takes place in 1995.

Dep. Gent (St. Pieters)	Frequent times from 05:47 to 22:47
Arr. Brussels (Midi)	30–35 minutes later
Arr. Brussels (Cen.)	6 minutes after arriving Midi station
Arr. Brussels (Nord)	3 minutes after arriving Central station

Brussels - Liege - Brussels 200

Dep. Brussels (Midi)	Frequent times from 05:47 to 23:15
Dep. Brussels (Central)	4 minutes later
Dep. Brussels (Nord)	6 minutes after departing Brussels (Central)
Arr. Liege (Guillemins)	72 minutes after departing Brussels (Midi)

Sights in **Liege**: There are many museums on and near Rue Feronstree. The wonderful collection of illuminated manuscripts, ancient Roman pottery, tapestries, medieval sculpture and ancient coins in the Musee Curtius (do not miss seeing the enormous twin fireplaces in the large hall on the second floor). In a building at the rear of the Curtius is the Musee du Verre, which has an incredible collection of ancient Egyptian and Roman glassware.

See the exhibit of very beautiful guns in the Musee d'Armes, on nearby Quai de Maestricht. The clocks, tapestries, wood paneling, chandeliers, leather covered walls, porcelain, kitchen utensils and furniture in the Musee d'Ansembourg. The collection of impressionist and expressionist paintings (Courbet, Corot, Chagall, Gauguin and Picasso) at the Musee des Beaux-Arts. The Aquarium.

The columned courtyard at the Palais des Princes-Eveques. Stroll La Roture, the city's old quarter. Visit the colorful Sunday market at La Batte. Shop the boutiques on Rue Pont de I'lle and Rue Vinave de I'lle.

Dep. Liege (Guillemins)	Frequent times from 05:46 to 22:02
Arr. Brussels (Nord)	60–70 minutes later
Arr. Brussels (Central)	6 minutes after arriving Nord station
Arr. Brussels (Midi)	3 minutes after arriving Central station

Brussels - Luxembourg - Brussels   210

Dep. Brussels (Midi/Zuid)	22 minutes after each hour, from 05:22 (1) to 20:22
Dep. Brussels (Cen.)	6 minutes after departing Brussels Midi-Zuid
Dep. Brussels (Nord)	3 minutes after departing Brussels Central
Arr. Luxembourg	2½ hours after departing Brussels Midi/Zuid
Dep. Luxembourg	31 minutes after each hour, from 06:31 (2) to 20:31
Arr. Brussels (Nord)	2¼ hours later
Arr. Brussels (Cen.)	5 minutes after arriving Brussels Nord
Arr. Brussels (Midi/Zuid)	4 minutes after arriving Brussels Central

(1) The 05:22 departure runs Monday–Friday, except holidays. Additional departures from Midi/Zuid station at 07:15 and 12:20 (both charge a supplement and have a restaurant car) do not stop at Central station. (2) There are additional departures from Luxembourg at 08:14, 12:06, 16:59 and 20:06 which (except for ther 20:06) do not stop at Brussels Central. All have a restaurant car (except the 08:14). The 16:59 and 20:06 departures charge a supplement.

Brussels - Namur - Brussels   210

Dep. Brussels (Midi)	Frequent times from 06:21 to 22:47
Dep. Brussels (Central)	4 minutes later (1)
Dep. Brussels (Nord)	6 minutes after departing Brussels Central
Arr. Namur	One hour after departing Brussels Midi

Sights in **Namur**: The silver art in Sisters of Our Lady Convent. The fortress. The baroque 18th century Cathedral. The Diocesan Museum. The extremely elegant Casino, featuring gastronomic feasts.

Dep. Namur   Frequent times from 06:24 to 22:24
Arr. Brussels (Nord)   47 minutes later
Arr. Brussels (Central)   6 minutes after arriving Nord station (1)
Arr. BRussels (Midi)   4 minutes after arriving Central station

(1) A few trains do not stop at Brussels' Central railstation.

Brussels - Paris - Brussels 18

Dep. Brussels (Midi)	07:04 (1)	08:00	10:06 (2)	11:54 (3)
Arr. Paris (Nord)	09:37	11:11	12:55	14:25

Dep. Paris (Nord)	14:33 (2)	16:36 (2)	17:25	18:38 (4+7)
Arr. Brussels (Midi)	17:42	19:49	20:01 (1)	21:10

(1) Supplement charged. Restaurant car. Runs daily, except Saturday and Sunday. Early July to early September: runs Monday–Friday. (2) Light refreshments. (3) Reservation required. Supplement charged. Runs daily, except Sunday. Restaurant car. (4) Reservation required. Supplement charged. Runs daily, except Saturday. Restaurant car. (5) Restaurant car. (6) Has couchettes. (7) Plus other Paris departures at 19:29 and 23:22 (7), arriving Brussels 22:30 and 04:32.

Brussels - Tournai - Brussels 214

Dep. Brussels (Nord)	06:57	08:01	09:01	10:01	11:01	12:01
Dep. Brussels (Cen.)	4 minutes after departing Nord station
Dep. Brussels (Midi)	6 minutes after departing Central station
Arr. Tournai	08:03	09:06	10:06	11:06	12:06	13:06

Sights in **Tournai**: One of Belgium's leading art towns. Pick up a free map and brochure at the city tourism center, at Vieux-Marche-aux-Poteries 14, open Monday–Friday 09:00–19:00, Saturday and Sunday 10:00–13:00 and 15:00–18:00. English speaking guides are available ($21 for a 2-hour tour in 1988).

Tournai is best seen on foot, and the place to start is at the Grand Place, a square that is lined with reconstructed medieval guild houses, of which the Cloth Hall is dominant. Nearby is the 236-foot-high 12th century Belfry. Its 16th century 43-bell carillon is played daily at 11:30.

Visit the 12th century 435-foot-long Romanesque Cathedral, particularly to see its 13th centuryIle-de-France Gothic choir and many fine paintings in several of its chapels. The remains of two 12th century murals there are extraordinary.

Also see the 13th century gilded copper Shrine of Our Lady, decorated with silver figures that depict scenes from the life of the Virgin...and a 7th century Byzantine cross studded with rubies, emeralds and pearls with what is said to be a fragment of the cross on which Jesus died imbedded in its back.

From Easter until the end of September, the Cathedral is open 08:30–18:00. The rest of the year: 08:30–16:30. Its Treasury is open from Easter until the end of September 10:00–12:00. Rest of the year: 10:00–12:00 and 14:30–16:30. Walk across the Scheldt River and see the earliest examples in Western Europe of bourgeouis houses of the Romanesque period as well as 14th and 15th century Gothic houses. From the Pont des Trous (one of the oldest bridges in Europe), view the 5 mammoth Cathedral towers at dusk, silhouetted against the sky.

Dep. Tournai	Every hour 05:34 to 22:34
Arr. Brussels (Midi)	56 minutes later
Arr. Brussels (Cen.)	5 minutes after arriving Midi station
Arr. Brussels (Nord)	3 minutes after arriving Central station

Luxembourg - Basel - Luxembourg   176

Prior to 1991, departure at 05:28 from Luxembourg made this excursion more practical than it has been since then.

Both of these trains charge a supplement and have a restaurant car.

Dep. Luxembourg	10:01		Dep. Basel (SNCF)	16:26
Arr. Basel (SNCF)	13:39		Arr. Luxembourg	19:56

Sights in **Basel**: Superb Holbein, Delacroix, Gaugin, Matisse, Ingres, Courbet and Van Gogh paintings in the Kunstmuseum on St. Alban Graben. The collection of 18th century clothing, ceramics and watches in the Kirschgarten. The Historical Museum in the Franciscan church in Barfusserplatz. Shop on Freiestrasse.

See the 16th century Town Hall. The fishmarket. The 15th century New University. Take a boat excursion from the pier in the back of Hotel Three Kings. See the view of the city from the Wettstein Bridge. Visit Munsterplatz.

Luxembourg - Bonn - Luxembourg

720			*710*		
Dep. Luxembourg	05:37 (1)	09:40	Dep. Bonn (Hbf.)	15:53	20:46
Arr. Koblernz	07:40	11:56	Arr. Koblenz	16:38	21:41
Change trains. 710			*Change trains. 720*		
Dep. Koblenz	08:17	12:21	Dep. Koblenz	16:56	22:19 (2)
Arr. Bonn (Hbf.)	09:12	13:12	Arr. Luxembourg	19:10	00:23

(1) Runs daily, except Sunday. (2) Runs daily, except Saturday.

Luxembourg - Brussels - Luxembourg 210

Dep. Luxembourg	06:27	07:07 (1)	07:31 (1)	08:14 (2)	08:27	09:27
Arr. Brussels (Nord)	09:11	09:33	10:11	10:40	11:11	12:11
Arr. Brussels (Cen.)	5 minutes after arriving Brussels Nord					
Arr. Brussels (Midi)	4 minutes after arriving Brussels Central					

Dep. Brussels (Midi)	13:21	14:21	15:21	16:21 (3)	17:21	18:21 (4)
Dep. Brussels (Cen.)	4 minutes after departing Brussels Midi					
Dep. Brussels (Nord)	5 minutes after departing Brussels Central					
Arr. Luxembourg	16:11	17:11	18:11	18:15	20:11	21:11

(1) Runs Monday-Friday, except holidaays. (2) Second-class only. (3) Restaurant car. (4) Plus other Brussels (Midi) departures at 19:13 and 19:21, arriving Luxemburg 21:49 and 22:15.

Luxembourg - Clervaux - Luxembourg 219

The best view (from the viaduct) as you depart Luxembourg City is from the left-hand side of the train.

Dep. Luxembourg	08:10	10:10	12:10
Arr. Clervaux	08:55	10:55	12:57

Sights in **Clervaux**: This is the Ardennes area, where the Battle of the Bulge was fought in December, 1944. It is a 15-minute walk from the railstation, along the river, to the center of town. You cross a bridge over the river in order to get to the office of the miniature golf course. This is also the tourist information office, open from late March to late September 10:00–12:00 and 14:00–18:00.

You can obtain a copy of the description they provide about the "Family of Man" exhibition of Edward Steichen photos. This world-famous American photographer was born in Luxembourg. Then, go to see that collection at DeLannoi Castle, which also has the Battle of the Bulge Museum and its monument—one of General Patton's U.S. army tanks. It also has an exhibit of castle models.

The Castle is open 10:00–17:00 June through September (13:00–17:00 on Sundays and bank holidays the rest of the year). It is pleasant to lunch at the Castle's restaurant.

See the view from the Benedictine Abbey of St. Maurice.

Dep Clervaux	12:51	14:51	17:51	19:36	20:51
Arr. Luxembourg	13:38	15:38	18:34	20:25	21:36

Luxembourg - Cologne (Koln) - Luxembourg

720			*710*		
Dep. Luxembourg	08:30 (1)	09:40 (2)	Dep. Cologne	16:19 (2)	18:19
Arr. Koblenz	10:38	11:55 (2)	Arr. Koblenz	17:38 (2)	19:41
Change trains. 710			*Change trains. 720*		
Dep. Koblenz	11:21	12:21	Dep Koblenz	17:19	20:17
Arr. Cologne	12:38	13:38	Arr. Luxembourg	19:23	22:29

(1) Changes train in Trier, Arr. 09:10—Dep. 09:15. (2) Direct train. No train change in Koblenz.

Luxembourg - Dusseldorf - Luxembourg

720			*650*		
Dep. Luxemb'g	05:37 (1)	10:33 (2)	Dep. Dusseldorf	15:45 (4)	18:28 (3)
Arr. Koblenz	07:40	12:37	Arr. Koblenz	-0- (4)	19:45
Change trains. 650			*Change trains. 720*		
Dep. Koblenz	07:48 (3)	09:48 (3)	Dep. Koblenz	-0-	20:17 (5)
Arr. Dusseldorf	09:11	11:11	Arr. Luxemb'g	19:23	22:29

(1) Runs daily, except Sunday. (2) Runs daily, except Sundays and holidays. Change trains in Trier (arr. 07:25-dep. 08:19). (3) Light refreshments. (4) Direct train. No train change in Koblenz. (5) Change trains in Trier (arr. 21:38—dep. 21:43).

Luxembourg - Frankfurt - Luxembourg

720			*650*		
Dep. Luxemb'g	05:37 (1)	10:33 (2)	Dep. Frankfurt	13:51 (3)	14:51 (3+5)
Arr. Koblenz	07:40	12:37	Arr. Koblenz	15:11	16:11
Change trains. 650			*Change trains. 720*		
Dep. Koblenz	07:46 (3)	09:46 (3)	Dep. Koblenz	15:19 (4)	17:19
Arr. Frankfurt	09:08	11:08	Arr. Luxemb'g	17:33	19:23

(1) Runs daily, except Sunday. (2) Runs daily, except Sundays and holidays. Change trains in Trier (arr. 07:25-dep. 08:19). (3) Supplement charged includes reservation fee. Restaurant car. (4) Change trains in Trier (arr. 16:40-dep. 16:43). (5) Plus other Frankfurt departures at 17:51 (3) and 19:51 (3), arriving Koblenz 19:13 and 21:13.

Luxembourg - Koblenz - Luxembourg 720

These schedules show that a stopover in Trier is possible in both directions.

Dep. Luxembourg	05:37 (1)	06:37 (2)	08:30	09:40	10:33	12:30
Arr. Trier	06:18	07:25 (3)	09:10 (3)	10:26	11:15	13:10 (3)
Arr Koblenz	07:40	09:41	10:38	11:55	12:38	14:38

Sights in **Koblenz**: A pedestrian tunnel goes from the front of the railstation to the city tourist information office, open mid-June to mid-October Monday–Saturday 08:30–20:00, Sunday 13:30–19:00. For a small fee you can obtain; hotel reservations, a city map and a "Tour of the City" brochure. See where the Moselle and Rhine rivers meet. Visit the Old Town, St. Castor's Church and the Middle Rhine Museum.

Dep. Koblenz	12:17 (3)	15:19	16:56	17:19	20:17	22:19 (4)
Arr. Trier	13:36	16:38 (3)	18:10	18:38	21:37 (3)	23:40
Arr. Luxembourg	14:31	17:33	19:10	19:23	22:29	00:23

(1) Runs daily, except Sunday. (2) Runs daily, except Sundays and holidays. (3) Change trains in Trier. (4) Runs daily, except Saturday.

Luxembourg - Liege - Luxembourg 219

Dep. Luxembourg	08:10	10:10	12:10	
Arr. Liege (Guillemins)	10:36	12:34	14:34	
Dep Liege (Guillemins)	13:08	16:08	17:48	19:08
Arr. Luxembourg	15:38	18:34	20:25	21:36

Luxembourg - Mainz - Luxembourg

720

Dep. Luxembourg	05:37 (1)	06:37 (2+3)	08:30 (3)	09:40	10:33
Arr. Koblenz	07:40	09:41	10:38	11:55	12:38
Change trains. 650					
Dep. Koblenz	07:52 (4)	09:52 (4)	10:52 (4)	12:22 (4)	12:52 (4)
Arr. Mainz	08:42	10:42	11:42	13:12	13:42

Sights in **Mainz**: The art collection in the Cathedral. The Museum of the Central Rhineland. The rare books in the World Museum of Printing in the Romischer Kaiser. The restored Baroque mansionns on the Schillerplatz and Schillerstrasse, in the Kirschgarten. Old Town. The sculptures in the Diocesan Museum.

Dep. Mainz	14:18 (4)	16:18 (4)	19:18 (4)	21:18 (4)
Arr. Koblenz	15:05	17:05	20:05	21:07
Change trains. 720				
Dep. Koblenz	15:19 (3)	17:19	20:17 (3)	22:19 (5)
Arr. Luxembourg	17:33	19:23	22:29	00:23

(1) Runs daily, except Sunday. (2) Runs daily, except Sundays and holidays. (3) Change trains in Trier. (4) Supplement charged includes reservation fee. Restaurant car. (5) Runs daily, except Saturday.

Luxembourg - Metz - Luxembourg   173 + 176

Dep. Luxembourg	05:26 (2) 07:11 (1) 07:44 (2) 10:01 (3)
Arr. Metz	45 minutes later

Sights in **Metz:** The fantastic railstation here looks like a castle because it was built for Kaiser Wilhelm II when he was Germanifying this region. The imperial apartments in the station were arranged for the Kaiser to enjoy his obsession with train-spotting.

See the oldest church in France, the 4th century Pierre-aux-Nonains.

The largest stained-glass windows in the world, in the 16th century Cathedral of Saint Etienne. The Cathedral was formed by the joining of two 12th century churches into a single building. Its contemporary Marc Chagall and Jacques Villon stained-glass are exceptional.

See the Gallo-Roman antiquities in the city's Museum. Walk across the 13th century Porte des Allemands (Gate of the Germans).

Dep. Metz	11:50 (1) 16:04 (5) 19:13 (3) 20:04 (4) 21:41 (6) 22:03
Arr. Luxembourg	45 minutes later

(1) Runs Sunday only. (2) Runs daily, except Sundays and holidays. Light refreshments. (3) Supplement charged. Restaurant car. (4) Supplement charged. (5) Restaurant car. (6) Runs daily, except Saturday. Supplement charged.

Luxembourg - Mulhouse - Luxembourg   176

Both of these trains charge a supplement and have a restaurant car.

Dep. Luxembourg	10:01	Dep. Mulhouse	16:50
Arr. Mulhouse	13:13	Arr. Luxembourg	19:56

Sights in **Mulhouse:** France's largest collection of antique cars, and one of the best collections in the world of old autos. The Musee Nationale de l'Automobile exhibits about 500 cars ranging from an 1878 steam-powered Jacquot to a magnificent 12-liter Bugati Royale. It is open daily except Tuesday 10:00–18:00.

The Museum of Fabric Printing (Musee de l'Impression sur Etoffes) has displays of textile arts (at 3 Rue des Bonnes-Gens). There are 8,000,000 fabric samples as well as drawings of printed and woven fabrics in its 1,700-volume library. April–December the museum is open daily 10:00–12:00 and 14:00–18:00. January–March: same hours, but closed on Tuesday.

Visit France's largest and best railroad museum, open daily at Rue Alfred de Glehn. Its exhibits include passenger cars, freight cars, and steam, diesel and electric locomotives.

Luxembourg - Paris - Luxembourg   173

Dep. Luxembourg	05:26 (1)	07:11 (2)	07:44 (3)
Arr. Paris (Est)	09:08	11:02	11:22
Dep. Paris (Est)	17:16 (4)	18:45 (5)	19:55
Arr. Luxembourg	20:45	22:31	23:54

(1) Supplement charged. Runs daily, except Sundays and holidays. Light refreshments. (2) Runs Sunday only. (3) Runs daily, except Sundays and holidays. Light refreshments. (4) Supplement charged. (5) Supplement charged. Runs daily, except Saturday.

Luxembourg - Saarbrucken - Luxembourg   — *via Trier*   720

These schedules allow stopping-over in Trier for sightseeing on the ride to/from Saarbrucken.

Dep. Luxembourg	06:37 (1)	08:30	09:40	10:33	12:30
Arr. Trier	07:25	09:10	10:26	11:15	13:10
Change trains.					
Dep. Trier	07:35 (2)	09:38	10:41	11:38	13:38
Arr. Saarbrucken	08:45	10:45 (4)	11:41	12:45	14:45

These schedules allow stopping-over in Trier for dinner en route back to Luxembourg:

Dep. Saarbrucken	11:12	12:15	15:12	17:12	20:10 (3)	22:10 (3)
Arr. Trier	12:19	13:15	16:19	18:19	21:10	23:12
Change trains.						
Dep. Trier	12:41	13:42	16:44	18:41	21:44	23:41 (5)
Arr. Luxembourg	13:23	14:31	17:33	19:23	22:29	00:23

(1) Runs daily, except Sundays and holidays. (2) Runs Monday-Friday except holidays.. (3) Light refreshments. (4) Runs Monday-Saturday (5) Runs daily, except Saturday.

Luxembourg - Saarbrucken — *via Metz* 173

These schedules allow stopping-over for sightseeing in Metz en route to/from Saarbrucken.

Dep. Luxembourg	05:26 (1)	07:11 (2)	07:44 (3)	10:01 (4)
Arr. Metz	06:11	07:58	08:31	10:43
Change trains.				
Dep. Metz	06:42 (5)	08:44 (6)	09:54 (7)	11:54 (8)
Arr. Saarbrucken	07:41	09:55	10:50	12:48

These schedules allow stopping-over in Metz for lunch or dinner en route back to
Luxembourg:

Dep. Saarbrucken	13:10 (4)	17:09 (9)	18:18 (5)	19:15 (6)	
Arr. Metz	14:03	18:06	19:28	20:22	
Change trains.					
Dep. Metz	16:04 (10)	19:13 (4)	20:06 (12)	21:49 (11)	23:03
Arr. Luxembourg	16:49	19:56	20:45	22:31	

(1) Supplement charged. Runs daily, except Sunday and holidays. (2) Runs Sunday only. (3) Runs daily,
except Sundays and holidays. Light refreshments. (4) Supplement charged. Restaurant car. (5) Runs
Monday-Friday, except holidays. (6) Operates late June to early September. (7) Runs daily, except Sundays (8) Light refreshments.(9) Supplement charged. Light refreshments. (10) Restaurant car. (11)
Supplement charged. Runs daily, except Saturday. (12) Supplement charged.

Luxembourg - Strasbourg - Luxembourg 176

Both of these trains charge a supplement and have a restaurant car.

Dep. Luxembourg	10:01		Dep. Strasbourg	17:48
Arr. Strasbourg	12:06		Arr. Luxembourg	19:56

Luxembourg - Trier - Luxembourg 720

Dep. Luxembourg	08:30	09:40	10:33	12:30	14:33
Arr. Trier	09:10	10:26	11:15	13:10	15:15

Sights in **Trier**: There are more Roman monuments here than in any other German city: the
4th century Porta Nigra (Black Gate), 2nd and 4th century baths, a 1st century amphitheater, and the 4th century Roman palace, Palastula (with its throne room of Roman emperors), now a Lutheran church. See the "Holy Coat of Trier," said to be Christ's robe, in the

Romanesque Cathedral, started in the 6th century.

Roman and medieval relics in the Municipal Museum. Peter's Fountain in the market square and, nearby, the 17th century Electoral Palace and 18th century Kasselstatt Palace.

Dep. Trier	13:42	16:44	18:41	21:44
Arr. Luxembourg	14:31	17:33	19:23	22:29

Luxembourg - Vianden - Luxembourg   217 + Government timetable

The Ettelbruck–Viandin bus leaves from the front of the Ettelbruck railstation. Re-check the bus schedules!!

Dep. Luxembourg	08:10	12:10	14:10
Arr. Ettelbruck	08:28	12:31	14:30
Change to bus.			
Dep. Ettelbruck	08:35	13:14	14:52
Arr. Vianden	09:03	13:38	15:15

Sights in **Vianden**: Leave the bus at the first stop, the Hotel Oranienburg. At the end of the day, don't fail to board the bus at Gare Routiere (the bus station) for the ride back to Ettelbruck. Most of the attractions in Vianden are closed 12:00–14:00.

Walk uphill from the Hotel Oranienburg to the large and very interesting castle, open daily March-December, only weekends in January and February.

Leave the castle at 12:00 and have lunch before visiting the home of Victor Hugo. Take the chairlift across the river to the top of a hill from which there are good views of the castle, dam and valley. After descending, walk across the top of the dam.

See the rococo altar in the 13th century Church of the Trinitarians. Visit the exhibits of folklore and ancient household items in the Museum of Rustic Arts.

Bus				
Dep. Vianden	14:34	16:26	18:10	20:31
Arr. Ettelbruck	15:05	16:55	18:38	21:01
Change to train.				
Dep. Ettelbruck	15:16	18:16	20:01	21:16
Arr. Luxembourg	15:38	18:34	20:25	21:38

SCENIC RAIL TRIPS

Most of the scenic rail trips of the Benelux countries are in Holland, and all of those are in-cluded in the list of one-day roundtrips from Amsterdam preceding this section. They are the train rides between Amsterdam and Delft, Den Haag, Leiden, Rotterdam and Utrecht.

The scenery on these trips is best from mid-March through May: fields of tulips, nar-cissus, crocus and other bulb flowers in bloom. The region is known as "Champs de Fleurs" (Fields of Flowers).

Three other scenic trips in the Benelux countries are listed in this section. All are note-worthy for beautiful river scenery.

Liege - Jemelle

This fine farm and river scenery can be seen by taking an indirect route from Brussels to Luxembourg.

200

Dep. Brussels (Midi)	10:18	11:18	12:18	13:18
Dep. Brussels (Cen.)	4 minutes after departing Midi station			
Dep. Brussels (Nord)	6 minutes after departing Central station			
Arr. Liege (Guill.)	11:40	12:40	13:40	14:40
Change trains. 215				
Dep. Liege (Guill.)	07:00	09:59	18:47	01:55 (1)
Arr. Namur	07:40	10:39	19:25	02:34
Change trains. 210				
Dep. Namur	13:12 (2)	14:22	15:22	16:22
Dep. Jemelle	-0-	15:00	16:00	17:00
Arr. Luxembourg	14:49	16:11	17:11	18:11

(1) Runs Monday–Friday, except holidays. (2) Supplement charged. Restaurant car. (3) Restaurant car.

Luxembourg - Liege 217

There is excellent farm and river scenery on this easy one-day roundtrip. See Luxembourg timetables above.

Namur - Dinant   210

This is a spur off the Brussels-Luxembourg route. The great farm and river scenery here can be seen either by breaking-up the ride from Brussels to Luxembourg (or vice versa) …or as an easy one-day roundtrip from Brussels.

For the first way (showing both directions):

Dep. Brussels (Midi)	08:44 (1)	09:44 (1)	Dep. Luxembourg	08:27	09:27
Dep. Brussels (Cen.)	08:46	09:46	Arr. Namur	10:19	11:02
Dep. Brussels (Nord)	08:53	09:53	*Change trains.*		
Arr. Namur	09:42	10:42	Dep. Namur	10:47 (1)	11:47 (1)
Arr. Dinant	10:13	11:13	Arr. Dinant	11:13	12:13
Change trains.			*Change trains.*		
Dep. Dinant	10:25 (1)	11:25 (1)	Dep. Dinant	11:27 (1)	12:25 (1)
Arr. Namur	10:55	11:55	Dep. Namur	12:00	13:00
Change trains.			Arr. Brussels (Nord)	12:49	13:49
Dep. Namur	11:24	12:24	Arr. Brussels (Cen.)	12:56	13:56
Arr. Luxembrg	13:11	14:11	Arr. Brussels (Midi)	13:00	14:00

(1) Runs Monday–Friday, except holidays.

Here is the Brussels one-day roundtrip   210
All of these trains run Monday–Friday except holidays.

Dep. Brussels (Midi)	08:44	09:44	Dep. Dinant	14:25	16:25
Dep. Brussels (Cen.)	08:46	09:46	Arr. Namur	15:00	17:00
Dep. Brussels (Nord)	08:53	09:53	Arr. Brussels (Nord)	15:49	17:49
Arr. Namur	09:42	10:42	Arr. Brussels (Cen.)	15:56	17:56
Arr. Dinant	10:13	11:13	Arr. Brussels (Midi)	16:00	18:00

INTERNATIONAL ROUTES
FROM BELGIUM

The Belgian gateway for rail travel to London, Amsterdam, Basel (and on to Zurich and Milan), Cologne (and on to Hamburg and Copenhagen) and Paris (and on to Madrid) is Brussels.

Brussels - Amsterdam   205

Many of these trains have light refreshments.

Dep. Brussels (Midi)	10 minutes after each hour, from 06:10 to 23:10
Dep. Brussels (Cen.	4 minutes after departing Midi station
Dep. Brussels (Nord)	4 minutes after departing Central station
Arr. Amsterdam	3 hours later

Brussels - Basel - Milan   43

Dep. Brussels (Midi)	07:15 (1)	19:13 (2)
Dep. Brussels (Nord)	8 minutes after departing Midi station	
Arr. Basel (S.N.C.F.)	13:56	02:00
Arr. Milan (Cen.)	19:15	07:10

(1) Supplement charged. Restaurant car. (2) Coaches are second-class. Runs Friday and Saturday only.

Brussels - Cologne (Koln)   200

Dep. Brussels (Midi)	06:47	07:47	09:47	10:47	12:03 (1)	13:47
Dep. Brussels (Cen.)	06:52	07:52	09:52	10:52	-0-	13:52
Dep. Brussels (Nord)	06:57	07:57	09:57	10:57	12:12	13:57
Arr. Cologne	09:42	10:42	12:42	13:42	14:42	16:42

Dep. Brussels (Midi)	15:47	16:55 (1)	18:08 (1)	18:47	20:03 (1)	21:25 (2)
Dep. Brussels (Cen.)	15:52	-0-	18:12	18:52	-0-	-0-
Dep. Brussels (Nord)	15:57	17:03	18:18	18:57	20:12	21:34
Arr. Cologne	18:42	19:42	20:42	21:39	22:42	00:17

(1) Supplement charged. Restaurant car. (2) Coach is second-class.

Brussels - London via Oostende   (Jetfoil)   12

The schedules shown below are for late May to late September, unless designated other-wise. All of these ships require reservation, charge a supplement and have light refresh-ments.

Dep. Brussels (Nord)	09:47	11:47	14:47	17:47 (1)
Dep. Brussels (Midi)	09:59	11:59	14:59	17:59
Arr. Oostende	11:09	13:09	16:09	19:09
Change to boat.				
Dep. Oostende	11:45	13:45	16:45	19:30 (1)
Set your watch back one hour, except from late September to late October.				
Arr. Dover (Western Docks)	-0-	-0-	-0-	-0- (2)
Arr. London (Vic.)	15:17	17:23	20:19	22:47

(1) The Oostende–London ship operates late June to late September. (2) Runs Sunday only.

Brussels - London via Oostende (Regular Ferry) 12

All ferries require reservation and have a restaurant.

Dep. Brussels (Nord)	11:47	22:47
Dep. Brussels (Midi)	11:59	22:59
Arr. Oostende	13:09	23:54
Change to a boat.		
Dep. Oostende	13:45	00:30

Set your watch back one hour, except from late September to late October.

Arr. Dover (Eastern Docks)	-0-	-0-

A free bus connects Eastern Docks with the railstation at Western Docks.

Dep. Dover (Western Docks)	-0-	-0-
Arr. London (Vic.)	17:23	06:30

Brussels - Luxembourg 218

See "Brussels-Luxembourg" under Luxembourg.

Brussels - Paris 18

Dep. Brussels (Nord)	01:27 (1)	-0-	07:44 (3)	09:45 (4)
Dep. Brussels (Midi)	01:53	07:04 (2)	08:00	10:04
Arr. Paris (Nord)	06:58	09:37	10:55	12:55

Dep Brussels (Nord)	11:32 (5)	13:46 (6)	15:50 (4)	16:23 (7)
Dep. Brussels (Midi)	11:54	14:13	16:00	17:10 (8)
Arr. Paris (Nord)	14:25	17:05	19:01	19:42

Dep. Brussels (Nord)	17:23 (7)	18:45 (10)	19:23 (7)	-0-
Dep. Brussels (Midi)	18:13 (9)	19:07	20:04 (6)	-0-
Arr. Paris (Nord)	20:43	22:05	23:01	-0-

(1) Has couchettes. (2) Runs Monday–Friday. Restaurant car. (3) Operates late August to late June. Runs Monday and Saturday. (4) Supplement charged. Restaurant car. (5) Reservation required. Supplement charged. Runs daily, except Sunday. Restaurant car. (6) Light refreshments. (7) Change trains at Midi railstation. (8)Supplement charged. Runs Monday-Friday. Restaurant car. (9) Runs daily. Supplement charged. Restaurant car. (10) Restaurant car.

INTERNATIONAL ROUTES
FROM HOLLAND

Amsterdam is the Dutch gateway for rail travel to London, Basel (and on to Zurich and Milan), Cologne, Hamburg (and on to Copenhagen) and Paris (and on to Madrid). Notes on the route to London appear under "London–Amsterdam" in Great Britain chapter.

Amsterdam - Brussels   205

Dep. Amsterdam	Frequent times from 06:23 to 22:15
Arr. Brussels (Nord)	3 hours later
Arr. Brussels (Cent.)	4 minutes after departing Nord station
Arr. Brussels (Midi)	4 minutes after departing Central station

Amsterdam - Cologne (Koln) - Mainz - Basel

Many castles are seen in the Koblenz–Mainz area as the train travels alongside the Rhine River. En route to Basel, sit on the left-hand side for the best views of marvelous Rhine River scenery.

All of these trains charge a supplement.

Dep. Amsterdam	06:02 (1)	07:06 (1)	08:00 (3)	09:00 (3)	11:06 (1+5)
Arr. Cologne	08:42 (2)	09:42 (2)	10:57	11:57	13:42 (2)
Dep. Cologne	09:00 (3)	09:50 (3)	11:07	12:07	14:00 (3)
Arr. Koblenz	09:51	10:51	11:51	12:51	14:51
Arr. Mainz	10:42	11:42	12:42	13:42	15:42
Arr. Basel (S.B.B.)	13:43	14:43	15:43	16:43	18:43

(1) Light refreshments. (2) Change trains in Cologne. (3) Restaurant car. (4) Carries a sleeping car. Also has couchettes. (5) Plus other Amsterdam departures at 13:06 (1+2), 15:06 (1+2) and 20:05 (4)…departing Cologne 16:00 (3), 18:00 (3) and 23:47…arriving Basel 20:43, 22:43 and 06:26.

Amsterdam - Osnabruck - Bremen - Hamburg - Copenhagen 22

Both of these trains have couchettes.

Dep. Amsterdam (Cen.)	20:09 (1)	19:06 (2)
Arr. Bremen	00:50	01:27
Arr. Hamburg (Hbf.)	01:54	02:35
Arr. Copenhagen	07:25	08:25

(1) Operates late June to early Sept. (2) Change trains in Duisburg.

Amsterdam - Luxembourg 38

Dep. Amsterdam	07:32 (1)
Arr. Maastricht	10:14
Change trains.	
Dep. Maastricht	10:14
Arr. Luxembourg	13:38

(1) Runs Saturday only June 4 - August 27.

Amsterdam - London via Hoek van Holland (regular ferry) 15

Dep. Amsterdam	09:32 (1)	19:48 (1)
Arr. Hoek van Holland	10:57	21:13
Change to ferry.		
Dep. Hoek van Holland	12:00	22:00 (2)
Set your watch back one hour.		
Arr. Harwich	18:00	07:00
Change to train		
Dep. Harwich	18:45	07:50
Arr. London (Liverpool)	20:00	09:00

(1) Light refreshments. (2) Reservation required.

Amsterdam - Brussels - Paris 18

Dep. Amsterdam (Cen.)	06:57 (1)	08:53 (2)	10:52 (3)	11:25 (3)	12:25 (3)
Dep. Antwerp (Berch.)	09:14	10:59	13:15	13:53	14:53
Dep. Brussels (Nord)	09:47	11:32	13:46	14:23	15:23
Arr. Brussels (Midi)	09:51	11:37	13:52	14:30 (4)	15:30 (4)
Dep, Brussels (Midi)	10:04	11:54	14:13	15:04 (5)	16:00 (5)
Arr. Paris (Nord)	12:55	14:25	17:05	17:43	19:01

Dep. Amsterdam (Cen.)	13:25 (3)	14:25 (3)	15:52 (8)	16:25 (3)	22:15 (9)
Dep. Antwerp (Berch.)	15:53	16:53	18:12	18:53	00:54
Dep. Brussels (Nord)	16:23	17:23	18:45	19:23	01:27
Arr. Brussels (Midi)	16:30 (4)	17:30 (4)	18:50	19:30 (4)	01:34
Dep. Brussels (Midi)	17:10 (6)	18:13 (7)	19:07	20:04 (3)	01:53
Arr. Paris (Nord)	19:42	20:43	22:05	23:01	06:58

(1) Supplement charged. Light refreshments. (2) Reservation required. Supplement charged. Runs daily, except Sunday. Restaurant car Brussels–Paris. (3) Light refreshments. (4) Change trains in Brussels-Midi. (5) Supplement charged. Restaurant car. (6) Supplement charged. Restaurant car. Early July to early

September: runs Monday–Friday. Early September to early July: runs daily, except Saturday. (7) Supplement charged. Restaurant car. (8) Restaurant car. (9) Has couchettes.

INTERNATIONAL ROUTES
FROM LUXEMBOURG

Luxembourg City is a gateway for rail travel to London, Amsterdam, Basel (and on to Zurich and Milan), Brussels, Cologne, Koblenz (and on to Frankfurt), and Paris. (Notes on the routes from Amsterdam, Brussels and Paris to London appear in Chapter 7.)

Luxembourg - Amsterdam   38

Dep. Luxembourg	16:10 (1)
Arr. Maastricht	19:21
Arr. Amsterdam	22:00

(1) Operates early June to late August. Runs Saturday only.

Luxembourg - Basel   40

Dep. Luxembourg	01:18 (1)	10:01 (2)	14:59 (2)	18:02 (3)
Arr. Basel (SBB)	05:16	13:39	18:25	21:30

(1) Carries a sleeping car. Also has couchettes. (2) Supplement charged. Restaurant car. (3) Restaurant car.

Luxembourg - Brussels   210

Dep. Luxembourg	04:09	05:27 (1)	06:27	07:07 (1)	08:14 (4)
Arr. Brussels (Nord)	6:40	08:11	09:11	09:33	10:40
Arr. Brussels (Cen.)	-0-	08:16	09:16	09:37	-0-
Arr. Brussels (Midi)	06:49	08:20	09:20	09:41	10:47

(1) Runs Monday–Friday, except holidays. (2) Second-class only. (3) Restaurant car. (4) Plus other departures from Luxembourg at 31 minutes after each hour from 08:31 to 20:31…also at 12:06 (3), 16:59 (3) and 20:06 (3).

Luxembourg - Cologne 720

Dep. Luxembourg	05:37 (1)	08:30	09:40 (2)	10:33 (3)	12:30 (4)
Arr. Trier	06:18	09:10	10:26 (2)	11:15 (3)	13:10
Change trains.					
Dep. Trier	07:17	09:15	10:36	11:17	13:17
Arr. Cologne	09:45	11:45	13:14	13:45	15:45

(1) Runs daily, except Sunday. (2) Direct train. No train change in Trier. Operates late June to mid-September. (3) Direct train. No train change in Trier. (4) Plus other departures from Luxembourg at 14:33 (3), 15:24 and 18:26, arriving Cologne 17:45, 19:45 and 21:45.

Luxembourg - Paris 173 *via Metz* 177 *via Rheims*

	173	*177*	*173*	*173*	*173*
Dep. Luxembourg	05:26 (1)	06:00 (2)	07:44 (3)	10:01 (4)	13:07 (5+9)
Dep. Rheims	-0-	10:01	-0-	-0-	-0-
Dep. Metz	06:11	-0-	08:35	10:53 (5)	14:15
Arr. Paris (Est)	09:08	11:27	11:22	13:40	17:10

(1) Supplement charged. Runs daily, except Sunday. Light refreshments. (2) Runs daily, except Sundays and holidays. Change trains in Longwy. (3) Runs daily, except Sundays and holidays. Light refreshments. (4) Supplement charged. Restaurant car. Change trains in Metz. (5) Supplement charged. Restaurant car. (6) Change trains in Longwy. (7) Runs daily, except Saturday. (8) Supplement charged. Light refreshments. (9) Plus other departures from Luxembourg at [173] 16:34 (7), [177] 17:18 (6) and [173] 17:25 (8), arriving Paris 20:22 (via Metz), 21:56 (via Rheims) and 21:04 (via Metz).

FRANCE

FRANCE

Overview

Travelers to Europe who return home without having ridden a French train are poorer for the experience. For over a decade the French State Railway, (Société Nationale de Chemins de Fer Français, SNCF) has been a leading force in international train travel, revolutionizing European rail with its streamline TGV (train à grande vitesse). The French high speed train has not only shrunk the country's borders, its cars are being exported and integrated into foreign rail systems as far and wide as China and Korea. The TGV has cut the traveling time in half between Paris and, for example, Marseilles, 900 kilometers away, to a little over four hours instead of eight. The TGV currently serves the Paris-Lyon-Marseilles line to the south with branches reaching Nice to the southeast and Perpignan to the southwest, Geneva and Lausanne in the east, Lille and Calais to the north, and the newer ultra high-speed Bordeaux Atlantic line to the southwest. High speed train travel is expanding rapidly in Europe with a network being prepared to tie in with London (via the EuroTunnel and Disneyland Paris) and several German, Belgian, and Dutch cities. The TGV requires reservations, which can be made in most travel agencies, all train stations, and at home with the Minitel, the home-style on-line computer that most French households and offices have perched in their hallways and desktops. Seat reservations for regular trains are also recommended during busy periods. Practically all French towns and cities and a large majority of even the rural villages are served by the SNCF. Although there has been a move away from Paris as the central transportation hub of France, the City of Lights still functions as the pivot point for much of French travel, especially internationally bound. New, smaller hubs are gaining importance, such as Lyon and Lille, which is particularly well situated for train traffic to the U.K., Belgium, Holland, and northern Germany. The Paris suburb to the south, Massy, now functions as a changing station for north-south passengers to avoid Paris. Marne la Vallée Chessy, TGV Hte Picardie, and Charles de Gaulle TGV, scheduled for opening in late 1994, have all been designed to move passengers across the country without having to transit in the already dense city of Paris.

In a nutshell, the train as a vehicle of transportation in France is both an excellent means of seeing some of the finest scenery in Europe and a model of contemporary European efficiency.

General Information

• Paris has nine main rail stations, six principal stations and three specialized stations designed for cars, etc., all of them connected to subway and commuter train (Métro and RER) lines. All offer a wide range of services: bars and restaurants, refreshment stands, lockers, business services, telephone and postal facilities, newsstands and information booths (sporadically staffed).

• SNCF Train Information

Information: 45.82.50.50

Reservations:

    Grandes Lignes (national & international lines): 45.82.50.50

Ile de France (regional lines): 45.65.60.00
Minitel: 36 15 SNCF
Open daily from 8h-20h

• French rail tickets purchased in France are valid for travel any day within two months from the date of purchase. Train tickets obtained before arrival in France are valid for six months.

• Passengers using a French train ticket purchased in Europe must validate it (composter) in one of the many orange-colored machines located at the entrance to the platforms before boarding a train. Failure to do so may result in a stiff fine—train travel within France is essentially based on the honor system. In most cases a conductor will check your tickets anyway. You can purchase tickets onboard, but you pay a supplement. A person holding a non-validated European ticket is subject to a fine. All tickets purchased outside Europe are exempt from having to be validated.

• As for time changes, travelers should note that France turns its clocks ahead on the last Sunday of March and converts back to Standard Time on the last Sunday of September.

• French train travel is graced by scores of internal regulations and new specialized services stipulating tariffs and days and times for reduced-fare travel. Children under four travel free. Half-fare for children from 4 to 11. Children 12 and over must pay full fare. (See Prix Joker details listed below.)

• Semi-Couchettes. Some compartments on French trains have eight semi-inclined bunks (instead of seats) on these routes: Paris-Brest, Paris-Bordeaux, Paris-Hamburg, Paris-Quimper, Paris-Strasbourg, Paris-Ventimiglia, and Rheim-Nice. For reservation purposes, these "Cabine 8" bunks are treated as seats and no supplement is charged.

Signs you are likely to see at rail stations in France:

arrivée	ARRIVAL
consigne	BAGGAGE CHECKROOM
dames	WOMEN
départ	DEPARTURE
entrée	ENTRANCE
fumeurs	SMOKING COMPARTMENT
gare	STATION
horaire	TIMETABLE
location de place assise	SEAT RESERVATION OFFICE
messieurs	MEN
quai	PLATFORM
renseignement	INFORMATION
sortie	EXIT
voie	TRACK
voiture-lit	SLEEPER CAR
voiture-retsa	RESTAURANT CAR

Connections with Great Britain

With the opening of the EuroTunnel underneath the English Channel, which accomodates train cars as well as private vehicles, the war for the passengers is on, with the ferry boat companies and hydrofoil services battling to maintain market share by reducing prices, offering attractive specials, and increasing services. The EuroTunnel option is undoubtedly the fastest and easiest way to go between England and France, but for the time being the price remains an obstacle for many. As of late 1994, private cars were grouped on a special shuttle train car that is pulled through the tunnel in some thirty minutes. Passenger train service through the tunnel on "Eurostar" began in late 1994 and there are now trains leaving almost every hour. For more information on UK-France connections, see the chapter for Great Britain. For EuroTunnel information write to BP 69, 62231 COQUELLES or telephone (33) 21.00.60.00 in France. An information and reservation number in Paris is: 44.94.80.80. U.S. toll-free information: 1-800-EUROSTAR.

Another option is the **"UK-France Sampler:"**
For any 3 days within one month, unlimited rail travel in France plus 3 consecutive days car rental in the UK plus the Eurostar journey (Paris-London or London-Paris). 1996 *first*-class per person price for two adults traveling in an "economy" car: $304.50 (additional car day $30). *Second*-class: $241, additional car day $30.

French Holidays

In that train schedules differ between working days and holidays, and many trains do not run at all on holidays, a list of such days in France can be especially useful. Also, those trains which operate on holidays are often filled, and it is necessary to make reservations for them long in advance. When at all possible, avoid train travel in France on holidays, long week-ends, and the first and last day of the Paris-region's school vacations!

Public Holidays

January 1	Jour de l'An (New Year's Day)
Late March/April	Pâques (Easter)
Monday after Easter	Lundi de Pâques (Easter Monday)
May 8	Victoire 1945 (V.E. Day)
Sixth Thursday after Easter	Ascension (Ascension Day)
Second Monday after Ascension	Pentecôte (Pentecost)
July 14	Fête nationale/14 juillet (Bastille Day)
August 15	Fête de l'Assomption (Feast of the Assumption)
November 1	Toussaint (All Saints' Day), Halloween
November 11	Fête de l'Armistice (Veteran's Day)
December 25	Noël (Christmas)

DISCOUNT TRAIN TRAVEL IN FRANCE

Additionally, the SNCF publishes a color-coded calendar of travel days and times and prices. Here, in order of largest discount to smallest, the days are listed: Jour bleue: Saturday noon through Sunday 15h.Jour blanche: Friday noon through Saturday noon, and Sunday 15h through Monday noon. Plus holidays. Jour rouge: Principal days of departure.

As of the end of May 1994, this system is no longer used for TGV service. The SNCF also publishes a free Guide des prix Réduits, Guide to Reduced Priced Train Travel. Here are the principal reduced ticket possibilities for those traveling without a Eurailpass: Discounts depend on destinations, dates, and times.

• **Carrissimo and Joker**: youth fares, 12-25 years old, up to 50%.

• **Carte Kiwi and Joker**: When traveling with children (even one child) discounts can go to 60%.

• **Carte Vermeil and Joker**: Senior citizens discounts for the over-60 bracket.

• The Joker 30 fare offers travelers up to 60% off when reservations are made between 60 and 30 days before departure.

• **The Joker 8** fare offers a 40% discount when reservations are made between 60 and 8 days before departure.

• Multiple subscription options are also available to SNCF train users. The EuroDomino is a three, five, or ten day coupon for unlimited train travel during one month; the Modulopass is a six month or one year subscription for unlimited travel on a certain line or on the whole network depending on your needs; the Businesspass is a pass in the name of your company or organization enabling businesses to profit from a 15% discount when 25 or more round-trip tickets are purchased. Two new subscriptions are now available on the TGV Nord Europe line: The Temporis, which offers discounts to travelers making at least 16 trips within a 19 to 31 day period, and ABO 8, a special offer of up to 75% off for travelers making at least one round-trip journey per week.

• Children under four years old travel free, but a child is not entitled to a seat.

• Animals pay half fare of a 2nd class ticket or 28 FF if the animal is under six kilos and is carried in a bag measuring not more than 45 x 30 x 25 cm.

• If you want to travel with your car or motorcycle on the train, the SNCF has a complete list of destinations applicable to this service. Motorail is a European network of special trains, generally overnight, carrying passengers with vehicles on journeys up to 900 miles. In Paris, reservations can be made by calling 45.65.60.60. Otherwise, inquire at:

Gare Austerlitz (Tolbiac): 45.82.73.62.

Gare de Lyon (Bercy): 40.19.60.11.

Gare Montparnasse (Vaugirard): 40.48.14.72.

THE FRENCH TGV:
FASTEST TRAINS ON EARTH

Since 1981, France has operated the world's fastest trains, the train a grande vitesse, which can run up to 320 kilometers per hour and are operated at the top speed of 186 mph on the 126-mile Paris-LeMans line, making that trip in 55 minutes versus the one hour and fifty minutes needed by regular trains! In the nineties, one speaks more of the opening of new services and lines than the high speed, which has become as a given and banal detail in daily European travel. Seat reservations are required for practically all TGV trains—and are particularly essential on peak days and at peak hours. Standing is not allowed on TGVs. Currently, the SNCF has 136 direct TGV destinations from Paris, Lyon, and Lille, five ultra-modern stations opened or opening in late 1994, including a TGV station at Paris' Charles de Gaulle Airport, Lyon's Satolas Airport, and Lille's "Europe" station, through which the Paris-London three hour jaunt will pass. Essentially, this network is progressing faster than any annual guidebook can accurately report on!

Although certain supplements for certain trains may be in effect, pass holders should only count on the modest reservation fee of 30 FF.

The usual composition for a TGV is 386 seats: 111 in first-class, 275 in second-class. Each TGV has a bar car with snack and drink services as well as providing international press and telephone cards. Meals are brought to seats in some of the first-class cars, however, in most cases, those interested in dining should indicate such and proceed to the dining car at the set dinner hour.

The initial 1982 TGV service (Paris-Lyon, Paris-Dijon and Paris-Geneva) was expanded in 1983 to include Paris-Marseilles, Paris-Montpelier and Paris-Annecy-Grenoble. A TGV service Paris-Lausanne (with cross-platform transfer in Lausanne for trains to Milan) began in 1984. Service Paris-Grenoble started in 1985, Paris-LeMans and Paris-Tours in 1989. The nineties has brought an excellent TGV Atlantic line serving Poitier, La Rochelle, Bordeaux, and Nantes. The northern route, one of the most promising extensions to the system in that it connects Paris with the cities of northern Europe, boasts of an exceptionally rapid and regular Paris-Lille service in one hour.

FRENCH TRAIN PASSES

The French national passes are sold everywhere in the world, except in France—at travel agencies and offices of Rail Europe (U.S.A. and Canadian addresses listed in introduction). Here are the most widely used and advantageous passes available for France:

France Railpass Unlimited train travel for any three days within one month. The 1996 prices are: $198 for first-class and $160 for second-class. Up to six additional days may be added at $30 per day for first-class, $30 per day for second-class. Half-fare for children age 4-11. Both passes include the following bonuses:

• Free round-trip train service between Orly or Charles de Gaulle Roissy airports and downtown Paris.

• A one-day Metropass valid in second-class within the city limits on the Paris subway and bus systems.

• 50% discount on the Nice-Digne scenic private rail line.

• 15% discount on the Train + Auto car rental system (Avis) available at most rail stations and airports.

• 15-20% discount on the entrance fee to numerous national museums.

• A gift from the Printemps Department Store!

• Irish Ferries ships from Le Havre to Rosslare and Cherbourg to Rosslare (late June to late August). On arrival in Ireland, the bus service (taking passengers from Rosslare pier to the Rosslare rail station) accommodates all passengers, and at no charge.

• Le Havre-Cork. (Port taxes are extra, payable in Irish Pounds. Reservations are required for cabins at all times, and for seats during July and August.

• The bus (7FF charge) that transports passengers from le Havre rail station to the boat pier takes people on a first-come-first-served basis. When the bus is filled, people left at the rail station must take a taxi to the pier.

France Rail N Drive   Unlimited three days of train travel plus three days of car rental (any six days) within one month. Prices vary depending on number of passengers and the category of car. Note that the third and fourth passenger needs to pay only for a three-day France Railpass.

The 1996 prices per person for two persons with a compact size car is: $189 for first-class train and $159 for second-class. Up to six more days of train travel may be added at $30 per day for first-class, $30 per day for second-class. Up to six more days of car rental may be added at $44 per day for the compact size. All prices include the French sales tax TVA (Value Added Tax) which is 18.6%, unlimited mileage, and the basic legal liability insurance, as well as free drop-off anywhere within continental France. Note: the car may be driven in other countries but must be dropped-off in France. Avis has more than 500 rental locations in France. When possible reservations for cars should be made at least seven days in advance and in your country of origin. (In the U.S.A., the toll free telephone number is (800) 331-1084. For making reservation after arriving in France, phone 05-05-22-11 at least 24 hours in advance. Note: experience shows that car rentals booked in the US tend to me less expensive than the same rentals booked in France.

France Rail N Fly   Unlimited three days of train travel plus one day of air travel anywhere in France (any four days) within one month.

The 1996 adult prices are: $295 for first-class, $255 for second-class. For children ages 2-11: $195 for first-class, $175 for second-class. Up to six more days of train travel may be added at $30 per day for first-class, $30 per day for second-class. For children age 2-11: $15 and $15. One additional day of air travel may be added at $99 for either first-class or second-class, for both adults and children.

Carte Vermeil Plein Temps   See Rail Europ Senior in the introduction.

Carte Vermeil Quatre Temps This senior citizen pass is available to persons aged 60 and older and may be purchased at major rail stations only in France. Those eligible for this card are able to purchase both first and second-class tickets at up to 50% discounts for travel on French trains. There are some restrictions though: travel cannot start between Noon Friday and Noon Saturday, from 15:00 Sunday to Noon Monday, and on certain holidays and periods of heavy train traffic. The Carte Vermeil Quatre Temps is valid for four rail trips within one year. The 1996 price of the card is 140 FF.

ONE DAY EXCURSIONS AND CITY TOURING

Here are 68 one-day round trip rail excursions that can be made comfortably from French cities, with return travel in most cases before dinner time. The comments provided on the major sites and events at each destination are designed to give travelers only a basic idea and a few suggestions of what to see. More specific guides are recommended for more in-depth and specialized discussion of these cities. Note that the number after the name of each route corresponds to the Thomas Cook Timetable of the same number.

Avignon

This walled city, the tourist capital of Province, can be entered through 14 different gates. You can obtain a city map or a personal guide at the Syndicat d'Initiative (41 Cours Jean-Jaurès). During the 14th century, Avignon was briefly the papal headquarters of the Roman Catholic Church when it was unsafe for a series of French popes to be in Rome. Take the one-hour tour of the Palace of the Popes, open daily January-March 09:00-12:45 and 14:00-18:00 April-late August 09:00-19:00 late August-September 09:00-20:00 October 09:00-19:00 November-December 09:00-12:45 and 14:00-18:00. Next to the Palace is the 12th century Cathedral of Notre-Dame-de-Doms. Outside the Palace you can board "Circuit #2" of a picturesque, 54-seater, trackless train pulled by a gasoline-powered locomotive that operates March through October, with daily departures every 15 minutes. This route is a climb to the top of a hill overlooking the Palace (a great view of the city and the Rhone Valley) and through the colorful Rocher Dom Gardens, where passengers can get off and return to the Palace by a later train. "Circuit #1" operates March through September and runs daily 10:00-19:00 for a 30-minute ride through the city's shopping streets and renovated old quarters. Initial boarding for this train (every 35 minutes) is at Palace Square. See the 13th to 16th century Italian-school religious paintings in the 14th century Petit Palais museum, open daily except Tuesday 9:30-11:30 and 14:00-18:00. Other medieval buildings worth seeing are the 12th century St. Ruff Church and the 14th century Gothic St. Didier Church. See the Roman sculptures and mosaics (some dating back 3,000 years) in the Lapidary Museum (housed in the 17th century Jesuit Church), open daily except Tuesday 10:00-11:55 and 14:00-18:00. Cross the Rhone River by walking or driving over the bridge to Villeneuve-les-Avignon and admire the view of Avignon from the other side of the river.

All-day bus tours from Avignon to many interesting places in this area can be taken from in front of the rail station. One tour includes Roman ruins at St. Remy, the village of Les Baux (sculptured during the Middle Ages from the top a stone hill), and the Roman theater in Arles. In nearby Orange, there is a Roman Triumphal Arch and an amphitheater built during the reign of Augustus. Don't forget that each summer in July and August Avignon hosts the most important theater festival in France. The population of the town multiply ten fold and its nearly impossible to find a room if you haven't booked in advance. But, the drama is excellent.

Bordeaux

Bordeaux turns its shoulders away from Paris and believes in its own supreme importance. A lively and wealthy port city, Bordeaux, of course, is one of the capitals of the French wine industry. Information about tours of the port and an excellent city map for making a walking tour of Bordeaux are available at the Tourist Office, 12 Cours du 30 Juillet. The opera, parks, hotels, Roman ruins and 18th century mansions are in the northern sector of the city. Museums, churches and fine shops are in the southern part of Bordeaux. See the Maritime Museum, on the Quai de la Douane, the wonderful Louis XV houses on rue Fernand Philippart, and the modern stained-glass in the 14th century St. Michel Church on Place Dubourg. The view of Bordeaux from the top of that church's tower shouldn't be missed. The large 15th century bell tower, Grosse Cloche, the 13th century Gothic St. Andres Cathedral, and the Musée des Beaux Arts, open daily except Tuesday 10:00-12:00 and 14:00-18:00, are key sites. Many tourists admire the fans with mother of pearl, ivory and silver handles (plus Medieval furniture, costumes and ceramics) in the Musée des Arts Decoratifs (39 rue Bouffard), open daily except Tuesday 14:00-18:00.

Do not miss seeing the array of fruits, cheeses, wild game and many exotic foods at the market on Place des Grands Hommes. The fantastic carved plants and the swan boat in the Jardin Public provide an easy-going afternoon activity. The Maison des Vins at 1 Cours du 30 Juillet, where you can obtain information on visiting nearby famous wineries, is a useful stop. See the lovely 18th century Opera House, the Grand Theatre, the Museum of Painting and Sculpture, the Numismatic Museum, the Museum of Old Bordeaux, and the Bonie Museum of Far Eastern Art.

Lyon

France's culinary capital, Lyon, is second to Paris in size and importance in the country. Occasionally, two trains depart from the same track at Lyon's Perrache rail station standing in opposite directions. Be sure to stand at the correct end (North or South) of the track in order to board the train you want to ride. Check the departure signs at the underground passageway. Do not rely merely on a track number when departing from Perrache rail station!

Next to the North passageway of Track A is a take-out restaurant, handy for provisioning your trip. A metropolitan train connects Lyon's Brotteaux and Perrache rail stations. The ride is 15 minutes.

If you try to keep from eating at the spectacular Nouvelle Les Halles food market: 65 tantalizing stalls of meat, poultry, fish, produce, cheese, bread, pastry, coffee, tea, spices, wine and candy, you are certain to fail. Too tempting. Open 07:00-19:00 Monday-Saturday and 07:00-12:00 on Sunday. Here, you can buy pheasants in plumage, partridges, wild ducks, quail, snipe, frog legs, four varieties of oysters, shrimp, eel, cod and sole. There are goose, duck and game patés. Do not fail to sample the three Lyon specialties: Morteau de Jesu (pork meat in a pig's foot casing), the peppery pink and white salami, and the garlicky Lyon sausage. The wine here is magnificent. It has been said that Lyon has three rivers: the Rhone, the Saone, and the Beaujolais. You are in Burgundy country.

Stroll for a few hours through the winding streets of the three-block wide half-mile long ancient section (Vieux Lyon) and see the magnificent 15th century Renaissance mansions. Much information is available in the booklet Guide du Vieux Lyon sold everywhere in the city. Take the funicular to the 19th century Basilica of Notre Dame de la Fourviere to see the extraordinary mosaics on its floors, walls and nave. The view from either the terrace behind it or from the observatory above it is marvelous. Then walk downhill to the Gallo Roman Museum (open daily except Monday and Tuesday 09:30-12:00 and 14:00-18:00), built into the side of a hill next to several Roman ruins. Its exhibits include objects from prehistory to the end of the Roman Empire, as well as elaborate floor mosaics and scale models of ancient Lyons. Walking further downhill brings you to the Cathedral of St. Jean, which has 13th century stained glass and a 500-year-old astrological clock that performs a tableau at 12:00, 13:00, 14:00 and 15:00. The exhibits in the History Museum at the nearby Palais Gadagne cover the period from where the Gallo Roman Museum leaves off, including carved Renaissance furniture, prints, Nevers glazed pottery, and documents from the French Revolution. The adjoining Puppet Museum at 10-14 rue de Gadagne, honors Laurent Mourguet, a destitute weaver who, in seeking to attract customers with a puppet show, invented the character Guignol, whose name has come to symbolize children's afternoon puppet theater everywhere in France. Both museums are open daily except Tuesday 10:45-18:00.

In the more modern area of the city, grab the Bus #13 from the rail station, through the main shopping streets, to the Place de la Croix Rousse and then proceed by foot to Place des Terreaux to see the 17th century City Hall, the 19th century Opera House and The Fine Arts Museum. This museum, featuring works of Rodin, Renoir, Gauguin, Monet, Delacroix, Courbet and Corot, is open daily except Monday and Tuesday 10:30-18:00. Do not miss the Italian fountain with its four bronze horses, sculptured by the same Bartholdi who created the Statue of Liberty. The Musée des Tissus (34 rue de la Charite), open daily except Monday 10:00-17:30, houses a nearly 2,000-year-old collection of Oriental and European silks and velvets. It displays Persian carpets hung in a room that is 28-feet high. Next door, there is a fine collection of silver objects, kitchen utensils, Louis XIV furniture, tapestries and enamels in The Museum of Decorative Arts, open daily except Monday 10:00-12:00 and 14:00-17:30. Visit The Museum of Printing and Banking (13 rue de la Poullaillerie), open daily except Monday and Tuesday 09:30-12:00 and 14:00-18:00, and The Museum of Medicine in Hotel-Dieu on rue de l'Hopital, closed Monday. And, certainly treat yourself to a full and leisurely Lyonnais lunch and dinner.

Marseilles

If scenes from The French Connection flutter to mind, you'd not be wholly wrong. Marseilles is a Mediterranean sea port with a strong flavor of North Africa, Italy, and the middle East. Yet it can only be French. Enjoy the sun, the pastis, the mixture of southern laziness and Latin fervor. There are plenty of fancy shops on Canebiere, the main street. Visit the dungeon from which Monte Cristo escaped, at Chateau d'If, reached by launch from the Quai des Belges. Most of the museums in Marseilles are closed Tuesday. The Maritime Museum, on the ground floor of the Palais de la Bourse (Stock Exchange), the Fine Arts Museum and Natural History Museum in the Palais de Longchamps, the Roman Docks Museum, the Museum of Old Marseilles, the Museum of Mediterranean Archaeology, and the Lapidary Museum, both in the Park of Borely. There are fine views of the harbor from Fort St. Jean and Fort St. Nicolas. Don't neglect just sitting out on a terrace and ordering a Ricard with ice and watching the people as you eat olives. This is the south of France.

Nice

Aside from being France's retirement enclave, Nice has lots to offer travelers. See the price-less antiques, lavish carpets and exceptional paintings and sculptures in the Hotel Negresco at 37 Promenade des Anglais, the long and delightful avenue that follows the sea. Hotels and out-door restaurants dot the wide boulevards. The Jules Cheret Museum of Fine Arts, 33 Avenue des Baumettes (behind the Promenade des Anglais), has many of Cheret's paintings. The Matisse Museum, 164 Avenue des Arenes, has guided tours in English. Note that most of the museums in Nice are closed either Monday or Tuesday.

Visits might also want to take in the War Memorial. The view of the Bay of Angels from the Naval Museum, and the Bellanda Tower are memorable things to see. The Marc Chagall National Museum, a short walk down the hill from the Arenes station, the Roman Baths, the Terra Amata Prehistory Museum, and the 15,000 species of seashells at the Musée Inter-nationale de Malacologie are definitely worth your time. Take the lift to the Colline du Cha-teau fortress ruins. One drawback about the Nice area and the famed Cote d'Azur is the nerve-raacking traffic in the summer months.

Try the Nicoise cuisine: pissaladiere (the local pizza), socca (a pancake), ratatouile (sau-teed eggplant, onions, tomatoes and squash), le poulet farci aux figues (roast chicken stuffed with fresh figs), and of course salade nicoise.

Paris

For travelers arriving in Paris for the first time, a more in depth guide book is advised. Paris is one of the few destinations on earth that continues to mesmerize visitors. The myths that Paris generate are all true. Paris enchants and it annoys, it fulfills all expectations, and it demands that you return. It is welcoming and it is cold. It is a city to fall in love in and a city that nur-tures melancholia.

As for getting around, the city is particularly fortunate in that its famous Métro is ubiqui-tous. There is virtually nowhere you can't get to by metro, and the prices are reasonable. Buy a day pass or a three day pass if you plan to stay for a short time and use the metro a lot. Otherwise, a carnet of 10 metro tickets are about half the price of buying one ticket at a time (7 FF). There is also an elaborate commuter rail service called the RER, which serves both major airports approximately every 15 minutes (05:00-24:00) in both directions: From the Gare de Nord rail station north to Roissy Aeroport/Charles de Gaulle (26 minutes), and from Gare de Nord rail station south to Antony, where one picks up the OrlyVal train to Aeroport d'Orly (23 minutes). For a more detailed discussion of Paris and its transportation, consult *Paris Inside Out* (Houghton-Mifflin, 1995).

Paris Train Stations and the Directions They Serve

(Always double-check the station for any departure from Paris!)

Gare du Nord: Serves the north, including the Channel ports, where trains connect with ferries and hover crafts from Britain; also services Belgium, Holland and the Scandinavian countries.

Gare de l'Est: Serves the east, Nancy and Strasbourg, and Germany and eastern Europe, including ex-Yugoslavia and Moscow. (The former Paris-Frankfurt train now continues to Leipzig.)

Gare d'Austerlitz: Serves the southwest; Bordeaux, Toulouse, and Spain and Portugal via Orleans, Tours, Poitiers and Angouleme.

Gare St. Lazare: Serves Normandy and boat trains to/from Dieppe.

Gare Montparnasse: Serves western France, especially Brittany.

Gare de Lyon: Serves southwestern France, Switzerland, Italy and Greece.

Bus service connects these Paris rail stations:

Between Gare Austerlitz and Gare de l'Est, Gare du Nord and Gare Saint Lazare, Gare de Lyon and Gare de l'Est, Gare du Nord and Gare Saint Lazare, Gare du Nord and Gare de Lyon and Gare Austerlitz, Gare de l'Est and Austerlitz, Gare du Nord and Gare Saint Lazare.

Cultural Sightseeing

Here are a few basic idea of things to see in Paris. Use this list simply as a jumping off point.

• Musée d'Orsay, the converted train station on the Left Bank which served the Paris-Orleans line in the 19th century and became a museum in 1987, now houses much of the impressionists and early 20th century French collection, and should excite train travelers and art lovers alike. Its main attractions: works by Monet, Van Gogh, Renoir, Pissarro. A great place to start your Parisian visit.

• Louvre (open Monday and Wednesday 09:00-21:45, Thursday-Sunday 09:00-18:00). The Pyramid, designed by I.M. Pei has modernized the feel of this classic world-important museum. New wings opened in 1994.

• Montmartre area and the stunning Sacre Coeur church. Do this at night.

• Eiffel Tower, which needs no introduction.

• The obelisk at Place de la Concorde where Marie Antoinette was guillotined. • Arch of Triumph, from which an excellent rooftop view of Paris can be experienced. At the top of the Champs-Elysée.

• Grande Arch at La Defénse.

• Stained-glass windows at St. Chapelle.

• Deportation Monument behind Notre Dame Cathedral.

• Luxembourg Gardens. Go for a stroll or a jog or a pony ride. Paris at its most Parisian.

• Pompidou Center (closed Tuesday). France's most significant cultural center, library, and public meeting place.

• Musée of the Renaissance in the 16th century Chateau d'Ecouen Castle, with its antique tapestries, ceramics, arms, furniture, outstanding carved white fireplace and painted ceilings.

• Orangerie Museum, with its 150 works of impressionist painters including Renoir, Matisse, Cezanne, Picasso and Utrillo.

• Les Invalides and its Army Museum, where the preserved body of Napoleon is on exhibit. Enormous collection of uniforms, weapons, war trophies, flags, books, manuscripts and paintings. And, the Eglise du Dome (containing Napoleon's Tomb). Open daily 10:00-18:00 April-September and 10:00-17:00 October-March. A fine sound-and-light show is presented nightly, April-September.

• Rodin Museum, at Hotel Biron, closed Tuesday. The gardens are delightful. Don't miss "The Thinker." The Rodin Museum, 77 rue de Varenne, is open daily except Tuesday 10:00-17:00. (Visitors are not admitted after 16:30.)

• Tour Montparnasse offers an excellent view of Paris from its 650-foot high observation deck.

• Flower markets on the Ile de la Cite, the rue de Buci, and rue Mouffetard in the Latin Quarter

• Flea Markets (marché aux puces) on Saturdays, Sundays, and Mondays at Porte de Clignancourt, Porte de Vanves, and Porte de Montreuil.

• Eugene Delacroix Museum, 6 Place Furstenberg, is open daily except Tuesday 09:45-17:15.

• Jewish Art Museum, 42 rue des Saules, is open Monday-Thursday 15:00-18:00. The collection of naive art in the Le Halle St. Pierre Museum, 1 rue Ronsard, can be viewed daily 10:00-18:00.

• Museum of Mechanical Musical Instruments at Impasse Berthaud, open Saturdays, Sundays and holidays 14:00-19:00. Exhibit of 19th century player pianos, violins and banjos

• The Tobacco Museum, 12 rue Surcouf, is open daily except Sunday 11:00-18:00.

• The Pasteur Museum, 25 rue du Docteur-Roux, is open daily except Saturdays, Sundays and holidays 14:00-17:30.

• Honoré de Balzac Museum, 47 rue Raynouard, is open daily except Mondays and holidays 10:00-17:40.

• Galerie des Monnaies, Medailles et Antiques (in the National Library at 58 rue de Richelieu) there are exhibits from its collection of 400,000 historic coins.

• Other noteworthy museums include the Musée de la Mode et du Costume, 10 Ave. Pierre Premier de Serbie, the Archaeological Museum, electronic exhibits at the Musée Branly, Chinese and Japanese artifacts at the Musée Dennery, the Museum of French Bread, the Museum of Police History, the Musical Instruments Museum, the large poster collection in the Musée de l'Affiche et la Publicité (at the Decorative Arts Museum, 107 rue de Rivoli). 17th and 18th century furniture in the Musée Carnavalet, 23 rue de Sevigne, open daily except Monday 10:00-17:40. For flea market enthusiasts, check out the Marchés aux Puces at Porte de Clignancourt and Porte de Montreuil.

Other Attractions

• The Marais district, the oldest section of Paris, a maze of narrow 16th century streets, should not be overlooked. It can be examined by starting at the Pompidou Center and walking along rue Rambuteau to rue des Francs-Bourgeois, a street named in the 15th century, describing its poor residents who were exempt from paying taxes. Interesting documents (the order sending Marie Antoinette to the guillotine, the 1944 law giving French women the right to vote, etc.) can be seen in the History of France Museum at 60 rue des Francs-Bourgeois, open daily except Tuesdays and holidays 14:00-17:00.

Among the many elegant town mansions (called hotels in the 15th century) worth seeing in the Marais are Hotel d'Albret, Hotel de Fourcy, and Hotel de Lamignon (all on rue des Francs-Bourgeois). Then take note of the Hotel Merle and Hotel de Chatillon (along rue Payenne), and follow the signs leading to the Hotel Sale on rue de Thorigny, which housed in great elegance and perfect sophistication the Picasso Museum, open Wednesday 10:00-22:00, Thursday-Monday 10:00-17:15. There is an extraordinary collection of stuffed animals, furniture carved with animal figures, and silver encrusted riffles at the Hunting and Nature Museum, in the Hotel Gueneguad at 60 rue des Archives, open daily except Mondays and holidays 10:00-17:30. By walking down rue du Parc Royal, you pass the pink and white Hotel Duret de Chevry. Turn right to go down rue de Sevigne so as to pass by Hotel Le Peletier St. Fargeau and Hotel Carnavalet, now the Museum of French Interior design, open daily except Monday 10:00-17:40. Then visit the Maison de Victor Hugo (6 Place des Vosges), situated in the corner of one of Paris's most charming and elegant old world squares, open daily except Mondays and holidays 10:00-17:40. Next, walk down rue de Birague and onto rue St. Antoine in order to see Hotel Sully (at Number 62). By walking rue Mahler until it reaches rue des Rosiers, you arrive at the center of the Jewish district and the most famous delicatessen in Paris, Jo Goldbergs, at Number 7. Don't miss Chez Marianne, slightly further down the rue des Rossiers, for it is here that you'll experience the soul (and Tunisian deli delights) of the neighborhood, under the welcoming acceuil of owners Marianne and her philosopher/poet/grocer husband André. Nearby is the unusual Art Deco synagogue on the rue Pavee. The rue Simon-le-Franc will lead you back to the Pompidou Center.

• At the 14-acre Pere Lachaise Cemetery are the graves of Edith Piaf, Gertrude Stein, Alice B. Toklas, Colette, Sarah Bernhardt, Isadora Duncan, Simone Signoret, Frederick Chopin, Oscar Wilde, Honore de Balzac, Ferdinand de Lesseps (promoter of the Suez Canal), and Jean Francois Champollion (interpreter of the Rosetta stone). Upstaging them all though is the cult hangout and graffiti-sprawled grave of myth-making rock star Jim Morrison, who came to Paris to attempt to become an obscure philosophical poet and died there in 1971. Opened in 1804, it is the oldest of the four main cemeteries in Paris. It is open mid-March to mid-November Monday-Saturday 07:30-18:00, the rest of the year 08:30-17:30. On Sundays and holidays: mid-November to mid-January 09:00-18:00, the rest of the year 08:30-17:30. Other cemeteries of note include Montparnasse cemetery in which such notables as Jean-Paul Sartre, Simone de Beauvoir, and Samuel Beckett rest in peace.

• For the recreation-minded traveler, Paris offers some prime swimming pools. Swimmers can chose from a wide variety of pools in this city. The 50-meter Piscine Georges-Vallerey, located next to the Porte des Lilas metro station. built for the 1924 Olympic Games, has a transparent roof that is opened in sunny weather. The underground Piscine Suzanne Berlioux at Les Halles, near the Pompidou Center, is another modern 50-meter facility. Aquaboulevard de Paris is an indoor-outdoor amusement park (sand beaches, wave machines, slides. toboggans, mock tropical islands and lagoons) is near the metro Balard. The former Piscine Pontoise re-opened after renovations in 1990 with the new name Piscine du Quartier Latin. The famous Piscine Deligny located on a moored barge on the Left Bank of the Seine, burned down in 1993 and has yet to be restored. Joggers can practice their habit in the Jardin du Luxembourg, Parc Monceau, or—although on the edges of town—the expansive and verdant Bois de Vincennes or Bois de Boulogne, which doubles up after dark as a commercial meeting grounds for amorous encounters of every sort.

• As for cuisine, not only is Paris a feast of fine dining, its gourmet shops have the power of overwhelming visitors with the elegance and beauty of its window presentations. The prices will send you spinning, but there's no charge to look. The most famous of these fine shops is Fauchon on the Place de la Madeleine and its neighbor Hediard. Across the Place is La Maison de Truffe (19 Place de la Madeleine), where truffles, foie gras and caviar are the rule, and next door you'll be amazed by the Creplet-Brussol fromagerie featuring a cool 250 varieties of cheeses. Caviar Kaspia hosts fine caviar from Iran and Russia, with the Marquise de Sevigne specializing in sinfully rich and stunning fine chocolates for nearly 100 years. All this on Place de la Madeleine, which houses as well a kiosque for same-day half price theater tickets.

For additional information on Paris and its surroundings contact:
Office du Tourisme et des Congrès de Paris
127, av des Champs-Elysées
75008 PARIS
Tel: 49.52.53.54
Fax: 49.52.53.00

Strasbourg

An historical pawn, Strasbourg was French until 1872. German 1871-1918, French 1918-1940, German 1940-1944, and has been French since 1944. Currently the seat of the European parliment, Strasbourg has gained continental importance over the last ten years. On rue de la Rape, visitors can observe the city's majestic 13th century Cathedral of Notre-Dame. All of its windows are 12th, 13th and 14th century stained-glass. Its famous 60-foot high astronomical clock, which calculates eclipses, sunrises and sunsets into eternity, comes alive on the hour and quarter-hour, when figures appear from and return into its interior. The clock's major performance is at 12:30. It is then that the Four Ages of Man pass before Death, and the 12 Apostles move past the figure of Jesus. As he blesses them, a mechanical rooster flaps its wings and crows three times.

There is an extraordinary view of the city from a platform 217 feet above street level, at the top of the Cathedral's 328-step spiral staircase. From April-September, a fabulous sound-and-light show is presented inside the Cathedral: illuminated stained-glass windows, bells tolling, organ music, the whole works for an enchanting Alsatian evening.

There are three fine museums in the 18th century Chateau des Rohans (next to the Cathedral): a collection of Monet, Renoir, El Greco, Goya and Tintoretto in the Art Gallery; the relics in the Archaeological Museum; and a display of clocks, ironwork, earthenware and porcelain in the Museum of Decorative Arts. More recently, Strasbourg opened up a new museum of contemporary works.

Next to the Rohans is a 14th century building that houses wonderful 11th to 17th century Alsatian art in the Musée de lOeuvre Notre-Dame. Next to it is the Modern Art Museum. All of these museums are open daily except Tuesday 10:00-12:00 and 14:00-18:00.

You might want to take the one-hour sightseeing mini-train ride that starts at the south side of the Cathedral. It runs every half-hour, late March to the end of October. There are also cruises on the Rhine (90 minutes, three hours, and 11 hours) starting in front of the Palais des Rohans, and nearby Musée Alsacien, 23 Quai St. Nicholas, which houses impressive rooms dating from the early 17th century (furnished with marvelous utensils, stoves, wooden molds and pottery from the same era).

In all cases, treat yourself to a choucroute garni, an elaborate and copious Alsatian dish of sauerkraut, sausage, potatoes, and pork. Order an Alsatian white wine and you'll never regret stopping in Strasbourg.

Tours

Although much of the old city was destroyed in the 1944 bombings, Tour is worth a stop. One option is to take a 90-minute walk by departing the Tours rail station along Boulevard Heurteloup to rue Nationale, then turning right and going up one side of rue Nationale to the bridge that stretches over the Loire, and by returning along the opposite side of rue Nationale, crossing Boulevard Heurteloup, going one block further, turning left onto rue de Bordeaux, and following it directly back to the rail station. This will give you a fine overview of the city. Stop in and see the fine collection of paintings in the Musée des Beaux-Arts.

A pamphlet called "The Loire Valley by Train" may be obtained from the information desk at many French rail stations. It shows schedules of trains from Tours (not provided in Cook) that stop at stations near 12 different castles. The train to Azay-le-Rideau continues to Chinon. Another train goes to Amboise, Chaumont (Onzain), Blois and Beaugency. A third goes to Villandry (Savonnieres), Langeais, Samur and Angers. A fourth train goes to Loches and a fifth goes to Chenonceaux. These train rides range from 10 to 70 minutes in each direction. Most are less than 30 minutes. There are also bus tours from Tours to the castles.

TIMETABLES

In the following tables, when cities host more than one rail station, the name of the particular station has been designated in parentheses after the name of the city. Don't assume that the station from where you depart is the same as the station where you arrived. Doing so may cause you to miss your train.

Note: Renovation of Paris's Gare du Nord was completed in late 1993. Now it serves two functions: one station handles all long-distance trains (including TGVs) servicing Lille and the northern regions of France. The other, exclusively designed for traffic to the Channel Tunnel, includes a duty-free area and a customs baggage check for passengers traveling to Great Britain.

Avignon - Antibes - Avignon   79

Dep. Avignon	04:44 (1)	05:14 (2)		Dep. Antibes	20:08 (3)	20:23 (4)
Arr. Antibes	08:55	09:21		Arr. Avignon	00:05	00:04

(1) Runs daily, except Friday and Saturday. (2) Runs Friday and Saturday. (3) Runs daily, except Saturday and Sunday. (4) Runs Saturday and Sunday.

Sights in **Antibes**: The exhibit of 231 Picasso paintings at the special Picasso Museum in Grimaldi Castle, on Place Mariejol. Open daily except Tuesday 10:00–12:00 and 15:00–18:00.

Avignon - Arles - Avignon   151

Dep. Avignon	08:05 (1)	09:51	12:08	15:06
Arr. Arles	20 minutes later			

Sights in **Arles**: The ancient Roman cemetery, Alyscamps, that contains 400,000 sarcophagi, hand-carved granite caskets. The 21,000-seat Roman arena (open 08:30-19:00 in Summer, 09:00-12:00 and 14:00-18:00 the rest of the year). The museum of Pagan Art, in St. Anne Church on Place de la Republique (open 09:00-12:30 and 14:00-19:00 in Summer, 10:00-12:30 and 14:00-17:30 the rest of the year). The Roman Theater, open 08:30-12:00 and 14:00-18:00. The Forum, built during Augustus' rule. The Thermae, from Constantine's era. The 12th century Cloister in the marvelous Romanesque Church of Saint-Trophime.

Dep. Arles	12:05	13:36 (2)	14:46	17:53	20:13	22:33 (3)
Arr. Avignon	20 minutes later					

(1) Runs daily except Sundays and holidays. (2) Runs Monday-Friday, except holidays. (3) Second-class.

Avignon - Lyon - Avignon   151

Dep. Avignon	06:53	07:39 (1)	08:04 (2)	10:39
Arr. Lyon (Part Dieu)	09:02	09:26	10:18	12:44
Dep. Lyon (Part Dieu)	14:05 (3)	17:17 (3)	18:44 (3)	19:00 (4+6)
Arr. Avignon	16:01	19:17	20:41	20:49

(1) Operates late August to early July. Runs Monday-Friday, except holidays. TGV. Reservation required. Supplement charged. Light refreshments. (2) Runs daily, except Sundays and holidays. (3) Light refresh-

ments. (4) TGV. Reservation required. Supplement charged. Restaurant car. (5) Operates September through June. Runs daily, except Saturday. TGV. Reservation required. Supplement charged. Restaurant car. (6) Plus other departures from Lyon at 20:20 (3), 22:03 (5) and 23:43, arriving Avignon 23:09, 23:56 and 01:41.

Avignon - Marseille - Avignon   151

Dep. Avignon	08:05 (1)	09:51		10:52 (2)	11:45 (4)	12:08
Arr. Marseille (St. Ch.)	50–60 minutes later					

Dep. Marseille (St. Ch.)	14:01 (3)	14:39 (3)		16:50 (4)	17:10 (3)	17:31 (4)
Arr. Avignon	50–60 minutes later					

Dep. Marseille (St. Ch.)	18:17 (5)	19:25 (3)		21:45 (6)	22:59 (6)	23:21 (6)
Arr. Avignon	50–60 minutes later					

(1) Runs daily, except Sundays and holidays. (2) Runs Monday–Friday, except holidays. TGV. Reservation required. Supplement charged. Restaurant car. (3) Light refreshments. (4) TGV. Reservation required. Supplement charged. Restaurant car. (5) Runs daily, except Saturday. TGV. Reservation required. Supplement charged. Restaurant car. (6) Second-class.

Avignon - Monaco (Monte Carlo) - Avignon

151			*164*	
Dep. Avignon	08:05 (1)	09:51	Dep. Monaco	19:29
Arr. Marseille	09:06	10:54	Arr. Nice	19:46
Change trains. 164			*No train change.*	
Dep. Marseille	09:18	11:04	Dep Nice	20:00
Arr. Nice	11:43	13:36	Arr. Marseille	22:41
Change trains.			*Change trains. 151*	
Dep. Nice	11:57	14:15	Dep. Marseille	22:59
Arr. Monaco	12:13	14:34	Arr. Avignon	00:05

(1) Runs daily, except Sundays and holidays. (2) Second-class.

Avignon - Nimes - Avignon   163

Dep. Avignon	07:35 (8)	11:00	11:48 (1)	12:17 (2)	14:13
Arr. Nimes	25 minutes later				

Sights in Nimes: Many Roman ruins in excellent condition, such as the 1st century amphitheater (seating 24,000 people) in the center of the city, used in recent years for bullfights to entertain Spanish migrant workers. The construction of the arena was done by fitting large stones together without the use of mortar. The Arena is open 08:00-19:00 in Summer, 09:00-12:00 and 14:00-17:00 the rest of the year. Also see the beautiful 1st century rectangular temple, Maison Carree, and its collection of Roman sculptures, open 09:00-20:00 in Summer, 09:00-12:00 and 14:00-18:00 the rest of the year. The view of Nimes from the oldest Roman building, Tour Magne, on a hill outside the city. A few miles away is the enormous Pont du Gard Roman aqueduct. Visit the collection of Iron Age and Roman objects in the Archaeological Museum. Stroll through the 18th century Garden of the Fountain.

Dep. Nimes	11:55	12:47(1)	13:29 (3)	14:29 (1)	15:05	15:39 (4)
Arr. Avignon	25 minutes later					
Dep. Nimes	16:28 (5)	17:44	18:29	20:29 (5)	23:02 (7)	
Arr. Avignon	25 minutes later					

(1) TGV. Reservation required. Supplement charged. Light refreshments. (2) Runs daily, except Sundays and holidays. Light refresments. (3) Runs daily, except Sundays and holidays. (4) Runs Monday-Thursday. (5) Runs Monday-Friday, except holidays. (6) Runs daily, except Saturday. (7) Second-class. (8) Sunday only

Avignon - Orange - Avignon 151

Dep. Avignon	08:04	10:27	12:29	14:05	15:07
Arr. Orange	15 minutes later				

Sights in **Orange**: See the 10,000-seat Roman Theater (open 09:00-18:30 in Summer, 09:00-12:00 and 13:00-17:00 the rest of the year) and the ancient walls of the old city. The Roman Triumphal Arch.

Dep. Orange	11:51	14:48	15:55	17:21 (1)	19:40 (2)	21:04 (3)
Arr. Avignon	15 minutes later					

(1) Runs Monday–Friday, except holidays. (2) Runs daily, except Saturday. (3) Runs daily, except Fridays.

Bordeaux - Bayonne and Biarritz - Bordeaux 137

Dep. Bordeaux (St. Jean)	07:24	10:33 (1)	11:14 (1+2)	13:08 (1)
Arr. Bayonne	09:13	12:05	13:50 (3)	14:37
Arr. Biarritz	10 minutes after arriving Bayonne.			

Sights in **Bayonne**: This is the Cote Basque's leading port and private yacht harbor. Visit the cathedral, The Basque Museum, Chateau-Viex, The Museum Bonnat. Exhibits tracing Basque history and customs (farm tools, household objects, costumes) are in the Musee Basque, at 1 Rue Marengo.

Sights in **Biarritz:** France's snootiest beach resort since 1854. Golf, tennis and every type of water sport are popular here. There are many spas offering thalassotherapy. See the food market. A small grocery store called Maison Arosteguy stocks 120 types of Scotch whiskey and what has been described as "a dizzying array" of Armagnacs.

Dep. Biarritz	14:50 (1)	17:47 (1+2)	18:02 (4)	18:39 (2)	20:23 (4)
Dep. Bayonne	10 minutes after departing Biarritz.				
Arr. Bordeaux (St. Jean)	16:35	19:36	20:30	21:20	22:46

(1) TGV. Reservation required. Supplement charged. Light refreshments. (2) Runs daily, except Sundays and holidays. (3) Change trains in Bayonne. (4) Runs Sunday only. (5) Operates early July to late August. (6) Plus other departures from Biarritz at and 23:24 (5), arriving Bordeaux 01:57.

Bordeaux - Carcassonne - Bordeaux 139

Bordeaux (St. Jean)	06:39 (1)	08:23 (2)	11:47 (1)
Arr. Carcassonne	09:50	12:17	14:59

Sights in **Carcassonne:** The most interesting walled city (actually double-walled) in France and Europe's best preserved relic of the Middle Ages. The inner wall, built by the Romans in the 2nd century, bears 29 towers. The 13th century French outer wall has 17 towers and barbicans (fortified castles). It is a 30-minute walk from the railstation to the walled city. There is both bus and taxi service.

Nearby are the ruins of 5 other walls, to the South, erected by France in medieval days as additional protection from attack by the Spaniards. As you stand on the walkways at the top of the French wall, it is easy to imagine yourself shooting arrows through the narrow slits or dropping hot oil on the marauders below.

See the Narbonnaise Gate and drawbridge. Nearby is a bust of Dame Carcas, for whom the city is named. Carcassonne had been under siege by Charlemagne. She gathered the little grain the starving people had and scattered it to livestock in view of the soldiers who were by then weary of the months they had been waiting for the people inside the impregnable walls to capitulate.

Her bold act convinced the soldiers that the people could last much longer, and Charlemagne abandoned his attempt to starve-out the town.

Inside the Basilica of St. Nazare are many stone carvings depicting scenes from the fort's history, magnificent stained-glass windows regarded by many as the finest in southern France, and the rectangular tombstone of Bishop Radulph. Also see the 12th century Countal Castle.

Dep. Carcassonne	15:52	17:52 (4)	20:17 (1)
Arr. Bordeaux (St. Jean)	19:04	21:53	23:35

(1) Light Refreshments. (2) Light refreshments. Change trains in Toulouse (arr. 11:04–dep. 11:29). (3) Operates early September to early July. Change trains in Toulouse (arr. 18:36–dep. 19:16). Light refreshments Toulouse-Bordeaux. (4) Operates early July to early September. Change trains in Toulouse (Arr. 18:36-dep 19:16). Light refreshments Toulouse-Bordeaux.

Bordeaux - Limoges - Bordeaux   140

Dep. Bordeaux (St. Jean)	06:16 (1)	07:47 (2)	10:30 (3)	12:00
Arr. Limoges	08:30	10:39	13:59	14:34

Sights in **Limoges**: Tours of the famous porcelain and enamel factories are free, by applying to the Syndicat de la Porcelain, 7 Rue du General Cerez. Visit the Adrien Dubouche Museum, with its great collection of ceramics. The Municipal Museum, to see its display of china made in Limoges from the 12th century to the present. The Cathedral of Saint Etienne.

Dep. Limoges	14:39 (4)	17:37 (5)	21:05 (6)
Arr. Bordeaux (St. Jean)	17:37	20:34	23:23

(1) Operates early July to late August. (2) Runs daily except Sundays and holidays. Change trains in Perigueux (arr. 09:05–dep. 09:31). (3) Change trains in Perigueux (arr. 11:56–dep. 12:39). (4) Operates late August to early July. Runs daily, except Sundays and holidays. (5) Change trains in Perigueux (arr. 18:55–dep. 19:15). (6) Light refreshments.

Bordeaux - Lourdes - Bordeaux   137

Dep. Bordeaux (St. Jean)	07:24 (1)	11:06 (2)	13:12 (3)	17:06 (4)	19:05 (11)
Arr. Lourdes	10:17	13:32	15:53	19:25	21:49

Sights in **Lourdes**: A 14-year-old girl, Bernadette Soubirous, had numerous visions here in 1858, in the Massabielle grotto. The underground spring in the grotto is believed by many to have miraculous qualities. About 3,000,000 people come here every year, many of them disabled or diseased and hoping to be cured.

The immense underground church seating 20,000 was innaugurated in 1958.

On the other side of the torrent called Gave de Pau there is an interesting 14th century castle which was used as a prison from 1643 until the early 19th century.

Dep. Lourdes	15:02	16:44 (5)	17:40 (6)	19:00 (7)	19:40 (8+10)
Arr. Bordeaux (St. Jean)	17:27 (4)	19:36	20:04	22:05	22:46

(1) Operates early July–late August. (2) TGV. Reservation required. Supplement charged. Runs Monday-Friday except holidays. Light refreshments. (3) Light refreshments. (4) TGV. Reservation required. Supplement charged. Light refreshments. Runs daily except Friday and Sunday. (5) Runs daily, except Sun. and holidays. Change trains in Dax (arr. 18:12–dep. 18:29). (6) TGV. Reservation required. Supplement charged. Runs Sun. only. Light refreshments. (7) Runs daily. (8) Runs Sun. only. (9) Plus another Bordeaux departure at 20:53 (4), arriving Lourdes 23:22. (10) Plus another Lourdes departure at 22:52, arriving Bordeaux 01:57. For those overnighting in Lourdes, there are other departures from Lourdes at 07:52 (4), 10:21 (3) and 11:20 (3). (11) TGV runs Friday only.

Bordeaux - Nantes - Bordeaux 134

Dep.Bordeaux (St. J.)	06:53	10:27 (1)
Arr. Nantes	11:05	14:29

• • •

Dep. Nantes	13:51 (1)	18:13	19:35 (2)
Arr. Bordeaux (St. J.)	18:06	22:15	23:26

(1) Light refreshments. (2) Early July to early September: runs daily, except Friday. Early September to early July: runs Friday and Sunday.

Sights in **Nantes**: This was a commercial center under the Romans. The Normans pillaged the town in 834. After having been partly destroyed in World War II, its railway was placed underground.

This is an important seaport and shipbuilding center. See the extraordinary white marble Renaissance tomb of Francois II, duke of Brittany, in the Cathedral that was bombed during World War II. The church was restored, only to have its roof almost entirely destroyed by fire in 1972. The tomb was not harmed.

Tour the medieval castle that was rebuilt in 1466, Chateau des Ducs de Bretagne and its museums (entrance on the Rue des Etats). Guided tours are offered every half-hour, daily during July and August from 10:00–12:00 and 14:00–18:00. The rest of the year there are only 3 tours a day, and the castle is closed on Tuesday. The castle is surrounded by a moat and has a drawbridge at its entrance.

Visit the Jules Verne Museum (the author was born in Nantes in 1828), open daily except Tuesday 10:00–12:00 and 14:00–17:00. See the exceptional paintings in the Fine Arts Museum (10 Rue Georges Clemenceau), open daily except Tuesday and national holidays 10:00–12:00 and 13:00–17:45.

Stroll through the Passage Pommeraye, a decorative 3 level shopping arcade. Visit the Jardin des Plantes, a botanical garden and formal French park, with grottos, waterfalls, statues, ponds, 400 varieties of camelias, and 19th century greenhouses, containing many orchids.

There are 3-hour boat cruises on the **Erbe River**, leaving from 24 Quai de Versailles at 12:30 (Lunch), 14:30 and 20:00 (dinner).

Bordeaux - Narbonne - Bordeaux 139

All of these trains have light refreshments.

Dep. Bordeaux (St. Jean)	06:39	08:23 (1)	Dep. Narbonne	19:47
Arr. Narbonne	10:20	12:26	Arr. Bordeaux (St. Jean)	23:35

Sights in **Narbonne**: The Cloister adjacent to the Palace of the Archbishops. The choir of the incomplete Cathedral of Saint-Just.

(1) Change trains in Toulouse (arr. 11:04-dep. 11:13).

Bordeaux - Toulouse - Bordeaux   139

Dep. Bordeaux (St. Jean)	05:54 (1)	06:39 (2)	08:23 (2)	10:06 (3)	11:02 (4)
Arr. Toulouse (Matabiau)	08:49	08:57	11:04	12:12	13:01

Sights in **Toulouse**:The Basilica of Saint Sernin, displaying the remains of 128 saints, including 6 of the apostles and a thorn from the Crown of Thorns. It also has 7 extraordinary 11th century marble bas reliefs and the Meigeville Door, a 12th century sculpture of apostles watching Christ ascend to heaven surrounded by angels.

The museum on the history of art and an exceptional collection of busts of Roman emperors at Musee Saint Raymond on Place St. Sernin. The Roman and medieval sculptures in the Musee des Augustins, 21 Rue de Metz. The beautiful 14th century Church of the Jacobins.

Popular art of the region and the history of Toulouse, at the Musee du Vieux-Toulouse, 7 Rue du May.

Chinese, Japanese and Indian art at the Musee Georges Labit, 43 Rue des Martyrs de la Liberation. St. Etienne Cathedral. Two 16th century homes: Hotel de Bernuy and Hotel d'Assezat, and the view of the city from the tower of the latter.

The Office de Tourisme (Donjon du Capitole, Square Charles de Gaule, 31000 Toulouse) offered in 1992 a 2–hour walking tour at 09:30 and 15:00 for $7.50, as well as a $10 city bus tour at 15:00.

Obtain the tourist office's brochure describing 16 different one-day bus sightseeing excursions to nearby interesting places ($25.50 each in 1994). All of these trips start at 08:00 and arrive back in Toulouse between 19:00–20:30.

One of these tours goes to the 16th century Chateau de Saint-Genies-Bellevue; to Cordes, a 13th century walled town, to see marvelous Gothic houses and the quality arts and crafts sold at 14th Marketplace; to see more than 600 works of Toulouse-Lautrec in Albi, where he was born in 1864; then to Chateau de Latours for tasting Gaillac wine.

Every year, from the end of June to late September, both an international Piano Festival featuring noted soloists and a series of orchestral concerts (jazz to Beethoven) are presented in Toulouse.

Barges can be rented to tour the 17th century Canal du Midi all the way to the Mediterranean. Visitors can also rent motorboats and rowboats.

Dep. Toulouse (Matabiau)	13:46 (5)	16:24 (4)	16:48	17:17 (6)	19:16 (2+7)
Arr. Bordeaux (St. Jean)	15:55	18:24	19:04	19:25	21:53

(1) Runs daily, except Sundays and holidays. (2) Light refreshments. (3) TGV. Reservation required. Supplement charged. Runs daily, except Sundays and holidays. Restaurant car. (4) Restaurant car. (5) TGV. Reservation required. Supplement charged. Light refreshments. (6) TGV. Reservation required. Supplement charged. Runs daily, except Saturday. Light refreshments. (7) Plus another departure from Toulouse at 21:14 (2), arriving Bordeaux 23:36.

Bordeaux - Tours - Bordeaux 136

All of the Bordeaux–St. Pierre-des-Corps and v.v. trains, are TGV, require a reservation, charge a supplement and have light refreshments, unless designated otherwise.

Dep. Bordeaux (St. Jean)	07:14	10:24 (1)
Arr. St. Pierre-des-Corps	09:40	12:57
Change trains (cross-platform).		
Dep. St. Pierre-des-Corps	09:43	13:06
Arr. Tours	09:51	13:08

Dep. Tours	14:43	16:13	19:37 (2)
Arr. St. Pierre-des-Corps	14:50	16:20	19:45
Change trains (cross platform).			
Dep. St. Pierre-des-Corps	14:54	16:23	19:47 (2)
Arr. Bordeaux (St. Jean)	17:25	18:53	22:22

(1) Change trains in Poitiers (arr. 12:05–dep. 12:11). (2) Runs daily, except Fri. Light refreshments.

Dijon - Beaune - Dijon 149

Dep. Dijon	07:40	09:04	11:17	11:30	12:11	14:40 (1)
Arr. Beaune	20 minutes later					

Sights in **Beaune**: The wine capital of Burgundy. Popular for its old houses along narrow, cobbled streets. Famous for Burgundian food: coq au vin, game birds, terines of veal and pork, snails, salamis, sausages, terines of salmon and sole. Hotels and restaurants here are booked months in advance.

Visit the many great wineries in this locale, such as Chateau de Meursault, Marche aux Vins and Maison Patriarche. Persuade your hotel to sell you $100 tickets to one of the 17 "grand dinners" at the Clos de Vougeot, sponsored by the Confrerie des Chevaliers de Taste-vin. See the priceless art collection in the 15th century Hotel-Dieu. The other attractions there are the 28 red-canopied and red-curtained beds that were used 5 centuries ago, the original 15th century furnishings in the 160-foot-long Paupers' Room, the ancient pharmacy and kitchen, fantastic tapestries and rare pewter.

See the 15th century tapestries in the Notre Dame Church.

Many hot-air balloon trips are available in this area.

Dep. Beaune	13:30 (1)	14:03 (2)	14:22 (3)	15:23	17:17	17:56 (1)	18:44 (5)
Arr. Dijon	20 minutes later						

(1) Runs daily, except Sun. and holidays. (2) Runs Sunday only. (3) Runs Mon.-Fri., except holidays. (4) Runs Sat., Sun. and holidays. (5) Plus other Beaune departures at 19:36 (3), 21:08 and 22:52.

Dijon - St. Claude - Dijon 157

Dep. Dijon	06:35 (1)	16:43	Dep. St. Claude	16:32 (2)	16:52 (1)
Arr. St. Claude	09:31	20:03	Arr. Dijon	18:32	19:49

(1) Runs daily, except Sundays and holidays. (2) Runs Sunday only. Change trains in Dole (arr. 17:49–dep. 18:06).

Sights in **St. Claude**: The 15 manufacturers of smoking pipes who are located here have made this "the pipe capital of France." They produce 1,600,000 briar pipes annually. A walk down Rue du Pre and its extension, Rue du Marche, takes you past many pipe shops to the Pipe Museum, at 1 Rue Gambetta, visited by 35,000 people June–September (the only months the museum is open), 09:30–11:30 and 14:00–19:00.

Across from the Pipe Museum is St. Claude's Cathedral.

The Genod factory, at 13 Fauborg Marcel, allows visitors daily except Saturdays, Sundays and holidays 09:30–11:30 and 14:00–18:00. One of the pipe shops, La Tabatiere at 8 Rue du Pre, has pipes ranging in price from $5 to $1,400.

Limoges - Les Eyzies de Tayac 138

Dep. Limoges	13:34	Dep. Les Eyzies	22:55
Arr. Les Eyzies	15:33	Arr. Limoges	01:00

Sights in **Les Eyzies de Tayac:** This is the prehistoric capital of Europe. The tourist information office and the famous cave paintings are a short walk from the railstation.

Lyon - Annecy - Lyon 167

En route, the train splits. Some cars go to Annecy, others to Grenoble. Be sure to sit in a car marked "Annecy" (pronounced Ahn-see).

Dep. Lyon (Part-Dieu)	06:59	09:09
Arr. Annecy	09:00	11:09

Sights in **Annecy**: This is a beautiful lake resort. See the 12th century Island Palace. The shops in the old quarter.

Dep. Annecy	12:39 (1)	15:57	17:11
Arr. Lyon (Part-Dieu)	14:38	18:11	19:20

(1) Light refreshments.

Lyon - Dijon - Lyon   149

Dep. Lyon (Perrache)	05:35	06:43 (2)	08:16	-0-	-0-
Dep. Lyon (Part-Dieu)	05:44 (1)	06:52	-0-	09:34	12:49
Arr. Dijon	07:30	08:35	10:32	11:15	14:32

Sights in **Dijon**: Town Hall, formerly the palace of those swashbuckling dukes of Burgundy and now one of the richest museums in France. The Church of Notre Dame. The 13th century Cathedral of St. Benigne archaeological museum. The Palace of Justice. The Magnin Museum. The 14th century Chartreuse de Champmol, with its famous chapel portrait and Moses Fountain. Rude Museum.

Don't fail to have lunch in Dijon, France's food and wine capital.

Dep. Dijon	12:17 (3)	15:44	16:57	19:14	20:43 (4+5)
Arr. Lyon (Part-Dieu)	14:01	17:44	18:40	20:57	22:26
Arr. Lyon (Perrache)	-0-	17:56	-0-	-0-	22:36

(1) Runs Monday–Friday, except holidays. (2) Runs daily, except Sundays and holidays. (3) Light refreshments. (4) Runs daily, except Saturday. (5) Plus another Dijon departure at 23:24 (runs Sunday only), arriving Lyon-Perrache 01:06.

Lyon - Geneva   159

There are many scenic canyons on this ride.

Dep. Lyon (Perrache)	07:30(1)	09:24(1)	12:13 (1)
Dep. Lyon (Part-Dieu)	07:39	09:33	12:23
Arr. Geneva (Cornavin)	09:38	11:26	14:16

Dep. Geneva (Cornavin)	16:30	19:29(1)	21:54(1)
Arr. Lyon (Part-Dieu)	18:18	21:25	23:39
Arr. Lyon (Perrache)	18:27	21:34	-0-

(1) Light refreshments.

Lyon - Grenoble - Lyon   154

Dep. Lyon (Part-Dieu)	07:05 (1)	08:18 (2)	10:12	12:12	14:14
Arr. Grenoble	08:23	09:40	11:43	13:35	15:30

Sights in **Grenoble**: The information office outside the railstation offers maps, guides and city bus tickets. See the monumental Calder sculpture at the railstation. The very rich (Utrillo, Picasso, Ruben) art museum in the 16th century Palace of Justice. The contemporary art museum's collection of Delaunay, Picasso, Matisse and many surrealists.

Fine paintings in the Musee des Beaux Arts at Place de Verdun (Corot, Renoir, Monet, Roualt, Picasso, Utrillo). The Stendahl Museum, devoted to Grenoble's native son and greatest writer, whose real name was Henri Beyle. The Museum of the Resistance, in the house where Stendahl was born on Rue Jean-Jacques Rousseau. At the Municipal Library, the "Catholicon" (printed by Gutenburg in 1460), Stendahl's manuscripts, and more historic papers.

The geometrical gardens and 3 fountains in Place Victor Hugo, Grenoble's prettiest square, locale of expensive shops and sidewalk cafes. The Natural History Museum, in the Jardine des Plantes. The 17th century Church of St. Laurent. The City Gardens.

Take the cable car ride up to Guy Pape Park for a marvelous view of the city below and the fields surrounding Grenoble. While at the top, visit the military museum in the 19th century fort, the Bastille, and the Auto Museum.

Walk back to Grenoble, downhill, through the Jardine des Dauphines.

Another walk on the way down leads to a collection of Alpine artificats from the past (antique cradles, beds, chests, backpacks, school rooms) at the Musee Dauphinois, in a 17th century cloister.

Dep. Grenoble	13:02	16:00	16:58	17:23	17:55 (4)
Arr. Lyon (Part-Dieu)	14:28	17:26	18:16	19:06 (3)	19:10
Dep. Grenoble	19:16	21:06	21:55 (5)		
Arr. Lyon (Part-Dieu)	20:44	22:54 (3)	23:24		

(1) Runs Monday–Friday, except holidays. (2) Runs daily, except Sundays and holidays. (3) Arrives at Lyon's Perrache railstation. (4) Runs daily, except Saturday. (5) Runs Monday-Friday except holidays July 11- August 26.

Lyon - Marseille - Lyon   151

Dep. Lyon (Perrache)	07:26	-0-(1)	09:59	12:04 (2)
Dep. Lyon (Part Dieu)	-0-	09:03	-0-	-0-
Arr. Marseille (St. Ch.)	10:54	11:46	13:08	15:00
Dep. Marseille (St. Ch.)	14:39	17:10 (2)	18:17 (3)	19:25 (6+7)
Arr. Lyon (Part Dieu)	17:38	20:38	21:07	23:02
Arr. Lyon (Perrache)	-0-	-0-	-0-	-0-

(1) TGV. Reservation required. Supplement charged. Runs Monday-Friday, except holidays. Restaurant car. (2) Light refreshments. (3) TGV. Reservation required. Supplement charged. Runs daily, except Saturdays and July 14, 15 and August 14. Restaurant car. (4) Second-class. (5) Arrives at Lyon's Perrache railstation. (6) Plus another Marseille departure at 21:45 (4), arriving Lyon 01:11 (5). (7) Runs daily except Firday. Light refreshments.

Lyon - Paris - Lyon 150

All of these trains are TGV, require reservation, charge a supplement and have a restaurant car or light refreshments.

Dep. Lyon (Per.)	05:39 (1)	06:19 (2)	06:46 (7)	07:49 (3)	08:45 (4)
Dep. Lyon (P-D)	05:50	06:30	06:57	08:00	09:00
Arr. Paris (Lyon)	08:06	08:34	08:59	10:10	11:02
Dep. Paris (Lyon)	14:00 (3)	15:00 (3)	16:49 (8)	17:00 (3)	17:27 (2+6)
Arr. Lyon (P-D)	16:02	17:00	18:57	19:02	19:31
Arr. Lyon (Per.)	16:17	17:10	-0-	19:12	-0-

(1) Runs Monday–Friday, except holidays. (2) Operates early September to early July. Runs Monday–Friday, except holidays. (3) Runs daily. (4) Runs daily, except Sundays and holidays. (5) Runs daily, except Saturday. (6) Plus other departures from Paris at 19:00 (3), 20:00 (3) and 21:00 (5), arriving Lyon (P-D) 21:04, 22:00 and 23:14. (7) Operates early September to early June. Runs Saturday only. (8) Runs Saturdays, Sundays and holidays.

Lyon - Tours - Lyon 128

Dep. Lyon (Perrache)	06:36 (1)	-0-
Dep. Lyon (Part-Dieu)	06:46	09:12 (2)
Arr. Tours	11:40	14:10
Dep. Tours	15:51 (2)	18:21 (3)
Arr. Lyon (Part-Dieu)	20:49	23:16
Arr. Lyon (Perrache)	20:59	23:25

(1) Runs Monday and Saturday only. (2) Light refreshments. (3) Runs Friday and Sunday. Light refreshments,

Lyon - Vienne - Lyon 151

| Dep Lyon (Perrache) | 07:26 | 12:31 |
| Arr. Vienne | 18 minutes later | |

Sights in **Vienne**: Many good Roman ruins. The Temple of Augustus and Livia, a large amphitheater, and the pyramid which once marked the center of a Roman coliseum. Ancient jewels and bronze and ceramic relics on exhibit at the Museum of Fine Arts. Try to dine at one of the world's most famous restaurants, Pyramide, open daily except Tuesday and closed November through mid-December.

Dep. Vienne	14:06	16:55	17:52	18:32 (1)	21:19 (2)	22:30(3)
Arr. Lyon (Perrache)		18 minutes later				

(1) Runs Monday–Friday, except holidays. (2) Runs Sunday only. (3) Runs Friday only.

Marseille to Aix-en-Provence   166

Dep. Marseille (St. Ch.)	07:49	12:28
Arr. Aix-en-Provence	35-40 minutes later	

Sights in **Aix-en-Provence**: See the remarkable Vasarely Museum and the 18th century quarter of the city.

Dep. Aix-en-Provence	11:34	16:23	20:44
Arr. Marseille (St. Ch.)	35-40 minutes later		

Marseille - Antibes - Marseille   164

Dep. Marseille	09:18	11:04	13:17
Arr. Antibes	11:20	13:21	15:25

Sights in **Antibes**: See notes under "Avignon–Antibes"

Dep. Antibes	14:00	14:51	16:54 (1)	18:47 (2)	20:42 (2)
Arr. Marseille	16:09	16:55	19:09	21:54	23:11

(1) Light refreshments. (2) Second-class.

Marseille - Cassis - Marseille   SNCF timetable

Dep. Marseille (St. Ch.)	08:40	09:45	11:10	12:15	14:42
Arr. Cassis	30 minutes later				

Sights in **Cassis:** A fishing village and beach resort. There are many small restaurants here offering "the catch of the day" prepared so as to please any gourmand. The activities in Cassis are topless sunbathing, sailing, swimming, snorkeling, diving and fishing.

The municipal Casino is open daily 15:00-20:00. The "calanques" (coves) of **Port Miou**, **Port Pin** and **En-Vau** can be visited by foot or by boat.

Dep. Cassis	12:23	13:10	13:42	14:27	15:30 (1)
Arr. Marseille (St. Ch.)	30 minutes later				

(1) Plus other departures from Cassis at 16:10, 17:34, 18:06, 19:07, 20:46 and 21:52.

Nice - Antibes - Nice   164

| Dep. Nice | Frequent times from 05:05 to 00:20 |
| Arr. Antibes | 16–30 minutes later |

| Dep. Antibes | Frequent times from 05:35 to 23:45 |
| Arr. Nice | 16–30 minutes later |

Nice - Cannes (and Grasse) - Nice   164

| Dep. Nice | Frequent times from 05:05 to 00:20 |
| Arr. Cannes | 40 minutes later |

Sights in **Cannes:** Stroll along Promenade de la Croisette to see the beautiful beach and splendid yachts, all the way to the Palm Beach Casino. Take boat rides on the Bay of Cannes or to the **St. Honorat** and **St. Marguerite** islands. On the latter, you can visit the prison that held the Man in the Iron Mask.

There is also a short boat trip to **Lerins**, where the 5th century Monastery of the Cistercians is located. It is said that St. Patrick began his evangelical tour of Europe from there. Visit the 10th century castle, Castrum Canois, on a mountain that overlooks Cannes. It houses the Museum of Mediterranean Civilization.

La Napoule is a few miles west of Cannes. The attraction there is the Chateau de la Napoule Art Foundation, one of the finest art galleries on the Riviera, open daily except Tuesday, with guided tours in the afternoon.

Sights in **Grasse:** Take the 50-minute bus ride from Cannes' railstation to nearby Grasse, the perfume capital of France. Many of the 35 perfume factories there are open to visitors. One of them, Parfumerie Fragonard, is only a 5-minute walk from the Grasse bus terminal. Near it is a Perfume Museum. The nearby hillsides are covered with wildflowers and jasmine every Spring.

| Dep. Cannes | Frequent times from 05:20 to 00:15 |
| Arr. Nice | 40 minutes later |

Nice - Marseille - Nice   164

These trains have light refreshments, unless designated otherwise.

Dep. Nice	06:00	06:37 (1)	08:25	09:10	10:38 (4)
Arr. Marseille (St. Ch.)	08:31	09:05	11:15	11:36	12:53
Dep. Marseille (St. Ch.)	13:17 (1)	15:20	15:52	16:39 (2)	17:25 (5)
Arr. Nice	15:40	17:55	18:30	19:05	20:10

(1) No light refreshments. (2) Restaurant car. (3) Supplement charged. Restaurant car. (4) Plus other Nice departures at 11:24 (3) and 11:59, arriving Marseille 13:43 and 14:29. (5) Plus other Marseille departures at 18:42, 20:35 and 22:03, arriving Nice 21:28, 23:02 and 00:25.

Nice - Monaco (Monte Carlo) - Nice   164

Dep. Nice	Frequent times from 06:05 to 00:35
Arr. Monaco	20–25 minutes later

* * *

Dep. Monaco	Frequent times from 05:23 to 23:55
Arr. Nice	20–25 minutes later

Nice - Saint Raphael - Nice   164

Dep. Nice	Frequent times from 06:00 to 22:32
Arr. St. Raphael	60 minutes later

Sights in **Saint Raphael**: An excellent Riviera beach resort. Good golfing, hiking and sailing here. There is a gambling casino.

Dep. St. Raphael	Frequent times from 06:40 to 23:34
Arr. Nice	60 minutes later

Paris - Angers - Paris   123

All of these trains are TGV, require reservation, charge a supplement and have light refreshments, unless designated otherwise.

Dep. Paris (Mont.)	07:50 (1)	08:50	09:50	11:30
Arr. Angers (St. L.)	09:19	10:21	11:25	12:59

Sights in **Angers**: Located on Promenade du Bout du Monde (Walkway of the World's End), is the massive 13th century castle (Chateau d'Angers), with its 17 towers. It houses the world's finest collection of medieval and Renaissance tapestries. Don't fail to see the supreme tapestry, "The Apocalypse."

It was 430 feet long and about 20 feet high when it was woven in the 14th century, unbelievably produced in less than 7 years. What we can view today is 350 feet long and 15 feet high 8,600 square feet. What remains are 67 of the original 84 panels and 4 of the original 6 scenes showing a bearded figure sitting on a stone dais.

The Angers tapestry illustrates the text of the Book of Revelation, complete with the 4 horsemen (the last of which is death), followed by hell.

It is in the second half of the tapestry that we are shown the ultimate destruction (Judgment Day): shipwrecks, rains of fire, many-headed beasts (including a dragon that has 7 heads and 10 horns), the fall of Babylon, the extinction of both the sun and the moon, and the descent of Jerusalem from heaven to earth, where it becomes the eternal dwelling of those who are blessed. The miracle of the tapestry is its survival.

Dep. Angers (St. L.)	12:02	14:14	15:17	17:09 (2)	18:08 (3+6)
Arr. Paris (Mont.)	13:35	15:50	16:50	18:45	19:45

(1) Operates late August to mid-July. Runs daily, except Sundays and holidays. (2) Runs daily, except Saturday. (3) Early July to early September: runs daily, except Sundays and holidays. Early September to early July: runs daily. (4) Runs Sunday only. (5) Runs daily, except Sundays & holidays. (6) Plus other Angers departures at 19:24 (4), 19:49 (5), 20:55 (7) and 21:13 (4). (7) Runs Monday-Friday except holidays.

Paris - Basel - Paris   171

Dep. Paris (Est)	07:30 (1)	08:39 (2)	11:50 (3)	13:41 (4)	17:00 (5+7)
Arr. Basel (SNCF)	12:11	14:07	16:36	18:34	21:40
Dep. Basel (SNCF)	00:28 (6)	08:23 (5)	12:48 (2)	16:48 (8)	18:30 (2)
Arr. Paris (Est)	06:47	13:12	18:05	21:29	23:41

(1) Supplement charged. Runs daily, except Sunday. Light refreshments. (2) Light refreshments. (3) Light refreshments. Early July to Early September: runs daily. Early September to early July: runs Friday and Saturday. (4) Runs Monday-Friday, except holidays. Light refreshments. (5) Supplement charged. Restaurant car. (6) Has second-class couchettes. (7) Plus another Paris departure at 22:40 (6), arriving Basel 05:30. (8) Runs daily except Satrudays. Supplement charged. Restaurant car.

Paris - Bayeux - Paris   120

All of these trains have light refreshments, unless designated otherwise.

Dep. Paris (St. Laz.)	06:55 (1)	09:02 (2)	11:29 (3)	12:48 (4)
Arr. Bayeux	09:28	11:25	13:52	15:16

Sights in **Bayeux**: The world-famous 230-foot long, 20-inch wide embroidered tapestry, sewn by Queen Mathilda (wife of William the Conqueror) and her friends for 10 years after the 1066 Battle of Hastings, both to commemorate the Norman conquest of England and her husband becoming king of England.

On public view in Bayeux since 1077, it consists of 58 scenes that include 626 people, 37 ships, 33 buildings and 730 animals while also depicting 11th century life.

The battle waged by Duke William of Normandy involved transporting 10,000 Normans across the English Channel in 400 ships.

One of the world's greatest works of art, "Queen Mathilda's Tapestry" has been exhibited daily 09:00–19:00 (except Christmas and New Year's Day) in a museum which opened in 1983 after 2 years of construction. As many as 2,300 people enter the museum on some days, including hordes of schoolchildren that begin arriving at 10:00.

The tapestry is mounted on a horseshoe-shaped frame, sealed inside unbreakable glass. Its humidity and temperature are regulated. Except for the light directed at the tapestry, the rest of the hall is entirely dark. A 15-minute description can be heard over earphones in many languages.

Other local attractions are the World War II Battle of Normandy Museum (next to the British Military Cemetery) and the 3-spired Notre Dame Cathedral. There are views of a magnificent seascape from its high center tower.

Dep. Bayeux	15:05 (5)	18:04 (7)	18:51 (8)	20:21 (9)
Arr. Paris (St. Laz.)	17:45 (6)	20:40	22:02	23:09

(1) Early July to early September: runs daily except Saturday. Early September to early July: Tuesday-Saturday. (2) Late June to early September: runs daily, except Sundays and holidays. Early September to late June: runs daily. (3) Runs Saturday only. (4) Runs daily except Saturdays. (5) No light refreshments. (6) Arrives 30 minutes later from late June to early September. (7) Runs daily, except Sundays and holidays. Supplement charged. (8) Runs Sunday only. No light refreshments. (9) Runs daily, except Sunday and Friday. No light refreshments. (9) Runs daily except Sundays and holidays July 8-September 1.

Paris - Bayeux - Caen - Paris   120

As shown below, it is possible to combine a visit from Paris to both Bayeux and Caen in one day.

Dep. Paris (St. Lazare)	06:55 (1)	09:02 (2)	Dep. Bayeux	15:17 (2)
Arr. Bayeux	09:28	11:45	Arr. Caen	15:32

Sights in **Bayeux**: See notes above.

Sights in **Caen**: Although much was destroyed here during the 1944 Normandy invasion battle, numerous historical buildings have been preserved. Hotel d'Escoville, the "Chateau." The 11th century Abbaye aux Hommes and Abbaye aux Dames. The Museum. The church of Saint Sauveur. The Palace of Justice. Try these regional specialties: *tripes, berlingots, cider, Calvados.*

Take Bus #12 from the railstation 3 miles to the "Normandy Memorial and Museum for Peace." It documents both the 1944 Battle of Normandy and the resulting Allied march from here to Berlin with original war films, photos, huge animated maps and vivid re-creations of battle scenes. Open daily except the first 2 weeks of January. The hours during June, July and August are 09:00-22:00. During the rest of the year: 09:00-19:00. The last entry allowed is 75 minutes before closing time.

Dep. Caen	19:17 (3)	19:39 (4)	20:20 (5)	20:45 (6)	21:43 (3)
Arr. Paris (St. Laz.)	22:02	22:13	22:48	23:09	00:12

Here are schedules leaving more time in Caen.

Dep. Paris (St. Laz.)	06:55 (1)	08:06 (7)	09:02 (2)	10:31 (8)
Arr. Caen	09:14	10:42	11:11	13:01

• • •

Dep. Caen	14:15 (9)	15:47	16:37 (11)	18:30 (13+14)
Arr. Paris (St. Laz.)	16:37	18:22 (10)	19:07	20:40

(1) Early July to early September: runs daily, except Saturday. Early September to early July: runs Tuesday-Saturday. (2) Runs daily. (3) Runs Sunday only. (4) Runs Sunday and Monday. (5) Runs Friday. Light refreshments. (6) Runs daily, except Monday,Friday and Sunday. (7) Runs daily. Light refreshments. (8) Runs daily, except Saturday. Light refreshments. (9) Light refreshments. Early July to early September: runs daily. Early September to early July: runs daily, except Sundays and holidays. (10) Runs daily June 25-Sept. 4 (11) Operates early September to late June. Runs Sunday only. Supplement charged. (12) Runs Tuesday, Wednesday, Thursday and Saturday. (13) Plus other Caen departures at 19:17 (3), 19:39 (3), 20:20 (5), 20:45 (12) and 21:42 (3), arriving Paris (St. Laz.) 22:02, 22:13, 22:48, 23:09 and 00:12. (14) Supplement charged.

Paris - Blois - Paris 135 a

Dep. Paris (Aust.)	07:33 (1)	09:48 (5)	12:00
Arr. Blois	09:05	11:19	13:29

Sights in **Blois**: St. Louis Cathedral. Church of Saint Nicolas. Church of Saint Vincent. Church of Saint Saturin, and its curious cemetery. The Alluye Manor.

Visit the Castle of Blois, the palace of Catherine de Medici during the 16th century. From late March to late September, a sound-and-light show is presented there every evening. The other 2 fine Chateaux here are Chambord and Bracieux (Herbault-en-Sologne). For lunch in Blois, try the regional specialties: Rillettes, Loire fish, great local wines and cheeses.

Dep. Blois	13:33 (2)	15:51	17:14 (1)	19:41 (3)	20:10 (4)	20:34 (6)
Arr. Paris (Aust.)	15:14	17:37	18:46	21:43	21:52	22:04

(1) Light refreshments. (2) Runs daily, except Sundays and holidays. (3) Runs Sunday only. Operates early July to late August. Runs Sunday only. (4) Operates late August to early July. Runs daily, except Friday & Saturday. (5) Runs daily July 9-August 28. (6) Runs Sunday only from July 1 to August 29.

Paris - Tours - Paris   135

Here are schedules for having more time in Tours than when combining a trip from Paris to both Blois and Tours.

All of these trains are TGV, require reservation, charge a supplement and have light refreshments, unless designated otherwise. They travel at 186 miles per hour on some portions of this route.

Dep. Paris (Mont.)	06:55(4)	07:45 (1)	09:00(4)	10:45	12:15
Arr. Tours	08:06	08:55	10:07	11:51	13:25

•   •   •

Dep. Tours	12:59	14:44	16:07	17:14 (2)	17:47
Arr. Paris (Mont.)	14:05	15:55	17:15	18:25	18:55

Dep. Tours	19:47 (3)	20:23 (1)	20:59 (3)	21:51 (1)	22:07 (3)
Arr. Paris (Mont.)	20:55	21:35	22:10	23:00	23:15

(1) Runs daily, except Sundays and holidays. (2) Runs daily, except Saturday. (3) Runs Sunday only. (4) Runs Saturday and Sunday only.

Paris - Bordeaux - Bayonne - Biarritz - Paris   136 + 137

All of these trains are TGV, require reservation, charge a supplement and have light refreshments, unless designated otherwise..

Dep. Paris (Mont.)	06:55	08:10 (1)	10:00
Arr. Bordeaux (St. Jean)	10:28	11:08 (2)	13:02
Arr. Bayonne	12:06	-0-	14:38
Arr. Biarritz	12 minutes after arriving Bayonne		

Dep. Biarritz	14:50	-0-	16:37 (3)	17:47 (1)	18:54 (3)
Dep. Bayonne	15:02	-0-	16:50	18:00	19:06
Dep. Bordeaux (St. Jean)	16:33	17:27	18:28	19:41	20:44
Arr. Paris (Mont.)	19:55	20:30	21:30	23:00	23:45

(1) Runs daily, except Sundays and holidays. (2) Terminates in Bordeaux. (3) Runs Sunday only.

Paris - Bourges - Paris   141

Dep. Paris (Austerlitz)	07:18 (1)	09:33 (2)
Arr. Vierzon	08:43	11:11
Change trains.		
Dep. Vierzon	08:50	11:20
Arr. Bourges	09:11	11:45

Sights in **Bourges**: A key gateway to the chateau area of the Loire Valley. Bourges is a living history museum.

The beautifully preserved stained glass windows in the Cathedral of St.-Etienne are a dazzling play of red against magenta and deep blue, located in a narrow halll that is 387 feet long, 136 feet wide, and an amazing 130 feet high. "Spellbinding" is the only way to describe these windows that depict the Bible's great morality stories. The Cathedral's restored 17th century organ is the best one of France. The l'Archeveche Garden is near the Cathedral. See the medieval houses below the Cathedral on a stroll along the town's winding, cobbled streets.

Visit the 15th century Palace of Jacques Couer, open daily 9:00–12:00 and 14:00–18:00 (closes at 17:00 November–March). See the collection of Roman artifacts and antique ceramics at the Musee de Berry in the 15th century Hotel Cujas (4 Rue des Arenes), open daily except Tuesday 10:00–12:00 and 14:00–18:00 (Sunday: only 14:00–18:00).

The Museum of Decorative Arts in the 16th century Hotel Lallemant (6 Rue Bourbonnoux), open daily except Tuesday 10:00–11:30 and 14:00–16:30. The Municipal Garden and the garden at the City Hall, formerly the residence of a 17th century archbishop.

Dep. Bourges	17:50 (3)	18:53 (5)	19:15 (4)
Arr. Vierzon	18:10(3)	19:22	19:43
Change trains.			
Dep. Vierzon	18:29	19:46 (4)	20:36(5)
Arr. Paris (Austerlitz)	20:22	21:34	22:20

(1) Runs daily, except Sun. and holidays. (2) Operates early July to early Sept. (3) Direct train to Paris. No train change in Vierzon. (4) Runs Mon.–Fri., except holidays. (5) Runs Saturday, Sunday and Holidays

Paris - Brussels - Paris   18

Dep. Paris (Nord)	07:05 (1)	07:50 (2)	10:08 (3)	10:23 (4)		
Arr. Brussels (Midi)	09:39	10:49	13:12	13:17		

Dep. Brussels (Midi)	14:13 (2)	15:04	16:00 (5)	17:10 (6)	18:13 (7)	19:07 (4+8)
Arr. Paris (Nord)	17:05	17:43(1)	19:01	19:42	20:43	22:05

(1) Supplement charged. Runs Monday–Friday. Restaurant car. (2) Light refreshments. (3) Operates late June to late August. Restaurant car. (4) Restaurant car. (5) Supplement charged. Restaurant car. (6) Supple-

ment charged. Runs Monday–Friday. (7) Supplement charged. Runs daily, except Saturday. Restaurant car. (8) Plus another departure from Brussels (Midi) at 19:57 (2), arriving Paris 22:59.

Paris - Chantilly - Paris   SNCF Timetable

| Dep. Paris (Nord) | Frequent times from 06:32 to 21:47 |
| Arr. Chantilly | 30–40 minutes later |

Sights in **Chantilly:** (Pronounced "Shawnteeyee") The 16th century castle, actually 2 chateaux, has been called "the most beautiful house in France." It stands in a lake and is surrounded by magnificent gardens and a large forest.

Of the 2 routes from the railstation to the castle, the shortest distance (and most pleasant stroll) is to walk 30 minutes via a trail through tall trees and then across the large lawn infield of the racecourse, locale during the first 2 weeks of June every year for a very elegant horse-racing meet.

The 2 attractions are the chateau's Conde Museum and its Living Museum of the Horse. Among the fine objects exhibited in the Conde are priceless collections of art spanning 1,000 years; 13,000 books beginning with 10th century manuscripts, paintings (Delacroix, Fouquet, Ingres, Rembrandt, Clouet, Raphael, Rosselli, Greuze) and furniture; all on an estate of 17,000 acres that contain forests, farms, a racetrack with stadium, and a golf course.

Between April 1 and September 30, the chateau is open daily except Tuesday 10:30–18:00 (until 17:00 the rest of the year).

Between April 1 and October 31, the Grand Stables are open daily except Tuesday 10:30–17:00 (13:00–17:00 the rest of the year). Riders wearing 18th century costumes perform at 12:00, 15:00 and 17:00 April 1 to October 31 (at 14:30 and 16:00 the rest of the year).

See the spectacle of the Tuesday and Saturday fox hunts.

| Dep. Chantilly | Frequent times from 05:53 to 23:19 |
| Arr. Paris (Nord) | 30–40 minutes later |

Paris - Chartres - Paris   125

| Dep. Paris (Montpar.) | 07:00 (1) 08:56 (2) 09:29 (3) 09:58 (2) 11:14 12:59 (4) |
| Arr. Chartres | 50–60 minutes later |

Sights in **Chartres:** The main attraction is the magnificent 13th century Cathedral, third largest in the world, exceeded in size only by St. Peter's and Canterbury. Its stained-glass is unrivaled. Open daily 07:30–19:30, it is a short stroll from the railstation.

Also see the ancient process that was used to make the Cathedral's stained glass, at the Stained Glass Center, next to the Cathedral, open daily except Monday 10:00–18:00.

A city map and details on a self-guided walking tour of Chartres is available at the Tourist Office, across from the Cathedral. The Tourist Office is open Monday–Saturday 09:30–

12:30 and 14:00–18:30, and on Sunday 10:00–12:00 and 15:00–19:00 (closed Sundays, November–April).

Malcom Miller has conducted his world-renowned English-language tour of the Cathedral since 1958 (at 12:00 and 14:45). He usually offers 2 different tours.

Other sights: the Former Collegiate Church, the Church of St. Aignan, the Church of St. Aignan, the Church of St. Martin-au-Val and the Church of St. Foy.

Picassiete's Garden was built by a street sweeper out of pieces of garbage (broken bottles, enameled tiles, stones)…similar to Watts Tower in Los Angeles. A bus goes within a few blocks of it, 2 miles north from the center of Chartres.

Dep. Chartres	11:21	14:04	15:10 (2)	16:56 (2)	18:41(7)
Arr. Paris (Montpar.)	50–60 minutes later				

(1) Runs daily, except Saturday and holidays. (2) Operates early July to early September. (3) Runs Monday-Friday except holidays. (4) Runs daily, except Sundays and holidays. Early September to early july, runs daily. (5) TGV. Supplement charged. Light refreshments. (6) Runs Sundays only. Light refreshments. (7) Plus other departures from Chartres at 19:37, 21:10(2), and 21:33 (6).

Paris - Cologne (Koln) - Paris   25

Both of these trains charge a supplement and have a restaurant car.

Dep. Paris (Nord)	07:31	Dep. Cologne	17:08
Arr. Cologne	12:48	Arr. Paris (Nord)	22:10

Paris - Compiegne - Paris   101

Dep. Paris (Nord)	07:10 (1)	07:52 (2)	12:16
Arr. Compiegne	50–60 minutes later		

Sights in **Compiegne**: Town Hall. Vivenel Museum. Hotel Dieu. The 7th century Beauregard Tower. The "Clairere de l'Armistice" in Compeigne Forest, where Marshal Foch signed the 1918 armistice for France…and Adolph Hitler received the June 21, 1940 surrender of France.

Beautiful furnishings and decorations can be seen in the first drawing room, family drawing room, Emperor's library, music room, Empress's bedroom, a series of dining rooms, the hunting gallery, and the ornate ballroom at the Chateau built by Louis XV in the late 18th century.

Dep. Compeigne	10:28	13:12	19:10	20:11 (3)	21:57 (4)
Arr. Paris (Nord)	50–60 minutes later				

(1) Runs daily, except Sundays and holidays. (2) Daily to June 30 to September 1.(3) Runs Sunday only. (4) Runs daily, except Saturday.

Paris - Dijon - Paris   157

All of these trains are TGV, require reservation, charge a supplement and have a restaurant car or light refreshments, unless designated otherwise.

Dep. Paris (Lyon)	07:14 (5)	08:05	09:28 (1)	10:32 (2)	12:21
Arr. Dijon	08:51	09:47	12:04	12:10	14:00

Dep. Dijon	14:44	16:50 (3)	18:30	19:57	22:16 (4)
Arr. Paris (Lyon)	16:28	18:35	20:19	21:39	23:55

(1) Not TGV. No reservation or supplement. Light refreshments. (2) Runs Monday–Friday, except holidays. (3) Early July to late August: runs daily, except Saturday. Late August to early July: runs daily. (4) Runs Friday and Sunday. (5) Runs Monday-Saturday except holidays.

Paris - Evreux - Paris   120

Dep. Paris (St. Laz.)	08:06 (1)	09:21 (2)	10:32	11:47 (3)	12:48 (4)
Arr. Evreux	09:10	10:36	11:37	12:44	13:44

Sights in **Evreux**: The Cathedral of Notre Dame, a jumble of architectural styles due to having been built over a period of 6 centuries: from the 11th to the 17th. Goldsmith work in the Church of Stain Taurin. The ancient Eveche. The tower of The Clock. For lunch, try the Norman cuisine.

Dep. Evreux	13:27	14:31 (5)	15:34 (6)	17:10 (7)	18:32 (5+8)
Arr. Paris (St. Laz.)	14:35	15:34	16:37	18:22	19:41

(1) Light refreshments. (2) Runs Saturday only. (3) Runs daily, except Sunday and holidays. (4) Runs daily, except Saturdays. (5) Runs Sunday only. (6) Light refreshments. Early July to early September: runs daily. Early September to early July: runs daily, except Sundays and holidays. (7) Operates late June to early September. Runs daily. (8) Runs daily except Sundays & holidaysto July 1 and to September 2. (9) Plus other departures from Evreux at 18:48 (8), 19:10 (5) and 23:04 (7), arriving Paris 19:57, 20:27 and 00:12.

Paris - Fontainebleau - Paris   151a

Dep. Paris (Lyon)	Frequent times from 06:02 to 22:33
Arr. Fontainebleau-Avon	40 minutes later

Take the 10-minute bus ride from the railstation to the palace, open 08:00 to sunset, daily except Tuesdays.

Sights in **Fontainebleau:** It is advisable to plan on an entire day here for seeing the magnificent 16th century palace that many kings of France occupied, and the parks and gardens surrounding it. There are guided tours of the palace 10:00–12:30 and 14:00–18:00. Many visitors bring a picnic lunch.

Dep. Fontainebleau-Avon   Frequent times from 05:20 to 20:44 (1)
Arr. Paris (Lyon)   30–40 minutes later

(1) Plus another departure from Fontainebleau on Sundays at 21:20.

Paris - Granville - Paris   117

Dep. Paris (Montpar.)	07:13 (1)	08:15 (2)
Arr. Granville	10:47	12:12

Sights in **Granville:** This is a lively seaside town near Mont.-st.-Michel, with remarkably high tides and sandy beaches. The marina here can accommodate 1,000 yachts. The Regional Nautical Center offers instructions in sailing and wind surfing.

The Aquarium (with exhibits of sea life, shells and mineral stones) is along the walk to the lighthouse. The **Chausey Islands** can be seen from the shore, and there is daily boat service to them.

Visit the Church of Notre Dame. Try your luck in the Casino.

Dep. Granville	14:11 (1)	14:25 (3)	18:09 (4)	19:14
Arr. Paris (Montpar.)	17:44	18:29	21:52	22:46(4)

(1) Runs Monday–Friday, except holidays. (2) Runs Saturdays, Sundays and holidays. Light refreshments. (3) Runs Saturday and Sunday. (4) Runs Sundays only. Light refreshments.

Paris - Limoges - Paris   138

Dep. Paris (Aust.)	07:02 (1)	07:18 (8)	09:33 (3)	10:09 (4)	10:24 (5)
Arr. Limoges	10:47	10:20	12:58	13:10	13:28
Dep. Limoges	14:41 (2)	17:01 (2)	18:27 (6)	19:46 (7)	20:54
Arr. Paris (Aust.)	18:33	20:22	21:23	23:08	23:56(9)

(1) Runs Sunday only to July 1 and from Sept. 2. (2) Light refreshments. (3) Operates late June to early September. (4) Operates early September to late June. Light refreshments. (5) Operates late June to early September. Light refreshments. (6) Runs daily except Saturday. Supplement charged. Light refreshments. (7) Runs Sunday only. Light refreshments. (8) Supplement charged. Runs daily except Sundays & holidays. Restaurant car. (9) Runs Friday, Saturday and Sunday.

Paris - Lyon - Paris   150

All of these trains are TGV, require reservation, charge a supplement and have a restaurant car or light refreshments.

Dep. Paris (Lyon)	06:15 (1)	06:45 (2)	07:00(7)	07:30	08:15 (3)
Arr. Lyon (P.D.)	08:23	08:45	09:00	09:30	10:15
Dep. Lyon (P.D.)	14:00 (4)	15:00	16:00	17:00	17:25 (1)
Arr. Paris (Lyon)	16:02	17:04	18:00	19:10	19:30
Dep. Lyon (P.D.)	18:00	18:47	20:00	21:10(8)	21:49 (6)
Arr. Paris (Lyon)	20:04	20:49	22:04	23:20	23:59

(1) Operates late August to late June. Runs Monday–Friday, except holidays. (2) Runs Monday-Friday, except holidays. (3) Operates late August to late June. Runs daily, except Sundays and holidays. (4) Operates late August to late June. Runs daily. (5) Operates late June to late August. Runs daily. (6) Runs Sunday only. (7) Runs daily except holidays. (8) Runs daily except Saturdays.

Paris - Nancy - Paris   173

Dep. Paris (Est)	06:53 (1)	07:47 (2)	07:59 (3)	09:02 (4)
Arr. Nancy	09:37	10:31	11:35	11:50

Sights in **Nancy:** The Ducal Palace, with its museum of this city's 2,000-year history at 64 Grande Rue, open daily except Tuesdays and holidays 10:00–12:00 and 14:00–18:00. Its exhibits include a room on the history of Jews in this region.

The Church of the Cordeliers. The 14th century Porte de la Craffe, oldest monument in Nancy. The wrought-iron grillwork and fountains in Place Stanislas. Lovely 18th century houses on Place de la Carriere.

Visit the model rooms of early 20th century interior decor at the Musee de l'Ecole, 36–38 Rue Sergent Blandan, open daily, except Tuesdays and holidays. April–September: 10:00–12:00 and 14:00–18:00. October–March: 10:00–12:00 and 14:00–17:00. Much work by Emile Galle, Jacques Gruber, Eugene Vallin and other Art Nouveau artisans is exhibited there: glass bowls, tables, fireplaces, tooled leather wall coverings, inlaid bed headboards and footboards, inlaid chests, Galle's fantastic glass mushroom lamp, and the extraordinary Louis Majorelle grand piano, inlaid with irises and waterlillies.

Majorelle's house, a few blocks away at 1 Rue Majorelle (open Monday-Friday except holidays 8:30–12:00 and 13:00–18:00), is well worth visiting to see the exterior and interior ceramic work and the Gruber stained glass windows there.

Visitors can also see examples of Galle and Daum vases, lamps and other glass objects at the Musee Beaux-Arts, Place Stanislas, open daily except Tuesdays and holidays 10:00–12:00 and 14:00–18:00.

Pepiniere is a 57-acre park with gardens, a small zoo, and a restaurant.

Dep. Nancy	13:34 (2)	14:33 (5)	14:55	17:21 (7)	18:33 (8+9)
Arr. Paris (Est)	16:20	18:00	18:32 (10)	20:05	21:14

(1) Supplement charged. Operates early September to mid-July. Runs Mon-Fir, except holidays. Restaurant car. (2) Supplement charged. Restaurant car. (3) Light refreshments. (4) Runs daily, except Sundays and holidays. Light refreshments. (5) Runs Sundays (daily from June 21), Light Refreshments. (6) Runs Monday–Friday, except holidays. Light refreshments. (7) Runs daily, except Saturday. (8) Operates late August to mid-July. Runs daily, except Saturday. (9) Plus another Nancy departure at 19:34 (2), arriving Paris 22:18. (10) Runs daily except Sundays and holidays to June 21.

Paris - Nantes - Paris   123

All of these trains are TGV, require reservation, charge a supplement and have light refreshments.

Dep. Paris (Mont.)	06:45 (1)	07:15 (2)	08:50	09:50	10:55 (3)
Arr. Nantes	08:45	09:26	10:58	12:02	12:57

Sight in **Nantes**: See notes under "Bordeaux–Nantes"

Dep. Nantes	13:36	14:40	16:31 (4)	17:31 (5)	18:20 (6)	19:05 (7+10)
Arr. Paris (Mont.)	15:50	16:50	18:45	19:45	20:25	21:10

(1) Operates late August to early July. Runs Monday–Friday, except holidays. (2) Early July to late August: runs daily, except Sundays and holidays. Late August to early July: runs Monday–Friday, except holidays. (3) Operates late June to late August. (4) Early July to early September: runs daily. Early September to early July: runs daily, except Saturday. (5) Early July to late August: runs daily, except Sundays and holidays. Late August to early July: runs daily. (6) Runs daily, except Saturday. (7) Runs Sunday only. (8) Runs daily, except Sundays and holidays. (9) Runs Monday–Friday, except holidays. (10) Plus other departures from Nantes at 19:11 (8), 20:18 (9), 20:55 (7) and 21:48.

Paris - Neuilly - Paris

Take the Metro from Paris' Champs-Elysees station. **Neuilly** is the fourth stop.

The attraction here is The Museum of Women at 12 Rue de Centre, open daily except Sunday 14:30–18:00. The one guided tour starts at 15:00. Among the exhibits is the lavishly decorated bed used by France's most famous prostitute during the reign of Napoleon III, the Marchioness de La Paiva. While the bed cost her 10,000 gold francs, she recovered this expense quickly. She charged her clients 10,000 gold francs a night.

There is also the corset that Marie Antoinette wore in prison while waiting to be guillotined, a bronze cast of ballet dancer-choreographer Katherine Dunham's feet, a silk jacket that belonged to the last empress of China, a letter written by Nobel prize-winner Marie Curie, and many other curiosities.

Paris - Rheims - Paris   177

Dep. Paris (Est)	07:13 (1)	08:04	11:00	13:01 (1)		
Arr. Rheims	08:46	09:55	12:36	14:40		

Sights in **Rheims**: See the 13th century Cathedral of Notre Dame (open daily 07:30–19:30), longer and higher than Notre Dame in Paris. Most of this city was destroyed in World War I, and restoration of the Cathedral was not completed until 1938.

See church treasures in the Palais du Tau (2 Place du Cardinal-Lucon), open 10:00–12:00 and 14:00–18:00. The Porte Mars 13th century Arch. Saint Remi Basilica (open daily 08:00–18:30). Nearby, the great collection of 16th–19th century weapons in the St. Remi Museum (53 Rue Simon), open daily 14:00–18:30.

The Church of St. Jacquet. The museum at the Church of St. Denis.

See champagne processed. The public is invited to visit the Taitinger and Pommery caves.

Dep. Rheims	12:24 (6)	16:06 (3)	17:11 (3)	17:47 (4)	18:03 (5)	20:27
Arr. Paris (Est)	13:59	17:38	18:50	19:32	19:38	21:56

(1) Runs daily, except Sundays and holidays. (2) Runs daily, except holidays. (3) Runs Monday–Friday, except holidays. (4) Runs Saturdays, Sunday and holidays. (5) Runs Monday–Friday, except holidays. (6) Departs 12:35 Mon-Friday except holidays from August 8.

Paris - Rouen - Paris   115

Dep. Paris (St. Laz.)	06:45 (1)	07:39 (2)	08:15 (3)	09:15 (8)
Arr. Vernon	07:27	08:23	09:04	-0-
Arr. Rouen (Rive Dr.)	08:00	09:03	09:47	10:24

Sights in **Rouen**: Walk out of the railstation and then down Rue de Jeanne D'Arc about 1½ miles. Turn right onto Rue de la Grosse Horloge and continue a short distance to the remodeled ancient, large central market, Vieux Marche, the place where Joan of Arc was tied to a stake and burned. This is now the Church of St. Joan, built in 1977. It is in the shape of an upside-down boat and has magnificent stained-glass windows that were saved from the Church of Saint-Vincent, bombed during World War II. Try the regional specialty (terrine of duck) in one of the nearby restaurants.

Then, go back along Rue de la Gross Horloge (crossing Rue de Jeanne D'Arc). Straight ahead is the gigantic, ornate clock for which the street was named. The clock presents a spectacle of moving figures when each hour strikes.

Past the famous clock is the Cathedral, with its renowned Carillon of 56 bells. Nearby, see the sculptures on the doors of the Church of Saint-Maclou.

See the stained-glass windows in the Church of St. Godard and the Church of St. Patrice.

Visit the remains of a building located below the Palace of Justice. It was either an 11th century Jewish school or a synagogue. See the Hebrew graffiti written on the walls there more than 900 years ago, the elaborate carved columns and the 2 inverted Lions of Judah. It is open only on Saturdays.

The rose window of the Gothic Church of St. Ouen. The collection of fine faience ware for which Rouen was once famous, in the Museum of Fine Arts. The Gallo-Roman artifacts in the Museum of Antiquities. The late Gothic and Renaissance Bourgtheroulde mansion. The collection of old street signs and other ironwork pieces in the Musee Le Secq.

From Rouen, it is an easy bus trip to the colorful harbor at **Honfleur**.

Take a bus ($1.00) or taxi ($7.50) from Vernon about 4 miles to Giverny, to visit the home and spectacular garden of painter Claude Monet, both of them open daily except Monday, 10:00-18:00 April 1 through October 31. Admission is $6.00.

Dep. Rouen (Rive Dr.)	12:05 (3)	12:46 (4)	14:10 (3)	14:51 (3)
Dep. Vernon	12:55	-0-	14:51	-0-
Arr. Paris (St. Laz.)	13:44	14:01	15:40	16:08

Dep. Rouen (Rive Dr.)	16:47	17:27 (1)	18:30 (2)	19:37 (7+9)
Dep. Vernon	-0-	18:12	19:12	20:24
Arr. Paris (St. Laz.)	18:16	18:58	20:00	21:19

(1) Runs Monday–Friday, except holidays. (2) Runs Sunday only. (3) Runs daily, except Sundays and holidays. (4) Runs daily. except Sundays and holidays. Light refreshments. (6) Runs Saturday and Sunday. (7) Runs Sunday only. (8) Plus other departures from Paris at 10:42 (7) and 12:00 (3), arriving Rouen 12:11 and 13:35. (9) Plus other departures from Rouen at 20:19 (7), 20:28 (7) and 21:21 (7), arriving Paris 21:37, 21:43 and 22:55.

Paris - Strasbourg - Paris 173

This ride is along the Marne, with clear views of the area near famous World War I battle fields.

Dep. Paris (Est)	06:53 (1)	07:47 (2)	08:06 (3)
Arr. Strasbourg	10:59	11:42	12:51

Dep. Strasbourg	16:00 (4)	17:07 (5)	18:19 (2)	19:06 (6)
Arr. Paris (Est)	20:05	21:14	22:18	23:20

(1) Supplement charged. Operates early September to early July. Runs daily, except Sundays and holidays. Restaurant car. (2) Supplement charged. Restaurant car. (3) Runs Sundays only. Light refreshments. (4) Runs daily except Saturday. Light refreshments. (5) Operates early September to early July. Runs daily, except Saturday. Light refreshments. (6) Runs Friday and Sunday. Light refreshments.

Paris - Tours - Paris

This one-day excursion appears immediately following "Paris–Blois–Tours–Paris"

Paris - Trouville and Deauville - Paris 120

Dep. Paris (St. Laz.)	07:44 (1)	08:29 (2)	10:25 (3)	12:18 (4)
Arr. Trou Deau	09:53	10:53	12:20	14:20

Sights in **Trouville**: There is no chance of obtaining hotel rooms here in Summer without advance reservation. One of France's most beautiful swimming beaches. A gambling casino. Marvelous seafood.

Sights in **Deauville**: One of France's most beautiful swimming beaches. Two racetracks. Lovely gardens. To explore the Norman countryside, you can rent a car at the Deauville railstation.

Take a bus 6 miles to **Honfleur**, the beautiful fishing village that inspired many Impressionist paintings. Very crowded in July and August. Stroll along the bank of its old harbor on the English Channel. Visit the Eugene Bodin Museum (paintings of the Saint Simeon school) and the Marine Museum in the 14th century Church of St. Etiene.

Dep. Trou Deau	13:20 (11)	15:54 (6)	17:16 (7)	18:39 (8+10)
Arr. Paris (St. Laz.)	15:34	17:55	19:41	20:35

(1) Operates late June to early September. Runs Monday-Friday, except holidays. (2) Runs Saturdays, Sundays and holidays. (3) Operates early July to late August. (4) Operates late June to late August. Runs daily, except Sundays and holidays. (5) Change trains in Lisieux (arr. 14:39-dep. 14:47). Early July to early September: runs daily. Early September to early July: runs daily, except Fridays, Sundays and holidays. (6) Operates early July to early September. (7) Runs Sunday only. Light refreshments. (8) Runs Sunday only. (9) Operates early July to late August. Runs Monday–Friday, except holidays. (10) Plus other departures from Trou Deau at 19:18 (9) and 19:59 (8), arriving Paris 21:26 and 22:43. (11) Runs Sunday only July 3-Aug 28.

Paris - Troyes - Paris 171

Dep. Paris (Est)	07:08 (1)	07:52 (2)	08:37 (3)	12:40	13:30 (4)
Arr. Troyes	08:36	09:34	10:12	14:11	14:53

Sights in **Troyes**: This is the Champagne area. The most interesting places here are located along the 30-minute walk from the railstation to St. Pierre Cathedral, which has marvelous 13th, 14th and 16th century stained glass.

See the museum of tools used in French crafts at the 16th century Hotel de Mauroy, on

Rue de la Trinite. The 16th century religious art and the hosiery museum, both at the Musee de l'Hotel de Vauluisant. The mansions of Autry, des Ursins and Marisy. The Museum of Fine Arts, with its solid collection of 17th–18th century paintings and 13th–14th century sculptures.

The 12th century manuscripts in the Library. The Pharmacy Museum. The Archaeology Museum. The Natural History Museum

Dep. Troyes	12:09 (5)	12:41 (6)	16:36 (3)	17:53 (7)	19:19 (6+9)
Arr. Paris (Est)	13:40	14:10	18:05	19:36	21:06

(1) Runs daily, except Sundays and holidays. (2) Runs Sunday only. (3) Light refreshments. (4) Runs Saturday, Sunday and holidays. (5) Runs Monday–Friday, except holidays. Light refreshments. (6) Runs Saturday only. (7) Runs Sunday only. (8) Supplement charged. Runs Sunday only. Light refreshments. (9) Plus other departures from Troyes at 20:34 (2), 20:55 (8) and 22:15 (3), arr. Paris 22:17, 22:22 and 23:41.

Paris - Versailles - Paris   125 a

To reduce the often long wait for a guided tour, phone 30-84-76-18 to get the schedule and arrive 90 minutes before the desired tour. Some of the tours (taking either one or 2 hours) are given in English.

Dep. Paris (Austerlitz)	Frequent times from 05:30 to 00:30.
Arr. Versailles	37 minutes later

Versailles is also reached by suburban trains that stop in Paris at the Pont St. Michel, Invalides and Pont d'Alma stations.

Sights in **Versailles**: The fabulous palace where Louis XV lived like a king, and the elegant 250 acres of gardens here. Open daily except Mondays and public holidays. Bring a picnic lunch and eat in the gardens, by the mile-long Grand Canal.

During the time of Louis XV, about 5,000 members of the nobility lived in the palace's private apartments. Versailles became a museum in 1837.

Among its highlights are: the 237-foot-long by 33-foot-wide Hall of Mirrors (in which 17 mirror-lined arcades reflect 17 corresponding arched windows), throne room, queen's chambers, chapel, theater, the apartments of Madame de Pompadour and Madame du Barry, and the rooms named for Venus, Mercury, Diana and Mars.

The private apartment of the king can be seen only as a part of the guided tours of the palace, which start at various times from 9:45 to 15:30. However, most of the great rooms, such as the Hall of Mirrors and the king's bedroom, can be visited without a guide from 9:45 until the palace closes at 17:00. Visitors can purchase a book here which makes it possible to see and appreciate the palace without a guide.

Dep. Versaille	Frequent times from 06:30 to 01:30
Arr. Paris (Austerlitz)	37 minutes later

If you visit Versaille in the morning, it is possible to also see Chartres in early afternoon. There are frequent trains for the 30-minute ride from Versaille to Chartres.

TRIPS TO THE RIVIERA

Unless designated otherwise, all of these trains are TGV, require reservation, charge a supplement and have light refreshments or restaurant car.

Paris - Marseille - Paris   151

Dep. Paris (Lyon)	07:00 (1)	07:40	10:23	11:40	13:29 (6)
Arr. Marseille (St. Ch.)	11:46	12:38	15:03	16:23	18:10

• • •

Dep. Marseille (St. Ch.)	06:42 (2)	08:06	08:44	12:13	14:58 (7+8)
Arr. Paris (Lyon)	11:33	12:49	13:34	16:59	19:46

(1) Runs Monday–Friday, except holidays. (2) Operates late August to early July. Runs daily, except Saturday. (3) A non-TGV train that has couchettes and a second-class coach. (4) A non-TGV train that carries a sleeping car and also has couchettes. No coaches. (5) Runs daily, except Saturday. (6) Plus other departures from Paris at 15:40, 16:49, 17:47, 20:29 (3) and 22:36 (4), arriving Marseille 20:25, 21:44, 22:36, 23:24, 04:44 and 07:10. (7) Plus other departures from Marseille at 17:31, 18:17 (5), 21:45 (3) and 22:36 (4), arriving Paris 22:22, 23:20, 06:24 and 07:42. (8) Runs daily except Saturday and daily July 3-Sept 2.

Paris - Nice - Paris   151

All of these trains are TGV, require reservation and charge a supplement, unless designated otherwise.

Dep. Paris (Lyon)	07:30 (1)	10:41 (2)	15:05 (3)	20:29 (4)	22:36 (5)
Arr. Nice	14:26	17:38	22:02	08:20	09:55

• • •

Dep. Nice	10:02	15:18 (1)	18:18 (4)	19:38 (5)	
Arr. Paris (Lyon)	17:09	22:18	06:24	07:42	

(1) Light refreshments. (2) Restaurant car. (3) Operates mid-June to late August. Light refreshments. (4) A non-TGV train that has couchettes and a second-class coach. (5) A non-TGV train that carries a sleeping car and also has couchettes. No coaches.

SCENIC RAIL TRIPS

Chamonix - Vallorcine - Chamonix 268

Good mountain scenery on this short ride. It is easy to combine this with the one-day roundtrip from Geneva to Chamonix.

Dep. Chamonix	07:54	09:04 (1)	09:59 (1)	11:34	13:44	14:50(2)	16:18(1)
Arr. Vallorcine	08:28	09:44	10:38	12:07	14:12	15:21	16:46
			• • •				
Dep. Vallorcine	09:18	10:01 (1)	11:19	12:54	14:32 (2)	15:38	17:10
Arr. Chamonix	10:03	10:39	12:08	13:33	14:58	16:28	17:39

(1) Operates late June to early September. (2) Operates early July to late September.

Limoges - Toulouse - Limoges 138

Recommended for mountain scenery. This can be seen either as an easy one-day roundtrip between Limoges and Toulouse or as a portion of the route from Paris to Toulouse (and v.v.) via Limoges.

Dep. Limoges	10:22(1)	13:01 (2)	13:13(3)		
Arr. Toulouse (Mat.)	13:48	16:42	16:55		
Dep. Toulouse (Mat.)	13:41 (4)	14:02 (5)	17:31 (6)	18:02 (7)	19:26 (8)
Arr. Limoges	17:00	17:36	21:06	21:39	22:57

(1) Runs Sunday only. (2) Operates early July to early September. (3) Operates early September to early July. Light refreshments. (4) Light refreshments. (5) Runs Friday & Sunday. (6) Runs Monday–Thursday. (7) Runs Friday only. (8) Runs Saturday, Sunday and holidays.

Here is the schedule for the Paris-Toulouse route:
All of the TGV trains in this table depart/arrive at Paris Montparnasse railstation. All of the TGVs require a reservation and charge a supplement.

138

Dep. Paris (Aust.)	07:02 (1)	11:15 (3)	13:45 (4)	17:00 (5)	17:45 (6)
Dep. Limoges	10:01 (2)	-0-	16:55	-0-	20:59
Arr. Toulouse (Mat.)	13:25	16:31	20:35	22:09	00:20

Dep. Paris (Aust.)	18:00 (7)	21:31 (8)	22:18 (9)	22:53 (10)
Dep. Limoges	20:59	01:14	02:12	-0-
Arr. Toulouse (Mat.)	00:20	04:40	07:03	07:00

Dep. Toulouse (Mat.)	00:35 (11)	01:41 (12)	06:08 (13)	07:31 (1)	10:32 (15)
Dep. Limoges	04:01	05:05	-0-	10:50 (3)	14:04
Arr. Paris (Aust.)	07:45	08:36	11:25 (14)	13:55	17:15

Dep. Toulouse (Mat.)	13:41 (15)	13:47 (16)	17:19 (5)	23:00 (10)
Dep. Limoges	17:05	-0-	-0-	-0-
Arr. Paris (Aust.)	20:22	19:00 (14)	22:30 (14)	07:06

(1) Runs Sundays only to July 1 and from Sept. 2. Light refreshments. (2)Change trains in Brive (arr. 11:00, dep. 11:10). (3) Supplement charged. Runs daily except Sundays & holidays. Restaurant car. (4) Supplement charged. Light refreshments. (5) TGV. Runs daily, except Saturday. Restaurant car. (6) Runs Friday and Sunday. Light refreshments. (7) Supplement charged. Runs daily, except Saturday. Light refreshments. (8) Has couchettes. (9) Runs daily, except Friday and Sunday. (10) Carries a sleeping car. Also has couchettes. No coaches. (11) Operates early September to early July. Has couchettes. (12) Operates early July to early September. Has couchettes. Coach is second-class. (13) TGV. Runs daily, except Sundays and holidays. Light refreshments. (14) Arrives at Paris' Montparnasse railstation. (15) Light refreshments.

Lyon - Geneva   159

This trip is noted for scenic canyons. See details under "Lyon."

Marseille - Monaco (Monte Carlo) 164

Great views of the Mediterranean seashore.

Dep. Marseille	06:15 (1)	09:18	11:04	13:17	15:52 (2)
Arr. Nice	8:58 (1)	11:43	13:36	15:40	18:30
Change trains.					
Dep. Nice	09:10 (1)	11:55	14:12	16:16	19:15
Arr. Monaco	10:00	12:16	14:37	16:37	19:39

• • •

Dep. Monaco	11:07 (1)	12:59	15:50	18:05 (1)	21:07 (1)
Arr. Nice	11:20 (1)	13:21	16:12	18:24 (1)	21:20 (1)
Change trains.					
Dep. Nice	11:24	13:41	16:38 (2)	18:35	22:32
Arr. Marseille	13:43	16:09	19:09	21:13	01:05

(1) Direct train. No train change in Nice. (2) Light refreshments.

Narbonne - Carcassonne 139

Outstanding farm and vineyard scenery. Easy to make as a one-day roundtrip or can be covered in the route from Narbonne to Toulouse and Bordeaux.

Dep. Narbonne	06:51 (1)	08:41	09:50	12:04 (2)	15:20 (2)
Arr. Carcassonne	40–45 minutes later				

Sights in **Narbonne**: The Cloister adjacent to the Palace of the Archbishops. The choir of the incomplete Cathedral of Saint-Just.

Sights in **Carcassonne**: See notes under "Bordeaux–Carcassonne."

Dep. Carcassonne	09:52 (2)	12:19 (2)	12:49 (2)	15:01 (2)	18:11 (3+4)
Arr. Narbonne	40–45 minutes later				

(1) Runs Monday-Friday, except Holidays. (2) Light refreshments. (3) Operates all year. Light refreshments early September to early July. (4) Plus other departures from Carcassonne at 18:03 (2), 19:46 (2) and 21:54 (2).

Here is the daytime viewing schedule for the Narbonne-Bordeaux route:

Dep. Narbonne	08:24	09:45	11:58	15:20 (1)
Dep. Carcassonne	08:54	10:16	12:28	15:52
Arr. Toulouse (Matabiau)	09:44	11:14	13:26	16:48 (1)
Arr. Bordeaux (St. Jean)	11:57	13:27	-0-	19:04
	•	• •		
Dep. Bordeaux (St. Jean)	06:39 (2)	08:23 (2)	11:47 (2)	14:48
Arr. Toulouse (Matabiau)	08:57	11:04 (3)	14:03	17:05
Dep. Carcassonne	09:52	11:13	15:01	18:03
Arr. Narbonne	10:20	12:26	15:29	18:31

(1) Light refreshments. Change trains in Toulouse at 16:36. (2) Light refreshments. (3) Change trains , departing Toulouse 11:13. Operates early July to early September. Light refreshments Toulouse–Narbonne.

Nice - Cuneo   356

There is spectacular scenery on the 74-mile long Nice–Cuneo rail route through the Alps and the **Roya Valley**, a service that first became operational in 1928. Severe damage during World War II caused it to be closed in 1940, and it was not re-opened until the Winter of 1979. An outstanding feat of engineering, this line is a succession of very high viaducts, bridges and 60 tunnels that span 27 miles of this route, interspersed with sections that look down into deep valleys. This route has attracted many tourists.

Dep. Nice	07:25	12:28(1)	Dep. Cuneo	10:32	16:16 (1)
Arr. Breil	08:29	-0-	Arr. Breil	12:14	-0-
Change trains.			*Change trains.*		
Dep Breil	10:08	-0-	Dep Breil	12:45	-0-
Arr. Cuneo	11:44	15:26	Arr. Nice	13:30	19:10

(1) Direct train. No train change in Breil.

Nice - Digne - Nice   151 d

This is a very scenic ride up the beautiful **Var Valley** on a self-propelled single car narrow-gauge train. The roundtrip ticket in 1993 cost $72 (U.S.) for first-class, $46 for second-class. Half-fare for holders of Eurailpass or any French pass. There is a great drop in temperature between sea-level Nice and 1,955-foot-high Digne. The scenery includes canyons, chateaus and forests. The train follows the route Napoleon took when he returned from exile in Elba in 1815. Plaques and monuments along the way mark that event.

Dep. Nice (Sud)	06:42	09:00	12:43
Arr. Digne	09:44	12:25	15:57

Sights in **Digne**: A popular mineral bath resort. See the 15th century Cathedral of Saint Jerome. Many fruit orchards. Digne is famed for the lavender cultivated here.

Dep. Digne	11:05	13:58	17:25
Arr. Nice (Sud)	14:17	17:15	20:35

Lyon - Torino (and Rome)   152 + 351

The Culoz-Modane portion of this trip offers outstanding lake and mountain scenery. The train goes through the 8.5-mile long Mont Cenis Tunnel, constructed in 1871.

Both of these trains have light refreshments.

Dep. Lyon (P-D)	06:59	Dep. Torino (P.N.)	12:22
Dep. Culoz	N/A	Dep. Modane	14:01
Arr. Modane	09:38	Dep. Culoz	N/A
Arr. Torino (P.N.)	11:16	Arr. Lyon (P-D)	16:40

Toulouse - La Tour-de-Carol - Toulouse   144

Excellent mountain and canyon scenery.

Dep. Toulouse (Mat.)	07:52	10:14	Dep. La Tour	10:40	13:35
Arr. La Tour	10:28	12:49	Arr. Toulouse (Mat.)	13:11	16:10

Toulouse - Limoges - Toulouse   138

Recommended for mountain scenery. This route can be seen either as an easy one-day roundtrip between Toulouse and Limoges or as a portion of the ride Toulouse–Paris and v.v. trip.

Dep. Toulouse (Mat.)	07:31 (1)	10:32 (2)	10:58 (3)	13:41 (2)	14:02 (4)
Arr. Limoges	10:48	14:04	14:21	17:00	17:36

• • •

Dep. Limoges	13:01 (5)	16:55 (6)	20:46 (6)
Arr. Toulouse (Mat.)	16:55	20:35	00:20

(1) Supplement charged. Runs daily, except Sundays and holidays. Light refreshments. (2)Runs daily. Light refreshments. (3) Operates mid-July to early September. Runs daily. (4) Runs Sunday and Friday only. (5) Runs daily. Light refreshments early September to early July. (6) Supplement charged. Runs Friday only. Light refreshments.

INTERNATIONAL ROUTES
FROM FRANCE

The French gateway for rail travel to Amsterdam, Bern (and on to Zurich and Vienna), Brussels, Cologne, Geneva, London and Madrid is Paris. Notes on the routes to London appear in Chapter 7.

From Marseille, there is rail service to Barcelona and Genoa (and on to Milan and Rome). From Paris, there are trains to Amsterdam, Barcelona, Bern, Brussels, Cologne, Geneva, Genoa, Lisbon, Madrid, Milan and Rome.

Nice - Marseille - Narbonne - Barcelona

163

Dep. Nice	06:00 (1)	-0-	-0-	11:56
Dep. Marseille	09:04	12:45 (1)	-0-	14:42
Arr. Narbonne	11:54	15:18	-0-	17:36
Change trains.				
162				
Dep. Narbonne	12:14	16:23	-0-	19:04
Arr. Port Bou	13:55	17:58	-0-	20:45
Change trains.				
416				
Dep. Port Bou	14:18 (2)	18:20 (2)	18:55 (4)	21:10 (2)
Arr. Barcelona (P. de G.)	16:50	21:32 (3)	20:50 (5)	23:22

(1) Light refreshments. (2) Second-class only. (3) Arrives at Barcelona's Sants railstation. (4) Restaurant car. (5) Arrives at Barcelona's Franca railstation.

Marseille - Nice - Genoa - Milan - Rome   90

There is marvelous Mediterranean coastal scenery on this route.

Dep. Marseille (St. Ch.)	-0-	05:00	06:15
Dep. Nice	07:15 (1)	08:08	09:10
Arr. Genoa (P.P.)	11:30	12:16	13:30
Arr. Milan (Cen.)	13:44	-0-	15:40
Arr. Rome	-0-	18:05	-0-
Dep. Marseille (St. Ch.)	16:39 (2)	17:28 (3)	20:35 (5)
Dep. Nice	19:10	20:29 (4)	23:12 (4)
Arr. Genoa (P.P.)	22:10	00:17	03:30
Arr. Milan (Cen.)	23:59	-0-	05:40
Arr. Rome	-0-	06:55	-0-

(1) Operates mid-July to late August. Second-class only. (2) Restaurant car. (3) Change trains in Nice at 20:19. (4) Carries a sleeping car. Also has couchettes. (5) Light refreshments. Change trains in Nice at 23:02.

Paris - Amsterdam 76

See "Amsterdam–Paris."

Paris - Basel 57

See "Paris–Basel."

Paris - Bordeaux - Lisbon 46

This train has couchettes Paris-Lisbon, plus a sleeping car, coaches and a restaurant car Irun-Lisbon.

Dep. Paris (Austerlitz)	13:54
Dep. Bordeaux (St. J.)	18:19
Set watch back one hour.	
Arr. Irun	20:51
Arr. Lisbon (S. Apol.)	13:05 Day 2

Paris - Bordeaux - Madrid 46

Dep. Paris (Aust.)	18:05 (1)	20:00 (2)
Dep. Bordeaux (St. J.)	22:35	00:26
Set your watch back one hour.		
Dep. Hendaye	01:57	02:37
Arr. Madrid (Cham.)	09:50	08:32

(1) Has only second-class couchettes. No coaches. Light refreshments Paris-Hendaye. (2) Has only first and second-class sleeping cars and a restaurant car. No couchettes or coaches.

Paris - Brussels - Amsterdam   18

Dep. Paris (Nord)	07:07 (1)	07:50 (3)	10:20 (3)	11:29 (4)	12:34 (5)	13:43 (6)
Arr. Brussels (Midi)	09:39	10:49 (3)	13:17 (3)	14:02	15:27	16:42
Change trains.						
Dep. Brussels (Midi)	10:10 (2)	11:04	13:29	14:10 (2)	16:10 (2)	17:10 (2)
Arr. Amsterdam	13:08	14:02	16:34	17:08	19:08	20:08

Dep. Paris (Nord)	14:33 (3)	16:36 (3)	17:25 (7)	18:38 (8)	23:22 (9)
Arr. Brussels (Midi)	17:42	19:49	20:01	21:10 (8)	04:32 (9)
Change trains.					
Dep. Brussels (Midi)	15:54	19:56	20:10	21:20	04:49
Arr. Amsterdam	21:01	22:47	23:08	23:59	08:05

(1) Supplement charged. Runs Monday–Friday. Restaurant car. (2) Light refreshments. (3) Direct train. No train change in Brussels. Light refreshments. (4) Supplement charged. Runs daily. Restaurant car. (5) Operates Monday-Friday late August to late June. Restaurant car. (6) Supplement charged. Restaurant car. (7) Restaurant car. Early September to early July: runs daily. Early July to early September: runs Monday-Friday. (8) Direct train. No train change in Brussels. Reservation required. Supplement charged. Runs daily, except Saturday. Restaurant car Paris–Brussels. (9) Direct train. No train change in Brussels. Has couchettes. (5) Runs Monday-Friday.

Paris - Cologne - Hamburg - Copenhagen   25

Dep. Paris (Nord)	07:31 (1)	13:43 (1)	16:32 (1)	21:30 (3)	23:14 (5)
Arr. Cologne	12:48	19:42	21:57	-0- (3)	05:52
Change trains.					
Dep. Cologne	13:10 (1)	20:10 (1)	-0-	-0- (3)	06:10 (1)
Arr. Hamburg (Hbf.)	17:11	00:11	-0-	07:11 (4)	-0-
Arr. Copenhagen	-0-	-0-	-0-	12:20	07:48

(1) Supplement charged. Restaurant car. (2) Direct train to Copenhagen. No train change in Cologne. Operates late May to late Ssptember. Carries a sleeping car. Also has couchettes. Coach is second-class. (3) Direct train to Hamburg. Does not call on Cologne. (4) Change trains in Hamburg, departing at 07:19 (1). (5) Carries a sleeping car. Also has couchettes and coaches. Light refreshments.

Paris - Geneva   159

All of these trains are TGV, require reservation and charge a supplement.

Dep. Paris (Lyon)	07:24 (1)	10:28 (1)	14:42 (2)	17:40 (1)	19:09 (1)
Arr. Geneva (Corn.)	10:51	-0-	18:14	21:11	22:45

(1) Restaurant car. (2) Light refreshments.

Paris - Dijon - Lausanne - Milan - Genoa - Rome or Venice 44

Dep. Paris (Lyon)	07:14 (1)	12:21 (1)	15:53 (1)	18:47 (3)	20:06 (3+8)
Arr. Lausanne	11:06	16:07	19:45	-0- (4)	-0- (4)
Change trains.					
Dep. Lausanne	11:13 (2)	16:13 (2)	19:53 (2)	-0-	-0-
Arr. Milan (Cen.)	14:40	19:45	23:40	-0-	04:43 (5)
Arr. Genoa (P.P.)	-0-	-0-	-0-	02:51	-0-
Arr. Rome (Ter.)	-0-	-0-	-0-	09:45	-0-
Arr. Venice (S.L.)	-0-	-0-	-0-	-0-	08:45

(1) TGV. Reservation required. Supplement charged. Restaurant car. (2) Restaurant car. (3) Light refreshments. This train has only sleeping cars and couchettes. No coaches. (4) Does not call on Lausanne. Direct train. (5) Arrives at Milan's Porta Garibaldi railstation. (6) Light refreshments. Carries a sleeping car. Also has couchettes. (7) Carries a sleeping car. Also has couchettes. Coach is second-class. (8) Plus another Paris departure at 20:56 (6), not calling on Lausanne, Genoa or Venice…arriving Rome's Ostiense railstaion at 14:19. There is also another Paris departure at 22:22 (4+7), terminating in Milan at 08:48.

THE FERRY-CROSSING TO IRELAND

Paris - Le Havre - Rosslare and Paris - Cherbourg - Rosslare

Operated by Irish Ferries Company. Passage *only* (without a seat or a berth) is free all year with a Eurailpass. The 1995 cost for "passage only" was $209 (U.S.) from July 10 to August 31, and was at lower prices in other times of the year.

Passage *plus a seat* was $217 (but only $10 with a Eurailpass) in mid-Summer when there are many more passengers than seats on the vessel and some passengers must sit on the deck for this 21-hour trip. Reserving and paying extra for a cabin is essential in Summer. A 6-berth cabin that was $221 per person in mid-Summer was onl y $13 with a Eurailpass. A 4-berth cabin with shower and private toilet (at $257 per person) was only $48 with a Eurailpass.

There are also sailings to and from Cork, Ireland during June, July and August.

Days of operation and departures times vary during 5 different periods of the year. For 1995 schedules, prices and reservations, contact the North American agent: Lynott Tours Inc., 350 Fifth Avenue, New York, NY 10118. Telephone: (212) 760-0101 or (800) 221-2474.

GERMANY

FLENSBURG
PUTTGARDEN
SASSNITZ
WARNEMÜNDE
STRALSUND
ROSTOCK
TRAVEMÜNDE
LUBECK
SCHWERIN
HAMBURG
LÜNEBURG
BERLIN
BREMEN
POTSDAM
CELLE
WARSAW
BENTHEIM
HANNOVER
BRAUNSCHWEIG
OSNABRÜCK
HELMSTEDT
ARNHEIM
HAMELN
HILDESHEIM
EMMERICH
BAD HARZBURG
GOSLAR
VENLO
DORTMUND
LEIPZIG
ESSEN
KASSEL
NAUMBURG
DÜSSELDORF
DRESDEN
KÖLN
SIEGEN
BEBRA
WEIMAR
AACHEN
ERFURT
BONN
CHEMNITZ
GIESSEN
(KARL-MARX-STADT)
PRAGUE
KOBLENZ
WIESBADEN
TRIER
FRANKFURT
BAMBERG
MAINZ
WÜRZBURG
MANNHEIM
HEIDELBERG
SAARBRÜCKEN
NÜRNBERG
KARLSRUHE
BADEN-BADEN
KEHL
STUTTGART
OFFENBURG
ULM
PASSAU
VIENNA
AUGSBURG
MÜNCHEN
SINGEN
FRIEDRICHSHAFEN
SALZBURG
SCHAFFHAUSEN
LINDAU
GARMISCH
VIENNA
BASEL
KUFSTEIN

GERMANY

Overview

Train travel in Germany has changed radically since the Berlin wall came down and the Bundesrepublik reunified with the former East Germany. Although tremendous building projects have begun to help the eastern part of the country catch up materially with the west, there is still a vast gully between the two. Trains equipped to go twice as fast must slow down in parts of the east due to old and ill-maintained tracks. Cities like Berlin, Leipzig, Weimar, and Dresden are now easily connected to the major western German cities of Munich, Frankfurt, Hannover, Hamburg, etc. The German national train company, (Deutsche Bundesbahn, DB) is highly efficient and well equipped. The new fast trains, not unlike the French TGVs, run regularly between the major cities in record time and are teched-out with business conference rooms and on-board telephones. In Germany the train station functions as the hub of most downtown areas and after 6:30 PM when stores close in German cities, the train station (hauptbahnhof) is pretty much the only place to buy groceries, wine, etc.

General Information

• Children under four travel free. Half-fare for children 4-11. Children 12 and over pay full fare.

• Fast InterCity and EuroCity trains, connecting 50 important cities along five major rail routes, have easy cross-platform connections in such cities as Cologne, Wurzburg, Mannheim and Dortmund. The 6 DM supplement charged for IC and EC trains includes the cost of a seat reservation. Where timetable footnotes indicate that a supplement is charged by a particular train, a passenger using a Eurailpass or German Flexipass does not have to pay the extra charge. (All of those passes are also valid on all commuter rail services in major German cities.) The IC supplement must be paid when using the Inter-Rail Card, available only to residents of Europe. Some of the InterCity trains have top speeds of 125 mph. A conference compartment in them can be rented for the cost of four first-class tickets. Worldwide telephone calls can be made from all IC trains.

• When entering or leaving Germany on an international train, the customs, passport and currency control are usually performed in the train. Because of this, passengers traveling across Germany (such as from Amsterdam to Copenhagen) are required to travel in a special car or compartment.

• Porter service may be reserved in advance at many rail stations, including those at the Dusseldorf and Frankfurt airports. A program began in 1987 to install conveyor belts at stairways in 130 rail stations as well as escalators which can accommodate baggage carts in all major stations.

• The signs you will see at rail stations in Germany are the same as those listed earlier in this chapter under Austria.

GERMANY'S TRAIN PASSES

EuroCity and InterCity supplements are included in the prices listed below for all German train passes. Travelers arriving in Germany by airplane can validate all of them and also Eurailpass at the airport rail ticket office after exiting the customs area and use them for the rail trip from the airport to the city.

Wunder Flexipass Sold worldwide outside Germany by travel agencies and Rail Europe (U.S.A. and Canadian offices listed under "France").

Unlimited 4 days of first-class train travel plus one day of car rental (any 5 days) within 21 days. Prices vary (a) whether for one person or for 2 persons, and (b) the category of car. A third and fourth passenger needs to pay only for a 5-day German Railpass (see below).

The 1996 prices were not set at the end of 1995. The 1995 price *per person* for 2 persons (using the smallest size car) was: $225. A third and fourth passenger had to pay only $215 per person. Up to 5 more rail days could be added at $42 per day. Unlimited additional car days could be added also at $42 per day.

All of the following passes are sold worldwide outside Germany by travel agencies and by GermanRail. All of them are 'flexible,' valid for one month (example: July 3 to August 2). These 1996 prices are shown in U.S. dollars.

German Railpass For first-class: $260 for any 5 days, $410 for any 10 days, and $530 for any 15 days. For second-class: $178, $286 and $386.

A second-class Youthpass (under age 26 on first day of travel) costs $138, $188 and $238.

German Rail Twinpass The first-class price per person when 2 persons travel together is $234 for any 5 days, $369 for any 10 days, $477 for any 15 days. For second-class: $160, $257 and $331.

German Rail & Car Pass Provides 5 days of unlimited rail travel within Germany plus 3 days of rental car with unlimited mileage. All supplements for travel on high speed trains and the Value Added Tax on car rental are included. Cars may be picked up at one Hertz location in Germany and dropped off at another Hertz location in Germany.

Not included: train reservation fees, auto insurance, and gas. GermanRail will make train reservations up to 10 days prior to departure at a charge of $10 per person, per train, plus $10 per order for mailing and handling. Car reservations must be made either up to 7 days prior to departure or in Germany up to 2 business days before rental is to begin.

Prices vary (a) whether for one person or for 2 persons, (b) whether the rail portion is for first-class or second-class, and (c) the category of car. A third and fourth adult passenger needs to pay only the rail portion $240 for first-class, $160 for second-class. Children under age 12 need to pay only the rail portion: $120 for first-class, $80 for second-class.

The prices for all travel completed by March 31, 1996 per person for 2 persons (using second-class train seats and the smallest size car) is $209 plus $3.75 handling charge. More car days can be added at $35 per day.

BAHNCARDS

They allow 50% discount. The 1996 *first*-class prices are shown below. *Second*-class is 50% less.

BahnCard   440DM.

BahnCard fur Ehepartner (for married couples)   220DM for first person, 110 DM for the partner.

BahnCard fur Familien (for families — parents and all children)   220DM.

BahnCard fur Kinder (for chidren age 4–11)   100DM

BahnCard fur Jugendliche/Teens (for youths age 12–17)   100DM

BahnCard fur Junioren (for youths age 18-22)   220DM.

BahnCard fur Senioren (for persons age 60 and older)   220DM.

ONE-DAY EXCURSIONS AND CULTURAL SIGHTSEEING

Here are 94 one-day rail trips that can be made comfortably from cities in Germany, returning to them in most cases before dinnertime. Notes are provided on a few possible recommended sights to see and do at each destination. The number after the name of each route corresponds to the Cook's Timetable. Details on 11 other rail trips recommended for exceptional scenery and schedules for international connections conclude this section. Sightseeing tours to Chemnitz (formerly Karl Marx Stadt), Dresden and Potsdam start in Berlin at Parkplatz Rankestrasse, near the Kurfurstendamm. For reservations, contact Deutsches Reiseburo, Kurfurstendamm 17, Berlin W.30, Germany.

The eight base cities for one-day excursions include Berlin, Cologne, Dresden, Frankfurt/Main, Hamburg, Hannover, Leipzig and Munich.

Berlin

Two-hour and 4-hour tours of West Berlin begin at 10:00 and occur at frequent intervals during the day, from 220 Kurfurstendamm, 216 Kurfurstendamm, and opposite from the bombed-out Gedachtniskirche (Memorial Church).

The stroll down tree-lined Kurfurstendamm is almost mandatory, to observe the city's fine stores, theaters, cafes, movie houses and bars. See the Zoo (started in 1843) and Aquarium, one of Europe's oldest and best animal exhibits, open daily until dusk. The New National Gallery, at Potsdamerstrasse 50, open daily except Monday 09:00–17:00.

The bust of Nefertiti and other important items in the Egyptian Museum at 70 Schloss Strasse, closed Friday. The rooms and gardens of Charlottenburg Castle, closed Monday, opposite the Egyptian Museum. The 1936 Olympic Stadium. The German History Museum, in the reconstructed Reichstag Building, on Paul-Lobe Strasse, open daily except Monday 10:00–17:00. The tent-shaped Philharmonic Hall. Take a boat ride on the Havel River.

See modern paintings at Brucke Museum, Bussardsteig 9, open Monday–Friday 11:00–17:00. Masterpieces by Durer, Cranach the Elder and Holbein the Younger, at the Dahlem Museum, Arnimallee 23–27, open Tuesday-Sunday 09:00–17:00. Models of everything that floats, flies or rolls, at the Transport Museum, Trebbinerstrasse 9, open Tuesday–Friday 09:00–18:00 and on Saturday and Sunday 10:00–18:00.

Exhibits about many modern architects in the Bauhaus Museum, Klingelhoferstrasse 13, open daily except Tuesday 11:00–17:00. The best collection of Durer drawings in Germany is at the Kupferstichkabinett.

Visit the sixth floor (called Feinschmecker Etage —"the gourmet's floor") of Kaufhaus des Westens (called KaDeWe "Kah-day-vay" by local people), a large department store on Tauentzienstrasse. It is the largest food store in Europe: 500 sales clerks dispensing 30,000 different products. Fruits and vegetables sold there include limes from Brazil, rare wild mushrooms from France and Poland, avocados from Israel, tiny beans from Kenya, tomatoes from Spain, apples from Hungary.

They sell 1,500 kinds of meats (250 varieties of salami). Then there are also eels, crawfish, catfish and carp. Live lobsters are delivered to the store in tank trucks. You will also find 400 types of bread. Three separate counters for 1,800 varieties of cheese from France, Italy and other countries. Eighteen kinds of herring salad. It also has 28 restaurants, counter services and stand-up bars.

Store hours are: 9:00–18:30 on Monday, Tuesday, Wednesday and Friday; 9:00–20:30 on Thursday; 9:00–14:00 on most Saturdays. KaDeWe has 30,000 customers on an ordinary day. Before holidays, there are 100,000 customers in a single day.

The Weissbierstube Restaurant in the Berlin Museum is acclaimed for its bounteous buffet tables. Both the Restaurant and the Museum are open daily except Mondays 11:00–18:00.

To see East Berlin, take the elevated railway from West Berlin's Zoo railstation to its Friedrichstrasse station. On leaving Friedrichstrasse station, turn right and walk 3 blocks to reach Berlin's famous boulevard, Unter den Linden, and the enormous Soviet embassy. A few blocks further, at the end of the boulevard, is the classical Brandenburg Gate and the ruins of the Berlin Wall.

Also see the reconstructed St. Hedwig's Cathedral. The National Gallery. The 18th century State Opera. The tremendous collection of Oriental, Greek and Roman antiquities, the Market Gate of Milet and the impressive Pergamon Altar, all at the Pergamon Museum on Bodestrasse, open Wednesday and Thursday 09:00–18:00 and Friday 10:00–18:00.

The Palace of the Republic. Bode Museum. The Altes Museum. The tiny 14th century church, Marienkirche. The Museum of German History.

Cologne (Koln)

All museums are closed on Monday.

It is a 10-minute bus ride from the Cologne/Bonn Airport to the center of Cologne.

Your city-sightseeing in Cologne should include, above all, the Cathedral, very near the railstation. Started in 1248 and not completed until 1880, it houses the world's largest reliquary, containing relics of the 3 kings, the Magi, as well as a splendid collection of illuminated books, vestments, ivories and liturgical articles. These can be seen Monday– Saturday 09:00–17:00, Sundays and holidays 12:30–17:00.

The best time to be inside the Cathedral is at the Sunday 10:00 mass, when the ceremony starts with a procession of church elders dressed in robes of burgundy, crimson and rose, and wearing white, embroidered, starched linen. If you climb the 502 steps to the top of the spire, past the 9 giant bells, you will see a magnificent view of Cologne, The Rhine River and the Rhine Valley.

Near the Cathedral, explore ancient Cologne. The Praetorium, a palace for Roman governors several centuries before Christ, located in the basement of the Town Hall, open daily 10:00–17:00. Its entrance, difficult to find, is across from the Restaurant-Bar-Cafe Oldtimer at 110 Kleine Budengasse. See the 3rd century Dionysus mosaic (once the dining hall floor of a Roman house) in the Roman Museum, open Tuesday–Sunday 10:00–20:00.

Also on view there is an outstanding collection of Roman glass, cooking utensils and 4th century jewelry. Visit the 3rd century Roman tower.

See the collection of paintings by Cologne masters of the 13th–17th and 19th centuries in the Wallraf Richartz Museum (1 Bischofsgartenstrasse, between the Cathedral and the Hauptbahnhoff), open Tuesday, Wednesday and Thursday 10:00–20:00. On Friday, Saturday and Sunday 10:00–18:00. Modern art is exhibited in the Ludwig Museum (same address and hours). Visit the Zoo. The 15th century Gurzenich. The Metropolitan Historical Museum. The Town Hall. St. Pantaleon Church. St. Andreas Church. Relics and treasures in the Golden Room at the Church of St. Ursula. The luxury shops on Hohestrasse and Schildergasse.

Dresden

Major works of Raphael, Rembrandt, Rubens, Tintoretto, Van Eyck, Vermeer and other great 16th and 17th century painters at the Picture Gallery in the Semper Building of Zwinger Palace. Another excellent collection of paintings in the National Gallery.

Hear the Silberman organ (235 years old in 1990) at the cathedral, Hofkirche. Visit the baroque Opera House. The Zoo in Stadtpark (also called Volkspark). The Block House.

Dresden Palace. The Japanese Castle. The treasures at the Albertinium Museum. The Palace of Culture. Take the cable car to Weisser Hirsch for the view of Dresden from the top of that hill.

It is a 17-mile ride by suburban railway from Dresdent to **Meissen**. See the 15th century castle (Albrechtsburg) and the Cathedral there. Shop in Meissen for Dresdent china and Albrecht porcelain.

Frankfurt

There is frequent rail service from Frankfurt's Hauptbahnhof railstation to the city's airport and vice versa (11-minute travel time) every 20 minutes from 04:14 to 23:54. From the airport to Frankfurt: every 30 minutes from 04:33 to 23:53 plus 00:33. Frequent trains per hour continue beyond the airport station to Mainz and Wiesbaden. Trains also depart the airport at frequent times for Bonn, Cologne, Dortmund, Dusseldorf, Koblenz, Ludwigshafen, Luxembourg, Mannheim, Nurnberg, Trier and Wurzburg.

Bus tours that cover in 2½ hours the city's most interesting places depart daily from the south side of the main railstation at 10:00 and 14:00. Most museums in Frankfurt are closed on Monday.

See the house where Goethe was born in 1749 (23 Grosser Hirschgraben), open daily, except Sunday: April–September, 09:00–18:00, October–March, 09:00–16:00. Next to it, the Goethe Museum (books, pictures, furniture and manuscripts associated with the writer) in the Grosser Hirschgraben, open Monday–Saturday 09:00–18:00, Sunday 10:00–15:00. The new (1991) Jewish Museum at 14–15 Untermainkal, in the former Rothschild Palace, is open daily except Monday.

The Zoo, one of the world's greatest, at Am Tiergarten, open 08:00–19:00 in Summer, 08:00–18:00 in October, 08:00–17:00 in Winter. Its Exoticarium (aquarium and reptile house) is open until 22:00. Buses #10, #13 and #15 go to the Zoo.

The emperor's coronation hall in the Romer complex at medieval Romerberg Square. The wonderful doors in the 13th century Leonhardskirche. The 13th century chapel of Saalhof in the remains of the palace of Frederick Barbarossa. Cloth Hall. The Botanical Garden. The pews and murals in the Cathedral of St. Bartholomew. The Church of St. Nicholas. The Church of St. Paul. Senckenberg Museum, the largest natural history museum in West Germany, open 09:00–16:00. The collection of Dutch primitives and 16th century German masters at the Stadel Art Institute and Municipal Gallery, open daily except Monday 10:00–17:00. The Liebighaus Exhibition of Sculpture.

The Museum of Plastic Art. The changing exhibits of European silver, porcelain, furniture and glass from the Middle Ages to the present time and also an Asian collection (3rd to 19th century) at the Museum of Arts and Crafts. The Henninger Tower in Sachsenhausen, the old quarter of the city (across the Main River, near the commercial district). The Postal Museum. The major shopping streets: Zeil and Kaiserstrasse.

The palm trees, other tropical plants, and Alpine gardens in the city's central park, Palmengarten. Nine miles away in **Offenbach,** center of West Germany's leather industry, is the German Leather Museum, open daily 10:00–17:00.

Hamburg

Most museums in Hamburg are closed Monday. See the port, one of the busiest in the world. There are splendid views of the enormous port from Stintfang Hill. Visit Hagenbeck Zoo, the first cageless zoo in the world, at Stellingen Gardens. St. James Church, with its famous organ, built in 1693. Rathausmarkt Square. The models of Old Hamburg, the port and the city's railway system, in the Museum of the History of Hamburg.

The Counting Houses in the business quarter, around Burchardplatz. The notorious Reperbahn. The view of the city from the Michel Tower of St, Michaelis Church. The Museum of Decorative Arts. The Art Gallery. The Botanical Garden. The "Sight and Sound" performances during Summer in the Planten un Blomen park. Take a flight over the city from Fuhlsbuttel Airport.

Hannover

The bus ride between Langenhagen Airport and Hannover's railstation takes 30 minutes. The bus terminal is located next to Track #14.

See the collection of art (from the Middle Ages to the beginning of the 20th century) in the Niedersachsische Landesgalerie. Modern painting and sculpture in the Sprengel Museum (Max Beckmann, Paul Klee, Pablo Picasso).

For an interesting 2-hour walking tour of Hannover, obtain the detailed brochure available at both of the railstation's 2 tourist information offices. Walk out of the station to the statue in front of it and start to follow the painted red line which leads to Passerelle (a pedestrian mall), the 19th century Opera House, the old city wall, Town Hall, and Hannover's oldest (16th century) half-timbered structure.

See the bronze doors by Marcks at Market Church. The outstanding collection of Egyptian antiquities in the Kestner Museum. The prehistoric objects in the Museum of Lower Saxony.

Take a short walk from the Central railstation to the station under Kropke Cafe and, from there, Tram #1 or #2 to the absolutely fantastic baroque Royal Gardens of Herrenhausen. Its ornamental fountains perform in Summer Monday–Friday, 11:00–12:00 and 15:30–16:30. On Saturdays and Sundays, they can be seen 10:00–12:00 and 15:30–17:30.

Next to Herrenhausen is the natural park, Georgengarten. Nearby, see the exotic plants in the greenhouses at Berggarten.

Take streetcar #6 from the Central railstation to Hannover's outstanding Zoo.

Leipzig

Concentrate on the area around Market Place. Visit the Museum of the History of Leipzig in the Renaissance Old Town Hall. The 17th century stock exchange (Alte Bourse), rebuilt in 1963. The weighinghouse (Alte Waage), where taxes were levied on imported goods. Auerbachs Keller, the old tavern on which Goethe based the locale of his Faust drama. Bach's tomb, at St. Thomas Church. The Museum of Fine Arts.

West of Market Place is the church where Johann Sebastian Bach is buried. Bach composed in that church the last 27 years of his life. Also see Gohliser Schlosschen, a rococo palace. Gohlis, the home of the poet Schiller. The Opera House in Karl Marx Platz. It is impossible to find a room in Leipzig during the semi-annual (March and September) trade fairs that attract visitors from all over the world.

Munich (Munchen)

A metropolitan train connects Munich's Hauptbahnhof and Ostbanhof railstations. It is a 10-minute bus ride between Munich's Riem Airport and the Hauptbahnhof railstation, where the city's monthly program of events (theaters, museums, exhibits, concerts, plays, etc.) can be obtained. The program is also sold at newsstands.

Most museums in Munich are closed on Monday. There are more than 50 — on coins, ethnology, theater, applied arts, hunting and fishing, folk music, graphic arts, mineralogy, Egyptian art, toys, fire fighting, beer making, prehistory, porcelains, paleontology, puppets, photography, even chamber pots.

See the works of Durer, El Greco, Raphael, Holbein, Rembrandt and many other great 14th to 18th century painters at Alte (Old) Pinakothek, at 27 Barer Strasse, open Tuesday-Sunday 09:00–16:30, and on Tuesday and Thursday 07:00–21:00. The Neue (New) Pinakothek at 29 Barer Strasse (same days and hours as the "Old" museum) has a collection of 19th and 20th century artists. The paintings of Kandinsky, Marcs and Klees in the Lenbachhaus, at 33 Luisen Strasse, open daily except Monday 10:00–18:00.

The 15th century Frauenkirche Cathedral, and the view of Munich from its north tower…and then later the view of Frauenkirche from the top of Neue Rathaus (New City Hall), where at 11:00 every day the mechanical figures in its bell tower perform a tournament of knights, a medieval royal wedding, and a dance. There are other fine views of Munich from Olympia Tower.

The paintings of Cezanne, Gauguin, Renoir and other impressionists at the Haus der Kunst at 1 Princregenten Strasse, open daily except Monday 09:00–16:30. On Thursday, it is also open 19:00–21:00. See Wittelsbach Fountain.

The fine exhibits and planetarium at Deutsches Museum, considered the best scientific museum in the world, open daily 09:00–17:00. It is across the Ludwigsbrucke, on an island in the Isar River. Displays of 16,000 items.

The view of the Alps from the top of Peterskirche. The best collection of tapestries and wood carvings in Germany, at the Bavarian National Museum. Munich's most famous beer palace, Hofbrauhaus.

The Schatzkammer in the Residenz palace (which houses the enormous Festaal and many museums that are open Tuesday–Saturday 10:00–16:30, Sunday 10:00–13:00), and the flower gardens in the park north of it. Words cannot describe the fabulous beauty of the Festaal.

At Schloss (Castle) Nymphenburg: the porcelain in the showrooms of Nymphenburger Porzellan Manufaktur, open daily except Monday 10:00–12:00 and 13:30–16:00. Also visit the park outside the castle. Located on the outskirts of Munich, Nymphenburg can be reached by taking the U-1 subway to the end of that line (Rotkreutzplatz) and transfering to the #12 streetcar. Alternate lines from the center of Munich are streetcars #17 or #21, or buses #41 or #42.

See the history of Munich in the Isartorplatz Museum. The impressive Renaissance Michalskirche on the Neuhauserstrasse pedestrian mall. Ancient Greek and Roman sculpture in the Glyptothek (Konigsplatz 3), open Tuesday, Wednesday, Friday and Sunday 10:00–16:30, on Thursday 12:00–20:30. Nearby, the Staatliche Antikensammlungen (State Collection of Antiquities) at Konigsplatz 1, open Tuesday and Thursday–Sunday 10:00–16:30, on Wednesday 12:00–20:30.

The collection of Medieval art and sculpture, arts and crafts, applied arts, folk art and folklore at the Bayerisches Nationalmuseum (Bavarian National Museum), at Prinzregenstrasse 3, open daily except Monday 09:30–17:00. Nearby, an exhibit of late 19th century Herman painters in Schackgalerie at Prinzregenstrasse 9, open daily except Tuesday 09:00–16:30.

Visit Schwabing, the Latin quarter. The palaces on Ludwigstrasse. The history of Bavarian Motor Works (aircraft, motorcycles, automobiles) in the BMW Museum, open daily 09:00–16:00.

Infamous Dachau is a 40-minute ride by commuter train #S-2 or bus #11. Although there are no guides at Dachau, an exhibit there details the operation of the concentration camp, and an English-language film is shown at 11:30 and 15:30.

Since 1870, an Alois Dallmayr food store has offered gourmet delicacies in Munich. It added a restaurant in 1978. As Fauchon's in Paris does, Dallmayr (15 Dienerstrasse) has a vast section of imported foods. Its most notable feature, however, is the enormous array it offers of West Germany's finest lunch meats, 22 varieties of smoked fish, and 27 types of bread.

Nearly everything edible can be found at Dallmayr's: local and imported fruits, cooked meats and poultry, live fish swimming in marble tanks, wines, more than 50 different salads, 200 different chocolates, 120 different sausages, 18 types of ham, and they also sell special cigars.

If you eat none of the splendid food there, at least see the statues, marble pillars and mounted deer heads that decorate the interior of the store. Another famous food emporium is Kafer's, at 73 Prinzregenten, Germany's largest delicatessen and caterer. Both stores have an excellent restaurant.

The Viktualienmarkt, behind St. Peter's Church, is one of Europe's largest outdoor food markets. Two blocks long, it has operated since 18:07: fruits, vegetables, poultry, cheeses, herbs, breads, pastries, wines, plants and flowers. It is open Monday–Friday 07:00–18:30, Saturday 07:00–17:00. Friday and Saturday are its busiest days. It is closed on Sundays.

The Most practical way to visit Neuschwanstein and Linderhof Castles is by taking the train-and-bus excursion operated by EurAide on Wednesday and Saturday during June, July and early August. Passsengers depart Munich at 07:35, returning there 17:30. For information and advisable advance reservations, write to EurAide, Bahnhofplatz 2, Am Gleissll, 80335 Munchen 2, Germnany. Telephone: (089) 59-38-89

**In the following timetables, where a city has more than one railstation we have desig-
nated the particular station after the name of the city (in parentheses).** Where no station is
designated for cities in Austria, Switzerland and Germany, the station is "Hauptbahnhoff."

Reservations are advisable on most German trains!

Berlin - Chemnitz (formerly Karl Marx Stadt) - Berlin   680

All of these trains have light refreshments. Reservation is advisable for them.

Dep. Berlin (Lichtenberg)	07:24	11:24
Dep. Berlin (Schonefeld) ·	07:43	11:43
Arr. Chemnitz	09:51	13:51

Sights in **Chemnitz:** This was an East German post-World War II showplace new city before
the 1990 unification of West and East Germany.

Dep. Chemnitz	14:17	16:17	18:17
Arr. Berlin (Schonefeld)	16:24	18:24	20:24
Arr. Berlin (Lichtenberg)	23 minutes later		

Berlin - Dresden - Berlin   680

*All of these trains charge a supplement that includes reservation fee and have a restaurant
car, unless designated otherwise.*

Dep. Berlin (Hbf.)	06:24	08:24	10:24	12:24
Arr. Dresden (Hbf.)	08:12	10:06	12:06	14:06
Dep. Dresden (Hbf.)	13:36	15:36	17:36	19:36	21:36
Arr. Berlin (Hbf.)	15:15	17:15	19:15	21:15	23:15

Berlin - Erfurt - Berlin   670

*Reservation is advisable for all of these trains. All of them have light refreshments, unless des-
ignated otherwise.*

Dep. Berlin (Lichtenberg)	06:18	08:18	10:18
Dep. Berlin (Schonefeld)	20 minutes after departing Lichtenberg railstation		
Arr. Erfurt	10:01	12:03	14:01

Sights in **Erfurt:** The exquisite Gothic and German Renaissance houses. The Cathedral, where Martin Luther was ordained in 1507. The bridge, on which 33 houses stand. St. Severin Church.

Dep. Erfurt	13:48	15:48	17:48	19:48
Arr. Berlin (Schonefeld)	17:06	19:06	21:06	23:06
Arr. Berlin (Lichtenberg)	20 minutes later			

Berlin - Frankfurt   750

All of these trains charge a supplement that includes reservation fee and have a restaurant car.

Dep. Berlin (Zoo)	05:48	07:48	09:48	11:48	13:48	15:48 (1)
Arr. Frankfurt (Hbf.)	10:39	12:39	14:39	16:39	18:39	20:39

Dep. Frankfurt (Hbf.)	07:18	09:18	11:18	13:18	15:18	17:18 (2)
Arr. Berlin (Zoo)	12:15	14:15	16:15	18:15	20:15	22:15

(1) Plus another Berlin departure at 17:48, arriving Frankfurt 22:41. (2) Plus another Frankfurt departure at 19:18, arriving Berlin 00:15.

Berlin - Hamburg   680

All of these trains charge a supplement that includes reservation fee and have a restaurant car.

Dep. Berlin (Hbf.)	05:40	07:40	09:40	11:40	13:40	15:40 (1)
Dep. Berlin (Zoo)	06:00	08:00	10:00	12:00	14:00	16:00
Arr. Hamburg (Hbf.)	08:59	10:59	12:59	14:59	16:59	18:59

Dep. Hamburg (Hbf.)	06:51	08:51	10:51	12:51	14:51	16:51 (2)
Arr. Berlin (Zoo)	09:45	11:45	13:45	15:45	17:45	19:45
Arr. Berlin (Hbf.)	10:04	12:04	14:04	16:04	18:04	20:04

(1) Plus other Berlin (Hbf.) departures at 17:40 and 19:40, arriving Hamburg 20:59 and 22:59. (2) Plus other Hamburg departures at 18:51 and 20:51, arriving Berlin (Hbf.) 22:08 and 00:04.

Berlin - Hannover   700

All of these trains charge a supplement that includes reservation fee and have a restaurant car, unless designated otherwise.

Dep. Berlin (Hbf.)	-0-	-0-	-0-
Dep. Berlin (Zoo)	07:23	09:07	11:07
Arr. Hannover	10:54	11:54	13:54

Dep. Hannover	16:04	18:04	19:04	20:04
Arr. Berlin (Zoo)	19:11	21:11	22:33	23:11
Arr. Berlin (Hbf.)	-0-	-0 -	-0-	-0-

Berlin - Leipzig - Berlin   670

Dep. Berlin (Licht.)	06:12 (1)	09:36
Dep. Berlin (Hbf.)	-0-	-0-
Arr. Leipzig	08:25	11:45

Dep. Leipzig	14:40 (2)	16:40 (2)
Arr. Berlin (Hbf.)	16:49	18:49
Arr. Berlin (Licht.)	-0-	-0-

(1) Reservation advisable. Light refreshments. (2) Supplement charged includes reservation fee. Restaurant car.

Berlin - Munich and Munich - Berlin   670

All of the day trains charge a supplement that includes reservation fee and have a restaurant car.

Dep. Berlin (Hbf.)	07:06	09:06	11:06	13:06	15:06
Arr. Munich	15:03	17:06	19:03	21:03	23:03

Dep. Munich	06:56	08:56	10:56	12:56	14:56
Arr. Berlin (Hbf.)	14:49	16:49	18:49	20:49	22:49

Berlin - Potsdam - Berlin 700

There are frequent trains from Berlin's Hauptbahnhoff and Zoo stations 05:57 to 23:12 for this 50-minute ride. From Potsdam: 06:13 to 22:09. Reservations are advisable.

Sights in **Potsdam:** The Concert Room and the great paintings in the Picture Gallery at the 18th century Sans Souci Palace. The 17th century Palace, Cecillienhof, where Truman, Attlee and Stalin signed the Potsdam Agreement in 1945.

Berlin - Rostock - Berlin 669

Reservation is advisable for all of these trains.

Dep. Berlin (Lichtenberg)	06:51 (1)	08:51 (2)	10:51	12:51 (1)	
Arr. Rostock	09:25	11:25	13:25	15:25	

Sights in **Rostock:** East Germany's largest seaport. See St. Mary's Church. The ancient Town Hall.

Dep. Rostock	12:32 (1)	14:32 (1)	16:32	18:32	20:32 (1)
Arr. Berlin (Lichtenberg)	15:07	17:07	19:07	21:07	23:07

(1) Light refreshments.

Berlin - Stralsund - Berlin 669

Dep. Berlin (Licht.)	06:51 (1)	08:51 (2)	09:20 (5)
Arr. Stralsund (Hbf.)	10:18	12:22	12:122

Sights in **Stralsund:** Many old red-brick buildings and churches along the city's quaint Hanseatic streets.

Dep. Stralsund (Hbf.)	14:27 (3)	16:16 (3)	17:08	18:14 (3)
Arr. Berlin (Licht.)	17:07	19:07	20:11	21:07

(1) Reservation is advisable. Light refreshments. Change trains in Neustrelitz. (2) Change trains in Neubrandenburg. (3) Change trains in Neustrelitz. (4) Plus another Stralsund departure at 19:01 (5), arriving Berlin 21:40 (5). (5) Direct train. No train change.

Berlin - Warnemunde - Berlin   669

Reservation is advisable for all of these trains.

Dep. Berlin (Licht.)	00:09 (1)	06:51 (2)	08:51 (3)	12:51 (4)
Arr. Warnemunde	03:10	09:56	11:45	15:56

Sights in **Warnemunde:** A famous beach resort. A ferry connection to Denmark.

Dep. Warnemunde	04:08 (1)	12:01	15:50 (3)	18:01 (2)
Arr. Berlin (Licht.)	07:04	15:07	19:07	21:07

(1) Carries a sleeping car. Also has couchettes. Coach is second-class. Light refreshments. (2) Light refreshments. (3) Operates late June to mid-August.

Cologne - Aachen - Cologne   700

Dep. Cologne	07:14 (1)	08:14 (2)	09:14 (2)	10:50	11:14 (1)
Arr. Aachen	08:02	08:58	09:58	11:45	12:02

Dep. Aachen	12:53 (1)	14:04 (2)	14:12	15:53 (1)	17:12	17:51 (1+3)
Arr. Cologne	13:42	14:42	15:09	16:42	18:09	18:42

(1) Light refreshments. (2) Supplement charged includes reservation fee. Restaurant car. (3) Plus other Aachen departures at 18:12, 18:56 (2), 19:12, 19:58 (2), 21:12 (2), 21:35 (1), 21:55 (2) and 22:04.

Cologne - Amsterdam - Cologne   28

All of these trains charge a supplement that includes reservation fee and have light refreshments.

Dep. Cologne	07:17	09:17	11:17	
Arr. Amsterdam	09:54	11:51	13:51	

Dep. Amsterdam	15:06	17:00	19:06	20:05	20:56 (1)
Arr. Cologne	17:42	19:42	21:42	23:47	00:22

(1) Coach is second-class.

Cologne - Bonn - Cologne 650 + 710

Dep. Cologne	Frequent times from 05:54 to 00:49
Arr. Bonn	22 minutes later

Sights in **Bonn:** Beethoven-Halle and the museum at Bonngasse 20, where Beethoven was born in 1770. Drachenfels Mountain and the castle ruins that Byron immortalized. The 13th century Remigius Church. Jesu Church. The view of the Rhine and Siebengebirge from Alte Zoll. The university in the Electors' Castle. Poppelsdorf Castle. The Rhineland Museum. The Collegiate Church and Cloister. Take a cruise boat on the Rhine River to see the Siebengebirge Mountains.

Dep. Bonn	Frequent times from 04:25 to 23:47
Arr. Cologne	22 minutes later

Cologne - Brussels - Cologne 200

Dep. Cologne	05:08 (1)	06:30 (2)	07:14	09:14 (2)
Arr. Brussels (Nord)	07:55	08:47	09:44	11:32
Arr. Brussels (Cen.)	-0-	-0-	09:49	11:36
Arr. Brussels (Midi)	08:06	09:01	09:59	11:42
Dep. Brussels (Midi)	12:03 (2)	13:47	15:47	16:55 (2)	18:08 (2+3)
Dep. Brussels (Cen.)	-0-	13:52	15:52	-0-	18:12
Dep. Brussels (Nord)	12:12	13:57	15:57	17:03	18:18
Arr. Cologne	14:42	16:42	18:42	19:42	20:42

(1) Coaches are second-class. (2) Supplement charged includes reservation fee. Restaurant car or light refreshments. (3) Plus other departures from Brussels Midi/Zuid at 18:47,20:03 (2), arriving Cologne 21:39.

Cologne - Dortmund - Cologne 650 + 700

Dep. Cologne	Frequent times from 05:03 to 23:16
Arr. Dortmund	70 minutes later

Sights in **Dortmund:** The view of the city from the top of the Television Tower. Westphalia Park. The Ostwall Museum.

Dep. Dortmund	Frequent times from 04:32 to 22:42
Arr. Cologne	70 minutes later

Cologne - Dusseldorf - Cologne   650 + 700

There is frequent rail service between Dusseldorf's railstation and its airport. Travel time is 12 minutes (Table 699).

Dep. Cologne	Frequent times from 05:03 to 26:16
Arr. Dusseldorf	24–28 minutes later

Sights in **Dusseldorf:** Many sensational modern buildings, replacing the 85 of the city that was destroyed in World War II. See the Paul Klee collection at Kunsttammlung Nordhein-Westfallen. The Aquarium at the Museumbunker am Zoo.

The collection of 18th century Meissenware and 20th century art (Kadinsky, Chagall, Braque, etc., with 90 works by Paul Klee) at the 18th century Jagerhof Castle in the 30-acre Hofgarten (park), open daily except Monday 10:00–17:00 (until 20:00 on Wednesday).

The large collection of Goethe memorabilia (30,000 items: first editions, paintings, manuscripts) at the Goethe Museum, also in Hofgarten, open daily except Monday 10:00–17:00. An enormous collection of paintings in the Kunstmuseum.

The more than 4,000 manuscripts in the Heinrich Heine Institute, Bilkerstrasse 14, open daily except Monday 10:00–17:00. Near Altstadt ("Old Town"), stroll the half-mile long shopping street, Konigsallee (called "the Ko").

Take the 75-minute boat trip on the Rhine to Zons. Boats leave every 60 minutes 13:30–17:30 from the Rathausufer, at the edge of Old Town.

Take the 30-minute tram ride (#1 and #18, from Jan-Welem-Platz) to the 18th century Benrath Castle, surrounded by spectacular English-style and French- style gardens.

Sample the 8 local beers in Old Town and try the local food specialties: reibekuchen, a potato pancake; halve hahn, a caraway cheese eaten with mustard on roggelchen, small loaves of rye bread; spanferkel brotchen, slices of roast suckling pig served on a roll; bratwurst with hot mustard; and blutwurst, a black pudding served with raw onions.

Dep. Dusseldorf	Frequent times from 05:17 to 23:56
Arr. Cologne	24–28 minutes later

Cologne - Frankfurt - Cologne   650

All of these trains have a restaurant car or light refreshments.

Dep. Cologne	Frequent times from 05:54 to 21:25
Arr. Frankfurt	2–2½ hours later
Dep. Frankfurt	Frequent times from 06:50 to 21:49
Arr. Cologne	2–2½ hours later

Cologne - Hamburg - Cologne 650

All of these trains charge a supplement that includes reservation fee and have a restaurant car, unless designated otherwise.

Dep. Cologne	06:26	07:09	08:09	09:09	10:10	11:10 (1)
Arr. Hamburg (Hbf.)	10:11	11:11	12:11	13:11	14:24	15:11

Dep. Cologne	12:33	13:10	14:09	15:10	16:10	17:09 (4)
Arr. Hamburg (Hbf.)	16:11	17:24	18:11	19:11	20:11	21:24

Dep. Hamburg (Hbf.)	03:12 (2)	04:47	05:47	06:47 (1)	07:47	08:47
Arr. Cologne	07:57	08:50	09:50	10:50	11:50	12:50

Dep. Hamburg (Hbf.)	09:47	10:47	11:47	12:47	13:47 (1)	14:47 (1+5)
Arr. Cologne	13:50	14:50	15:50	16:50	17:50	18:50

(1) Light refreshments. (2) Reservation advisable. Light refreshments. (3) Runs daily, except Saturday. (4) Plus other Cologne departures at 18:09, 19:09, 20:10 and 22:00 (1). (5) Plus other Hamburg departures at 15:47, 16:47, 17:57 (3), 18:47 and 19:47.

Cologne - Heidelberg - Cologne 730

Reservation is advisable for all of these trains, and they have light refreshments.

Dep. Cologne	07:11	09:11
Arr. Heidelberg	09:59	11:57

Sights in **Heidelberg:** Take a short cable-car ride from the town center to see the gardens, Library, Great Terrace, Fat Tower, Elizabeth Gate, Freidrich's Wing, the Otto-Heinrich Wing, the Mirror Room Wing, the 10-room German Pharmaceutical Museum and the Great Vat (said to be the world's largest wine barrel, holding 55,000 gallons), all at Heidelberg Castle.

Visit Germany's oldest (13th century) university, immortalized in "The Student Prince" opera. The astounding 16th century carved wood Altar of the Twelve Apostles in the Kurpfalzisches Museum. The Jesuit Church. The Church of the Holy Ghost, where visitors often hear impromptu organ concerts.The 16th century wood-carved Windsheim Altar (Christ and the Twelve Apostles) plus many rooms furnished with period pieces and paintings in the Palatine Museum at the Palais Morass. Knight's Mansion. Student's Jail.

From Easter into October, there are boat trips on the **Neckar River** that begin each morning and afternoon, with views of many medieval villages and fortresses. It is only a 20-minute bus ride to **Neckargemund**, where you can wander ancient cobbled streets and see the view of the river and the countryside from Zum Ritter, a restaurant operating since 1579.

| Dep. Heidelberg | 13:58 | 17:58 |
| Arr. Cologne | 16:45 | 20:45 |

Cologne - Koblenz - Cologne 650

Most of these trains charge a supplement that includes reservation fee and have a restaurant car.

| Dep. Cologne | Frequent times from 05:54 to 00:49 |
| Arr. Koblenz | 60 minutes later |

Sights in **Koblenz:** Where the Rhine and Moselle rivers meet. See Old Town. St. Castor's Church. The Middle Rhine Museum. Stolzenfels Castle. The 18th century Prince Electors' Palace. The regional and Rhenish museums in the 19th century Ehrenbreitstein Fortress. The wine village.

The 13th century Old Castle. The 18th century Mint Master's House. The 18th century Baroque Franconian Royal Palace. The 13th century Romanesque Church of Our Lady. The 15th century Altes Kaufhaus. The 16th century Schoffenhaus.

The very scenic 4½-hour Koblenz–Cochem boat trip on the Mosel Rivel is covered by Eurailpass. Views include hillside vineyards and quaint "wine villages." There is a magnificent castle in Cochem.

A popular detour is to get off the boat before it arrives in Cochem—at Moselkern—and walk 45 minutes through the forest to Burg Eltz, one of Europe's loveliest castles. Then take a train from Moselkern to Cochem, and return to Koblenz from Cochem either by boat or by a 45 minute train ride.

| Dep. Koblenz | Frequent times from 03:50 to 23:15 |
| Arr. Cologne | 60 minutes later |

Cologne - Luxembourg - Cologne 720

Reservation is advisable for these trains, unless designated otherwise.

| Dep. Cologne | 06:11 | 08:11 (1) | 10:11 |
| Arr. Luxembourg | 09:23 | 11:27 | 13:23 |

| Dep.Luxembourg | 12:30 (1) | 14:33 | 18:26 (1) |
| Arr. Cologne | 15:45 | 17:45 | 21:45 |

(1) Change trains in Trier.

Cologne - Mainz - Cologne   Boat   714

Here is a way to combine a cruise on the Rhine with a scenic rail trip.

Have lunch and Rhine wine on board the 09:00 boat just before arriving Mainz. Early in the trip, you can see Drachenfels Castle, near Bonn. During the Koblenz–Bingen portion of this cruise, you will see the best scenery on the Rhine, many hilltop castles, and the Lorelei.

Dep. Cologne (Rheingarten)	09:00 (1)	14:15
Dep. Bonn	09:40	14:55
Dep. Koblenz	11:05	11:00 (2)
Dep. Bingen	12:28	16:20
Arr. Mainz	13:10	18:45

(1) Hydrofoil boat express service. *Not* covered by Eurailpass. Supplement charged. Operates mid-April to late October. Runs daily, except Monday. (2) Operates May 1 to June 30 and September 1 to early October. Runs daily.

Sights in **Mainz:** The art collection in the 1,000-year-old Cathedral. Adjacent to it is the Gutenberg Museum, with the first printed bible and where a movie on the inventor's life can be viewed. Also visit the Museum of the Central Rhineland. Rare books in the World Museum of Printing in the Romischer Kaiser. Restored Baroque mansions on the Schillerplatz and Schillerstrasse, in the Kirschgarten. Old Town. Sculptures in the Diocesan Museum.

Then for the train ride back to Cologne:
All of these trains charge a supplement that includes reservation fee and have a restaurant car.

650

Dep. Mainz	14:18	19:48(1)	21:24	22:24
Arr. Koblenz	15:05	20:35	22:05	23:13
Arr. Bonn	15:37	21:07	22:37	23:45
Arr. Cologne	15:59	21:29	22:59	00:07

(1) Daily except Saturday.

Here is the schedule for visiting Mainz by taking the train both ways:

650

Dep. Cologne	Frequent times from 05:54 to 21:00
Arr. Mainz	2 hours later

• • •

Dep, Mainz	Frequent times from 06:36 to 20:37
Arr. Cologne	2 hours later

Cologne - Mannheim - Cologne   650

All of these trains charge a supplement that includes reservation fee and have a restaurant car, unless designated otherwise.

Dep. Cologne	06:30	07:00	07:30	08:00	08:30 (1)
Arr. Mannheim	08:53	09:22	09:52	10:22	10:53

(1) Plus other frequent departures from Cologne at 09:00 to 21:00.

Sights in **Mannheim:** The Squared Town. The first thing that strikes you about Mannheim is its "Squareness." Built to be a fortified town, it was designed as a chessboard of 144 residential blocks, each known by a letter and number that identifies its position on the grid.

See the Fine Arts Museum. The Reiss Municipal Museum. The Cathedral, Europe's largest Romanesque Church. The Water Tower. The old Town Hall and parish church in the Marketplatz. The Castle.

Dep. Mannheim	Frequent departures from 06:36 to 20:37.
Arr. Cologne	2½ hours later

Cologne - Siegen - Cologne   709

Dep. Cologne	Every hour 07:10-22:19
Arr. Siegen	1½ hours later

Sights in **Siegen:** The Upper Castle, with its Reubens paintings (he was born here) in the Siegerland Museum, which also offers the history of this region and a tour of the old iron mine under the Castle's cellar. See the crypts of the Princes of Nassau-Orange in the Castle.

Dep. Siegen	Every hour 08:10-21:10
Arr. Cologne	1½ hours later

Cologne - Trier - Cologne   720

Dep. Cologne	06:11	08:11	10:11	Dep. Trier	15:17	17:17
Arr. Trier	08:38	10:38	12:38	Arr. Cologne	17:45	19:45

Dresden - Berlin - Dresden   680

All of these trains charge a supplement that includes reservation fee and have a restaurant car, unless designated otherwise.

Dep. Dresden (Hbf.)	07:36	09:36	11:36		
Arr. Berlin (Hbf)	09:15	11:15	13:15		

Dep. Berlin (Hbf.)	12:24	14:24	16:24	18:24	20:24
Arr. Dresden (Hbf.)	14:06	16:06	18:06	20:06	22:06

(1) Reservation advisable. Light refreshments.

Dresden - Chemnitz (formerly Karl Marx Stadt) - Dresden   780

Reservation is advisable for all of these trains, unless designated otherwise.

Dep. Dresden (Hbf.)	07:52 (1)	09:52 (1)	10:40 (2)	11:52 (1)	12:40 (4)
Arr. Chemnitz	09:03	11:03	12:03	13:05	14:03

Sights in **Chemnitz**: An East German post-World War II showplace *new* city.

Dep. Chemnitz	11:53 (2)	12:58 (1)	13:53 (2)	14:58 (1)	15:53 (2+3)
Arr. Dresden (Hbf.)	13:07	14:06	15:07	16:06	17:29

(1) Light refreshments. (2) Reservation not available. (3) Plus other Chemnitz departures at 16:59 (1), 18:58 (1), 19:53 (2), 20:26 (1) and 21:53 (2), arriving Dresden 18:07, 20:06, 21:07, 21:34 and 23:07. (4) Runs daily except Sundays & holidays.

Dresden - Leipzig - Dresden   674

Dep. Dresden (Hbf.)	07:11 (1) 10:11 (2)				
Dep. Dresden (Neu.)	8 minutes after departing Hauptbahnhof.				
Arr. Leipzig	08:45 11:45				

Dep. Leipzig	13:07 (2)	14:01 (2)	17:07 (2)	18:01 (2)	21:07 (1)
Arr. Dresden (Neu.)	14:40	15:30	18:34	19:33	22:34
Arr. Dresden (Hbf.)	8 minutes later				

(1) Reservation advisable. Restaurant car. (2) Reservation advisable. Light refreshments.

Frankfurt - Basel - Frankfurt   730

All of these trains charge a supplement that includes a reservation fee and have a restaurant car, unless designated otherwise.

Dep. Frankfurt (Hbf.)	05:40 (1)	07:43	08:43	09:43	10:09 (1)
Arr. Mannheim	-0- (1)	08:24	09:24	10:24	-0- (1)
Change trains.					
Dep. Manheim	-0-	08:31	09:31	10:31 (1)	-0-
Arr. Basel (Badisch.)	08:34	10:36	11:35	12:35	13:01
Arr. Basel (S.B.B.)	7 minutes later				
Dep. Basel (S.B.B.)	14:17	15:17	16:17	17:17	18:17 (2)
Dep. Basel (Badisch.)	7 minutes later				
Arr. Mannheim	16:27	17:27	18:27	19:27	20:27
Change trains.					
Dep. Mannheim	16:35	17:35	18:35	19:35	20:35
Arr. Frankfurt	17:14	18:14	19:14	20:14	21:14

(1) Direct train. No train change in Mannheim. (2) Plus other departures from Basel at 19:17 and 20:20, arriving Frankfurt 22:15 and 23:15.

Frankfurt - Bremen - Frankfurt

All of these trains charge a supplement that includes a reservtion fee, unless designated otherwise. Unless designated otherwise, the Frankfurt–Hannover (and v.v.) trains have a restaurant car — and the Hannover–Bremen and (v.v.) trains have light refreshments.

750

Dep. Frankfurt	06:17	08:18	08:51	10:18
Arr. Hannover	08:38	10:38	11:06	12:38
Change trains. 652				
Dep. Hannover	09:43	11:43 (1)	12:17 (1)	13:43
Arr. Bremen	10:48	12:48	13:37	14:48

Sights in **Bremen:** It is an easy walk, down Bahnhofstrasse, from the railstation to the fine buildings in Market Square. Starting there at the 18-foot-high statue of Roland (Sculpted in 1404), following the white dots on the sidewalk will lead you to most of the city's important places. The statue faces the 11th century St. Peter's Cathedral, open daily to tourists, except Saturday afternoon and Sunday morning.

Close by the Cathedral, the 17th century City Hall offers free guided morning tours daily, except Sunday. The interesting features in its upstairs hall are the oak-beamed ceiling, portraits of Holy Roman emperors from Charlemagne to Sigismund, and ship models. Also see the exceptional woodcarving in its Golden Chamber.

The largest rathskeller in Europe, serving only German wine (500,000 bottles a year), located under the City Hall, has been a tavern, restaurant and wine cellar for over 500 years. More than 800 people can be seated there. Very crowded at noon, it offers a choice of more than 500 wine varieties and vintages from Germany's 11 main wine areas. Its bottles and casks include vintages from as far back as 16:53.

Behind the City Hall is the 13th century Liebfrauenkirche (Church of Our Lady), whose 7 new stained glass windows were installed in 1966. It is open daily, but closed 12:30–14:00.

Walk from Market Square down Bottcherstrasse to see the Porcelain Carillon and Atlantic House, decorated with Zodiac signs.

The Ubersee (Overseas) Museum, across from the railstation at 13 Bahnofplatz, has exhibits of ethnology, world trade and natural history, gathered in the Middle Ages by Bremen ships. It is open daily, except Monday 10:00–18:00.

Visit the Focke Museum of Folklore and the Municipal Weights and Measures Office. See the old workshops, inns and houses in the Schnoor residential area.

Near Martini Church, 90-minute boat tours of Europe's third largest port depart 5 times a day in summer, at the river end of Bottcherstrasse.

In Bremerhaven, 36 miles away where the Weser River meets the North Sea, there is a maritime museum called Schiffahrts on Van Ronzelenstrasse. It is open daily, except Monday.

Dep. Bremen	13:10 (1)	14:21 (1)	15:10	16:21	17:10 (2)
Arr. Hannover	14:16	15:41	16:16	17:41	18:16
Change trains. 750					
Dep. Hannover	14:51	15:51	16:51	17:51	19:20
Arr. Frankfurt	17:06	18:06	19:06	20:06	21:39

(1) No supplement. (2) Plus another Bremen departure at 19:10, arriving Frankfurt 23:41.

Frankfurt - Brussels - Frankfurt 33

Dep. Frankfurt	06:50 (1)	08:50 (2)	Dep. Brussels (Midi)	15:47	16:55 (1+4)
Arr. Cologne	09:05	11:05	Arr. Cologne	18:42	19:42
Change trains.			*Change trains.*		
Dep. Cologne	09:14 (1)	11:14	Dep. Cologne	18:54 (3)	19:54 (1)
Arr. Brussels (Midi)	11:42	13:55	Arr. Frankfurt	21:08	22:08

(1) Supplement includes a reservation fee. Restaurant car. (2) Supplement includes reservation fee. (3) Supplement includes reservation fee. (4) Plus another Brussels departure at 18:08 (1), arriving Frankfurt 23:08.

Frankfurt - Cologne - Frankfurt   650

From Mainz to Bonn, the cliffs on both sides of the Rhine are topped by ruins of ancient castles. This portion of the river is crowded with barges, sailboats, recreational motorboats, ferries and cruise ships.

All of these trains charge a supplement that includes a reservation fee and have a restaurant car, unless designated otherwise.

Dep. Frankfurt	06:50	07:49	08:50	09:49	10:49		
Dep. Mainz	07:24	08:24	09:24	10:24	11:24		
Dep. Bonn	08:45	09:45	10:45	11:45	12:45		
Arr. Cologne	09:05	10:05	11:05	12:05	13:05		
Dep. Cologne	12:54	13:54	14:54	15:54	16:54	17:54	18:54 (2)
Dep. Bonn	13:14	14:14	15:14	16:14	17:14	18:14	19:14
Dep. Mainz	14:38	15:38	16:38	17:38	18:38	19:38	20:38
Arr. Frankfurt	15:08	16:08	17:08	18:08	19:08	20:08	21:08

(1) No supplement. Light refreshments. (2) Plus other departures from Cologne at 19:54, 20:37 (1), 20:54 and 21:33, arriving Frankfurt 22:08, 23:07, 23:08 and 23:30.

Frankfurt - Dusseldorf - Frankfurt   650

All of these trains charge a supplement that includes a reservation fee and have a restaurant car, unless designated otherwise.

Dep. Frankfurt	06:50	09:49 (1)			
Arr. Dusseldorf	09:31	12:31			
Dep. Dusseldorf	13:28	15:28	18:28 (1)	19:21 (2)	20:05 (3+5)
Arr. Frankfurt	16:08	18:08	21:08	22:08	23:07

(1) Light refreshments. (2) Light refreshments. Change trains in Cologne. (3) No supplement charged. Light refreshments. (4) Runs daily except Saturdays. Change trains in Cologne. No supplement charged. Light refreshments. (5) Plus another Dusseldorf departure at 20:56 (4), arriving Frankfurt 23:54.

Frankfurt - Essen - Frankfurt   650

All of these trains charge a supplement that includes a reservation fee and have a restaurant car, unless designated otherwise.

Dep. Frankfurt	06:50	07:49 (1)	10:04 (2)
Arr. Essen	09:57	11:22	12:59

Sights in **Essen**: One of the leading German collections of 18th, 19th and 20th century art (Menzel, Delacroix, Renoir, Gaugin, Vlaminck, Kandinsky, Klee, Rothko, Rodin) at the Folkwang Museum. The 10th century Cathedral and its collection of priceless 10th and 11th century processional crosses, the 9th century Golden Madonna (oldest Western statue of the Virgin Mary), and the sword of Cosmas and Damian, the martyr saints.

The chronicle of the Krupp family and business in the Annex at Villa Hugel, former residence of the Krupp family. The 12th century castle, Burg Altendorf. The Four Horsemen bronze door on the 11th century Marktkirche, Protestant since 1563.

Dep. Essen	15:01	15:35 (1)	16:35 (1)	18:01	19:31 (2)
Arr. Frankfurt	18:08	19:08	20:08	21:08	23:07

(1) Change trains in Cologne. (2) No supplement. Light refreshments.

Frankfurt - Hamburg - Frankfurt   750

All of these trains charge a supplement that includes a reservation fee and have a restaurant car, unless designated otherwise.

Dep. Frankfurt (Hbf)	06·17	07:51	08:18	09:50	
Arr. Hamburg (Hbf.)	09:56	11:21	11:56	13:21	
Dep. Hamburg (Hbf.)	14:37	15:37	16:02	18:02	20:02 (2)
Arr. Frankfurt (Hbf.)	18:06	19:06	19:39	21:39	23:41

(1) Runs daily, except Sunday. (2) Runs daily, except Saturday.

Frankfurt - Hannover - Frankfurt   750

All of these trains charge a supplement that includes a reservation fee and have a restaurant car, unless designated otherwise.

Dep. Frankfurt	06:17	07:51	08:18	08:51	09:50	10:18
Dep. Hannover	08:38	10:06	10:38	11:06	12:06	12:38
Dep. Hannover	14:51	15:20	15:51	16:51	17:20	17:51 (2)
Arr. Frankfurt	17:06	17:39	18:06	19:06	19:39	20:06

(1) Runs daily, except Saturday. (2) Plus other Hannover departures at 18:51 (1), 19:20 and 21:23 (1), arriving Frankfurt 21:02, 21:39 and 23:41.

Frankfurt - Heidelberg - Frankfurt   730

Reservation is advisable for all of these trains, and they have light refreshments.

Dep. Frankfurt	Every 2 hours from 07:47 to 21:47
Arr. Heidelberg	One hour later
Dep. Heidelberg	Every 2 hours from 07:16 to 21:16 + 23:10
Arr. Frankfurt	One hour later

Frankfurt - Kassel - Frankfurt   750

All of these trains charge a supplement that includes a reservation fee and have a restaurant car.

Dep. Frankfurt (Hbf.)	Every hour from 06:18 to 21:18
Arr. Kassel (Wil.)	1½ hours later

Sights in **Kassel**: Take the bus #13 to see the enormous 233-foot high copper statue of Hercules, the 19th century Wilhelmshohe Castle, and the art museums (Rembrandt, Durer, Rubens) inside the Castle. Open daily except Monday, March–October, 10:00–17:00. Also see the collection of Brothers Grimm memorabilia in the City Museum. They wrote their fairy tales here. Other interesting sights are the 18th century Orangery Palace in Karlsaue Park. The paintings in the Landesmuseum. The Tapestry Museum. The Fredericianum Museum. The world's only Wallpaper Museum.

Dep. Kassel (Wil.)	Every hour from 06:15 to 22:15
Arr. Frankfurt (Hbf.)	1½ hours later

(1) Runs daily, except Saturday. (2) Plus other departures from Kassel at 19:16 (1), 20:16, 21:16 and 22:36, arriving Frankfurt 20:42, 21:42, 22:42 and 00:08.

Frankfurt - Luxembourg - Frankfurt

All of the Frankfurt–Koblenz (and v.v.) trains charge a supplement that includes reservation fee. Reservation is advisable for the Koblenz-Luxemburg (and v.v.) trains, unless designated otherwise.

650			*720*		
Dep. Frankfurt	07:49 (1)	09:51 (2)	Dep. Luxembourg	14:33	17:19 (4+5)
Arr. Koblenz	09:11	11:11	Arr. Koblenz	16:38	19:42
Change trains. 720			*Change trains. 650*		
Dep. Koblenz	09:19 (3)	11:19	Dep. Koblenz	16:46 (1)	19:46 (1)
Arr. Luxembourg	11:27	13:23	Arr. Frankfurt	18:08	21:08

(1) Restaurant car. (2) Light refreshments. (3) Change trains in Trier (arr. 10:38—dep. 10:44). (4) Reservations not available. Runs daily, except Sundays and holidays. Change trains in Trier (arr. 18:06—dep. 18:21). (5) Plus another departure from Luxembourg at 18:26. Change trains in Trier at 19:10 and in Koblenz at 20:38, departing Kolbenz 20:47, arriving Frankfurt 22:08.

Frankfurt - Mainz - Frankfurt   650

All of these trains charge a supplement that includes a reservation fee and have a restaurant car or light refreshments.

Dep. Frankfurt	49 minutes past each hour from 06:49 to 23:47
Arr. Mainz	30 minutes later
Dep. Mainz	38 minutes past each hour from 06:38 to 22:38
Arr. Frankfurt	30 minutes later

Frankfurt - Mannheim - Frankfurt   730

All of these trains charge a supplement that includes reservation fee and have a restaurant car or light refreshments.

Dep. Frankfurt	Frequent times from 05:42 to 22:58.
Arr. Mannheim	40 minutes later
Dep. Mannheim	Frequent times from 05:08 to 22:35.
Arr. Frankfurt	40 minutes later

Frankfurt - Munich - Frankfurt   760

All of these trains charge a supplement that includes reservation fee and have a restaurant car.

Dep. Frankfurt	06:31 (1)	07:43	08:43	09:43			
Arr. Munich	09:42	11:17	12:17	13:17			

Dep. Munich	12:46	13:46	14:46	15:46	16:46	17:46 (2)	18:46 (3)
Arr. Frankfurt	16:14	17:14	18:14	19:14	20:14	21:14	22:15

(1) Runs Monday–Friday. (2) Runs daily, except Saturday. (3) Plus another Munich departure at 19:46 (2), arriving Frankfurt 23:15.

Frankfurt - Nurnberg (and Bayreuth) - Frankfurt   740

All of these trains charge a supplement that includes reservation fee and have a restaurant car or light refreshments.

Dep. Frankfurt	Every hour form 06:22 to 21:22
Arr. Nurnberg	2 hours and 20 minutes later

Sights in **Nurnberg**: The bronze and silver Sebaldusgrab, excellent stained glass and the carved tomb of the Saint for whom it is named in the 13th century St. Sebaldus Church. Take a guided tour of the Kaiserburg (Imperial Castle), Burggrafenburg and Imperial Stables in the fort. See the Albrecht Durer Haus, with copies of his paintings. The kitchen is as it was, when the artist lived there from 1509 to 1528. It is open daily except Monday 10:00–13:00 and 14:00–17:00. The Rosette window, wood carving and statues in St. Lorenz Kirche.

Visit the 14th century Frauenkirche in the marketplace, where the moving figures in the clock perform every day at 12:00. Then lunch at a bratwurst restaurant. One is located next to St. Sebaldus Church; another is behind the rebuilt 17th century Rathaus (City Hall). There are guided tours of 14th century catacombs (torture chamber and dungeons) in the Rathaus.

The Alstadt Museum. The collection of toys, doll houses and other works in the German National Museum. The 40 gold figures of artists, emperors, philosophers, prophets and popes around the 14th century Schoner Brunnen (Beautiful Fountain) at Hauptmarkt, where farmers sell their produce from stalls.

On the little island in the Pegnitz River is the Holy Ghost Hospital, locale of the legendary Till Eulenspiegel. Disguised as a doctor, this is where the 14th century peasant clown told the man in charge of the hospital that he could cure all the patients in one day. The hospital authorities believed Till was a miracle worker when the patients rose from their beds and left the hospital after he whispered in each one's ear. He told the patients: "Those of you who are the most sick are going to be burned into a powder the hospital will use to heal the others."

Visit the collection of porcelains and the model of Old Nurnberg at Fembo House (The City Historical Museum), 15 Burgstrasse, open daily except Monday 10:00–17:00. The best collection of old trains in West Germany (including Germany's first locomotive) is in Nurnberg's Transport Museum, open Monday-Saturday 10:00–17:00 (closes at 16:00 in Winter) and Sunday 10:00–13:00. Toys from all over the world are exhibited at Spielzeug Museum, open daily except Monday 10:00–17:00.

From Nurnberg, it's a short trip to Bayreuth, site of a 5-week annual (over 100 years) Wagner opera festival at Festspielhaus, every year from late July to late August at 16:00.

Marvelous sights in nearby **Bayreuth**: Haus Wahnfried, Wagner's home. The breathtaking opera house. The Orangerie castle, open daily 10:00–11:30 and 13:30–15:00. Eremitage Park.

Dep. Nurnberg	Every hour form 05:17 to 21:17
Arr. Frankfurt	2 hours and 20 minutes later

Here are the connections between Nurnberg and Bayreuth:
There is great river and canyon scenery on the Nurnberg-Pegnitz portion of this trip.

778

Dep. Nurnberg	49 minutes after each hour from 05:49 to 23:49	Dep. Bayreuth	10 minutes after each hour from 05:10 to 22:10
Dep. Pegnitz	40 minutes later	Arr. Pegnitz	18 minutes later
Arr. Bayreuth	16 minutes after Pegnitz	Arr. Nurnberg	1 hour after Bayreuth

Frankfurt - Siegen - Frankfurt   709

Dep. Frankfurt	08:55	09:55 (1+2)	Dep. Siegen	13:54	15:54 (3)
Arr. Giessen	08:35	10:35	Arr. Giessen	14:48	16:48
Change trains.			*Change trains.*		
Dep. Giessen	09:08	11:08	Dep. Giessen	15:21 (1)	17:21 (1)
Arr. Slegen	10:05	12:05	Arr. Frankfurt	16:01	18:01

(1) Light refreshments. (2) Plus another departures from Frankfurt at 11:55 (1), arriving Siegen 14:05. (3) Plus other departures from Siegen at 17:54 and 19:54, departing Giessen 19:21 (1) and 21:21 (1), arriving Frankfurt 20:01 and 22:01.

Frankfurt - Strasbourg - Frankfurt

730			*727*		
Dep. Frankfurt	07:47 (1)	11:47 (1)	Dep. Strasbourg	09:21	17:57 (3)
Arr. Offenburg	09:51	13:51	Arr. Offenburg	09:47	18:31
Change trains. 727			*Change trains. 730*		
Dep. Offenburg	11:31	17:31	Dep. Offenburg	16:06 (1)	18:06 (1)
Arr. Strasbourg	12:04	18:05	Arr. Frankfurt	18:09	20:09

(1) Reservation advisable. Light refreshments. (2) Plus other departures from Strasbourg at 21:44 (3), departing Offenburg 22:17 (1), arriving Frankfurt 24:15. (3) Change trains in Kehl.

Frankfurt - Stuttgart - Frankfurt   760

All of these trains charge a supplement that includes reservation fee and have a restaurant car.

Dep. Frankfurt	Every hour from 07:43 to 21:43
Arr. Stuttgart	One hour and 20 minutes later

Sights in **Stuttgart:** Outstanding contemporary architecture, built since World War II. The Schillerplatz flower and vegetable market (Tuesday, Thursday and Saturday). Also on Schillerplatz, Swabian art and culture from the Middle Ages to Art Nouveau, at the Wuerttemberg Provincial Museum in the Altes Schloss. Europe's most modern planetarium, opened in 1977.

The largest Picasso collection in Germany (among the 4,000 paintings from the 14th to 20th century), at the State Gallery, Konrad Adenauer Strasse 32. The Daimler-Benz Automobile Museum, admission only by advance appointment. The Museum of Natural History, in Rosenstein Palace.

Dep. Stuttgart	Every hour from 05:53 to 21:53
Arr. Frankfurt	One hour and 20 minutes later

Frankfurt - Wiesbaden   717

Dep. Frankfurt	Frequent times from 05:18 to 00:18
Arr. Wiesbaden	33-40 minutes later

Sights in **Wiesbaden:** One of Europe's top mineral bath resorts. See Brunnenkolonnade, the longest colonnade in Europe.

Dep. Wiesbaden	Frequent times from 07:07 to 00:07
Arr. Frankfurt	33-40 minutes later

Hamburg - Berlin - Hamburg   665

See "Berlin-Hamburg."

Hamburg - Bremen - Hamburg 650

All of these trains charge a supplement that includes reservation fee and have a restaurant car or light refreshments.

Dep. Hamburg (Alt.)	Every hour from 05:33 to 20:33
Dep. Hamburg (Hbf.)	14 minutes later
Arr. Bremen	70 minutes after departing Altona railstation.

Dep. Bremen	Every hour from 07:16 to 20:16
Arr. Hamburg (Hbf.)	55 minutes later
Arr. Hamburg (Alt.)	13 minutes after arriving Hauptbahnhof railstation.

Hamburg - Munich and Munich - Hamburg 750

Germany inroduced its 165-miles-per-hour air-conditioned luxury trains on this route in 1991. All of its coaches have phone service, and the seats are fitted with earphones that carry a choice of music. These trains charge a supplement that includes the reservation fee and have a restaurant car.

Dep. Hamburg (Hbf.)	07:05	10:02	11:07	12:02	13:07 (3)
Dep. Hannover	08:28	11:28	12:21	13:15	14:21
Dep. Kassel	09:23	12:23	13:23	14:23	15:23
Dep. Augsburg	12:17	15:33	16:33	17:33	18:33
Arr. Munich	12:49	16:05	17:05	18:05	19:05
Dep. Munich	07:21 (1)	09:21	09:54	10:54	11:21 (4)
Dep. Augsburg	07:44	09:26	10:26	11:26	12:26
Dep. Kasse	10:37	12:37	13:37	14:37	15:37
Dep. Hannover	11:37	13:37	14:43	15:37	16:43
Arr. Hamburg (Hbf.)	12:51	15:05	15:56	16:51	16:51

(1) Runs daily, except Saturday. (2) Runs daily, except Sunday. (3) Plus other Hamburg departures at 14:02, 15:07 and 17:07 (1). (4) Plus other Munich departures at 13:21, 13:54, 15:21, 17:12 and 17:54.

Hamburg - Lubeck - Hamburg 665

Dep. Hamburg (Hbf.)	Frequent times from 06:02 to 00:34
Arr. Lubeck	40 minutes later

Sights in **Lubeck**: All museums here are closed Monday. April–September, they are open other days 10:00–17:00, October–March 10:00–16:00. It is an easy walk from the railstation down Konrad Adenauer Strasse, over the Puppenbrucke bridge, and straight ahead to the museum of the city's history in Holstentor, the immense 15th century fort. Particularly interesting there is the model of the town as it was in 1650.

Nearby, just off Holstenstrasse, is the 15th century St. Peter's Church. There is a marvelous view of the city and its harbors from the top of the church's 165-foot-high tower. Also see the elegant chapel in the 14th century St. Mary's Church. Across the square from it is Buddenbrookshaus, at 4 Mengstrasse, where Thomas Mann was born. Although it is now a bank, some of the upstairs rooms can be visited during the hours the bank is open.

There are dozens of interesting alleys and little passageways here with lovely cottages, shops and restaurants. See the mansions on Grosse Petersgrube, Engelsgrube, Fischergrube and Mengstrasse. See the 19th and 20th century paintings, handicrafts and sculptures in the Bennhaus, a magnificent 18th century merchant's house. The city's main museum is in St. Anne's Convent.

Cruise boats that go around the city and harbor leave from the front of Hotel Jensen (Trave Landing) daily in Spring, Summer and Fall every half hour from 10:00 to 18:00.

Dep. Lubeck	Frequent times from 05:24 to 24:00
Arr. Hamburg (Hbf.)	40 minutes later

Hannover - Berlin - Hannover   700

All of these trains charge a supplement that includes reservation fee and have a restaurant car, unless designated otherwise.

Dep. Hannover	06:00 (1)	07:46 (2)	09:04		
Arr. Berlin (Zoo)	08:58	10:40	12:53		
Dep. Berlin (Zoo)	14:34	16:32	17:07	18:47 (2)	20:38 (1)
Arr. Hannover	17:54	19:54	20:54	21:54	23:54

(1) No supplement. No restaurant car. Light refreshments. (2) Runs daily, except Sunday.

Hannover - Bremen - Hannover   652

Dep. Hannover	07:43 (1)	08:17	09:43 (1)	10:17	11:43 (1)	12:17
Arr. Bremen	08:48	09:37	10:48	11:37	12:48	13:37
Dep. Bremen	13:10 (1)	14:21	15:10 (1)	16:21	17:10 (1)	18:21 (2)
Arr. Hannover	14:16	15:41	16:16	17:41	18:16	19:41

(1) Supplement charged which includes a reservation fee. Light refreshments. (2) Plus other departures from Bremen at 19:10 (1), 20:21, 21:10 (1), 22:21 and 23:17.

Hannover - Celle - Hannover 750

Reservation is advisable for most of these trains.

Dep. Hannover   Frequent times from 05:21 to 22:49
Arr. Celle   25 minutes later

Sights in **Celle:** The beautifully decorated chapel and wonderful French Garden at the 13th century Duke's Palace. The 14th century Marienkirche. The exhibit of the local life and farm culture in the Bomann Museum. The heavy wood-beamed ceilings and quality wood panelling in the 14th century Rathaus (Town Hall), oldest tavern in Northern Germany. The Lower Saxony stud farm, home of the famous Hannoverian horses.

The 480 half-timbered houses, some dating back to the 15th century, many with carved beams. The Apiary Museum at the Institute for Bee Research. The nearby Wienhausen Monastery. Regional food specialties are *heidschnuckenbraten* (roasted lamb), *meissendorfer spiegelkarpfen* (carp) and *burgdorfer spargel* (asparagus). There are steamer cruises on the **Aller River.**

Dep. Celle   Frequent times from 05:45 to 22:57
Arr. Hannover   25 minutes later

Hannover - Dortmund - Hannover 700

All of these trains charge a supplement that includes reservation fee and have a restaurant car.

Dep. Hannover	06:57	07:57	08:57	09:57	10:57	11:57	
Arr. Dortmund	08:33	09:33	10:33	11:33	12:33	13:33	
Dep. Dortmund	13:27	14:27	15:27	16:27	17:27	18:27	19:27 (1)
Arr. Hannover	15:03	16:03	17:03	18:03	19:03	20:03	21:03

(1) Plus other departures from Dortmund at 20:27 and 21:27.

Hannover - Dusseldorf - Hannover 700

Dep. Hannover	09:57 (2)	11:57	13:57	
Arr. Dusseldorf	12:23	14:28	16:28	
Dep. Dusseldorf	15:33 (2)	16:33 (1)	19:45 (1)	20:33 (2)
Arr. Hannover	18:03	19:03	22:25	23:06

(1) Reservation advisable. Light refreshments. (2) Supplement includes reservation fee. Restaurant car.

Hannover - Frankfurt - Hannover   750

All of these trains charge a supplement that includes reservation fee and have a restaurant car.

Dep. Hannover	07:20	08:51	09:20	09:51	10:51	11:20
Arr. Frankfurt	09:39	11:06	11:39	12:06	13:06	13:39

Dep. Frankfurt	13:51	14:18	14:51	15:51	16:18	16:51	17:51 (3)
Arr. Hannover	16:06	16:38	17:06	17:52	18:38	19:06	20:06

(1) Runs daily, except Sunday. (2) Runs daily, except Saturday. (3) Plus other departures from Frankfurt at 18:18, 18:51 (2), 20:18 and 21:18 (2), arriving Hanover 20:38, 21:06, 22:38 and 23:38.

Hannover - Goslar - Hannover   697

Dep. Hannover	06:33	07:33	08:33	09:33	10:18 (1)	11:33
Arr. Goslar	07:57	08:57	09:57	10:57	11:45	12:57

Sights in **Goslar**: The many 13th–16th century half-timbered buildings and 19th century houses. The Eagle Fountain. The five 13th century churches. The chandeliers of reindeer horns in the 15th century Town Hall. The 16th century towers and old city walls. The 11th century Imperial Palace. The museums of natural science and antiquities.

Goslar is a popular base for touring the Harz Mountains.

Dep. Goslar	12:00	13:00	14:00	14:24 (1)	16:00	17:00 (2)	18:24 (3+4)
Arr. Hannover	13:25	14:25	15:25	15:40	17:25	18:25	19:40

(1) Light refreshments. (2) Runs Monday–Friday, except holidays. (3) Reservation advisable. Light refreshments. (4) Plus other departures from Goslar at 19:00 and 21:00.

Hannover - Hamburg - Hannover   750

All of these trains charge a supplement that includes reservation fee and have a restaurant car, unless designated otherwise.

Dep. Hannover	06:49 (1)	07:37	08:03 (1)	08:43	09:37	10:07
Arr. Hamburg (Hbf.)	08:16	08:51	10:01	09:56	10:51	11:21

Dep. Hamburg (Hbf.)	14:23	15:23	16:23	17:23	18:02 (5)
Arr. Hannover	15:49	16:49	17:49	18:49	19:15

(1) No supplement. Reservation advisable. Light refreshments. (2) Runs daily, except Sunday. (3) Runs daily, except Saturday. (4) No Supplement. No restaurant car. Reservation advisable. (5) Plus other departures from Hamburg at 19:02, 19:42 (1), 20:02 (3) and 21:42 (4), arriving Hannover 20:21, 21:09, 21:51 and 23:19.

Hannover - Hameln - Hannover   702

Dep. Hannover   Every hour from 06:48 to 22:48
Arr. Hameln   47 minutes later

Sights in **Hameln:** Every Sunday at Noon (mid-May through mid-September), see the reenactment of the Pied Piper leading children through the Town Square. Approximately 80 actors in historical costumes participate in the 30-minute performance.

Take the 90-minute guided walking tour (10:00–11:30) from the tourist information office. A stroll through the surrounding woods is pleasant. Or, try a steamboat trip on the **Weser River**.

Dep. Hameln   Every hour from 08:23 to 22:23
Arr. Hannover   47 minutes later

Hannover - Hildesheim - Hannover   697

Dep. Hannover   Every hour from 05:34 to 21:34
Arr. Hildesheim   30 minutes later

Sights in **Hildesheim**: The supposedly 1,100-year old rose tree (probably 300–500 years old) which survived World War II bombings that literally destroyed the city, on the grounds of the 11th century Cathedral.

The Cathedral houses marvelous 11th century art, particularly the 2 wings of the bronze door cast in 1015, showing 8 scenes from the Old and New Testaments.

Also see the Egyptian and Greco-Roman objects, as well as the collection of episcopal silverware and Chinese porcelain, in the Roemer und Pelizaeus Museum. The 12th century painted ceiling in the 11th century St. Michael's Church. The 15th century Tempelhaus.

The Gothic Town Hall. The collection of 15th century books and official records dating back to the 12th century at the Stadtarchiv.

Take a local train for the short ride to **Nordstemmen** and then it is a 20-minute walk from that railstation to see the medieval castle, Schloss Marianburg.

Dep. Hildesheim   Every hour from 05:54 to 21:54
Arr. Hannover   30 minutes later

Hannover - Kassel - Hannover   750

There is beautiful **Fulda River Valley** scenery 20 minutes before arriving in Kassel.

All of these trains charge a supplement that includes reservation fee. Most of them have a restaurant car.

Dep. Hannover	Frequent times from 06:28 to 21:20
Arr. Kassel (Wil.)	60 minutes later

Dep. Kassel (Wil.)	Frequent times from 06:34 to 22:44
Arr. Hannover	60 minutes later

Hannover - Luneburg - Hannover   750

Dep. Hannover	07:42	08:03 (1)	08:49 (2)	09:42	10:49 (1)	11:42
Arr. Luneburg	09:13	09:19	09:44	11:07	11:44	13:07

Sights in **Luneburg**: The 18th century crane at the waterfront. Guided tours of Town Hall, constructed over 5 centuries (1300-1800). The 17th century Ducal Palace. The view of the town from Kalkberg (Chalk Mountain).

The 15th–16th century wood carvings and paintings and the 16th–18th century organs in the 3 churches that have survived out of the city's 14 original churches: St. Johannis, St. Michaelis and St. Nicolai. There are magnificent tombs of the town's most important citizens inside St. Johannia, the oldest church here. The sound of its organ is unique.

Don't miss seeing the 12th century Monastery, slightly more than one mile northeast of the town.

Dep. Luneburg	14:12 (2)	14:45	16:12 (2)	16:45	18:12 (2+3)
Arr. Hannover	15:09	16:16	17:09	18:16	19:09

(1) Reservation advisable. Light refreshments. (2) Supplement charged which includes a reservation fee. Light refreshments. (3) Plus other departures from Luneburg at 18:45, 20:12 (1) and 20:33 (1), arriving Hannover 20:16, 21:09 and 21:57.

Leipzig - Berlin - Leipzig   670

Dep. Leipzig	06:22 (1)	06:48 (2)	08:48	10:40 (6)
Arr. Berlin (Hbf.)	08:39	09:09	11:07	12:49

Dep. Berlin (Licht.)	13:36 (6)	14:45 (6)	17:36 (6)	20:29 (1)
Arr. Leipzig	15:45	17:04	19:45	22:43

(1) Reservation advisable. Light refreshments. (2) Supplement charged which includes reservation fee. Light refreshments. (3) Runs daily, except Sunday. Supplement charged which includes reservation fee. Restaurant car. (4) Reservation advisable. (5) Depart/Arrive Berlin's Lichtenberg railstation. (6) Supplement charged which includes reservation fee. Restaurant car.

Leipzig - Chemnitz (formerly Karl Marx Stadt) - Leipzig   777

| Dep. Leipzig | 08:28 | 10:28 | 12:28 | Dep. Chemnitz | 12:41 | 14:41 | 16:41 (1) |
| Arr. Chemnitz | 10:00 | 12:00 | 14:00 | Arr. Leipzig | 14:10 | 16:10 | 18:10 |

(1) Plus other departures from Chemnitz at 18:41, 19:39 and 20:41, arriving Leipzig 20:10, 22:10 and 24:10.

Sights in **Chemnitz**: An East German post-World War II showplace new city.

Leipzig - Dresden - Leipzig   660 + 775

Dep. Leipzig	06:52	08:07 (1)	09:18 (2)	09:52 (3)	10:07 (2)	12:07 (3)
Arr. Dresden (Neu.)	08:40	09:32	10:48	11:17	11:38	13:32
Arr. Dresden (Hbf.)	9 minutes later					

Dep. Dresden (Hbf.)	12:22 (2)	14:22 (2)	14:45 (3)	15:25 (2)	16:22 (3)	18:22 (2+7)
Dep. Dresden (Neu.)	8 minutes later					
Arr. Leipzig	13:51	15:51	16:09	16:52	17:51	19:51

(1) Reservation advisable. Restaurant car. (2) Reservation advisable. Light refreshments. (3) Supplement charged includes reservation fee. Restaurant car. (4) Supplement charged includes reservation fee. Light refreshments. (5) Runs daily, except Saturday. (6) Reservation advisable. (7) Plus other departures from Dresden (Hbf.) at 20:22 arriving 21:51.

Leipzig - Erfurt - Leipzig   775

| Dep. Leipzig | 08:12 (1) | 10:12 (1) | 12:12 (1) | |
| Arr. Erfurt | 09:32 | 11:32 | 13:32 | |

| Dep. Erfurt | 14:20 (1) | 16:20 (1) | 18:20 (1) | 20:20 (1+3) |
| Arr. Leipzig | 15:43 | 17:43 | 19:43 | 21:43 |

(1) Supplement charged includes reservation fee. Restaurant car. (2) Reservation advisable. Restaurant car. (3) Plus another departure from Erfurt at 22:37 (1), arriving Leipzig 23:55.

Leipzig - Naumburg - Leipzig   770

All of these trains charge a supplement that includes reservation fee and have a restaurant car, unless designated otherwise.

Dep. Leipzig	07:13	09:13	11:13	13:13
Arr. Naumburg	40 minutes later			

Sights in **Naumburg**: A gem of a Medieval village.

Dep. Naumburg	12:02	14:02	16:02	18:02	20:02	22:02	23:16
Arr. Leipzig	40 minutes later						

Leipzig - Rostock - Leipzig   674

Reservation is advisable for all of these trains. All of them have light refreshments.

Dep. Leipzig	06:53	10:53 (1)	Dep. Rostock	15:38 (2)	17:50
Arr. Rostock	11:37	16:03	Arr. Leipzig	21:09 (1)	22:49

(1) Change trains in Magdeburg (arr. 09:39-dep. 09:50). (2) Change trains in Ludwigslust (arr. 17:48–dep. 17:54).

Sights in **Rostock**: Eastern Germany's largest seaport. St. Mary's Church. The ancient Town Hall.

Leipzig - Schwerin - Leipzig   674

Reservation is advisable for all of these trains, and all of them have light refreshments, unless designated otherwirs.

Dep. Leipzig	06:53	08:53 (1)	Dep. Schwerin	14:54	18:54 (2)
Arr. Schwerin	10:28	12:54	Arr. Leipzig	18:49	22:49

(1) Change trains in Magdeburg (arr. 09:39-dep. 09:54). (2) Reservations not available. No light refreshments. Change trains in Ludwigslust (arr. 17:48–dep. 17:54 restaurant car).

Sights in **Schwerin**: The Opera House. The fine castle.

Munich - Augsburg - Munich 750 + 760

Most of these trains charge a supplement that includes reservation fee and have a rest- aurant car or light refreshments.

| Dep. Munich (Hbf.) | Frequent times from 04:54 to 23:10 |
| Arr. Augsburg | 30–40 minutes later |

Sights in **Augsburg**: An ancient castled city, complete with splendid Gothic gate, moat, tower and ramparts. The Tourist Information Office, 7 Bahnhofstrasse, is open Monday-Friday 09:00–18:00, Saturday 09:00–13:00.

See the palatial, 8-story, 17th century City Hall. Next to it is the 11th century Perlachturm, a belltower. The oldest (12th century) Romanesque stained-glass in the world, great 11th century bronze doors, 4 altarpieces by Holbein and a huge 11th century bronze portal with scenes from the Old Testament in the 10th century Cathedral.

Just north of the Cathedral, on Frauentorstrasse, is the Mozart Museum (closed on Tuesday) in the house where the composer's father lived.

Schaezlerpalais, at 46 Maximilianstrasse, is an 18th century 60-room mansion that houses the Municipal Art Collections (Rubens, Rembrandt, Veronese, Tiepolo) and has a richly ornamented rococo ballroom on the second floor. The ballroom leads to an adjacent building that has a dazzling collection: Lucas Cranach, Holbein the Elder, Albrecht Durer. Both museums are open daily except Monday 10:00–16:00.

Also see the 15th century Basilica of St. Ulrich and St. Afra, the largest and most impressive church in Augsburg. The collection of manuscripts and drawings in the Municipal Library. The city's three 16th century fountains. Maximilianstrasse is considered by many to be the best Renaissance street in Germany.

| Dep. Augsburg | Frequent times from 05:43 to 23:38 |
| Arr. Munich (Hbf.) | 30–40 minutes later |

Munich - Bamberg - Munich 770

All of these trains charge a supplement that includes reservation fee and have a restaurant car.

Dep. Munich (H.)	06:56	08:56	10:56	Dep. Bamberg	16:44	18:44	20:44
Arr. Bamberg	09:12	11:12	13:12	Arr. Munich (H.)	19:15	21:15	23:15

Sights in **Bamberg**: A major port on the Rhine-Main-Danube Canal that connects the North Sea with the Black Sea. One of the few towns not damaged in World War II.

Visit the Town Hall, located in the center of the bridge that crosses the Regnitz River. The 16th century Geyerworth Castle. A History Museum is located in the 16th century Ratsstube. Nearby is the Old Imperial Court, The 17th cnetury Concordia House.

Walk 10 minutes up the hill to Domplatz (Cathedral Square), location of the 13th century Imperial Cathedral, to see many masterpieces of German medieval and early Renaissance sculpture (especially the 13th century life-size Knight of Bamberg astride his horse)... the 16th century tomb of Henry II with sculpted bas-relief panels showing scenes from his and his wife's life...the dazzling carved wood Marienaltar...the tile floors, frescoes and 18th century French tapestries in the Neue Residenz, the 15th and 16th century German paintings in the Museum there, and its 18th century rose garden.

The Cathedral is open dawn to sunset, daily except holidays. The Neue Residenz is open 09:00–12:00 and 13:30–17:00 (16;00 October through March). See the paintings of more than 600 different medicinal herbs in the ceiling of St. Michael, an 11th century church.

Munich - Bayreuth - Munich

All of the Munich–Nurnberg (and v.v.) trains charge a supplement that includes reservation fee and have a restaurant car.

770			778		
Dep. Munich (Hbf.)	06:56	08:56 (1)	Dep. Bayreuth	14:10	16:10 (2)
Arr. Nurnberg	08:40	10:40	Arr. Nurnberg	15:09	17:09
Change trains. 778			*Change trains. 770*		
Dep. Nurnberg	08:49	10:49	Dep. Nurnberg	15:18	17:18
Arr. Bayreuth	09:46	11:46	Arr. Munich (Hbf.)	17:15	19:15

(1) Plus another departure from Munich at 10:46, arriving Nurnberg 12:49, arriving Bayreuth 13:46. (2) Plus other departures from Bayreuth at 18:10 and 20:10, arriving Nurnberg 19:09 and 21:09, arriving Munich 21:15 and 23:15.

Sights in **Bayreuth**: Sight of a 5-week annual (over 100 years) Wagner opera festival at Festspielhaus, every year from late July to late August, at 16:00. See Haus Wahnfried, Wagner's home. The breathtaking opera house. Eremitage Park. The Orangerie castle, open daily 10:00–11:30 and 13:30–15:00.

Munich - Frankfurt - Munich   760

All of these trains charge a supplement that includes reservation fee and have a restaurant car.

Dep. Munich (Hbf.)	06:44	07:44	08:44	09:44	
Arr. Frankfurt	10:14	11:14	12:14	13:14	
Dep. Frankfurt	15:43	16:43	17:43	18:43	19:43
Arr. Munich (Hbf.)	19:17	20:17	21:17	22:17	23:19

Munich - Heidelberg - Munich   760

All of these trains charge a supplement that includes reservation fee and have a restaurant car.

Dep. Munich (Hbf.)	06:48	08:46	09:46
Arr. Heidelberg	09:52	11:52	12:52

Sights in **Heidelberg**: See notes under "Cologne–Heidelberg"

Dep. Heidelberg	14:07	15:07	16:07	17:07	18:07
Arr. Munich (Hbf.)	17:11	18:11	19:11	20:11	21:11

Munich - Innsbruck - Munich   70 + 795

Dep. Munich (Hbf.)	07:00 (1)	08:30 (2)	09:30 (1)	11:30 (1)		
Arr. Innsbruck	08:36	10:11	11:18	13:20		

Dep. Innsbruck	12:41 (1)	14:41 (1)	15:39 (1)	16:41 (1)	18:37 (2)	21:03 (1)
Arr. Munich (Hbf.)	14:30	16:30	17:30	18:30	20:30	22:40

(1) Supplement charged that includes reservation fee. Restaurant car. (2) Reservation advisable. Light refreshments.

Munich - Lindau - Munich   765

There are good views of the Allgau region and fine mountain scenery on this easy one-day roundtrip.

Dep. Munich (Hbf.)	06:19	06:52	08:10 (1)	08:19
Arr. Lindau	09:14	09:50	10:22	11:14

Sights in **Lindau**: An island resort town in the Bodensee (Lake Constance), third largest lake in central Europe and actually a part of the Rhine River. Departure times for the sightseeing boat can be obtained at the tourist information office across from the railstation.

See the 13th century lighthouse, Mangturm. The beautiful 15th century Old Town Hall on the Reichplatz. The Fountain of Linavia. The casino. The collection of furniture, arms, paintings and folk art in the 18th century mansion that now houses an art museum called Stadtische Kunstsammlungen, open Tuesday–Saturday 09:00–12:00 and 14:00–17:00, also Sunday 10:00–12:00.

The 15th century homes on Hauptstrasse, a pedestrian-only road. Enjoy a mid-day repast at one of the many sidewalk cafes along that street. The only existing wall mural by Hans Holbein The Elder, done between 1485 and 1490, depicting the Passion of Jesus, can be seen in the 11th century St. Peter's Church. Visit the wine tavern in the 16th century Pulverturm (Gun Powder Tower). Walk on the breakwater to the New Lighthouse and climb its 108-foot-high tower for a breathtaking view of the Alps.

Dep. Lindau	12:45	15:37 (2)	18:46 (6)
Arr. Munich (Hbf.)	15:29	17:51	21:29

(1) Supplement charged includes reservation fee. Restaurant car. (2) Change trains in Buchloe. (3) Runs Monday-Friday, except holidays. (4) Plus other departures from Lindau at 19:37 (2), 19:46 and 20:44 (3), arriving Munich 21:45, 22:29 and 23:31.

Munich - Mainz - Munich 650

All of these trains charge a supplement that includes reservation fee and have a restaurant car.

Dep. Munich (Hbf.)	06:48	08:48	09:48		
Arr. Mainz	10:46	12:46	13:46		
Dep. Mainz	14:12	15:12	16:12	17:12	19:12
Arr. Munich (Hbf.)	18:11	19:11	20:11	21:11	23:11

Munich - Mannheim - Munich 760

All of these trains charge a supplement that includes reservation and have a restaurant car.

Dep. Munich (Hbf.)	Frequent times from 05:40 to 19:05
Arr. Mannheim	3 hours later
Dep. Mannheim	Frequent times from 06:27 to 20:58
Arr. Munich (Hbf.)	3 hours later

Munich - Nurnberg - Munich 750

All of these trains charge a supplement that includes reservation and have a restaurant car, unless designated otherwise.

Dep. Munich (Hbf.)	07:54	08:54	09:54	10:54	11:54		
Arr. Nurnberg	09:32	10:32	11:32	12:32	13:32		
Dep. Nurnberg	13:24	14:24	15:24	16:24	17:24	18:24	19:24 (1+3)
Arr. Munich (Hbf.)	15:05	16:05	17:05	18:05	19:05	20:05	21:15

(1) Light refreshments. (2) Plus other departures from Nurnberg at 20:24, 21:23 and 22:24, arriving Munich 22:05, 23:05 and 00:05.

Munich - Oberammergau - Munich

There is very good mountain and lake scenery on the Murnau–Oberammergau portion of this trip.

785

Dep. Munich (Hbf.)	08:00	09:00	10:00	11:00	12:00
Arr. Murnau	08:52	09:56	10:52	11:56	12:52
Change trains. 786					
Dep. Murnau	08:57	10:06	10:57	12:07	13:09
Arr. Oberammergau	40 minutes later				

Sights in **Oberammergau**: Every year ending in zero (1990, 2000, etc.), the famous Passion Play. Three hundred years ago the villagers here promised to produce this play every 10 years if the Black Plague ended. In the interval between decades, you can still see the unique theater and enjoy this interesting woodcarving capital of Bavaria. There is time to take a bus trip and see the lapis lazuli, gilt and crystal in King Ludwig II's glorious palace, Schloss Linderhof.

786

Dep. Oberammergau	10:57	12:07	13:09	14:07	15:07	16:10	17:07 (1)
Arr. Murnau	11:36	12:50	13:50	14:45	15:47	16:49	17:47
Change trains. 785							
Dep. Murnau	11:58	12:54	13:58	14:54	15:58	16:54	18:00
Arr. Munich (Hbf.)	12:51	13:51	14:51	15:51	16:51	17:53	18:53

(1) Plus other departures by bus from Oberammergau at 18:07 and 20:07 that connect with trains departing Murnau 18:58 and 20:54, arriving Munich 19:56 and 21:51.

Munich - Regensburg - Munich   779

Dep. Munich (Hbf.)	07:48	09:48	11:48		
Arr. Regensburg	09:13	11:13	13:13		
		•	•	•	
Dep. Regensburg	13:37	14:44	16:44	19:37	21:37
Arr. Munich (Hbf.)	15:01	16:11	18:11	21:01	23:01

Sights in **Regensburg:** Founded by the Celts in about 500 B.C. It was made into an impregnable fort by the Romans in 179 A.D. How amazing that it still exists, intact! Its locat-ion on the Danube River made this city Germany's gateway to the Balkans and the Orient for several centuries.

Undamaged during World War II, this is the largest (130,000 population) and most perfectly preserved medieval city in Germany.

Because most of the streets here are too narrow for modern vehicles and also because its size is only one mile by a half-mile, Regensburg is ideal for strolling. A half-day guided walking tour is offered by the municipal tourist office, located in the 14th century Rathaus (City Hall). Many guided tours of the City Hall's ornate rooms are offered daily.

The ancient Roman 23-foot-high wall surrounding the city is built of enormous limestone blocks without mortar, and it runs more than a mile long. Christian tombstones here date back to the 4th century. The city's forum, temples, mint, and pottery and tile factories served a population of 12,000 in Roman times. This was also one of the most important cities in the German Holy Roman Empire from the 10th through the 18th centuries.

You will not even scratch the surface in a one-day visit. In order to see all of the 26 Romanesque and Gothic churches and the wonderful artwork displayed in them would require several weeks…and there is much more than those churches to see here.

Walk over the 12th century Steiner Brucke (Stone Bridge), one of the greatest engineering marvels of the Middle Ages. Riverboat rides on the Danube start near the Stone Bridge.

Visit St. Peter's Cathedral to see its lacework spires and its collection of sacral art dating back to the Middle Ages and the Renaissance, especially the 13th century gem-and-pearl-encrusted crucifix.

Hear the boys' choir (called "cathedral sparrows," they sing both secular and liturgical songs) in the adjacent Niedermunster. Famous since the year 975, the choir can be heard Sundays and holidays at the 9:00 a.m. mass.

See the 20 medieval tower houses (some are 12 stories high), especially the 13th century Goldener Turm on Wahlenstrasse and the Bamberger Turm on Watmarkt, near the City Hall. The Golden Cross, a magnificent hotel since the 16th century.

The Municipal Museum at Dachauplatz has several paintings by Albrecht Altdorfer, considered to be the world's first landscape painter and founder of the Danubian School in the 16th century. The collection there also includes Celtic, Roman, early German and medieval artifacts.

The 9th and 10th century sculptures and tombs in the 5th century St. Emmeramskirche are notable. There are many illuminated manuscripts and more than 200,000 ancient books in the adjacent abbey.

The enormous monastery at St. Emmerams's (named for a martyred 7th century missionary monk) is presently the palace of the princes of Thurn-und-Taxis. After Napoleon secularized the abbey in 1808, that family bought it and converted it into their palace. It is worth visiting to see the priceless art in its many lavishly decorated rooms.

The Thurn-und-Taxis family invented postal service in the 15th century and used a network of stage coaches. There is a very interesting stable museum across from St. Emmeram's, with exhibits of silver and gold harnesses, equestrian paintings and 19th century coaches.

Also near this church is the Diozesan Museum, which houses 1,000 years of ecclesiastical art.

The Shipping Museum is located on the other side of the Danube River. Weinstube zur

Stritzelback at No. 6 Watmarkt has been an inn since the 13th century. (Stritzel is a salty roll.)

There is an exhibit of 17th century mathematical instruments, astronomical tools and manuscripts that were used by the mathematician and astronomer Johann Kepler at No. 5 Keplerstrasse, the house in which he died in 1630.

Sample the chocolate pralines called "Barbara's kisses" at Cafe Prinzess (No. 2 Rathausplatz), Germany's oldest pastry shop and coffeehouse. It opened in 1686.

Try the fist-sized, white radishes that the locals eat as beer snacks.

Munich - Salzburg - Munich   790

These trains charge a supplement that includes reservation fee and have a restaurant car, unless designated otherwise.

Dep. Munich (Hbf.)	07:51	08:25	09:51 (1)	10:50 (2)
Arr. Salzburg	08:55	09:55	11:40	12:45

Dep. Salzburg	13:05	13:18 (2)	14:18 (1)	15:05	16:18 (1)	17:18 (2+4)
Arr. Munich (Hbf.)	14:35	15:10	16:07	16:34	18:07	19:10

(1) No supplement charged. Reservation advisable. Light refreshments. (2) Reservation not available. No supplement. No restaurant car. (3) No supplement charged. Reservation advisable. No restaurant car. (4) Plus other departures from Salzburg at 18:05, 18:18 (1), 19:05, 19:18 (2), 20:18 (1) and 22:15 (3), arriving Munich 20:07, 20:36, 21:10, 22:00 and 24:00.

Munich - Stuttgart - Munich   760

Many of these trains charge a supplement that includes reservation fee and have a restaurant car.

Dep. Munich (Hbf.)	Frequent times from 05:40 to 20:18
Arr. Stuttgart	2–3 hours later

Dep. Stuttgart	Frequent times from 05:02 to 22:01
Arr. Munich (Hbf.)	2–3 hours later

Munich - Tegernsee and Schliersee - Munich   759

Take a local train from Starnberger Bahnhof (the northern annex of Munich's Hauptbahnhof station) for this 37-mile ride that takes 66 minutes.

At the northern end of Tegernsee (an exceptionally beautiful lake) is **Gmund**, not to be confused with the 2 Austrian villages also named Gmund. A mile away from this Gmund is a smaller lake, **Schliersee**. It is only a 4-mile walk around Schliersee.

There is a lovely view of the lake from the ruins of Hohenwaldeck Castle and also from one of the many benches along the lake's shore. Sports (tennis, sailing, swimming)are very popular in this area.

The Taubenstein mountain railway goes to an area that provides extensive mountain hiking. Wandering through the Weissachau wildlife preserve, with its rare flowers, is worthwhile. Local food specialties in this region are white sausage, liver loaf, big white radishes and spicy Miesbacher cheese.

Sights in **Tegernsee**: The concerts (May–September) in the enormous Baroque dining hall of the Castle. The large collection of rustic furniture, weapons, craft utensils, traditional costumes and ancient books in the Tegernsee Museum. Try the beer in the Hofbrauhaus, located in the Museum building. Ludwig Schieffer of Cologne tells us the beer there is better than which is sold at Munich's famous Hofbrauhaus.

See the drawings, illustrations, sketches and caricatures by Olaf Gulbransson at the Kurpark Museum. Visit the lakeside gambling casino at **Wiessee,** across the lake.

Take the 10-minute boat trip (every half hour) across the lake to Wiessee. Both Tegernsee and Wiessee have been popular for centuries for their curative mineral waters, laden with iodine and sulphur. Swimming in the pristine lake is marvelous.

Take the cable car from nearby **Rottach-Egern** to the top of **Wallberg** for a view of the Tegernsee Valley and Austria's highest peak, the **Grossglockner**.

Munich - Ulm - Munich   760

All of these trains charge a supplement that includes reservation fee and have a restaurant car or light refreshments.

Dep. Munich   Frequent times from 05:40 to 22:18
Arr. Ulm   70–80 minutes later

Sights in **Ulm**: The Bakery Museum (tools, library, artwork pertaining to bread) on Fuersteneckerstrasse. The display there includes breads made in ancient Egypt and in the Middle Ages. Open Monday-Friday 10:00–12:00 and 15:00–17:30.

The 14th century Gothic Cathedral has one of the highest towers in the world (528 feet) and a ceiling that is 100 feet above the central nave. When you hear an organ recital here (8,000 pipes !), you will experience an incredible affect from the exceptional acoustics. Don't miss seeing the magnificent 15th century carving on the choir stalls.

The views of the Alps while climbing the 528-feet-high tower are breathtaking. (You don't have to make the entire ascent.)

The 17th century Schworhaus, where Town Council members once took their oaths to perform their duties (where they were "sworn in").

Arts and crafts from this region are displayed in the Ulmer Museum, open Tuesday–Saturday 10:00–12:00 and 14:00–17:00, Sunday 10:00–13:00 and 14:00–17:00. See the 15th century fountain, Fischkasten, at the Marktplatz. Also on that square is the 14th century Town

Euralpass Europe—Germany 237

Hall with an exceptional astronomical clock on its east wall.

Visit Metzgerturm, Ulm's 14th century leaning tower. Cross the bridge to New Ulm and walk along the Jahnufer promenade to see good views of the old city.

Dep. Ulm — Frequent times from 06:05 to 22:56
Arr. Munich — 70–80 minutes later

Munich - Wurzburg - Munich 750

All of these trains charge a supplement that includes reservation fee and have a restaurant car.

Dep. Munich (Hbf.)	07:21	07:54	09:54	10:38 (1)
Arr. Wurzburg	09:32	10:32	12:32	13:13

Sights in **Wurzburg**: Vineyards and wineries galore. The tourist information center is located in Falcon House, on the square where bratwurst, vegetables, fruits and flowers are sold. See the Main-Franconia Museum (sculptures, wine presses, etc.) in the 13th century Miarienberg Fortress.

The view of the city from the restaurant at the Fortress. The rococo garden in the nearby Schloss Veitshochheim. The 12 statues of saints on the Old Main Bridge. Pilgrimage Church. The Tiepolo ceiling and the Emperor's Hall, in the Residenz. Neumunster Church. The Cathedral. The fine sculptures in the Mainfrankisches Museum at the Festung. Take a boat trip on the River Main to see **Randersacker** and **Sommerhausen**, both of them located in one of Germany's most important wine regions. Pfuelben, Sonnenstuhl and Tuefelskeller are among the leading wineries here.

Sights in **Randersacker**: There are many scenic walking tours near the **Main River** and through vineyards. Stroll the narrow Medieval streets lined with baroque houses. Many sculptures here (madonnas and pietas). See the Balthasar garden-pavilion. Try the delicious franconian meat and sausages. Fishing and many other watersports here.

Sights in **Sommerhausen:** Famous since the Middle Ages for winemaking. Its coat-of-arms features a radiant sun above a cluster of grapes. Its old town walls, gates and towers make it one of the most beautiful towns in the region. Sailing and motorboating are popular here. Visit the Rechteren-Limpurgsche Castle. The ancient City Hall.

Dep. Wurzburg	12:23	13:23	14:23	15:23	16:23	17:23 (4)
Arr. Munich (Hbf.)	15:05	16:05	17:05	18:05	19:05	20:05

(1) Runs daily, except Sunday. (2) No supplement. Reservation advisable. No restaurant car. (3) Runs daily, except, Saturday. (4) Plus other Wurzburg departures at 18:23, 19:23, 20:23 (3),and 21:23 (3), arriving Munich 20:49, 22:05, 23:05 and 00:05.

Munich - Zurich - Munich   768

Both of these trains charge a supplement that includes reservation fee and have a restaurant car.

Dep. Munich (H.)	08:11	Dep. Zurich	17:40
Arr. Zurich	12:21	Arr. Munich (H.)	21:45

SCENIC RAIL TRIPS

Cologne - Koblenz - Bullay - Cologne   720

There is beautiful farm, mountain and vineyard scenery on this easy one-day trip through the Moselle Valley. Very good river scenery on the Koblenz–Bullay portion.

Reservation is advisable for all of these trains.

Dep. Cologne	08:11	10:11	12:11	14:00
Dep. Koblenz	09:19	11:19	13:19	15:19
Arr. Bullay	50 minutes later			

* * *

Dep. Bullay	09:54	11:54	13:54	15:54
Arr. Koblenz	10:38	12:38	14:38	16:38
Arr. Cologne	57 minutes later			

Cologne - Mainz

See the fine mountain, vineyard and Rhine river scenery. Complete schedules appear under the "Cologne–Mainz–Cologne" one-day excursion.

Cologne - Giessen - Frankfurt - Koblenz - Cologne

View excellent mountain scenery on this ride, which can be made as a circle trip from either

709

Dep. Cologne	08:19	10:19	12:19			
Arr. Giessen	10:48	12:48	14:48			
Change trains.						
Dep. Giessen	11:21 (1)	13:21 (1)	15:21 (1)			
Arr. Frankfurt	12:01	14:01	16:01			
Change trains.	650					
Dep. Frankfurt	11:51 (2)	13:51 (2)	15:51 (2)	16:51 (2)	17:51 (2)	18:51 (2+3+4)
Dep. Koblenz	13:13	15:13	17:13	18:13	19:13	20:13
Arr. Cologne	14:05	16:05	18:05	19:05	20:05	21:05

(1) Light refreshments. (2) Supplement charged includes reservation fee. Restaurant car. (3) Plus other departures from Frankfurt at 19:51 (2), 20:51 (2) and 21:51 (2), arriving Cologne 22:05, 23:05 and 00:07. (4) runs daily except Saturday.

Dresden - Bad Schandau - Dresden

For best views of the **Elbe River** en route to **Bad Schandau**, sit on the left side of the 50-minute suburban train as it goes down the **Elbe Canyon**. Then, take a local tramway from the center of Bad Schandau into the mountains of the Sachsischer Schweiz to the **Lichtenhainer Waterfall**.

Frankfurt - Koblenz - Cologne - Giessen - Frankfurt

Here is the Frankfurt version of the circle trip shown on the previous trip.

650

Dep. Frankfurt		07:51 (1)	09:51 (1)	11:51 (1)	14:51 (1)
Dep. Koblenz		09:13	11:13	13:13	15:13
Arr. Cologne		10:05	12:05	14:05	16:05
Change trains.	709				
Dep. Cologne		10:19	12:19	14:19	16:19
Arr. Giessen		12:48	14:48	16:48	18:48
Change trains.					
Dep. Giessen		13:21 (2)	15:21 (2)	17:21 (2)	19:21 (2)
Arr. Frankfurt		14:01	16:01	18:01	20:01

(1) Supplement charged includes reservation fee. Restaurant car. (2) Supplement charged includes reservation fee. Light refreshments.

Freiburg - Donaueschingen

The train runs through the heart of the Black Forest. Very good mountain scenery on this spur of the Frankfurt–Basel route.

730			*732*		
Dep. Frankfurt	10:09 (1)	11:43 (1+2)	Dep. Donau.	14:49	16:49
Arr. Freiburg	12:27	14:01	Arr. Neu. Schwarz.	15:25	17:25
Change trains. 731			*Change trains. 731*		
Dep. Freiburg	12:41	14:41	Dep. Neu. Schwarz.	15:31	17:31
Arr. Neu. Schwarz.	13:24	15:24	Arr. Freiburg	16:17	18:17
Change trains. 732			*Change trains. 730*		
Dep. Neu. Schwarz.	13:30	15:30	Dep. Freiburg	16:29 (1)	18:29 (1)
Arr. Donau.	14:10	16:08	Arr. Basel (SBB)	17:11	19:11

(1) Supplement charged includes reservation fee. Restaurant car. (2) Change trains in Mannheim (arr. 12:24-dep. 12:31).

Koblenz - Giessen   713

There is fine river scenery on this easy one-day roundtrip. This area can also be seen by taking an *indirect route* from Koblenz to Frankfurt. For the first way:

Dep. Koblenz	08:43 (1)	09:53 (2)	10:43 (1)	12:43	14:43
Arr. Giessen	10:39	12:14	12:39	14:39	16:39
Dep. Giessen	11:15	12:15 (3)	13:15	15:15	17:15
Arr. Koblenz	13:08	14:35	15:08	17:08	19:08

Here is the long route to Frankfurt which offers the same scenery:

713					
Dep. Koblenz	08:43 (1)	10:43 (1)	12:43	14:43 (4)	16:43 (4)
Arr. Giessen	10:39	12:39	14:39	16:39	18:39
Change trains. 709					
Dep. Giessen	11:21 (5)	13:21 (5)	15:21 (5)	17:21 (5)	19:21 (5)
Arr. Frankfurt	12:01	14:01	16:01	18:01	20:01

(1) Runs daily, except Sundays and holidays. (2) Runs Sunday only. (3) Runs Saturdays, Sundays and holidays. (4) Runs daily, except Saturday. (5) Reservation advisable. Light refreshments.

Here is the schedule for the reverse of the Koblenz–Frankfurt trip on previous page:

709

Dep. Frankfurt	07:55 (1)	09:55	-0-	-0-	11:55	13:55 (5)
Arr. Giessen	08:35	10:35	-0-	-0-	12:35	14:35

Change trains. 713

Dep. Giessen	09:15 (2)	11:15	11:55 (3)	12:15 (4)	12:35 (3)	13:15
Arr. Koblenz	11:08	13:08	14:15	14:35	15:02	15:08

(1) Light refreshments. (2) Runs daily, except Sundays and holidays. (3) Runs Monday-Friday, except holidays. (4) Runs Saturdays, Sundays and holidays. (5) Plus other Frankfurt departures at 14:22, 15:22 and 16:22, arriving Koblenz 17:08, 18:35 and 19:08.

Munich - Garmisch - Innsbruck - Munich

There is fine mountain scenery on this easy one-day circle trip.

785

Dep. Munich (Hbf.)	09:00	11:00	12:00	14:00
Arr. Garmisch	10:23	12:23	13:16	15:16
Arr. Mittenwald	10:46 (1)	12:47	13:43	15:39
Arr. Innsbruck	11:57	14:02	14:49	16:39

Change trains. 795

Dep. Innsbruck				
(via Kufstein)	12:41 (3)	14:41 (3)	15:39 (3)	16:41 (3+7)
Arr. Munich (Hbf.)	14:30	16:30	17:30	18:30

(1) Change trains in Mittenwald. (2) Change trains in Garmisch. (3) Supplement charged includes reservation fee. Restaurant car. (4) Reservation advisable. (5) Rervation advisable. Light refreshments. (6) Arrives at Munich's Ost railstation. (7) Plus other departures from Innsbruck at 17:05 (4), 18:37 (4), 21:03 (3) and 22:48 (5), arriving Munich 19:03, 20:30, 22:40 and 01:55 (6).

Garmisch - Zugspitzplatt - Zugspitzgipfel (summit) - Garmisch 783

The following schedule allows one to take one route to the summit of Zugspitze and a different route back to Garmisch.

Cook did not carry Schneefernerhaus schedules in 1994. Shown below are 1993 times.

Cog train.

Dep. Garmisch	07:35	08:35	09:35	10:35	11:35	12:35	13:35	14:35	15:35
Arr. Eibsee	08:15	09:15	10:15	11:15	12:15	13:15	14:15	15:15	16:15
Arr. Zugspitzplatt	08:40	09:40	10:40	11:40	12:40	13:40	14:40	15:40	16:40

Change to cable car.

Dep. Zugspitzplatt	08:45	09:45	10:45	11:45	12:45	13:45	14:45	15:45	16:45
Arr. Zugspitzgipfel	09:05	10:05	11:05	12:05	13:05	14:05	15:05	16:05	17:05

• • •

Dep. Zugspitzgipfel	09:15	10:15	11:15	12:15	13:15	14:15	15:15	16:15	17:05
Arr. Zugspitzplatt	09:35	10:35	11:35	12:35	13:35	14:35	15:35	16:35	17:35

Change cable cars.

Dep. Zugspitzplatt	09:45	10:45	11:45	12:45	13:45	14:45	15:45	16:45	17:45
Arr. Schneefernerhaus	09:49	10:49	11:49	12:49	13:49	14:49	15:49	16:49	17:49

Change to cog train.

Dep. Schneefernerhaus	10:00	11:00	12:00	13:00	14:00	15:00	16:00	17:00	18:00
Arr. Garmisch	11:20	12:20	13:20	14:20	15:20	16:20	17:20	18:20	19:20

Munich - Nurnberg - Heilbronn - Heidelberg

This schedule follows the route of the "Castle Road" and "Romantic Road" bus trips.

The 09:54 and 11:54 Munich departures must be made only Monday–Friday except holidays because of connection in Crailsheim.

750

Dep. Munich	07:56 (1)	09:56 (1)	11:56 (1)
Arr. Nurnberg	09:32	11:32	13:32

Change trains. 745

Dep. Nurnberg	09:45 (2)	11:45 (2)	13:45 (2)
Arr. Crailsheim	10:35	12:35	14:35

Change trains. 744

Dep. Crailsheim	10:48	12:48 (3)	14:48 (3)
Arr. Heilbronn	12:00	14:00	16:00

Sights in **Heilbronn**: More than 80% of the pre-World War II buildings in this city of 110,000 in the heart of Germany's wine country was obliterated by Allied bombing planes in 1944. The Wine Festival (one week in September) attracts 300,000 people every year.

742

Dep. Heilbronn	12:40	14:40	16:40
Arr. Heidelberg	13:59	16:13	17:59

(1) Supplement charged includes reservation fee. Restaurant car. (2) Reservation advisable. Light refreshements. (3) Runs Monday–Friday, except holidays.

Munich - Salzburg

This route offers good mountain scenery and is an easy one-day roundtrip. See schedules earlier in this section, under "One-Day Excursions."

Offenburg - Konstanz - Offenburg 730

This trip is recommended for exceptional mountain scenery.

Dep. Offenburg	07:02 (1)	07:56 (1)	08:37	09:53 (1)	10:37	11:53 (1)
Arr. Konstanz	09:17	10:11	11:18	12:11	13:18	14:11
Dep. Offenburg	12:37	13:53 (1)	14:37	15:53 (1)		
Arr. Konstanz	15:18	16:11	17:18	18:11		

* * *

Dep. Konstanz	09:49 (1)	10:50	11:49 (1)	12:50	13:49 (1)	14:50
Arr. Offenburg	12:04	13:18	14:04	15:18	16:04	17:18
Dep. Konstanz	15:49 (1)	16:45	17:49 (1)	18:50	19:49 (1)	20:55 (1)
Arr. Offenburg	18:04	19:18	20:04	21:15	21:44	23:09

(1) Reservation advisable. Light refreshments.

Offenburg - Singen - Schaffhausen - Offenburg

Excellent Black Forest scenery on this route. This trip can also be made as a detour en route from Frankfurt to Basel.

Reservation is advisable for all of the Offenburg-Singen (and v.v.) trains, and all of them have light refreshments.

730

Dep. Offenburg	07:56	09:53	11:53	13:53	15:53
Arr. Singen	09:48	11:47	13:47	15:47	17:47

Change trains.
734

Dep. Singen	12:14	14:14	16:14	18:14
Arr. Schaffhausen	12:32	14:32	16:32	18:32

Dep. Schaffhausen	11:29	13:29	15:29	17:29	19:29
Arr. Singen	11:45	13:45	15:45	17:45	19:45

Change trains.
730

Dep. Singen	12:13	14:12	16:13	18:13	20:13
Arr. Offenburg	14:04	16:04	18:04	20:04	21:44

Here is the detour from the Frankfurt-Basel ride:

730			734		
Dep. Frankfurt	07:47 (1)	09:47 (1)	Dep. Singen	12:14	14:14
Arr. Offenburg	09:51	11:51	Dep. Schaffhausen	12:34	14:34
Arr. Singen	11:47	13:47	Arr. Basel (Bad.)	13:48	15:48
Change trains.					

(1) Reservation advisable. Light refreshments.

Wurzburg - Zurich

There is exceptional Black Forest scenery on this ride.

741

Dep. Wurzburg	06:52 (1)	08:01 (2)	10:40	12:40		
Arr. Stuttgart	09:15	10:21	12:58	14:58		

Change trains. 74

Dep. Stuttgart	09:42 (3)	11:42 (3)	13:42	15:42	16:52 (4)	17:42
Arr. Zurich	12:47	14:47	16:47	18:47	19:50	20:47

(1) Runs daily, except Sunday. (2) Runs Sunday only. (3) Light refreshments. (4) Runs Monday-Friday. Supplement charged includes reservation fee. Restaurant car.

RHINE RIVER CRUISES

A variety of cruising on the Rhine is offered. The complete 5-day *down*stream route (from Basel to Amsterdam or Rotterdam) and the complete 6-day *up*stream route (Amsterdam or Rotterdam to Basel) are offered April to October.

A shorter portion (Rotterdam-Strasbourg and vice versa) is also available April to October. It is 4 days downstream and 5 upstream.

Still another service (3 days downstream and 4 upstream), between Amsterdam or Rotterdam and Mainz, is offered April to September.

On any of these, passengers may stop-over at points en route and resume the journey later (Cologne, Koblenz, etc.).

The most popular stretch of the Rhine (Koblenz to Mainz and Frankfurt) is covered by the Eurailpass. This is the portion famed for scenic vineyards and hilltop castles. The *entire* Rhine trip is *not* covered by Eurailpass. However, with a Eurailpass there is *no* charge for either the boat trip or train ride Mainz–Cologne or Cologne–Mainz.

The scenery between Mainz and Koblenz can be seen as well from a train as from a boat because the track on this run goes along the river bank.

Here are the schedules for taking the boat *Mainz–Cologne* and returning to Mainz by train the same day:

714 (Boat)		650 (Train)	
Dep. Mainz	08:45 (1)	Dep. Cologne (Hbf.)	19:54 (2)
Arr. Koblenz	13:50	Dep. Koblenz	20:47
Arr. Cologne (Rheing'n)	18:50	Arr. Mainz	21:33

(1) Operates May 1 to October 3. (2) Supplement charged includes reservation fee. Restaurant car.

Here are the schedules for taking the hydrofoil *Cologne-Mainz* and returning to Cologne by train the same day:

714 (Hydrofoil)		650 (Train)	
Dep. Cologne (Rheing'n)	09:00 (1)	Dep. Mainz	14:18 (2)
Arr. Koblenz	11:00	Dep. Koblenz	15:07
Arr. Mainz	13:10	Arr. Cologne (Hbf.)	15:59

(1) Operates April 1 to October 23. Runs daily, except Monday. Supplement charged. (2) Supplement charged includes reservation fee. Restaurant car. Plus other departures from Mainz at frequent times from 14:24 to 22:24.

THE ONE-DAY RHINE HYDROFOIL CRUISE ROUNDTRIP

Cologne - Mainz - Cologne   714

Operates April 1 to October 23. Runs daily, except Monday. Supplement charged.

Dep. Cologne (Rheing'n)	09:00	Dep. Mainz	14:25
Arr.. Koblenz	11:00	Dep. Koblenz	16:20
Arr. Mainz	13:10	Arr. Cologne (Rheing'n)	18:05

SCENIC BUS TRIPS COVERED BY EURAILPASS

Both of these extremely popular bus trips are covered by Eurailpass: "Roman tische Strasse" (**Romantic Road**) and "Burgenstrasse" (**Castle Road**). Advance seat reservations should be made at least 3 days before travel date. They can be obtained at no cost by writing to: Deutsche Touring GmbH, Am Roemerhof 17, D-6000 Frankfurt/M. 90, Germany, or by phoning: (069) 790-32-56. Be sure to indicate the dates you want to journey, which of the 2 different lines you want to travel, where you will start and end your trip, and the number of seats you want.

Passengers are allowed to break the journey at as many stops as they desire on both bus lines, and we recommend some specific places to do so in the text that follows. If that is your plan, be sure to provide all the specific dates this will involve when requesting a reservation.

The 2 lines connect in **Rothenburg**, making it easy to ride on all or part of both trips. Lodging in Rothenburg is good quality, but the supply is small and the demand very great. The Encyclopedia Britannica calls Rothenburg "probably the finest surviving example of a medieval town." It has been there for 1,000 years. Its 30 watchtowers and many dungeons, churches, patrician homes, ornamental fountains and market squares are perfectly preserved.

The town's most important buildings are on the old Market Square: Town Hall, Virgin's Pharmacy (Marienapotheque), the lovely stone fountain (Herterichbrunnen), the ancient city council drinking hall, and the mechanical clock that performs at 11:00, 13:00 and 14:00.

The Meistertrunk Legend When the town was under siege in the 17th century, the commander of the victorious Imperial Army was given his first taste of wine by the inhabitants. He offered to spare the lives of the city officials if any of them could empty in one drink the content of a tankard holding almost one gallon. One burgermeister rose to the challenge, accomplished the feat, and even quaffed more. The 3.24 liter Meistertrunk tankard is on display in the town's Reichstadt Museum. The legend is recreated every year in a pageant held on Whitsunday, 7 weeks after Easter.

Statues of the 7 deadly sins and 7 virtues adorn the Baumeisterhaus, on Schmiedgasse, near Market Square. This chiseled house is well worth seeing. The torture museum at the Dominican Nunnery is another attraction in the town.

Rothenburg has 15 hotels with 11 to 145 rooms each. It is an ideal stopover either for breaking the Romantische Strasse ride into 2 days or for transferring from or to the Burgen-strasse ride.

Also a recommended stopover on the Romantische Strasse ride is **Dinkelsbuhl,** another finely preserved medieval town with a surfeit of gates, bastions, towers, a moat equipped with floating swans and a sharp sense of ancient history. Its major pageant is every July, complete with sword dances and historic tableaux.

Augsburg is an ancient castled city. See notes under "Munich–Augsburg."

Castle Road 748

This bus trip operates from mid-May to late September.

Dep. Mannheim	08:37		Dep. Rothenburg	17:00
Dep. Heidelberg	08:56		Arr. Heidelberg	20:45
Arr. Rothenburg	13:27		Arr. Mannheim	21:10

Romantic Road 748

The portion of this bus trip which has the principal sights is Wurzburg–Augsburg (and v.v.). A stewardess-guide is provided for that part of the 2 schedules shown below.

These buses operate April 1 to October 31.

Dep. Frankfurt	08:15	-0-	Dep. Munich	09:00	-0-
Dep. Wurzburg	09:45	-0-	Dep. Fussen	-0-	08:00
Arr. Rothenburg	12:15 (1)	-0-	Dep. Augsburg	10:30	10:45
Dep. Rothenburg	13:00	14:45	Arr. Dinkelsbuhl	11:55 (1)	12:15
Arr. Dinkelsbuhl	13:40 (1)	15:25 (1)	Dep. Dinkelsbuhl	12:05	12:25
Dep. Dinkelsbuhl	16:20	16:15	Arr. Rothenburg	12:45 (1)	13:00 (2)
Arr. Augsburg	18:00	18:00	Dep. Rothenburg	17:00	17:00
Arr. Fussen	-0-	20:00	Arr. Wurzburg	18:25	18:25
Arr. Munich	19:15	-0-	Arr. Frankfurt	20:00	20:00

(1) Meal stop. Time to stroll. (2) Change buses.

SPECIAL RAIL TRIP FROM FUSSEN

For a marvelous extension from Fussen, here is a train trip that offers superb scenery: alpine meadows, deep river gorges, mountains. One of the most spectacular one-day rail routes in Europe.

Bus. German table.

Dep. Fussen	09:30	12:50
Arr. Reutte	10:03	13:43
Change to train.		
785		
Dep. Reutte	12:00 (1)	14:08
Arr. Garmisch	12:57 (1)	15:06
Change trains		
Dep. Garmisch	13:26	15:26
Arr. Innsbruck	14:41	16:43
Change trains.		
800		
Dep. Innsbruck	15:02 (2)	17:02 (2)
Arr. Salzburg	17:00	19:00

(1) Direct train Reutte–Innsbruck. No train change in Garmisch. (2) Supplement charged includes reservation fee. Restaurant car.

INTERNATIONAL ROUTES
FROM GERMANY

The German gateway for travel to Amsterdam and Brussels (and on to London) is Cologne. Frankfurt and Cologne are the access points to Paris (and on to Barcelona and Madrid). Frankfurt is also the starting point for travel to Basel and Zurich (and on to Milan and Genoa)…as well as to Warsaw.

Munich and Nurnberg are gateways for trips to Vienna (and on to Belgrade and Budapest), and Bologna (and on to Rome or Venice). Nurnberg and Berlin are departure points for getting to Prague. Berlin and Hamburg are the gateways to Copenhagen (and on to Oslo and Stockholm).

Berlin - Copenhagen   51

Dep. Berlin (Lichtenberg)	08:51 (1)	14:51 (2)	23:52 (3)
Arr. Copenhagen	16:55	22:55	08:31

(1) Carries first and second-class sleeping car. Also has second-class couchettes. Coach is second-class only. Runs June 23-August 20. (2) Operates late June to mid-August. (3) Restaurant car 16:00-20:55.

Berlin - Prague   680

Reservation is advisabe for all of these trains and they have a restaurant car, unless designated otherwise.

Dep. Berlin (Licht.)	02:14	09:24	17:23	18:48
Dep. Berlin (Sch'fld)	-0-	09:43	17:42	19:07
Arr. Prague (Hole.)	07:14	14:59	21:41	22:47
Arr. Prague (Hlavni)	-0-	-0-	-0-	-0-

Dep. Berlin (Licht.)	22:24	23:48
Dep. Berlin (Sch'fld)	22:43	00:07
Arr. Prague (Hole.)	01:59	05:14
Arr. Prague (Hlavni)	-0-	-0-

Berlin - Warsaw   56

Dep. Berlin (Hbf.)	08:10 (1)	-0-	-0-	16:32 (1)	-0-
Dep. Berlin (Licht.)	-0-	10:39 (2)	11:40 (3)	-0-	22:07 (4)
Arr. Warsaw (Centralna)	14:25	19:25	20:07	22:40	06:15
Arr. Warsaw (Wschodnia)	14:44	19:39	20:21	22:54	06:29

(1) Supplement charged includes reservation fee. Restaurant car. (2) Train has only first and second-class sleeping cars. *No* coaches. (3) Train has only second-class sleeping cars. *No* coaches. (4) Carries a sleeping car. Also has couchettes.

Cologne - Amsterdam   28

Sit on the right-hand side for best views of the marvelous Rhine River scenery.

All of these trains charge a supplement that includes reservation fee and have light refreshments, unless designated otherwise.

Dep. Cologne	07:17	09:17	11:17	13:17	15:17	17:17	18:02 (1+2)
Arr. Amsterdam	09:54	11:51	13:51	15:51	17:51	19:51	20:51

(1) Restaurant car. (2) Plus other departures from Cologne at 19:02 (1), and 21:17, arriving Amsterdam 21:51 and 23:51.

Cologne - Basel - Zurich   77

Dep. Cologne	07:00 (1)	08:00 (1)	09:00 (1)	11:00 (1)	12:00 (1+4)
Arr. Basel (S.B.B.)	11:43 (2)	12:43 (2)	13:43	15:43 (2)	16:43
Arr. Zurich	13:00	14:00	15:00	17:00	18:03

(1) Supplement charged includes reservation fee. Restaurant car. (2) Change trains in Basel. (3) Carries a sleeping car. Also has couchettes. (4) Plus other Cologne departures at frequent times from 13:00 to 17:00 plus 23:59 (3).

Cologne - Brussels   20

Dep. Cologne	05:08	06:30 (1)	07:14	11:14	12:14 (2)
Arr. Brussels (Nord)	07:55	08:50	09:44	13:44	14:14
Arr. Brussels (Midi)	08:04	09:01	09:55	13:55	14:55

(1) Supplement charged includes reservation fee. Restaurant car. (2) Plus other departures from Cologne at 13:14 (1), 14:14, 15:14 (1), 16:14, 18:14 and 20:14, arriving Brussels Nord 15:48, 16:44, 17:49, 18:44, 20:44 and 22:44.

Cologne - Paris   25

Dep. Cologne	00:07 (1)	05:46 (2)	08:14 (3)	13:14 (3)	17:08 (3)
Arr. Paris (Nord)	06:25	11:20	13:31	19:01	22:10

(1) Carries a sleeping car. Also has couchettes. Light refreshments. (2) Operates late May to late September. Coach is Second-class. (3) Supplement charged includes reservation fee. Restaurant car.

Munich - Bologna - Florence - Rome   76

Dep. Munich (Hbf.)	08:30	09:30 (1)	20:30 (2)	21:43 (3)	23:30 (2)
Arr. Bologna	16:14	17:16	04:08	05:32	07:47
Arr. Florence (S.M.N.)	-0-	18:23	-0-	-0-	09:06
Arr. Rome (Ter.)	-0-	20:30	08:15	-0-	-0-

(1) Supplement charged includes reservation fee. Restaurant car. (2) Carries a sleeping car. Also has couchettes. Coach is second-class. (3) Has couchettes. Coach is second-class.

Munich - Salzburg - Vienna 67

Dep. Munich (Hbf.)	06:50 (1)	08:25 (2)	09:51 (1)	10:50 (5)
Arr. Salzburg	08:45	09:55	11:40 (3)	12:45 (3)
Arr. Vienna (Westbf.)	-0-	13:25	15:25	16:25

(1) Reservation advisable. Light refreshments. (2) Supplement charged includes reservation fee. Restaurant car. (3) Change trains in Salzburg. (4) Has couchettes. (5) Plus other Munich departures at 12:25 (2+3), 13:25 (2+3), 13:51 (1+3), 15:25 (2+3), 16:25 (2), 16:50, 18:25 (2) and 23:19(4).

GREECE

GREECE

Overview

In the days before the conflicts in Yugoslavia, many Eurailpass travelers took the train to Athens via Belgrade and Thessaloniki. Today most train to the Italian port of Brindisi and ferry across to Corfu and then continue by rail to the Greek capital via Patras. This is a long but not unpleasant ride.

General Information

• Children under four travel free if they do not occupy a separate seat.
• Greece changes to summer time on the last Sunday of March and converts back to standard time on the last Sunday of September.

Greek Holidays

January 1	New Year's Day	May 1	Labor Day
January 6	Epiphany	August 15	Virgin Mary's Day
	Ash Monday	October 28	National Day
March 25	Independence Day	December 25	Christmas
	Greek Good Friday	December 26	Boxing Day
	Greek Good Saturday		
	Greek Easter		
	Greek Easter Monday		

GREECE'S TRAIN PASSES

Sold worldwide outside Greece by travel agencies and Rail Europe (U.S.A. and Canadian offices listed under "France").

Greek Railpass Unlimited *first-class* train travel. The 1996 adult prices are: $80 for any 3 days within 15 days, $130 for any 5 days within 15 days, $223 for any 10 days within one month. Half-fare for children age 4-11.

Greek Rail'N Drive Unlimited 5 days of first-class train travel plus 3 days of car rental (any 8 days) within 15 days. Prices vary (a) whether for one person or for 2 persons, (b) the category of car, and (c) the season. High Season is July, August and September. The 1996 price *per person* for 2 persons (using the smallest size car) in High Season was: $132. A third and fourth passenger had to pay only for the Greek Railpass. And, more days of car rental could be added in increments of two or more consecutive days at $65 per day.

Greek Flexipasses Unlimited *first-class* train travel. The 1996 adult prices are: $86 for any 3 days in one month, $120 for any 5 days in one month. Children: $58 and $85.

The passes described below can be purchased only in Greece, at travel agencies and main railstations. Prices shown are for 1996 and are in drachmas.

Greek Tourist Card   Unlimited *second*-class travel on trains and CH buses.

Persons	10 days	20 days	30 days
1	6,000	9,000	10,000
2	10,000	15,000	22,000
3	13,000	21,000	20,000
4	15,000	25,000	34,000
5	17,000	27,000	37,000

Greek Senior Card   Valid for one year from date issued (except 10 days before and after Easter, 10 days before and after Christmas, and July 1 to September 30. For persons age 60 or older on the day that identity card or passport is presented. Allows 5 free journeys plus 50% discount for unlimited number of journeys after the first 5. The 1996 prices are: 6,000 drachmas for first-class; 4,000 drachmas for second-class.

Group Discount   A 30% discount is granted to groups of 10 or more persons.

EURAILPASS BONUSES IN GREECE

• The ferry crossing from Patras to Brindisi (see note under "Italy").
• There is also a 30% reduction on Adriatica di Navagazione Line for ships between Piraeus–Venice (and v.v.) and Piraeus–Alexandria (and v.v.).

ONE-DAY EXCURSIONS AND CITY-SIGHTSEEING

Here are 8 one-day rail trips that can be made comfortably from Athens and Thessaloniki, returning to them in most cases before dinnertime. Notes are provided on what to see and do at each destination. The number after the name of each route is the Cook's timetable.

Details on 2 longer rail trips in Greece follow the one-day excursions. Schedules for international connections conclude this section.

Athens (Athinai)

From 07:30 to sunset, and from 21:00 to 24:00 on nights of a full moon, visit the Parthenon, the elegant temple of the Wingless Victory and the Erechtheion at the ancient Acropolis. The monuments there can be seen 07:30–16:45 daily. The adjacent museum is closed Tuesday. Then walk northwest to the partly restored ancient Agora to see the best preserved Doric temple in Athens, the Hephaistos, also known as the Thesseion.

Also near the Acropolis are: The old theater of Dionyssos. The gravestones and sculptures in Kerameikos, the city's ancient cemetery. The Corinthia-style columns of the Temple of Olympian Zeus. Hadrian's Arch. The all-marble Athenian Stadium, where the Olympic Games were revived in 1896. The Clock of Kyrrestos, showing the prevailing wind on each of its 8 sides, standing in Aerides Square, named for the function of the clock. The Roman Forum.

Walk downhill to the Monastiraki area, where the daily "Flea Market" is held. See the view of Athens from the white chapel of Agios Georgios on the Hill of Lycabettus, climbed either by foot or by cable car.

Athens' best-known museums are the National Archaeological Museum at 1 Tositza Street; the collection of ancient coins at the Numismatic Museum, next to the Archaeological Museum; the Acropolis Museum (noted above), the Byzantine Museum at 22 Vassilis Sophias Avenue (closed Monday), for its collection of icons; the Museum of Greek Popular Art (closed Monday); the Museum of the Ancient Agora excavations in the Stoa, an ancient commercial community at Attalus (closed Tuesday). The work of contemporary Greek painters and sculptors in the National Gallery at 60 Vas Constantinou (closed Monday). The more than 2,000 items relating to the social and religious customs of Romanlot and Sephardic Jews in the Jewish Museum (third floor at 36 Amalias Avenue), open daily except Saturday 09:00–13:00. Displays include the reconstructed interior of a provincial synagogue, religious articles, costumes and objects of everyday life.

The 28 exhibit rooms at the fantastic Benaki Museum in central Athens (Vasilisis Sophias Avenue at Koumbari Street), arranged chronologically, cover the entire spectrum of Greek culture from the early Bronze Age to the start of the 20th century: gold, ornaments, jewelry, portraits, statues, embroidery, icons, rare 17th and 18th century bibles, and 8 centuries (10th to 18th) of Islamic art that includes ceramics, textiles and wood carvings. The Benaki is open daily except Tuesday 08:00 to 14:00.

Figurines of white marble from the Cycladic islands (in the Aegean Sea), created 5,000 years ago, in the Goulandris Museum of Cycladic Art (4 Neophytou Douka Street), open Monday–Friday 10:00-16:00, Saturday 10:00–15:00.

A collection of weapons since the Neolithic Age in the War Museum (Vasilisis Sophia Avenue at Rizari Street), open Tuesday-Saturday 09:00–14:00, Sunday 9:30–14:00. Nineteenth century arts and crafts (woodcarving, needlework, naive painting) at the Museum of Greek Folk Art (17 Kydathineon Street), open daily except Monday 10:00–14:00.

The collection (from the Archaic period through the Middle Ages) of stone sculptures, ceramics, bronzes and exceptionally beautiful icons in the Canellopoulos Museum (below the Acropolis, at Theorias and Panos streets), closed Tuesday, open other weekdays 08:45–15:00, Sundays 09:30–14:30.

There are sound-and-light performances in English at Pnyx Hill every night at 21:00. When it ends, cross the road and see native dances of Greece, performed nightly at 22:15 on the Hill of Philopappus.

For Greek arts and handicrafts (ceramics, hand-woven fabrics, alabaster articles, embroideries, hand-carved wood furniture), shop on the streets around Syntagma Square, the center of the city.

Athens - Arghos - Athens   980

| Dep. Athens | 06:30 | 08:30 | 09:28 | 14:59 | 16:09 |
| Arr. Arghos | 09:18 | 11:10 | 12:18 | 17:50 | 19:03 |

Sights in **Arghos:** The Museum, with its archaeological exhibits. From there, it is a 15-minute walk to the ancient theater, carved into the hillside, and to some Roman ruins. A 5-mile taxi ride to the 800 B.C. ruins of Tiryns is well worth the small fare. At the birthplace of Hercules you will see the ruins of Greece's oldest recognizable temple: underground galleries polished for many centuries by the woolly backs of innumerable sheep who sought shelter there during storms. Massive Cyclopean walls.

| Dep. Arghos | 10:18 | 13:53 | 17:51 | 19:25 |
| Arr. Athens | 13:02 | 16:38 | 20:46 | 22:13 |

Athens - Corinth (Korinthos) - Athens   980

Watch 80 minutes after departing Athens for the same view described above, under "Athens–Arghos." The arrival in Corinth is in the "modern" Corinth, built after the 1858 earthquake.

| Dep. Athens | 06:30 (1) | 07:56 | 08:30 (1) | 08:54 | 09:28 (3) |
| Arr. Corinth | 08:06 | 09:27 | 10:14 | 10:24 | 11:19 |

Sights in **Corinth:** The 2500-year old Temple of Apollo. The Kato Pirini Fountain. The rostrum from which St. Paul preached Christianity to the Corinthians.

| Dep. Corinth | 11:20 (2) | 11:56 | 12:36 (1) | 14:31 | 14:53 (1) | 15:57 (1) | 17:46 (2+4) |
| Arr. Athens | 13:08 | 13:50 | 14:27 | 15:58 | 16:38 | 17:42 | 19:12 |

(1) Light refreshments. (2) Restaurant car. (3) Plus other departures from Athens at 09:50 (1) and 12:02. (4) Plus other departures from Corinth at 18:47, 19:55, 20:31 and 21:31.

Athens - Kalamata - Athens   980

| Dep. Athens | 06:30 (1) | 08:50 (2) | 09:20 (2) | 14:32 |
| Arr. Kalamata | 13:00 | 15:55 | 20:03 | 21:30 |

Sights in **Kalamata:** The exhibits at the Museum in the Kyriakos mansion, ranging from Stone Age weapons to Venetian mirrors and coins as well as relics from the 1821 War of Independence. The Byzantine-style Church of Aghii Apostoli. The splendid view from the Frankish castle and, descending from there, see the handmade silk articles at the Convent. Aghios Haralambos, one of the finest Byzantine churches in the area, is a short distance east of the

Convent. Stroll along the seafront.

Dep. Kalamata	06:30 (2)	10:00	15:40
Arr. Athens	14:25	16:38	22:13

(1) Via Xylocastron. (2) Via Arghos. (3) Light refreshments. Change trains in Patras (arr. 15:28-dep. 15:55). (4) Via Xylocastron. Change trains in Patras (arr. 15:10-dep. 15:50 light ref.).

Athens - Pirghos - Olympia - Athens

Most of this trip is alongside the sea, through green fields of citrus and olive trees. Between Athens and Corinth, the train goes across a bridge that spans the Korinthos Canal, which separates northern Greece from Peloponesia.

All of the trains Pirghos–Olympia (and v.v.) are second-class.
980

Dep. Athens	08:54 (1)	13:43
Arr. Pirghos	13:50	18:38
Change trains. 977		
Dep. Pirghos	14:40	20:00
Arr. Olympia	15:16	20:36

Sights in **Olympia:** The first Olympic Games (776 B.C.) were held here and continued here every 4 years for the next 12 centuries. See the Stadium. The fine Olympic Museum, with its marvelous Hermes of Praxiteles sculpture. The temples of Hera and Zeus.

Dep. Olympia	07:30	11:00	16:00
Arr. Pirghos	08:06	11:36	16:36
Change trains. 980			
Dep. Pirghos	09:10 (1)	11:08 (2)	16:29 (1)
Arr. Athens	14:02	17:53	21:22

(1) Light refreshments. Supplement charged. (2) Change trains in Patras (arr. 15:10-dep. 15:50 light refreshments).

Athens - Patras - Athens 980

Dep. Athens	06:30 (1)	08:54	09:50	12:02 (1)	13:43 (3+5)	
Arr. Patras	10:39	12:15	14:38	15:28 (5)	17:05	

• • •

Dep. Patras	06:00 (1)	09:35 (2)	10:42 (1)	13:25 (1)	15:57 (2)	18:03 (1+4)
Arr. Athens	09:20 (5)	13:42	14:02 (5)	17:53	19:12	21:20 (5)

(1) Light refreshments. (2) Restaurant car. (3) Plus other departures from Athens at 14:59 (2), 17:09 (1) and 19:19 (1+5), arriving Patras 19:05, 20:19 and 22:53. (4) Plus other departures from Patras at 19:16, arriving Athens 23:22. (5) Supplement payable.

Sights in **Patras:** Cross the street in front of the railstation to the park. Then walk from the Trion Fountain along Ayiou Nijulauo to the steps that ascend to the Patras Acropolis for a fine view of Patras, the surrounding mountains and the port, third largest of Greece.

After descending the steps, go to the left along Georgiou Street to the old Roman Theater, the Odeon. Another walk from the Trion Fountain is to the Archaeological Museum to see its collection of exhibits from the Mycenean, Geometric, Archaic and Roman periods. Also worth seeing are the Venetian castle and Greece's largest church, St. Andrews's. See the Clock of Patras, made entirely of flowers. Visit the century-old Achaia Clauss Winery, the leading producer of Greek wines.

Athens - Piraeus - Athens

Subway trains depart every few minutes from the southbound section of a combined north-and-south platform at Athens' Omonia Square railstation for the 20-minute ride to Piraeus. Be certain, at the same platform, you are not boarding the northbound train for Kifissia. There is also ordinary train service from Athens to Piraeus.

Sights in **Piraeus:** One of the largest ports on the Mediterranean. Ships sail daily from here to almost all the Aegean islands and to many other Greek ports. The 2 small adjoining ports of Zea and Mikrolimano are for pleasure craft. Bus #20 goes to those ports. The bus terminal is to the left of the railstation. See the neo-classical style Municipal Theater and the exhibits in the Archaeological Museum. The Maritime Museum, closed Monday, exhibits 13,000 items reflecting 5,000 years of Greek seafaring. Plays are performed at the open-air Theater of Kastella in the Summer.

Thessaloniki - Kavala - Thessaloniki

All of the Thessaloniki-Drama (and v.v.) trains have light refreshments.

974

Dep. Thessaloniki	07:50 (1)	09:31	13:30 (1+2)
Arr. Drama	11:32	13:00	16:11
Change to bus. (G.T.O. advice)			
Dep. Drama	10:00	16:00	18:00
Arr. Kavala	10:30	16:30	18:30

Sights in **Kavala:** The view from the Byzantine Fort. The colossal 16th century aqueduct, Kamares. Imaret, the group of Moslem buildings constructed a short time prior to the 1821 War of Independence. The ancient relics in the Archaeological Museum. Beautiful beaches.

Dep. Kavala	08:00	12:00	16:00	18:00
Arr. Drama	08:30	12:30	16:30	18:30
Change to train. 974				
Dep. Drama	10:03 (1)	13:01	17:08 (1)	01:56
Arr. Thessaloniki	12:43 (2)	16:39	20:42	05:20

(1) Reservations recommended. (2) Supplement payable.

SCENIC RAIL TRIPS

Athens - Thessaloniki and Thessaloniki - Athens

970 + Greek Timetable

From **Tithorea** to **Domokos,** the train winds along **Mt. Iti** and **Mt. Orthrys,** providing a panoramic view of many valleys and high mountains and, at one point, of the sea in the distance. Then the train goes along **Pinios River** and passes through **Tembi Valley.** About one hour before arriving **Katerini** (Athens–Thessaloniki), you can see on the left side of the train 9,000-foot-high **Mt. Olympus.**

Dep. Athens (Larissa)	07:00 (1)	08:10	10:00 (2)	13:00 (2)	15:00	17:00 (2+4)
Dep. Tithorea	N/A	N/A	N/A	N/A	N/A	N/A
Dep. Domokos	N/A	N/A	N/A	N/A	N/A	N/A
Dep. Katerini	11:55	14:27	14:50	18:08	20:45	22:02
Arr. Thessaloniki	12:55	15:32	15:51	19:15	21:58	23:13

Sights in **Thessaloniki:** Second largest city in Greece. See the ruins of the Roman Baths, north of the Church of Agios Demetrios. The Roman Market and Theater. Nym- phaion, the ancient circular building. The Arch of Galerius. The unique mosaics in the 4th century Rotunda, at the intersection of Agiou Georgiou and Filippou streets.

The 2 surviving early Christian churches: the 4th century Ahiropiitos and the 5th century Osios David. The 15th century White Tower. The collection of pre-historic to Byzantine items in the Archaeological Museum on YMCA Square. Articles from the past 3 centuries at the Folklore and Ethnological Museum, 68 Vasilisais Olgas.

Dep. Thessaloniki	08:00	13:07	17:07 (2)
Dep. Katerini	N/A	14:40	-0-
Dep. Domokos	N/A	N/A	N/A
Dep. Tithorea	N/A	N/A	N/A
Arr. Athens (Larissa)	15:19	18:58	23:16

Dep. Thessaloniki	18:00	22:04 (2)	23:30 (1)
Dep. Katerini	19:08	23:14	00:46
Dep. Domokos	N/A	N/A	N/A
Dep. Tithorea	N/A	N/A	N/A
Arr. Athens (Larissa)	00:58	05:45	07:26

(1) Carries a sleeping car. Also has couchettes. (2) Reservation required. Supplement charged. Light refreshments. (3) Reservation required. Supplement charged. (4) Plus other departures from Athens at 22:00 (1) arriving Thessaloniki 05:17.

INTERNATIONAL ROUTES FROM GREECE

Thessaloniki is Greece's gateway to Central Europe (and on to Western Europe), as well as to Turkey (and on to the Middle East).

Athens - Belgrade - Budapest

...Plus Salzburg, Vienna, Munich or Venice

	97 b +970	97 b +61	
Dep. Athens	10:00 (1)	23:30 (2)	
Arr. Thessaloniki	15:51	07:50 (3)	
Dep. Thessaloniki	-0-	08:26	

Set your watch back one hour from late September to early April, 2 hours from early April to late September.

	97 b +970	97 b +61	
Arr. Belgrade	-0- (3)	21:23	
Change trains.			
Dep. Belgrade	-0-	21:45	
Arr. Budapest (Keleti)	-0-	05:55 (4)	
Change trains.		61	61
Dep. Budapset (Keleti)	-0-	05:55	12:25 (7)
Arr. Vienna (Westbf.)	-0-	09:20	15:50
Arr. Salzburg	-0-	-0-	19:00
Arr. Munich	-0-	-0-	20:36
Arr. Venice (S.L.)	-0-	-0-	-0-

(1) Carries a sleeping car. Also has couchettes. (2) Day 2. (3) Direct train Athens–Vienna. No train change in Belgrade or Budapest. Carries a sleeping car. Also has couchettes. Arrives Budapest and Vienna on day 2. (4) Day 3. (5) Restaurant car. (6) Arrives at Vienna's Sud railstation. (7) Supplement charged. Restaurant car.

Athens - Patras - Brindisi   980

The Patras-Brindisi boat trip is covered by Eurailpass and Eurail Youthpass but only if you go on Adriatica di Navagazione.

WARNING: The employees of other lines intimate that their ships honor the 2 passes and then charge fees after the boat leaves the pier.

With or without a Eurailpass or Eurail Youthpass, a reservation theoretically can be made on day of departure or day before departure but it is very unlikely that space will be available (particularly during July and August) unless a reservation is made many weeks in advance of departure date.

Those gambling on making a reservation after arriving in Patras can make application January 1 to June 9 and October 1 to December 31 only at the Adriatica di Navagazione embarkation office, located at Othonos Amalias Street 8.

From June 10 to September 30, those without advance reservations can apply also to any Patras travel agency that displays in its window the green badge "Eurail Information—Eurailpass."

Holders of advance reservations must go at all times directly to the Adriatica di Navagazione embarkation office to have their tickets checked, settle port taxes due and obtain the required Embarkation Ticket. That office is open 09:00–13:30 and 16:00–22:00.

Advance reservations before you start your trip can be made by contacting Extra Value Travel, 683 So. Collier Blvd., Marco Island, Florida 33937, U.S.A. Telephone: (813) 394-3384.

Another fee is charged for such special accommodations as aircraft type seats, pullman berths and cabins. There is also a port tax of 180 Drachmas that is not covered by Eurailpass and must be paid in Drachmas.

Passengers without advance reservations must obtain the Embarkation Ticket at least 2 hours prior to the ship's departure time. The ships reserve the right to cancel a reservation when that is not done and to give the space to a standby passenger.

Readers reported to us in 1990 that conditions on the boat were unsatisfactory.

For a view first of the Corinthian Canal and then the Corinthian Gulf, sit on the right side of the train Athens–Patras.

Dep. Athens	06:30	08:54 (1)	09:50	12:02 (1)	13:43 (3+4)
Arr. Patras	09:55	12:15	14:38	15:28 (4)	17:30

It is a 20-minute walk from the railstation to the harbor. A taxi costs about $5.00 (U.S.).

Change to boat. Check Cook's table 1490 for sailing dates.

Dep. Patras Harbor	19:00	22:00	
Arr. Brindisi	10:00	17:00	Both arrivals are on day 2

(1) Light refreshments. (2) Restaurant car. (3) Plus other departures from Athens at 14:59, 17:09 (4) and 19:19 (4), arriving Patras 19:05, 20:27 and 22:37. (4) Supplement payable.

Athens - Thessaloniki - Istanbul

Both of these trains have light refreshments.

970

Dep. Athens	07:00
Arr. Thessaloniki	12:55

Change trains.

974

Dep. Thessaloniki	15:04
Arr. Istanbul	07:20 Day 2. (Reservation recommended.)

IBERIAN PENINSULA
(SPAIN AND PORTUGAL)

Overview

It has become increasingly difficult to speak of Spain and Portugal as a single entity, as each country's tourist industry and infrastructure has progressed independently. Spain, of course, had a big year in 1992 when it hosted the Olympics in Barcelona, the World Expo in Seville, and the seat of the European Cultural Capital in Madrid, as so modernized considerably for the festivities. Lisbon has been the Cultural Capital of Europe in 1994 and some development and expansion has occurred.

Train travel in Spain is highly varied in that you can zoom across central and south Spain from Madrid to Seville in rocket time or take what seems like days to creek 50 kilometers across the Basque country or Galicia. Spain and Portugal have the broadest gauge railroad tracks in Western Europe It is therefore necessary in most crossings from Spain into France (at Irun/Hendaye, Port Bou/Cerbere, or La Tour-de-Carol) to change trains. A few trains running between Spain and France are adaptable to either gauge.

General Information

• Children under four travel free in Portugal and Spain if they do not occupy a separate seat. Half-fare for children 4-11 includes use of a separate seat. Children 12 and over must pay full fare.

• First-class sleeping cars in Spain have single-berth and two-berth compartments. Second-class sleeping cars have three-berth tourist compartments, except the Paris-Madrid and Barcelona Talgos, which have tourist compartments with four berths. There is a supplemental charge for air-conditioned sleeping cars. Neither berths nor this supplement are covered by Eurailpass. Some Spanish trains have second-class couchette cars, with six-berth compartments, as are also available in other Western European countries.

• First-class sleeping cars in Portugal have single and double-berth compartments. Second-class Portuguese sleeping cars have 3-berth compartments.

• Many Spanish train tickets include the price of a lunch or dinner, a fact that is wise to determine this in advance of a trip.

• For most Spanish trains, it is necessary to reserve a seat and have ones ticket stamped with the train number and departure date. Even when traveling with a Eurailpass or a Spanish pass, an endorsed ticket should be obtained for trains requiring them.

• Do not discard a ticket during the journey. Frequently, the ticket is collected at the termination of a ride. If it is not presented at the destination rail station, the passenger must purchase a second ticket.

• Every year, some tourists using Eurailpass or a Spanish pass report being ejected from a Spanish train either just before its departure or at a station en route to their destination for failing to obtain the required endorsed tickets. A person using a pass has been indoctrinated

SPAIN & PORTUGAL

with the idea that he or she need not have either a ticket or (when riding an ordinary train) a seat reservation. This is confirmed everywhere in Europe outside Spain. Unaware of the Spanish Railway regulation, the passenger blithely steps aboard a train in Spain without having the ticket and seat reservation required there and a ticket can be obtained without charge upon presenting a Eurailpass or a Spanish pass. If the train is not exceptionally crowded that day and the conductor appears before the train departs, the passenger is told to get off the train, go back into the rail station, and obtain the required endorsed ticket. Frequently, the notice to do this is given so close to the departure time that the train leaves before the passenger is able to return to it. If the train departs before the conductor has discovered the omission of an endorsed ticket, often the passenger is forced to leave the train at the next stop to obtain a ticket. If that stop is typically brief, the train leaves that station before the passenger is able to return to the train.

• The justification for the Spanish ticket-and-reservation requirement is that Spain's first-class fares are substantially lower than those about 60% of what French National Railroads charges for the 7-hour trip from Paris to Avignon or what Norwegian State Railways charges for the 8-hour Bergen-Oslo trip. The demand for Spain's limited number of express train seats far exceeds the supply. Only by issuing endorsed tickets can they control the situation. The Spanish name for its national company is Red Nacional de los Ferrocar- riles Espanoles. Abbreviation: RENFE. Reservations can be made at RENFE offices both in the major rail stations and at numerous locations outside the station, as well as at various travel agencies in Spanish cities. Making train reservations in Spain is very easy. More than 90% of the stations in Spain are hooked-up with a computer in Madrid, making it usually possible to arrange at one time all of your reservations for train trips in Spain. Reservations can be made as much as two months in advance. Timetable information can be obtained at offices of RENFE and at Spanish travel agencies. Tell the clerk at the train information window your departure date, train number (which you can find in the rail station on the list of departures) and/or departure time, destination and number of seats required. You will be handed a form which you then take to a ticket window, where you will be handed a seat reservation computer card. It will show either an exact seat number or the symbol SR (Seat Reserved) under the column Asiento. If it is marked SR, the conductor will tell you which seat to occupy after you board the car designated on the reservation computer card.

Do not board a Spanish non-local train without a seat reservation!

• To ride without a Eurailpass or a Spanish pass on Spanish trains classified Rap, one must pay a supplement. An even higher supplement must be paid when riding a train classified Talgo, E.L.T. or T.E.R., all of which are air-conditioned. A Eurailpass or a Spanish pass entitles the bearer to ride these special trains without having to pay their supplemental charges, the same as when riding EuroCity or InterCity trains.

• In Spain, Rail Club Lounges are special rail station waiting rooms that have television sets, a bar, telephones, magazines and daily newspapers. These lounges are located at Madrid's Chamartin and Atocha stations, Barcelona's Sants, Valencias Termino, and at the rail station in Bilbao, Cordova, Malaga, Vigo and Zaragoza. These lounges are available to passengers who are ticketed for international trains: Madrid-Paris, Barcelona-Geneva, Barcelona-Paris, Barcelona-Bern...and also for domestic travelers holding first-class tickets for sleeping compartments as well as for coach seats on any Talgo or InterCity train.

In order to avoid waiting in the wrong line for Spanish tickets and seat reservations, take note of these signs you will find in large Spanish railstations:

TRENES DE SALIDA INMEDIATE   trains ready to depart
VENTA PARA HOY   trains leaving later in the day
VENTA ANTICIPADA   for trains leaving on a future day

Other **Spanish** railstation signs:

ANDEN	PLATFORM
ASIENTO	SEAT
BILLETTE	TICKET
CABALLEROS	MEN
COCHE-CAMA	SLEEPING CAR
COCHE-LITERA	COUCHETTES
COCHE-COMEDOR	RESTAURANT CAR
ENTRADA	ENTRANCE
ESTACION	STATION
HOMBRES	MEN
HORARIOS DE TRENES	TIMETABLES
LARGO RECORRIDO	LONG DISTANCE
LLEGADA	ARRIVAL
OFICINA DE INFORMACION	INFORMATION OFFICE
RESERVA	SEAT RESERVATION
SALA DE CONSIGNA	BAGGAGE CHECKROOM
SALIDA	DEPARTURE (EXIT)
SENORAS	WOMEN
TREN CON SUPLEMENTO	TRAIN WITH SURCHARGE
VIA	TRACK

Signs you will find in **Portuguese** railstations:

CARRUAGEM-CAMA	SLEEPING CAR
CARRUAGEM-RESTAURANTE	RESTAURANT CAR
CHEGADA	ARRIVAL
ESTACAO	STATION
HOMENS	MEN
HORARIO DOS CAMINHOS	TIMETABLES
PARTIDA	DEPARTURE
PLATAFORMA	PLATFORM (TRACK)
SAIDA	EXIT
SENHORAS	WOMEN

Spanish Holidays

A list of holidays is helpful because some trains will be noted later in this section as *not* running on holidays. Also, these trains which operate on holidays are filled, and it is necessary to make reservations for them long in advance.

January 1	New Year's Day		Ascension Day
January 6	Epiphany		Corpus Christi Day
March 19	Saint Joseph's Day	June 29	St. Peter and St. Paul
	Maundy Thursday	July 18	National Holiday
	Good Friday	July 25	Saint James' Day
	Easter	August 15	Assumption Day
	Easter Monday (Barcelona)	October 12	Columbus Day
April 1	Victory Day	November 1	All Saints Day
May 1	St. Joseph Artisan Day	December 8	Immaculate Conception
		December 25	Christmas Day

Portuguese Holidays

January 1	New Year's Day	August 15	Assumption of Our Lady
	Shrove Tuesday	October 5	Anniversary of the
	Good Friday		Proclamation of the
	Easter		Portuguese Republic
May 1	Labor Day	November 1	All Saints Day
	Corpus Christi Day	December 1	Restoration of Independence
June 10	Day of The Race	December 8	Immaculate Conception
	(Portuguese National Day)	December 25	Christmas
	Saint Anthony's Day (Lisbon)		

Summer Time

Portugal is one hour earlier than Spain all year. Portugal is on the same time as England nearly all year, except for a few weeks in the Spring and Fall. Both Portugal and Spain change to Summer Time on the last Sunday of March and convert back to Standard Time on the last Sunday of September. During Summer Time, when it is 12:00 in England, it is 12:00 in Portugal and 13:00 in Spain.

SPAIN'S TRAIN PASSES

Spain Flexipass and Spainrail'N Drive are sold both in Spain (at travel agencies and the offices of RENFE — the Spanish Railway) and also outside Spain worldwide by travel agencies and Rail Europe (U.S.A. and Canadian offices listed under "France"). Purchasers must prove by passport that they are *not* residents of Spain.

Spain Flexipass Unlimited train travel. The 1996 *first*-class prices are: $180 for any 3 days within one month. *Second*-class: $144. Additional days: $40 for *first*-class, $32 for *second*-class.

Spain Rail'N Drive Unlimited 3 days of train travel plus 3 days of car rental (any 6 days) within one month. Prices vary (a) whether for one person or for 2 persons, and (b) the category of car. A third and fourth passenger needs to pay only for a 3-day Flexipass.

The 1995 prices *per person* for 2 persons (using the smallest size car) are: $249 for *first*-class train, $219 for *second*-class. More days of car rental could be added ($49 per day for smallest size).

All of the following are sold only in Spain, at main railstations and travel agencies.

Family Card For at least 3 persons from the same family or living at the same address, a discount is given on train tickets for "Blue " periods of the day or all-day to certain destinations on certain trains. Not valid for high speed or inter-regional trains. The passholder pays full fare. All adults except the passholder receive 50% discount on tickets. For children 4–11 the discount is 75%. Valid for one year from date of purchase. Proof by marriage certificate or any other certifying documents is required. The 1996 price is 300 pesetas.

Golden Pass (Senior Citizen and Disabled Person Discount) For persons 60 and older and disabled persons of any age —*and who are residents of Spain*. One must first purchase a "Tarjeta Dorada" (Gold Card) for 300 pesetas at any railstation or Renfe ticket office. Proof of age (passport, etc.) required. Valid for one year. With the Gold Card, there is a 40% discount in "Blue " periods of the day or 25% discount all-day.

Under 26 For travelers under age 26. Valid for 2 months. Cannot be used for high speed trains. Allows discounts up to 15%. The 1996 price is 3,000 pesetas.

Roundtrip Discount A 30% discount on both first-class and second-class roundtrips on high speed trains if both trips are on the same day, 20% discount if both trips are on different days within 2 months. There is a 10% discount for inter-regional trains. The discounts for other trains depends on destination and period of the day.

PORTUGAL'S TRAIN PASSES

Portuguese Railpass Unlimited *first*-class train travel. The 1996 prices are: $99 for any 4 days within 15 days, $155 for any 7 days within 21 days.

Portuguese Rail'N Drive Unlimited 3 days of *first*-class train travel plus 3 days of car rental (any 6 days) within one month. Prices vary (a) whether for one person or for 2 persons, and (b) the category of car. The 1996 prices were not set at the end of 1995. The 1995 price *per person* for 2 persons (using the smallest size car) was $135 and $45 per day for each additional day of car rental. Up to 5 more days of car rental could be added at $20 per day for each person. A third passenger had to pay only $65 for a 3-day *first*-class train pass.

All of the following are sold only in Portugal, at main railstations and travel agencies:

Tourist Ticket Unlimited train travel for any class. The 1995 price was: 15,200 escudos for 7 days, Esc-24,200 for 14 days, and Esc-34,600 for 21 days.

Senior Citizen Discount Persons 60 or older receive 30% reduction.

Family Ticket For 3 or more persons. Valid only for trips of more than 149 km. (92 miles). Passports and documents proving family relationship must be presented. One person must pay full fare. Half-fare for others who are age 13 or older. One-quarter fare for children 4–12. Children under 4 travel free.

EURAILPASS BONUSES

There are no Eurailpass bonuses in Portugal or Spain.

ONE-DAY EXCURSIONS AND CITY SIGHTSEEING

Here are 67 one-day rail trips that can be made comfortably from 13 major Spanish and Portuguese cities, returning to them in most cases before dinner-time. Notes are provided on what to see and do at each destination. The number after the name of each route is the Cook's timetable.

The 13 base cities are: Barcelona, Cordoba, Granada, Leon, Lisbon, Madrid, Porto, Regua, San Sebastian, Seville, Tarragona, Valencia and Vigo.

This section concludes with details on 12 rail trips recommended for exceptional scenery plus 6 trips to/from Madrid, the schedules for 2 other major routes (Barcelona-Valencia and Lisbon-Seville), and the international rail connections from Portugal and Spain.

Barcelona

There is rail service (Table 414) between the center of Barcelona (Sants railstation) and the city's airport every 30 minutes from 05:44 to 22:14. The rail service from the airport to the city is every 30 minutes from 06:12 to 22:42.

Local trains, not requiring seat reservations, depart from Barcelona's underground Pas de Gracia and Sants railstations. Faster express trains, requiring seat reservations, also depart from Pas de Gracia and from Sants, as well as from Barcelona's Termino station.

A guided walking-tour audiocassette (and Walkman adaptable to one or 2 headphones) can be rented from Libreria de la Virreina, at Rambla 99. It is closed Sunday of one week and Saturday of the alternate week. Open 10:00-14:00 and 16:30-20:30.

Your sightseeing here can be divided into covering 4 separate areas of Barcelona. In the Gothic Quarter: The cloisters in the 14th century Cathedral (La Seu), the Episcopal Palace, Palacio de la Generalidad, many elegant 14th and 15th century palaces, the Federico Mares Museum. The Picasso Museum.

In the Montjuich area: the Museum of Catalan Art in the National Palace, the collection of El Greco, Velasquez and Rembrandt paintings at the Archaeological Museum in Palacio Real, handicrafts and architecture representing every region of Spain in the Spanish Village.

In the Tibidado area: Pedralbes Palace, Pedralbes Monastery, and the view all the way to Montserrat and the Pyrenees.

In the modern city center: Stroll the mile-long Ramblas, from Plaza de Cataluna to Plaza Puerta de la Paz at the waterfront, with its Columbus monument. You will enjoy seeing the numerous stalls selling hundreds of varieties of birds, the many stands with flowers and plants, the very large central food market, cafes offering tapas (the local and varied between-meal snacks), and at least half the population of Barcelona. Visit the Picasso Museum, for exhibits of his early Impressionist works.

Another rewarding walk, in the opposite direction, is along beautiful Paseo de Gracia, from Plaza de Cataluna to Avenida del Generalismo Franco (also called "Diagonal," its original name), to see luxury shops, decorative sidewalks designed by Dali, and several buildings created by Barcelona's most radical and inventive architect, Antonio Gaudi.

In Plaza Gaudi, you must see the uncompleted and absolutely unique church, La Sagrada Familia, the architect's most important work. It was started in 1884. Because of lack of funds, Barcelonians believe construction will not be finished until 100 years from now.

What has been constructed in the last 100 years is well worth seeing: the 4 lofty towers (nearly 300 feet tall), the Nativity and Passion facades with the Tree of Life supported by the central arch, and the wrought-iron plants in the side chapels of the completed crypt.

Although public transportation is not available to the Gaudi-designed park, Parque Guell, we suggest you take a taxi there to see it and to see the view of Barcelona from its elevated plaza. The paths in this park are decorated with concrete pillars that imitate trees and vines. Also see the colorful undulating bench surfaced with broken ceramic pieces, on the plaza. And the gigantic tiled frog fountain on the steps leading down from the park's plaza.

Regular city tours include only the church and one apartment building designed by Gaudi. A guided tour of most of his projects is offered by the Municipal Tourist Office (Avenida Paralelo 202) for both individuals and groups.

Lisbon

Santa Apolonia is Lisbon's railstation for departure to Madrid and beyond (to France and the rest of Europe). It has currency exchange and hotel reservation services.

See the beautiful Avenida de Liberdade. The Tower of Belem (monument to Portugal's sailors). The view from the bi-cultural St. George's Castle, built by the Visigoths in the 5th century and by the Moors in the 9th century. Largo das Portas do Sol (Sun Gateway), one of the 7 gates into the ancient Arab City. Santa Cruz quarter. Alfama Quarter. Salazar Bridge.

The lovely Praco de Rossio. The marvelous collection of priceless Middle Eastern and European tapestries, jewelry, ceramics, and Dutch, Spanish, Italian and 15th to 18th century Portuguese paintings in the Ancient Art Museum (9 Rua das Janelas Verdes). The more than 3,000 art treasures (Rembrandt, Fragonard, Corot, many Impressionists, Egyptian sculpture, Persian art) in the Gulbenkian Museum (45 Avenida de Berna). Across the park from it is the Gulbenkian Center of Modern Art (Rua Dr. Nicolau Bettencourt).

Edward VII Park. The Zoological Garden. The Botanical Garden. The Museum of Modern Art. The Municipal Museum. The greatest collection in the world of royal coaches in the Belem Palace at Praca Afonso de Albuquerque. The Flea Market. The Military Museum. The collection of 17th and 18th century Portuguese and Indo-Portuguese furnishings in the Museum of Decorative Arts (2 Largo das Portas do Sol).

The Maritime Museum, in the West wing of Jeronimos Monastery. Jeronimo's Church. The Cathedral. House of Facets, its front entirely faced with dark stones that have been cut into diamond-like facets.

Madrid

There is train service connecting Madrid's Chamartin and Atocha stations. A Eurailpass *can* be used on it. At Chamartin station, look for the track marked "Linea de Atocha y Guadalajara." At Atocha, go to the separate small station, a short walk from the main station. "Atocha-Apeadero" is a lower level at Atocha railstation.

See the Prado Museum, with its breathtaking collection of great paintings (open Tuesday–Saturday 09:00–19:00, Sunday 09:00–13:45). Puerta del Sol. The Goya Pantheon. Plaza Mayor. San Miguel Basilica. San Isidor Cathedral.

Two-hour, guided tours of the Royal Palace take you nearly a mile through 52 sumptuously furnished rooms on the main floor. Open Monday-Saturday 09:30–17:15, Sundays and holidays only 09:30–12:45.

CAUTION: the Palace is closed to the public about 60 days a year for official functions. Check in advance about the day you plan to tour it.

At the Palace, you will see more than 400 antique clocks (keeping perfect time), paintings (Velasquez and Goya), and 15th and 18th century Flemish tapestries. Then, spend more hours seeing the magnificent Armory. Also, visit the Carriage Museum, near the west gate.

The Music Museum has 5 instruments made by Stradivari. Other fascinating rooms in the Palace are the State Apartments and Chapel, Apartments of Queen Maria Cristina of Hapsburg, the Private Apartments, Royal Pharmacy, Library, Numismatic Museum and Music Museum.

Additional interesting sights in Madrid are the Botanical Garden. The Bullfighting Museum. Descalzas Reales Convent. The Archaeological Museum. The Folk Museum. The Americas Museum. Retiro Park. University City. Plaza de Espana, with its stone monument to Cervantes. The Royal Tapestry Factory, closed Sunday during August.

For the best food in Spain, and it is moderately priced, dine at Restaurante Botin, at Calle de Cuchilleros 17. Every dish is marvelous. Their specialties are roast suckling pig and roast baby goat. These and many other foods are cooked there with oak wood in the original 16th century tiled oven. Botin is run by a very handsome gentleman, Antonio Gonzalez Jr. His family has operated Botin for more than 90 years.

San Sebastian

Excellent beaches. The Goya and El Greco collection at San Sebastian Picture Gallery. Santa Maria Church. San Telmo Museum. The Aquarium and Oceanographic Museum in Sea Palace, open daily 10:00–3:30 and 15:00–20:00. The picturesque fishing village nearby. Climb up Mount Urgull for a view of the bay from the Castle of Santa Cruz de la Mota.

Seville

The city of Don Juan and Carmen. You must not miss seeing Corpus Christi Cathedral, largest Gothic cathedral in the world and the site of Columbus' tomb.

The 14th century Alcazar Palace with its magnificent chambers, particularly the room where foreign ambassadors were received. Its colorful mosaics and tiles, delicate wrought-iron and carved wood ceilings are spellbinding. You can see nearby Segovia from the tower of Isabella's castle. Allow time to stroll through the elaborate gardens there: bronze and marble statues, lovely fountains and the extraordinary Pavillion of Carlos V.

On one side of the Alcazar is a university, formerly Antigua Fabrica de Tobacos, the tobacco factory Bizet immortalized in his opera, Carmen. On the other side of the Alcazar is Barrio de Santa Cruz, with its ancient buildings and narrow streets. Once a refuge for Jews fleeing the Inquisition, now it is a fashionable residential section of Seville.

You can enjoy spending many hours in Maria Luisa Park, seeing the beautiful buildings, gardens, pools and fountains there. Particularly noteworthy is the magnificent Plaza de Espana.

Other notable sights in Seville: The 12th century La Giralda Tower, a minaret when the Moors ruled here (open only on Sundays and holidays 11:00–14:00). The 12-sided Tower of Gold. Meander along the city's cobbled streets to see many picturesque homes.

RESERVATIONS ARE STRONGLY ADVISED
ON ALL SPANISH TRAINS!!

In the following timetables, where a city has more than one railstation we have designated the particular station (in parentheses).

Barcelona - Blanes - Barcelona   417 Costa Brava Resorts

Go to the "Estacion de Cercanias" (suburban section of Barcelona's Termino railstation) to board the train for Blanes. Seat reservations are *not* required for this ride. Board well before departure time to avoid standing for 70 minutes.

All of these trains are second-class only.

Take a bus or taxi from Blanes' railstation to the center of the village. It is a half-mile walk there from the station.

Dep. Barcelona (Sants)	Every 30 minutes from 06:12 to 22:12
Arr. Blanes	90 minutes later

Sights in **Blanes**: Stroll the waterfront. See the Aquarium and Botanical Garden, near the location of the daily fish auction, at 17:00. The Gothic fountain. The Church of Santa Maria. The view of the Bay of Blanes from the ruins of the castle on San Juan Mountain. it is a short drive to many popular beaches: Santa Catalina, Fanals, Lloret and Tossa.

Sights in **Lloret de Mar**: See the remains of the Tower of the Moors. The colored tiles that decorate the Church of San Roman. The 11th century castle at the beach. There is an active nightlife here (discotheques, nightclubs and casinos).

Sights in **Tossa de Mar**: Exhibits of Roman archaeology, modern paintings and sculptures (Catalan and foreign), and a 1933 painting of the town by Marc Chagall in the Town Museum, open 10:00–13:00 and 17:00–20:00. See the view from the lighthouse.

Dep. Blanes	Every 30 minutes from 06:00 to 21:30
Arr. Barcelona (Sants)	90 minutes later

Barcelona - Girona - Barcelona   416

All of these trains are second-class, unless designated otherwise.

Dep. Barcelona (Sants)	07:00 (1)	08:10	09:10	10:10 (2)	10:15
Dep. Barcelona (P. de G.)	-0-	08:15	09:15	-0-	10:20
Arr. Girona	08:32	09:32	10:19	11:12	11:27

Sights in **Girona**: The collection of paintings, sculptures, ceramics, glass objects, coins and silverware at the Art Museum in the former Episcopal Palace, open 10:00–13:00 and 16:30–19:00. Exhibits of local history and art in the Museum of the History of the city, open Monday–Saturday 10:00–14:00 and 17:00–19:00, Sundays and holidays 9:30–14:30.

The Museum in the magnificent 14th century Cathedral has such outstanding exhibits as the 11th century Tapestry of Creation. the 10th century Book of the Apocalypse, and the 10th century Arab chest of Hisham II, the oldest Hispanic-Arab work of silver. It is open daily 10:00–13:00 and 15:30–18:00.

The Provincial Archaeological Museum is open daily 10:30–13:00 and 16:30–19:00.

Visit the 12th century Arab Baths. See Sobreportes, the ancient gate. Stroll on the narrow 17th century streets.

Dep. Girona	11:36	12:30	13:29	14:34 (3)	15:26 (5)
Arr. Barcelona (P. de G.)	12:52	13:40	14:50	15:50	16:50
Arr. Barcelona (Sants)	12:57	13:45	14:55	14:55	16:55

(1) Reservation advisable. Has a first-class coach. Restaurant car. (2) Departs/arrives Barcelona's Estacio de Franca railstation. Reservation advisable. Supplement charged. Has a first-class coach. Restaurant car. (3) Has a first-class coach. (4) Light refreshments. Has a first-class coach. (5) Plus other departures from Girona at 16:24 (3), 17:28, 18:27, 19:23, 19:41 (2), 20:35 (4), 20:42 and 22:05, arriving Barcelona (Sants) 17:45, 18:55, 19:59, 21:32, 20:50 (2), 21:45, 22:16 and 23:28.

Barcelona - Lerida - Barcelona   410

It is advisable to make a reservation for this ride well in advance of departure date. Although departures are from other stations, go to Barcelona's Triunfo railstation to make this reservation. On boarding, find a seat on the left side so as to have a good view of the restored 13th century Seo Antiqua Cathedral before the arrival in Lerida.

Reservation advisable for all of these trains, unless designated otherwise.

Dep. Barcelona (Paseo de Gracia)	-0-	08:15 (2)
Dep. Barcelona (Sants)	07:30 (1)	08:30
Arr. Lerida	09:19	10:12

Sights in **Lerida**: The Archaeological Museum, in the Antiguo Hospital de Santa Maria, where the tourist office is located. A walking tour is easy with the city map available there. See the old Byzantine-Gothic-Moorish 13th century Cathedral. The Palacio de la Paheria. Stroll the maze of narrow streets in the interesting old section on the right bank of the Segre River, and visit the 12th century Alcazaba (castle).

Dep. Lerida	15:43 (3)	18:40 (2)	20:34 (2)	21:04 (1)
Arr. Barcelona (Sants)	18:00	20:35	22:35	23:04
Arr. Barcelona (Paseo de Gracia)	18:10	20:46	22:46	-0-

(1) Light refreshments. (2) Reservation advisable. Supplement charged. Restaurant car. (3) Restaurant car.

Barcelona - Montserrat - Barcelona   Barcelona T.O.

This trip is not covered by Eurailpass.

Dep. Barcelona (P. Espanya)	Every 2 hours from 09:11 to 15:11
	(Summer: until 17:11)
Arr. Martorell-Enllac	50–60 minutes later
Change to cable car.	
Dep. Martorell-Enllac	Every 15 minutes from 10:00 to 17:45
Arr. Monistrol (Monastery)	5 minutes after departing Martorell-Enllac

Sights in **Montserrat**: The 9th century Monastery, still occupied by hundreds of Benedictine monks, is 3700 feet above a valley. It ranks with Zaragoza and Santiago de Compostela as one of the most important pilgrimage sites in Spain. See the Grotto of the Virgin, the Mirador, the Chapel of San Miguel and the Chapel of Santa Cecilia. Then take a funicular to the Grotto of San Juan Garin and an aerial tram to the 4,000-foot-high Hermitage of San Jeronimo, from where you will have a view of the Eastern Pyrenees.

Dep. Monistrol (Monastery)	Every 15 minutes from 10:00 to 17:45
Arr. Martorell-Enllac	5 minutes after daparting Monistrol
Change to train.	
Dep. Martorell-Enllac	Every 2 hours from 11:26 to 19:26
	(Summer: from 09:26)
Arr. Barcelona (P. Espanya)	50–60 minutes later

Barcelona - Sitges - Barcelona

Frequent local trains run from Barcelona's Paseo de Gracia and Sants stations to Sitges, a 30-minute trip.

Sights in **Sitges:** The 18th century furnishings at Casa Llopis. Antique dolls collected from every part of Europe, in the Lola Anglada Museum. El Greco paintings at the Cap Ferrat Museum.

Barcelona - Tarragona - Barcelona

Frequent local trains run from Barcelona's Paseo de Gracia and Sants stations to Tarragona, a 90-minute trip.

Sights in **Tarragona:** Relics of pre-Roman, Roman, Visigothic and Moorish cultures.

It is a short, but severely uphill, walk from the railstation to the long promenade, Balcon del Mediterraneo, from which there is a marvelous view of the sea. Two strolling streets start at each end of the "balcony." The first is Rambla del Generalismo. The other is Rambla de San Carlos.

We suggest you rest a while at one of the many sidewalk cafes on either Rambla. Then, start your walking tour of Tarragona by going 2 blocks from the "balcony," down Rambla de San Carlos to where it intersects with San Augustin. Turn right (the street name changes to "Mayor") and walk one-quarter mile to the 12th century Cathedral, worth seeing for its large and architecturally unique Cloisters, influenced by Roman, Gothic and Moorish styles.

Next, return to Rambla de San Carlos and turn right. Walk down it 2 blocks until it intersects with Abalto. Turn right and walk uphill, alongside the Roman wall.

You will then be on the semi-circular Paseo Arqueologico walk, from which there are excellent views of the countryside surrounding Tarragona.

At the end of this walk, bear to the right and come downhill on Avenida de la Victoria for 5 minutes until you reach Plaza del Rey. There, you can visit both the museum in the 1st century B.C. Pretoria and also the marvelous mosaics and ancient coins in the Archaeological Museum.

Across from Plaza del Rey is the Roman Amphitheater. Having completed a circle, you will again be at Balcon del Mediterraneo, and it is all downhill to return to the railstation.

Granada - Malaga - Granada   426

Between Bobadilla and Malaga, the train travels through the spectacular **El Chorro Gorge**.

All of these trains are second-class.

Dep. Granada	08:20		Dep. Malaga	13:55	17:35
Arr. Bobadilla	10:05		Arr. Bobadilla	14:58	18:34
Change trains.			*Change trains.*		
Dep. Bobadilla	10:25		Dep. Bobadilla	15:20	18:40
Arr. Malaga	12:10		Arr. Granada	17:47	20:29

Sights in **Malaga**: Winter sun. The 9th century Alcazaba Moslem palace and the ruins of Gibralfaro Castle, 2 fortresses which made Malaga a major stronghold in the Middle Ages. The Fine Arts Museum. Sagrario, an unusual rectangular church that was originally a mosque. The Cathedral.

Lisbon - Algarve Resorts

The 100-mile Algarve (Lisbon-Vila Real de Santo Antonio) coastline, famous for its many popular resorts, consists of several centuries-old fishing villages and offers championship golf courses, tennis, horseback riding and all the watersports (windsurfing, fishing, water skiing, yachting).

Lisbon - Vila Real or Lagos   449

There is a bridge from **Vila Real** to **Ayamonte** (Spain) every 30 minutes. Summer: 08:30-23:30. Winter: 09:00-18:00.

Boat			Train		
Dep. Lisbon			Dep. Vila Real	-0-	06:03 (5)
(Ferry Ter.)	07:25 (1)	07:55 (2)	Dep. Faro	-0-	07:15
Arr. Barreiro	07:55 (9)	08:25	Dep. Albufeira	-0-	07:43
Change to train.			Dep. Lagos	06:10 (4)	-0-
Dep. Barreiro	08:05	08:35	Arr. Tunes	07:27 (3)	07:48
Arr. Tunes	11:0	12:17 (3)	Dep. Tunes	-0-	08:03
Dep. Tunes	11:05	12:29	Arr. Barreiro	-0-	11:11
Arr. Lagos	-0-	13:23	*Change to boat.*		
Arr. Albufeira	11:13	-0-	Dep. Barreiro	-0-	11:25
Dep. Faro	11:40	-0-	Arr. Lisbon		
Arr. Vila Real	-0-	-0-	(Ferry Ter.)	-0-	11:55

(1) Plus other Lisbon departures for Tunes, Albufeira, Faro and Vila Real at 13:25 (6), 17:30 (6), 18:50 (7) and 23:10. (2) Plus other departures for Tunes and Lagos at 17:30, 18:50 and 23:10, all requiring train change in Tunes. (3) Change trains in Tunes. (4) Plus other Lagos departures at 13:30 (8), 17:00 (8) and 22:30. (5) Plus other Via Real departures at 06:35 (8) and 21:35. (6) Reservation required. (7) Reservation advisable. (8) Light refreshments. (9) Runs daily July 1-August 31.

Sights in **Lagos**: This historic town was the center for the Portugal–Africa trade. See the marvelous tiles in the Baroque Chapel of San Antonio.

Sights in **Albufeira**: The Moorish ambiance here is striking. This is a very "arty" place. Has a colorful market.

Sights in **Faro**: The ancient church. The old quarter.

Lisbon - Setubal and Lisbon - Evora   448

Boat					
Dep. Lisbon (Ferry Ter.)	05:45	07:25	15:15	19:20	23:10 (5)
Arr. Barreiro	06:15	08:15	15:45	19:50	23:40
Change to train.					
Dep. Barreiro	06:20	08:20 (2)	16:00	20:05 (3)	23:50
Arr. Setubal	-0-	-0-	-0-	-0-0	-0-
Arr. Evora	-0-	10:30	18:10	-0-	-0-

Sights in **Setubal**: The paintings in the Town Museum. Next to it, the lovely Church of Jesus. The view from the 16th century Saint Philip's Castle, while having lunch there.

Many sardine canneries, some of them open to the public. The Maritime Museum. Take an inexpensive taxi ride to the nearby (5½ miles) Palmela Castle.

Sights in **Evora**: Portugal's "Museum City." The Tourist Information Office faces the main square, Praca Do Giraldo. See the beautiful Temple of Diana, oldest Roman remains on the Iberian Peninsula. Visit the excellent regional museum in what was once the Bishop's Palace. The 17th century monastery, now an inn called Pousada dos Loios. The Church of St. Francis, where the walls are decorated with the skulls and bones of nearly 5,000 monks.

Dep. Evora	-0-	-0-	19:25 (2)	23:03
Dep. Setubal	12:57 (3)	-0- (3)	-0-	-0-
Arr. Barreiro	15:10	15:10	21:41	00:12
Change to boat.				
Dep. Barreiro	15:20	15:12	21:50	00:40
Arr. Lisbon (Ferry Ter.)	30 minutes later			

(1) Runs Monday–Friday, except holidays. (2) Reservation advisable. Light refreshments. (3) Second-class.

Lisbon - Coimbra - Lisbon   445

Reservation is advisable for all of these trains and all of them have light refreshments, unless designated otherwise.

Dep. Lisbon						
(S. Apol.)	07:22 (1)	08:05	08:10	09:00	11:00	11:35 (2)
Arr. Coimbra	09:46	10:13	10:45	11:21	13:14	14:08

Sights in **Coimbra**: Walk uphill to the 13th century Old Cathedral, one of the finest Romanesque buildings in Portugal. Continue to the treasures at the Machado do Castro Museum. At the top of the hill is the 13th century University, where you must see the gilded carved stone and wood and the Baroque library. Also see the silver shrine in the magnificent interior of the New Convent of St. Clara. The Almedina Gate. Nearby, the Roman ruins at Conimbriga. Try the local food specialty, roasted suckling pig (leitao).

Dep. Coimbra	12:19	15:49 (3)	17:02 (1)	17:22	18:19 (3)	19:14 (5)
Arr. Lisbon						
(S. Apol.)	14:25	17:50	19:15	19:50	20:20	21:35

(1) Reservation *required*. (2) Runs Friday and Saturday. Reservation *required*. Supplement charged. (3) Reservation *required*. Supplement charged. (4) Reservation not available. No refreshments. (5) Plus other departures from Coimbra at 19:26 (4), 20:19 (6) and 21:29, arriving Lisbon 22:38, 22:23 23:35. (6) Runs Sunday.

Lisbon - Estoril and Cascais - Lisbon   P142

A scenic seashore ride that costs about one U.S. dollar.

All of these trains run daily, except Sundays and holidays.

Dep. Lisbon (Cais do Sodre)	Frequent times from 05:30 to 02:30
Arr. Estoril	35 minutes later
Arr. Cascais	4 minutes after departing Estoril

Sights in **Estoril:** Portugal's major beach resort. Try your luck in the gambling Casino.

Sights in **Cascais:** Bloodless bullfights on Summer Sundays. Surf fishing. Wednesday is market day, on the street that veers right from the railstation. There are taxis that will take you to Sintra (see "Lisbon–Sintra").

Dep. Cascais	Frequent times from 05:30 to 02:30.
Dep. Estoril	3 minutes later
Arr. Lisbon (Cais do Sodre)	35 minutes after departing Estoril

Lisbon - Fatima - Lisbon   P100-A

Dep. Lisbon (S. Apol.)	07:29	10:33	Dep. Fatima	14:33	20:38 (1)
Arr. Entroncamento	09:06	12:25	Arr. Entroncamento	14:52	-0- (1)
Change trains.			*Change Trains.*		
Dep. Entroncamento	09:43	12:56	Dep. Entroncamento	15:13	-0-
Arr. Fatima	10:05	13:16	Arr. Lisbon (S. Apol.)	17:00	22:38

(1) Direct train. No train change in Entroncamento.

Sights in **Fatima:** Millions of pilgrims have come here from all over the world to worship at one of the world's most famous Marian Shrines.

Lisbon - Porto (Oporto) - Lisbon   445

Reservation is required for all these trains and they have light refreshments, unless designated otherwise.

Dep. Lisbon (S. Apol.)	07:00 (1)	08:05	09:00 (2)	11:00 (3)
Arr. Porto (Campanha)	10:00	11:30	13:15	14:25

Sights in **Porto**: The more than 80 wine stores occupying all of the Vila Nova de Gaia quarter. The 12th century Cathedral. The 3 great bridges: Dom Louis, Dona Maria and Ponte da Arrabida. Portugal's oldest chapel, Sao Martinho de Cedofeita. The gilded wood-carvings in the Church of San Francisco.

The Church of the Clerigos, with its 10-story tower. The city's many beautiful gardens. The 15th century Church of Santa Clara. The Moorish Hall of the Stock Exchange. The 14th century convent-fortress, Leca do Bailio Abbey. The fine paintings, sculpture, porcelain and jewelry at the Soares dos Reis Museum. The folklore objects of this region in the Ethnological Museum.

Dep. Porto (Campanha)	14:30 (4)	15:30 (3)	17:00 (4)	19:00 (3)	20:10
Arr. Lisbon (S. Apol.)	17:50	19:50	20:20	22:20 (7)	23:20

(1) Runs Monday-Friday except holidays. Supplement charged. Restaurant car. (2) Runs daily, except Sundays and holidays. Supplement charged. (3) Reservation advisable. (4) Supplement charged. (5) Restaurant car. (6) Runs Monday-Friday and Sunday, except holidays.

Porto - Braga - Porto   446

Dep. Porto (Cam.)	06:27 (4)	09:34
Arr. Braga	08:16	11:14

Sights in **Braga**: The most interesting buildings are on the narrow street that runs from Arco da Porta Nova to the Praca da Republica. (It changes its name along the way.)

See the beautiful Santa Barbara Gardens. The treasury at the Cathedral (gold and ivory crosiers, also damask and velvet vestments embroidered with heavy gold thread). The museum in the Casa dos Biscainhos. The terraced gardens that ascend uphill to the church of Bom Jesus.

Dep. Braga	12:16	14:29 (3)	17:25 (2)	21:02 (3)
Arr. Porto (Cam.)	13:23	15:53	18:30	22:40

(1) Change trains in Nines. (2) Reservation *required*. Light refreshments. (3) Runs daily, except Saturday. (4) Runs daily except Sundays and holidays.

Lisbon - Sintra - Queluz - Lisbon   P 141

All of these trains run daily, except Sundays and holidays.

Dep. Lisbon (Rossio)	Frequent times from 05:56 to 02:00
Arr. Sintra	45 minutes later

Sights in **Sintra**: An outstanding old town, nestled on a mountaintop. There are many antique and craft shops on this village's winding, narrow streets. Take the "Sintra–Vila" bus from the railstation to the city's tourist office, where guide books and maps are available.

Use inexpensive taxis to see the view from the 19th century Palacio de Pena, the Moorish Castle, the Palacio Real, and the marvelous gardens at the Palacio de Monserrate. The palaces are closed on Tuesday.

Dep. Sintra	Frequent times from 05:15 to 01:15
Arr. Queluz	12 minutes later

Sights in **Queluz**: The beautiful gardens, the monument to Maria I and the exquisite restaurant at the 18th century Palacio de Queluz, a miniature Versailles.

Dep. Queluz	Frequent times from 05:39 to 01:38
Arr. Lisbon (Rossio)	37 minutes later

Madrid - Aranjuez - Madrid

	420	420	425	419
Dep. Madrid (Cham.)	08:00 (1)	09:00 (1)	09:05 (2)	-0-
Dep. Madrid (Atocha-Cer.)	08:15	09:15	09:20	-0-
Dep. Madrid (P. de Atocha)	-0-	-0-	-0-	09:35
Arr. Aranjuez	08:42	09:44	09:53	10:09

Sights in **Aranjuez**: The Museum of Royal Robes, the luxurious interiors of the Porcelain Room (walls and cielings covered with red and green figures depicting Chinese and Japanese themes), the intricately chiseled Moorish interior of the Arab Chamber, the more than 200 drawings from the Ching Dynasty in the Chinese Print Room, and the Throne Room all in the Royal Palace, which has guided tours that are usually in Spanish. See the bed of Queen Isabella II, inlaid with carvings, floral decorations and bronze ornaments.

There are guided tours of the magnificent furnishings in the 18 rooms at the 18th century Casa del Labrador, where a 19th century clock in the form of Hadrian's Column is exhibited in the sculpture gallery. (A ruby and pearl-studded star strikes the hour by spiraling up and down the column.) Platinum, gold and bronze decorations are displayed in the Platinum Chamber. There are many silk wall tapestries in this palace.

The Pastere and Island gardens. The collection of royal ships in the Casa de Marinos. The 300-acre forest, called Jardin del Principe (Prince's Garden). The Fountain of Hercules and the Fountain of Bacchus in the park called Jardin de la Isla.

	419	425	419	433	419
Dep. Aranjuez	14:08	15:00	15:57 (4)	16:11 (2)	17:18 (6)
Arr. Madrid (P. de Atocha)	14:48	-0-	16:34	-0-	17:55
Arr. Madrid (Atocha-Cer.)	-0-	15:52	-0-	16:46	-0-
Arr. Madrid (Ch.)	-0-	16:07	-0-	16:59	-0-

(1) Suppplement charged. Light refreshments. (2) Second-class. (3) Restaurant car. (4) Runs Monday-Friday, except holidays. (5) Light refreshments. (6) Plus other Aranjuez departures at [420] 19:26 (2), [419] 20:02, [433] 20:15 and [420] 20:25 (1).

Madrid - Avila - Madrid   431

Dep. Madrid (Cham.)	08:00 (1)	09:00 (1)	10:00	11:30	13:30
Arr. Avila	09:23	10:19	11:24	12:54	14:52

Sights in **Avila**: There are bus and inexpensive taxi services from Avila's railstation to the city center, about one mile from the station. Take a stroll on the 1½-mile long 11th century walls that circle Avila to see best the 88 semi-circular towers and more than 2,300 battlements (11:00–13:00 and 16:15–18:00, closed weekday afternoons from October through April).

Also see the El Greco painting and the enormous (nearly 200 pounds) silver monstrance in the fortress Cathedral. The baroque 17th century Convent of St. Teresa. The Basilica of St. Vincent.

Dep. Avila	13:25 (2)	16:15 (2)	17:50 (3)	18:34	19:52 (4+5)
Arr. Madrid (Cham.)	14:53	17:42	19:21	20:13	21:20

(1) Supplement charged. Light refreshments. (2) Light refreshments. (3) Second-class. (4) Supplement charged. (5) Plus other Avila departures at 20:57 (2) and 21:46, arriving Madrid 22:34 and 23:20.

Madrid - Burgos - Madrid   431

Dep. Madrid (Ch.)	09:20 (1)	10:00	Dep. Burgos	17:18 (1)	19:03 (2)	19:15
Arr. Burgos	12:25	13:32	Arr. Madrid (Ch.)	21:05	22:09	23:20

(1) Second-class. (2) Supplement charged. Light refreshments.

Sights in **Burgos**: The many interesting chapels in the magnificent 13th century Cathedral of Santa Maria, where the remains are of Spain's greatest hero, El Cid, and those of his wife. The Archaeological Museum. Stroll 15 minutes on Paseo del Espolon, from the 14th century Arch of Santa Maria to the statue of El Cid.

To see the Royal Monastery of Las Huelgas, only a few minutes outside Burgos, take a bus from Plaza de Jose Antonio.

Madrid - Cuenca - Madrid   419

Dep. Madrid (Ato.)	09:35	11:30	Dep. Cuenca	15:29	18:07 (2)
Arr. Cuenca	12:03	14:10	Arr. Madrid (Ato.)	17:55	20:49

(1) Runs Friday and Sunday. (2) Plus another Cuenca departure at 20:05 (1), arriving Madrid 22:46.

Sights in **Cuenca**: The Tourist Information Office (Calderon de la Barca 28) is only a 5-minute walk from the railstation.

Strolling down the winding lanes and narrow footpaths is marvelous. See the old houses hanging from sheer cliffs in this 15th century setting. The best modern art museum in Spain, Museo de Arte Abstrato. Wonderful El Greco paintings and 15th and 16th century altarpieces in the cathedral. A few steps away from the Cathedral, the collection of coins, statues and Roman mosaics at the Archaeological Museum in a restored 14th century granary.

Paleolithic red paintings of bison, wild boars, horses and archers at La Pena del Escrito National Monument.

Madrid - Escorial - Madrid

Timetables for this trip were were deleted from Cook's in 1992. The travel time is one hour. Below are 1991 schedules.

Dep. Madrid (Ato.)	09:15 (1)	12:05 (1)	Dep. Escorial	16:30	19:30 (1)
Dep. Madrid (Ch.)	09:30	12:20	Arr. Madrid (Ch.)	17:13	20:10
Arr. Escorial	10:14	13:07	Arr. Madrid (Ato.)	17:29	20:25

(1) Second-class only.

Sights in **Escorial**: Burial place of Spanish kings and queens. The Royal Monastery of San Lorenzo del Escorial, an enormous granite fortress (300 rooms), has more than 1,600 paintings (many of the finest Velasquez and El Greco) and murals, and it houses the Charter Hall Royal Library, containing 60,000 volumes.

See the Phillip II Apartments, the Throne Room, Apartments of the Bourbon kings, Whispering Hall, Casita del Principe, and the Basilica.

The Basilica was intended to copy St. Peter's in Rome, filled with gilt and marble carvings. Its 4 enormous pillars are 100 feet in circumference and support a cupola more than 300 feet high. Life-size bronze figures (royal families) surround the 100-foot-high altar.

The 18th century Prince's Cottage has 9 elaborately furnished rooms. Don't miss seeing the famous cross by Benvenuto Cellini and paintings by El Greco, Ribera and Velasquez in the church.

The circular, domed Royal Pantheon, crypt for most of the Spanish kings since the 17th century. Thirty feet underground, it contains 26 charcoal-gray marble coffins, in 5 tiers, and is illuminated by Italian baroque candelabra. Lesser royalty rest in white marble coffins in other rooms.

In planning a visit here, keep in mind that this enormous 16th century building covers 8 acres. It is open 10:00–13:00 and 15:30–18:30 (18:00 in Winter).

Also visit the nearby monumental Valley of the Fallen, memorializing those who died in Spain's civil war. A 492-foot-high cross of concrete faced with stone marks this crypt containing more than 100,000 bodies. Its 900-foot-long Basilica is a tunnel into the mountain. You can ride to the top of the cross in an elevator.

Madrid - Salamanca - Madrid   432

All of these trains are second-class only.

Dep. Madrid (Ch.)	09:35	Dep. Salamanca	17:35	20:10 (1)
Arr. Salamanca	12:55	Arr. Madrid (Ch.)	20:55	23:30

(1) Runs Sunday only.

Sights in **Salamanca:** The Convent of San Sebastian. The church and cloister at St. Stephens Monastery. The 15th and 16th century houses around the beautiful Plaza Mayor.

The oldest part of the city is the area between Plaza Mayor and the Tormes River. En route to the river, the 12th century Church of St. Martin is on Plaza del Corrillo. Opposite it is the 15th century Casa de las Conchas, named so because its facade is covered with 400 stone conch shells.

A few minutes walk from it is the third oldest university in Europe (after Oxford and Bologna), founded in 1218. A stone staircase leads to the university's magnificent Old Library which has 60,000 books from the 16th to 18th centuries and ancient manuscripts going as far back as 1059.

The city's Old and New cathedrals stand side by side behind the university. A magnificent altar and an elaborate ceiling are the highlights of the New Cathedral, begun in 1513. Its 16th century organ still works.

Madrid - Segovia - Madrid   432

All of these trains are second-class only. The arrivals are estimated.

Dep. Madrid (Chamartin)	06:25 (1)	09:16	10:16	12:16 (1)	
Arr. Segovia	08:05	10:56	11:56	13:56	
		•	•	•	
Dep. Segovia	12:55	14:55	16:55	18:55	19:36 (2)
Arr. Madrid (Chamartin)	14:35	16:35	18:35	20:35	21:16

(1) Runs daily, except Sundays and holidays. (2) Plus another Segovia departure at 20:55, arriving Madrid 22:35.

Madrid - Toledo - Madrid   432

Seat reservations are not required or obtainable for this ride. Board well before departure time to avoid standing for entire ride. The walk from Toledo's railstation to the center of that city is long. It is best to take a bus or taxi.

Most of these trains are second-class. The arrivals are estimated.

Dep. Madrid (Atocha-Cercarias)	07:20	09:09	10:50	12:20
Arr. Toledo	09:30	10:19	12:00	13:30

Sights in **Toledo**: The most spectacular Cathedral in Spain (750 stained-glass windows, priceless church clothing, jeweled ornaments, hundreds of tapestries, and paintings by Goya, El Greco, Velasquez, Tintoretto, Murillo and Titian). The house of El Greco, with a superb collection of his paintings. The 15th century Palace of the Duchess of Lerma. The Church of Santo Tome, containing El Greco's "Burial of the Count of Orgaz."

The Sefardi Museum in the 14th century El Transito Synagogue. The Provincial Museum of Archaeology and Fine Arts in the 16th century Hospital de Santa Cruz. The Army Museum in the Alcazar (fortress).

The Museum of Santa Cruz. Cristo de la Luz, the church first built in the 11th century as a Mosque (on the site of the ruins of a Visigothic church). It was then converted into a Catholic church in the 12th century. The works of Spain's leading modern sculptor, in the Vitorio Macho Museum.

Dep. Toledo	12:15	14:20	16:30	17:50	19:25 (1)
Arr. Madrid (Atocha-Cercarias)	13:25	15:30	17:40	19:00	20:35

(1) Plus another Toledo departure at 21:30, arriving Madrid 22:40.

Madrid - Valladolid - Madrid   431

Dep. Madrid (Cham.)	08:00 (1)	09:00 (1)	10:00
Arr. Valladolid	10:27	11:25	12:30

Sights in **Valladolid**: The National Museum of (Wood) Sculpture in San Gregorio College, founded in the 15th century by the confessor to Isabella, one of the finest museums in Spain, open Tuesday–Saturday 10:00–14:00 and 16:00–19:00. Its life-size 15th–16th century carvings are famous for their emotive and natural expressions, swirling draperies, and their realistic, vivid colors.

These sculptures were carved for religious processions and also to fill many of the magnificent and very complex altars that still remain in churches and museums throughout Spain. Visit the adjacent Church of San Pablo.

Sculptures, carvings and massive gold and silver objects are exhibited at the Cathedral in a museum that is open Tuesday–Friday 10:00–13:30 and 16:30–19:00; on Saturdays, Sundays and holidays 10:00–14:00.

See Vivero Palace, where Ferdinand and Isabella were married in 1474. The magnificent ceilings and wood sculptures at the National Museum of Sculpture, in the 15th century Colegio de San Gregorio. The wood sculptures in the 15th century Convent of Santa Clara. The 15th century Palace of Santa Cruz.

Cervantes' House, where he spent the last years of his life. Simancas Castle, 7 miles from Valladolid. Charles V converted the castle into a storehouse for state records. It holds 8,000,000 documents that provide a history of Spanish administration from the 16th through the 20th century.

Dep. Valladolid	15:00 (1)	16:35 (2)	17:30	18:45 (3)	19:55 (4+5)
Arr. Madrid (Cham.)	17:42	19:21	20:13	21:20	22:34

(1) Supplement charged. Light refreshments. (2) Second-class. (3) Supplement charged. (4) Light refreshments. (5) Plus another Valladolid departure at 20:40, arriving Madrid 23:20.

Madrid - Zaragoza - Madrid   410

All of these trains charge a supplement.

Dep. Madrid (Chamartin)	07:00 (1)	09:00 (1)	11:00 (2)
Arr. Zaragoza (Portillo)	10:00	12:10	14:13

Sights in **Zaragoza**: The Tapestry Museum in the Cathedral. The Exchange. Aljaferia, an 11th century Moorish palace. The Basilica de Pilar. The Goya and El Greco paintings at the Museo de Pintura.

Dep. Zaragoza (Portillo)	14:13 (3)	16:00 (2)	17:00 (1)	18:00 (1)	20:00 (1)
Arr. Madrid (Chamartin)	18:41	19:30	20:35	21:10	23:05

(1) Light refreshments. (2) Restaurant car. (3) Second-class.

San Sebastian - Biarritz - Bayonne - San Sebastian

46
Dep. San Sebastian (Donastia)   08:32
Arr. Hendaye   09:10
Change trains.
137
Dep. Hendaye   09:39 (1)
Arr. Biarritz   10:00
Arr. Bayonne   10:10

Dep. Bayonne   14:15   14:40 (1)   15:53 (2)   20:40 (1)
Dep. Biarritz   14:24   14:53   16:05   20:53
Arr. Hendaye   14:49   15:16   16:29   21:17
Change trains.
46
Dep. Hendaye   -0-   15:20 (1)   21:25 (1)
Arr. Irun   -0-   15:25   21:26
Change trains.
Dep. Irun   -0-   15:35   22:15 (4)
Arr. San Sebastian (Donastia) -0- 15:50   22:30

(1) TGV. Reservation required. Supplement charged. Light refreshments. (2) Light refreshments. (3) Direct train to San Sebastian. No train change in Irun. (4) Second-class.

San Sebastian - Bilbao - San Sebastian   436

*This second-class narrow-gauge rail trip is **not** covered by Eurailpass. Other (slower) trains, which depart/arrive Bilbao's Concordia railstation, run on this route at frequent times not listed in Cook.*

Dep. San Sebastian (Amara) 08:35 | Dep. Bilbao (Axturi)   13:30   19:30
Arr. Bilbao (Axturi)   10:25 | Arr. San Sebastian (Amara) 14:40   20:40

 Sights in **Bilbao**: The Fine Arts Museum. The Biscay Historical Museum. The Begona Sanctuary.

San Sebastian - Burgos - San Sebastian   430

All of these trains have light refreshments.

Dep. San Sebastian	08:32	09:04
Arr. Burgos	11:11	12:20
Dep. Burgos	17:46	18:24 (1)
Arr. San Sebastian	21:05	21:17

(1) Supplement charged.

San Sebastian - Pamplona - San Sebastian   412

All of these trains have light refreshments.

Dep. San Sebastian (Dona.)	10:30 (1)	Dep. Pamplona	19:38
Arr. Pamplona	12:15	Arr. San Sebastian (Dona.)	21:28

(1) Operates June 25-September 25. Runs Monday, Wednesday, Friday and Sunday. (2) Runs Monday, Wednesday, Friday and Sunday.

Sights in **Pamplona**: The 14th century Gothic Cathedral, with its cloisters and Diocesan Museum. The Navarre Museum. The running of the bulls through the city's streets, every year between July 6 and July 15.

Seville - Cadiz - Seville   425

All of these trains are second-class, unless designated otherwise.

Dep. Seville (S.Justa)	07:30	08:20 (1)	08:45	10:00
Arr. Cadiz	09:57	10:28	10:47	12:02

Sights in **Cadiz**: The African environment. The Fine Arts Museum. The Museum of Archaeology and Art. The Cathedral, with its monumental Silver Tabernacle, decorated with almost 1,000,000 jewels. The Historical Museum.

Dep. Cadiz	13:05	15:05	16:30	18:20 (3)
Arr. Seville (S.Justa)	15:02	17:02	17:55	20:15 (4)

(1) Runs June 24-September 5 only.(2) Supplement charged. Restaurant car. (3) Plus other departures from Cadiz at 18:55 and 20:30 arriving Seville 20:49 and 22:35. (4) Runs Tuesday, Thursday and Sunday June 2- September 25.

Seville - Cordoba - Seville   425

Dep. Seville (S. Justa)	07:00 (1)	08:00 (2)	08:45 (1)	09:45 (1)	11:00 (1+5)
Arr. Cordoba	07:42	08:42	10:14	10:43	11:42

Sights in **Cordoba**: One thousand years ago, this was the most important city west of Constantinople (today's Istanbul). Its 200,000 houses *then* were double those of today. See the array of marble, jasper, onyx and granite on the 80 marble columns in the 8th century Mosque, built on top of what was first a Roman temple and later a Catholic church, before the Moors seized Cordoba.

Following the recapture of the city by the Spaniards and in the conversion of the building to a church again, most of the original 1,000 marble columns were removed to provide space for a nave and a high altar. Called "Mezquita," its interior is illuminated by 4,000 bronze and copper lamps. Its ceiling is carved cedar. Its mosaics are made from 35 tons of glass bits. The Mosque is closed 12:00–16:00, and the Alcazar palace fortress is closed 12:00–17:00.

Also see the 14th century Synagogue. The Fine Arts Museum. The Museum of Julio Romero de Torres. The Museum of Cordoban art, with its Bullfight Museum. The Provincial Archaeological Museum, one of the most important archaeological collections in Spain. The Roman Bridge, built in the time of Emperor Augustus. The home of the Marques de Viana, with its 14 flower-filled patios.

Dep. Cordoba	12:47 (1)	13:50 (3)	15:20 (3)	15:38 (1)	16:50 (3+6)
Arr. Seville (S. Justa)	13:40	15:43	17:13	16:25	18:43

(1) Supplement charged. Restaurant car. (2) Runs daily except Sundays and holidays. Supplement charged. Restaurant car. (3) Second-class. (4) Light refreshments. (5) Plus another Seville departure at 11:40 (3), arriving Cordoba 13:20. (6) Plus other departures from Cordoba at 18:00 (3), 18:49 (1), 20:20 (3), 20:40 (1) and 22:49 (1), arriving Seville 19:40, 19:45, 22:13, 21:35 and 23:40. (7) Does not run May 29-September 24 and December 16-January 9.

Seville - Granada - Seville   426

Both of these trains are second-class only.

Dep. Seville (S.Justa)	08:15	Dep. Granada	16:45
Arr. Granada	12:10	Arr. Seville (S. Justa)	20:46

Sights in **Granada**: The indescribable Alhambra complex, consisting of the Royal Palace, adjacent Partal Gardens, the 9th century Alcazaba watchtower fortress and, a quarter of a mile away, the Generalife (summer palace of Moorish caliphs), one of Europe's greatest gardens.

At the Royal Palace, be sure to see the Court of the Mexuar, the Hall of the Ambassadors, the Court of the Myrtle Trees, the Hall of the Two Sisters, the Court of the Lions, the

Royal Baths and the Daraxa courtyard. The Mocarabes Gallery and Abencerrrajes Gallery are near the Court of the Lions.

The Partal Gardens are a series of terraces featuring roses, poinsettias, orange and lime trees, lilies, bouganvillea and carnations.

Also see the crypts of Ferdinand and Isabella in the Cathedral's Royal Chapel. The Fine Arts Museum and Hispano-Moorish Museum in Charles V's Palace. The Royal Hospital. Casa Castril.

Seville - Jerez - Seville   425

All of these trains are second-class.

Dep. Seville (S. Justa)	07:50	08:20 (4)	08:45	10:00 (5)
Arr. Jerez	09:07	09:30	10:05	11:17

Sights in **Jerez**: A 3,000-year old city, famous for its horses, beautiful women and sherry wine. Its renowned Andalusian horses, bred from Spanish mares and stallions which the Moorish invaders brought here more than 1,500 year ago, do not date as far back as the wine does. Phoenicians started the vineyards here in 1100 B.C. Later Romans began the vinting of sherry. Many of the best wineries offer tours that conclude with tasting.

See the annual September Wine Festival. Its opening ceremony takes place on the steps that lead into the 17th century Collegiate Church of Santa Maria. Next to it is the 11th century Moorish fort, the Alcazar.

Also visit the 15th century San Dionisio Church. See the exhibit of Punic, Roman and Arabic pottery, tombstones, household implements and statues in the Archaeological Museum that occupies 2 small rooms inside Chapter House on tiny Plaza de la Asuncion, across from San Dionisio Church.

Look for the 7th century BC Corinthian helmet, believed to be the oldest Greek artifact ever found in Spain.

Dep. Jerez	13:43	15:48	17:17	18:55 (3+6)
Arr. Seville (S. Justa)	15:02	17:02	18:35	20:08

(1) Supplement charged. Light refreshments. (2) Restaurant car. (3) Plus other Jerez departures at 19:33, 21:15, and 22:58 (2), arriving Seville 20:49, 22:35 and 23:15. (4) Runs June 24-September 5 only. (5) Runs June 24-September 4, December 15-January 8. (6) Runs Tuesday, Thursday and Sunday June 2-September 25 and December 18-January 8. Also runs Sundays October 2-December 17 and January 15-May 25.

Seville - Malaga (via Bobadilla) - Seville 426

Both of these trains are second-class.

Dep. Seville (S. Justa)	08:15		Dep. Malaga	17:35
Arr. Malaga	11:20		Arr. Seville (S.Justa)	20:46

Sights in **Bobadilla:** An elegant modern resort, designed to resemble an Andalusian village. Recitals on a pipe orgen that has 1,595 pipes are presented in a copy of a 16th century church.

Seville - Torremolinos - Seville

426			*427 Electric train.*	
Dep. Seville (S.B.)	08:15		Dep. Torrenmolinos	17:04
Arr. Malaga	11:20		Arr. Malaga	17:22
Change to electric train.			*Change to ordinary train.*	
427			*426*	
Dep. Malaga	11:30		Dep. Malaga	17:35
Arr. Torremolinos	11:48		Arr. Seville (S.B.)	20:46

Sights in **Torremolinos:** Characters from all over the world, on and around this resort's 5-mile beach.

Tarragona - Tortosa - Tarragona 415

Dep. Tarragona	08:00 (1)	08:58	09:11	09·58 (1)	12·08 (3)
Arr. Tortosa	08:43	09:41	10:18	10:42 (2)	13:11

Sights in **Tortosa:** St. Louis College, founded in 1554 by Charles V for Moors converting to Christianity. The Cathedral. The Bishop's Palace.

Dep. Tortosa	13:15	15:06 (1)	15:45	17:00	18:40 (1+6)
Arr. Tarragona	14:19	15:53	16:53	17:57	20:12

(1) Supplement charged. Light refreshments. (2) Runs May 29-September 24 and December 15-January 8. (3) Second-class. (4) Runs daily, except Sundays and holidays. Supplement charged. Light refreshments. (5) Operates late June to early September. (6) Plus other Tortosa departures at 19:55 (2) and 21:10 (1), arriving Tarragona 20:55 and 22:00.

Valencia - Alicante - Valencia   415

Dep. Valencia (Ter.)	08:00	10:50 (2)	Dep. Alicante (Ter.)	17:05	18:34 (3+4)
Arr. Alicante (Ter.)	10:15	12:50	Arr. Valencia (Ter.)	19:05	21:19

(1) Operates late June to late September. Light refreshments. (2) Supplement charged. Light refreshments. (3) Second-class. (4) Plus other Alicante departures at 19:30 (1) and 20:25 (3), arriving Valencia 21:50 and 23:10.

Sights in **Alicante**: The avenue lined with date palms, part of the complete African atmosphere. The huge Moorish castle. Take the 26-mile bus trip to Elche to see the only palm forest in Europe.

Alicante - Benidorm - Denia - Alicante   418

There is marvelous scenery on a one-class narrow-gauge train that runs from Alicante (via **Benidorm**), to **Denia** and the time to take it (13:15–17:57) before returning to Valencia. *Not covered by Eurailpass.*

A special tourist train called "Limon Express" (*not covered by Eurailpass* and for which Cook's does not carry a timetable) runs between Benidorm and **Gata de Gorgos** on Wednesday and Friday. Taking "Limon Express" requires arriving Alicante the prior day and overnighting in Alicante.

Departing 08:15 from Alicante's FGV railstation, arriving Benidorm 09:21. Change to "Limon Express." Depart Benidorm 09:50 for this roundtrip, arriving back in Benidorm 13:50. Depart Benidorm 14:51, arriving Alicante (FGV) 15:57.

Tickets for "Limon Express" (sold by Alicante travel agencies) include visiting a guitar factory, and visiting Gata de Gogos, and a half-bottle of sparkling wine. The 1994 prices were: 1,250 pesetas for an adult, 650 pesetas for a child.

Valencia - Cuenca - Valencia   419

Dep. Valencia (Ter.)	08:40	11:50	Dep. Cuenca	14:15	18:30
Arr. Cuenca	11:58	15:27	Arr. Valencia (Ter.)	17:25	21:34

Sights in **Cuenca**: See notes under "Madrid–Cuenca"

Valencia - Murcia - Valencia   415

All of these trains are second-class.

Dep. Valencia (Ter.)	07:50	Dep. Murcia	17:14	22:15 (1)
Arr. Murcia	11:58	Arr. Valencia (Ter.)	21:19	02:00

(1) Light refreshments. Runs daily except Saturdays.

Sights in **Murcia**: The Moorish granary. The 14th century Gothic-Romanesque Cathedral. Glass, pottery and leather factories.

Valencia - Tarragona - Valencia   415

Dep. Valencia (Ter.)	06:30 (1)	08:15	09:45 (2)
Arr. Tarragona	09:50	10:59	12:22

Dep. Tarragona	15:28 (2)	18:28 (2)	19:35 (1)
Arr. Valencia (Ter.)	18:25	21:20	22:35

(1) Second-class coach. Restaurant car. (2) Supplement charged. Light refreshments.

SCENIC RAIL TRIPS

Here are 16 exceptionally scenic rail trips in Spain and Portugal.

Barcelona - La Tour-de-Carol - Villefranche - Perpignan - Barcelona

Passengers on the famous La Tour-de-Carol to Villefranche narrow-gauge service (called "The Yellow Train") may ride either in modern cars, an antique car or a completely open car, which John Zucker of New York City recommends for best glimpses of beautiful Pyrenees mountain scenery.

This very scenic route can be traveled either as a one-day circle trip from Barcelona (see schedules below) or when going from Spain to France. (A direct train Perpignan–Marseille [Table 162] departs Perpignan 20:01.)

You pass the popular **Mont-Louis** and **Font-Romeu** ski resorts and then ride alternately along very narrow ledges and also on very high bridges as the line criss-crosses canyons before arriving in the ancient walled-city of **Villefranche-de-Conflans**, a few miles from the **Vernet les Bains** sulfur-bath spa. The train-change in Villefranche is an easy cross-platform transfer.

The One-Day Circle Trip

All of these trains are second-class.

413				143		
Dep. Barcelona (Sants)	06:15	09:18		Dep. Villefranche	13:16	17:16 (2)
Arr. La Tour	09:59	12:48		Arr. Perpignan	14:03	18:04
Change to narrow-gauge				*Change trains.*		
"Yellow Train"				163		
143				Dep. Perpignan	17:11	18:25
Dep. La Tour	10:36	14:04		Arr. Port Bou	17:58	19:10
Dep. Font-Romeu	11:38	15:15		*Change trains.*		
Arr. Villefranche	12:53	16:42		416		
Change trains.				Dep. Port Bou	17:25	19:35 (1)
				Arr. Barcelona (P. de G.)	19:54	-0-
				Arr. Barccelona (Sants)	19:59	22:00

(1) Light Refreshments. (2) Plus another Villefranche departure at 18:24, arriving Barcelona (Sants) 23:28.

Barcelona - Massanes - Blanes - Barcelona   416

Fine coastline and mountain scenery on this easy one-day circle excursion. There are no tourist restaurants in Massanes or Blanes.

(Via Granollers)

Dep. Barcelona (Sants)	06:53 (1)	08:10 (2)	09:10	10:15	11:12 (2)	12:10
Arr. Massanes	08:00	09:08	10:00	11:08	12:59	13:03

Second-class only.

Dep. Massanes	08:00	09:52	11:58	12:50	13:53	15:52
Dep. Blanes	-0-	-0-	-0-	-0-	-0-	-0-
Arr. Barcelona (Sants)	09:02	10:54	12:57	13:45	14:55	16:55

(1) Runs daily, except Sundays and holidays. Second-class. (2) Second-class.

Barcelona - Zaragoza - Madrid 410

There are many ancient towns, castles, mountains and gorges to see on this route.

Dep. Barcelona (Sants)	08:30 (1)	10:00 (2)	12:00 (1)	15:30 (1)	23:10 (4)
Arr. Zaragoza	11:51	13:56	15:58	18:55	03:50
Arr. Madrid (Cham.)	15:05	17:45	19:30	22:10	08:00

(1) Supplement charged. Restaurant car. (2) Light refreshments. (3) Carries a sleeping car. Also has second-class couchettes. Restaurant car. (4) Carries a sleeping car. Coach is first-class. Restaurant car.

Barcelona - Puigcerda

There is beautiful Pyrenees mountain scenery on this portion of the Barcelona–Toulouse route. As shown below, this trip also can be made as a one-day excursion from Barcelona.

All of these trains are second-class, unless designated otherwise.

413

Dep. Barcelona (Sants)	06:15	09:18	15:06
Arr. Puigcerda	09:53	12:42	18:21
Arr. La Tour-de-Carol	09:59	12:48	18:26
Change trains. 144			
Dep. La Tour-de-Carol	10:40 (1)	13:35 (1)	19:17 (1)
Arr. Toulouse (Mat.)	13:11	16:10	22:17

(1) Has first class.

Here is the easy one-day excursion 413
All of these trains are second-class only.

Dep. Barcelona (Sants)	06:15	09:18	15:06
Arr. Puigcerda	09:53	12:42	18:21
Arr. La Tour-de-Carol	09:59	12:48	18:26
	•	•	•
Dep. La Tour-de-Carol	10:52	13:19	18:50
Dep. Puigcerda	10:58	13:25	18:56
Arr. Barcelona (Sants)	14:29	16:38	22:08

Barcelona - Tarragona

This trip is noted for excellent scenery along the Mediterranean coastline. Complete schedules can be found with "Barcelona" schedules.

Barcelona - Valencia

There are good views of the Mediterranean shoreline on this ride.
    Schedules appears with "Barcelona" schedules.

Cordoba - Malaga - Cordoba   426

Scenic canyons can be seen on this trip, an easy one-day excursion from Cordoba.

All of these trains are second-class, unless designated otherwise.

Dep. Cordoba	06:50	12:13 (1)
Arr. Malaga	09:35	14:45

Sights in **Malaga**: See notes under "Granada–Malaga"

Dep. Malaga	13:55	16:10 (2)	19:40 (3)	20:10	22:35 (4)
Arr. Cordoba	16:46	18:28	22:28	23:10	01:28

(1) Light refreshments. Subject to confirmation. Has both first and second-class coaches. (2) Restaurant car. Subject to confirmation. Has both first and second-class coaches. (3) Restaurant car. (4) Light refreshments.

Leon - Oviedo - Leon   435

Very good mountain scenery on this one-day roundtrip.

Sights in **Leon**: The stained-glass windows in the Cathedral and the 11th century Church of San Isidoro.

Dep. Leon	05:45 (1)		Dep. Oviedo	11:12 (1)	11:38 (2)
Arr. Oviedo	08:25		Arr. Leon	13:05	13:28

(1) Second-class. (2) Supplement charged. Light refreshments.

Leon - Monforte   440

The Leon–Monforte portion of the Leon–Vigo route is recommended for mountain scenery.

Both of these trains are second-class only.

Dep. Leon	08:05	Dep. Monforte	16:31
Arr. Monforte	12:03	Arr. Leon	20:55

Lisbon - Porto - Vigo - Santiago de Compostela...Lisbon

This table shows both extending the Leon-Vigo trip (above) from Vigo to Santiago de Compostela and also the route from Lisbon to Santiago. Notes on this marvelous attraction appear under "Madrid–Santiago."

445		*439*	
Dep. Lisbon (S. Apol.)	11:00	Dep. Santiago	08:40 (3)
Arr. Porto (Campanha)	14:25	Arr. Vigo	10:15
Change trains. 446		*Change trains. 446*	
Dep. Porto (Campanha)	15:09 (2)	Dep. Vigo	12:55
Set watch forward one hour		*Set watch back one hour*	
Arr. Vigo	18:42	Arr. Porto (Campanha)	16:05
Change trains. 439		*Change trains. 445*	
Dep. Vigo	20:12 (3)	Dep. Porto (Campanha)	17:00 (4)
Arr. Santiago	22:13	Arr. Lisbon (S. Apol.)	20:20

(1) Runs daily, except Sundays and holidays. Reservation required. Light refreshments. (2) Reservation advisable. Light refreshments. (3) Second-class. (4) Reservation required. Supplement charged. Light refreshments.

Porto - Viana do Castelo - Vigo   446

Schedules allow stopping over in Viana on the Porto–Vigo route.

Reservation is advisable for all of these trains. All of these trains have light refreshments.

Dep. Porto (Camphanha)	07:39	15:09	18:57
Arr. Viana do Castelo	-0-	16:39	20:15
Arr. Vigo	11:05	19:10	22:57

Sights in **Viana do Castelo**: A pretty, little fishing resort. Walk along the twisting road lined with pine and eucalyptus trees, up to the Basilica of Santa Luzia for marvelous views (or take the funicular).

See a collection of ceramics for which Portugal is famous, at the Municipal Museum. The Renaissance buildings in the Praca da Republica. The church of Sao Domingos.

Dep. Vigo	07:20
Arr. Viana do Castelo	09:18
Arr. Porto (Camphanha)	10:42

Porto - Regua - Porto   447

There is good river scenery on this easy one-day roundtrip.

Dep. Porto (S. Bento)	08:45	10:48 (1)	12:15 (2)	13:18	14:35 (1+4)
Dep. Porto (Campanha)	08:52	10:56	12:23	13:26	14:42
Arr. Regua	11:21	12:54	14:47	16:02	16:44
		•	•	•	
Dep. Regua	11:22 (1)	13:16	14:50 (3)	16:02 (1)	17:54 (5)
Arr. Porto (Campanha)	13:27	15:12	16:38	18:21	19:55
Arr. Porto (S. Bento)	13:35	15:18	16:45	18:30	20:02

(1) Reservation advisable. Light refreshments. (2) Runs daily, except Sundays and holidays. (3) Reservation advisable. (4) Plus another daytime Porto (S. Bento) departure at 16:15, arriving Regua 18:37. (5) Plus other Regua departures at 19:07 and 21:10 (1), arriving Porto (S. Bento) 21:41 and 23:30.

Madrid - Barcelona   Barcelona - Madrid   410

Many ancient towns, castles, mountains and canyons to see on this route.

Dep. Madrid (Cham.)	01:00 (1)	11:00 (2)	12:00 (4)	14:00 (2)	16:00 (2+8)
Arr. Barcelona (Franca)	08:50	18:00 (3)	20:20	20:55	22:55
		•	•	•	
Dep. Barcelona (Franca)	08:05 (2)	09:35 (5)	15:10 (2)	21:50 (1)	
Arr. Madrid (Cham.)	15:05	17:4	22:10	05:40 (1)	

(1) Departs/Arrives Madrid's Puerto de Atocha railstation. Carries only sleeping cars. (2) Supplement charged. Restaurant car. (3) Departs/Arrives Barcelona's Sants railstation. (4) Second-class. Light refreshments. (5) Light refreshments. (6) Carries a sleeping car. Also has couchettes. Light refreshments. (7) Carries a sleeping car. Also has couchettes. Coaches are first-class only. Light refreshments. (8) Plus other Madrid departures at 22:00 (6) and 23:10 (7), arriving Barcleona 07:00 (Sants) and 08:00 (Sants).

THE MAJORCA ONE-DAY RAIL TRIP

If you are planning on visiting the island of Majorca, you will enjoy this trip.

This narrow-gauge, easy one-day trip goes through olive groves before tunneling through a mountain and emerging high above **Soller**. At the tunnel exit, the train stops for 10 minutes to allow passengers to enjoy the view before the train spirals downhill to Soller. A quaint tram makes the short ride from Soller to the seaside **Puerto de Soller**.

Palma - Soller   422

*This ride is **not** covered by Eurailpass.*

Dep. Palma	08:00	10:40	13:00	15:15	19:45 (1)
Arr. Soller	55 minutes later				

• • •

Dep. Soller	06:45	09:15	11:50	14:10	18:30 (1)
Arr. Palma	55 minutes later				

(1)January 1-April 30 and November 1-December 31.

THE TRIP TO ANDORRA

Barcelona - La Tour-de-Carol - Andorra la Vella

All of these trains are second-class only.

413 Train

Dep. Barcelona (Sants)	06:15	-0-	15:06
Arr. La Tour-de-Carol	09:59	-0-	18:26

Change to a bus (weather permitting).   144 a

Dep. La Tour-de-Carol	11:10 (1)	12:00 (2)	18:35 (3)
Arr. Andorra la Vella	13:15	14:00	20:35

Sight in **Andorra la Vella**: Capital of the quaint, tiny (50,000 population) co-principality, governed jointly by the French government and the Spanish Bishop of Urgel. Both the Spanish peseta and the French franc are legal currency here.

The country's main export is postage stamps, created for philatelists. Small ski resorts and duty-free shops are the main attraction for the 6,000,000 tourists who come here every year. Located in the eastern Pyrenees, the country's mountain peaks reach heights of 9,800 feet.

Lying in one of Andorra's 6 valleys, this is the market town for the entire country (179 square miles). Catalan (the language of the Barcelona area), Spanish and French are spoken here.

Dep. Andorra la Vella	07:45	08:15 (5)	14:30 (3)
Arr. La Tour-de-Carol	10:00	10:30	17:00
Change to train. 413			
Dep. La Tour-de-Carol	-0-	10:52	18:50
Arr. Barcelona (Sants)	-0-	14:29	22:08

(1) Operates June 1 to September 30. (2) Operates October 1 to May 31. (3) Operates July 1 to September 30. (4) Operates May 1 to October 31. (5) Operates May 1-October 31.

THE MADRID ROUTES

Madrid is the hub of the Iberian Peninsula, with spokes going from it to the major cities of Spain and Portugal: Barcelona, Bilbao, Cordoba, Lisbon, San Sebastian, Santiago de Compostela, Seville and Valencia. Here are the schedules for reaching those cities from Madrid:

Madrid - Barcelona   Barcelona - Madrid

Covered under the description of scenic trips.

Madrid - Bilbao   430

Dep. Madrid (Chamartin)	15:30 (1)	23:00 (2)
Arr. Bilbao (Abando)	21:15	07:55

Sights in **Bilbao**: This is the largest Basque city. A major port and industrial city.

Dep. Bilbao (Abando)	16:25	23:00 (2)
Arr. Madrid (Chamartin)	22:09	07:45

(1) Supplement charged. Light refreshments. (2) Carries a sleeping car. Also has couchettes. Coaches are second-class.

Madrid - Lisbon   80 + 433

Both of these trains charge a supplement and have light refreshments.

Dep. Madrid (Chamartin)	-0- (2)	22:30 (1)
Dep. Madrid (Atocha)	14:00	-0-
Set your watch back one hour.		
Arr. Lisbon (S. Apolonia)	21:45	08:33

• • •

Dep. Lisbon (S. Apolonia)	11:55 (2)	22:05 (1)
Set your watch forward one hour.		
Arr. Madrid (Atocha)	19:56	-0-
Arr. Madrid (Chamartin)	-0-	08:40

(1) Carries a sleeping car. Also has couchettes. (2) Runs daily except Saturday.

Madrid - San Sebastian   430

Dep. Madrid (Cham.)	10:00 (1)	15:30 (1)	18:15 (2)	23:00 (3)
Arr. San Sebastian	16:16	21:27	01:35	07:55
Dep. San Sebastian	08:32 (4)	13:33 (5)	16:01 (1)	22:45 (3)
Arr. Madrid (Cham.)	14:53	20:25	22:09	07:45

(1) Light refreshments. (2) Coach is second-class. (3) No supplement charge. Carries a sleeping car. Also has couchettes. Coaches are second-class. (4) No supplement charged. (5) Operates late September to late May. Coaches are second-class.

Madrid - Santiago de Compostela   441

Dep. Madrid (Cham.)	14:00 (1)	21:45 (2)
Arr. Santiago	21:15	07:40

• • •

Dep. Santiago	09:49 (3)	13:40 (4)	22:18 (2)
Arr. Madrid (Cham.)	17:35	21:30	08:45

(1) Supplement charged. Light refreshments. (2) Carries a sleeping car. Also has couchettes. Coaches are second-class. Restaurant car. (3) Runs Saturday only. Supplement charged. Light refreshments. (4) Runs daily, except Saturday. Supplement charged. Light refreshments.

Sights in **Santiago de Compostela**: One of the 3 most sacred places in Christendom, ranking equally with Jerusalem and Rome since 812. It is believed that this is the repository of St. James (Santiago), a cousin of Jesus, son of Mary's sister, and the first follower of Jesus to attain martyrdom.

After witnessing the crucifixion, James came to Spain in A.D. 44, converted 9 Iberians to Christianity, was visited at Zaragoza by the Virgin Mary, returned to the Holy Land, and was beheaded there by King Herod Agrippa.

The legend which has generated the pilgrimage to Santiago de Compostela for the past 1,100 years is that, after the decapitation in Jerusalem, his body was disinterred and found to have the head intact. The body was brought to Spain's West Coast in A.D. 44.

Eight centuries later, a hermit saw a bright star (stela) over a vacant field (compo). Excavations were conducted, and the remains of James were found. Since that event, pilgrims have come to this shrine by horse and in vehicles, as well as on foot (from as far as Scandinavia) to pray and meditate here.

You would stop here to see the majestic Cathedral built in the 12th century.

See its beautiful Baroque sculptured Obradoire facade. The carved Romanesque 12th century Door of Glory. Touch the grooves left in the central pillar by the fingers of millions of pilgrims over the centuries.

Visit the Archaeological Museum in its basement, the art pieces in its Treasury, the collection of tapestries with designs by Goya and Rubens in the many halls of the Cathedral's Tapestry Museum.

Also see the gigantic 6-foot tall, 118-pound brass censer in the Library of the Cathedral.

In the early pilgrimage years, it was difficult for priests to tolerate the odor of worshippers from afar who had gone unbathed for weeks and months. The censer here, called Botafumeiro (smoke-thrower), masked the noxious odors.

A custom that originated in the early days of pilgrimages here is perpetuated today. On feast days, this censer is brought into the Cathedral, filled with incense, hung by ropes from the dome 104 feet above the floor, and swung in an arc, barely passing over the heads of people standing in the Cathedral. It is easy to explore Santiago de Compostela on foot. See the marvelous view of the town from Alameda Park. Santa Maria del Sar, one of the more than 40 churches here, is a splendid example of 12th century Romanesque architecture.

Madrid - Seville   425 + Government timetable

The introduction of high-speed trains (in excess of 156 mph) on this route in 1992 reduced this trip from 6 hours to 2½ hours. Called AVE (Tren de Alta Velocidad Espanola), they go between Madrid's Atocha railstation and Seville's Santa Justa station, on the grounds of the 1992 World Expo.

The 3 classes on an air-conditioned AVE train are: "Club" (the most luxurious, with boutiques and fax, video and secretarial services), "Preference" (equivalent to first-class on a French TGV), and "Tourist" (similar to TGV second-class, but with larger and lower windows. Each AVE has a cafeteria and a bar.

Each of these 3 classes is available on all of 3 types of trains (making 9 prices for the same journey!) — "Valle" stops in Cordoba and also in 2 other towns. Some "Llano" make the same 3 stops, while other "Llano" stop only in Cordoba. All of the "Punta" trains stop only in Cordoba.

As an example of the range of cost for 9 possible AVE services, the 1994 price of a one-way Tourist ticket on a "Valle" train was 6,000 pesetas. For a Club ticket on a "Punta" train it was 16,500 pesetas!

There was a 40% discount for children age 4-11. Holders of Eurailpass, Eurodomino and Tarjeta Turistica (Tourist Card) were given 60% discount for a Club ticket, 65% discount for Preference, and 85% discount for Tourist.

In North America, tickets and reservations can be obtained from Rail Europe.

Reservation is required for all of these AVE trains. All of them charge a higher supplement than other Spanish express trains. The AVE supplement includes a reservation fee and mandatory travel insurance. All have a restaurant car.

Dep. Madrid (Atocha AVE)	10:00 (3)	11:00	14:00	16:00 (4)		
Arr. Seville (S. Justa)	13:25	13:40	16:25	18:35		

Dep. Madrid (Atocha AVE)	17:00	18:00 (2)	19:00	20:00	21:00	
Arr. Seville (S. Justa)	19:45	20:35	21:35	22:35 (4)	23:40	

Dep Seville (S. Justa)	07:00	08:00	09:00	11:00	14:00	16:00
Arr. Madrid (Atocha AVE)	09:45	10:25(5)	11:45	13:35	16:25	18:35

Dep. Seville (S.Justa)	17:00	18:00 (2)	19:00	20:00 (1)	21:00	
Arr. Madrid (Atocha AVE)	19:45	20:35	21:35	22:35 (4)	23:40	

(1) Does not operate in August. (2) Runs Friday and Sunday. Does not operate in August. (3) Subject to confirmation. (4) Runs daily except Saturdays. (5) Runs daily except Sundays and holidays.

Madrid - Valencia - Madrid   420

All of these trains charge supplement and have light refreshments, unless designated otherwise.

Dep. Madrid					
(Atocha-Cer.)	07:15(2+6)	09:15 (6)	13:15 (1+6)	15:15 (1+6)	16:45 (5+6)
Arr. Valencia (Ter.)	11:10	13:10	17:10	19:10	20:40 (4)

Sights in **Valencia**: See the Holy Grail, the chalice used at the Last Supper, exhibited in the 13th century Cathedral. The great art collection in the Convent of Pio V. The Orange Court at the 15th century Lonja del Mercado. The popular beaches: Arenas, Nazaret and Pinedo y Saler. The scent of the vast surrounding orange groves, perfuming the night.

Dep. Valencia (Ter.)	07:00 (2)	09:00	13:00 (1)	15:00 (1)	16:30 (5)
Arr. Madrid (Atocha-Cer.)	10:55	12:55	16:55	18:55	20:25

(1) Runs daily, except Saturday. (2) Runs daily, except Sundays and holidays. (3) No supplement charged. Has couchettes. Coach is second-class. (4) Plus other departures from Madrid (Chamartin) at 18:45 (6) and 20:15 (2), arriving Valencia 22:40 and 00:50. (5) Plus other departures from Valencia at 18:30 and 20:00 (1), arriving Madrid 22:25 and 23:55(Chamartin). (6) Arrives/departs Madrid Puerta de Atocha.

Barcelona - Valencia - Barcelona   415

Dep. Barcelona (Franca)	06:40 (1)	-0-	-0-
Dep. Barcelona (P. de G.)	06:50	-0-	-0-
Dep. Barcelona (Sants)	07:00	08:00 (2)	09:00 (3)
Arr. Valencia (Termino)	10:55	11:45	12:50

Dep. Barcelona (Franca)	14:10 (1)	17:10 (1)
Dep. Barcelona (P. de G.)	14:20	17:21
Dep. Barcelona (Sants)	14:30	17:30
Arr. Valencia (Termino)	18:25	21:20

Dep. Valencia (Termino)	02:20 (7)	06:30 (6)	09:45 (1)
Arr. Barcelona (Sants)	07:30	11:00	13:30
Arr. Barcelona (P. de G.)	-0-	-0-	13:41
Arr. Barcelona (Franca)	-0-	-0-	13:50

Dep. Valencia (Termino)	13:15 (1)	15:10 (1)	16:30 (3+10)
Arr. Barcelona (Sants)	17:03	19:03	20:40
Arr. Barcelona (P. de G.)	17:11	19:11	-0-
Arr. Barcelona (Franca)	-0-	-0-	-0-

(1) Reservation *required*. Supplement charged. Light refreshments. (2) Restaurant car. (3) Operates late May to late September. Reservation *required*. Supplement charged. Light refreshments. (4) Second-class. (5) Reservation *required*. Supplement charged. Runs Monday-Friday, except holidays. Light refreshments. (6) Second-class. Restaurant car. (7) Runs daily, except Saturday. Carries a sleeping car. Also has couchettes. Coach is second-class. Light refreshments. (8) Operates late June to early September. Second-class. (9) Plus other departures from Barcelona (Sants) at 18:30 (1), 19:45 (8) and 22:45 (7), arriving Valencia 22:30, 00:45 and 03:25. (10) Plus other departures from Valencia at 18:00 (2) and 19:15 (1), arriving Barcelona (Sants) 22:05 and 23:07.

INTERNATIONAL ROUTES
FROM PORTUGAL

The 2 routes to France and beyond are Lisbon-Madrid and Lisbon-San Sebastian (see below).

The only practical way from Lisbon to southwestern Spain has been very indirect since 1991 — via Madrid. Lisbon-Madrid schedules appear under "Madrid-Lisbon."

Lisbon - San Sebastian - Bordeaux - Paris   46

The 2-hour stop in Hendaye is for changing the train's wheels to conform with the narrower track in France.

"Sud Express." Carries a sleeping car and restaurant car Lisbon-Irun. Hascouchettes Lisbon-Paris.

Arrival in Paris can be 4 hours earlier by changing in Hendaye to a TGV.

Dep. Lisbon (S. Apol.)	17:03 (1)	
Set your watch forward one hour.		
Dep. Salamanca	02:05	-0-
Dep. San Sebastian	08:32	-0-
Arr. Irun	09:00	-0-
Arr. Hendaye	09:10	-0-
Dep. Hendaye	09:34 (3)	09:49 (2)
Arr. Bordeaux	11:52	12:10
Arr. Paris (Austerlitz)	-0-	17:15
Arr. Paris (Montparnasse)	15:00	14:55

(1) "Sud Express." See headnote. (2) TGV. Supplement charged. Light refreshments. (3) Change trains in Hendaye.

INTERNATIONAL ROUTES
FROM SPAIN

Spanish National Railways (RENFE) makes reservations for only 4 trips to other countries: Madrid–Lisbon, Madrid–Paris, Barcelona–Geneva–Zurich and Barcelona–Milan.

When traveling by train from another country to Spain, if you want to travel later from Spain back into France and/or beyond France, it is necessary to book the trip from Spain to another country *before you enter Spain*.

The Spanish gateway for rail travel to London, Paris, Brussels and Amsterdam is Madrid.

From Barcelona, there is rail service to southwestern France (via Toulouse) and to southeastern France (Avignon, Marseille and Nice), from where there are connections to Italy, Austria and Switzerland (and on to Germany and Denmark)...plus Barcelona–Zurich and Barcelona–Milan on the fabulous "Pablo Casals" (see "Barcelona–Milan").

Seville - Lisbon

The only practical way to make this trip has been very indirect since 1991: Seville–Madrid–Lisbon.

Madrid - Bordeaux - Paris   46

All arrivals in Paris are on Day 2.

Dep. Madrid (Chamartin)	10:00 (5)	18:15 (6)	19:30 (7)	23:00 (8)
Arr. Hedaye	16:50	02:08 (6)	-0- (7)	08:30
Change trains.				
Dep. Hendaye	18:32 (2+4)	-0-	-0-	09:34
Arr. Bordeaux	20:39	05:51	03:55	11:50
Arr. Paris (Austerlitz)	-0-	10:55	08:30	-0-
Arr. Paris (Montparnasse)	23:45	-0-	-0-	14:55

(1) Second-class. (2) TGV. Reservation required. Supplement charged. (3) Runs daily, except Sundays and holidays. (4) Runs Sundays and holidays only. (5) Supplement charged. Light refreshments. (6) Direct train. No train change in Hendaye. Has only couchettes. No coaches. Light refreshments Hendaye-Paris. (7) Direct train. No train change in Hendaye. Has only sleeping cars and a restaurant car. (8) Carries a sleeping car. Also has couchettes. Coaches are second-class.

Barcelona - Avignon - Geneva - Bern - Zurich   81

The "Pablo Casals" began in 1990 to carry one "Gran Clase" sleeping car, the most luxurious cleeping car in Europe. Each of its large single and double 'staterooms' has a private, adjoining bathroom (circular shower stall, toilet and washbasin). Two armchairs are converted into beds by the compartment attendant.

Compartments in the first-class cars also have seating that converts to beds at night and a washbasin with towels. Second-class cars contain 4 berths and a washbasin. The 1994 second-class price (Barcelona-Geveva, Barcelona-Zurich or Barcelona-Milan) was 15,350 Pesetas Thursday-Saturday and 12,300 Pesetas Sunday-Wednesday.

Talk about secrecy! Spanish Railways flatly refused to divulge to the National Tourist Office of Spain what the 1995 price was for a full-course dinner, wine and dessert. It was $25-$40 in 1992, when the 2 government offices spoke to each other. Dinner is served in the restaurant car. Beverages and snacks are served in the bar car.

Substantial discounts are given to holders of Eurailpass and Eurodomino.

Dep. Barcelona (Franca)	-0-	10:10 (1)	20:15 (2)
Dep Barcelona (Sants)	08:02	-0-	-0-
Arr. Cerbere	10:45	12:30	-0-
Arr. Avignon	-0-	15:14	-0-
Arr. Geneva (Cornavin)	-0-	19:28	05:52
Arr. Bern	-0-	-0-	07:51
Arr. Zurich	-0-	-0-	09:15

(1) Supplement charged. Restaurant car. (2) "Pablo Casals." See description in headnote.

Barcelona - Torino - Milan   90

This is the second route of "Pablo Casals." A $10 continental breakfast can be purchased in one's compartment or the restaurant car.

Reservations for "Pablo Casals" can only be made in Spain. Substantial discounts are given to holders of Eurailpasses and Eurodomino passes.

Dep. Barcelona (Franca)	20:15
Arr. Torino (Porta Susa)	07:30
Arr. Milan (Centrale)	09:03

Barcelona - Paris   47

Dep. Barcelona (Sants)	07:10 (1)	17:16 (3)	17:35 (4)	18:40	21:00 (7)
Arr. Cerbere	09:50	20:25	19:35	20:50	- 0 - (7)
Change Trains					
Dep. Cerbere	10:27	- 0 -	20:40 (5)	22:13	0
Arr. Paris (Aus.)	20:22 (2)	- 0 -	07:33	08:36	08:15

(1) Second-class. (2) Arrives 20:45 on Saturday. (3) Departs from Barcelona's Franca railstation. Second-class. (4) Supplement charged. Light refreshments. (5) Carries only sleeping and couchette cars. (6) Operates early July to early September. Has couchettes. (7) Direct train. No change in Cerbere. Reservation can only be made in Spain. Carries only sleeping cars and a restaurant car. No coach cars.

Barcelona - Rome   90

This car has second-class couchettes.

Dep. Barcelona (Sants)	19:45
Arr. Rome (Termini)	18:05 Day 2

IRELAND

- BELFAST
- SLIGO
- CARRICK
- WESTPORT
- CLAREMORRIS
- MULLINGAR
- ATHLONE
- GALWAY
- PORTARLINGTON
- DUBLIN
- DUN LAOGHAIRE
- → *HOLYHEAD*
- BRAY
- WICKLOW
- SHANNON
- KILKENNY
- LIMERICK
- LIMERICK JUNCTION
- TRALEE
- WEXFORD
- WATERFORD
- ROSSLARE HARBOUR
- MALLOW
- → *FISHGUARD HARBOUR*
- KILLARNEY
- CORK

REPUBLIC OF IRELAND

Overview

Ireland is not really known for its train system, but nonetheless a network sprawls from Cork in the south to Belfast in Northern Ireland with Dublin acting as the country's hub with some highly scenic lines stretching to Westport, Killarney, and Silgo.

General Information

• Children under five travel free. Half-fare for children 5-15. Children 16 and ocer must pay full fare.

• Ireland changes to summer on the last Sunday of March and coverts back to standard time on the last Sunday of October.

• Eurailpass Bonuses in Ireland: See introductory chapter on Eurail pass bonuses.

IRISH TRAIN PASSES

All of these passes are sold at rail and bus stations throughout the Irish Republic and in North America at CIE Tours, 108 Ridgedale Ave., P.O. box 2355, Morristown, NJ 07962. All of them provide unlimited second-class travel. Children age 5-15 pay half-fare.

Irish Explorer Rail (Republic of Ireland) Valid for any 5 days of train travel witin 15 days. The 1996 adult price is $102.

Irish Explorer Rail/Bus (Republic of Ireland) Valid for any 8 days within 15 days. The 1996 adult price is $153.

Irish Rover Rail (Republic of Ireland and Northern Ireland) Valid any 5 days within 15 days. The 1996 adult price is $128.

Emerald Card Rail/Bus (Republic of Ireland and Northern Ireland) The 1996 adult prices are: $179 for any 8 days within 15 days, and $306 for any 15 days within 30 days.

Dublin

Capital of the Irish Republic. See the outstanding Bronze Age gold ornaments, the 9th century Derrynaflan Chalice and the 12th century Cross of Cong, in the National Museum, open Tuesday-Saturday 10:00–17:00 and Sunday 14:00–17:00. The collection of paintings (Rubens, Rembrandt, Goya. Reynolds, Gainsborough) at the National Gallery of Art, open Monday–Saturday 10:00–18:00 and Sunday 14:00–17:00.

The 8th century Book of Kells, a richly illuminated bible regarded as one of the most beautiful books ever made, on view in the Old Library of Trinity College. The Hugh Lane Municipal Gallery of Modern Art.

The pulpit from which Jonathan Swift preached, at the 12th century St. Patrick's Cathedral, and a performance of the young boys' choir there. The collection of oriental manuscripts at Chester Beatty Library. The Zoo, in the 1,760-acre Phoenix Park. The 13th century Dublin Castle. Leinster House. The restored 12th century Christ Church Cathedral.

The 18th century mansions on St. Stephen's Green. Window-shop on Grafton Street. Stroll on O'Connell Street. See the historic General Post Office, site of the 1916 uprising. The Georgian houses on Parnell Square. The house where George Bernard Shaw was born. Take a tour of the facilities of the Irish Sweepstakes. A tour of Guinness's Brewery.

Belfast

This is the capital of Northern Ireland. A major port. See the elegant Queen's University. The collection of antique locomotives and train cars in the Transport Museum. The richly marbled interior of the 19th century City Hall. The beautiful Grand Opera House. Across the street, the decorative interior of the Crown Bar. Palm House and the collection of modern Irish paintings, silver and glass and exhibits of the history, geology and botany in Ulster Museum, both at the Botanic Gardens. Tour the Harland and Wolff Shipyard, location of the world's largest drydock and where many of the world's great ocean liners were built.

See the display of everything produced in Ulster factories (old farm implements, stagecoaches, a schooner, antique locomotives and train cars, modern aircraft) at the 180-acre open-air Ulster Folk and Transport Museum, a complex of 18 exhibit buildings. It also has cottages in styles spanning several centuries (some with original furniture), water-powered mills, and demonstrations of such traditional crafts as spinning and thatching.

Genealogical research can be done at the Public Record Office, 66 Balmoral Avenue as well as by mail with the Irish Genealogical Association, 164 Kingsway, Dunmurry, Belfast BT17 9AD.

Birth and death records since 1864 and copies of marriage registrations since 1922 can be obtained at General Register Office, Oxford House, 49-55 Chichester Street, Belfast BT1 4HL.

ONE-DAY EXCURSIONS AND
CITY SIGHTSEEING

Here are 8 one-day rail trips that can be made comfortably from Belfast, Cork, Dublin, Galway and Limerick, returning to them in most cases before dinnertime. Notes are provided on what to see and do at each destination. The number after the name of each route is the Cook's timetable.

Dublin - Belfast - Dublin   630

Dep. Dublin (Con.)	07:55 (1)	10:30 (2)	11:00 (1)	13:00 (3)	15:00 (1+7)
Arr. Belfast (Cen.)	10:10	13:05	13:32	15:20	17:16

• • •

Dep. Belfast (Cen.)	08:00 (1)	09:00 (3)	10:15 (2)	11:00 (1)	15:00 (5+8)
Arr. Dublin Con.)	09:58	11:32	12:40	13:22	17:15

(1) Runs daily, except Sundays and holidays. Restaurant car. (2) Runs Sunday only. Light refreshments. (3) Runs daily, except Sundays and holidays. Light refreshments. (4) Runs daily. Restaurant car Monday–Saturday. Second-class and light refreshments on Sunday. (5) Runs daily, except holidays. Restaurant car. (6) Runs daily, except Sundays and holidays. Second-class. (7) Plus other Dublin departures at 18:20 (2), 18:34 (6) and 20:15 (3), arriving Belfast 20:18, 21:45 and 22:38. (8) Plus other Belfast departures at 17:00 (3) and 18:00 (4), arriving Dublin 19:20 and 20:00 (20:25 on Sunday).

Dublin - Cork - Dublin   640

This is a train ride through Ireland's lush southern area.

Dep. Dublin (Heu.)	07:30 (1)	08:15 (2)	10:15 (3)	10:45 (4)	13:20 (4+10)
Arr. Cork (Kent)	10:05	10:50	13:30	13:45	16:20

Sights in **Cork:** Parnell Bridge. The Customs House, the finest building in Cork. The collection of 19th and 20th century works by leading Irish and English painters, in the Crawford Gallery on Emmet Place. Visit the shops on Paul Street and Patrick Street. The perpetual flea market and vegetable stands on Corn Market Street.

Dep. Cork (Kent)	05:20 (5)	07:35 (4)	09:00 (6)	11:20 (4)	14:45 (7+11)
Arr. Dublin (Heu.)	08:40	10:05	12:10	14:25	17:35

(1) Runs Monday–Friday, except holidays. Restaurant car. (2) Runs Saturday only. Restaurant car. (3) Runs Sunday only. Second-class. Restaurant car. (4) Runs daily, except Sundays and holidays. Restaurant car. (5) Runs daily, except Sundays and holidays. Second-class. (6) Runs daily, except holidays. Restaurant car. Second-class on Sunday. (7) Runs daily, except holidays. Monday–Saturday: restaurant car. Sunday: light refreshments. Departs and arrives 15 minutes earlier on Sunday. (8) Runs Sunday only. Second-class. (9) Runs Sunday only. Second-class. Light refreshments. (10) Plus other departures from Dublin at 14:55 (4), 17:30 (4), 18:30 (3), 18:55 (4) and 21:15 (8). (11) Plus other departures from Cork at 17:30 (7) and 18:30 (9).

Cork - Killarney - Tralee - Cork   647

There is much beautiful scenery throughout this fertile area.

These trains run daily, except Sundays and holidays, unless designated otherwise.

Dep. Cork	09:15	11:25	12:15 (1)	14:45 (1)	19:15 (2)
Dep. Killarney	11:10	13:20	14:16	16:40	21:05
Arr. Tralee	11:45	13:55	14:45	17:15	22:40
			• • •		
Dep. Tralee	08:50 (2)	12:00	14:00 (2)	16:05	18:00 (2)
Dep. Killarney	09:25	12:35	14:35	16:40	18:35
Arr. Cork	11:20	14:30	16:30	18:30	20:30

(1) Runs Sunday only. (2) Runs daily. Second-class.

Sights in **Killarney**: It is 85 miles from Shannon Airport. See the sculpture by Seamus Murphy, called The Shy Woman of Kerry. The marvelous garden and the exhibit of early crafts and housing at Muckross House, a 19th century mansion on the outskirts of Killarney. Shop here for linens, glassware and crocheted women's clothing.

Take the 112-mile, all-day "Ring of Kerry" bus sightseeing trip, a popular excursion. You will see many lakes and mountains.

Dublin - Galway - Dublin   645

The are many beautiful lakes in this area.

All of these trains run daily except Sundays and holidays, are second-class and have light refreshments, unless designated otherwise.

Dep. Dublin (Heu.)	08:00 (1)	09:20 (2)	11:00	14:10 (3)	18:45 (4)	20:20 (6)
Arr. Galway	10:55	12:20	13:50	16:55	21:15 (5)	23:05

Sights in **Galway:** The 14th century St. Nicholas' Church. The ruins of a 13th century Franciscan friary. The 13th century town walls.

Dep. Galway	08:00 (1)	08:50 (2)	11:35 (1)	14:50 (2)	15:15	18:05 (7)
Arr. Dublin (Heu.)	10:30	11:40	14:20	17:45	18:10	21:10

(1) Restaurant car. (2) Runs Sunday only. (3) Runs daily, except holidays. No light refreshments on Sunday. (4) Runs daily, except holidays. Also has first-class coach and restaurant car Monday–Saturday. (5) Arrives 25 minutes later on Sunday. (6) Runs Sunday only. No light refreshments. (7) Runs daily, except holidays. Departs 5 minutes later on Sunday.

Dublin - Kilkenny - Dublin 642

Dep. Dublin						
(Heuston)	07:35 (1)	09:50 (2)	11:35 (3)	14:50 (2)	15:00 (1)	18:10 (4+6)
Arr. Kilkenny	09:30	11:43	13:20	16:35	16:48	20:00

• • •

Dep. Kilkenny	08:17 (4)	10:32 (5)	11:39		15:26 (2)	16:02	18:50 (2+7)
Arr. Dublin							
(Heuston)	09:50	12:15	13:25	17:20	17:50	20:35	

(1) Runs daily, except Sundays and holidays. Second-class. Light refreshments. (2) Runs Sunday only. Second-class. (3) Runs daily, except Sundays and holidays. Light refreshments. (4) Runs daily. Restaurant car. (5) Runs Sunday only. Second-class. Light refreshments. (6) Plus another Dublin departure at 18:15 (5), arriving Kilkenny 20:04. (7) Plus another Kilkenny departure at 19:13, arriving Dublin 21:00.

Sights in **Kilkenny:** The formal gardens and the 150-foot-long hall at Kilkenny Castle. The 13th century Saint Canice Cathedral, one of the loveliest in Ireland from that era. The 13th century Kytler's Inn, now a restaurant. The 19th century Saint Mary's Cathedral.

Dublin - Limerick - Dublin 638

There is bus service between Limerick and Shannon Airport.

Dep. Dublin (Heuston)	09:00 (1)	17:40	18:30 (4+5)	
Arr. Ballybrophy	10:15	18:50	-0- (4)	
Change trains.				
Dep. Ballybrophy	10:20 (2)	18:55 (2)	-0-	
Arr. Limerick	11:54	20:20	20:55	

• • •

Dep. Limerick	07:00 (2+4)	08:20 (1+4)	15:45 (2)	19:00 (3+4)
Arr. Ballybrophy	-0- (4)	-0- (4)	17:05	-0- (4)
Change trains.				
Dep. Ballybrophy	-0-	-0-	17:10 (2)	-0-
Arr. Dublin (Heuston)	09:25	10:25	18:20	22:30

(1) Runs daily, except Sundays and holidays. Restaurant car. (2) Runs daily, except Sundays and holidays. Second-class. (3) Runs Friday only. Second-class. (4) Direct train. No train change in Ballybrophy. (5) Runs Sunday only. Second-class.

THE FERRY-CROSSINGS
TO FRANCE

Rosslare - LeHavre - Paris and **Rosslare - Cherbourg - Paris**

Operated by Irish Ferries Company. Passage only (without a seat or a berth) is free all year with a Eurailpass. The 1993 cost for "passage only" was $209 (U.S.) from July 10 to August 31 and was lower prices in other times of the year. Passage *plus* a seat was $217 (but only $10 with Eurailpass) in mid-Summer when there are many more passengers than seats on the vessel and some passengers must sit on the deck for this 21-hour trip.

Reserving and paying extra for a cabin is essential in Summer. A 6-berth cabin that was $221 per person in mid-Summer was only $13 with a Eurailpass. A 4-berth cabin with shower and private toilet at $257 per personwas only $48 with a Eurailpass.

There are also sailings to and from Cork, Ireland during June, July and August.

Days of operation and departure times vary during 5 different periods of the year. For 1994 schedules, prices and reservations, contact the North American agent: Lynott Tours Inc., 350 Fifth Avenue, New York, NY 10118. Telephone: (212) 760-0101 or (800) 221-2474.

RAIL CONNECTIONS WITH ENGLAND
See Chapter 7.

ITALY

Overview
Italian train travel belongs to several centuries at once, depending where you are and how you are traveling. Trains south of Rome can be snail-like whereas Rapidos live up to their name and the pendolinos have been the most chic trains in Europe since 1990. To accommodate curves at very high speeds, Pendolinos tilt—using the motion of a pendulum.

General Information
• Except for EuroCity trains: children under four travel free. Half-fare for children 4-11. Children 12 and over must pay full fare.
• Italy has four types of fast trains: Pendolino (first-class only), EuroCity, InterCity, and Rapido. Passengers using individual tickets (not traveling with first-class Italian passes or one of the first-class Eurailpasses) must pay a supplemental charge when riding on all Pendolinos and most of the other three. The supplement includes a seat reservation and a meal. Reservations are required on all EuroCity and most InterCity trains.
• Sleeping-car service is offered by Wagon-Lits Company in first- and second-class compartments, first- and second-class couchette. All should be reserved in advance.
• Few Italian trains offer full meal services.
• The signs you will see at railstations in Italy are:

ARRIVI	ARRIVAL
BINARIO	TRACK
CARROZZA LETTI	SLEEPING CAR
CARROZZA RISTORANTE	RESTAURANT CAR
DONNE	WOMEN
ENTRATA	ENTRANCE
ORARIO FERROVIARIO	TIMETABLE
PARTENZE	DEPARTURE
PIATTAFORMA	PLATFORM
PRENOTAZIONE POSTI	SEAT RESERVATION
SCOMPARTIMENTO PER FUMATORI	SMOKING COMPARTMENT
STAZIONE FERROVIARIO	RAILSTATION
UFFICIO BAGAGLI	BAGGAGE CHECKROOM
UFFICIO BIGLIETTO	TICKET OFFICE
UOMINI	MEN
USCITA	EXIT

ITALY

Italian Holidays

A list of holidays is helpful because some trains will be noted later in this section as *not* running on holidays. Also, those trains which operate on holidays are filled, and it is necessary to make reservations for them long in advance.

January 1	New Year's Day		Proclamation of the Republic
January 6	Epiphany		(First Monday in June)
	Easter	August 15	Assumption Day
	Easter Monday		Victory Day (World War I)
April 25	Liberation Day		(First Monday in November)
May 1	Labor Day	December 8	Immaculate Conception
		December 25	Christmas Day
		December 26	St. Stephen's Day

Summer Time

Italy changes to Summer Time on the last Sunday of March and converts back to Standard Time on the last Sunday of September. Many Italian trains and international trains originating or terminating in Italy have different schedules during Summer Time than they do the balance of the year.

EURAILPASS BONUSES IN ITALY

A 30% reduction from the fare for the Venice–Piraeus (and v.v.) and Venice–Alexandria (and v.v.) boat trips.

The Brindisi-Patras boat trip (see schedules next page) is covered by the Eurailpasses — but only if you go on Adriatica di Navagazione Line or Hellenic Mediterranean Line. A bench seat or sitting on the deck is covered by Eurailpasses for this trip (the 1994 cost *without* Eurailpass was $108). However, pass holders are charged $14 for travel June 10 to September 30.

Other fees are charged for such special accommodations as aircraft type seats, pullman berths and cabins. There is also a port tax (10,000 Lira in 1993) that is *not* covered by Eurailpass and must be paid in Lira.

WARNING: The employees of other lines intimate that their ships honor the 2 passes and then charge fees after the boat leaves the pier.

With or without a Eurailpass, a reservation theoretically can be made on day of departure or day before departure — but it is very unlikely that space will be available (particularly during July and August) unless a reservation is made many weeks in advance of departure dates.

Those gambling on making a reservation after arriving in Brindisi can make application January 1–June 9 and October 1–December 31 only at the Adriatica di Navagazione embarkation office, located at Maritime Station, a 15-minute walk from Brindisi's Central railstation, along Corso Umberto and Corso Garibaldi. Taxis are available at the railstation.

From June 10 to September 30, those without advance reservations can apply also to any Brindisi travel agency that displays in its window the green badge "Eurail Information Euraipass."

Holders of advance reservations must go at all times directly to the Adriatica di Navagazione embarkation office to have their tickets checked, settle port taxes due and obtain the required Embarkation Ticket. That office is open 08:30–13:00 and 15:30–22:30.

Advance reservations before you start your trip can be made by contacting Extra Value Travel, 683 South Collier Boulevard, Marco Island, Florida 33937, U.S.A. Telephone: (813) 394-3384.

Passengers with advance reservation must obtain the Embarkation Ticket at least 2 hours prior to the ship's departure time. The ships reserve the right to cancel a reservation when that is not done and to give the space to a standby passenger.

The trains from northern Italy to Brindisi, timed to connect with the ferry departures, are frequently late. For that reason, it is *advisable* to arrive Brindisi the day before a ferry departure to Patras.

Brindisi - Patras - Athens   For sailing dates, see Cook's Table 1490.

Dep. Brindisi Harbor	20:00	22:30	
Arr. Patras	13:00	18:00	

It is a 20-minute walk from Patras' dock to its railstation. A taxi costs about $7 (U.S.)
Change to train. 980
For a view of the Corinthian Gulf and then the Corinthian Canal, sit on the left side of the train.

Dep. Patras	15:57 (1)	18:03 (1+2)	19:16
Arr. Athens	19:12	21:22	23:22

(1) Light refreshments. (2) Supplement payable.

ITALIAN TRAIN PASSES

When ordering any number of train tickets or any train pass *except Eurailpass* from the Italian State Railways, there is a $20 processing fee per order for ordinary tickets and a $10 fee per pass on all Italian train passes.

Anyone who purchases an Italian train pass may obtain a 10% discount on city sightseing and excursion tours by presenting the pass at any Compagnia Italiana Turismo (CIT) office in Florence, Milan, Naples, Rome and Venice.

Both the Italian Train Pass and Italy Flexi Railcard offer unlimited travel on all Italian trains (including InterCity and EuroCity trains), including free seat reservations (*which can be made only in Italy*) *on trains for which reservations are compulsory. If you choose to make a reservation on a train for which reservations are not compulsory, you must pay an additional reservation fee.* Sleeper and couchette services are *not* included. Both passes are available at travel agencies worldwide *outside* Italy and at all offices worldwide of CIT, including those in Italy.

Italian Railpass The 1995 prices were not available at the first printing of this book. The 1995 *first*-class prices were: $226 for 8 days, $284 for 15 days, $330 for 21 days, and $396 for 30 days. For *second*-class: $152, $190, $220, and $264. The 15, 21 and 30-day tickets can be extended to double their initial period. Half-fare for children 4–12 years old. Children under 4 travel free.

Italy Flexi Railcard The 1995 prices were not available at the first printing of this book. The 1995 *first*-class prices were: $176 for any 4 days within 9 days, $258 for any 8 days within 21 days, and $324 for any 12 days within 30 days. For *second*-class: $120, $168 and $216.

Kilometric Ticket Permits travel up to a maximum of 20 single trips totaling 3,000kms (1,875 miles) within 60 days. When used on a train that charges a supplement, the passengers using the Ticket must pay the supplement. Can be used by more than one person at a time, to a maximum of 5 persons. When a child 4–12 years old travels on this ticket, only half the mileage used is counted. Children under 4 travel free. Available before you leave home at both Italian State Railways and from travel agents worldwide. Also available in Italy at all railstations and from Italian travel agencies.

The 1996 prices were not available at the first printing of this book. The 1995 prices were: $264 for *first*-class, $156 for *second*-class.

ONE-DAY EXCURSIONS AND
CITY SIGHTSEEING

Comprehensive maps which make it easy to find the worthwhile sights there can be obtained in most Italian cities in offices marked "Azienda Autonoma di Turismo" or "Ente Provinciale di Turismo," located on a principal street.

Here are 70 one-day rail trips that can be made comfortably from Agrigento, Bologna, Catania, Florence (Firenze), Genoa, Messina, Milan, Naples (Napoli), Palermo, Rome and Torino (Turin), returning to those cities in most cases before dinnertime. Notes are provided on what to see and do at each destination. The number after the name of each route is the Cook's timetable.

Bologna

See the dissection theater in the ancient medical school. The fantastic inlaid wood panels in the Chorus at San Domenico Church. (Be sure to turn on the electric lights there in order to get a good look at the marvelous woodwork.) The Church of San Petronio. The Art Gallery. Neptune's Fountain, wherePiazza Maggiore and Piazza Nettuno connect.

The 2 leaning towers in Piazza di Port Ravegnana: 165-foot tall Garisenda and the 330-foot high Asinelli. Climb the 486 steps of the Asinelli for the splendid view from the top of the tower. Visit the churches on Santo Stefano. The Municipal Archeological Museum. The Communale, Podesta, Mercanzia, Re Anzio and Bevilacqua palaces. Try the marvelous Bolognese food.

Florence (Firenze)

The 14th century Cathedral of Santa Maria del Fiore (open daily 07:00–12:00 and 14:30–18:00) is where most visitors begin sightseeing in Florence. Ascend its 292-foot high bell-tower for a great view of the city. Across from the Cathedral, see the magnificent sculptured bronze Ghiberti doors ("Gates of Paradise" was Michelangelo's description) on the octagonal Baptistry of San Giovanni (open 09:30–12:30 and 14:30–17:30).

See the 14th–19th century furniture and utensils representing domestic life in those eras, in the Davanzati Palace.

There is much more to see, in 2 different directions from the Cathedral-Baptistry complex. Facing the Baptistry, you proceed North on Via Ricasoli to visit Area #1. You go South, toward the Arno River, for the sightseeing in Area #2.

Area #1: See the Michelangelo sculptures and breathtaking marble floors, walls and crypts at the Medici Chapel. The street behind the Chapel is lined with vendors. On the other side of the street is an enormous food market where game with colorful furs and feathers make an unusual display.

An easy walk from the Chapel is the Academia (closed Monday), housing the stupendous statue of David. Nearby is the Fra Angelico Museum in the Church of San Marco, with its interesting frescoes and monk's cells.

Across the street from the Academia, you can board a city bus for the 20-minute ride uphill to the village of Fiesole, where there are Etruscan ruins, a Roman amphitheater, a 13th century Cathedral, the Convent of St. Francis, and a splendid view of Florence.

Area #2: The Piazza della Signoria and, next to it, the thousands of great art treasures in the 29 exhibit rooms of the Palazzo degli Uffizi (open Tuesday–Saturday 09:00–19:00, Sunday 09:00–13:00). Nearby is the Franciscan Church of Santa Croce, where Michelangelo, Machiavelli, Rossini and Galileo are buried. Also see the sculptures (Donatello's bronze David and the della Robbia glazed terra cottas) at the Bargello Palace and Museum, in a 13th century palace. Next, cross to the other side of the Arno River, over the Ponte Vecchio (lined with tiny jewelry shops) to visit the outstanding paintings, statues, tapestries and furniture in the 28 exhibit rooms and galleries of the Palazzo Pitti (closed Monday).

The Pitti is a complex of 5 different museums. The Palace itself contains the Palatine Gallery (noted for its Raphaels), the Modern Art Gallery, and the Silver Museum. Two other museums are located in the Boboli Gardens behind the Palace: the Costume Museum and the Porcelain Museum, both of which are open only on Tuesday, Thursday and Saturday (hours during May and June are 09:00–19:00).

The Medici Chapel, Academia, Bargello, Uffizi and Pitti are open Tuesdays–Saturdays 09:00–14:00 and Sundays and feast days from 09:00–13:00.

Genoa

Italy's largest port. See the house where Columbus is said to have been born, at Piazza Dante.

St. Lawrence Cathedral. *Do not fail* to walk down the 15th century streets near the waterfront, too narrow for a tour bus and unfortunately not seen by many visitors to Genoa. The incredible Monumental Cemetery, with its vast number of dramatic statues of many of the people buried there. The landscaped hillside with colorful plants painting a flowering tapestry of Columbus' fleet: the Nina, the Pinta and the Santa Maria.

The 16th century palaces on Via Garibaldi. The 17th century palaces on Via Balbi. The Cathedral of San Lorenzo, constructed from 1099 to 1250.

Milan

The Duomo Cathedral, holding more than 20,000 people, begun in 1386 and taking 5 centuries to complete. There are more than 3,000 statues on its exterior. Then go through the incredibly beautiful shopping arcade, the Galleria Vittorio Emanuele, to La Scala Opera House—one of the world's greatest theaters, accommodating 3,600 people, it was first constructed in 1776. Its opera museum is open Tuesdays–Saturdays 09:00–12:00 and 14:00–18:00.

Exhibited in the museum are old paintings and engravings of the opera house before its destruction by bombs in 1943 and its reconstruction in 1946, portraits of many famous singers, several of Verdi's pianos and such other Verdi memorabilia as his manuscripts and death mask.

Opposite La Scala, behind a statue of da Vinci, is the 16th century Palazzo Marino, now the City Hall. Just past the gate (Porta Nuova) at the end of Via Manzoni are the Museum of Natural History, the Zoo and the Planetarium.

See da Vinci's "Last Supper" at Santa Maria delle Grazie. It can be viewed daily 09:00–13:15 and 14:00–18:15. *Do not fail to see* the enormous and elaborate crypts at the Monumental Cemetery. Visit the Palazzo Dugnani, on Via Manin, to see the Tiepolo ceiling fresco there.

It is a short taxi ride from the Dugnani to the enormous Castello Sforzesco, which has a vast collection of paintings (including Michelangelo's last work, the Rondanini Pieta) and exhibits of harpischords, wrought iron, tapestries and ceramics. The Castle is open daily except Monday 09:30–12:00 and 14:30–17:00.

See the collection of sculpture, Flemish and Persian tapestries, paintings, scientific instruments, glass and armor at Museo Poldi-Pezzoli, at 12 Via Manzoni, open Tuesday–Sunday 09:30–12:30 and 14:30–17:30. Many great paintings (Raphael, Tiepolo, Canaletto) are exhibited in the Accademia di Brera on Via Brera, open Tuesday–Saturday 09:00–14:00, and on Sunday 09:00–13:00.

Both the Modern Art Gallery (16 Via Palestra) and the Archaeological Museum (15 Corso Magenta) are open Wednesday–Saturday 09:30–12:30 and 14:30–17:30; on Sunday 09:30–13:00. There are marvelous paintings by Raphael, Caravaggi and Botticelli in the Ambrosian Library, open Mondays–Fridays except holidays 10:00–12:00 and 15:00–17:00 and Saturdays, Sundays and holidays 15:00–17:00.

Gourmets will want to visit the fantastic food store called Peck's, at No. 9 Via Spadari, opened in 1892 by a Czechoslovak named Frank Peck. It is the Italian equivalent of Hediard, described under "Paris" in the section of this chapter on France. What you will see at Peck's are: large wedges of parmigiano and reggiano cheese, Italian wines, roasts, loins, saddles and breasts of white veal, caviar, numerous cold seafood salads, mussels, langouste, squid, lobster, celery remoulade, pates, head cheese, scampi, sturgeon, hot vegetable dishes (baked fennel, baby zucchini, asparagus milanese), roasted quail skewered with sausages and wrapped in bacon, tripe in tomato sauce, a wide range of pasta (green ravioli al forno, tortellini, ravioli alla contadina), paella with saffron rice, white mushrooms in oil, many sausages and many fish (herring, smoked salmon, smoked eels, smoked trout).

If that is not enough, across the street from Peck's is a famous pork store, La Bottega del Maiale, with an enormous display of whole baby pigs, pork parts (loins, ears, fillets, tongue, liver) and such sausages as sopresa Calabra, salame Toscana, coppa, cacciatorini, stagionata, capocolla and finocchiona.

Next door to the pork store is Peschere Spadari, a great fish store, selling nearly everything that swims: scampi, Channel sole, mackerel, scampi, squid, mussels. A short distance down the street, at No. 1 Via Speroni, is a large cheese store.

Naples

Most museums in Naples are closed on Monday. See the view from Certosa de San Martino monastery and, inside, its National Museum. The 13th century Castel Nuovo. The National Library. The Archaeological Museum, with its great Grecian and Roman sculptures. The Capodimonte Park, Palace and Art Gallery. The Teatro San Carlo, home of Neapolitan opera. The Royal Palace and scores of other palaces. The Botanical Garden. There are good views of Naples Bay from the gardens of the Duca di Martina Museum of Ceramics at the Villa Floridiana. Splendid views of Mount Vesuvius from the quay at Santa Lucia. Nearby **Herculaneum** (now called **Ercolano**) is as interesting as Pompeii.

Rome

There is nonstop train service between Rome's da Vinci airport and the cities of Naples and Florence. Eurailpasses and Italian passes cover the train service from the airport to both the city's Ostiense and Termini railstations.

Visit St. Peter's, the most wonderful work by man in all the world. Take an elevator to the dome for views of Vatican City and Rome. Tour the Vatican to see the Sistine Chapel, Raphael Rooms, Pio-Clementino Museum, Picture Gallery, Tapestry Gallery, Map Gallery and Candelabra Gallery (all of them closed on Sunday, except the last Sunday of each month).

See Capitoline Hill. The Roman Forum. Palatine Hill. The Imperial Fora.

Marcellus Theatre. The Jewish Synagogue. The Temple of Avesta. Aventine Hill. St. Paul's Gate. The view of Rome from the Villa Borghese Park. The Protestant cemetery, with the graves of Keats and Shelley. The Colosseum. The Arch of Constantine. The Basilica of St. Paul Outside the Walls. Michelangelo's statue of Moses in the Church of St. Peter in Chains. The Pantheon. The mosaics at the Baths of Caracalla.

Castel Sant'Angelo (closed Monday). Trevi Fountain. The Zoo. The Etruscan Museum (closed Monday). The Napoleon Museum (closed Monday). The Spanish Square, Steps and Fountain. The National Modern Art Gallery (closed Monday). Diocletian's Baths.

The House of the Vestal Virgins. Marvelous views of Rome from Janiculum Hill. The Monument to Vittorio Emanuele. The Bernini sculptures in the Borghese Gallery (Villa

Borghese), open daily 09:00–13:30. The magnificent Velazquez portrait of Pope Innocent X in the Doria Gallery (Piazza del Collegio Romano), open Tuesday, Friday, Saturday and Sunday 10:00–13:00.

Displays of Etruscan art at the National Museum of Villa Giulia (Piazza di Villa Giulia), open daily except Monday 09:00–19:00, holidays 09:00–13:00. Exhibits of ancient Rome at the National Museum of Rome (in the Baths of Diocletian), open Tuesday–Saturday 09:00–14:00, Sunday 09:00–13:00. The Museum of Folklore (Piazza Sant' Egidio, in Trastevere), open Tuesday–Sunday 09:00–13:00, also Thursday evenings 17:00–19:30.

In the following timetables, where a city has more than one railstation we have designated the particular station after the name of the city (in parentheses).

Bologna - Florence - Bologna   375

Exceptional mountain scenery on this easy one-day roundtrip.

The train goes through the 11.5-mile long Apennine Tunnel, Italy's longest tunnel. Some trains stop almost midpoint in the tunnel at an underground station called **Precendenze**. Residents of a small village at the crest of the mountain, in order to return home, must climb 1,863 steps inside a diagonal shaft that was used for constructing the tunnel.

All of these trains require reservation and charge a supplement, unless designated otherwise.

| Dep. Bologna | 07:38 (1) | 08:44 (2) | 10:35 | 12:30 (4) | 16:30 (4) |
| Arr. Florence (S.M.N.) | 08:36 | 09:53 (3) | 11:44 | 13:56 | 17:27 (3) |

| Dep. Florence (S.M.N.) | 14:17 | 16:21 (4) | 18:17 | 20:17 (1) | 20:52 (3+4) |
| Arr. Bologna | 15:27 | 17:36 | 19:27 | 21:27 | 21:51 |

(1) Light refreshments. (2) "Pendolino." Supplement includes reservation fee and meal. First-class only. (3) Arrives/departs Florence's Rifredi railstation. (4) Restaurant car.

Bologna - Milan - Bologna   370

| Dep. Bologna | 07:46 | 08:16 | 08:38 | 09:16 (2) | 09:48 (1) | 10:00 |
| Arr. Milan (Cen.) | 09:50 | 09:55 (3) | 10:30 | 10:50 | 11:50 | 12:05 |

| Dep. Milan (Cen.) | 15:00 | 16:00 | 16:05 (3) | 16:35 | 17:05 | 17:50 (1+5) |
| Arr. Bologna | 16:52 | 17:42 (3) | 18:22 | 18:55 | 19:08 | 20:10 |

(1) Reservation *required*. Supplement charged. Light refreshments. (2) "Pendolino" Reservation *required*. Supplement includes reservation fee and meal. First-class only. (3) Light refreshments. (4) Reservation *required*. Supplement charged. Restaurant car. (5) Plus other departures from Milan at 17:55, 18:45, 19:40 (2), 20:00 and 22:05, arriving Bologna 20:20, 21:34, 21:16, 22:21 and 00:47.

Bologna - Parma - Bologna   374

Dep. Bologna	Frequent times from 02:04 to 22:41
Arr. Parma	50-65 minutes later

• • •

Dep. Parma	Frequent times from 06:45 to 02:55
Arr. Bologna	50-65 minutes later

Sights in **Parma:** The 19th century Teatro Reggio opera house. Nearby, the Lombardi Museum in the Palazzo di Riserva. The restored Palazzo della Pilotta, which houses the Farnese Theater, National Gallery, Palatina Library and the National Museum of Antiquities. The latter, Italy's most modern museum, has an outstanding collection of Etruscan, Roman, medieval and Renaissance works of art, including larger-than-life-size statues of members of the Julian-Claudian family (Britannicus, the 2 Drussii, Livia and Claudius) that are familiar to viewers of the "I Claudius" television program.

More than 40,000 rare books are displayed in the Library (Biblioteca). Particularly interesting are the De Rossi collection of Oriental manuscripts and the Bodoni Museum, a complete collection of all the volumes of the great 19th century typographer for whom it is named.

Visit the Cathedral to view the marvelous Assumption of the Virgin fresco by Correggio in the dome. Also the Camera di Corregio, a room near the Cathedral he frescoed in 1518. The 12th century sculptures by Benedetto Antelami, in the 5-story red marble Baptistry, one of Italy's finest buildings. See the early 19th century sculpture by Lorenzo Bartolini in the Madonna della Steccata church. Toscani's room at the Conservatory.

Bologna - Pisa - Bologna

All of the Florence–Pisa (and v.v.) trains shown here are second-class only.

375

Dep. Bologna	07:38 (1)	09:42 (2)	10:35 (2)	12:30 (2)	16:30 (2)
Arr. Florence (S.M.N.)	08:36 (3)	10:46	11:44	13:56	17:27 (3)
Change trains. 369					
Dep. Florence (S.M.N.)	09:40	11:40	12:40	13:40	14:06
Arr. Pisa	10:32	12:32	13:32	14:32	15:11

The #1 Bus takes you from the Pisa railstation to the Piazza del Duomo in 10 minutes.

• • •

Dep. Pisa	13:22	14:22	15:22	16:22	17:22
Arr. Florence (S.M.N.)	14:15	15:15	16:15	17:15	18:315
Change trains. 375					
Dep. Florence (S.M.N.)	14:17	16:21 (2)	17:15 (1)	18:17	20:17 (2)
Arr. Bologna	15:27	17:27	18:09	19:27	21:27

(1) Reservation *required.* Supplement charged. Light refreshments. (2) Reservation *required.* Supplement charged. Restaurant car. (3) Departs/arrives Firenze Rifredi.

Sights in **Pisa**: The Piazza del Duomo, with 4 major attractions. Walk up the spiral stairs of the Leaning Tower to its roof and see the view from there. A few feet from the base of the Tower is the majestic 11th century striped marble Cathedral. Key features of it are the magnificent bronze entrance doors and, inside, paintings, statues, mosaics, a fantastic pulpit, and Galileo's lamp. While watching the lamp swing, Galileo timed each arc by his pulse and observed that every swing, long or short, took the same time span. By that, he postulated "the isochronism of the pendular movement."

Next, walk the short distance from the Cathedral to the beautiful, enormous 11th century circular marble Baptistry to see its font and its 6 columns of porphyry, marble and oriental granite. Three of the columns rest on carved lions. Biblical scenes are carved on each panel.

A very short walk from the Baptistry is a large building with a cemetery in its central court. Each section of the building exhibits many frescoes. See the 50-foot by 19-foot "Triumph of Death" in the North Gallery.

Before the train from Florence reaches Pisa, it stops 2 minutes in **Campiglia Marittima**, which has a large statue of a mongrel dog at its railstation. The dog (named Lampo) appears to watch the procession of arriving and departing trains.

Lampo ("flash of lightning") liked train travel as much as we do. He learned the train schedules and took a trip every day—more than 3,000 train trips in his lifetime.

Owned by the assistant stationmaster, Lampo escorted his master's daughter to school every morning. For that reason, he made short rail trips on schooldays, longer journeys on weekends. Always, he would go only such distances and make the necessary connections so as to return home every day before dawn.

Prior to Lampo's death in 1961 (under a freight train), he had become known not only by every trainman in Italy but by the Italian public as well, through reports of his love of train travel that appeared on Italian television and in Italy's newspapers.

Local railway workers say only a person with a printed timetable could have equaled the dog's feat, when he once went past his stop on a certain trip and then managed to return home by taking a complex series of connecting trains to get back to Campiglia Marittima.

Bologna - Ravenna - Bologna   388

All of these trains are second-class.

| Dep. Bologna | 06:13 | 08:21 | 10:48 |
| Arr. Ravenna | 07:33 | 09:33 | 11:43 |

Sights in **Ravenna**: The marvelous 5th century monuments, the Mausoleum of Galla Placidia and the Orthodox Baptistry. Just behind the Mausoleum, see the mosaics at the Church of San Vitale. Great mosaics also in Sant'Appollinare Nuovo Church, where it is helpful to use binoculars or even an opera glass in order to see those mosaics that are at the top of the walls. There are more dazzling mosaics in the Archiepiscopal Chapel.

See the ivory pulpit in the Archbishop's Palace. Dante's Tomb. The Museum of Antiquities. The exhibits at the Academy of Fine Arts.

Dep. Ravenna	13:00	14:31	17:30	20:06 (1)
Arr. Bologna	14:35	15:44	18:52	21:18

(1) Runs daily, except Sundays and holidays.

Bologna - Rome   375

Dep. Bologna	05:40	07:38 (3)	08:44 (3)	10:35 (4)
Arr. Rome (Ter.)	09:30	10:15	11:55	13:45

Dep. Rome (Ter.)	14:15 (5)	16:15 (2)	18:15	19:15 (5)	19:20 (4)
Arr. Bologna	17:36	19:27	21:27	21:51	23:00

(1) Reservation *required*. Supplement charged. Light refreshments. (2) Light refreshments. (3) "Pendolino" Reservation *required*. Supplement includes reservation fee and meal. First-class only. (4) Second-class. (5) Reservation *required*. Supplement charged. Restaurant car.

Bologna - Siena - Bologna

375				*373*		
Dep. Bologna	06:27 (1)	08:44		Dep. Siena	15:45 (1)	15:45 (1+3)
Arr. Florence (S.M.N.)	07:53	09:53		Arr. Florence (S.M.N.)	17:13	17:30
Change trains. 373				*Change trains. 375*		
Dep. Florence (S.M.N.)	08:10 (1)	09:15 (1)		Dep. Florence (S.M.N.)	18:17 (2)	20:17 (2)
Arr. Siena	09:48	10:42		Arr. Bologna	19:08	21:27

(1) Second-class. (2) Reservation *required*. Supplement charged. Restaurant car. (3) Plus other departures from Siena at 17:40 (1), 18:38 (1) and 19:55 (1), departing Florence 20:28 (1) and 21:48, arriving Bologna 21:31 and 22:47.

Sights in **Siena:** The pervasive color, named for Siena, that dominates this hill town. The view of Italy's most unique square, Piazza del Campo, from the top of the Mangia Tower of the Palazzo Publico (with its marvelous 14th century murals) or from a window of the Palazzo Publico (open daily except Sunday 9:00–13:00), where records in unbelievably beautiful calligraphy going back to the 12th century are exhibited with 15th century costumes and fine frescoes. The Pisano sculpture and mosaic floors at the Cathedral, on Piazza del Duomo. The paneled Duccio Crucifixion in the Museum of the Cathedral. Climb from there to the top of Facciatone, the skeleton for a new cathedral whose construction ceased when the Black Death of 1348 ravished Siena.

Pinacoteca, the art museum, on a street that is down from the Cathedral. Fontebranda, the old fountain with 3 arches. The ancient houses along Via degli Archi, Vicolo della Fortuna, and Vicolo delle Scotto, all of these streets radiating out from the Piazza del Campo.

Bologna - Venice - Bologna   375

Dep. Bologna	06:02	07:40	08:40 (1)	11:29 (3)	11:40 (1)	
Arr. Venice (S.L.)	08:10	09:45	10:44	13:09	13:42	

• • •

Dep. Venice (S.L.)	13:20(1)	14:20 (1)	14:42 (3)	16:20	17:20	18:20 (5)
Arr. Bologna	15:23	16:33	16:23	18:27	19:23	20:22

(1) Light refreshments. (2) Reservation *required*. Supplement charged. Restaurant car. Change trains at Venice's Mestre railstation. (3) "Pendolino" Reservation *required*. Supplement includes reservation fee and meal. First-class only. (4) Reservation *required*. Supplementt charged. Restaurant car. (5) Plus other departures from Venice at 19:20, 20:20 and 20:54, arriving Bologna 21:28, 22:25 and 23:10.

Sights in **Venice**: After the obligatory gondola ride, stand at either end of Piazza San Marco and try to cope with the enormity and beauty of the most impressive square in the world. Next visit St. Mark's Cathedral, the most wonderful Byzantine structure in Europe. Next door, see the Doge's Palace. Then relax at one of the outdoor cafes on St. Mark's Square and take in the wonder of it all while waiting for the figures on the enormous 15th century clock to emerge and strike the bell.

For another view of St. Mark's Square and the entire Lagoon, go to the top of the Bell Tower. Walk through the colorful, narrow streets of shops to the 16th century Rialto Bridge and, standing there, watch the canal traffic. The Rialto is lined with stores selling jewelry, linens, hand-blown glass, clothing, gloves and fabrics. After crossing over the Bridge, walk a short distance to the extraordinary fish market, which is the most lively 07:00–11:00 and particularly on Friday.

Among the score of churches to see in Venice are: San Giuliano, Santa Maria Formosa, Santa Maria dei Miracoli, San Giovanni e Paolo, San Francesco della Vigna, San Zaccaria, Santo Stefano, Santa Maria Gloriosa dei Frari, Santa Maria del Carmine, San Sebastiano, Madonna dell'Orto and Santi Apostoli. There are also 5 synagogues here: the German (oldest), Spanish (most beautiful), Levantine, Italian and Canton.

See the Archaeological Museum (closed Monday) in the Old Library. The many beautiful palaces on the Grand Canal. The exquisite 18th century decor of the most beautiful small opera house in the world, the Gran Teatro La Fenice.

A 15-minute boat ride takes you to the **Lido**, Venice's beach resort and site of its largest gambling casino and a 14th century Jewish cemetery. It is only a 3-minute boat ride to the beautiful, white Church of Santa Maria della Salute, built on more than one million wood pilings.

It is a 15-minute boat ride to the island of **Murano** to watch glass-blowing and visit the Glassworks Museum (closed Tuesday) in Palazzo Giustiniani. Boats for Murano leave from the Fondamenta Nuove vaporetto dock. We recommend you get off the boat at the second stop, tour the Glassworks Museum, and then walk past many interesting shops to the first landing for the return ride to Venice. The Glassworks Museum displays ancient Roman work and many excellent glass pieces from the Middle Ages

To see lacemaking (tablecloths, handkerchiefs, bedspreads, dresses) and buy fine lace, take a 30-minute boat ride to **Burano**. It is only a few minutes by boat from Burano to **Torcelo**, a small island of orchards, vineyards and artichoke farms. The 11th century basilica there has splendid mosaics. Another sight on Torcello that interests some tourists is the display of the small skeleton of the martyr Santa Fosca in a glass coffin at the church there that is named for her.

Bologna - Verona - Bologna 380

| Dep. Bologna | 06:43 | 08:45 | 10:38 (3) | 11:45 | 12:44 |
| Arr. Verona | 08:18 | 10:33 | 12:41 | 13:40 | 14:40 |

Sights in **Verona:** The large and excellently preserved first century Arena. Then take Via Mazzini (Verona's main shopping street) to Piazza della Herbe (Herb Square), where you will find a marvelous display of fruits, vegetables, live pet birds, and dead game birds. Only a few minutes walk from there, the Veronese marble lobby of the Hotel Due Torri is worth seeing.

At Piazza dei Signori are the tombs of the Della Scala Family, once rulers of Verona. La Scala Opera House in Milan is named after them. See the paintings in the Church of Sant'Anastasia. Visit the Cathedral and the Museum of Art in Castelvecchio, on Corso Cavour.

The main attraction in Verona, since Shakespeare, has always been Juliet's balcony, at Via Cappelo 17–25 (Shakespeare's "Capulet.")

| Dep. Verona | 12:23 | 13:30 | 15:01 (5) | 15:18 | 15:30 | 17:29 (6) |
| Arr. Bologna | 14:00 | 15:14 | 16:50 | 17:16 | 17:24 | 19:22 |

(1) Operates late May to late July and most of September. Runs Monday-Friday, except holidays. (2) Early September to late July: runs Saturday and Sunday. Late July to early September: runs daily. (3) Reservation *required.* Supplement charged. Restaurant car. (4) Reservation *required.* Supplement charged. Frist-class only. (5) Light refreshments. (6) Plus other departures from Verona at 19:30 and 21:56, arriving Bologna 21:14 and 23:42.

Florence - Arezzo - Florence 385

| Dep. Florence (S.M.N.) | 06:30 | | 06:50 | 08:15 | 10:15 (2) | 11:15 | | 14:15 (2) |
| Arr. Arezzo | | 07:07 | 08:00 | 08:56 | 10:56 | | 12:15 | 14:56 |

Sights in **Arezzo:** The 15th century Piero frescoes of the Legend of the True Cross that can be seen 12:00–14:30 and 19:00–21:30 in the Church of San Francesco. The carvings on the facade of the 11th century Church of Santa Maria della Pieve. Behind Pieve, the marvelous Piazza Grande, with its medieval palaces. There are many other fine palaces on Corso Italia.

The musical scale and staff of 4 lines was invented in the 10th century by Guido Monaco of Arezzo. The Piazza Guido Monaco is named for him.

See the 16th century stained glass and the great Renaissance organ in the Cathedral. Walk across the park to the enormous fortress, Medicea, built in the 16th century by the Medici family. See the collection of Etruscan and Roman artwork in the Archaeological Museum at the Convent, including the ancient Corallini vases. The remains of a Roman amphitheater can be seen in the park next to the Museum. A library and museum is maintained in the home where Petrarch was born.

The collection of ivories, goldsmith work, coins, furniture, weapons, ceramics and 13th–20th century sculptures and paintings (including Vasari's huge fresco "Feast in the House of Ahasuerus") in the Galleria e Museo Medievale e Moderno at the Bruni-Ciocchi Palace.

Other frescoes by Vasari are exhibited in the Casa del Vasari, on Via 20 Settembre.

See the 17th century frescoed dome of the Badia Church.

Dep. Arezzo	13:46	15:03	15:53	17:05	19:05	20:00 (5)	21:05 (4)
Arr. Florence (S.M.N.)	14:47	16:11	16:48	17:45	19:45	21:25	21:50

(1) Reservation *required*. Supplement charged. Light refreshments. (2) Reservation *required*. Supplement charged. Restaurant car. (3) Light refreshments. (4) Plus another departure from Arezzo at 22:08, arriving Florence 22:48. (5) Runs Monday-Friday except holidays.

Florence - Assisi - Florence

385			*385*		
Dep. Florence (S.M.N.)	06:50	10:15	Dep. Assisi	14:22	17:00
Arr. Terontola	08:27	11:20	Arr. Terontola	15:26	18:07
Change trains. 385			*Change trains. 385*		
Dep. Terontola	08:50	12:48	Dep. Terontola	16:41	18:41
Arr. Assisi	09:50	13:48	Arr. Florence (S.M.N.)	17:45	19:57

Sights in **Assisi**: St. Francis' tomb in the 13th century Basilica on the Hill of Paradise, and the many outstanding paintings there, considered to be the greatest museum of Italian Renaissance mural painting. St. Claire's Church. The medieval Castle. Piazza del Commune. The upper and lower churches at the Convent of St. Francis, with their many frescos. Prison Hermitage. The 16th century Church of Santa Maria degli Angeli. The 12th century Cathedral of St. Ruffino. The 14th century La Rocca Maggiore fortress. The Temple of Minerva.

Florence - Bologna - Florence   375

See Bologna schedules.

Florence - Livorno - Florence 369

On the departures from Livorno, there is time to taxi 10 minutes from Pisa's station to the Leaning Tower and return to the station for a later departure to Florence.

All of these trains are second-class, unless designated otherwise.

Dep. Florence (S.M.N.)	07:15	11:40	Dep. Livorno	13:05	15:05 (3)
Arr. Pisa	08:10	12:32	Arr. Pisa	13:15	15:17
Dep. Pisa	08:12	12:35	Dep. Pisa	13:17	15:19
Arr. Livorno	08:27	13:50	Arr. Florence (S.M.N.)	14:15	16:57

(1) Has a first-class coach. (2) Runs Saturdays, Sundays and holidays. (3) Plus other Livorno departures at 16:05, 18:05, 20:05, 21:05 and 21:45, departing Pisa 16:22, 18:22, 20:22, 21:22 and 22:12, arriving Florence 17:15, 19:15, 21:15, 22:20 and 23:35.

Sights in **Livorno**: The old and new forts, both from the 16th century. The marble statue of Ferdinand. Tacca's 17th century bronze statues of "The Four Moors." Villas once occupied by Shelley and Byron. Italy's Naval Academy. The paintings and the Communal Library, both in the Civic Museum.

Florence - Milan - Florence 370

Dep. Florence (S.M.N.)	06:58 (1)	07:23	08:35 (2)	09:04	10:07 (3)
Arr. Milan (Centrale)	09:55	10:30	11:50	12:15	13:10

Dep. Milan (Centrale)	15:00 (1)	16:00 (1)	17:00 (3)	17:55 (1)	20:00 (2)
Arr. Florence (S.M.N.)	17:46	18:46	19:46	21:19	22:58

(1) Reservation *required*. Supplement charged. Light refreshments. (2) "Pendolino." Reservation *required*. Supplement includes reservation fee and meal. First-class only. Departs/arrives Florence's Rifredi railstation. (3) Reservation *required*. Supplement charged. Restaurant car.

Florence - Padua - Florence 390

Dep. Florence (S.M.N.)	07:15 (1)	10:32 (2+4)	Dep. Padua	15:12 (3)	18:27 (5)
Arr. Padua	09:46	12:37	Arr. Florence (S.M.N.)	17:27 (6)	20:53

(1) Reservation *required*. Supplement charged. (2) "Pendolino." Reservation *required*. Supplement includes reservation fee and meal. First-class only. Departs from Florence's Rifredi railstation. (3) Reservation *required*. Supplement charged. Restaurant car. (4) Plus another departure from Florence at 14:17, arriving Padua at 16:46. (5) Plus another departure from Padua at 20:16, arriving Florence 22:54. (6) Arrives Florence's Rifredi station.

Sights in **Padua:** The 13th century university where Petrarch lectured and Galileo taught (on the Via 8 Febraio) has guided tours on each hour, 09:00-12:00 and 15:00-17:00. It is open daily, except Saturday afternoon and all day Sunday.

Scrovegni Chapel, noted for its Giotto frescoes, is open April-September 09:00-12:30 and 14:30-17:30. From October through March, it is open 09:00-12:30 and 13:30-16:30 daily, except Sunday afternoon, Christmas, New Year's Day and Easter.

The Church of Eremitani.

The Basilica of Sant'Antonio, a major Roman Catholic shrine with several statues by Donatello, is open daily 06:30-19:45. The Cathedral is open daily 08:00-12:00 and 16:00-19:00. The Art Gallery (Pinacoteca) is open daily except Sunday, 09:00-13:30;.

The Oratorio di San Giorgio and the Scuola di San Antonio are open daily except Monday, Easter and Christmas. April-September: 09:00-12:00 and 14:30-18:30. October-March: closes at 18:00.

Santa Giu stina is open daily 07:30-12:00 and 15:30-19:30.

Florence - Parma - Florence   370

Dep. Florence (S.M.N.)	07:15	08:35	09:04
Arr. Bologna	08:23	09:11 (3)	10:18
Change trains.			
Dep. Bologna	08:38	09:38	10:30
Arr. Parma	09:30	10:31	11:24

Sights in **Parma:** See notes about Parma under "Bologna–Parma"

Dep. Parma	15:26 (2)	16:26	17:26 (2)	19:07 (3)
Arr. Bologna	16:18	17:27	18:22	-0- (3)
Change trains.				
Dep. Bologna	16:44 (4)	17:40 (4)	18:34	-0-
Arr. Florence (S.M.N.)	17:46	18:46	19:56	21:19

(1) "Pendolino" Reservation *required.* Supplement includes reservation fee and meal. First-class only. Departs/arrives Florence's Rifredi railstation. (2) Light refreshments. (3) Direct train. No train change in Bologna. Reservation *required.* Supplement charged. Light refreshments. (4) Reservation *required.* Supplement charged. Light refreshments.

Florence - Perugia - Florence   374

Dep. Florence (S.M.N.)	11:15	13:10 (2)	Dep. Perugia	16:34 (2)	17:30 (1+3)
Arr. Terontola *Change trains.*	-0-	-0- (2)	Arr. Terontola *Change trains.*	-0- (2)	18:11
Dep. Terontola	-0- (2)	-0-	Dep. Terontola	-0-	18:41
Arr. Perugia	13:26	15:20	Arr. Florence (S.M.N.)	18:46	19:45

(1) Second-class. (2) Direct train. No train change in Terontola. (3) Plus another Perugia departure at 19:28 (1), arriving Florence 21:50 (change trains in Terontola).

Sights in **Perugia:** Take a bus from the railstation rather than walk the steep climb uphill to the town. Visit the Municipal Palace, to see the magnificent carved and inlaid wood panels in the Library, the chapel of the Stock Exchange, and the great paintings in the National Gallery (Pinacoteca). On display to the left of the main door of the Stock Exchange chapel is the white onyx ring with which the Virgin Mary was married.

Also visit the 13th century Church of San Ercolano. Galleng Palace, with its Foreign University. The Pisano sculptures at the Fontana Maggiore in beautiful Piazza 4 Novembre. The fine collection of Tuscan paintings in the museum of the 13th century Palazzo dei Priori. Stroll along Maesta della Volte, Via dei Priori (to the Oratory of San Bernardino), Via Bagliona and Corso Vannucci, the main street.

Florence - Pisa - Florence   370

Dep Florence (S.M.N.)	Frequent times from 05:55 to 22:30
Arr. Pisa	50–60 minutes later

Sights in **Pisa**: See notes about Pisa under "Bologna–Pisa"

Dep. Pisa	Frequent times from 05:49 to 23:57
Arr. Florence (S.M.N.)	50–60 minutes later

Florence - Ravenna - Florence

375			388		
Dep. Flor. (S.M.N.)	07:15	09:47 (3)	Dep.Ravenna	13:00 (2)	14:31 (2+4)
Arr. Bologna	08:27	10:58	Arr. Bologna	14:35	15:44
Change trains. 388			*Change trains. 375*		
Dep. Bologna	08:21 (2)	10:48	Dep. Bologna	16:30 (3)	17:06 (3)
Arr. Ravenna	09:33	11:43	Arr. Flor. (S.M.N.)	17:27 (5)	18:16

(1) Reservation *required*. Supplement charged. Light refreshments. (2) Second-class. (3) Reservation *required*. Supplement charged. Restaurant car. (4) Plus another departure from Revenna at 17:30…departing Bologna 20:20…arriving Florence 21:19. (5) Arrives Florence's Rifredi station.

Florence - Rome - Florence   375

Dep. Florence (S.M.N.)	06:56 (1)	08:36 (3)	09:53 (3)	11:44	13:56 (4)
Arr. Rome (Ter.)	09:30	10:15	11:55	13:45	16:05

Dep. Rome (Ter.)	16:15 (2)	18:15	19:15 (3)	19:20 (4)
Arr. Florence (S.M.N.)	18:17	20:17	20:52 (3)	21:48

Dep. Rome (Ter.)	19:00 (3)	19:10 (3)	19:15	19:45 (3)	20:00 (1)
Arr. Florence (S.M.N.)	20:34 (3)	20:47 (3)	21:39	21:22 (3)	22:16

(1) Reservation *required*. Supplement charged. Light refreshments. (2) Light refreshments. (3) "Pendolino" Departs/arrives Florence's Rifredi railstaion. Reservation *required*. Supplement includes reservation fee and meal. (4) Reservation *required*. Supplement charged. Restaurant car.

Florence - Siena - Florence   373

All of these trains are second-class only.

Dep. Florence (S.M.N.)	06:35	08:10	09:15	11:45	13:25	14:13 (1)
Arr. Siena	08:02	09:48	10:42	13:25	15:05	15:33

Dep. Siena	13:35	15:45	16:33 (2)	17:37 (2)	18:38	19:55	21:15
Arr. Florence (S.M.N.)	15:05	17:30	18:20	19:22	20:00	21:24	22:33

(1) Runs daily, except Sundays and holidays. Change trains in Empoli. (2) Change trains in Empoli.

Florence - Verona - Florence

375

Dep. Florence (S.M.N.)	07:15	09:47	10:32	14:17 (2)
Arr. Bologna	08:27	10:58	11:30	15:27
Change trains. 380				
Dep. Bologna	08:45	-0-	11:45	12:44
Arr. Verona (P.N.)	10:33	12:41	13:40	14:40

Dep. Verona (P.N.)	15:18 (1)	15:30	17:29	
Arr. Bologna	-0- (1)	17:24	19:22	
Change trains. 375				
Dep. Bologna	-0-	17:46 (2)	19:44 (4)	
Arr. Florence (S.M.N.)	18:23	18:46	20:58	

(1) Reservation *required*. Supplement charged. Direct train. No train change in Bologna. Restaurant car. (2) Reservation *required*. Supplement charged. Light refreshments. (3) Late July to early September: runs daily. Early September to late July: runs Saturday and Sunday. (4) Second-class. (5) Arrives/departs Florence's Rifredi station.

Genoa - Bologna - Genoa   354

Dep. Genoa (Piazza Principe)	07:04	16:21	18:23
Arr. Bologna	10:08	19:20	21:36

Dep Bologna	07:38	13:38	17:38
Arr. Genoa (Piazza Principe)	10:35	16:48	20:35

Genoa - Cremona - Genoa

355

Dep. Genoa (P.P.)	05:48	09:13	11:54
Arr. Milan (Centrale)	07:40	10:50	13:44
Change trains. 363			
Dep. Milan (Centrale)	08:20	12:20	14:20
Arr. Cremona	09:32	13:33	15:27

Sights in **Cremona**: One of Italy's most impressive squares, the Piazza del Commune, with its octagonal Baptistry, 12th century Duomo Cathedral, Loggia de Militi, and the Gothic Torrazzo (tallest bell tower in Italy).

Cremona is where the art of violin-making reached its apex, with the works of Amati, Stradivari and Guarneri. It is possible to watch young violin makers following that great tradition by visiting La Scuola Internazionale de Liuteria, in a renovated 16th century palace.

At the City Museum every day at 11:00, an outstanding violin made by Stradivari is played by the museum curator. Located near the Liuteria are many shops which will make a special violin to order. On view at the City Hall are 2 original Stradivari, 2 Amatis and a Sacconi.

Dep. Cremona	12:37	15:42	17:58 (1)	-0-
Arr. Milan (Centrale)	13:50	16:45	19:22	-0-
Change trains. 356				
Dep. Milan (Centrale)	14:05	18:05	21:35	22:15
Arr. Genoa (P.P.)	15:49	19:55	22:47	00:04

(1) Arrived Milano Porta Garibaldi.

Genoa - Milan - Genoa   355

Genoa (P.P.)	07:13 (1)	07:54	09:13	11:13	11:54
Arr. Milan (Centrale)	08:47	09:40	10:50	13:05	13:45
Dep. Milan (Centrale.)	14:15	15:10	16:15	17:05	18:05
Arr. Genoa (P.P.)	16:10	16:45	18:00	18:44	19:55

(1) Reservation *required*. Supplement charged. Light refreshments. (2) Reservation *required*. Supplement charged. (3) Plus other departures from Milan at 19:05, 20:10 and 22:15, arriving Genoa 20:44, 21:54 and 00:05.

Genoa - Nice   90

Dep. Genoa (P.P.)	05:55	08:22 (1)	Dep. Nice (Ville)	19:10 (2)	20:29
Arr. Nice (Ville)	10:15	11:20	Arr. Genoa (P.P.)	22:10	00:17

(1) Reservation *required*. Supplement charged. Restaurant car. (2) Restaurant car.

Sights in **Nice**: See notes about Nice under France.

Genoa - Pisa - Genoa   355

There is exceptional mountain and Mediterranean coastline scenerey on this ride.

Dep. Genoa (P.P.)	06:17 (1)	12:16 (2)	13:05 (2)
Arr. Pisa (Cen.)	08:11	14:30	15:31

Sights in **Pisa:** See notes about Pisa under "Bologna–Pisa"

Dep. Pisa (Cen.)	15:00 (3)	16:02 (1)	21:27 (1)
Arr. Genoa (P.P.)	17:25	18:11	23:23

(1) Reservation *required.* Supplement charged. Light refreshments. (2) Light refreshments. (3) Operates late May to late September. Light refreshments. (4) "Pendolino" Reservation *required.* Supplement includes reservation fee and meal. First-class only.

Genoa - Rome   355

Dep. Genoa (P.Prin.)	00:40 (1)	06:17 (3)	12:16 (6)	13:05 (5)
Arr. Rome (Ter.)	06:55	10:35	18:05	19:20

(1) Carries a sleeping car. Also has couchettes. (2) "Pendolino" Reservation *required.* Supplement includes reservation fee and meal. First-class only. (3) Reservation *required.* Supplement charged. Light refreshments. (4) Change trains in Pisa. (5) Light refreshments.

Genoa - Torino - Genoa   360

Dep. Genoa (P.P.)	06:39	09:00	11:00 (1)	11:41 (2)
Arr. Torino (P.N.)	08:40	10:35	12:38	13:33

Sights in **Torino:** The marvelous facade of the Porta Nuova railstation, built in the 1860's. The beautiful Piazza Carlo Felice park, near the railstation.

Piazza San Carlo (considered second only to St. Mark's in Venice), dominated by a large statue (called "the bronze horse") of Emanuele Filiberto, hero king of the mid-16th century. In Piazza dello Statuto, the large monument dedicated to the completion of the Frejus rail tunnel between Italy and France in the late 19th century.

The imposing Palazzo Madama, with its enormous marble staircase and Royal Armory, in Piazza Castello, which is the heart of the city. (It is a museum.) The Museo Egizio in Palazzo Carignano, the third most important (after London and Cairo) Egyptian collection in the world. he university in Piazzo Carlo, where Erasmus of Rotterdam earned his doctorate in 1506. The view from the top of Mole Antonelliani, on Via Montebello. Parco del Valentino, with its splendid gardens and buildings.

The frescos in the Castello del Valentino. It is an easy walk from the Castle to Borgo

Medievale, a village built in 1884 to depict the lifestyle of this area in the year 1400. The Church of the Great Mother of God, patterned after Rome's Pantheon.

The 17th century Royal Palace. Near it, the black and white marble Chapel of the Holy Shroud in the Church of San Lorenzo. An urn holding what is believed to be the shroud placed on Jesus when he was taken from the cross is the major attraction there. The Auto Museum on Corso Unita d'Italia, with models going back to 1893.

Dep. Torino (P.N.)	12:28 (1)	13:28 (1)	14:28 (1)	16:28 (1)	17:28 (1)	18:28 (3)
Arr. Genoa (P.P.)	14:18	14:58	16:18	18:18	18:58	20:18

(1) Reservation *required*. Supplement charged. Light refreshments. (2) Operates mid-June to mid-September. (3) Plus other departures from Torino at 19:28 (2), 20:28, 22:00 and 23:05, arriving Genoa 20:58, 22:18, 23:53 and 00:56.

Milan - Bologna - Milan 370

Most of these trains charge a supplement and have either a restaurant car or buffet.

Dep. Milan (Cen.)	06:55 (1)	07:05 (2)	07:50 (2)	08:00 (4)	09:05 (2)	10:00 (2+6)
Arr. Bologna	08:31	08:57	09:28	09:44	10:52	11:42

Dep. Bologna	12:58 (2)	14:04 (2)	14:15 (2)	15:16 (2)	15:46 (2)	16:04 (4+7)
Arr. Milan (Cen.)	15:05	15:55	16:05	17:00	17:35	18:00

(1) "Pendolino" Reservation *required*. Supplement includes reservation fee and meal. First-class only. (2) Reservation *required*. Supplement charged. Restaurant car. (3) Light refreshments. (4) Reservation *required*. Supplement charged. Light refreshments. (5) Runs daily, except Sundays and holidays. Light refreshments. (6) Plus other departures from Milan at 11:05 (2) and 12:05 (2), arriving Bologna 12:56 and 13:42. (7) Plus other departures from Bologna at 17:16 (2), 18:16 (2), 19:16 (2) and 21:20 (2) arriving Milan 19:15, 20:07, 21:00 and 23:45.

Milan - Como - Milan 290

Reservation is required or advisable on most of these trains. All of them charge a supplement.

Milan (Cen.)	Frequent times from 07:25 to 21:25
Arr. Como (S.G.)	35–45 minutes later

Sights in **Como**: Take Bus #4, marked "Piazza Cavour," from the railstation to reach both the lakeshore and the cable car which ascends the 2300-foot high **Mount Brunate** in 7 minutes. At the peak, there is a wonderful view of **Lake Como** and the Alps.

Dep. Como (S.G.)	Frequent times from 06:12 to 22:56
Arr. Milan (Cen.)	35–45 minutes later

Milan - Faenza - Milan   390

| Dep. Milan (Cen.) | 08:05 | 10:05 (2) |
| Arr. Faenza | 11:12 | 13:09 |

Sights in **Faenza**: This has been Italy's city of ceramics since 1100. See the collection in the Ceramics Museum.

Many of the factories have showrooms: Mazzotti (Via Firenze 240), Gatti (Pompignoli 4), Navarra (Via XX Septembre 42A) and Morigi (Via Barbavara 7). A wide selection of ceramics is sold at the Coopertiva Artigiana Ceramisti Faentini.

| Dep. Faenza | 13:43 | 15:53 (1) | 17:43 (1) | 19:43 |
| Arr. Milan (Cen.) | 16:53 | 19:08 | 20:50 | 23:05 |

(1) Light refreshments. (2) Runs Monday-Saturday only.

Milan - Cremona - Milan   363

| Dep. Milan (Cen.) | 08:20 | 12:20 | Dep. Cremona | 12:37 | 15:42 | 19:34 |
| Arr. Cremona | 09:29 | 13:02 | Arr. Milan (Cen.) | 13:50 | 16:45 | 20:45 |

Sights in **Cremona**: See "Genoa–Cremona."

Milan - Florence - Milan   375

| Dep. Milan (Cen.) | 06:55 (1) | 07:55 (2) | 08:55 (3) | 09:55 (2) | 10:35 (2) |
| Arr. Florence (S.M.N.) | 09:24 (1) | 10:46 | 11:46 | 12:46 | 13:51 |

| Dep. Florence (S.M.N.) | 14:11 (2) | 15:10 (3) | 16:15 (2) | 17:05 (3) | 18:10 (2+4) |
| Arr. Milan (Cen.) | 17:00 | 18:00 | 19:15 | 20:07 | 21:00 |

(1) "Pendolino" Supplement includes reservation fee and meal. First-class only. Departs/arrives Florence's Rifredi railstation. (2) Reservation *required.* Supplement charged. Restaurant car. (3) Reservation *required.* Supplement charged. Light refreshments. (4) Plus other departures from Florence at 19:23 (2) and 21:27 (1), arriving Milan 22:40 and 23:59.

Milan - Genoa - Milan   355

See schedule under "Genoa-Milan."

Milan - Locarno - Milan

The Camedo–Locarno portion of this trip is one of the 5 most scenic rail trips in Europe, with outstanding mountain, canyon and river scenery.

365

Dep. Milan (Cen.)	07:23 (1)	08:25 (1)	09:05 (2)	10:25 (2)	12:25 (2)	14:00 (2)
Arr. Domodossola	09:00	09:58	10:33	11:58	13:58	15:31

Change trains.
Walk outside the Domodossola railstation and go to the underground track
in order to board the Centovalli narrow-gauge local railway.
272

Dep. Domodossola	09:02	10:18	11:12	12:16	15:16	16:00
Dep. Camedo	10:05	11:22	12:14	13:20	16:22	17:02
Arr. Locarno	10:40	11:55	12:48	13:55	16:55	17:37

Sights in **Locarno**: Stroll the gardens along the shore of **Lake Maggiore** and take the funicular ride to **Orselin** to see the art treasures in the Madonna del Sasso (Madonna of the Rock) church high above the village and, from there, the fine view of Locarno and Lake Maggiore. From Orselin, ride the cable-car to 4,400-foot-high **Cardada**. Then take the chair lift from **Cardada** to **Cimetta**, more than a mile high.

In nearby **Ascona,** see the frescoes depicting scenes of the Old and New Testament in the 14th century church of Santa Maria Misericordia and the adjoining cloisters of Collegio Papio.

Dep. Locarno	12:22	13:50	15:28	16:28	17:28	19:05
Dep. Camedo	12:57	14:23	16:01	17:01	18:01	19:40
Arr. Domodossola	14:00	15:30	17:00	18:00	19:00	20:46

Change trains. Walk from the underground Centovailli track, up to the main Domodossola railstation.
365

Dep. Domodossola	15:15 (2)	16:02 (4)	17:45 (3)	18:20 (2)	19.45	22:02 (2)
Arr. Milan (Cen.)	16:50	17:45	19:15	19:45	21:10	23:40

(1) Reservation *required*. Supplement charged. (2) Reservation *required*. Supplement charged. Light refreshments. (3) Reservation *required*. Supplement charged. Restaurant car. (4) Light refreshments.

CRUISING THE BORROMEAN ISLANDS ON LAKE MAGGIORE

An overnight stay in Locarno is worthwhile, in order to have a complete day for touring the **Borromean Islands** on Lake Maggiore.

Isola Madre is a fantastic garden island. See the 18th century palace and stroll through the lush gardens there (palm trees, orange and grapefruit trees, magnolias, roses, camelias, azaleas, and many gold and silver Chinese pheasants).

On **Isola Bella**, the fascinating and very unique 17th century palace where European leaders met in 1925 to sign the Locarno Pact is the attraction. You will be enchanted by the palace's 6-room Neptune Grotto, decorated with enormous plaster seashells, walls that simulate white coral, and floors that are mosaics of small pebbles. Stroll through the lavish 10-terrace garden.

The only schedule which allows visiting both islands in one day is to take the 10:30 hydrofoil (reservation required) from Locarno Pier. Arrive Isola Madre 11:45. Depart Isola Madre 13:00, arriving Isola Bella 13:20. Lunch there. Depart Isola Bella 16:35. Arrive back in Locarno at 18:30.

Milan - Lugano - Milan   290

Dep. Milan (Cen.)	07:25 (1)	08:25 (2)	09:20 (2)	10:25 (2)	11:25 (2)	12:25 (1)
Arr. Lugano	08:52	09:55	10:55	11:55	12:55	13:55

Sights in **Lugano:** Take the cable car from the railstation to Piazza Cioccaro. Walk downhill from there to the city center, Piazza Riforma. See the view of the city from the Cathedral of San Lorenzo. The collection of over 700 masterpieces (Rubens, Goya, Durer, Raphael, Tiepolo, Tintoretto, and some Americans) in the Thyssen Art Gallery of La Villa Favorita, open only from Easter to October.

Stroll the shore of lovely **Lake Lugano**.

It is 15 minutes by boat, bus, taxi or private car to **Campione** on the eastern shore of Lake Lugano, where a small gambling casino has operated since 1933. People under 18 years old are not admitted. Men must wear neckties and jackets. The Casino is open daily from 15:15 until dawn the next day.

Although Campione is located in Italian territory, no passport or any other identity document is required, and there is no customs checking.

Other sights in Campione are the frescoes in the church called Sanctuary of the Madonna dei Ghirli (Our Lady of the Swallows), first built in the Middle Ages and then rebuilt in the 18th century.

Another of the many boat trips on the lake is to the ceramic, clothing and craft shops in **Gandria**.

Dep. Lugano	14:06 (2)	15:06 (2)	16:32 (2)	17:06 (2)	18:06 (1+4)
Arr. Milan (Cen.)	15:35	16:35	17:35	18:35	19:35

(1) Reservation *required*. Supplement charged. Light refreshments. (2) Reservation *required*. Supplement charged. Restaurant car. (3) Light refreshments. (4) Plus other departures from Lugano at 19:06 (2), 20:06 (1), 21:19 (3) and 22:06 (2), arriving Milan 20:35, 21:30, 22:40 and 23:35.

Milan - Rome and Rome - Milan 370

Dep. Milan (Cen.)	06:55 (1)	07:50 (1)	09:00 (2)	10:00 (2)	10:55 (2)
Arr. Rome (Ter.)	11:05	12:48	14:00	15:05	16:15 (10)

Dep. Milan (Cen.)	12:55 (2)	14:00 (4)	15:00 (4)	16:00 (4)	17:00 (2+8)
Arr. Rome (Ter.)	17:50	18:50	19:52 (3)	20:50	21:50

• • •

Dep. Rome (Ter.)	06:55 (1)	08:05 (2)	09:05 (4)	11:05 (2)	12:05 (2)
Arr. Milan (Cen.)	10:50	13:10	14:32	16:05	17:00

Dep. Rome (Ter.)	13:05 (4)	14:05 (2)	15:05 (4)	16:05 (2)	17:05 (2+9)
Arr Milan (Cen.)	18:00	19:15	20:07	21:00	22:40

(1) "Pendolino." Reservation *required*. Supplement includes reservation fee and meal. First-class only. (2) Reservation *required*. Supplement charged. Restaurant car. (3) Depart/Arrive Rome's Tiburtina railstation. (4) Reservation *required*. Supplement charged. Light refreshments. (5) Has couchettes. (6) Carries a sleeping car. Also has couchettes. Coach is second-class. (7) Operates early September to late July. Carries only sleeping cars. (8) Plus other Milan departures at 17:50 (4), 19:30 (1), 19:40 (1), 22:15 (5), 22:55 (6) and 00:15. (9) Plus other Rome departures at 19:45 (1), 22:30 (5) and 22:50 (5). (10) Runs Sunday only.

Milan - Torino - Milan 350

Dep. Milan (Cen.)	07:10 (1)	08:20 (2)	09:10 (1)	11:20 (1)	12:20 (2)
Arr. Torino (P.N.)	08:45	09:58	10:55	13:13	13:58

Sights in **Torino**: See notes under "Genoa–Torino"

Dep. Torino (P.N.)	13:08 (1)	13:50 (2)	15:08 (1)	15:50	16:53 (2+5)
Arr. Milan (Cen.)	14:45	15:40	16:40	17:40	18:40

(1) Reservation *required*. Supplement charged. Light refreshments. (2) Light refreshments. (3) Depart/arrive Milan's Porta Garibaldi railstation. (4) Reservation *required*. Supplement charged. (5) Plus other Torino departures at 17:50, 19:08 (4), 19:50 (2), 21:32 (1), 21:50 and 22:50, arriving Milan 19:40, 20:50, 21:40, 23:05, 23:45 and 00:40.

Milan - Venice - Milan 350

Dep. Milan (Cen.)	06:10	07:05 (1)	08:10	11:05 (1)	11:10 (3)	12:10
Arr. Venice (S.L.)	09:16	09:52	11:18	13:59	14:25	15:25

Sights in **Venice**: See notes under "Bologna–Venice"

Dep. Venice (S.L.)	Frequent times from 05:10 to 00:05
Arr. Milan (Cen.)	3 hours later

(1) Reservation *required*. Supplement charged. Light refreshments. (2) Departs from Milan's Porta Garibaldi station. (3) Light refreshments.

Milan - Verona - Milan 350

Dep. Milan (Cen.)	06:10	07:00 (1)	08:10	09:05 (2)	11:05 (2)	12:10 (3)
Arr. Verona (P.N.)	07:44	08:26	09:44	10:27	12:27	13:53

Sights in **Verona**: See notes about Verona under "Bologna–Verona"

Dep. Verona (P.M.)	Frequent times from 05:35 to 22:14
Arr. Milan (Cen.)	1½ hours later

(1) Reservation *required*. Supplement charged. Restaurant car. (2) Light refreshments. (3) Restaurant car.

Naples - Bari - Naples 400

Dep. Naples (P. Garibaldi)	07:33	Dep. Bari	17:06
Arr. Bari	12:00	Arr. Naples (P. Garibaldi)	21:20

Naples - Pompeii - Naples 392

The standard-gauge trains that depart from Naples' Centrale railstation, (shown below) *are* covered by Eurailpass.

The narrow-gauge trains that leave from Naples' F.S. railstation are operated by Circumvesuviana Railway (Table 401) and are *not* covered by Eurailpass.

Salerno is as convenient a base for visiting Pompeii as Naples is.

Dep. Naples (Cen.)	07:10	08:05	11:41	13:10	14:10	15:10
Arr. Pompeii	25 minutes later					

Sights in **Pompeii:** See where 20,000 people were living and how they lived 1900 years ago when this city was buried within a few minutes under a volcanic rain of ashes from nearby (still active) Vesuvius, when it was young and strong.

Dep. Pompeii	11:19	14:39	15:42	17:22	20:19	22:00
Arr. Naples (Cen.)	25 minutes later					

Naples - Rome - Naples   405

Dep. Naples (Cen.)	06:47	07:05	07:47 (1)	08:35	08:57
Dep. Naples (P.G.)	-0-	-0-	-0-	-0-	-0-
Dep. Naples (Mer.)	-0-	-0-	07:50 (1)	-0-	-0-
Dep. Naples (C. Fl.)	-0-	-0-	07:54	-0-	-0-
Arr. Rome (Ter.)	09:10	09:20	09:50	10:45	10:50
Dep. Rome (Ter.)	13:20 (2)	14:00 (3)	15:15	16:10 (4)	17:10 (1+5)
Arr. Naples (C. Fl.)	15:18	-0-	-0-	-0-	-0-
Arr. Naples (Mer.)	15:24	-0-	-0-	-0-	17:42
Arr. Naples (P.G.)	-0-	-0-	-0-	-0-	17:53
Arr. Naples (Cen.)	15:53	16:18 (6)	17:26	18:08 (6)	19:00

(1) Reservation *required.* Supplement charged. Light refreshments. (2) Reservation *required.* Supplement charged. Light refreshments. First-class only. (3) Light refreshments. (4) Runs daily, except Sundays and holidays. (5) Plus other departures from Rome Termini at frequent times from 16:20 to 21:20. (6) Arrives Napoli Piazza Garibaldi.

Rome - Anzio - Rome   393

All of these trains are second-class only.

Dep. Rome (Ter.)	07:55	09:55	11:35	12:55	13:50	14:45	15:35 (1+2)
Arr. Anzio	66 minutes later						

Sights in **Anzio:** Has been a beach resort since ancient times. Many Americans visit the nearby military cemeteries, holding those killed in the January 22, 1944 Allied invasion.

Dep. Anzio	13:14	14:12 (1)	15:16	16:08	18:14	19:18	21:59
Arr. Rome (Ter.)	66 minutes later						

(1) Runs daily, except Sundays and holidays. (2) Plus other departures from Rome at 16:45, 17:45, 18:55, 20:15 and 22:00.

Rome - Assisi - Rome   385

Dep. Rome (Ter.)	07:00 (1)	07:30 (3)	10:15 (1)
Arr. Foligno	08:42	09:21	11:57
Change trains			
Dep. Foligno	08:45 (2)	09:35 (2)	12:02
Arr. Assisi	08:55	09:52	12:11

Sights in **Assisi**: See notes under "Florence-Assisi"

Dep. Assisi	11:51 (2)	14:44 (2)	17:41	18:51 (2)	20:38
Arr. Foligno	12:10	15:02	-0-	19:05	20:50
Change trains					
Dep. Foligno	12:32 (3)	15:58 (1)	17:56 (4)	19:38	21:17 (1)
Arr. Rome (Ter.)	14:30	17:45	19:40	21:40	23:10

(1) Reservation *required*. Supplement charged. Light refreshments. (2) Second-class. (3) Light refreshments. (4) Reservation *required*. Supplement charged. (5) Reservation *required*. Direct train.

Rome - Florence - Rome   375

Dep. Rome (Termini)	07:45 (1)	08:55 (1)	12:15 (3)	14:15 (3)
Arr. Florence (S.M.N.)	09:47 (2)	10:32 (2)	14:17	16:21 (2)
Dep. Florence (S.M.N.)	11:44 (3)	13:56 (3)	17:27 (1)	18:16 (3)
Arr. Rome (Termini)	13:45	16:05	19:05 (2)	20:20

(1) "Pendolino" Reservation *required*. Supplement includes reservation fee and meal. First-class only. (2) Arrives/Departs Florence's Rifredi railstation. (3) Reservation *required*. Supplement charged. Restaurant car. (4) Reservation *required*. Supplement charged. Light refreshments. (5) Operates late August to late July. Runs daily, except Saturday.

Rome - Genoa   355

Dep. Rome (Ter.)	-0-	-0-	-0-	-0-	07:20 (4)
Dep. Rome (Ost.)	00:20 (1)	01:04	03:23 (2)	05:05 (3)	07:30
Arr. Genoa (Brig.)	05:44	06:13	08:46	10:50	12:37
Arr. Genoa (P.Prin.)	05:52	06:23	08:56	10:58	12:45

Dep. Rome (Ter.)	-0-	12:25 (4)	12:40 (5)	14:50 (4)	-0- (7)
Dep. Rome (Ost.)	08:50 (4)	12:35	-0-	15:00	16:13 (5)
Arr. Genoa (Brig.)	14:02	17:37	18:18	20:00	21:36
Arr. Genoa (P.Prin.)	14:10	17:45	18:26	20:08	21:46

(1) Carries a sleeping car. Also has couchettes. (2) Has couchettes. (3) Operates mid-June to mid-September. Has couchettes. (4) Reservation *required*. Supplement charged. Light refreshments. (5) Light refreshments. (6) "Pendolino" Reservation *required*. Supplement includes reservation fee and meal. (7) Plus other departures from Rome (Termini) at 16:30 (4), 19:00 (6), 23:15 (1) and 23:30 (1), arriving Genoa (P. Principe) 21:54, 23:16, 04:50 and 05:35.

Rome - Naples - Rome   394

Dep. Rome (Ter.)	07:00 (1)	07:20 (2)	08:00 (3)	09:10 (2)	10:30 (4)
Arr. Naples (Mer.)	08:55	-0-	09:53	-0-	-0-
Arr. Naples (P.G.)	09:07	-0-	10:06	-0-	-0-
Arr. Naples (Cen.)	-0-	10:00	-0-	11:29	12:25
Dep. Naples (Cen.)	13:00 (3)	13:52 (2)	14:15 (2)	15:15 (7)	16:00(8+9)
Arr. Rome (Ter.)	15:05 (5)	16:03 (6)	16:55	18:00	17:40

(1) Runs daily, except Sundays and holidays. Reservation *required*. Supplement charged. (2) Light refreshments. (3) Reservation *required*. Supplement charged. Light refreshments. (4) Runs daily, except Sundays and holidays. Reservation *required*. Supplement charged. Light refreshments. (5) Arrives at Rome's Tiburtina railstation. (6) Arrives at Rome's Ostiense railstation. (7) Departs from Naples' Piazza Garibaldi railstation. (8) Departs from Naples' Mergelina railstation. First-class only. Light refreshments. (9) Plus other departures from Naples' Centrale at 16:37 (3+7), 17:15, 17:58 (2), 18:42 (3+7), 19:10, 19:20, 19:50, 20:04 (3), 20:23 and 21:28, arriving Rome's Termini 18:40, 19:55, 20:15, 20:50, 21:41 (5), 22:10, 22:25, 22:00, 23:00 and 00:04 (6).

Rome - Pisa - Rome   360

Dep. Rome (Ter.)	06:30	07:40 (2)	10:00 (3)	10:30		
Arr. Pisa	10:25 (1)	10:37 (1)	12:53 (1)	14:26 (1)		

Sights in **Pisa:** See notes about Pisa under "Bologna–Pisa"

Dep. Pisa	13:04 (2)	13:45	14:35 (5)	15:04	15:31	17:45 (2+7)
Arr. Rome (Ter.)	16:20	17:40	18:05	18:20 (3)	19:20 (5)	21:10 (8)

(1) The Leaning Tower is only 10 minutes by bus or taxi from the railstation. (2) Reservation *required*. Supplement charged. Light refreshments. (3) Reservation *required*. Supplement charged. Light refreshments. (4) Operates late May to late September. Light refreshments. (5) Light refreshments. (6) Arrives at Rome's Tiburtina railstation. (7) Plus another departure from Pisa at 19:45 (2), arriving Rome 23:40. (8) Arrives Rome's Ostiense station.

Rome - Pompeii - Rome   394 + 392

Trains departing Rome's Termini railstation at 07:00, 08:00, 08:55 and 09:10 arrive 2 hours later at Naples' Centrale or Piazza Garibaldi stations. Garibaldi is next to Centrale. A travel-ator provides transportation from Centrale to the F.S. station, from which it is a short walk to the Circumvesuviana station.

The ride from Circumvesuviana station to Pompeii is only 30 minutes, arriving there about 4 hours after having departed Rome.

Departures from Pompeii are at frequent times from noon to aproximately 20:00, arriving Rome 4–5 hours later.

Sights in **Pompeii**: See notes under "Naples–Pompeii"

Rome - Spoleto - Rome   385

Dep. Rome (Ter.)	07:00 (1)	07:30 (2)	10:15 (1)
Arr. Spoleto	08:19	08:58	11:24

Sights in **Spoleto:** The tourist office in the Piazza della Liberta has many brochures, including a town map and offers 3 half-day walking tours.

Dep. Spoleto	12:52 (2)	15:01 (2)	16:20 (1)	18:14 (1)	20:01	21:40 (1)
Arr. Rome ("Ter.)	14:30	16:40	17:45	19:38	21:40	23:10

(1) Reservation *required*. Supplement charged. Light refreshments. (2) Light refreshments.

Rome - Florence - Venice   390

Dep. Rome (Ter.)	07:45	08:55 (1)	-0-	12:15 (3)
Dep. Florence (S.M.N.)	09:47	10:32 (2)	11:30	14:17
Arr. Venice (S. Lucia)	-0-	13:09	14:40	17:15

Dep. Rome (Ter.)	14:15 (4)	16:15 (3)	18:15 (3)	19:15 (1)	19:20 (9)
Dep. Florence (S.M.N.)	16:21	18:20 (6)	20:17	20:52 (8)	21:48
Arr. Venice (S. Lucia)	19:45	21:40	23:15	23:38	-0-

(1) "Pendolino" Reservation *required*. Supplement includes reservation fee and meal. First-class only. (2) Departs from Florence's Rifredi railstation. (3) Reservation *required*. Supplement charged. (4) Reservation *required*. Supplement charged. First-class only. Change trains in Venice's Mestre railstation. (5) Departs from Rome's Ostiense railstation. Reservation *required*. Supplement charged. (6) Change trains in Venice's Mestre railstation (arr. 21:04-dep. 21:31). (7) Reservation *required*. Supplement charged. Restaurant car. (8) Arrives at Florence's Rifredi railstation. (9) Carries a sleeping car. Also has couchettes.

ROUTES TO THE TOE OF ITALY

Here is the rail route to southern Italy: along the Adriatic Sea from Pescara to Bari and the Ionian Sea from Taranto to Reggio di Calabria…and also north from Reggio di Calabria to Pescara.

See following page for the route to southern Italy along the Tyrrhenian seacoast from Rome to Naples and on to Reggio di Calabria…and north from Reggio to Rome.

Milan - Bologna - Pescara - Foggia - Barletta - Bari - Brindisi - Taranto - Catanzaro - Reggio di Calabria

---

This trip offers beautiful coastal scenery along both the Adriatic Sea (Pescara–Bari) and the Mediterranean (Taranto–Reggio di Calabria).

390

Dep. Milan (Cen.)	07:05 (1)	11:05 (1)	13:05 (1)	19:50 (10)	22:00 (3+9)
Dep. Bologna	09:01	13:00	14:59	22:11	00:15
Dep. Pescara	12:26	16:35	16:28	02:28	03:55
Dep. Foggia	14:28	18:32	20:27	04:30	06:13
Dep. Barletta	15:04	-0-	21:00	05:09	06:53
Arr. Bari	15:39	19:40	22:34	06:04	07:33
Dep. Bari	15:59	20:02	-0-	06:25	07:53
Arr. Brindisi	17:10	21:13	-0-	08:08	09:48

Change trains. 403

Dep. Brindisi	17:27(4)	21:29 (4)	-0-	-0-	08:28 (4)	10:29 (5)
Arr. Taranto	19:08	23:14	22:45	-0-	10:13	12:10

Change trains. 398

Dep. Taranto	-0-	-0-	23:05 (6)	09:59	-0-	14:08
Arr. Catanzaro	-0-	-0-	03:30	13:29	-0-	18:04
Arr. Reggio	-0-	-0-	06:14	15:41	-0-	20:13

(1) Reservation *required*. Supplement charged. Restaurant car. (2) Reservation *required*. Supplement charged. Light refreshments. (3) Train has only sleeping cars and couchettes. No coach cars. (4) Second-class. (5) Runs daily, except Sundays and holidays. Second-class. (6) Carries a sleeping car. (7) Carries a sleeping car. Also has couchettes. (8) Has couchettes. (9) Plus other departures from Milan at 00:05 (8), terminating in Brindisi at 11:42. (10) Only takes passengers for Rimini or beyond.

Sights in **Bari**: Much wine, olive oil and almonds in this area. Bari is actually a complex of 3 different cities. The "old town" is a peninsula which was the ancient port, rivaling Venice 900 years ago. Both the 11th century St. Nicola Basilica and the 12th century Romanesque Cathedral are located there.

"New Bari," built in the 19th century, is where the Archaeological Museum, the Picture Gallery, concert halls and fine restaurants are located. Industrial Bari encircles the other 2 areas (factories, oil refineries, low-income apartments).

Don't fail to visit the rebuilt Norman Castle.

Sights in **Barletta**: The 13th century S. Sepolcro Church. The Norman castle. The 12th century Gothic Cathedral.

Sights in **Brindisi:** Many Crusaders set out from here for Jerusalem. See the Roman column that marks the end of the Appian Way. The Civic Museum in the 11th century circular S. Giovanni al Sepolcro Church. Frederick II's 13th century castle. The rebuilt 11th century Cathedral.

Sights in **Catanzaro**: The Baroque S. Domenico Church. The paintings in the Museum.

Sights in **Foggia**: Much wool has been marketed here for centuries. See the ancient records of sheep tax at the Library. The city has an Art Gallery, a Museum and a Cathedral.

Sights in **Pescara**: A nice beach resort on the Adriatic coast.

Sights in **Reggio di Calabria**: A very popular tourist resort. Founded by the Greeks in 720 B.C. See the fine archaeological collection in the Museo Nazionale della Magna Grecia. The 15th century Aragonese Castle. The reconstructed Romanesque-Byzantine Cathedral. There are many Greek and Roman ruins in this area.

Sights in **Taranto**: A swing bridge connects the "old" city (on an island) with the new Taranto on the mainland. See the 15th century Aragonese castle. The 14th century S. Domenico Maggiore Church. The exhibit of Greek vases and statues in the Museo Nazionale. The early 19th century Arsenal. The 11th century Cathedral.

The Northbound Trip

398

Dep. Reggio	07:00 (1)	-0-	-0-	-0-	15:24 (1)	23:15
Dep. Catanzaro	09:13	-0-	-0-	-0-	17:33	01:55
Arr. Taranto	12:53 (1)	-0-	-0-	-0-	21:05	06:39
Change trains. 403						
Dep. Taranto	13:29	06:13 (4)	06:53 (4)	11:44 (4)		
Arr. Brindisi	15:00	08:00	08:42	13:30		
Change trains. 390						
Dep. Brindisi	13:13 (3)	16:57	20:02 (5)	21:52		
Arr. Bari	14:29	19:00	21:41	23:01		
Dep. Bari	14:48 (3)	19:49	21:57	23:20 (6)		
Dep. Barletta	15:19	20:23	22:30	-0-		
Arr. Foggia	15:57	21:06	23:13	00:31		
Arr. Pescara	17:44	23:24	01:26	02:38		
Arr. Bologna	21:16	03:30	05:23	06:38		
Arr. Milan (Cen.)	23:15	06:05	08:40	09:50		

(1) Reservation *required*. Supplement charged. Direct train to Bari. No train change in Taranto. Does not call at Brandisi. (2) Change trains in Bari. (3) Reservation *required*. Supplement charged. (4) Runs daily, except Sundays and holdays. Second-class. (5) Train has only sleeping cars and couchettes. No coach cars. (6) Carries a sleeping car. Also has couchettes. (7) Has couchettes. Light refreshments.

Rome - Naples - Villa San Giovanni - Reggio di Calabria and v.v. 400

There is great Tyrrhenian coastal scenery between Rome and Reggio.

Dep. Rome (Ter.)	-0-	-0-	08:10 (4)	12:10 (4)
Dep. Rome (Tib.)	03:30	04:24 (2+3)	-0-	-0-
Dep. Naples (Cen.)	05:36 (1)	06:46 (1)	10:10	13:42
Dep. Salerno	06:35	07:42	10:53	14:20
Arr. V.S. Giovanni	10:25	12:12	14:30	17:51
Arr. Reggio di Cal.	10:55	12:30	14:58	18:35

Dep. Rome (Ter.)	14:00 (4)	16:10 (4)	22:00	-0- (12)
Dep. Rome (Tib.)	-0-	-0-	-0-	22:30
Dep. Naples (Cen.)	16:05 (5)	17:57 (5)	00:57	00:46 (11)
Dep. Salerno	16:49	18:08	-0-	01:45
Arr. V.S. Giovanni	20:23	22:15	05:56	05:51
Arr. Reggio di Cal.	20:38	22:50	06:15	06:20

Dep. Rome (Ter.)	22:20 (3)	23:20 (7)
Dep. Rome (Tib.)	-0-	-0-
Dep. Naples (Cen.)	00:57	-0-
Dep. Salerno	01:35	02:33
Arr. V.S. Giovanni	05:20 (8)	08:31
Arr. Reggio di Cal.	06:28	02:45

The Northbound Return Trip

Dep. Reggio di Cal.	07:15 (4)	12:05	
Dep. V.S. Giovanni	07:49	12:27 (4)	
Dep. Salerno	11:20	15:55	
Arr. Naples (Cen.)	11:49 (5)	16:33	
Arr. Rome (Tib.)	-0-	-0-	
Arr. Rome (Ter.)	13:50	18:40	
Dep. Reggio di Cal.	14:15 (4)	15:05 (4)	17:20
Dep. V.S. Giovanni	14:24	15:40	17:40
Dep. Salerno	18:02	19:14	21:32
Arr. Naples (Cen.)	18:38 (5)	19:52	22:56 (11)
Arr. Rome (Tib.)	-0-	-0-	01:04
Arr. Rome (Ter.)	20:50	22:00	-0- (2)
Dep. Reggio di Cal.	19:30 (7)	20:27 (7)	20:42 (10)
Dep. V.S. Giovanni	19:58	21:04	21:30
Dep. Salerno	01:06	03:00	01:18
Arr. Naples (Cen.)	-0-	03:42	01:58
Arr. Rome (Tib.)	03:34	-0-	05:40
Arr. Rome (Ter.)	-0-	06:20	-0-

(1) Departs/Arrives Naples' Campi Flegrei railstation. (3) Has couchettes. (4) Reservation *required*. Supplement charged. Light refreshments. (5) Departs/Arrives Naple's Piazza Garibaldi railstation. (6) "Pendolino" Reservation *required*. Supplement includes reservation fee and meal. (7) Carries first and second-class sleeping cars. Also has first and second-class couchettes. (8) Change trains in Villa San Giovanni. (9) Second-class. (10) Carries only coach cars. (11) Departs Napoli Campi Flegrei. (12) Runs Friday, Saturday only.

THE RAIL TRIP TO SICILY

Milan, Florence, Rome and Naples to Messina and Palermo or Messina - Taormina - Catania - Siracusa   400

This trip includes a 35-minute ride on the ferry boat that runs between Villa S. Giovanni and Messina (Maritima).

There is beautiful seacoast scenery on this journey's Messina–Siracusa portion.

Dep. Milan (Cen.)	19:55 (1)	21:00 (2)	-0-	-0-	-0-
Dep. Florence (Campo)	23:34	00:34	-0-	-0-	-0-
Dep. Rome (Ter.)	-0-	-0-	04:29(3)	04:29 (3)	08:10 (4)
Dep. Rome (Tibur.)	-0-	03:30	-0-	-0-	-0-
Dep. Naples (Cen.)	-0-	05:46	06:56	06:56	-0-
Dep. Naples (C. Fleg.)	04:30	-0-	-0-	-0-	10:10 (5)
Arr. Messina (Cen.)	11:15	12:20	13:15	13:15	16:25
Arr. Palermo	-0-	16:55	-0-	17:38	-0-
Arr. Taormina	12:16	-0-	14:09	-0-	17:25
Arr. Catania	13:16	-0-	15:03	-0-	18:15
Arr. Siracusa	15:13	-0-	16:45	-0-	18:50

Dep. Milan (Cen.)	-0-	-0-	-0-	-0-	-0-
Dep. Florence (Campo)	-0-	-0-	-0-	-0-	-0-
Dep. Rome (Ter.)	08:10 (4)	12:10 (4)	12:10 (4)	19:35 (6)	20:40 (6)
Dep. Rome (Tibur.)	-0-	-0-	-0-	-0-	-0-
Dep. Naples (Cen.)	10:10 (5)	13:42	13:42	21:54	22:52
Dep. Naples (C. Fleg.)	-0-	-0-	-0-	-0-	-0-
Arr. Messina (Cen.)	16:25	19:50	19:50	03:55	05:20
Arr. Palermo	19:55	-0-	23:30	07:50	-0-
Arr. Taormina	-0-	20:31	-0-	-0-	06:27
Arr. Catania	-0-	21:30	-0-	-0-	07:25
Arr. Siracusa	-0-	22:50	-0-	-0-	09:05

Dep. Milan (Cen.)	15:59 (7)	16:35 (6)	-0-	-0-	22:46
Dep. Florence (Campo)	19:28	20:05	-0-	-0-	22:51 (6)
Dep. Rome (Ter.)	-0-	-0-	22:20 (8)	22:20 (9)	-0-
Dep. Rome (Tibur.)	21:53	23:23	-0-	-0-	-0-
Dep. Naples (Cen.)	-0-	-0-	00:57	00:57	-0-
Dep. Naples (C. Fleg.)	00:05	-0-	-0-	-0-	-0-
Arr. Messina (Cen.)	06:40	08:00	08:30	07:05	-0-
Arr. Palermo	10:30	-0-	-0-	-0-	-0-
Arr. Taormina	-0-	07:37	-0-	08:13	-0-
Arr. Catania	-0-	08:28	-0-	09:04	-0-
Arr. Siracusa	-0-	11:45	-0-	10:35	14:410

The Northbound Trip

Dep. Siracusa	08:15 (4)	-0-	-0-	10:50	12:30 (2)
Dep. Catania	09:25	-0-	-0-	12:00	14:05
Dep. Taormina	10:02	-0-	-0-	12:46	14:49
Dep. Palermo	-0-	08:00 (4)	10:35 (4)	-0-	-0-
Dep. Messina (Cen.)	11:05	10:40	13:40	13:50	15:55
Arr. Naples (C. Fleg.)	-0-	-0-	-0-	-0-	-0-
Arr. Naples (Cen.)	16:45	16:33	19:52	19:52	-0-
Arr. Rome (Tibur.)	-0-	-0-	-0-	-0-	01:04
Arr. Rome (Ter.)	18:50	18:40	22:00	22:00	-0-
Arr. Florence (Campo)	-0-	-0-	-0-	-0-	-0-
Arr. Milan (Cen.)	-0-	-0-	-0-	-0-	-0-

Dep. Siracusa	-0-	-0-	15:15 (6)	-0-
Dep. Catania	-0-	-0-	16:50	-0-
Dep. Taormina	-0-	-0-	17:31	-0-
Dep. Palermo	12:00 (2)	13:30 (6)	-0-	15:40 (6)
Dep. Messina (Mari.)	15:55	16:45	18:30	19:05
Arr. Naples (C. Fleg.)	-0-	-0-	-0-	-0-
Arr. Naples (Cen.)	-0-	-0-	-0-	-0-
Arr. Rome (Tibur.)	01:04	-0-	03:31	03:53
Arr. Rome (Ter.)	-0-	-0-	-0-	-0-
Arr. Florence (Campo)	-0-	-0-	05:42	05:59
Arr. Milan (Cen.)	-0-	-0-	09:05	09:45

Dep. Siracusa	-0-	18:10 (9)
Dep. Catania	-0-	19:40
Dep. Taormina	-0-	20:37
Dep. Palermo	16:30 (10)	-0-
Dep. Messina (Mari.)	20:20	21:45
Arr. Naples (C. Fleg.)	-0-	-0-
Arr. Naples (Cen.)	02:28	-0-
Arr. Rome (Tibur.)	04:42	-0-
Arr. Rome (Ter.)	-0-	-0-
Arr. Florence (Campo)	07:22	08:55 (12)
Arr. Milan (Cen.)	11:20	12:15

(1) Operates late July to early September. (2) Carries only coach cars. (3) Departs/Arrives Rome's Ostiense railstation. Carries only coach cars. (4) Reservation *required.* Supplement charged. Light refreshments. (5) Departs/Arrives Naples' Piazza Garibaldi railstation. (6) Train has only sleeping cars and couchettes. (7) Carries first and second-class sleeping cars. Also has first and second-class couchettes. Coach cars are second-class. (8) Carries a sleeping car. (9) Has couchettes. (10) Carries a sleeping car. Also has couchettes. (11) Arrives at Rome's Ostiense railstation. (12) Arrives at Florence's S.M.N. railstation.

Sights in **Messina**: The Cathedral and the Annunciata dei Catalani Church, both rebuilt in the 12th century by Norman occupiers. The beautiful astronomical clock in the modern Bell Tower, next to the Cathedral. The art in the Museo Nazionale. The Botanical Gardens.

Sights in **Catania**: Founded 729 B.C. by Greek settlers. Now a very busy seaport and a popular Winter beach resort. Whatever could happen to a city happened here in the 16th and 17th centuries: famines, civil wars, epidemics, pirate raids, earthquakes, and the eruption of Mt. Etna in 1693, after which Catania was almost completely rebuilt. The dark gray color of the city results from the use of volcanic matter in constructing buildings.

See the Greek and Roman theaters, aqueducts and baths. The excellent collection of art and archaeological relics in the Civic Museum of the 13th century Castello Ursino. The tomb of the composer Vincenzo Bellini in the rebuilt 11th century Cathedral, also containing relics of St. Agatha. Sicily's largest church, San Nicolo. Next to it, the Benedictine San Nicolo Monastery, started in the 14th century.

The medieval manuscripts in the library of the University. The royal chapel, Collegiata. The 18th century palaces circling the Piazza del Duomo, with its Elephan Fountain. The museum at the birthplace of Bellini. The Astronomical Observatory.

Sights in **Siracusa**: Settled by Greeks in 734 B.C., 5 years after the founding of nearby Catania. An earthquake that destroyed much of Catania leveled Siracusa in 1693, after which Siracusa was rebuilt.

A comprehensive tour of Siracusa starts by visiting on the hill of Neapolis the Roman Amphitheater (which held 15,000 people attending gladiator fights), constructed during the reign of Augustus, before the birth of Christ. This structure was severely stripped in 1526 for the building of the city's defensive walls.

Above the Amphitheater is the 600-foot-long altar of Hieron II, where 450 oxen were simultaneously sacrificed on pagan religious days. Nearby is the ancient Paradise Quarry in which the cave called "the ear of Dionysius" is located. Next to it is the 5th century B.C. Greek Theater, where Plato and Aeschylus performed.

Behind the Theater is the "Grotto of the Nymphs." The views are wonderful from the walkway to the Paradise Grotto and from the Viale Rizzo, looking down into the Greek Theater and out toward the harbor. The archaeological area is open daily except Monday 09:00–17:00 (later in Summer).

Five miles further, on the hill of Epipoli overlooking Siracusa, is the Castle of Euryalus, the mightiest and most complete fortress of Greek times.

Returning downhill, along Corso Gelone, you come to the ruins of the Roman Forum, at Piazzale Marconi. Go along Corso Umberto I and cross the Ponte Nuovo to reach the island of **Ortygia**. There, in Piazza Pancali, are the remains of the Temple of Apollo, which the conquering Arabs turned into a mosque.

Other sights in Ortygia are the 16th century Santa Maria dei Miracoli church, the 15th century arch (Porta Marina), the Maniace Castle, and the 13th century Bellomo Palace, which houses a museum of medieval and modern art. The 17th century Palazzo del Municipo (Town Hall), the 18th century Palazzo of Benevantano del Bosco.

The National Archaelogical Museum, which has one of the most important collections

(Greek, Roman and Byzantine) of sarcophagi, pottery, coins and bronzes in Italy. Its most famous treasure is the 2nd century B.C. Venus Landolina sculpture.

The ancient Cathedral is dominated by the Doric columns of the original Temple of Minerva, where many works of art are exhibited.

Sights in **Palermo**: This city was entirely Arabic in ancient times. It is the modern capital of Sicily. Severely damaged by bombs in July of 1943. Most museums and galleries here are closed on Monday. Their hours are 09:00 to 12:30 or 13:30. Most of them re-open from 15:00 to 18:00 on certain days. All are open Sunday 09:00 to 12:00 or 13:00.

See the exhibits of carretti (Sicilian horsecarts) and many other phases of traditional Sicilian life (bridal dresses, fishing boats, whips used for self-flagellation during Holy Week processions) at the Pitre Ethnological Museum. The fine archaeological collection in the Museo Nazionale on Via Roma. The Risorgimento Museum at Piazza San Domenico. The International Museum of Marionettes (located at Via Butera 1), open daily 10:00–13:00 and 17:00–19:00.

Watch tin, copper and iron being shaped into utensils in the stalls along Via dei Calderai, near Piazza Bellini. See tombs of important Sicilians, in the San Domenico Church.

The 800-year old Cathedral and, next to it, The Archepiscopal Palace, both on Vittorio Emanuele. Nearby, the marvelous Oriental garden at the Church of San Giovanni degli Eremiti, a converted mosque.

See statues of former Spanish rulers in the Quattro Canti (Four Corners), a small octagonal piazza. Near it are 2 very interesting street markets, Vucciria and Il Capo. Located on a small, twisting street, Vucciria offers Sicilian pastries, cheeses and many foods that are exotic to non-Mediterranean tastebuds: fried lungs and spleen, sea urchins, pork sausage encased in the skin of a pig's foot.

The great array of food at Il Capo (which starts at the intersection of Via Volturno and Via Carini) includes squash, cheese, mounds of tomato paste, grapes, melons, swordfish, eggplant as well as shirts, blouses, sweaters, leather handbags, etc.

See the antiques sold at Il Papireto, the flea market. Decorative tiles, Italian Victorian furniture, filigree jewelry, coins, religious art.

One of the most splendid opera houses in Europe, the Teatro Massimo, built in 1897. The 12th century Royal Palace. The Cuba and Zisa palaces. The catacombs under the Convent of the Capuchin Friars.

There are dazzling mosaics at the 12th century Sala di re Roggero, open to the public on Monday, Friday and Saturday mornings if no official meetings of the Regional Assembly are taking place. This is only one of the many local churches and palaces built when Norman knights returned to Europe from the Crusades, ending Saracen rule of Sicily. Additional ancient mosaics can be seen in the Martorana Church in Piazza Bellini.

Don't fail to see other Norman mosaics in the Palace of the Norman Kings and at the 12th century Arabic-Norman Palatine Chapel in nearby **Monreale**, a 5-mile bus ride (#9) from Palermo. It is one of the most outstanding architectural achievements in Italy, open in the morning on Wednesday and Sunday, all other days 09:00–13:00 and 15:00–17:30 (hours vary in Winter). Also the excellent mosaics in the 12th century Cathedral there.

Take the #14 or #77 bus to the bathing beach, Mondello. There are half-day bus excursions and local train service to **Segesta** and **Selinunte**, sites of substantial Greek ruins.

A local train leaves almost hourly for the 15-minute ride to **Bagheria**, where the eccentric 18th century Villa Palagonia and the beautiful Villa Valguarnera are located.

There is hydrofoil service in the Spring and Summer to 2 interesting islands. The Blue Grotto on **Ustica** attracts many visitors. The Archaeological Museum on **Lipari** is worthwhile. From Lipari, there is boat service to other nearby islands: **Alicudi, Filicudi, Salina, Stromboli** (immortalized by Ingrid and Roberto with more passion off the silver screen than they invested in the motion picture) and **Vulcano**.

Passenger ships run from Palermo to Tunisia.

TRAIN ROUTES IN SICILY
(INCLUDING ONE-DAY EXCURSIONS)

Messina - Milazzo - Palermo 400

Dep. Messina	05:30	06:10 (1)	07:07	08:10	10:05
Dep. Milazzo	06:00	06:52	08:05	09:32	10:42
Arr. Palermo	09:10	09:40	10:30	11:35	13:35
Dep. Messina	11:00	13:40	16:10 (2)	18:15	20:05 (2)
Dep. Milazzo	11:32	14:12	16:40	18:50	20:37
Arr. Palermo	14:25	17:38	19:10	21:50	23:30

Sights in **Milazzo**: Founded 7 centuries before Christ. An important naval victory over the Carthaginians was won by the Romans in Milazzo's bay more than 2,200 years ago. See the 13th century Norman castle and the 16th century Spanish walls at the old town, on a hill above the modern city.

Dep. Palermo	04:20 (3)	06:20	08:00 (2)	10:10 (2)	10:40	11:30 (3)
Dep. Milazzo	07:18	09:01	10:15	12:52	13:45	14:41
Arr. Messina	09:35	09:35	10:50	13:30	14:30	15:23
Dep. Palermo	12:00	13:30	13:50 (3)	15:40	18:10	20:40
Dep. Milazzo	15:00	16:05	16:35	18:14	20:55	23:25
Arr. Messina	15:40	16:42	17:20	18:50	21:35	23:59

(1) Second-class. (2) Reservation *required*. Supplement charged. Light refreshments. (3) Runs daily, except Sundays and holidays.

Messina - Taormina - Catania - Siracusa   400

There is beautiful seacoast scenery on this route.

Dep. Messina (Cen.)	07:07	08:20 (1)	11:05	13:35	15:32 (4)
Arr. Taormina	-0-	08:50	11:40	14:10	16:10
Arr. Catania	-0-	09:45	12:38	15:03	17:02
Arr. Siracusa	-0-	11:45	14:30	16:45	18:30

Sights in **Taormina**: A year-around resort, with very mild Winter weather, consisting mainly of 3 streets, each on a different level, connected to each other by many stairways, all on one side of Mont Venere. One funicular provides access to the beaches below the little town (4,000 population).

Stroll and shop for pottery, embroidery and carved wood figures along Corso Umberto, the main street. See the 3rd century Roman theater, facing Mt. Etna. The medieval great halls in the 15th century Palazzo Corvaja. The 14th century Palace of the Duke of St. Stephen. The 13th century Cathedral.

Dep. Siracusa	05:10 (4)	07:00 (7)	08:15 (3)	10:50 (3)	12:30	15:15 (6)
Arr. Catania	06:24	07:55	09:25	11:56	13:46	16:30
Arr. Taormina	07:08	08:49	10:02	12:42	14:45	17:27
Arr. Messina (Cen.)	07:55	10:00	10:48	13:30	15:38	18:15

(1) Operates late July to early September. (2) Change trains in Catania. From Siracusa: runs daily. From Catania: runs daily, except Sundays and holidays. (3) Reservation *required.* Supplement charged. Light refreshments. (4) Runs daily, except Sundays and holidays. (5) Plus other departure from Messina at 20:10 (3), arriving Siracusa 22:50. (6) Plus other departures from Siracusa at 18:14 (1) arriving Messina 18:50. (7) Runs Sunday only.

Palermo - Agrigento - Palermo   407

Dep. Palermo	07:35	10:05	11:05	13:02	14:20	16:20 (2)
Arr. Agrigento	09:32	12:10	13:10	15:05	16:20	18:35

Sights in **Agrigento**: Founded by Greeks in 581 B.C. See the extremely fine Greek ruins: 7 Doric temples in the Valley of the Temples, many ancient aqueducts and cemeteries. The 14th century Cathedral. The 13th century churches: S. Nicola, Santa Maria dei Greci and S. Spirito. Baroque palaces. There is an especially good Archaeological Museum here.

Dep. Agrigento	06:45	08:22 (1)	10:12	11:35	13:30	16:35 (3)
Arr. Palermo	08:50	10:18	12:15	13:40	15:30	18:35

(1) Runs daily, except Sundays and holidays. (2) Plus other departures from Palermo at 17:20, 18:55 (1) and 20:10, arriving Agrigento 19:15, 20:55 and 22:05. (3) Plus other Agrigento departures at 17:50 and 20:00, arriving Palermo 19:50 and 22:00.

Palermo - Caltanissetta - Palermo 407

| Dep. Palermo | 05:55 (1) | 08:10 | 12:05 (1) | 14:00 | 16:10 (1) | 18:20 |
| Arr. Caltan. (Xirbi) | 07:36 | 10:00 | 14:06 | 15:46 | 18:00 | 20:02 |

Sights in **Caltanissetta**: The Greek, Arabic and Norman ruins at the Pietrarossa Castle. The excellent archaeological collection in the Civic Museum. The Baroque Cathedral and Palazzo Moncada.

| Dep. Caltan. (Xirbi) | 07:41 (1) | 10:04 | 13:00 (1) | 16:02 (1) | 18:17 | 21:05 |
| Arr. Palermo | 09:20 | 11:40 | 14:50 | 17:40 | 20:05 | 22:50 |

(1) Runs daily, except Sundays and holidays.

Palermo - Catania - Siracusa

407

Dep. Palermo	05:55 (1)	08:10	09:20 (2)	12:05 (1)	14:00	16:01 (1)
Arr. Catania	09:30 (1)	11:50	13:25	16:05	17:35	20:00
Change trains. 400						
Dep Catania	10:00	12:50	15:14	17:05 (1)	18:40	21:32 (4)
Arr. Siracusa	11:45	14:00	16:45	18:30	20:05 (1)	22:50
Dep. Siracusa	-0-	06:40	12:27	14:10	15:15 (7)	
Arr. Catania	-0-	07:55	13:46	15:30	16:30	
Change trains. 407						
Dep Catania	05:50 (1)	08:07	14:06 (1)	16:05	18:05 (7)	
Arr. Palermo	09:20	11:40	17:33	20:00	21:55	

(1) Runs daily, except Sundays and holidays. Direct train (no train change) late July to early September. (2) Change train in Agrigento. (3) Operates late July to early September. (4) Reservation *required.* supplement charged. Light refreshments.

Palermo - Trapani - Palermo 392

| Dep. Palermo | 05:20 | 07:10 (1) 09:00 | 10:40 | 13:00 (1) 13:50 (3) |
| Arr. Trapani | 07:26 | 08:56 11:06 | 12:46 | 15:06 15:56 |

Sights in **Trapani**: A major Carthaginian and Roman naval base in the 3rd century B.C. See the outstanding 14th century Santuario dell'Annunziata, rebuilt in the 18th century. The 14th century Santa Agostino Church. The excellent sculpture and paintings in the Museo Nazionale Pepoli. The 17th century Cathedral. The Baroque Palazzo della Giudecca. The 15th century Santa Maria di Gesu Church.

Dep. Trapani	04:25	04:55 (1)	08:00	09:25	11:00	12:35	16:08 (4)
Arr. Palermo	06:31	07:01	10:06	11:31	13:06	14:41	18:14

(1) Runs daily, except Sundays and holidays. (2) Runs Sunday only. (3) Plus other departures from Palermo at 14:55 (1), 16:05, 17:20, 18:50 and 20:35, arriving Trapani 17:01, 18:11, 19:26, 20:56 and 22:41. (4) Plus other departures from Trapani at 17:10 and 19:10, arriving Palermo 19:21 and 21:16.

Agrigento - Caltanissetta - Agrigento   407

Dep. Agrigento	06:55 (1)	10:00	15:20	17:20
Arr. Caltanissetta (Cen.)	08:22	11:14	16:45	18:45
Arr. Caltanissetta (Xirbi)	10 minutes after arriving Centrale station			

Sights in **Caltanissetta:** See "Palermo–Caltanissetta"

Dep. Caltanissetta (Xirbi)	07:41 (1)	10:04	10:40	12:40	17:20 (1)	20:10 (3)
Dep. Caltanissetta (Cen.)	-0-	10:16	11:00	12:43	17:35	20:20
Arr. Agrigento	-0-	11:35	12:45	14:40	19:00	21:45

(1) Runs daily, except Sundays and holidays. (2) Runs daily, except Sundays and holidays. Second-class. (3) Second-class.

Catania - Caltanissetta - Catania   407

Dep. Catania	05:50 (1)	08:05	08:27	10:35	13:10	14:13 (1+3)
Arr. Caltanissetta (Xirbi)	07:35	10:04	10:40	12:40	15:05	15:55

Sights in **Caltanissetta:** See "Palermo–Caltanissetta"

Dep. Caltanissetta (Xirbi)	07:38 (1)	08:35	10:01	11:35	14:12 (1)	15:46 (4)
Arr. Catania	09:30	10:45	11:50	13:25	16:05	17:25

(1) Runs daily, except Sundays and holidays. (2) Second-class. (3) Plus other departures from Catania at 16:14, 18:15, 18:10 and 21:40, arriving Caltanissetta 18:14, 20:05, 20:58 and 23:45. (4) Plus other departures from Caltanissetta at 16:10, (1), 19:10 and 20:08, arriving Catania 19:15, 21:20 and 21:50.

The Malta Cruise

Reggio di Calabria, Catania and Siracusa are gateways for the boat trip to Malta.

1476

Dep. Reggio	08:30 (1)		Dep. Malta	05:30 (2)
Dep. Catania	11:00 (1)		Arr. Siracusa	14:00
Dep. Siracusa	16:30		Dep. Catania	17:45
Arr. Malta	21:30		Arr. Reggio	22:00

(1) Runs Tuesday + Saturday July 19-September 4. (2) Runs Tuesday + Saturday April 1-May 31; Tuesday, Friday + Saturday June 1- October 10.

SCENIC RAIL TRIPS

Arona - Brig 82

There is beautiful lake and mountain scenery on this portion of the Milan–Lausanne route.

Dep. Milan (Cen.)	07:23	09:10 (1)	14:00 (1)	15:25 (1)	17:25 (5)
Dep. Arona	08:16	09:53	14:43	17:16 (3)	18:15 (4)
Dep. Brig	09:48	11:16	16:15	18:48	19:48
Arr. Lausanne	11:27	12:40	17:40	20:27	21:11

(1) Reservation *required*. Supplement charged. Light refreshments. (2) Reservation *required*. Supplement charged. Restaurant car. (3) Change trains in Brig. (4) Reservation *required*. Supplement charged. (5) Plus another Milan departure at 19:05 (4), arriving Lausanne 22:55.

Bologna - Florence 374

Excellent mountain scenery on this ride.

The train goes through the 11.5-mile long Apennine Tunnel, Italy's longest tunnel.

Complete schedules appear under the "Bologna–Florence" and "Florence–Bologna"one-day excursions.

Bolzano - Brennero

Beautiful views of medieval castles and wild alpine mountain scenery on this portion of the route from Verona to Innsbruck, and on to Munich.

Sights in **Bolzano**: Has been Italian since only 1919. The language spoken here (called "Bozen" during the nearly 6 centuries it was ruled by the Hapsburgs, from 1363 until World War I) is German.

Take at least one of the 3 funiculars that climb up the Alps. See the 16th to 18th century house on both Bindnergasse and Silbergasse. The vegetable and fruit market on Piazza delle Erbe. The 18th century Neptune fountain.

The exceptional carved altar depicting the Nativity, in the Holy Virgin Chapel of the Franciscan church. The frescoes at both the Cathedral and the Dominican church.

Stroll along the Talvera River first to the 13th century Maretsch Castle and then to Runkelstein Castle, whose lovely frescoes can be seen on guided tours Tuesday–Saturday, 10:00–12:00 and 15:00–18:00.

Buses are available to make short trips of less than an hour to many vineyard villages. Traminer and Gewurtztraminer are produced in this area.

Verona - Innsbruck - Munich   76

Dep. Verona (P.N.)	08:32 (1)	10:54 (1)	12:55 (1)	14:06
Dep. Bolzano	10:20	12:30	14:28	16:00
Arr. Fortezza	11:06 (3)	13:06 (3)	15:03 (3)	16:45 (3)
Dep. Brennero	12:04	14:04	16:04	17:50
Arr. Innsbruck	12:37	14:37	16:37	18:28
Arr. Munich	14:30	16:30	18:30	20:30

(1) Reservation *required*. Supplement charged. Restaurant car. (2) Light refreshments. 3) Estimated. Cook deleted Fortezza from this timetable in 1993.

Fortezza - Dobbiaco

Very good mountain scenery on this spur off the Bolzano–Brennero route, appearing above. The following schedule shows how the Verona–Innsbruck–Munich trip can accommodate this en route detour.

380		*381*	
Dep. Verona (P.N.)	08:32 (1)	Dep. Dobbiaco	12:55 (3)
Arr. Fortezza	11:04	Arr. Fortezza	14:02
Change trains. 381		Arr. Bolzano	14:54
Dep. Fortezza	11:24	*Change trains. 76*	
Arr. Dobbiaco	12:32	Dep. Bolzano	16:00
		Arr. Innsbruck	18:28
		Arr. Munich	20:30

(1) Reservation *required*. Supplement charged. Restaurant car. (2) Restaurant car. (3) Runs daily except Sundays & holidays.

Torino - Cuneo - Breil - Nice 356

There is spectacular scenery on the 74-mile-long Cuneo–Nice rail route through the Roya Valley and the Alps, a service that first became operational in 1928. Severe damage during World War II caused it to be closed in 1940, and it was not re-opened until the Winter of 1979.

An outstanding feat of engineering, this line is a succession of very high viaducts, bridges and 60 tunnels that span 27 miles of this route, interspersed with sections that look down into deep valleys. This route has attracted many tourists.

Dep. Torino (P.N.)	08:59 (2)	10:10 (3)
Arr. Cuneo	10:24	11:00
Change trains.		
Dep. Cuneo	10:39	14:00 (2)
Arr. Breil	11:38	15:32 (2)
Change trains.		
Dep. Breil	12:45	18:05
Arr. Nice	13:43	19:10

(1) Departs from Torino's Porta Susa railstation. (2) Direct train to Breil. (3) This schedule includes a Breil-Nice train that runs only on Sunday.

Sights in **Cuneo:** The 10th century Cathedral. The 13th century Church of San Francesco. The marvelous viaduct over the Stura di Demonte. The Civic Museum in the 18th century Palazzo Audiffredi. The 18th century Town Hall.

The magnificent Cuneo–Breil scenery can also be seen on the following easy one-day roundtrip from Torino.

Torino - Cuneo - Torino 356

All of these trips require changing trains in Cuneo.

Dep. Torino(P.N.)	08:59	07:45 (1)	Dep. Breil	17:44 (1)	16:29
Arr. Cuneo	10:24		Arr. Cuneo	19:12	18:00
Dep. Cuneo	10:39	08:44	Dep. Cuneo	15:58	18:12
Arr. Breil	12:08	10:07	Arr. Torino (P.N.)	20:16	19:18

(1) Direct train, no change in Cuneo.

Genoa - Torino - Cuneo - Ventimiglia - Genoa and v.v.

The right-hand column allows a layover in Torino (see footnote #4) for sightseeing and for dinner.

360		*355*	
Dep. Genoa (P.P.)	06:39 (1)	Dep. Genoa (P.P.)	12:05 (1)
Arr. Torino (P.N.)	08:50	Arr. Ventimiglia	15:10
Change trains. 356		*Change trains. 356*	
Dep. Torino (P.N.)	08:59	Dep. Ventimiglia	15:29
Arr. Cuneo	13:35	Arr. Breil	16:24
Dep. Breil	10:13	Arr. Cuneo	18:00 (2)
Arr. Ventimiglia	12:01	Arr. Torino (P.N.)	19:18 (5)
Change trains. 3555		*Change trains. 360*	
Dep. Ventimiglia	13:15	Dep. Torino (P.N.)	19:33 (1+4)
Arr. Genoa (P.P.)	15:40	Arr. Genoa (P.P.)	21:27

(1) Reservation *required*. Supplement charged. Light refreshments. (2) Change trains in Cuneo. (3) Operates mid-June to mid-September. (4) Plus other departures from Torino at 17:28, 18:26 (1), 19:28 (3), 20:28 and 22:20, arriving Genoa 19:10, 20:31, 20:04, 21:00, 22:27 and 00:25. (5) Arrives on Sunday only.

Brindisi - Reggio and Reggio - Brindisi

There is splendid coastline scenery on this trip.

404		*398*		
Dep. Brindisi	06:14	Dep. Reggio (Cen.)	07:00 (1)	-0-
Arr. Taranto	07:50	Arr. Taranto	12:53	-0-
Change trains. 398		*Change trains. 403*		
Dep. Taranto	09:59 (1)	Dep. Taranto	13:29	14:35
Arr. Reggio (Cen.)	15:52	Arr. Brindisi	15:15	16:20

(1) Reservation *required*. Supplement charged. (2) Runs daily, except Sundays and holidays.

Genoa - Pisa

There is exceptional mountain and Mediterranean coastline scenery on this ride. Complete schedules appear under the "Genoa–Pisa" one-day excursion.

Genoa - Nice - Cannes - Marseille   90

A close look at more than 100 miles of outstanding seashore resorts along the Mediterranean's Ligure coastline: the Savona and San Remo beaches (on the Italian Riviera) and the Monaco, Nice, Antibes, Cannes and St. Raphael beaches (on the French Riviera).

Dep. Genoa (P.P.)	05:55	08:22 (3)	16:20	18:16
Arr. Nice	10:15 (1)	11:20	19:46	22:00
Dep. Nice	10:38 (2)	11:25	19:51	22:05
Arr. Cannes	11:01	11:47	20:30	22:45
Arr. Marseille (St. Ch.)	12:53	13:43	22:41	01:00

(1) Change trains in Nice. (2) Light refreshments. (3) Reservation *required*. Supplement charged. Restaurant car.

Milan - Barcelona   90

The "Pablo Casals" (20:00 departure) began in 1990 to carry one "Gran Clase" sleeping car, the most luxurious sleeping car in Europe. Each of its large single and double compartments has a shower and toilet. The train also has ordinary sleeping compartments and 4-berth tourist compartments. There are *no* coach seats. The train has a restaurant car. Substantial discounts are given to holders of Eurailpass and Eurodomino. Reservation is required but can be made only in Spain!

Dep. Milan (Cen.)	18:15 (1)	20:00 (2)
Arr. Barcelona (Sants)	09:35 (3)	09:10

(1) Operates mid-July to late August. Has couchettes. (2) "Pablo Casals" (see description above the time-table). Arrives Barcelona Franca. (3) Change trains in Porto Bou.

Milan - Bern   82

The Brig–Bern portion of this ride is one of the 5 most outstanding scenic rail trips in Europe, with a fabulous array of lakes, mountains and rivers.

Dep. Milan (Cen.)	07:25	08:25 (2)	10:25 (2)	12:25 (3)	14:00 (4+7)
Dep. Brig	10:01 (1)	10:43	12:46	14:43	16:22 (5)
Arr. Bern	11:38	12:12	14:38	16:12	18:04

(1) Change trains in Brig. Light refreshments Brig-Bern. (2) Reservation *required*. Supplement charged. Restaurant car. (3) Reservation *required*. Supplement charged. Light refreshments. (4) Reservation *required*. Supplement charged. (5) Light refreshments. (6) Restaurant car. (7) Plus other Milan departures at 15:25 (3), 16:25 (1) and 17:25 (2), arriving Bern 19:38, 20:38 and 21:38.

Milan - Genoa   356

Great views of marble quarries, mountains, farms and the Mediterranean coast, all in 2 hours. An easy one-day roundtrip.

Milan - Locarno

Great canyon, mountain and river scenery is seen from a narrow-gauge local train over the Domodossola-Locarno portion of this route. This Centovalli (one hundred valley) ride is one of the 5 most outstanding scenic rail trips in Europe. Complete schedules appear under the "Milan–Locarno" one-day excursion.

Milan - Zurich   84

This is one of the 5 most outstanding scenic rail trips in Europe.

A feast of beautiful farms, lakes, mountains, rivers and vineyards. You go through the 9.3-mile long Gotthard Tunnel. Before it was opened to traffic in 1882, there was no direct rail route from Italy to eastern Switzerland through the Alps.

Prior to entering the Gotthard, the train goes through the beautiful Ticino Valley.

Immediately upon exiting the first of a series of 9 tunnels, you first see the small, white Wassen Church on your right, 170 feet below the track. The next time the church comes into view, after exiting tunnel #4, the church is to your left and nearly level with the track.

Later, after exiting tunnel #6, you have a third view of the church, again to your left, this time nearly 230 feet above the track, but you will see it there only if you look far ahead and before being alongside the church. (The train is in the Kirchberg Tunnel when it is directly alongside the church.)

The turns inside 3 semi-circular tunnels in this area (Leggistein, Wattinger and Pfaffensprung) are engineered so well that there is no sensation of the curves that the train is making inside those tunnels.

Try this interesting experiment: make a pendulum of any object, holding the top of a weighted string, chain or handkerchief against the inner face of a train window (a left-hand window when inside Leggistein, and a right-hand window when inside Wattinger and Pfaffensprung). As the train goes around a curve, the weighted bottom will move away from the window.

The Mediterranean climate on the Italian end of the tunnel is usually much warmer than the Alpine temperature on the Swiss end. The train makes 3 gradients at 45–50 miles per hour.

Dep. Milan (Cen.)	08:25 (1)	10:25	12:25	14:25	15:00 (2+5)
Arr. Zurich	12:57	14:57	16:57	18:57	19:28
		•	•	•	
Dep. Zurich	13:33 (3)	15:03 (4)	17:03 (2)	19:03 (2)	-0-
Arr. Milan (Cen.)	17:35	19:30	21:30	23:35	-0-

(1) Restaurant car. (2) Reservation *required*. Supplement charged. Restaurant car. (3) Reservtion *required*. Supplement charged. Light refreshments. (4) Reservation *required*. Supplement charged. (5) Plus other Milan departures at 16:25, 17:20 (2) and 19:25 (3), arriving Zurich 20:57, 21:48 and 23:36.

Milan - Tirano - St. Moritz - Chur - Zurich

This is an alternate route from Milan to Zurich. Many rivers and lakes are seen between Milan and Tirano. There is great mountain scenery on the Tirano-St. Moritz narrow-gauge portion of this easy one-day excursion. The track reaches 7,405-foot altitude going through the Bernina Pass, Europe's highest main rail line. The descent from St. Moritz to Chur is spectacular.

362

Dep. Milan (Cen.)	05:04 (1)	06:15 (2)	08:15	-0-	09:15
Arr. Tirano	08:23	08:23	10:20	-0-	12:06
Change trains. 328					
Dep. Tirano	-0-	08:40	10:30	11:30	12:24
Arr. St. Moritz	-0-	10:58	13:02	13:56	14:56
Change trains. 330					
Dep. St. Moritz	-0-	11:00 (8)	13:00 (4)	14:00	15:00 (4)
Arr. Chur	-0-	13:07	15:07	16:07	17:07
Change trains. 310					
Dep. Chur	-0-	13:15	-0-	16:23 (6)	17:15 (7)
Arr. Zurich	-0-	14:50	-0-	17:50	18:50

(1) Runs daily, except Sundays and holidays. (2) Runs only on Sunday. (3) Runs daily, except Sundays and holidays. (4) Runs Saturday, Sunday and holidays. (5) Late May to late October: runs daily. Late October to mid-May: runs daily, except Sundays and holidays. (6) Reservation *required*. Supplement charged. Restaurant car. (7) Light refreshments. (8) Runs Saturdays, Sundays & holidays except Saturdays June 18-September 24.

Milan - St. Moritz - Milan

Very good river and lake scenery Milan-Tirano. Great mountain scenery on the Tirano-St. Moritz narrow-gauge portion of this one-day roundtrip. The track reaches 7,405-foot altitude going through the Bernina Pass, Europe's highest main rail line.

362

Dep.Milan	05:04 (1)	06:15 (2)	08:15	09:15	12:05	14:05
Arr. Tirano	08:23	08:23	10:20	12:06	14:42	16:36
Change trains. 328						
Dep. Tirano	-0-	08:40	13:30	12:24	15:30	17:30
Arr. St. Moritz	-0-	10:58	13:02	14:56	17:56	19:56

•   •   •

Dep. St. Moritz	11:05	16:00	17:00
Arr. Tirano	13:30	18:28	19:28
Change trains. 362			
Dep. Tirano	15:02	19:02 (1)	20:02 (2)
Arr. Milan	17:30	21:40	22:30

(1) Runs daily except Sundays and holidays. (2) Runs only Sunday. (3) Runs daily, except Sundays and holidays. Change trains in Sondrio at 11:12.

Naples - Siracusa

There is wonderful Mediterranean coastline scenery on this trip. See details earlier in this section, under "The Rail Trip To Sicily."

Naples - Sorrento   401

There is excellent Mediterranean coastline scenery on this ride.

Dep. Naples (Circumvesuviana) and Naples (F.S.) at one or 2 times per hour from 05:31 until 22:48 for the 55–65 minute ride to Sorrento.

•   •   •

Dep. Sorrento at one or 2 times every hour from 04:13 to 22:41 for the ride back to Naples. (There are stops in both directions at Pompeii.) A travolator provides transportation between Naples' F.S. station and Naples' Centrale station.

Naples - Taranto

There is very good mountain scenery on this route.

390		398	
Dep. Naples (P. Gari.)	07:33	Dep. Taranto	20:24
Arr. Bari	12:00	Arr. Bari	23:04
Change trains. 398		*Change trains. 390*	
Dep. Bari	12:35 (1)	Dep. Bari	22:31
Arr. Taranto	14:08	Arr. Naples (P. Gari.)	05:00

(1) Reservation *required*. Supplement charged.

Reggio Calabria - Taranto - Brindisi

There is excellent coastline scenery on this ride, which allows a sightseeing stopover in Taranto.

Brindisi is the gateway for the cruise to Greece.

398						
Dep. Reggio Calabria (Cen.)	07:00 (1)	15:24 (1)				
Arr. Taranto	13:09	21:08				
Change trains. 403						
Dep. Taranto	13:29	14:35	16:43	17:45	19:00	21:38
Arr. Brindisi	15:15	17:20	18:17	19:21	20:25	23:25

(1) Reservation *required*. Supplement charged. (2) Runs daily, except Sundays and holidays.

Rimini - Pescara - Brindisi 390

The excellent scenery on this route includes olive groves, vineyards and superb beaches on the Adriatic coastline. This can be broken into a 2-day trip by *stopping in Pescara one night and then continuing on to Brindisi the next day*.

Also, this trip can be extended by continuing on from Brindisi to Reggio di Calabria, a ride that offers fine coastline scenery.

Dep. Rimini	09:00 (1)	10:07 (2)	14:09 (2)
Arr. Pescara (Cen.)	11:46	12:22	16:30
Dep. Pescara (Cen.)	11:49	12:26	16:35
Arr. Brindisi (Cen.)	16:30	17:15	21:18

(1) Operates late June to early September. (2) Reservation *required*. Supplement charged. Restaurant car.

Rome - Foligno - Terontola - Foligno - Rome   385

Between Foligno and Terontola, there are magnificent views of vineyards, olive groves, the hillside towns of **Spello** and **Assisi, Lake Trasimente**, and the city of **Perugia**.

These Schedules allow a sightseeing stopover in Foligno or Perugia.

Dep. Rome (Ter.)	10:15 (1)	13:25	14:20 (1)
Arr. Foligno	11:46	15:16 (1)	16:30
Change trains			
Dep. Foligno	12:00	16:00	16:44
Dep. Perugia	12:36	16:34	17:21
Arr. Terontola	13:17	17:22	18:07

Sights in **Foligno**: An ancient Roman city that was badly damaged by earthquake in 1832 and then by heavy bombing during World War II. See the restored 12th century Cathedral. The archaeological museum and picture gallery, in the 14th century Palazzo Trinci.

You can go by bus from Foligno 8 miles to the mountain-top 14th century village called **Montefalco**. Its main attraction is the vista from the top of its Communal Tower (Torre Comunale). Also see the interiors of St. Augustine's Church and St. Francis's Church.

Sights in **Perugia**: see notes under "Florence–Perugia"

Dep. Terontola	13:33 (3)	17:44	18:46 (3)
Dep. Perugia	14:27	18:25	19:36
Arr. Foligno	15:02	19:05	20:18
Change trains.			
Dep. Foligno	15:58 (1)	19:40	21:20 (1)
Arr. Rome (Ter.)	17:45	21:30	23:03

(1) Reservation *required.* Supplement charged. Light refreshments. (2) Light refreshments. (3) Second-class.

Udine - Trieste

This portion of the Venice-Trieste ride has excellent scenery of the Adriatic coastline. Sit on the right side for best viewing. The schedules allow a sightseeing stopover in Udine.

377

Dep. Venice (S. L.)	06:34	09:10 (2)	11:10	11:47 (2)	14:10
Arr. Udine	08:48	10:50	13:03	13:50	16:00
Change trains. 378					
Dep. Udine	09:50 (3)	12:35	13:30 (2)	17:01 (3)	17:40 (2+4)
Arr. Trieste (Cen.)	10:48	13:45	15:06 (3)	18:21	19:07

(1) Restaurant car. (2) Second-class. (3) Runs daily, except Sundays and holidays. Second-class. (4) Plus other departures from Udine at 18:50 (2), 19:45 (3) and 20:45, arriving Trieste 19:58, 20:54 and 21:53.

Sights in **Udine**: see notes under "Trieste–Udine"

INTERNATIONAL ROUTES
FROM ITALY

The primary Italian gateway for rail travel to Switzerland, western Germany, Luxembourg, Belgium, Holland and northeastern France (Paris) is Milan. A secondary gateway for rail travel from Italy to Switzerland is from Torino, via Aosta, to either Brig or Geneva.

There is rail service to southern France (Nice, Marseille and Avignon), Paris, and to Spain from Milan and Genoa.

The gateways for travel to Austria, Germany and Denmark are Verona and Venice.

Venice is also the starting point for trips to Yugoslavia, Czechoslovakia, eastern Germany and the rest of Eastern Europe (Bulgaria, Greece, Romania, Hungary, Poland and Russia).

Milan - Genoa - Nice - Marseille - Barcelona 90

"Pablo Casals" (departing Milan 20:00) began in 1990 carrying one "Gran Clase" sleeping car, called by Cook "probably the most luxurious sleeping car in Europe." Each of its large single and double compartments has both a shower and a toilet. Substantial discounts are given to holders of Eurailpass and Eurodomino. Reservation is required but can be made only in Spain!

Dep. Milan (Cen.)	06.40 (1)	07:10 (2)	14:15	-0-	20:00 (5)
Dep. Genoa (P. Principe)	08:22	-0-	16:10	18:16 (3)	-0-
Arr. Nice	11:20	-0-	19:46	22:00	-0-
Arr. Marseille	13:43	-0-	22:41	01:00	-0-
Arr. Port Bou	-0-	-0-	-0-	05:52 (4)	-0-
Arr. Barcelona	-0-	20:50	-0-	09:35	09:10

(1) Reservation *required*. Supplement charged. Restaurant car. (2) Reservation *required*. Supplement charged. Light refreshments. Change trains in Chambery at 11:38. Depart Chambery 12:48 (1). (3) Has couchettes Genoa–Port Bou. (4) Change trains. Depart Port Bou 07:15. (5) "Pablo Casals" (see note above the timetable.). Reservation *required*. Supplement charged. Train has only sleeping cars. (No coaches.) Offers 4 different classes of accommodation: Gran Clase, single, double and 4-berth tourist compartments. Restaurant car.

Milan - Luzern - Basel   290

Dep. Milan (Cen.)	07:25 (1)	09:20 (2)	11:25 (2)	13:25 (2)
Arr. Luzern	11:46	13:39	15:39	17:39
Arr. Basel (S.B.B)	13:09	14:53	16:53	18:53

Dep. Milan (Cen.)	15:25 (2)	17:25 (1)	18:25	19:03
Arr. Luzern	19:39	21:39	22:39	-0-
Arr. Basel (S.B.B.)	20:53	22:53	23:59	00:08

(1) Reservation *required*. Supplement charged. Light refreshments. (2) Reservation *required*. Supplement charged. Restaurant car.

TORINO - AOSTA
GATEWAYS TO SWITZERLAND

(1) Via Le Grand St. Bernard

Torino - Aosta - Martigny - Brig or Lausanne

All of the Torino-Aosta trains are second-class.

353
Dep. Torino (Porto Nvova)	06:30 (1)	11:20	13:20
Arr. Aosta	08:55	13:32	15:20

Change to a bus.
269
Dep. Aosta (Place Narbonne)	10:00 (3)	14:15 (3)	16:25 (5)
Arr. Orsieres	-0-	17:19	17:58

Change to a train.
Dep. Orsieres	-0- (3)	17:24 (8)	18:03
Arr. Martigny	11:10	17:58	18:44

Change trains.
270
Dep. Martigny	11:25	14:21 (6)	18:25 (6)
Arr. Brig	12:23	15:12	19:23

OR

Dep. Martigny	11:34	15:34	19:38 (7)	20:37 (9)
Arr. Lausanne	12:27	16:27	20:27	21:27

(1) Runs daily, except Sundays and holidays. (2) Runs only Sunday. (3) Runs June 10-September 18. (4) Operates mid-June to mid-September. (5) Via the St. Bernard Tunnel. (6) Light refreshments. (7) Restaurant car. (8) Runs daily June 10- October 9. (9) Runs Saturdays, Sundays and holidays June 5-September 24.

(2) Via Mt. Blanc Tunnel

Torino - Aosta - Chamonix - Geneva

A layover in Chamonix (11:30–16:31) allows for sightseeing there.

353

Dep. Torino (Place Nvova)	06:30 (1)	09:01	13:20
Arr. Aosta	08:55	11:00	15:20
Change to bus.			
192			
Dep. Aosta	09:40 (2)	11:30 (2)	12:15 (2)
Arr. Courmayeur	10:40	12:20	14:05
Change buses.			
Dep. Courmayeur	10:50	12:30	14:15
Arr. Chamonix	11:30	13:10	14:55

All of the Chamonix–Geneva train changes are "cross-platform," each taking less than one minute.

268

Dep. Chamonix	12:12 (5)	13:27	16:16
Arr. St. Gervais	12:52	14:06	16:55
Change trains. 167			
Dep. St. Gervais	13:07 (6)	14:32 (6)	17:23 (6)
Arr. La-Roche-sur-Foron	13:58	15:20	18:08
Change trains. 167			
Dep. La-Roche-sur-Foron	14:00 (7)	15:30	18:15 (4)
Arr. Geneva (Eaux-Vives)	14:32	16:03	19:06

(1) Runs daily, except Sundays and holidays. (2) Operates early July to mid-September. (3) Runs Monday-Friday, except holidays. (4) Change trains in Annemasse at 18:36. (5) Runs daily. July 4-28 runs 16 minutes earlier. (6) Does not run July 4-28. (7) Runs 5 minutes earlier July 4-28.

ROUTES TO OTHER COUNTRIES

Rome - Milan - Genoa - Lausanne - Dijon - Avignon - Lyon - Paris

44

Dep. Rome (Ter.)	-0-	-0-	08:05 (1)	-0-
Dep. Florence (SMN)	-0-	-0-	10:16	-0-
Arr. Bologna	-0-	-0-	11:10	-0-
Dep. Bologna	-0-	-0-	11:20	-0-
Dep. Genoa (P.P.)	-0-	07:05 (3)	-0-	11:50
Arr. Milan (Cen.)	-0-	08:47 (4)	13:10 (4)	13:44 (4)
Dep. Milan (Cen.)	07:10 (1)	09:10 (1)	→	14:00 (1)
Arr. Lausanne	-0-	12:40 (4)		17:40 (4)
Dep. Lausanne	-0-	12:46		17:54 (2)
Arr. Dijon	-0-	14:44		19:57
Arr. Paris (Lyon)	16:02	16:28		21:39

Dep. Rome (Ter.)	-0-	16:22 (6)	-0-	19:10 (7)
Dep. Florence (SMN)	-0-	-0-	19:43 (7)	-0-
Arr. Bologna	-0-	-0-	-0-	-0-
Dep. Bologna	-0-	-0-	21:00	-0-
Dep. Genoa (P.P.)	-0-	22:04	-0-	00:18
Arr. Milan (Cen.)	21:10 (5)	-0-	-0-	-0-
Dep. Milan (Cen.)	-0-	-0-	-0-	-0-
Arr. Lausanne	-0-	-0-	04:02	-0-
Dep. Lausanne	-0-	-0-	04:07	-0-
Arr. Dijon	04:32	05:58	06:39	07:37
Arr. Paris (L yon)	07:22	08:52	09:21	10:07

(1) Reservation *required*. Supplement charged. Restaurant car. Change trains in Lyon (2) TGV. Reservation *required*. Supplement charged. Light refreshments. (3) Reservation *required*. Supplement charged. (4) Change trains. (5) Carries a sleeping car. Also has couchettes. Coach is second-class. (6) Departs from Rome's Ostiense railstation. Carries a sleeping car. Also has couchettes Light refreshments Rome-Genoa. (7) Train carries only sleeping cars and couchettes. No coach cars. Light refreshments.

Rome - Venice - Budapest - Kiev to St. Petersburg or Moscow 88

This train carries only sleeping cars. It does not have coach cars. Runs Monday, Wednesday and Friday.

Dep. Rome (Termini)	19:20	Day 1
Dep. Venice (Santa Lucia)	-0-	Day 2
Arr. Budapest (Keleti)	-0-	
Train divides		
Dep. Budapest (Keleti)	16:15	
Arr. St. Petersburg	-0-	Day 3
Arr. Kiev	17:38	Day 3
Arr. Moscow (Kievski)	11:21	Day 4

Milan - Venice - Innsbruck - Munich 76

Dep. Milan (Cen.)	-0- (4)	07:00 (2)	-0-	15:30 (2)
Dep. Venice (S.L.)	06:25 (3)	-0-	08:55 (2+7)	-0-
Arr. Innsbruck	-0-	12:37	14:37	20:58
Arr. Munich (Hbf.)	14:30	14:30	16:30	22:40

(1) Carries a sleeping car. Also has couchettes. Coach is second-class. (2) Reservation *required*. Supplement charged. Restaurant car. (3) Change trains in Verona. (4) Reservation *required*. Supplement charged. Light refreshments. (5) Light refreshments. (6) Has couchettes. Coach is second-class. (7) Plus other Venice departures at 10:25 (3), 12:05 (3+4), 15:25 (2) and 22:05 (6), arriving Munich 18:30, 20:30, 22:40 and 06:35.

Venice - Milan - Geneva 83

Dep. Venice (Santa Lucia)	10:25	12:25 (2)	14:05 (3+4)	22:05 (3+5)
Arr. Milan (Cen.)	13:54	15:50	17:20 (3)	-0- (3)
Change trains.				
Dep. Milan (Cen.)	14:00 (1)	16:25 (2)	17:25	-0-
Arr. Geneva	18:17	21:12 (1)	21:48	06:39

(1) Reservation *required*. supplement charged. (2) Restaurant car. (3) Direct train to Geneva. No train change in Milan. (4) Reservation *required*. Supplement charged. Restaurant car. (5) Carries a sleeping car. Also has couchettes. Coaches are second-class.

Bologna - Venice - Milan - Lausanne - Paris 44

Dep. Bologna	11:16 (1+2)	-0-	-0-	-0-
Dep. Venice (S.L.)	-0-	10:25	-0-	20:10 (6)
Arr. Padua	-0- (1)	10:54	-0-	-0- (6)
Change trains.				
Dep. Padua	-0-	11:00 (3)	-0-	-0-
Arr. Milan (Cen.)	13:10	13:40	-0-	23:08 (7)
Change trains.				
Dep. Milan (Cen.)	-0-	14:00 (2)	21:10 (5)	23:13 (7)
Arr. Lausanne	-0-	17:40	-0-	-0- (6)
Change trains.				
Dep. Lausanne	-0-	17:54 (4)	-0-	-0-
Arr. Paris (Lyon)	-0-	21:39	07:22	08:25

(1) Direct train to Milan. No train change in Padua. (2) Reservation *required*. Supplement charged. Restaurant car. (3) Lignt refreshments. (4) TGV. Reservation *required*. Supplement charged. Restaurant car. (5) Direct train to Paris. No train change in Lausanne. Carries a sleeping car. Also has couchettes. Coach is second-class. (6) Direct train to Paris. No train changes en route from Venice. Train has only sleeping cars and couchettes. No coach cars. Has light refreshments. (7) Arrives/departs Milan's Porta Garibaldi railstation. (8) Direct train to Paris. No train changes en route from Venice. Operates late June to early September. Carries a sleeping car. Also has couchettes. Coach is second-class.

Venice - Salzburg 88

Dep. Venice (S. Lucia)	07:30
Arr. Villach (Hbf.)	11:33
Change trains.	
Dep. Villach (Hbf.)	16:00 (2)
Arr. Salzburg	18:53

(1) Restaurant car. (2) Reservation *required*. Supplement charged. Restaurant car. (3) Departs from Venice's Mestre railstation. Direct train to Salzburg. No train change in Villach.

Venice - Vienna 88

Dep. Venice (S. Lucia)	07:30	-0-	20:50 (3)	23:55 (4)
Dep. Venice (Mestre)	07:42	12:41 (2)	21:01	00:06
Arr. Vienna (Sud.)	16:40	20:40	06:23	08:49

(1) Restaurant car. (2) Reservation *required*. Supplement charged. Restaurant car. (3) Carries a sleeping car. Also has couchettes. Coach is second-class. (4) Runs daily.

SCANDINAVIA
(DENMARK, FINLAND, NORWAY, AND SWEDEN)

Children under 4 travel free on trains in Denmark and Norway, under 6 in Finland, and under 12 in Sweden.

SCANRAILPASS

Unlimited travel on all trains and several ferries throughout Denmark, Finland, Norway and Sweden — such as Stockholm–Turku, Rodby–Puttgarden and Trelleborg–Sassnitz. Also allows 50% discount on such ferries as Copenhagen–Malmo, Stockholm–Helsinki and Bergen–Flam.

Both "Scanrailpass" and "Scanrail'N Drive" (below) are sold worldwide (except Scandinavia) by travel agencies, tour operators, and Rail Europe (U.S.A. and Canadian offices listed under "France").

The 1996 *first*-class prices are $222 for any 5 days within 15 days, $346 for any 10 days within one month. For *second*-class: $176 and $278. First-class youth:$167 and $260. Second-class youth: $132 and $209. Children under 4 travel free.

For passengers aged 55 and over, the following prices apply: $193 for *first*-class for any 5 days within 15, *second*-class $153. For any 10 days within one month: $301, $242 respectively.

SCANRAIL'N DRIVE

Unlimited 5 days of train travel plus 3 days of car rental (any 8 days) within 15 day. Prices vary (a) whether for one person or for 2 persons, and (b) the category of car. A third and fourth passenger needs to pay only for a Scanrailpass. The 1996 prices *per person* for 2 persons (using the smallest size car) with the 8-day pass are: $289 for *first*-class train, $249 for *second*-class. Unlimited additional car rental days can be added to either pass at $55 per day.

NORDTURIST RAIL TICKET

Sold only in Denmark, Finland, Norway and Sweden — at all railstations. Unlimited travel for 21 consecutive days on all government railways and on the Oslo–Copenhagen (and v.v.) and the Stockholm–Helsinki (and v.v.) ferries, plus 50% discount on the Bodo/Fauske–Kirkenes (and v.v.) bus in Norway. Depending on the currency exchange rate, the approximate 1996 first-class prices are: $430 for adults, $332 for youths age 12–25, and $215 for children age 4–11. For second-class: $332, $250 and $166.

376

NORWAY
SWEDEN
DENMARK

MIDNIGHT SUN CALENDAR

An average June day has over 17 hours of daylight in Copenhagen and almost 19 in Helsinki, Oslo and Stockholm. Above the Arctic Circle, the whole disc of the sun remains visible throughout the night for periods of 30 to 120 days, depending how far north a city is. Some of the best vantage points are:

NORWAY					SWEDEN				
Green Harbor	April	21	– Aug	23	Bjorkliden	May	26	– July	19
North Cape	May	14	– July	30	Abisko	May	31	– July	14
Hammerfest	May	17	– July	28	Kiruna	May	31	– July	14
Tromso	May	21	– July	23	Gallivare	June	2	– July	12
Harstad	May	26	– July	19	Boden	June	4	– July	10
Narvik	May	26	– July	19					
Svolvaer	May	26	– July	19	FINLAND				
Bodo	June	5	– July	9	Utsjoki	May	22	– July	24
Trondheim	June	8	– July	6	Kilpisjarvi	May	27	– July	18
Andalsnes	June	5	– July	3	Pallastunturi	May	30	– July	15

Gallivare, Kiruna and Abisko are on the rail route from Boden to Narvik. Andalsnes, Trondheim and Bodo can be reached by train service from Oslo. Trondheim also can be reached by rail from Stockholm.

DENMARK

General Information

• Children under four travel free. Half-fare for children 4-11. Children 12 and over must pay full fare. Denmark's two categories of fast trains are IC (Intercity Trains) and EC (EuroCity Trains).

• Seats are reserved on IC and EC trains, and reservations are required between Copenhagen-Frediricia-Aalburg, Copenhagen-Fredericia-Herning and Copenhagen-Fredericia-Esbjerg. Ferry service to England operates from Esbjerg.

The signs you will see at rail stations in Denmark:

AFGANG	DEPARTURE
ANKOMST	ARRIVAL
BANEGARDEN	RAILSTATION
BILLETKONTORET	TICKET OFFICE
DAMER	WOMEN
GARDEROBEN	CHECKROOM
HERRER	MEN
INDGANG	ENTRANCE
KOREPLAN	TIMETABLE
LYNTOG	FAST INTERCITY TRAIN
OPLYSNING	INFORMATION
PLADSBESTILLINGEN	RESERVATIONS
PERRON	TRACK
RYGEKUPES	MOKING COMPARTMENT
SOVEVOGN	SLEEPING CAR
SPISEVOGN	RESTAURANT CAR
TIL PERRONERNE TO	THE PLATFORMS
TOG AFGAR	DEPARTURE TIMETABLE
TOG ANKOMMER	ARRIVAL TIMETABLE
UDGANG	EXIT

Danish Holidays

A list of holidays is helpful because some trains will be noted later in this section as *not* running on holidays. Also, those trains which operate on holidays are filled, and it is necessary to make reservations for them long in advance.

January 1	New Year's Day	June 5	Constitution Day
	Maundy Thursday		(from Noon)
	Good Friday		Whit Sunday
	Easter		Whit Monday
	Easter Monday	December 24	(From Noon)
	Prayer Day	December 25	Christmas Day
	(4th Fri. after Easter)	December 26	Boxing Day
	Ascension Day		

Summer Time

Denmark, Finland, Norway and Sweden change to Summer Time on the last Sunday of March and convert back to Standard Time on the last Sunday of September. Finland is one hour ahead of Denmark, Norway and Sweden all year.

DENMARK'S TRAIN PASSES

All of Denmark's passes must be purchased in Denmark.

Cheap Day Discount Allows discount of about 20% on *first-class* tickets only, on distances of over 100kms (62 miles). Valid all year on Tuesday, Wednesday, Thursday and Saturday.

Child's Discount One child plus one adult traveling a minimum of 100kms in *second-class* only pay the price of 2 children's tickets. On a "cheap day" (see above), the price is even lower. Children under 4 travel free. Half-fare for children 4–11.

65-Ticket Persons 65 and older receive discounts of 25–40% on both first and second-class tickets, depending on the day of the week. Valid most days except Fridays, Sundays, the Wednesday before Easter, Maundy Thursday, Easter Monday, Common Prayer Eve, Ascension Eve, and Dec. 22 to Jan. 2. Can be used in combination with the Cheap Day Discount (which includes Mondays when using 65 Ticket).

Group Ticket Discounts of 20% and more on tickets. The group must be a minimum of 3 adults traveling together in second-class.

ONE-DAY EXCURSIONS AND CITY-SIGHTSEEING

Here are 12 one-day rail trips that can be made comfortably from Copenhagen and Odense, returning to them in most cases before dinnertime. Notes are provided on what to see and do at each destination.

Copenhagen

Travel on commuter trains is covered by train passes. Trains depart every 20 minutes to most commuter stations.

City tours start from Town Hall Square, in front of the Palace Hotel. To get to the Mermaid or Amalienborg Castle (changing of the guard daily at 12:00) on your own, take bus #1 or #6. For brewery visits, take bus #6 to Carlsberg, or take bus #1 to Tuborg.

Tivoli Gardens, one of the world's most famous amusement parks, is open eaarly April to mid-September. Fireworks are presented several nights each week.

Also see Thorvaldsen Museum, with his sculptures and tomb. Christiansborg Palace, where the Danish Parliament meets. The Danish Resistance Museum. The Zoo. Windowshop in the walking area, Stroget.

The vast collection in the National Museum (12 Frederiksholms Kanal) reflecting Danish life from the Ice Age to the late 17th century plus Danish sculptures and paintings by European artists, open daily except Monday. From mid-June to mid-September: 10:00–16:00. From mid-September to mid-June: 11:00–15:00 Tuesday–Friday and 12:00–16:00 on Saturday and Sunday.

Danish and European paintings (an excellent Matisse collection) at the Royal Museum of Fine Arts, on Solvgade, open daily 10:00–17:00. An exhibit of superb French Impressionists and also Egyptian, Greek, Roman and French sculptures at Carlsberg Glypotek (behind Tivoli Gardens), open daily except Monday. From May through September: 10:00–16:00. From October through April: 12:00–15:00 (10:00–16:00 on Sunday).

The Toy Museum is open all year Wednesday-Sunday 10:00–16:00. There is a good collection of weapons and uniforms in the Royal Arsenal. From May through September: 13:00–16:00 on weekdays, 10:00–16:00 on Sunday. From October through April: 13:00–15:00 on weekdays, 11:00–16:00 on Sunday.

The City Museum, at 59 Vesterbrogade. The view from the top of Town Hall's 350-foot-high tower. Borsen, the oldest stock exchange in the world, still functioning.

The gilded spiral staircase of the Old Saviour's Church (Vor Frelsers Kirke), and the view at the top, from its tower. Regensen, a residential university since 1623. Thorvaldsen's marble statues of Christ and the Apostles in Our Lady's Church (Vor Frue Kirke).

The picturesque buildings along Nyhavn Canal. The line of foreign naval ships along Langelinie Promenade.

The crown jewels and other possessions of Danish monarchs in the museum at Rosenborg Palace (open daily in Summer, only on Tuesday, Friday and Sunday the rest of the year), particularly the pearl-encrusted saddle of Christian IV. Nearby, the 25-acre Botanical Garden and the National Art Gallery.

The Frilandsmuseet open-air museum of Danish houses and farms in suburban **Sorgenfri**, open daily except Monday 10:00–17:00. mid-March to the end of September and 10:00–15:00 the first half of October. the excellent English-language guidebook sold at the ticket counter is essential for understanding the exhibits. Allow at least 2 hours here to stroll the 2 miles of paths.

The farms here are complete with livestock. You will see sheep being sheared, the carding of wool and the spinning of cloth. There are folk dances on Saturday and Sunday.

Commuter trains run 3 times every hour during the day for the 30-minute ride.

In the following timetables, where a city has more than one railstation we have designated the particular station after the name of the city (in parentheses).

Copenhagen - Alborg - Copenhagen   450

All of these trains require reservation and have light refreshments.

Dep. Copenhagen	06:55	07:55	08:55
Arr. Alborg	12:46	13:46	14:46

Sights in **Alborg**: This thousand-year old town is the most important in the north Jutland area. You will find many medieval houses, down the lanes that wind off the modern boulevards. The early 15th century Monastery of the Holy Ghost. The early 16th century Aalborghus Castle.

The basement Duus Wine Cellar in the outstanding ornate, 5-story, 17th century Jens Bang House. The 16th century paintings, depicting the Ten Commandments, in the 12th century Budolphi Cathedral.

The oak-paneled room from 1602 in the Historical Museum, open daily June through August 10:00–19:00 (48 Algade). Works by Scandinavian modern artists in the North Jutland Museum of Modern and Contemporary Art, open daily except Monday 10:00–17:00 (50 Kong Christians Alle).

The more than 300 restaurants (Greek, Italian, Lebanese, Danish) on Jomfru Ane Gade. The Shipping and naval Museum, open daily 10:00–19:00 (75 Vestre Fjordvej). Lindholm Hoje, a museum devoted to Viking archaeology, open daily 10:00–19:00 (11 Vendilavej).

Dep. Alborg	15:51	16:51	17:51	18:51
Arr. Copenhagen	21:48	22:48	23:48	01:05

Copenhagen - Aarhus - Copenhagen

There are 2 ways to make this trip. The first is by train between Copenhagen and Kalundborg, then by boat between Kalundborg and Aarhus. The boat has a smorgasbord cafeteria, and the scenery on the cruise is good.

The second way to Aarhus, entirely by train, is via Fredericia.

382   *The Eurail Guide to Train Travel in the New Europe*

It makes an interesting day to go to Aarhus by the combination of train and boat via Kalundborg and return to Copenhagen by train via Fredericia.

Boat - via Kalundborg 451

The tickets for the ferry must be purchased before boarding the train.

Train			Boat		
Dep. Copenhagen (H.)	06:58 (1)	08:50 (8)	Dep. Aarhus (Pier)	12:40 (1)	14:40 (4+7)
Arr. Kalundborg	08:34	10:11	Arr. Kalundborg	14:10	16:10
Change to boat.			*Change to train.*		
Dep. Kalundborg	09:10 (1)	10:25 (8)	Dep. Kalundborg	14:23 (1)	16:23 (5)
Arr. Aarhus (Pier)	12:20	11:55	Arr. Copenhagen (H.)	15:42	17:42

(1) Runs daily, except Sundays and holidays. (2) Reservation *required*. Runs Monday-Friday, except holidays. (3) Runs Monday-Friday, except holidays. (4) Runs Sunday only. (5) Reservation *required*. Runs Sunday only. (6) Runs daily except Saturdays. (7) Plus other Aarhus departures at 16:05 (6) and 18:40 (5), arriving Copenhagen 21:17 and 21:42. (8) Runs Saturday only. Reservation required.

Sights in **Aarhus**: Board the train at the Aarhus pier and take it to Aarhus' railstation. Don't fail to visit the 17th century Clausholm Castle and its Italian garden. The owners have been restoring their home since 1965 in order to make its extraordinary interior accessible to the public.

The magnificent decor, paintings, tapestries and furnishings of the Castle are worth going to Aarhus.

It is a one-hour drive from the city to the Castle, which is open only Easter to October 15. In Spring and Autumn, it is open only on Saturday and Sunday. From June 1 to August 15, Clausholm is open daily 11:00–17:00.

See the 60 completely furnished medieval houses and the 400-year-old mayor's residence at the Old Town open-air museum (Den Gamle By) in the Botanical Gardens. The 15th century Cathedral, noted for the magnificent tones of its twin organs and for the altar's woodcarvings. The ancient University. The Tivoli Friheden amusement park in Marselisborg Woods.

Take bus #6 from the railstation for the 5-mile drive to see the great collection of primitive relics (Stone Age to Viking Era) in the Prehistoric Museum at **Moesgaard**, open daily in Summer 10:00–17:00. It is closed Mondays the rest of the year.

Train - via Fredericia 450

All of these trains require reservation and have light refreshments.

Dep. Copenhagen (H.)	05:55 (1)	06:55	07:55	08:55	09:55
Arr. Aarhus	10:15	11:15	12:15	13:15	14:15
		• • •			
Dep. Aarhus	13:26	14:26	15:26	16:26	17:26 (3)
Arr. Copenhagen (H.)	17:48	18:48	19:48	20:48	21:48

(1) Runs daily, except Sundays and holidays. (2) The Friday departure from Aarthus arrives Copenhagen 00:48 on Saturday morning. (3) Plus other departures from Aarhus at 18:26, 19:26 and 20:26 (2), arriving Copenhagen 22:48, 23:48 and 01:05 (2)

THE TRIP TO LEGOLAND

Copenhagen - Billund - Copenhagen

All of these trains require reservation and have light refreshments.

Train 450

Dep. Copenhagen	05:55	06:55	07:55	08:55	09:55 (2)
Arr. Vejle	09:25	10:25	11:25	12:25	13:25

Change to bus.

Dep. Vejle	Frequent times from 10:00 to 24:00
Arr. Billund	55 minutes later

Sights in **Billund**: Although the visit to Legoland can be made as a one-day excursion, an overnight stay in or near Billund is recommended so as to have adequate time to see everything at this 21-acre park that features the world's most popular toy.

The outdoor exhibit of buildings, monuments, cities and villages modeled after sites from all over the world (including the Statue of Liberty and Mount Rushmore sculptures in the U.S.A., the Rhine River and an African wildlife scene) is constructed from more than 33 million plastic interlocking pieces. It is open May 1 to mid-September, 10:00–20:00.

Both a monorail and a small train provide overviews of the park to see details one might miss while walking. Children can make projects at several large playrooms on tables equipped with Legos kits.

Dep. Billund	Frequent times from 05:00 to 24:00
Arr. Vejle	55 minutes later

Change to train.

Dep. Vejle	18:13	19:13	20:13	21:13 (3)
Arr. Copenhagen	21:48	22:48	23:48	01:05

(1) Runs daily, except Sundays and holidays. (2) Plus other departures from Copenhagen every hour 10:55 to 19:55. (3) Friday departure arrives Copenhagen 00:48 Saturday morning.

Copenhagen - Frederickshavn and Frederickshavn - Copenhagen   450

Most of these trains require reservation and have light refreshments.

Dep. Copenhagen (H.)	05:55 (1)	06:55	07:55	08:55	09:55 (6)
Dep. Odense	08:35	09:35	10:35	11:35	12:35
Dep. Fredericia	09:13	10:13	11:13	12:13	13:13
Arr. Arhus	10:15	11:15	12:15	13:15	14:15
Arr. Alborg	11:46 (2)	12:46	13:46 (2)	14:46	15:46 (2)
Arr. Frederickshavn	13:00	13:53	15:00	15:53	17:00

Signts in **Frederickshavn**: The military museum at the 17th century fort. The museum in the 18th century manor house called Bangsbo.

Dep. Frederickshavn	04:40 (3)	05:39 (1)	06:38(2)	07:16 (1)	08:47 (7)
Dep. Alborg	05:51 (1)	06:51	07:51	08:51 (2)	09:51
Dep. Arhus	07:27	08:27	09:27	10:27	11:27
Dep. Fredericia	08:33	09:33	10:33	11:33	12:33
Dep. Odense	09:08	10:08	11:08	12:08	13:08
Arr. Copenhagen (H.)	11:48	12:48	13:48	14:48	15:48

(1) Runs daily, except Sundays and holidays. (2) Change trains. (3) Runs Monday-Friday, except holidays. (4) *No* reservation required. Train has only sleeping cars and couchettes. *No* refreshments. Coach cars are second-class. (5) Runs daily, except Saturday. (6) Plus other departures from Copenhagen every hour from 10:55 to 18:55 and 23:30 (4). (7) Plus other Frederickshavn departures at 09:36, 10:47, 11:36, 12:47, 14:47, 15:36 (5), 16:47, 17:36 (5) and 22:07 (4).

Copenhagen - Helsingborg - Copenhagen   463

Train

Dep. Copenhagen (H.)	07:25 (3)	07:55	08:25	08:55	09:25	09:55 (1)
Arr. Helsingor	08:20	08:50	09:20	09:50	10:20	10:50
Change to ferry						
Dep. Helsingor	08:30	09:10	09:30	10:10	10:30	11:10
Arr. Helsingborg	25 minutes later					

Sights in **Helsingborg:** Stained-glass windows, depicting the city's 900 years of history, in the Radhuset (Town Hall). Karnan, the 14th century fort with walls up to 15 feet thick, one of the best preserved Medieval buildings in Scandinavia. To reach it, take the elevator at the left of The Terrace, from the Main Square.

See the view of the Sound from Rosengarden, and the beautiful roses there. The Municipal Museum. The magnificent pulpit in the 15th century Mariakyrkan (Church of St. Mary). The handsome Concert Hall in Stadsbiblioteket (Town Library). The bronze statue in Hamntoget (Harbor Square).

Ferry

Dep. Helsingborg	13:10	13:30	14:10	14:30	15:10	15:30 (2)
Arr. Helsingor	13:35	13:55	14:35	14:55	15:35	15:55
Change to train						
Dep. Helsingor	13:44	14:14	14:44	15:14	15:44	16:14
Arr. Copenhagen (H.)	14:39	15:09	15:39	16:09	16:39	17:09

(1) Plus other departures from Copenhagen at 10:25, 10:55 and 11:25, arriving Helsingborg 1½ hours later. (2) Plus other departures from Helsingborg at 10 and 30 minutes after each hour until 23:30 (less frequent after 23:30), arriving Copenhagen 1½ hours later. (3) Runs Monday-Friday except holidays.

Copenhagen - Helsingor - Copenhagen 463

Dep. Copenhagen (H.)   07:25 (1)   07:55   08:25   08:55 (2)
Arr. Helsingor   55 minutes later

Sights in **Helsingor**: Kronborg Castle (of Shakespeare's Hamlet). The stained-glass, depicting the town's history, in the Council Chamber of the Radhus (Town Hall). If time allows you to visit only Helsingor or Hillerod (described in the next listing), do *not* choose Helsingor. Fredericksborg Castle at Hillerod is by far the more interesting of the two.

Dep. Helsingor   12:14   12:44   13:14   13:44 (3)
Arr. Copenhagen (H.)   55 minutes later

(1) Runs Monday to Friday, except holidays. (2) Plus other Copenhagen departures at the same frequencies until 18:25, then every 30 minutes until 22:55, plus 23:55 and 00:55. (3) Plus other Helsingor departures at the same frequencies until 18:14, then every 30 minutes until 21:44, plus 22:44 and 23:44.

Copenhagen - Hillerod - Copenhagen STB

This is an excellent one-day trip by local commuter train on which Eurailpass is valid. We recommend leaving Copenhagen (Central) between 08:00 or 09:00 for the 50-minute ride. (There is service 3 times every hour during the day.) It is a 25-minute walk from the **Hillerod** railstaion, through the village, past the lake and market square, to the 17th century Fredericksborg Castle and its National Historic Museum of both worldwide art and Danish history. One of the most beautiful castles in Europe, it is located on an island in a small lake, reached by walking over a short bridge. You could spend many days enjoying its contents. A full morning will fly by.

The Castle is open 10:00–17:00 May through September, 10:00–16:00 April and October, and 10:00–15:00 November through March.

Market days in Hillerod are Monday, Thursday and Saturday (09:00–13:00).

You can eat lunch at the Castle's restaurant or in the village on your walk back to the railstation, for departures to Copenhagen every hour at 8 minutes past the hour (05:08–00:08).

By leaving Copenhagen early in the day, it is easy to combine a visit to both Hillerod and **Gilleleje**, a colorful fishing port that is 40 minutes beyond Hillerod. The attractions in Gilleleje are the daily fish auction and the famous Adamsens Fiske-Udsalgr take-out stand which sells fish salads and sandwiches made of fresh-caught crab, shrimp, cod and tuna. It is only a 5-minute walk from Gilleleje's railstation to its port.

The train for Gilleleje leaves Hillerod's track #14 hourly Monday–Friday, every 90 minutes on Saturday and Sunday.

Copenhagen - Humlebaek - Copenhagen STB

Dep. Copenhagen	Frequent times from 05:25 to 00:55
Arr. Humlebaek	30 minutes later

Sights in **Humlebaek**: Exhibits of Giacometti sculptures, painters of the "Cobra" group, and post-1950 art (Warhol, Picasso, Lichtenstein, Calder) in the Louisiana Museum of Modern Art, open daily except Wednesday 10:00–17:00, on Wednesday 10:00–22:00. It is a 15-minute walk from the railstation to the Museum.

Dep. Humlebaek	Frequent times from 05:05 to 00:05
Arr. Copenhagen	30 minutes later

Copenhagen - Malmo - Copenhagen 1215

This popular roundtrip ferry-boat ride to Sweden's West Coast is inexpensive (1994: $44-U.S. for first-class, $28 for second-class), and a 50% discount from first-class is given to holders of a Eurailpass, 25% discount from second-class for Eurail Youthpass.

There are 16–22 sailings daily from Copenhagen (Havnegade) and Malmo for this 45-minute cruise.

Sights in **Malmo**: The Art, Archaeology, Military, Technical and Carriage Museums, all in the Castle. Town Hall. St. Peter's Church. The Sailor's House (3 Fiskehamnsgatan). The 17th and 18th century houses on Lilla Torg (Small Square). Malmo is the gateway to Skane, the beautiful chateau country of Sweden.

Copenhagen - Odense - Copenhagen 450

En route, the train drives onto a ferry for the 65-minute boat ride between Korsor and Nyborg. Passengers can leave the train and stroll on the boat for fine views of the shoreline.

All of these trains require reservation and have light refreshments.

Dep. Copenhagen (H.)	Every hour from 06:55 to 19:55
Arr. Odense	2½ hours later

Sights in **Odense**: The home of Hans Christian Andersen, now a museum, on Hans Jensen-straede. You can visit another Andersen Museum at Munkemollestraede 3. Also see the National Railway Museum in the Dannebrogsgade. The 13th century Cathedral of St. Knud.

Dep. Odense	Every hour from 06:08 to 22:08
Arr. Copenhagen (H.)	2½ hours later

Copenhagen - Roskilde - Copenhagen   450

All of these trains require reservation and have light refreshments.

Dep. Copenhagen (H.)	Frequent times from 06:55 to 19:55
Arr. Roskilde	18 minutes later

Sights in **Roskilde:** The 40 tombs of Denmark's kings and queens, a 500-year old clock, and the post on which such royalty as Peter the Great and the 20th century Duke of Windsor marked their heights (some of them with humorous exaggeration), all in the red brick Cathedral. Open for tours weekdays April–September 09:00–17:45 and October–March 10:00–15:45. Also on Sundays and holidays 12:30–17:45 June–August and 12:30–15:45 September–May.

Also see the exhibits of 5 ancient boats (39 to 59-feet long) in the Viking Ship Museum. Open daily 09:00–17:00 April-October, 10:00–16:00 November-March. It is a 20-minute walk from the town center.

The town center and the Cathedral are a short walk from the railstation. The tourist office (near the Cathedral) supplies an excellent English-language brochure, a city map, and a printed description of a walking tour that includes the town's most important sights.

Dep. Roskilde	Frequent times from 08:29 to 00:41
Arr. Copenhagen (H)	18 minutes later

SCENIC RAIL TRIPS

Jaegersborg–Naerum

Called "Denmark's most scenic train ride" by Danish State Railways, this trip begins at Copenhagen's Central railstation. Change trains 30 minutes after departing Copenhagen, at Jaegersborg.

The 30-minute rail trip Jaersborg–Naerum (frequent departures) is along meadows, forests and small lakes. It is covered by train passes.

Naerum is a modern town.

Odense - Fredericia - Odense   450

There is fine coastline scenery on this easy one-day roundtrip. This can also be seen as a portion of the Copenhagen–Frederickshavn route.

All of these trains require reservation and have light refeshments..

Dep. Odense	35 minutes after each hour, from 07:35 to 22:35
Arr. Fredericia	35 minutes later

•   •   •

Dep. Fredericia	33 minutes after each hour, from 06:33 to 22:33 (1)
Arr. Odense	39 minutes later

(1) Plus another departure from Fredericia at 23:33 daily except Saturday.

INTERNATIONAL ROUTES
FROM DENMARK

Copenhagen is the gateway for travel from Denmark, Norway and Sweden to Western Europe, starting with its connections to Berlin and Hamburg, and then on from those cities to the rest of Western Europe.

Copenhagen - Berlin - Prague   51

The trains are carried Gedser–Warnemunde (a 2-hour trip) by ferries that have a restaurant.

Dep. Copenhagen (Hovedbanegard)	07:20	12:41 (2)	22:30 (3)
Dep. Gedser	09:25	15:25	01:00
Arr. Warnemunde	11:20 (1)	17:20	03:05
Arr. Berlin (Lichtenberg)	15:07 (4)	21:07	07:04
Arr. Prague (Holesovice)	20:59	-0-	-0-

(1) Restaurant car Warnemunde-Prague. (2) Operates late June to mid-August. (3) Carries a sleeping car. Also has couchettes. Coach is second-class. (4) Change trains.

Copenhagen - Hamburg   460

The trains are carried Rodby–Puttgarden (a 65-minute trip) by ferries that have a restaurant.

Dep. Copenhagen (H.)	07:30 (1)	09:20 (1)	12:30	15:20
Dep. Rodby Ferry	09:30	11:30	14:30	17:30
Arr. Hamburg (Hbf.)	12:29	14:29	17:22	20:27
Dep. Copenhagen	17:30 (1)	19:05 (4)	20:05 (5)	21:05 (6+9)
Dep. Rodby Ferry	19:30	21:30	22:30	23:30
Arr. Hamburg (Hbf.)	22:29	00:40	01:35	02:40

(1) Reservation advisable. Supplement charged. Light refreshments. (2) Operates early June to late September. (3) Operates late June to mid-August. (4) Second-class. (5) Operates June 17-September 11. Coach is second-class. (6) Has couchettes. Light refreshments. Coach is second-class. (7) Operates late June to late August. Has couchettes. Coach is second-class. (8) Opearates late May to late September. Has couchettes. (9) Plus other Copenhagen departures at 22:05 (7), arriving Hamburg 04:10.

Copenhagen - Oslo   466

Dep. Copenhagen (H.)	09:45 (1)	21:45 (2)
Arr. Oslo (Sen.)	19:43	07:10

(1) Restaurant car. (2) Runs May 29-August 28. Carries a sleeping car. Also has couchettes. Coach is second-class.

Copenhagen - Stockholm   465

All of these trains require reservation.

Dep. Copenhagen (H.)	11:15 (1)	15:15 (1)	22:15 (2)
Arr. Stockholm (Cen.)	19:35	23:26	07:47

(1) Restaurant car. (2) Carries a sleeping car. Also has couchettes. Coach is second-class.

FINLAND

FINLAND

Overview

Many Eurailpass holders arrive in Finland via the country's ancient capital of Turku and connect with the train immediately to the contemporary capital of Helsinki. Finland's national timetable is called Suomen Kulkuneuvot.

The northern line is dependable and mostly tree-lined.

General Information

• Travel on Finnish trains titled EP or IC requires payment of a supplement.

• The tracks in Finland are constructed with the wide Russian gauge of 50". This makes for spacious cars. The rail service extends as far north as Lapland. Service is maintained during severe Winter weather. All major Finnish Express trains are equipped with radiotelephones for passenger use.

• The signs you will see at railstations in Finland are:

AIKATAULUT	TIMETABLE
LAHTO	DEPARTURE
LAITURILTA	TRACK
LIPPULUUKKU	TICKET OFFICE
MAKUUVAUNU	SLEEPING CAR
MATKALIPPUJEN MYYNTI	RESERVATIONS
MIEHILLE	MEN
NAISILLE	WOMEN
NEUVONTA (TOIMISTO)	INFORMATION
ODOTUSSALI	CHECKROOM
RAUTATIEASEMALLE	RAILSTATION
RAVINTOLAVAUNU	RESTAURANT CAR
SAAPUMINEN	ARRIVAL
SISAAN	ENTRANCE
TUPAKOITSEVILLE	SMOKING COMPARTMENT
ULOS	EXIT

FINLAND'S TRAIN PASSES

Finnrailpass Unlimited rail travel. Can be purchased worldwide and at railstations and ports of arrival in Finland. Sales agents in North America are Holiday Tours of America (425 Madison Ave., New York, N.Y. 10017) Rahim Tours (12 S. Dixie Highway, Suite #203, Lake Worth, FL 33460), Scantours Inc. (1535 Sixth St., Suite #205, Santa Monica,

CA 90401), and Rail Europe (U.S.A. and Canadian offices listed under "France"). Valid for one month, the 1996 *first*-class prices are: $179 for any 3 days, $249 for any 5 days, and $339 for any 10 days. For *second*-class: $119, $169 and $229. Half-fare for children age 6–16. Children under 6 travel free.

Senior Citizens Rail Card Available at railstations. Buyer must pay 50 Finnish marks and provide photo. Allows persons over 65 a 50% discount on each trip that is at least 48 miles.

Group Reduction Groups of 3 or more persons traveling together on a trip of at least 48 miles are allowed discounts of 20% on ticket prices, 25–50% discount for groups of 11 or more.

Child Reduction Tickets are half-price for children 6–16. Children under 6 travel free.

FINNISH HOLIDAYS

A list of holidays is helpful because some trains will be noted later in this section as *not* running on holidays. Also, those trains which operate on holidays are filled, and it is necessary to make reservations for them long in advance.

January 1	New Year's Day	Whit Saturday
	Epiphany	Whit Sunday
	Good Friday	June	Midsummer Eve
	Easter	Midsummer's Day
	Easter Monday	All Saint's Day
May 1	May Day	December 6	Independence Day
	Ascension Day	December 25	Christmas Day
		December 26	Boxing Day

ONE-DAY EXCURSIONS AND CITY-SIGHTSEEING

Here are 7 one-day rail trips that can be made comfortably from Helsinki, returning there in most cases before dinnertime. Notes are provided on what to see and do at each destination. The number after the name of each route is the Cook's timetable.

Helsinki

Helsinki's single most inspiring sight is Temppeliaukio Church, known since its 1969 dedication as the "Rock Church." This fantastic structure was quarried on its site, out of the bedrock in the middle of one of the oldest residential districts of Helsinki. Because the area occupied by worshipers is below the street level, all that can be seen as you walk toward the church is a low rock wall and the massive (70-foot diameter) copper dome.

Also see the large tubular steel sculpture, symbolizing music, in Sibelius Park. Tapiola, the model "new town." Finlandia Hall. The National Museum (closed Mondays September through May). The floral cemetery. The onion towers on the Greek Orthodox Uspenski Cathedral.

It is best to visit Market Square before Noon, to see the flowers, fish and mountains of berries. Also see the Town Hall. The Empress Stone obelisk. (Ferries from a pier near the obelisk go every hour to the island Suomenlinna Fortress.) See the impressive columns of Parliament House. The University Library and the Cathedral, in Senate Square.

The paintings and sculptures in the National Art Gallery. The National Theater. The Elaintarhantie shopping complex, opposite the railstation. The Botanical Gardens, in Elaintarha Park. The Linnanmaki amusement center, closed Mondays. The collection of Finnish wood houses at the open-air Museum of Seurasaari.

The Ateneum Art Gallery. The Gallen-Kallela Museum. The art and furniture at the Helsinki Municipal Museum. Old-fashioned and modern farm tools and implements in the Agricultural Museum. The Military Museum (Maurinkatu 1.) There are good views of the South Harbor and the waterfront from Observatory Hill (Tahtitornin Vuori). See the displays in the Architectural Museum of Finland (Puistokatu 4).

Take the #6 tram to Arabia and see the original site of Helsinki, Old Town. Take the ferry from North Harbor to the Korkeasaari Island Zoo. See the displays in the Architectural Museum of Finland (Puistokatu 4).

Helsinki - Hameenlinna - Helsinki   495

All of these trains have light refreshments, unless designated otherwise.

Dep. Helsinki	06:58	07:58 (1)	08:58	09:58	10:58	11:58 (5)
Arr. Hameenlinna	65 minutes later					

Sights in **Hameenlinna**: The medieval castle. Ahvenisto Tower. The Art Museum. The City Museum.

Dep. Hameenlinna	11:46	12:42 (2)	13:46	14:46	15:46 (3)	17:08 (6)
Arr. Helsinki	74 minutes later					

(1) Reservation *required.* (2) Reservation *required.* Restaurant car. (3) Restaurant car. (4) Runs daily, except Sundays and holidays. (5) Plus another departure from Helsinki at 12:58 (3). (6) Plus other departures from Hameenlinna at 18:48 (3), 19:46 (4), 20:41, 21:46 and 22:58 (2).

Helsinki - Hanko - Helsinki   490 + Finnish timetable

A beautiful ride through woods and along lakes,

All of the trains Helsinki–Karjaa and v.v. have light refresments.

Dep. Helsinki	06:50	09:02	12:02
Arr. Karjaa	07:50	10:00	13:00
Change to local train.			
Dep. Karjaa	07:52	10:02	13:02
Arr. Hanko	08:42	10:52	13:57

Sights in **Hanko**: The southernmost town in Finland. The tourist office is open all year Monday–Friday, 09:00–16:00 and in Summer also on Saturday 09:00–16:00, Sunday 11:00–15:00. Take a 2-hour cruise, leaving from the eastern harbor, operating June through mid-August. There is good fishing here. See the statue dedicated to the many Finns who disembarked from here to migrate to the United States between 1880 and 1930. Dance or try your luck at the Casino.

Dep. Hanko	14:10	16:10	21:18
Arr. Karjaa	14:52	16:52	22:02
Change to a standard train.			
Dep. Karjaa	15:02	17:02	22:09
Arr. Helsinki	16:02	18:02	23:10

Helsinki - Lahti - Helsinki   496

All of these trains have light refreshments, unless designated otherwise.

Dep. Helsinki	07:04	08:04	09:10 (1)	10:26	11:26	12:26 (2)
Arr. Lahti	08:23	09:23	10:52	11:45	12:45	13:45

Sights in **Lahti**: A Winter sports center. The tourist office (closed Sunday) is in the rear of the Town Hall (intersection of Vesijarvenkatu and Aleksanterinkatu). See the view from the top of the 90-meter high ski jump, its elevators operating June through September, 10:00–19:30. It is only a 10-minute walk from the Town Hall.

Visit the Art Gallery. The Ethnographic Museum. The Radio Museum, open Sundays 13:00–15:00. In Summer, there are open-air concerts at the Mukkula Tourist Center. Shop here for marvelous Finnish glassware.

Dep. Lahti	12:07	14:03 (1)	14:58	16:30 (2)	17:55	18:30 (5)
Arr. Helsinki	13:32	15:50	16:34	17:54	19:56	19:54

(1) Second-class. No light refreshments. (2) Runs daily, except Saturday. No light refreshments. (3) Runs Sunday only. Second-class. No light refreshments. (4) Runs Sunday only. Reservation *required*. (5) Plus other Lahti departures at 19:36 (3), 19:53 (4), 20:30 and 21:41.

Helsinki - Riihimaki - Helsinki   495 + 496

Dep. Helsinki	Frequent times from 06:26 to 23:04
Arr. Riihimaki	50 minutes later

Sights in **Riihimaki**: The wood-working mills of H. G. Paloheimo. The glass factories of Riihimaen Lasi Oy. The Museum Peltosaari. The Municipal Museum.

Dep. Riihimaki	Frequent times from 05:58 to 23:20
Arr. Helsinki	50 minutes later

Helsinki - Rovaniemi   495

A trip to Lapland.

Dep. Helsinki	07:00 (1)	09:58 (1)	19:26 (2)	22:00 (2)
Arr. Rovaniemi	16:40	20:05	07:42	11:09
		• • •		
Dep. Rovaniemi	07:00 (3)	13:00 (1)	18:05 (2)	20:10 (5+6)
Arr. Helsinki	16:58	22:58	07:10	08:15

(1) Light refreshments. (2) Carries a sleeping car. Coaches are second-class. Light refreshments. (3) Restaurant car. (4) Runs Sunday only. Carries a sleeping car. Coaches are second-class. (5) Runs Friday and Sunday. Carries a sleeping car. Coaches are second-class. Light refreshments. (6) Plus another Rovaniemi departure at 21:05, arriving Helsinki 08:27.

Helsinki - Savonlinna   499

Dep. Helsinki	07:02 (1)	10:26 (1)	17:02 (2)
Arr. Parikkala	10:47	14:19	20:44
Change trains.			
Dep. Parikkala	10·52	14:24 (4)	20:49
Arr. Savonlinna	11:45	15:41	21:45

Sights in **Savonlinna**: A charming town in the Lake Region, near the Russian border. The Tourist Office (Olavinkatu 35) is open in Summer daily 07:15–22:00. There is an English-language guided tour at Olavinlinna, a medieval castle. Shop for food at the open-air market.

Dep. Savonlinna	06:20 (2)	16:25 (3)	16:47
Arr. Parikkala	07:16	16:23	16:48
Change trains.			
Dep. Parikkala	07:20 (2)	16:25 (3)	16:50 (1+5)
Arr. Helsinki	11:02	20:56	21:58

(1) Light refreshments. (2) Reservation *required*. Restaurant car. (3) Runs Sunday only. Reservation required. Light refreshments.(4) Runs May 29-August 14 only. (5) Runs daily except Sundays and holidays.

Helsinki - Tampere - Helsinki   495

All of these trains have light refreshments, unless designated otherwise.

Dep. Helsinki	06:58	07:58 (1)	08:58	09:58	10:58	11:58
Arr. Tampere	2 hours later					

Sights in **Tampere**: The aquarium, planetarium, children's zoo, amusement park, observation tower and planetarium at the Sarkanniemi Recreation Center. The more than 30,000 objects exhibited in the Hame Museum, particularly the handwoven rugs and tapestries. Many excellent artworks, frescoes and the altarpiece in the Cathedral, completed in 1907. The fine modern architecture of Kaleva Church. The National history Museum. The Haihara Doll Museum. The largest church bells in Finland, at the Orthodox Church.

See a performance at Tampere's Summer Theater in Pyynikki Park, from a seat in the unique bowl-shaped auditorium that rotates 360 degrees. Everyone sitting in the last row at the beginning of a performance also has a front-row seat during the show.

Dep. Tampere	12:00 (2)	12:58	13:58	15:00 (3)	16:00 (1)	16:20 (5)
Arr. Helsinki	2 hours later					

(1) Reservation *required*. (2) Reservation *required*. Restaurant car. (3) Restaurant car. (4) Reservation *required*. Runs daily, except Saturday. Restaurant car. (5) Runs, daily, except Sundays and holidays. (6) Runs Friday and Sunday. Reservation *required*. (7) Plus other departures from Tampere at 18:04 (3), 18:58 (5), 19:56, 20:10 (6), 20:58 and 22:10 (2).

Helsinki - Turku - Helsinki   490

All of these trains have light refreshments.

Dep. Helsinki	06:50	09:02	12:02
Arr. Turku (Stn.)	09:12	11:16	14:16

Sights in **Turku**: A "Turku Card," good for city buses, museum admissions and discounts in restaurants and shops is sold at the City Tourist Office, near Market Square, at Kasityolaiskatu 4.

See the Provincial Museum and the marvelous Banquet Hall in the 13th century Castle, a short walk from the Silja Lane railstation, only a few minutes ride past the Main railstation. The Castle is open 10:00–18:00 May–September, 11:00–15:00 the rest of the year. The great organ (6,057 pipes) in the 13th century Cathedral.

The composer's instruments and personal possessions in the Sibelius Museum. The cobbled marketplace (fruits, flowers, fish and produce), Monday Saturday 08:00–14:00

Dep. Turku (Stn.)	13:43	15:43	17:00	19:35	20:55
Helsinki	16:02	18:02	19:18	22:00	23:10

INTERNATIONAL ROUTES
FROM FINLAND

Helsinki is the gateway both to Russia (Leningrad, and on to Moscow) and Western Scandinavia (Stockholm, and on to Oslo and Copenhagen). Oulu is the starting point for trips to northern Sweden (Boden) and northern Norway (Narvik).

Helsinki - St. Petersburg 902

These trains require reservation and have a restaurant car.

Dep. Helsinki	06:26	15:32
Arr. St. Petersburg (Fin.)	13:55	23:20

Helsinki - Moscow 902

This train carries a sleeping car and a restaurant car.

Dep. Helsinki	17:08	Arr. Moscow	09:10

Helsinki - Stockholm 490

The price for the cruise across the Gulf of Bothnia (Turku-Stockholm) on the comfortable and pleasant Silja Line ships is $46 for first-class and $37 for second-class in 1994. This passage *is* covered by Eurailpass. The fare for a sleeping cabin is *not* covered by Eurailpass — but only for those who reserve and pay for a bed. Food on the ship is varied and delicious.

We recommend the daytime sailing in order to see the thousands of tiny islands on the ride through this extremely interesting archipelago. During the daytime cruise, there is a good smorgasbord for both lunch and dinner. On the night cruise, a live band plays music in the ship's nightclub. On both day and night cruises, the major activity is duty-free shopping.

490 Train			*1250 Ship*		
Dep. Helsinki	06:50 (1)	17:06 (1)	Dep. Turku (Abo)	10:00 (2)	20:00 (3)
Arr. Turku (Harbor)	09:27	19:26	*Set watch back one hour.*		
Walk to Abo Pier.			Arr. Stockholm (Var.) 19:00		07:00

(1) Light refreshments. (2) Runs daily except January 1,3,10,17,24, April 17-21, September 12,13 and December 24, 25. (3) Runs daily except May 29, 30, September 4-8, December 24, 25, 31.

Helsinki - Oulu - Haparanda - Boden - Narvik

495

Dep. Helsinki	06:58 (1)	-0-	12:58 (2)	19:26 (3)	22:00 (3)
Arr. Oulu	13:52	-0-	20:05	04:20	07:33

Sights in **Oulu:** The Art Museum. The Zoological Museum. The Cathedral. The Water Tower, on top of Puolivalinkangas, open May-October. Picturesque, ancient waterfront warehouses. The Church and Open Air Museum. Kastelli Church.

Dep. Oulu	13:57	-0-	04:25	07:38
Arr. Kemi	15:09	-0-	05:55	09:18
Change to bus. 474				
Dep. Kemi	15:15	-0-	06:42 (4)	09:23 (4)
Arr. Torino	15:43	-0-	06:58	09:55
Change buses. 474				
Dep Torino	-0-	-0-	-0-	-0-
Set your watch back one hour.				
Arr. Haparanda	-0-	-0-	-0-	-0-
Change buses. 474				
Dep. Haparanda	14:25	-0-	-0-	10:10 (5)
Arr. Boden	16:45	-0-	-0-	12:35
Change to train. 475				

We recommend stopping-over in Boden for the night so as to travel Boden–Narvik during the daylight hours in order to be able to see the fine mountain scenery on that route. You cross the Arctic Circle going from Boden to Narvik.

Dep. Boden	07:35 (6)	10:43 (7)	-0-	-0-	-0-
Arr. Kiruna	11:03	14:12	-0-	-0-	-0-
Dep Kiruna	11:18 (6)	14:23 (7)	-0-	-0-	-0-
Arr. Narvik	14:23	17:34	-0-	-0-	-0-

(1) Light refreshments. (2) Restaurant car. (3) Carries a sleeping car. Coach is second-class. Light refreshments. (4) Runs daily, except Sundays and holidays. (5) Runs Monday-Friday, except holidays. (6) Reservation *required*. Coach is second-class. (7) Reservation *required*. Coach is second-class. Light refreshments.

NORWAY

Overview

Norway's train service extends to the very top of the country in the Land of the Midnight Sun and to the western port of Bergen. A delightful way of touring the country, train travel in Norway can boast of the most number of scenic rail trips of any Scandinavian country.

General Information

• Children under four travel free. Half-fare for children 4-15. Children 16 and over must pay full fare.

• Norway is the most glorious places in which to experience the wonder of the Midnight Sun.

• Norwegian State Railways have one coach on the Oslo-Bergen and Bergen-Oslo runs (and similar service on other long-distance routes) designed for conveying handicapped persons and other passengers requiring special care, such as mothers traveling with young children. These special cars have a compartment accommodating two wheel chairs that are lifted aboard. An 8-seat compartment in these cars, equipped for mothers and their infants, is provided with a baby-chair, bottle heater, and other equipment helpful when caring for small children. This compartment is adjacent to a space with fitted toilets and a diaper-changing table. The car also has oxygen tanks, a stretcher and a small wheel chair for handicapped persons to use in moving about inside the train.

• From Dombas and on north, you are in the land of the Midnight Sun. (See Midnight Sun Calendar.)

The signs you will see at railstations in Norway are:

ANKOMIST	ARRIVAL
AVGANG	DEPARTURE
BANESTASJONEN	RAILSTATION
BILLETLUKEN	TICKET OFFICE
DAMER	WOMEN
GARDEROBEN	CHECKROOM
HERRER	MEN
INFORMASJON	INFORMATION
INGANG	ENTRANCE
RESERVASJONSLUKEN	RESERVATIONS
ROKERE	SMOKING COMPARTMENT
SOVEVOGN	SLEEPING CAR
SPISEVOGN	RESTAURANT CAR
SPOR	TRACK
TIL PLATTFORMENTE	TO THE PLATFORMS
TOGTABELL	TIMETABLE
UTGANG	EXIT
VEKSLIGSKONTOR	CURRENCY EXCHANGE
VINDUSPLASS	WINDOW SEAT

Norwegian Holidays

A list of holidays is helpful because some trains will be noted later in this section as *not* running on holidays. Also, those trains which operate on holidays are filled, and it is necessary to make reservations for them long in advance.

January 1	New Year's Day		Ascension Day
	Maundy Thursday	May 17	Constitution Day
	Good Friday		Whit Monday
	Easter	December 25	Christmas Day
	Easter Monday	December 26	Boxing Day
May 1	Labor Day		

EURAILPASS BONUSES

A 30% reduction on the fares of the Color Line Steamship Company for the cruise between Kristiansand and Hirtshals (Denmark).

NORWAY'S TRAIN PASSES

Norway Rail Pass Unlimited train travel. The *second-class* prices during May-September are: $190 for 7 days, $255 for 14 days. During October-April, 1996: $150 and $205. Half-fare for children age 4-15. *First-class* 1996 prices: May-September $250 for 7 days, $330 for 14 days. October-April $200 for 7 days, $265 for 14 days. Sold in North America by travel agencies and Scanam World tours, 933 Highway 23, Pompton Plains, NJ 07444. Telephone: (800) 545-2204. **Flexipasses** also available: *First-class* for any 3 days in one month: May-September $190; October-April $170. *Second-class:* $135 and $120.

All of the following train passes can be purchased only at Norwegian railstations.

"Green Departures" are at times when traffic volume is low. All of the following discounts are restricted to "Green Departures," marked with a green dot in Norwegian timetables.

Senior Citizen Discount Persons over 67 years old are allowed a 50% discount on both first-class and second-class tickets. Must obtain an ID card, available at railstations.

Mini-Price Tickets A one-way, *second*-class train ticket available either (a) at discount for a *specific* trip, such as $51 Oslo–Bergen versus $66 normal fare for an ordinary second-class ticket, or (b) at $67 for an *unlimited* distance. Must be purchased at least one day in advance.

The Oslo–Bodo–Tronheim 1,282 km trip (797 miles) costs about $246 for an ordinary second-class ticket. This $492 roundtrip can be covered with 2 "Mini-Price Tickets" for only $164.

ONE-DAY EXCURSIONS AND CITY-SIGHTSEEING

Here are 11 one-day rail trips that can be made comfortably from Bergen, Oslo and Stavanger, returning to them at or shortly after dinnertime. Notes are provided on what to see and do at each destination. The number after the name of each route is the Cook's timetable.

In the following timetables, where a city has more than one railstation, we have designated the particular station after the name of the city (in parentheses).

Oslo

Free admission to most Oslo museums and the Tusen Fryd amusement park; 50% discount on sightseeing by bus and boat; free travel on public city boats, buses, trams and trains; and discounts at cinemas, theaters and opera with "Oslo Card." Sold at most Oslo hotels, the Tourist Offices, Norway Information Center, and Oslo's Central railstation.

The 1995 prices are: Adult one-day: $16; two-day:$27; three-day: $34. Children one day: $8; two-day:$12; three-day:$16.

Walk from the railstation, up Karl Johansgate, to the Royal Palace. En route, you will pass the National Theater. Behind it is the underground suburban train station. See the massive mural, in the post World War II City Hall, commemorating the Nazi occupation of Norway.

From the pier behind City Hall, take the 4-minute boat ride to Bygdoy (or take Bus #30 from the center of town) to see the 4 interesting museums there: Viking ships (daily 09:00–18:00); the balsa Kon Tiki and reed Ra II rafts used by Thor Heyerdahl to recreate ancient voyages (daily 09:00–18:00); Roald Amunden's polar exploration ship Fram in the National Maritime Museum (daily 09:00–17:45); and the outdoor collection of 170 historical buildings brought to Oslo from all over Norway along with more than 80,000 items exhibited in the Norwegian Folk Museum (daily 10:00-18:00).

The walk from the Maritime Museum to the Viking ships and the Folk Museum takes only 20 minutes.

Later, see the bronze and granite sculptures of Gustav Vigeland in Frogner Park. Its highlight is a 55-foot-high monolith that has 121 intertwined figures. The Vigeland Museum at Nobelsgate 32. The collection of 1,100 Munch paintings and 18,000 Munch prints in the Edvard Munch Museum (53 Toyengata). The Historical Museum. Norway's largest art collection, at the National Gallery (13 Univesitetsgaten), open Monday and Wednesday-Saturday 10:00-16:00, Sunday 11:00-14:00. Oslo Cathedral.

Visit Aker Brygge (pier), a huge entertainment, shopping and residential project. The Museum of Applied Art. The 12th century, stone Gamle Aker Church (open Tuesday and Thursday in Summer).

The Resistance Museum and Defense Museum (commemorating the German occupation of Norway during World War II) in the Hjemmefront, at the 14th century Akershus Castle and Fortress, only a 5-minute walk from City Hall.

The Sonja Henie-Nils Onstad collection of modern paintings at Henie-Onstad Art Center (Monday-Saturday 09:00–22:00, Sunday 11:00–22:00). The Museum of Contemporary Art, opened in 1991. Marvelous views of Oslo and the Fjord from the Ski Jump and Ski Museum at

Holmenkollen. Take the trolley to the Merchant Marine Academy at Sjomannsskolen.

Take Bus #36 from Town Hall Square for a one-hour ride to **Sundvollen**. Beautiful Tyri Fjord scenery.

Oslo - Goteborg - Oslo   480

All of these trains require reservation and have a restaurant car.

Dep. Oslo (Sen.)	08:10 (1)		Dep. Goteborg	14:48 (2)	18:00(1)
Arr. Goteborg	12:10		Arr. Oslo (Sen.)	19:43	22:10

(1) Second class only. (2) Runs Friday, Saturday and Sunday (daily May 29-Sept. 24)

Oslo - Hamar - Oslo   483

Be sure to sit on the left side for the best view of the fantastic scenery along the western shore of **Lake Mjosa**. Norway's largest lake (75 miles long).

All of these trains have light refreshments and are second-class, unless designated otherwise.

Dep. Oslo (Sen.)	08:00 (1)	09:05	10:05	11:00 (2)	13:05
Arr. Hamar	09:26	10:40	11:43	12:36	14:47

Sights in **Hamar**: The enormous outdoor Hedmark Museum complex of more than 40 buildings, most of them from the 18th and 19th century, brought here from other places. One of the buildings is a house built in 1871 in North Dakota, U.S.A., by a Norwegian emigrant.

Also visit the 7½-acre Railway Museum, open May–September, to see many early coaches and locomotives as well as Norway's first railstation.

Dep. Hamar	13:56 (4)	15:09 (2)	16:26 (8)	17:15 (2)	19:17 (2)	20:23 (6+7)
Arr. Oslo (Sen.)	14:27	16:55	18:25	18:55	20:55	22:07

(1) Reservation *required*. Has first-class coach seats. Restaurant car. (2) Reservation *required*. (3) Runs daily, except Saturday. (4) Reservation *required*. Has first-class seats. (5) Restaurant car. (6) Runs Sunday only. (7) Plus another Hamar departure at 20:58 (4), arriving Oslo 22:28. (8) Runs Friday and Sunday.

Oslo - Lillehammer - Oslo   483

All of these trains have light refreshments and are second-class, unless designated otherwise.

Dep. Oslo (Sen.)	08:05 (1)	09:05	11:05 (2)
Arr. Lillehammer	10:09	11:36	13:23

Sights in **Lillehammer**: Site of the 1994 Winter Olympic Games. Visit the Sandvig collection of more than 100 old buildings and craftwork demonstration at the 100-acre open-air Maihaugen Museum, open daily 11:00–19:00 from late June to early August and 11:00–14:00 the rest of the year. See the "White Swan" paddle-wheel steamboat, Skibladner, at the city's dock.

Dep. Lillehammer	12:12 (3)	14:13 (1)	16:30 (2)	18:29 (2)	20:15 (3)
Arr. Oslo (Sen.)	14:27	16:46	18:55	20:55	22:28

(1) Reservation *required*. Has first-class coach. Restaurant car. (2) Reservation *required*. (3) Reservation *required*. Has first-class coach. (4) Restaurant car.

Oslo - Vinstra - Oslo   483

All of these trains have light refreshments and are second-class, unless designated otherwise

Dep. Oslo (Sen.)	08:05 (1)	09:05	11:05 (2)
Arr. Vinstra	11:05	12:47	14:27

Sights in **Vinstra:** A mountain resort. Home of the legendary Peer Gynt. See the memorial over his grave in the village church. Cross-country skiing is popular here.

Dep. Vinstra	11:07 (3)	13:06 (1)	17:13 (2)	18:08 (5)	19:15 (2)
Arr. Oslo (Sen.)	14:27	16:46	20:46	22:07	22:28

(1) Reservation *required*. Has first-class coach seats. Restaurant car. (2) Reservation *required*. (3) Reservation *required*. Has first-class coach. (4) Restaurant car. (5) Runs Sunday only.

THE FJORD TRAIN ROUTE

Oslo - Drammen - Tonsberg - Sandefjord - Larvik - Skien - Nordagutu - Oslo   488

This one-day excursion offers great views of several fjords (starting with the Oslofjord), wooded countryside, and lovely lakes. As the schedules indicate, stops can be made for sightseeing in several of the towns on this route.

All of these trains are second-class and have light refreshments Oslo-Skien (and v.v.), unless designated otherwise.

  A train change in Skien is necessary in both directions.

Oslo (Sen.)	06:21 (9)	09:09 (9)	11:09 (9)	13:09 (9)	14:18 (3+7)
Arr. Drammen	07:04	09:37	11:37	13:38	14:37
Arr. Tonsberg	08:02	10:31	12:31	14:32	15:33
Arr. Sandefjord	08:25	10:58	12:55	14:56	15:57
Arr. Larvik	08:43	11:14	13:11	15:12	16:18
Arr. Skien	09:28	11:58	13:56	15:57	17:02
Dep. Skien	09:49	-0-	-0-	16:12	18:36 (2)
Arr. Nordagutu	10:21	-0-	-0-	17:11	19:10
	• • •				
Dep. Nordagutu	-0-	10:28	12:42 (1)	14:45 (1)	16:48 (8)
Arr. Skien	-0-	10:52	13:35	15:18	17:20
Dep. Skien	09:50 (9)	11:38 (4)	13:40	15:40 (4)	17:35
Dep. Larvik	10:23	12:23	14:23	16:23	18:23
Dep. Sandefjord	10:39	12:39	14:39	16:39	18:39
Dep. Tonsberg	11:02	13:02	15:02	17:02	19:02
Dep. Drammen	12:01	14:02	16:02	18:02	20:02
Arr. Oslo (Sen.)	12:43	14:43	16:43	18:43	20:43

(1) No light refreshments. (2) Skien–Nordagutu (and v.v.): runs daily, except Saturday. No light refreshments. (3) Runs Monday–Friday, except holidays. (4) Runs daily. (5) Runs daily, except holidays Nordagatu–Skien. No light refreshments. (6) Runs daily, except Saturday. No light refreshments. (7) Plus another departure from Oslo at 15:09, arriving Skien 17:56, Nordagutu 19:10 (2). (8) Plus another departure from Nordagutu at 18:50 (6+9), arriving Oslo 22:51. (9) Reservation required.

Sights in **Drammen**: The activity along the busy docks. Many attractive old buildings. Watching the Drommensfjorden meet the Drammen River.

Sights in **Tonsberg**: Norway's oldest town. See today's whaling ships and the ruins of an ancient Viking castle, Tonsberghus. Also, the Vestfold Museum, the 12th century St. Michael's Church, the 12th century Sem Church, and the 13th century Royal Castle.

Sights in **Sandefjord**: The main port for Norway's whaling ships. See the whaling monument in the square. The Whaling Museum. Nearby are the mouth of the Oslofjorden and the head of the Sandefjorden.

Sights in **Larvik**: The Museum. The fjord.

Sights in **Skien**: The large sawmill operations. The meeting of Skien River and Lake Hjelle.

"NORWAY IN A NUTSHELL"

The easiest way to take the Myrdal-Flam scenic train ride is to buy either one of the one-day "Norway In A Nutshell" packages. The Bergen roundtrip, which cost 390 Norwegian Kroner in 1994 (NOK-195 for children under 16), includes the train Bergen–Myrdal, the "Flam Line" cogwheel train Myrdal–Flam, the fjord boat trip Flam–Gudvangen, the bus Gudvangen–Voss, and the train from Voss back to Bergen = 7 to 9 hours.

The Oslo roundtrip, which cost 596 Norwegian Kroner in 1994 (NOK-298 for children under 16), includes the train Oslo–Myrdal, the "Flam Line" cogwheel train Myrdal–Flam, the fjord boat trip Flam–Gudvangen, the bus Gudvangen–Voss, and the train from Voss back to Oslo =15 hours.

Both the one-way Bergen-Oslo "Nutshell" (13-15 hours) and the one-way Oslo-Bergen "Nutshell" (11 hours) cost NOK-557 for an adult in 1994, and NOK-278 for a child age 4-15.

For North American booking of "Nutshell," phone Passage Tours of Scandinavia at (800) 548-5960 or Nordique Tours at (800) 995-7997.

When these packages are purchased in Norway, either a Eurailpass or a Scanrailpass can be used for all of the train rides, reducing the prices above substantially.

Sights in **Bergen**: Free admission to most Bergen museums, rides on the funicular to the top of Mt. Flojen, and discounts at cinemas, theaters, concerts, sightseeing, boat excurions, parking and car rental with "Bergen Card." Sold at Bergen hotels, Tourist Information and the bus station.

The 1995 adult prices are: 100 Norwegian Kroner for one day, NOK-150 for 2 days. For children age 4-15: NOK-50 and NOK-75.

Visit Torget, a fish market that has been operating for 9 centuries (weekdays: 08:30–15:00). See Bergenhus Fortress, with its 13th century Hakon Hall. The 12th century Maria-kirken (St. Mary's Church). Europe's most modern aquarium and the collection of 19th century houses in Gamle Bergen (Old Bergen). Edvard Grieg's home in **Troldhaugen**.

Take the 5-minute funicular ride to the top of 2,000-foot-high **Mt. Floien**. See the Hanseatic Museum. The Maritime Museum. The Arts and Crafts Museum. The Bryggen Museum. The Leprosy Museum. Take the cable car to the top of **Mt. Ulriken**.

It is only 22 minutes for the bus ride and short walk to see the 13th century Fana Church and Fantoft, the 12th century Stave Church.

SCENIC RAIL TRIPS

Bergen to Oslo...and The Stalheim-Flam Detour   481

Indisputably, the most scenic rail route in Europe. There are several ways to make the detour, either in a single day or by adding one or 2 days to the Bergen-Oslo trip.

The most carefree way to make the detour in a single day is to check baggage direct from Bergen to Oslo, rather than be bothered with it all day.

The complete Bergen–Oslo line was opened in 1909 as the only year-round land transportation between Norway's 2 larges cities. It was electrified in 1964. Terrain and climate both caused construction problems which prior to then had never been encountered in building a railway line. The 300-mile length of track must pass through 200 tunnels and 18 miles of snow sheds in addition to crossing more than 300 bridges.

The first 40 minutes after leaving Bergen is along the lovely Sorfjorden. Travelers are frustrated by the interruptions of viewing the scenery caused by the many snow sheds.

However, it would be impossible for the trains to operate daily year round on this route and stick to a strict timetable if it were not for these structures.

When taking the Voss-Stalheim–Flam–Myrdal detour we have been recommending since 1971, you omit the 63-minute Voss–Myrdal portion of the main Bergen–Oslo line.

Voss - Stalheim - Flam - Myrdal Detour

The Gudvangen-Flam cruise on the Sognefjord (called "King of the Fjords") is the most scenic fjord trip in Norway.

481		*481*	
Dep. Bergen	07:33 (1)	Dep. Oslo (Sen.)	07:42 (1)
Arr. Voss	08:39	Arr. Myrdal	12:17
Change to bus. (Nor.)		*Change to narrow-gauge train (481)*	
Dep. Voss	09:50	Dep. Myrdal	12:25
Arr. Stalheim	10:25	Arr. Flam	13:25
Dep. Stalheim	10:35	*Change to fjord boat.*	
Arr. Gudvangen	11:20	Dep. Flam	14:30 (2)
Change to fjord boat.		Arr. Gudvangen	16:35
Dep. Gudvangen	11:30 (2)	*Change to bus. (Nor.)*	
Arr. Flam	13:30	Dep. Gudvangen	16:55
Change to narrow-gauge train (481)		Arr. Stalheim	17:40
Dep. Flam	15:00	Dep. Stalheim	17:50
Arr. Myrdal	15:55	Arr. Voss	18:10
Change trains. 481		*Change to train. 481*	
Dep. Myrdal	16:58 (3+5)	Dep. Voss	18:46 (4)
Arr. Oslo (Sen.)	21:55	Arr. Bergen	20:01

(1) Reservation *required*. Light refreshments. (2) Operates mid-April to mid-October. (3) Reservation *required*. Light refreshments. Plus another Myrdal departure (reservation *required*, runs daily, restaurant car) at 17:21, arriving Oslo 22:12. (4) Second-class. (5) Runs daily except Sat. May 29-Sept. 28 and Fridays + Sundays Sept. 19-May 27.

Sights in **Voss**: The 13th century church. The restored farmhouses and other buildings in the outdoor folk museum.

NOTE: On the Oslo-Bergen route (right-hand column above), there are only 8 minutes to change trains in Myrdal. *In mid-Summer, hundreds of people compete for the few seats on the Flam Line train.* Bus tour groups which board the Flam Line in Vatnahalsen (3 minutes after Myrdal) have to stand, which is very difficult on this route.

En route Bergen-Oslo, the one-hour bus ride from Voss to **Stalheim** passes (on your left) the spectacular Tvinde waterfall. At Stalheim there is only a Norwegian village museum and a hotel—which we recommended with high praise for 23 years.

Reports we received from readers in 1993, sadly, told us that the hotel is concentrating its services on tour groups. Its management is discouraging individual travelers.

Those traveling independently were told there were no porters to help with luggage and that they could not be seated in the dining room until groups were finished with lunch, by which time the fabled smorgasbord had been decimated.

The jouney via Stalheim is still recommended. The change is withdrawing our recommendation about staying or dining at the hotel. We also no longer recommend staying at the Fretheim Hotel in Flam.

There is a view here of such magnificence that Kaiser Wilhelm II came to Stalheim annually for 25 years to look at it.

The land here has been farmed since 400 A.D. Some facility for food and lodging has existed here since 1647 when mail was carried by Norway's "pony express" from Bergen to Oslo, and Stalheim was one of the stations for changing horses and riders, right up until 1900.

An inn was operated at Stalheim before 1700. The first hotel here, constructed in 1885, burned in 1900. A second hotel, built in 1901, met the same fate in 1902. Another hotel, constructed and used first in Voss, was moved to Stalheim in 1906, enlarged in 1912, and burned down in 1959.

The present Stalheim Hotel was built in the Winter of 1959–60 and enlarged in 1967 to its present capacity of 130 units, ranging from single rooms to doubles and then suites consisting of a double room plus sitting-room with fireplace. Stalheim can accommodate 219 guests, and it is filled nearly every day in its April-September operation with tour groups.

The terrace of the hotel provides a view over the Naro, Brekke and Jordal valleys, the Sivle and Stalheim waterfalls, and the conical peak of Mt. Jordal.

Two mounds on the right-hand side of the hotel's terrace date from 800 A.D. These were opened in 1890, revealing the remains of a woman who had been buried with her frying-pan, loom, bronze brooches and bracelets and the remains of a man, with his sword, axes and other utensils. These relics were given to the museum in Bergen. The mounds have been reconstructed, and photos of the relics are displayed in the hotel's entrance hall.

The hotel will arrange (for guests) a tour of its open air Ancient Village Museum. A commentary is on the old log buildings, the lives that were led in them, the white mansion of the landowner who built it in 1726, and the contents of all the structures. These objects dramatize the contrasting life-style between the rich and the poor of that era. Among the contents are antique Norwegian furniture, arms, glass, silver, pewter and brass, some of which are also displayed in the hotel lobby.

If your schedule does not allow staying overnight at Stalheim, from mid-June to mid-August a boat leaves Gudvangen (only a 30-minute bus ride from Stalheim) at 16:50 and 19:50 for a cruise along the Sognefjord, all in Midnight Sun daylight, arriving Aurland at 18:15 and 21:20.

You can leave Stalheim by bus on Day 2 at 10:35 to connect with the Gudvangen–Flam boat ride on the **Sognefjord**, starting at 11:35 for arrival in Flam at 13:30. Snacks and beverages are available on the boat, or you can have lunch after you reach **Flam**.

On the morning of the following day, start the 12½-mile "Flam Line" railway ride to Myrdal (Table 481) late May to mid-September at 10:00 or mid-September to late May at 10:40, arriving Myrdal 10:55 or 11:35, changing to the 12:25 departure for Oslo, and arrive Oslo 18:10.

The 41-minute Flam-Myrdal trip is one of the 5 most beautiful train rides in Europe.

"Flam Line" goes along the **Aurlandsfjord**, a branch of the Sognefjord. Watch for sturdy, wild mountain goats that often cluster on huge granite boulders only a few feet from the track. There is an ascent of 2,845 feet from sea level in the first 12 miles. This railway has the greatest incline of any Norwegian track, 5.5 percent at one stretch.

The descent is so steep that the train takes a longer time to go downhill than it does to go up. It has 5 different braking systems, any one of which is sufficient to stop the train.

The mountainside is so steep along one stretch that the train has to go through reverse tunnels. In one particular short distance, the track must go on 3 different levels on one side of Kjosfossen Gorge and on 2 levels on the other side of the Gorge. There are 20 tunnels with a combined length of 3.7 miles in the 12½-mile route.

The train proceeds slowly or stops completely at the finest scenic sections in order for passengers to have the best possible views of magnificent scenery and of a road that was built in 1895 to supply materials for building the railway. This road has 21 hairpin bends. Along another stretch, the train crosses a 110-yard-long embankment and stops there for several minutes so that passengers can get off and walk closer to the enormous raging Kjos waterfall that cascades close to the train. Its force is marvellous to see and hear.

The first stop en route from Myrdal to Oslo is at **Finse**, highest elevation (4,267 feet) of the entire Bergen–Oslo line. Workers are stationed permanently at Finse to fight snow on the tracks 9 months out of the year and repair the snow sheds during the 3-month Spring-Summer-Autumn there.

Between Finse and Oslo, the scenery changes from glacier to ski resorts, waterfalls, and then beautiful valley farms and fast-moving rivers.

If time does not permit going to Stalheim, you can leave Bergen (late May to mid-September) at 08:45, terminating in Myrdal at 11:00. Depart Myrdal 11:45 on "Flam Line," arriving Flam 12:45. Depart Flam 15:00 for the ride back to Myrdal, arriving Myrdal 15:55 and connecting with the train that departed Bergan at 15:30. Depart Myrdal on that train at 17:21 (reservation required). Arrive Oslo at 22:12. Despite the late arrival, you will see all of the interesting scenery between Myrdal and Oslo in daylight if you are taking this trip in Summer.

Oslo to Bergen with Myrdal-Flam Detour 481

Depart Oslo (Sentral) 07:42, 10:48, 14:55 (daily except Saturday) or 16:09 for the direct trip to Bergen, arriving there 14:07, 18:26, 20:45 and 22:14. The 07:30 has light refreshments. the other 3 trains have a restaurant car. All 4 trains require reservation.

To take the Myrdal–Flam–Myrdal roundtrip detour, leave Oslo 07:30 or 10:30, arriving Bergen 18:26 or 20:45. The 14:30 and 15:42 Olso departures reach Myrdal too late for making the detour.

For a 2-day Oslo-Bergen trip, overnight in Flam. Then, on the morning of Day 2, leave Flam Pier 08:45 for the boat trip on Sognefjord to Gudvangen, take the bus Gudvangen-Stalheim-Voss, and then by train Voss to Bergen.

All of these trains are second-class, unless designated otherwise.

Dep. Voss	06:33 (1)	08:42 (1)	10:30	12:30 (2)	13:16 (3+5)
Arr. Bergen	07:51	09:56	12:07	13:44	14:07

(1) Runs daily, except Sundays and holidays. (2) Runs Monday–Friday, except holidays. (3) Reservation *required*. Light refreshments or restaurant car. Has a first-class coach. (4) Operates late June to mid-September. Runs daily. (5) Plus other departures from Voss at 14:55, 16:00, 17:20 (3), 18:46, and 21:37 (3), arriving Bergen 16:03, 17:30, 18:26, 19:47 and 22:42.

Hotel Grand Terminus is a 2-minute walk from the Bergen railstation.

If time does not permit going to Stalheim on Day 2, you can depart Flam by fjord boat [table 481a] at 14:35 (early June to mid-September), arriving Bergen at 20:35 the same day.

Oslo - Dombas - Andalsnes 483

This 71-mile "Rauma Line" detour off the "Dovre Line" (Oslo to Trondheim) is, mile for mile, one of the 5 greatest scenic rides in Europe.

Even for one who is not going further north than Dombas, the 2-day roundtrip is well worth the time involved. There is no question that the route is worth seeing twice, and from 2 perspectives.

Be sure to obtain a free brochure at Oslo's Central railstation before beginning the trip. We would enjoy riding "Rauma Line" every day of our lives. Depart Oslo (Sentral) at 08:55 or 14:27. Arrive Andalsnes 15:30 or 20:50. In the Summer, you can read a newspaper there by sunlight at Midnight.

Soon after the train leaves Dombas it crosses the granite Jora Bridge, which spans a 120-foot deep gorge. At **Bjorli,** the Romsdal Valley comes into view, and you will see (at least in late Spring and early Summer) unmatched foaming torrents of thawed- glacier water, rushing at 80 miles an hour down vertical mountain slopes and through the boulder-strewn Rauma River bed.

The descent from Bjorli involves a double spiral through 2 circular mountain tunnels, first the 1,550-yard-long Stavem Tunnel, then through the 500-yard-long Kylling Tunnel.

Between these 2 tunnels, at **Verma** railstation, there is a monument that commemorates the opening of the Rauma Line by King Haakon in 1924. Along the opposite side of the Rauma River are small, well-kept farms, lush from the benefit of the warmth of the Gulf Stream, which keeps temperatures moderate along most of the coast of Norway.

The train next crosses Kylling Bridge, 200 feet above a thundering run of the Rauma River through a steep, narrow gorge. You are now approaching the valley floor.

Near **Flatmark,** you cross Foss Bridge and see Bridal Veil, best known of the numerous waterfalls on this route. At **Marstein** railstation, the sun is visible only 7 months of the year due to the combination of the tall surrounding mountains and the arc of the sun at this latitude.

After passing along the glaciated foot of the majestic Romsdalshorn Montain, whose peak rivals the Matterhorn as a climber's challenge, one can see on the left the highest vertical rock face in northern Europe, the "Troll's Wall" (Trollveggen), which is 3,000 feet high.

The "Rauma Line" reaches sea level in the Romsdall Valley before ending at **Andalsnes** (population 2,500) on the shore of Isfjord, at the head of the Romsdallfjord.

There is a bus connection between Andalsnes and **Alesund.** At Alesund, one can make flights to Oslo, Bergen or Trondheim, or make coastal express boat trips to Bergen or Trondheim.

The Rauma River is fished by sportsmen for salmon and trout.

To return to Oslo, depart Andalsnes 10:05. Depart Dombas 11:53. Arrive Oslo 16:46... or, depart Andalsnes 16:25, change trains in Dombas at 18:00, depart Dombas 18:06, arrive Oslo 22:16. Both trains require reservation and have light refreshments.

The Oslo-Andalsnes-Oslo roundtrip can be made without stopping overnight in Andalsnes. There is a night departure from Andalsnes at 23:10 [table 483], arriving Oslo the next morning at 07:16. What a shame, to take this ride at night!

The only overnight lodging we know of in **Andalsnes** is at the 65-room Grand Hotel Bellevue. Advance room reservations are recommended.

There is a 2-hour bus/ferry connection [483] from Andalsnes to **Molde**, Norway's "town of roses" located on a fjord and surrounded by 87 beautiful snowcapped peaks. In Molde, see the many ancient wood buildings from the 11th century. The Romsdal Museum, largest Norwegian provincial museum. The floral decorations in the modern concrete and glass Town Hall. The view of the Norwegian Sea and the countryside from the Varden Restaurant, 1300 feet above the town. An International Jazz Festival (music, art, poetry and theatrical events) has been held in Molde the first week of August every year since 1960.

Take the Eide bus 18 miles to visit the grottos and caves at the Troll's Church and the waterfall that tumbles against a marble mountain.

Oslo - Andalsnes - Trondheim - Bodo - Narvik

This is a marvelous 5-day rail trip up Norway's Gulfstream-warmed coastline. There is very good mountain and lake scenery Oslo–Trondheim, and excellent mountain, lake and seacoast scenery Trondheim-Bodo.

Keep in mind when reading the timetables that there is constant daylight on this route during June and July.

A transplanted herd of gigantic musk oxen live along the Dombas–Trondheim route, Day 2 of this journey. On one of our trips, we saw a mother and baby grazing late at night on a grassy slope near the train track.

The scenery of forests, rich valleys, waterfalls, rivers and farms is lovely almost all the way to the crossing of the Arctic Circle, on the ride from Trondheim to **Bodo.**

Passengers are given a brochure with details about the Arctic Circle trip. Announcements during the ride over a public address system alert passengers to approaching points of interest. A steward or hostess is on board to provide information.

Upon reaching the stone monument that marks the Arctic Circle, the train stops there for 5 minutes, allowing passengers adequate time to take photographs.

We were fortunate that it was snowing on our first crossing of the Arctic Circle one June, giving the trip the feeling of a polar environment. A few hours later, as the train's route came close to the coastline, and when we were considerably north of the Arctic Circle, the weather was sunny and warm.

Because of the sunny, balmy weather that day, there was no sensation of being so far north, nor was there in Narvik the next day, by which time we were 700 miles above the Arctic Circle.

The northernmost rail service from Oslo is to Bodo. Passage from Bodo to Narvik is via an all-day bus trip through beautiful countryside interspersed by 3 ferry-boat crossings.

There are schedules on this page for a recommended rail trip from Oslo to Narvik, and then from Narvik across northern Norway to northern Sweden and then south to Stockholm. On the trip from Narvik to Sweden (Boden), you cross the Arctic Circle north-to-south, although without the interesting ceremony that is presented on the south-to-north Trondheim–Bodo ride.

Day 1 (*table 483*)		*Day 3* in *Trondheim*	
Dep. Oslo (Sen.)	09:05 (1)		
Arr. Andalsnes	15:30	*Day 4* (*table 484*)	
		Dep. Trondheim	08:55 (4)
Day 2 (*table 483*)		*Cross the Arctic Circle.*	16:10
Dep. Andalsnes	16:35 (2)	Arr. Bodo	18:40
Arr. Dombas	18:00		
Change trains.		*Day 5* *Bus.*	
Dep. Dombas	18:52 (3)	Dep. Bodo	07:30 (5)
Arr. Trondheim	21:50	Arr. Narvik	14:35

(1) Second-class. Light refreshments. (2) Second-class. (3) Second-class. Restaurant car. (4) Reservation *required.* Restaurant car. (5) Food is available at occasional stops.

Keep in mind that during late June, all of July and most of August, the Midnight Sun allows you to see the scenery all the way to Trondheim, despite the 21:50 arrival time there. The light is not blinding, but you can read a newspaper by it straight through the night.

Deleting Overnight in Andalsnes and Trondheim

Here are schedules for those wishing to continue on from Andalsnes to Narvik without spending 21 hours in Andalsnes or a night in either Trondheim or Bodo and who don't mind missing a daytime view of the Andalsnes–Dombas "Rauma Line." The bus Fauske–Narvik is *not* covered by Eurailpass. Its cost in 1994 was 245 Norwegian kroner.

483		
Dep. Oslo (Sen.)	09:05 (1)	14:205 (5)
Arr. Dombas	13:51	19:08
Arr. Andalsnes	15:30	20:15
Return to Dombas.		
Dep. Andalsnes	16:35 (2)	23:15 (4)
Arr. Dombas	18:00	01:00
Change trains.		

483		
Dep. Dombas	18:41 (4)	04:26 (4)
Arr. Trondheim	21:20	07:20
Change trains. 484		
Dep. Trondheim	23:00 (4)	08:55 (5)
Cross the Arctic Circle.		
Arr. Fauske	09:05	17:55
Change to a bus.		
Dep. Fauske	09:10	18:15
Arr. Narvik	13:55	22:55

(1) Second-class only. Light refreshments. (2) Second-class only. (3) Second-class only. Restaurant car. (4) Reservation *required*. Carries a sleeping car. Coach is second-class only. (5) Reservation *required*. Has a first-class coach. Restaurant car.

Sights in **Trondheim**: This is the gateway for northern cruises. See the old Nidaros Cathedral, the largest medieval structure in Scandinavia. The 18th century rococo Strift-sgarden royal residence. The Bishop's Palace. The open-air Folk Museum, open daily 10:00–18:00. The dazzling array of unusual musical instruments in the Ringve Museum of Musical History (including an Eskimo drum made from a walrus stomach, a Tibetan trumpet, a violin made of matches).

Sights in **Narvik:** The second (after Murmansk) most northern rail passenger terminus in the world.

Founded in 1901 at the western tip of **Ofot Fjord** to provide an ice-free port for the mid-Winter export of iron ore from Swedish mines which cannot ship via the frozen Bay of Bothnia during Winter.

For the most breathtaking view of Midnight Sun sky, fjords, mountains and the town of Narvik, take the 10-minute walk from Grand Hotel Royal to the base of the cable that lifts you 2,000 feet in 13 minutes to the top of **Mt. Fagernesfjell**.

Food and beverages are sold in the Fjellsheimen restaurant on the peak, an ideal site for taking spectacular photos and watching the sun revolve clockwise around the horizon.

A crucial British-German naval battle (commemorated at a small museum in the center of town) was fought in Narvik's fjords during World War II. Destroyed in 1940, Narvik was completely rebuilt after the war.

The Direct Trip

Oslo - Trondheim and Trondheim - Oslo   483

Dep. Oslo (Sen.)	08:00 (1)	10:05 (2)	14:05 (1)	16:05 (1)	22:30 (4+7)
Arr. Trondheim	14:45	18:20	21:20	22:35	07:05

• • •

Dep. Trondheim	07:45 (1)	09:20 (1)	09:25 (6)	15:50 (1)	22:45 (1+8)
Arr. Oslo (Sen.)	14:46	16:46	17:46	22:28	06:55

(1) Reservation *required*. Restaruant car or light refreshments. (2) Second-class. Light refreshments. (3) Second-class. Restaurant car. (4) Runs daily, except Saturday. Reservation *required*. Carries a sleeping car. Coach is second-class. (5) Runs daily. Reservation *required*. Coach is second-class. (6) Restaurant car. (7) Plus another Oslo departure at 23:00 (5), arriving Trondheim 07:20. (8) Plus another Trondheim departure at 22:25 (4) (5), arriving Olso 07:16.

Narvik - Boden - Stockholm   476

There is fine mountain scenery Narvik–Kiruna.

Day 6

Dep. Narvik	13:45	Day 6 of the Oslo–Narvik–Stockholm trip.
Arr. Kiruna	16:25	
Dep. Kiruna	17:05 (1)	
Arr. Boden	20:20	
Arr. Stockholm (Cen.)	10:45	Day 7 of the Oslo–Narvik–Stockholm trip.

(1) Reservation *required*. Carries a sleeping car. Also has couchettes. Restaurant car.

Oslo - Kritiansand - Stavanger   482

There is excellent mountain scenery between Kristiansand and Stavanger.

Dep. Oslo (Sen.)	07:18 (2)	15:39 (2)	22:39 (3)	22:48 (4)
Dep. Kristiansand	12:02	20:26	04:10	04:30
Arr. Stavanger	14:48	23:15	07:32	07:56

Sights in **Stavanger**: Many old streets and houses in this 1100-year old town. See the market of fruits, vegetables, flowers and fish. The 11th century Cathedral. Outside the city, see the prehistoric Viste Cave. Try a deep-sea fishing trip.

Dep. Stavanger	07:00(2)	12:06 (1)	22:00 (4)
Arr. Kristiansand	09:40	15:17	01:25
Arr. Oslo (Sen.)	14:21	20:42	07:18

(1) Reservation *required*. Second-class. Light refreshments. (2) Reservation *required*. Restaurant car. (3) Operates all year except most of July. Runs Sunday only. Carries a sleeping car. Coach is second-class. (4) Carries a sleeping car. Coach is second-class. Runs daily, except Saturday.

Stavanger - Kristiansand - Stavanger   482

From Stavanger, it is an easy one-day roundtrip to see the fine mountain scenery en route to Kristiansand.

All of these trains require reservation and have light refreshments, unless designated otherwise.

Dep. Stavanger	07:00 (1)	12:06		Dep. Kristiansand	12:02 (2)	20:26 (1)
Arr. Kristiansand	09:140	15:17		Arr. Stavanger	14:48	23:15

(1) Restaurant car. (2) Second-class.

Voss - Ulvik

This spur off the Bergen–Oslo route affords great farm, mountain and river scenery. It is an easy one-day roundtrip.

481 Train			
Dep. Bergen	10:20 (1)	13:30 (2)	15:45 (1)
Arr. Voss	11:25	14:42	16:47
Change to bus. 489			
Dep. Voss	11:40 (3)	15:40 (3)	17:20 (4)
Arr. Ulvik	12:45	16:45	18:25

• • •

Dep. Ulvik	13:55 (4)	16:50 (4)	18:45 (3)
Ar. Voss	15:00	17:55	19:50
Change to train. 481			
Dep. Voss	16:00 (2)	18:46 (2)	21:37 (1)
Arr. Bergen	17:15	20:01	22:42

(1) Reservation *required*. Restaurant car. (2) Second-class. (3) Runs daily, except Sundays and holidays. (4) Runs daily, except Saturday. (5) Runs daily, except Sundays and holidays. Second-class.

INTERNATIONAL ROUTES
FROM NORWAY

Bergen is Norway's starting point for *cruises* to England. Oslo is the gateway for *rail* trips to Sweden (Stockholm, and on to Finland) and Denmark (Copenhagen, and on to Germany and the rest of Western Europe).

Bergen - Newcastle   1050

The arrivals in Newcastle are on Day 2 after departing Bergen.

Dep. Bergen	11:00 (1)	11:00 (2)	14:30 (3)	17:00 (4)	17:00 (5)
Dep. Stavanger	17:45	18:00	21:15	23:30	23:59
Arr. Newcastle (Tyne)	12:00	12:00	14:30	16:45	19:00

(1) Operates late Monday only Jan 1 - June 3 and Sept 3 - December 31. Runs Friday only. (2) Runs Friday only June 4-Sept 2. (3) Operates June 4-Sept 2. Runs Sunday only. (4) Operates June 4 - Sept 2. Runs Tuesday only. (5) Runs Thursday only.

Narvik - Boden - Haparanda - Kemi - Oulu - Helsinki

The schedule below indicates that it is necessary to layover one night in Boden when going from Narvik to Helsinki. In order to see the entire Boden–Oulu portion during daylight, take the 08:00 departure from Boden. To see the entire Oulu–Helsinki portion during daylight, layover one or more nights in Oulu and on Day 3 or later depart Oulu 09:56.

475 Train					
Dep. Narvik	010:05 (1)	13:45 (2)			
Arr. Boden	16:56	20:11			
Change to bus. 474					
Dep. Boden	08:05	10:55 (4)	13:35 (3)		
Arr. Haparanda	10:20	13:30	15:55		
Change buses. 474					
Dep. Haparanda	11:05 (3)	13:50 (4)	16:05		
Set your watch forward one hour.					
Arr. Kemi	12:50	15:35	17:52		
Change to a train. 495					
Dep. Kemi	14:22 (5)	-0-	20:10 (6)	22:43 (6)	08:30 (7)
Dep. Oulu	16:03	-0-	22:10	00:12	09:56
Arr. Helsinki	22:58	-0-	07:10	08:27	16:58

(1) Reservation *required*. Second-class. Light refreshments. (2) Reservation *required*. Second-class. (3) Runs daily, except Sundays and holidays. (4) Runs Monday-Friday, except holidays. (5) Light refreshments. (6) Carries a sleeping car. Coach is second-class. Light refreshments. (7) Restaurant car.

Oslo - Stockholm   470

| Dep. Oslo (Sen.) | 08:20 (1) | 16:20 (1) | 22:50 (3) |
| Arr. Stockholm | 14:41 | 22:41 | 06:47 |

(1) Reservation *required*. Restaurant car. (2) Restaurant car. Mid-June to mid-August: runs daily. Mid-August to mid-June: runs daily, except Saturday. (3) Carries a sleeping car. Also has couchettes. Coach is second-class.

Oslo - Copenhagen   466

All of these trains require reservation.

Dep. Oslo (Sen.)	10:15 (1)	22:43 (2)
Arr. Helsingborg	18:20	05:58
Arr. Copenhagen (H.)	20:15	08:20

(1) Restaurant car. (2) Carries a sleeping car. Also has couchettes. Coach is second-class. Runs May 29-August 28.

SWEDEN

Overview

Most train travelers coming into Sweden cross over on one of the quick ferries from Denmark (Helsingborg-Helsingor) which connects to the Stockholm line.

General Information

• Children under 12 travel free when accompanied by an adult (to a maximum of two children for each adult). Half-fare for children 12-15. Children 16 and over must pay full fare.

• The signs you will see at railstations in Sweden are:

ANKOMST	ARRIVAL
AVGANG	DEPARTURE
BILJETTLUCKAN	TICKET OFFICE
DAMER	WOMEN
GARDEROBEN	CHECKROOM
HERRAR	MEN
JARNVAGSTATION	RAILWAY STATION
INGANG	ENTRANCE
INFORMATIONSDISKEN	INFORMATION
LIGGPLATSVAGN	COUCHETTE CAR
PLATSBILJETTER	RESERVATIONS
RESTAURANGVAGN	RESTAURANT CAR
SOVVAGN	SLEEPING CAR
SPAR	TRACK
TILL SPAREN	TO THE PLATFORMS
UTGANG	EXIT
VAXELKONTORET	CURRENCY EXCHANGE

Swedish Holidays

A list of holidays is helpful because some trains will be noted later in this section as *not* running on holidays. Also, those trains which operate on holidays are filled, and it is necessary to make reservations for them long in advance.

January 1	New Year's Day		Ascension Day
	Epiphany		Whit Monday
	Good Friday		Midsummer Day
	Easter		All Saint's Day
	Easter Monday	December 25	Christmas Day
May 1	Labor Day	December 26	Boxing Day

EURAILPASS BONUSES IN SWEDEN

These boat trips: Goteborg–Fredrickshavn, Helsingborg–Helsingor, Stockholm––Helsinki, Stockholm–Turku and Stockholm–Aland Islands–Turku. There is also a 50% reduction of the fares of the ferries between Malmo and Lubeck-Travemunde (Germany) and between Trelleborg and Sassnitz (Germany). From Stockholm or Oslo, Sassnitz is the most direct gateway to Berlin, with both day and night trains operating Sassnitz–Berlin.

SWEDEN'S TRAIN PASSES

All of Sweden's passes are sold *only* in Sweden, at main railstations and travel agencies.

Reslust Card Entitles the holder to 25% discount on *all* trains on Tuesday, Wednesday, Thursday and Saturday — plus other advantages such as restaurant car discounts and special Summer rates. The 1996 price is $18 (only $6 for persons over 67).

Red Departure Discount Ticket The holder is allowed 50% discount for trains marked in red on Finnish timetables on *second*-class tickets that are valid for 36 hours. No stopovers. The minimum ticket must be $14, or $10 for persons holding the "Reslust Card" (see above). If the station's ticket office is closed when the train departs, "Red Departure" can be purchased on the train. Seat reservation, at $3 each, is required for InterCity trains and for many long distance trains.

ONE-DAY EXCURSIONS AND CITY SIGHTSEEING

Here are 9 one-day rail trips that can be made comfortably from Stockholm and Goteborg, returning to them in most cases before dinnertime. Notes are provided on what to see and do at each destination. The number after the name of each route is the Cook's timetable.

Goteborg

A great seaport. The one-hour sightseeing bus tour leaves from Stora Teatern. There are one-hour boat trips covering the 7-mile harbor and its canals, leaving from Kungsportsbron. See the view of the harbor and city from the Sailor's Tower near the Maritime Museum at Gamla Varvsparken. The Liseberg amusement park. The magnificent City Theater, Concert House and Art Museum, all in the large square, Gotaplatsen. Antikhallarna, Scandinavia's largest permanent antiques and collectors market.

The view from Ramberget, highest point on the Hisingen side of Goteborg. The Botanical Garden. The 07:00 fish auction, weekdays, at Scandinavia's largest fish market. The 17th century Elfsborg Fortress. The historical and archaeological collections at the Goteborg Museum, located in the city's oldest (1643) building. Art from all over the world, at the Rohss Museum. Slottsskogen Zoo. The view of the harbor and city from the top of Sjomanjtornet, a 193-foot-high tower. Stroll down the broad Kungsportsavenyn, hub of the city.

Stockholm

Maps, literature and advice can be obtained at the Stockholm Tourist Association in Sweden House (Hamngatan 27), in the central business-shopping district (open Monday–Friday 08:30–18:00, Saturday and Sunday 08:00–17:00).

Bus connections to the city's airport are available at a terminal across the street from the Central railstation. Stockholm's subways depart from the same level as the Tourist Information Office in Central railstation. A Tourist Ticket, good for rides on both buses and subways, is sold for 2 periods: one day and 3 days. These can be purchased at the Tourist Information Office in Central railstation.

Bus #47 can be taken from across the street from Central railstation to the 75-acre Skansen amusement park, open 08:00–23:30 June through August. Its prime attraction is the Vasa Museum (open daily 09:30–19:00 June through mid-August, 10:00–17:00 the rest of the year), where a 17th century battleship is on exhibit. This ancient ship sank in Stockholm harbor at the moment she set forth on her first voyage as flagship of the Swedish Navy and rested in 100 feet of water from 1628 until it was raised in 1956, restored and turned into a museum.

Located near the Nordic Museum in the Galarvarv area of Djurgarden Island, the Vasa Museum can be reached by bus or by ferries that leave continuously from Nybroplan and from the end of Gamla Stan. It is an easy 5-minute walk from where the ferries dock at the island to the Vasa Museum.

Also popular are Skansen's Zoo and its outdoor museum of life in early Stockholm (more than 150 buildings from the 18th and 19th centuries).

At the Royal Palace, the treasury and Armory are open in Summer 10:00–16:00. The king's silver throne in the Hall of State can be seen 12:00–15:00. Also see the Bernadotte and Festival suites. The historic and art treasures in the Royal Chapel. The Changing of the Guard in the courtyard takes place daily at 12:10.

Other sights: the 15th century Storkyrkan Cathedral, with its sculpture of St. George and the Dragon, is a short walk from the Palace. The tall old houses and Stock Exchange on Stortorget, the city's oldest square. The modern architecture in Skarholmen, a suburb

The collection of Carl Milles statues at Millesgarden sculpture park. Fine views of the city and the archipelago from the 504-foot-high Kaknas television tower, open May through August 09:00–24:00. The exhibit of 16th through 19th century paintings by European masters at the National Museum of Fine Arts, open daily 10:00–16:00 (see the 9 Rembrandts on the second floor). Rosendal Palace, closed Monday. The Chinese Pavilion, Court Theater and Museum, all at Drottingholm Palace, open April through October.

Do not miss seeing the Golden Hall, Blue Hall, Prince's Gallery, Terrace and the view from the Tower, all at Town Hall (1 Hantverkgatan), one of Europe's most famous buildings, where guided tours are offered daily at 10:00 (plus 12:00 on Sundays and holidays). The Nobel festivities take place there.

Goteborg - Kalmar - Goteborg   467

Dep. Goteborg	08:00 (1)	Dep. Kalmar	17:26 (2)
Arr. Kalmar	12:37	Arr. Goteborg	22:00

(1) Runs Saturdays only. (2) Runs daily, except Saturday. Light refreshments.

Sights in **Kalmar**: The moat, courts and towers of the Castle. A bus trip to the nearby glassworks.

Stockholm - Eskilstuna - Stockholm   471 Bus

Dep. Stockholm	08:10	10:10	12:10	14:10
Arr. Eskilstuna	10:25	12:15	14:15	16:25

Dep. Eskilstuna	13:30	15:30	17:30 (1)	19:30
Arr. Stockholm	15:35	17:50	19:35	21:40

(1) Runs Saturdays, Sundays and holidays.

Sights in **Eskilstuna**: The 6 Rademacher Forges that are more than 300 years old, on display in the center of town. Eskilstuna is the capital of Sweden's steel industry. Also see the wooden Fors Church and the statue of the 10th century English missionary, Saint Eskil, for whom the town was named in 1659, one year after Reinhold Rademacher built the forges which launched the local industry.

The Zoo and Amusement Park. The 12th century church. The wonderful collection of Scandinavian art in the Art Museum. Take a local bus 8 miles to Sundbyholm Castle. Shop for gold, iron and copper souvenirs.

Stockholm - Gavle - Stockholm   476

All of these trains require reservation.

Dep. Stockholm (Cen.)	05:40 (1)	07:13 (2)	08:13 (4)	10:13 (12)	12:13 (13)
Arr. Gavle	07:47	09:11	10:19	12:06	14:15

Sights in **Gavle**: The Swedish Railway Museum.

Dep. Gavle	11:49 (4)	13:49 (9)	15:49 (4)	16:47 (2)	19:11 (4+11)
Arr. Stockholm (Cen.)	13:44	15:44 (9)	17:44	18:44	21:30

(1) Runs Monday–Friday, except holidays. Light refreshments. (2) Restaurant car. (3) Runs Saturday only. Light refreshments. (4) Light refreshments. (5) Runs Monday-Thursday. Restaurant car. (6) Runs daily, except Saturdays and Sundays. (7) July: runs daily. August-June: runs Friday, Saturday and Sunday. Resaurant car. (8) Operates August-June. Runs Monday-Thursday. Restaurant car. (9) Runs daily, except Saturday. Light refreshments. (10) Plus another Stockholm departure at 12:13 (7), arriving Gavle 14:08. (11) Plus other departures from Gavle at 20:34 (2) and 21:106 (14), arriving Stockholm 22:27 and 22:57. (12) Runs Friday, Saturday only. (13) Runs Friday, Saturday and Sunday only. (14) Runs Sunday only.

Stockholm - Goteborg - Stockholm   469

All of these trains require reservation and have a restaurant car, unless designated otherwise.

Dep. Stockholm (Cen.)	07:00 (1+3)	08:00 (1+2)	08:12	
Arr. Goteborg (Cen.)	10:10	11:04	12:55	
Dep. Goteborg (Cen.)	15:10	16:05 (4)	17:05 (1+3)	17:10 (9)
Arr. Stockholm (Cen.)	19:47	19:17 (5)	20:11	21:35

(1) X2000 high speed train. Supplement charged includes reservation fee and meal. Operates mid-August to early June. (2) Runs daily except holidays. (3) Runs Monday–Thursday. (4) X2000 high speed train. Supplement charged includes reservation fee and meal. Operates all year. (5) Runs daily , except Saturday. (6) Runs Friday and Sunday. (7) Runs Monday-Thursday and Sunday. (8) Train carries only sleeping car and couchettes. Reservation *not* required. *No* restaurant car. (9) Plus other Goteburg departures at 19:10 (6),   and 23:55 (5), arriving Stockholm 23:33, and 06:17.

Stockholm - Malmo - Stockholm   465

This trip is impratical as a one-day Stockholm excursion.

All of these trains require reservation and have a restaurant car., unless designated otherwise.

Dep. Stockholm (Cen.)	06:12	08:06	10:06	12:06	14:06	16:12 (6)
Arr. Malmo (Cen.)	12:48	14:50	10:58	18:53	20:45	22:37
Dep. Malmo (Cen.)	05:15 (2)	07:14	09:17	11:17	13:17	15:00 (7)
Arr. Stockholm (Cen.)	11:53	13:53	15:53	17:53	19:35	21:53

(1) Runs Saturday only. (2) Runs Monday–Friday, except holidays. (3) Runs daily, except Saturday. (4) Runs Saturday only. Train carries only sleeping cars and couchettes. No coaches. Reservation *not* required. *No* restaurant car. (5) Early June to mid-August: runs daily. Mid-August to early June: runs daily, except Saturday. Train carries only sleeping cars and couchettes. No coaches. Reservation *not* required. *No* restaurant car. (6) Plus other departures from Stockholm at and 23:12 (5), arriving Malmo 06:45. (7) Plus other departures from Malmo at 17:17 and 23:00 (5), arriving Stockholm 23:26 and 06:47.

Stockholm - Borlange - Mora - Stockholm   478

There is excellent lake and mountain scenery Borlange-Mora.

All of these trains require reservation and have light refreshments, unless designated otherwise.

Dep. Stockholm (Cen.)	06:10 (7)	09:32	Dep. Mora	11:38 (2)	14:29 (6+7)
Arr. Borlange	08:52 (2)	11:51 (4)	Arr. Borlange	13:23	15:53 (2)
Arr. Mora	10:33	13:35	Arr. Stockholm (Cen.)	16:02	18:57 (4)

(1) Runs Monday-Friday, except holidays. (2) Change trains in Borlange. (3) Mid-June to mid-August: runs daily. Mid-August to mid-June: runs Saturday and Sunday. (4) Runs Sunday only. (5) Mid-June to mid-August: runs daily, except Saturday. Change trains in Borlange on Friday and Sunday. Mid-August to early June: runs Monday and Thursday.(6) Plus other departures from Mora at 17:51 arriving Stockholm 22:44. The 17:51 train runs daily except Saturday. (7) Runs daily except Sundays and holidays. (8) Runs July 4-31 only.

Sights in **Mora**: The outdoor museum of 40 timber buildings, some 600 years old. The collection of Anders Zorn, Swden's most famous painter.

Stockholm - Norrkoping - Stockholm   465

All of these trains require reservation and have a restaurant car, unless designated otherwise.

Dep. Stockholm (Cen.)	06:12	08:06	10:30	12:06
Arr. Norrkoping	08:05	10:05	12:15	14:05

Sights in **Norrkoping**: The amazing collection of more than 25,000 cactus plants in beautiful Karl Johans Park. Take the short sightseeing trip by boat, from the pier at the end of this park.

See the 3,000-year old Bronze Age carvings and also the display of roses in Himmelstalund Park, to the right of the railstation. On the other (east) side of the railstation, visit the ruins of the star-shaped Johannisborg Fort. See the Lindo Canal.

Hear the bell-chiming at 13:00 in front of the Radhuset (Council House). See Hedvigs Kyrka, the German Church.

See the demonstration of antique textiles (from rugs to doilies) and textile machinery in the museum of old factory buildings and tour the restored residence of the factory owner, the Stadsmuseet, a short walk from the railstation. Also exhibited there are interesting scale models of the city as it was in various past centuries.

Dep. Norrkoping	11:55	13:55	15:55	17:05 (1)	17:55 (4)
Arr. Stockholm (Cen.)	13:53	15:53	17:53	19:11	19:35

(1) Runs Monday-Friday except holidays. Reservation not required. No restaurant car.(2) Runs Friday only. *No* restaurant car. (3) Runs Sunday only. *No* restaurant car. (4) Plus other departures from Norrkoping at 18:55 (3), 19:55, 21:40 arriving Stockholm 20:53, 21:53, 23:26.

Stockholm - Uppsala - Stockholm

All of these trains require reservation, unless designated otherwise.

	476	478	476	476
Dep. Stockholm (Cen.)	08:13 (1)	09:32 (2)	10:13 (11)	12:13 (5)
Arr. Uppsala	40–50 minutes later			

Sights in **Uppsala:** The Cathedral, a short walk from the railstation, is the largest church in Scandinavia.

England's Princess Louise (after whom Lake Louise in Canada is named) visited it in 1929. An anecdote about that occasion has been passed on to generations of Britains:

The Swedish bishop whose command of the English language was imperfect, led the Princess on a tour of the church. After having shown her many priceless religious objects in several areas of the Cathedral, he led her into the sacristry where he conducted her to a large cabinet of severals drawers and began to open one of them. In halting English, he announced to her: "I will now open these trousers and show your Royal Highness even more precious treasures."

Also visit Sweden's largest library, Carolina Rediviva, with more than 20,000 hand-illuminated medieval manuscripts, including the only book in existence that is written in pure Gothic, the famous Codex Argentus, the 5th century Silver Bible. The Great Hall of State in the old red Castle, open 11:00–18:00 from mid-May to mid-September.

The 18th century Linnaeus Garden at 27 Svartsbacksgatan (open May–December 09:00–21:00) was created for the study of plant species by Karl von Linne, Sweden's "Prince of Botanists." The present collection numbers 1,300 plants. It was Linne who originated the system of sexual plant classification and the dual nomenclature for natural science.

Take a bus marked "Gamla Uppsala" for a 2-mile ride to see relics of heathen worship going back to the 5th century.

	476	476	478	476
Dep. Uppsala	12:57 (6)	14:57 (9)	15:28	17:57 (10)
Arr. Stockholm (Cen.)	40–50 minutes later			

(1) Runs Saturday only. Light refreshments. (2) Runs daily except Sundays and holidays. (3) Runs Monday–Friday, except holidays. Light refreshments. (4) Operates August through June. Runs Monday-Thursday. Restaurant car. (5) Runs Friday, Saturday and Sunday. (6) Light refreshments. (7) Runs Sunday only. Light refreshments. (8) Restaurant car. (9) Runs daily, except Saturday. Light refreshments. (10) Plus other Uppsala departures (all table 476) at 21:40 (8) and 22:10 (7). (11) Runs Monday-Saturday.

INTERNATIONAL ROUTES
FROM SWEDEN

Stockholm is the gateway for rail trips to northern Norway (Trondheim and Narvik) and to northern Finland (Oulu), as well as by boat to Helsinki, and on to Leningrad. It is also the gate-

424   *The Eurail Guide to Train Travel in the New Europe*

way for travel to southern Norway (Oslo, and on to Bergen or Stavanger). Malmo is the starting point for rail travel to Denmark, (Copenhagen, and on to Germany and the rest of Western Europe).

There is fine lake scenery on the Ostersund–Storlien portion of this route.

Stockholm - Trondheim

476

Dep. Stockholm (Cen.)	07:13 (1)	11:45 (2)	12:13 (3)	22:10 (4)
Dep. Ostersund	13:26	18:15	18:42	06:35
Arr. Storlien	15:51	21:22	21:28	09:34
Change to a bus. 484				
Dep. Storlien	16:10	21:35	21:35	10:05
Arr. Trondheim	18:25	23:25	23:25	12:00

(1) Reservation *required*. Restaurant car. (2) Runs Monday-Thursday. Restaurant car. (3) Runs Friday, Saturday and Sunday. (4) Carries a sleeping car. Also has couchettes. Coach is second-class only.

Stockholm - Copenhagen   465

All of these trains require reservation and have a restaurant car, unless designated otherwise.

Dep. Stockholm (Cen.)	06:12	10:30	22:12
Arr. Copenhagen (Hoved.)	14:51	18:51	07:05

Stockholm - Helsinki   Boat and Train

This is the short route to Helsinki, *across* the Gulf of Bothnia.

The price for the cruise across the Gulf of Bothnia on the comfortable and pleasant Silja Line ships in 1995 is $46 for first-class and $37 for second-class. Passage is free on day sailings of the Silja Line ferry for Eurailpass holders. On night sailings a bed in at least a 4-bed cabin must be used, at $12. It can be upgraded to higher cabin class at extra charge. The fare for a sleeping cabin is *not* covered by Eurailpass. Food on the ship is varied and delicious.

We recommended the 08:00 sailing in order to see the thousands of tiny islands on the ride through this extremely interesting archipelago. During the daytime cruise, there is a good smorgasbord for both lunch and dinner.

A small band plays music in a delightful bar area. Movies are shown in a small theater. There is a duty-free shop on board. The ships ferry autos.

All of the Turku–Helsinki trains have light refreshments.

1250 Boat

Dep. Stockholm (Var.)	08:00 (1)	20:00 (2)
Arr. Turku (Harbor)	19:00	08:00

Walk to either railstation.

493

Dep. Turku (Harbor)	-0-	08:30
Dep. Turku (Stn.)	19:35	08:43
Arr. Helsinki	22:00	11:02

(1) Runs daily except January 1,3,10,17,24; May 30,31;September 5-9; December 24,25. (2) Runs daily except April 17-21, September 11,12 and December 24,25.

Stockholm - Narvik

There is good mountain scenery on the Kiruna–Narvik portion of this trip.

Both of these trains require reservation. Coach cars on both trains are second-class.

476		*475*	
Dep. Stockholm (Central)	17:30 (1)	Dep. Lulea	10:00 (2)
Arr. Lulea	07:53	Arr. Boden	10:23
Change trains.		Arr. Kiruna	14:12
		Arr. Narvik	17:34

(1) Carries a sleeping car. Also has couchettes. Restaurant car. (2) Light refreshments.

Stockholm - Oslo   470

Dep. Stockholm (Cen.)	07:36 (1)	15:35 (1)	23:00 (3)
Arr. Oslo (Sen.)	14:00	21:50	07:35

(1) Reservation *required*.Restaurant car. (2) Early June to mid-August: runs daily. Mid-August to early June: runs daily, except Saturday. (3) Carries a sleeping car. Also has couchettes. Coach is second-class.

Stockholm - Oulu - Helsinki

By stopping-over one night in Oulu, the Oulu-Helsinki trip can be made the next day in daylight by departing Oulu 07:15, 09:56 or 12:52.

476

Dep. Stockholm (Cen.)	17:30 (1)	20:10 (1)	-0-
Arr. Boden	07:14	10:30	-0-
Change to bus. 474			
Dep. Boden	08:05	10:55 (3)	13:35 (3)
Arr. Haparanda	10:20	13:30	15:55
Change buses.			
Dep. Haparanda	11:05 (2)	13:50 (3)	16:05 (2)
Set your watch forward one hour.			
Arr. Kemi	12:50	15:35	17:52
Change to a train. 495			
Dep. Kemi	14:22 (4)	17:23 (5)	20:10 (6)	-0-
Arr. Oulu	15:58	18:45	22:05	-0-
Dep. Oulu	16:03	-0-	22:10	07:15 (7+8)
Arr. Helsinki	22:58	-0-	07:10	13:54

(1) Reservation *required.* Carries a sleeping car. Also has couchettes and a cinema/bistro car. Coach is second-class. (2) Runs daily, except Sun. and holidays. (3) Runs Mon.-Fri., except holidays. (4) Runs daily. Light refreshments. (5) Second-class. (6) Carries a sleeping car. Coach is second-class. Light refreshments. (7) Restaurant car. (8) Plus other Oulu departures at 9:56 (7), 12:52 (7) and 16:03 (4), arriving Helsinki 16.58, 19:58 and 22:58.

SWITZERLAND

Overview
Switzerland is the scenic treasure that it is made out to be, although its people and their traditions are relatively little known outside of the country. Train travel here is easy and predictably efficient, with a range of modern and rather traditional train services available to Eurailpass holders. Switzerland is one country where the train can get you places that the automobile could not.

General Information
• See "Swiss Family Card" for children's free fares.
• The signs you will see at rail stations in Switzerland are those you would see in France, Germany or Italy depending on the section of the country you are in.
• French is the language south and southwest of Bern. Italian is dominant in the southeast corner of Switzerland. Elsewhere, the prevailing language is German.
• There are free timetables distributed at most rail stations.
• Seat reservations are advised for most EuroCity and Intercity trains.
• A traveler with a confirmed flight reservation for a departure from Zurich or Geneva airport can check bags at a special counter in the rail station at nearly 100 Swiss cities.
• Unencumbered with luggage, the passenger using "Fly Luggage Service" rides a train from places such as Bern, Locarno, and Luzern directly to the airport, checks-in at the airport's "Express" counter, boards the airplane and claims the luggage at the end of the flight. The time required for baggage deposit in advance of train departure varies from one Swiss rail station to another. Be sure to obtain that information before departure day. Because of USA security procedures, "Fly Luggage Service" is not available to passengers who are departing on a US airline.

SWITZERLAND'S TRAIN PASSES

These passes are good for unlimited travel on all trains covered by Eurailpass, *plus* many expensive trains that do *not* honor Eurailpass, and on lake steamers and postal buses *not* covered by Eurailpass…plus local subways, buses and trams in 25 major Swiss cities.

Swiss Pass Sold worldwide, including in Switzerland. In addition to the services described above, also provides either free travel or discounts up to 50% on many extremely scenic and very expensive privately-owned mountain railroad and aerial cable car routes that are *not* covered by a Eurailpass. Valid for consecutive days.

The 1996 *first*-class prices for one adult are: $316 for 8 days, $368 for 15 days, and

SWITZERLAND

$508 for one month. *Second*-class: $220, $256 and $350. Children under age 16 with an adult travel free. For two adults traveling together (**"Swiss Pass Companion"**) 1996 *first*-class for 8 days, 15 days, and one month respectively: $237, $276, $381 for each adult.

Swiss Flexipass Allows unlimited travel any 3 days within a 15-day period. Includes everything covered by Swiss Pass. The 1996 prices for one adult are: $264 for *first*-class, $176 for *second*-class. For two adults traveling together, (**"Swiss Couples Flexi Pass"**), 1996 prices are as follows: *first*-class $198, *second*-class $132 each.

Swiss Card A free one-day trip from any entry point (airport or border station) to any single destination in Switzerland and a free one-day trip from any place in Switzerland to any departure point. In addition, the holder can purchase an unlimited number of both roundtrip and one-way tickets for Swiss trains postal buses and lake steamers at 50% discount (25% discount on some mountain railroads). Valid for one month, the 1996 prices are: *first*-class $142, *second*-class $116.

Swiss Rail'N Drive 3 days of unlimited train travel plus 3 days of car rental (any 6 days) within 15 days. Prices vary (a) whether for one person or for 2 persons, (b) time of year, and (c) the category of car. A third and fouth passenger needs to pay only for a 3-day Swiss Flexipass.

The 1996 prices *per person* for 2 persons (using the smallest size car trav eling between May 1-October 31) were: $275 for *first*-class, $205 for *second*-class. More days of car rental could be added at $55 per day. All prices include all of the Swiss government railways, most of the private mountain railroads and aerial cable cars (except some short routes), lake steamers and distance buses, plus ocal buses and trains in 25 major Swiss cities. All prices for Hertz auto rental include Value-added Tax, unlimited mileage, basic liability insurance, and free drop-off in Switzerland.

Swiss Family Card Children under 16 travel free if accompanied by at least one parent and holder of a Swiss Pass, Swiss Flexi Pass or Swiss Card. If the Swiss Family Card is purchased in Switzerland (sold at rail stations), it costs 20 Swiss francs. There is no charge for this card when it is obtained from Rail Europe in conjunction with the purchase of a Swiss train ticket or a Swiss train pass.

Regional Passes Sold only in Switzerland. For details on 8 separate passes, obtain a brochure from Swiss National Tourist Office (U.S.A. and Canadian listed in introductory material).

SWISS HOLIDAYS

A list of holidays is helpful because some trains will be noted later in this section as not running on holidays. Also, those trains which operate on holidays are filled, and it is necessary to make reservations for some Inter-City, Euro City and TGV trains.

January 1	New Year's Day		Ascension Day
January 2			Whit Monday
	Good Friday	December 25	Christmas Day
	Easter Monday	December 26	

ONE-DAY EXCURSIONS AND CITY-SIGHTSEEING

Here are 129 one-day rail trips that can be made comfortably from cities in Switzerland, returning to them in most cases before dinnertime. Notes are provided on what to see at each destination. The number after the name of each route is the Cook's timetable. The 13 base cities are: Basel, Bern, Brig, Chur, Geneva, Interlaken, Lausanne, Locarno, Luzern, St. Moritz, Spiez, Zermatt and Zurich. When no station is designated for cities in Austria, Switzerland and West Germany, the station is "Hauptbahnhof."

Basel (Appears as *Bale* in French timetables)

The superb Picasso, Holbein, Delacroix, Gauguin, Matisse, Ingres, Courbet and Van Gogh paintings in the Kunstmuseum. The Historical Museum in the Franciscan Church in Barfusserplatz. The Municipal Casino. The collection of 18th century clothing, ceramics and watches in the Kirschgarten mansion. Shop on Freiestrasse. See the 16th century Town Hall. The fishmarket. The 15th century New University.

The beautiful Munsterplatz. Fifteenth century tapestries in the 14th century Barfuserkirche. The tombs of Queen Anne and Erasmus of Rotterdam at Munster, the 13th century Cathedral. Nearby, the Folk Art Museum.

The more than 100,000 rarities from every continent (particularly those from New Guinea and the South Seas) in the Ethnological Museum at Augustinerstrasse 2. In the same complex, the extraordinary geological section at the Museum of Natural History.

The Jewish Museum of Switzerland, at Kornhausgasse 18, where Theodore Herzl presided over the first Zionist Congress, in 1897. One of the world's greatest collection of animals, at the Zoo (Binningerstrasse 40), open 08:00–18:30 in Summer, 08:00–17:30 in Winter. Switzerland's largest, it is a short stroll from the SNCF and SBB railstations. Or, take Trolleys #4 and #7 from the stations.

Take a boat excursion from the pier in the back of the Hotel Three Kings. See the view of the city from the Wettstein Bridge.

Bern

The capital of Switzerland. See the comic antics of the denizens of the Bear Pit. How they love figs! The Rose Gardens, north of the Bear Pit. The performance of the 16th century clock tower, the Zytglockenturm, at 11:57. The nearby old arcaded streets. Lunch on the terrace of the Casino restaurant and enjoy the view from there of the River Aare. The Art Museum, with the largest Klee collection in the world.

Climb the 254 steps to the top of one of the towers of the Cathedral for a marvelous view. Play chess with people-size chessmen on the huge slate chessboard near the Cathedral. The elaborate statue honoring the world postal system, without which it would be impossible to have one country handle and deliver to an addressee a mailing for which another country had been paid the postage by the addressor.

One of the world's largest stamp collections, at the Swiss PTT Museum. The view of the Alps from the terrace of the Federal Palace, and the nearby open-air flower and produce market (Tuesday and Saturday mornings). The Swiss Alpine Museum. The Natural History Museum. Prison Tower. Holy Ghost Church. The Botanical Gardens. The many window-boxes with flowering geraniums throughout the streets in the city center.

Geneva

The 6-minute train ride [table 250] *from* the airport to the center of Geneva runs 05:39 to 23:46. From the center of Geneva *to* the airport, it runs 06:14 to 23:12.

Walk from the railstation, down Rue du Mont Blanc, to the shore of Lake Leman. See the enormous Jet d'Eau (water fountain). Walk on the bridge across the lake to the Jardin Anglais. It has a fabulous clock of living flowers and plants and a monument to international Protestantism. It is on that side of the lake you will find the city's old narrow streets and, in St. Peter's Cathedral, the pulpit from which Calvin preached. See the view of Geneva and Lake Leman from the top of the Cathedral's North Tower, a climb of 153 steps.

In modern Geneva: Palais des Nations, today the European headquarters of the United Nations Organization. The chinaware collection in the Ariana Museum, open daily except Monday during Summer. The Far East art (Japanese jade, Chinese porcelain, many pieces from Sri Lanka) at the Baur Collection. The Botanical Garden. The Museum of Historic Musical Instruments, open Tuesday, Thursday and Friday. The Ethnographic Museum, closed Monday.

The Art and History Museum, 2 Rue Charles-Galland (Bus #1 from the railstation) has an archaeological collection, paintings, decorative art and sculptures, open daily except Monday 10:00–17:00. The National History Museum, 11 route de Malagnou (Bus #5 from the railstation), one of the most modern museums in Europe, open Tuesday–Sunday 10:00–12:00 and 14:00–18:00, on Monday 14:00–18:00. Nearby, at 15 route de Malagnou, is the Watch and

The Voltaire Museum, 25 rue des Delices (Bus #6 from the railstation), open Monday-Friday 14:00–17:00. The world-famous Davidoff's Cigar Store at Rue de Rive 2, open Monday-Friday 08:30–18:45 and Saturday 08:00–17:00, where the No. 2 coronas sold for $8.00 (U.S.) each in 1993. Also in stock there: the world's biggest choice of cigars and enormous ebony and mahogany humidors.

Luzern

Walk across the 14th and 15th century bridges spanning the Reuss River and see the 120 paintings on the ceiling of Kappelbrucke depicting Luzern's history and the 45 "Dance of Death" paintings inside the Spreuerbrucke.

See the immense 30-foot high, 42-foot long Lion of Luzern, carved in 1821 into a sandstone cliff which became in 1872 the entrance to the Glacier Gardens outdoor museum. The lion commemorates the bravery of those Swiss soldiers who defended Marie Antoinette during the French Revolution.

You will see at the Glacier Museum, open 08:00–18:00, the absolute proof that palm trees grew here 20,000,000 years ago when this area was tropical. A bank manager, planning to augment his income by turning a meadow into a vineyard, blasted this area so as to make a wine cellar in the rock. A geologist friend spotted a bowl-like recess in the sandstone and convinced the banker to cease the blasting. The 32 round holes found there were made by the erosion from ice-age waterfalls.

The old railway cars, locomotives, trolley cars, buses, autos, many scale models, and the simulated ride in an engine cab at the Swiss National Transport Museum at Lidostrasse 5, largest museum of its kind in Europe. There is also a very interesting model of the Gotthard Tunnel (see "Zurich–Lugano"). The museum is open 09:00–18:00 March-October, 10:00–16:00 November–February. Next door is a Planetarium. Visit the Art Museum, near the railstation. The August Music Festival.

The giant (12,000 square foot) canvas Grand Panorama, depicting the Winter campaign of the 1870–71 Franco-Prussian War.

Zurich

There is 12-minute rail service [Table 310] *from* the airport to Zurich's Hauptbahnhof (Main Railstation) from 06:05 to 23:40. From Zurich's Hauptbahnhof *to* the airport, it runs 07:00 to 23:00. A cruise on Lake Zurich is covered by Eurailpass. Board the boat at the lake end of Bahnhofstrasse.

Here is a great 2-hour walk: Upon arriving at the main Zurich railstation, take the escalator down one level and enjoy a snack or meal in Shopville, the enormous underground shopping center beneath Bahnhof Platz, the square in front of the station. Come up from Shopville on the other side of Bahnhof Platz. Walk one mile down one side of Bahnhofstrasse, lined with smart stores. When this city's Fifth Avenue ends at the shore of Lake Zurich, take in the lakeside promenade before returning to the railstation by walking along the opposite side of Bahnhofstrasse that you walked earlier.

Upon returning to the station, go all the way through it, cross Museumstrasse, and visit the National Museum to see its collection of medieval and Renaissance art, prehistoric artifacts, elaborately carved ancient peasant furniture and much more. Open Tuesday- Friday and Sunday 10:00–12:00 and 14:00–17:00, on Saturday 14:00–16:00.

Other sights: The Bellevue Platz amusement center. The paintings and sculptures at the Kunsthaus. African and Asian art at the Rietberg Museum. Kunstgewerbemuseum (The Museum of Applied Arts): handicrafts, architecture and industrial design. The Zoo. The Botanical Garden. The 5 Chagall stained-glass windows (red, blue and green) in the 13th century Fraumunsterkirche, open Monday–Saturday 10:00–16:00, Sunday 14:00–16:00.

Basel - Baden Baden - Basel   730

Reservation is advisable for all of these trains and all of them have a restaurant car, unless designated otherwise.

Dep. Basel (S.B.B.)	-0-	07:17 (1)	08:17 (1)	08:51 (1)	09:17
Dep. Basel (Bad. Bf.)	06:20	07:58	08:24	08:58	09:24
Arr. Baden-Baden	07:40	09:06	10:02	10:21	10:40

Sights in **Baden-Baden:** Praised for its hot salt springs since the Romans discovered the curative water in this area nearly 2,000 years ago. The illnesses treated here include rheumatism, abnormal blood pressure, metabolic disturbances, respiratory ailments, and problems caused by lack of physical exercise.

Nearly 300 prominent European families once had their permanent homes here. Fantastic landscape. The Oos Valley has been called the most beautiful valley in the world. Exotic trees include the Japanese maple, American tulip, East Asian ginkgo, Chinese trumpet, magnolia and fig. The colors of many deciduous trees make Autumn glorious here.

See the Louis XIII and Louis XIV decor of the halls in the casino. The fancy boutique shops. Exhibitions of international art in the Staatliche Kunsthalle (City Art Gallery).

Motorized vehicles are not permitted in the central area of Baden-Baden. There is a constant schedule of balls, fashion shows and concerts. Food specialties here are Grunkernsuppe (a vegetable soup), game pate, pike dumplings, Blaufelchen (a kind of whitefish, from Lake Constance), raspberry schnapps and kirsch with smoked bacon, bread baked by charcoal, and pate of truffled goose-liver from nearby Strasbourg.

Dep. Baden-Baden	11:11	11:30 (2)	13:11	13:47 (1)	15:11 (3)
Arr. Basel (Bad Bf.)	12:35	13:01	14:35	15:36	16:35
Arr. Basel (S.B.B.)	8 minutes later				

(1) Change trains in Offenburg. (2) Change trains in Offenburg. Light refeshments Offenburg-Basel. (3) Plus other Baden Baden departures at 15:47 (1), 17:30 (1), 19:11, 19:47 (1), 21:11.

Basel - Bern - Basel 280

Reservation is advisable for most of these trains.

Dep. Basel (S.B.B.)	07:01 (1)	07:23 (2)	08:01 (1)	08:11	09:01 (2+3)
Arr. Bern	08:12	08:36	09:12	09:36	10:12

Dep. Bern	11:48 (2)	12:48 (1)	13:48 (2)	14:48 (1)	15:48 (2+4)
Arr. Basel (S.B.B.)	12:59	13:59	14:59	15:59	16:59

(1) Restaurant car. (2) Light refreshments. (3) Plus other departures from Basel at 10:01 (2), 11:01 (1) and 12:01, arriving Bern 11:12, 12:12 and 13:12. (4) Plus other departures from Bern at 16:48 (1), 17:48 (2), 18:48 (1), 19:48, 20:48 (1), 21:48 (2) and 22:45, arriving Basel at 17:59, 18:59, 19:59, 20:59, 21:59, 22:59 and 23:59.

Basel - Interlaken - Basel 280

Reservation is advisable for most of these trains, and most of them have light refreshments, unless designated otherwise.

Dep. Basel (S.B.B.)	07:01 (1)	08:01 (2)	09:01 (3)	10:01	11:01 (1+5)
Arr. Interlaken (West)	09:12	10:12	11:12	12:12	13:12
Arr. Inerlaken (Ost)	5 minutes later				

Sights in **Interlaken**: A fine Summer resort and health spa. Take the funicular to **Heimwehfluh** for a marvelous view of the mountains.

Dep. Interlaken (Ost)	12:39	13:39 (3)	14:39 (3)	15:39 (3)	16:39 (6)
Dep. Interlaken (West)	5 minutes later				
Arr. Basel (S.B.B.)	14:59	15:59	16:59	17:59	18:59

(1) Restaurant car. Change trains in Speiz. (2) Restaurant car. (3) Change trains in Speiz. (4) No light refreshments. (5) Plus another departure from Basel at 12:01 (4), arriving Interlaken (West) 14:12. (6) Plus other departures from Interlaken (Ost) at 17:39 (3), 18:39 (3), 19:39 (2) and 20:40 (3+4), arriving Basel 19:59, 20:59, 21:59 and 22:59.

Basel - Luxembourg - Basel 176

Dep. Basel (SNCF)	08:32 (1)	Dep. Luxembourg	14:59 (2)	18:02	20:43 (3)
Arr. Luxembourg	12:00	Arr. Basel (SNCF)	18:25	21:30	00:35

(1) Restaurant car. (2) Reservation advisable. Supplement charged. Restaurant car. (3) Runs Friday only.

Basel - Luzern - Basel 290

| Dep. Basel (S.B.B.) | 06:00 (1) | 07:07 (2) | 07:51 (1) | 09:07 (3) | 09:51 (1+4) |
| Arr. Luzern | 70 minutes later | | | | |

| Dep. Luzern | 09:56 | 10:56 (1) | 11:56 (2) | 12:56 (1) | 13:46 (3+5) |
| Arr. Basel (S.B.B.) | 70 minutes later (6) | | | | |

(1) Light refreshments. (2) Reservation advisable. Light refreshments. (3) Reservation advisable. Restaurant car. (4) Plus other departures from Basel at 11:07 (3), 11:51 (1) and 13:07 (3). (5) Plus other departures from Luzern at 14:56 (1), 15:46 (3), 15:56, 16:56 (1), 17:46 (3), 17:56, 18:56 (1), 19:46 (3), 19:56, 20:56 (1), 21:46 (2) and 22:46. (6) Supplement charged.

Basel - Rheinfelden - Basel 300

| Dep. Basel (S.B.B.) | Every hour from 07:49 to 22:49 + 23:32. |
| Arr. Rheinfelden | 15 minutes later |

Sights in **Rheinfelden**: This has been a world-famed health spa since 1844. There are tours of the Cardinal and Feldschlosschen breweries. Visit the island park on the Rhine River.

| Dep. Rheinfelden | 07:28 + every hour from 07:58 to 22:58 and 00:36. |
| Arr. Basel (S.B.B.) | 15 minutes later |

Basel - Strasbourg - Basel 176

| Dep. Basel (SNCF) | 07:04 (1) | 08:32 (2) | 09:33 (3) | 11:12 (6) | 12:30 (3) |
| Arr. Strasbourg | 08:41 | 09:54 | 10:50 | 12:36 | 13:48 |

| Dep. Strasbourg | 14:01 (4) | 16:28 (4) | 17:07 (5) | 17:14 (7) | 19:22 (6) |
| Arr. Basel (SNCF) | 15:50 | 18:02 | 18:25 | 18:44 | 20:39 |

(1) Runs Monday-Friday, except Sundays and holidays. (2) Restaurant car. (3) Runs daily, except Sundays and holidays. (4) Change trains in Mulhouse. Runs Monday-Friday, except holidays. (5) Reservation advisable. Supplement charged. Restaurant car. (6) Runs daily, except Saturday. (7) Runs daily except holidays.

Basel - Zurich - Basel   310

Dep. Basel (S.B.B.)	Frequent times from 05:49 to 21:17
Arr. Zurich	60 minutes later

Dep. Zurich	Frequent times from 06:51 to 23:50
Arr. Basel (S.B.B.)	60 minutes later

Bern - Basel - Bern   280

Dep. Bern	Frequent times from 06:48 to 22:51
Arr. Basel (S.B.B.)	70–80 minutes later

Dep. Basel (S.B.B.)	Frequent times from 05:50 to 21:52
Arr. Bern	70–80 minutes later

Bern - Geneva - Bern   260

Dep. Bern	06:10	06:38 (1)	07:18 (2)	08:18 (2)	08:38 (3+4)
Arr. Geneva (Corn.)	08:02	08:34	09:02	10:02	10:34
Dep. Geneva (Corn.)	11:48 (2)	12:48 (2)	13:15 (3)	13:48 (2)	14:48 (2+5)
Arr. Bern	13:42	14:42	15:22	15:42	16:42

(1) Runs daily, except Sundays and holidays. (2) Reservation advisable. Restaurant car. (3) Light refreshments. (4) Plus other Bern departures at frequent times from 09:18 to 23:26. (5) Plus other Geneva departures at frequent times from 15:25 to 21:57.

Bern - Interlaken - Bern   280

Dep. Bern	06:56 (1)	07:28	08:28 (2)	09:28 (3)	10:28 (2+4)
Arr. Interlaken (West)	07:41	08:13	09:13	10:13	11:16
Arr. Interlaken (Ost)	8 minutes later				

Dep. Interlaken (Ost)	Frequent times from 05:31 to 22:32
Dep. Interlaken (West)	4 minutes after departing Ost railstation
Arr. Bern	55 minutes after departing Interlaken (Ost)

(1) Reservation advisable. Light refreshments. (2) Light refreshments. (3) Reservation advisable. Restaurant car. (4) Plus other departures from Bern at frequent times from 11:28 to 22:28.

Bern - Lausanne - Bern   260

Dep. Bern   Frequent departures from 06:10 to 23:26
Arr. Lausanne   70 minutes later

Sights in **Lausanne:** The Cathedral. The Castle of St. Maire. City Hall. The Federal Palace of Justice. There are 13 museums here, including the collection of photographs at Musee Cantonal de l'Elysee (18 Avenue de l'Elysee), and the Pipe Museum (7 Rue de l'Academie).

Dep. Lausanne   Frequent departures from 05:31 to 22:33
Arr. Bern   70 minutes later

Bern - Fribourg - Lausanne - Bern   260

It is possible to stop and sightsee in both Fribourg and Lausanne on the same one-day excursion.

Dep. Bern	08:18	08:38	09:18	10:18	10:38	11:18	12:18
Arr. Fribourg	08:39	08:59	09:39	10:39	11:59	11:39	12:39

Sights in **Fribourg**: The 17th century altar in the Church of the Augustines. Farmers and their wives in traditional local dress, at the Wednesday and Saturday markets. The many stone fountains in the winding streets that lead to the 16th century Town Hall.

Dep. Fribourg	10:41	11:01	11:41	12:41	13:01	13:41	14:41
Arr. Lausanne	12:26	11:50	12:26	13:26	13:50	14:26	15:26

Dep. Lausanne   Frequent times from 05:31 to 22:33
Arr. Bern   70 minutes later

Bern - Fribourg - Bern   260

Here are the schedules for a one-day excursion involving only Fribourg.

Dep. Bern   Frequent times from 06:10 to 23:26
Arr. Fribourg   20 minutes later

Sights in **Fribourg**: See notes in preceding listing.

Dep. Fribourg   Frequent times from 06:18 to 23:20
Arr. Bern   20 minutes later

Bern - Luzern - Bern   265

Outstanding farm and forest scenery as you travel through Switzerland's beautiful Emmental (valley of the Emme River).

All of these trains have light refreshments.

Dep. Bern	06:48	07:31	08:48	09:31	10:48	11:31	12:48 (1)
Arr. Luzern	08:12	08:46	10:12	10:46	12:12	12:46	14:12

Dep. Luzern	11:13	11:56	13:13	13:46	15:13	15:46	17:13 (2)
Arr. Bern	12:24	13:36	14:29	15:12	16:24	17:12	18:24

(1) Plus frequent other Bern departures from 13:31 to 22:45. (2) Plus frequent other Luzern departures from 17:46 to 23:20.

Bern - Langnau - Luzern - Bern   265

It is possible to stop and sightsee in both Langnau and Luzern on the same one-day excursion.

All of these trains have light refreshments, unless designated otherwise.

Dep. Bern	07:31	09:31	11:31	13:31
Arr. Langnau	25 minutes later			

Sights in **Langnau:** The antique household utensils and local industry products (linen-weaving, tanning embroidery) in the museum housed in a 16th century wood building.

Dep. Langnau	10:00	12:00	14:00	16:00	17:00		
Arr. Luzern	10:46	12:46	14:46	16:46	17:46		

Dep. Luzern	13:13	15:13	15:46	17:13	17:46	18:13	19:13 (2)
Arr. Bern	14:24	16:24	17:12	18:24	19:12	19:29	20:24

(1) No light refreshments. (2) Plus other departures from Luzern at 19:46, 21:01, 22:01 (1), 22:46 arriving Bern 21:12, 22:15, 23:15, 00:25.

Bern - Langnau - Bern 265

Here are the schedules for a one-day excursion involving only Langnau.

All of these trains have light refreshments, unless designated otherwise.

| Dep. Bern | 07:31 | 09:31 | 11:31 | 13:31 | | | |
| Arr. Langnau | 30 minutes later | | | | | | |

| Dep. Langnau | 10:01 | 12:01 | 14:01 | 16:01 | 18:01 | 19:01 | 20:01 |
| Arr. Bern | 30 minutes later | | | | | | |

(1) No light refreshments.

Bern - Neuchatel - Bern 255

| Dep. Bern | Frequent time from 06:05 to 23:46 |
| Arr. Neuchatel | 40–60 minutes later |

Sights in **Neuchatel:** The 16th and 17th century houses, fountains and towers. Painted, carved 16th century statues. The exhibit of androids, a seated draftsman, scribe and musician, that have been performing since 1774 and attracting tourists from all over the world since then.

After many years of recommending a visit to the Suchard chocolate factory, we received a letter from the Suchard people telling us it *does not offer tours during July and August* when its employees take vacations and it slows down production during those months. At any time of year, Suchard requires advance notice "of at least a couple of days" before it can provide a factory tour. For chocolate maniacs such as we are, if a tour of Suchard is imperative try phoning them at (038) 21-11-55.

Failing the Suchard tour, see the city's museum of mechanical dolls and music boxes. Take a stroll up winding streets, past elegant Renaissance and 17th century houses, to the hilltop Castle. Visit the Fine Art Museum. Take the funicular to the top (3,839 feet) of Chaumont for a view of the Alps.

Boat rides on the 2 nearby lakes (Biel and Neuchatel) *are* covered by Eurailpass.

Try the great Fondue Neuchatelois, made from white wine and kirsch schnapps. On the first Sunday of October, the local grape harvest is celebrated with a colorful Parade and Battle of Flowers. On this day, wine flows from the city's outdoor fountains instead of water.

| Dep. Neuchatel | Frequent times from 07:02 to 23:10 |
| Arr. Bern | 40–60 minutes later |

Bern - Zurich - Bern   260

Most of these trains have a restaurant car or light refreshments.

Dep. Bern	Frequent times from 04:51 to 23:50
Arr. Zurich	60–90 minutes later

Dep. Zurich	Frequent times from 04:45 to 0:03
Arr. Bern	60–90 minutes later

Chur - Andermatt - Chur   320

Not covered by Eurailpass. The 1995 prices for a roundtrip ticket *without* a Swiss Pass: 109.20 Swiss francs for first-class, Sfr-64.80 for second-class. *With* a Swiss Pass: Free.

Dep. Chur	05:45 (1)	06:48	08:11	09:03 (2)	09:45	10:55 (2)
Arr. Disentis	07:17	08:15	09:32	-0- (2)	11:08	-0- (2)
Change trains.						
Dep. Disentis	07:22	08:22	09:36	-0- (2)	11:35	-0- (2)
Arr. Andermatt	08:29	09:37	10:58	11:34	12:46	13:25

Sights in **Andermatt:** A great ski resort. See the rock crystal altar crucifix and other treasures in the baroque St. Peter and St. Paul Church.

Dep. Andermatt	08:29	10:30	12:00 (2)	12:18	13:34 (2)	14:18 (3)
Arr. Disentis	09:36	11:34	-0- (2)	13:33	-0- (2)	15:26
Change trains.						
Dep. Disentis	09:40	11:40	-0- (2)	13:40	-0- (2)	15:40
Arr. Chur	11:03	13:03	14:18	15:03	16:10	17:03

(1) Runs daily except Sundays and holidays. (2) "Glacier Express." Runs May 29-October 16 only. Reservation required (tel. 081-22-1425), Supplement charged. Direct train to and from Anermatt. No train change in Disentis. Light refreshments. (3) Plus other departures from Andermatt at 16:18(4), and 18:18(4), arriving Chur 19:03, and 21:03. (4) Runs May 14-October 16 only.

Chur - Arosa - Chur   324

These are cogwheel trains that leave from the front of the Chur railstation. A very scenic ride.

Dep. Chur	06:31	08:13	09:00	09:55	10:55	11:55	12:55 (1)
Arr. Arosa	61 minutes later						

Sights in **Arosa**: Great Summer and Winter sports. Fantastic mountain scenery.

Dep. Arosa	07:45	09:05	10:05	11:05	12:05	13:05	14:05 (2)
Arr. Chur	61 minutes later						

(1) Plus other departures from Chur every hour 13:55–17:55, plus 19:07, 19:55, 21:05 and 23:00. (2) Plus other departures from Arosa every hour 15:05–21:05.

Chur - Filisur - St. Moritz - Chur 330

Dep. Chur	06:40	08:08 (1)	09:00 (1)	09:52 (1)	10:52	11:52 (2+3)
Arr. Filisur	08:00	09:15	10:14	11:00 (5)	12:00	13:00 (5)
Arr. St. Moritz	09:00	10:18	11:18	11:58	12:58	13:58

•   •   •

Dep. St. Moritz	10:00 (2)	11:00 (1)	12:00 (1)	13:00 (5)	14:00	15:00 (1+4)
Arr. Filisur	11:02	12:02 (5)	13:02	14:02	15:02	16:02 (5)
Arr. Chur	12:07	13:07	14:07	15:07	16:07	17:07

(1) Light refreshments. (2) Restaurant car. (3) Plus other departures from Chur at 12:52 (1), 13:52, 14:52 (2), 15:52, 16:52, 17:52, 18:52, 19:52 and 20:57. (4) Plus other departures from St. Moritz at 05:45, 07:05, 08:05, 09:00, 16:00 (1), 17:00 (1), 18:00 (2), 19:00 and 20:00 (5) Runs Fridays, Saturdays and Sundays.

Sights in **Filisur:** Near a very high railway bridge, Filisur is located in a narrow valley. The Hotel Grischuna, close to the railstation, has some rooms with a view of the village and the valley. Train fans might prefer other rooms that face the rail line.

It is only a 30-minute walk to the edge of the roaring **Landwasser River**, where you can look up at the trains going over the bridge.

Chur - Zurich - Chur 310

Dep. Chur	06:13 (1)	07:15 (1)	08:23 (2)	09:15 (3)	10:23 (2)	11:15 (3)
Arr. Zurich	07:51	08:50	09:50	10:50	11:50	12:50

Dep. Zurich	11:10 (1)	12:10 (4)	13:10 (3)	14:10 (2)	15:09 (2)	16:10 (4+5)
Arr. Chur	12:45	13:37	14:45	15:37	16:37	17:37

(1) Restaurant car. (2) Reservation advisable. Restaurant car. (3) Light refreshments. (4) Reservation advisable. Light refreshments. (5) Plus other departures from Zurich at 17:10 (3), 18:10 (2), 19:10 (1), 20:10 (3), 21:10 (1) and 22:10.

Geneva - Annecy - Geneva   167

The train changes in La Roche-sur-Foron are easy cross-platform transfers.

Dep. Geneva (Eaux-Vives)	08:27 (6)	11:10 (1)	13:20 (6)
Arr. La Roche-sur-Foron	08:57	11:46 (6)	13:56
Change trains.			
Dep. La Roche-sur-Foron	09:04 (2)	11:57 (2)	14:06 (7)
Arr. Annecy	09:48 (6)	12:30 (6)	14:41

Sights in **Annecy**: Pronounced "Ahn–see." This is a beautiful lake resort. See the 12th century Island Palace. The shops in the old quarter.

Dep. Annecy	11:14 (6)	12:42 (3)	14:48 (6)	16:41 (6)	17:31 (4)
Arr. La Roche-sur-Foron	11:46	13:17 (6)	15:21	17:13	18:13 (6)
Change trains.					
Dep. La Roche-sur-Foron	11:56 (6)	13:21 (3)	15:30	-0-	18:15 (4+5)
Arr. Geneva (Eaux-Vives)	12:36	13:52 (6)	16:03	-0-	19:06

(1) Runs Saturdays, Sundays and holidays. (2) Light refreshments. (3) Runs daily, except Sundays and holidays. (4) Runs Monday-Friday, except holidays. (5) Change trains in Annemasse (arr. 18:36-dep. 18:56). (6) Does not run July 5-29. (7) Does not July 4-28.

Geneva - Basel - Geneva   260

Dep. Geneva (Corn.)	07:38 (1)	08:15 (2)	09:44	10:15 (2)	11:44 (2)
Arr Basel (S.B.B.)	10:37	11:37	12:37	13:37	14:37
Dep. Basel	13:23 (1)	14:23	15:23 (1)	16:23	17:23 (4+6)
Arr. Geneva (Corn.)	16:06	17:34	18:06	19:34	20:06

(1) Reservation advisable. Light refreshments. (2) Light Refreshments. (3) Reservation advisable. (4) Reservation advisable. Restaurant car. (5) Change trains in Biel. (6) Plus other departures from Basel at 18:23, 19:23 (5), 20:23 and 21:23 (5), arriving Geneva 21:34, 22:37, 23:37 and 00:34.

Geneva - Bern - Geneva   260

All of these trains have a restaurant car, unless designated otherwise.

Dep. Geneva (Corn.)	06:25 (1)	06:57 (2)	07:57 (3)	08:57 (3)	09:25 (3+5)
Arr. Bern	08:22	08:42	09:42	10:42	11:22
Dep. Bern	13:18 (3)	14:18 (3)	14:38 (4)	15:18 (3)	16:18 (3+6)
Arr. Geneva (Corn.)	15:02	16:02	16:34	17:02	18:02

(1) No restaurant car or light refreshments. (2) Reservation advisable. (3) Reservation advisable. Restaurant car. (4) Light refreshments. (5) Plus other departures from Geneva at 09:57 (3) and 10:57 (3). (6) Plus other departures from Bern 16:38, 17:18 (3), 18:18 (3), 18:38 (4), 19:18 (3), 20:18 (3), 20:38, 21:18 (3), 22:21 (3) and 23:26.

Geneva - Dijon - Geneva

250

Dep. Geneva (Corn.)	06:38	08:48 (1)	11:48 (1)
Arr. Lausanne	07:27	09:31	12:31

Change trains. 157

Dep. Lausanne	07:31 (2)	10:15 (3)	12:46 (2)
Arr. Dijon	09:42	12:16	14:45

Dep. Dijon	14:00 (2)	17:31 (3)	19:46 (2)
Arr. Lausanne	16:07	19:45	21:57

Change trains. 250

Dep. Lausanne	16:28 (1)	19:55	22:28 (1)
Arr. Geneva	35-50 minutes later		

(1) Reservation advisable. Restaurant car. (2) TGV. Reservation advisable. Restaurant car. (3) TGV. Reservation advisable. Light refreshments. (4) Restaurant car.

Geneva - Grenoble - Geneva   165

Dep. Geneva (Corn.)	09:44	10:34 (2)	11:32 (1)
Arr. Grenoble	11:39	12:47	13:29

Dep. Grenoble	15:07	17:29 (1)	18:25 (2)
Arr. Geneva (Corn.)	17:18	19:28	20:44

(1) Supplement charged. Restaurant car. (2) Operates early July to early September. Light refreshments.

Geneva - Lausanne - Montreux - Geneva   270

As these schedules indicate, a stopover in Lausanne en route to Montreux is possible.

Dep. Geneva (Corn.)	07:38 (1)	08:38 (1)	09:38 (1)	10:38	11:38 (1)	12:38 (1+2)
Arr. Lausanne	08:30	09:30	10:30	11:30	12:30	13:30
Arr. Montreux	23 minutes later					

Sights in **Montreux:** The casino offers gambling, a cabaret and a disco. The 13th century Chillon Castle, about 1½ miles from Montreux, was immortalized by Byron. Its dungeon, used as a model for many movies, is the attraction. Board the bus to Chillon across from the Montreux railstation.

Dep. Montreux	11:07	12:07	13:07 (1)	14:07	15:07 (1)	16:07 (3)
Dep. Lausanne	11:30	12:30	13:30	14:30	15:30	16:30
Arr. Geneva (Corn.)	50 minutes later					

(1) Light refreshments. (2) Plus another departure from Geneva at 13:38. (3) Plus other departures from Montreux at frequent times from 17:07 to 22:07.

Montreux - Gstaad - Zweisimmen - Montreux   275

This is the scenic route of both the "Panoramic Express" and "Crystal Panoramic Express." See details about these special Observation Trains as well as the scenery and interesting places on this line under "Geneva–Montreux–Zweisimmen – Geneva"

Reservations for "Crystal Panoramic Express" are accepted only for groups, but individuals may ride if there are any vacant seats.

Dep. Montreux	09:00 (1)	08:54	10:00 (2)	11:00	12:21 (3)
Dep. Gstaad	10:11	10:30	11:18	12:30	13:42
Arr. Zweisimmen	10:36	11:00	11:45	13:00	14:10

Sight in **Gstaad:** A *very* expensive ski village.

Dep. Zweisimmen	10:43 (1)	10:50	12:00	12:50	14:00 (4)
Dep. Gstaad	11:14	11:20	12:32	13:20	14:32
Arr. Montreux	12:30	12:38	14:00	14:38	16:00

(1) Reservation required. Supplement charged. "Crystal Panoramic Express." First-class only. Runs Saturdays, Sundays and holidays. (2) Reservation required for first-class, advisable for second-class. Supplement charged. "Panoramic Express." Runs daily. (3) Plus other Montreux departures at 14:00 (1), 14:21 (2) and 15:00. (4) Plus other Zweisimmen departures at 14:50 (2), 16:00, 16:50, 17:15 (1), 18:00 and 20:00, arriving Montreux at 16:38, 18:00, 18:38, 19:00, 20:00 and 22:00.

Geneva - Lyon - Geneva   159

The first 90 minutes from Geneva is noted for scenic canyons. Occasionally, 2 trains depart from the same track at Lyon's Perrache railstation, heading in opposite directions. Be sure to stand at the correct end (North or South) of the track in order to board the train you want to ride. Check the departure signs at the underground passageway. Do not rely merely on a track number when departing from Perrache railstation!

Next to the North passageway of Track "A" is a take-out restaurant, handy for provisioning your trip.

Dep. Geneva (Corn.)	07:04	10:22	12:54
Arr. Lyon (Part-Dieu)	08:53	12:12	14:46
Arr. Lyon (Per.)	9 minutes later		

Dep. Lyon (Per.)	12:13 (1)	17:10	19:21
Dep. Lyon (Part-Dieu)	9 minutes later		
Arr. Geneva (Corn.)	14:16	19:08	21:29

(1) Light refreshments.

Geneva - Neuchatel - Geneva 260

Dep. Geneva (Corn.)	07:54 (1)	08:54 (1)	09:54	10:54 (1)	11:54 (1+6)
Arr. Neuchatel	09:04	10:04	11:04	12:04	13:04

Sights in **Neuchatel:** See notes under "Bern–Neuchatel"

Dep. Neuchatel	12:55 (1)	13:01 (3)	13:55 (4)	14:55 (1)	15:55 (4+7)
Arr. Geneva (Corn.)	14:06	14:34	15:06	16:06	17:06

(1) Reservtion advisable. Light refreshments. (2) Reservtion advisable. (3) Change trains in Lausanne. (4) Reservtion advisable. Restaurant car. (5) Restaurant car. (6) Plus another departure from Geneva at 12:54(4). (7) Plus other departures from Neuchatel at 16:01,16:55 (1), 17:55 (1), 18:55 (4), 19:01 (3), 19:55 (1), 20:01, 21:01 (5), 22:01 and 23:01 (1).

Geneva - Zurich - Geneva 260

Reservation is advisable for all of these trains and all of them have a restaurant car or light refreshments.

Dep. Geneva (Cor.)	Frequent times from 04:49 to 21:57
Arr. Zurich	3 hours later

Dep. Zurich (Hbf.)	Every hour from 06:00 to 21:06
Arr. Geneva (Cor.)	3 hours later

Interlaken - Bern - Interlaken   280

Dep. Interlaken (Ost)	Every hour from 05:31 to 22:32
Dep. Interlaken (West)	5 minutes after departing Ost railstation
Arr. Bern	53 minutes after departing Interlaken (Ost)

Dep. Bern	Every hour from 06:56 to 23:28
Arr. Interlaken (West)	48 minutes after departing Bern
Arr. Interlaken (Ost)	5 minutes later

Interlaken - Lausanne - Interlaken

280

Dep. Interlaken (Ost)	07:11 (1)	07:39 (2)	08:11 (3)	08:39 (3)	09:39 (1)
Dep. Interlaken (West)	5 minutes later				
Arr. Bern	08:04	08:32	09:04	09:32	10:32
Change trains. 260					
Dep. Bern	08:18 (1)	08:38 (2)	09:18 (1)	10:18 (1)	10:38 (2)
Arr. Lausanne	09:26	09:50	10:26	11:26	11:50
Dep. Lausanne	12:33 (1)	13:33 (1)	14:10 (2)	14:33 (1)	15:33 (1+5)
Arr. Bern	13:42	14:42	15:22	15:42	16:42
Change trains. 280					
Dep. Bern	13:56 (4)	15:28 (2)	-0-	16:28 (2)	17:28 (1)
Arr. Interlaken (West)	14:44	16:16	-0-	17:16	18:16
Arr. Interlaken (Ost)	5 minutes later				

(1) Reservation advisable. Restaurant car. (2) Light refreshments. (3) Reservation advisable. Light refreshments. (4) Reservation advisable. (5) Plus other Lausanne departures at 16:10 (2), 16:33 (1), 17:10 (2), 17:33 (1), 19:10 and 21:10, arriving Interlaken (West) 18:16, 19:00, 19:16, 20:21, 21:23 and 23:23.

Interlaken - Murren - Jungfraujoch - Interlaken

This one-day trip covers the heart of the Bernese Oberland area. *It is not covered by Eurailpass.* The 1995 total price of tickets *without* a Swiss Pass: 170.80 Swiss francs for first-class, and Sfr-161.40 for second-class. *With* a Swiss Pass: Sfr-95.10.

All of the train changes shown here take less than one minute.

Hiking and trout fishing are Summer activities in **Murren**. Both it and **Wengen** are postcard Alpine villages. There have been top ski resorts in this area since 1906. **Jungfraujoch** is the highest (11,333 feet) railstation in Europe. From there, you can see the Jungfrau, Eiger and Monch peaks. The highest waterfall in Europe (2,000-foot drop) is spectacular there in late Spring and early Summer.

287

Dep. Interlaken (Ost)	08:32 (1)	Dep. Scheidegg	11:30 (3)
Arr. Lauterbrunnen	08:54	Arr. Jungfraujoch	12:22
Change to funicular. 289		*Change trains*	
Dep. Lauterbrunnen	09:02	Dep. Jungfraujoch	12:30 (2)
Arr. Murren	09:32	Arr. Scheidegg	13:21
Return to Lauterbrunnen.		*Change trains. 288*	
Dep. Murren	09:45	Dep. Scheidegg	14:00
Arr. Lauterbrunnen	10:15	Arr. Grindelwald	14:45
Change to a train. 287		*Change trains. 288*	
Dep. Lauterbrunnen	10:35	Dep Grindelwald	14:50
Dep. Wengen	10:55	Arr. Interlaken (Ost)	15:27
Arr. Scheidegg	11:20 (3)		
Change trains.			

(1) Plus other circle trips departing Interlaken at 09:02(3), 10:02(3), 10:32(3), 11:02, 11:32 and 12:32, arriving back in Interlaken at 15:57, 16:27, 17:57, 18:27 and 19:27. (2) Plus other departures from Jungfraujoch (via Grindelwald) at 13:00, 14:00, 14:30, 15:30, 16:00, 17:00 and 18:00, arriving Interlaken (Ost) at 15:57, 16:27, 16:57, 17:57, 18:27, 19:27 and 20:27. (3) Does not run May 29-June 23.

Interlaken - Luzern - Interlaken   285

There is a very scenic 48-mile panorama of the Alps on this trip along the shore of Lake Brienz.

Dep. Interlaken (Ost)	06:32	07:37	08:44	09:37	10:44 (1)
Arr. Luzern	08:36	09:36	10:36	11:36	12:36
Dep. Luzern	11:24	12:24 (2)	13:24 (1)	14:24 (2)	15:24 (2+3)
Arr. Interlaken (Ost)	13:16	14:23	15:16	16:23	17:16

(1) Restaurant car. (2) Light refreshments. (3) Plus other departures from Luzern at 16:24, 17:24, 18:24, 19:09 and 20:09, arriving Interlaken 18:23, 19:20, 20:23, 21:25 and 22:25.

Lausanne - Sion - Lausanne   270

Dep. Lausanne	08:09(1)	08:32 (2)	09:00 (2)	09:32 (2)	09:56 (2)	10:32 (4)
Arr. Sion	09:02	09:40	10:08	10:41	11:04	11:41

Sights in **Sion**: Ruins of the 13th century Valere Castle and the 4th–11th century religious art in the museum there. The world's oldest operable pipe organ (built in 1390), carved and painted wood chests and 15th century frescoes in the Church of Our Lady of Valere, open daily except Monday, 9:00–12:00 and 14:00–18:00.

The collection of Roman antiquities in the Cantonal Archaeological Museum on rue des Chateaux. Paintings by artists of this area in the Majorie Fine Arts Museum. Both museums are open daily except Monday 9:00–12:00 and 14:00–18:00.

The astronomical clock and carved doors of the 17th century City Hall. The ancient Tour de Sorciers (Tower of the Wizards). The 9th century Romanesque bell-tower of the Cathedral. Supersaxo, the 16th century mansion of a Renaissance nobleman.

Dep. Sion	13:23	14:17	15:17	15:52	16:17 (2+5)
Arr. Lausanne	14:27	15:27	16:27	17:03	17:27

(1) Reservation advisable. Light refreshments. (2) Light refreshments. (3) Reservation advisable. Restaurant car. (4) Plus other departures from Lausanne at 11:13 (3), 11:32, 11:56 (2) and 12:32 (2). (5) Plus other departures from Sion at frequent times from 16:45 to 22:03.

Luzern - Andermatt - Luzern

The Goschenen-Andermatt-Goschenen portion of this one-day excursion (a thrilling ride in the Schollenen Canyon) is by rack railway and is *not* covered by Eurailpass. The 1994 price of a roundtrip ticket *without* a Swiss Pass: 20.80 Swiss francs for first-class, Sfr-12.40 for second class. *With* a Swiss Pass: free.

290

Dep. Luzern	08:14 (1)	10:19 (1)	12:19 (2)	13:14 (3)
Arr. Goschenen	09:45	11:45	13:45	14:45
Change trains. 320				
Dep. Goschenen	09:55	11:55	13:55	15:55
Arr. Andermatt	10:06	12:06	14:06	16:06

Sights in **Andermatt**: A great ski resort.

Dep. Andermatt	12:50	16:50 (4)	18:50
Arr. Goschenen	13:05	17:05	19:05
Change trains. 290			
Dep. Goschenen	13:13 (3)	17:13 (5)	19:13
Arr. Luzern	14:46	18:46	20:46

(1) Reservation advisable. Light refreshments. Change trains in Arth-Goldau. (2) Reservation advisable. Restaurant car. Change trains in Arth Goldau. Supplement charged. (3) Light refreshments. (4) Operates late May to late October. (5) Light refreshments. Change trains in Arth Goldau.

Luzern - Basel - Luzern 290

Dep. Luzern	06:35 (1)	07:56 (1)	08:56	09:56	10:56 (1)
Arr. Basel (S.B.B.)	07:49	09:09	10:09	11:09	12:09

Dep. Basel (S.B.B.)	11:07 (2)	11:51 (1)	13:07 (2)	13:51 (1)	15:07 (2+3)
Arr. Luzern	12:12	13:04	14:12	15:04	16:12

(1) Light refreshments. (2) Reservation advisable. Supplement charged. Restaurant car. (3) Plus other departures from Basel at frequent times from 15:51 to 23:02.

Luzern - Bern - Luzern 265

Most of these trains have light refreshments.

Dep. Luzern	06:35	07:13 (1)	07:56		08:13 (2)	08:46	09:13 (1)	09:56
Arr. Olten	07:15	-0- (1)	08:37		-0- (2)	09:25	-0- (1)	10:37
Change trains.								
Dep. Olten	07:29	-0-	08:48		-0-	09:29	-0-	10:48
Arr. Bern	08:12	08:27	09:36	09:29		10:12	10:27	11:36

Dep. Bern	13:31 (1)	14:48		15:31 (1)	16:31 (1)	16:51	18:31 (1+3)
Arr. Olten	-0- (1)	15:30		-0- (1)	-0- (1)	17:39	-0- (1)
Change trains.							
Dep. Olten	-0-	15:35	-0-		-0-	17:49	-0-
Arr. Luzern	14:46	16:12	16:46		17:46	18:27	19:46

(1) Direct train. No train change in Olten. (2) Direct train. No train change in Olten. Runs Saturdays, Sundays and holidays. (3) Plus other departures from Bern at 18:51, 19:31 (1), 19:51 (1), 20:51, 21:48 (1), 22:21 (1) and 22:45, arriving Luzern 20:27, 20:46, 21:41, 22:52, 22:59, 23:57 and 00:16.

Luzern - Interlaken - Luzern 285

Dep. Luzern	06:03 (1)	07:24 (2)	08:24 (3)	09:24 (2)	10:24 (4)
Arr. Interlaken (Ost)	08:23	09:16 (6)	10:23	11:16	12:23

Dep. Interlaken (Ost)	10:44 (3)	11:37	12:44 (2)	13:37	14:44 (5)
Arr. Luzern	12:36	13:36	14:36	15:36	16:36

(1) Runs daily, except holidays. (2) Light refreshments. (3) Restaurant car. (4) Plus other departures from Luzern at frequent times from 11:24 to 20:09. (5) Plus other departures from Interlaken at frequent times from 15:37 to 20:37. (6) Reservation recommended.

Luzern - Neuchatel - Luzern

265

| Dep. Luzern | 06:35 (1) | 07:13 (2) | 08:46 (1) | 09:13 (2) | 09:56 (1) | 11:56 (1) |
| Arr. Bern | 08:12 | 08:27 | 10:12 | 10:27 | 11:36 | 13:36 |

Change trains. 255

| Dep. Bern | 08:22 | 09:22 | 10:22 | 11:22 | 12:22 | 14:22 |
| Arr. Neuchatel | 08:57 | 09:57 | 10:57 | 11:57 | 12:57 | 14:57 |

| Dep. Neuchatel | 14:02 | 15:02 | 16:02 | 17:02 | 18:02 | 19:02 (3) |
| Arr. Bern | 14:38 | 15:38 | 16:38 | 17:38 | 18:38 | 19:38 |

Change trains. 265

| Dep. Bern | 14:48 (1) | 16:31 (2) | 16:51 | 18:31 (1) | 18:51 (2) | 19:51 (1) |
| Arr. Luzern | 16:12 | 17:46 | 18:27 | 19:46 | 20:27 | 21:41 |

(1) Change trains in Olten. Light refreshments. (2) Light refreshments. (3) Plus other departures from Neuchatel at 21:08 and 22:06, arriving Luzern 23:57 and 00:16.

Luzern - Schwyz - Luzern   290

| Dep. Luzern | 08:14 (1) | 09:14 (2) | 10:19 (3) | 11:14 (2) | 12:19 (3) | 13:14 (2) |
| Arr. Schwyz | 50 minutes later | | | | | |

Sights in **Schwyz:** Visit the Staatsarcivmuseum (National Archive Museum), to see the 13th century Oath of Eternal Alliance, the document which marks the founding of Switzerland. This village's name became the name of the country (Schweiz). The Museum is one mile (uphill) from the railstation. A bus meets every train. There are also nicely restored 17th and 18th century patrician homes here.

| Dep. Schwyz | 12:01 (2) | 13:01 (4) | 14:01 (1) | 15:01 (4) | 16:01 (2) | 17:01 (4+5) |
| Arr. Luzern | 50 minutes later | | | | | |

(1) Change trains in Arth Goldau. (2) Light refreshments. (3) Reservation advisable. Restaurant car. Change trains in Arth Goldau. (4) Light refreshments. Change trains in Arth Goldau. (5) Plus other departures from Schwyz at 18:01 (2), 19:01 (4), 20:01 (4), 22:01 and 22:55.

Luzern - Zurich - Luzern   295

Most of these trains have light refreshments.

Dep. Luzern	Frequent times from 06:04 to 23:08
Arr. Zurich	50 minutes later
Dep. Zurich	Frequent times from 07:07 to 00:13
Arr. Luzern	50 minutes later

Zurich - Andermatt - Zurich

The Goschenen–Andermatt–Goschenen portion of this one-day excursion (a thrilling ride down the **Schollenen Canyon**) is by rack railway and is not covered by Eurailpass. The 1995 prices of a roundtrip ticket without a Swiss Pass were: 20.80 Swiss francs for first-class, Sfr-12.40 for second-class. *With* a Swiss Pass: free.

*All of the trains **Zurich–Gochenen** and vice-versa, have light refreshments, unless designated otherwise.*

290
Dep. Zurich	08:03 (1)	10:03 (2)	12:03 (3)
Arr. Goschenen	09:45	11:45	13:47
Change trains. 320			
Dep. Goschenen	09:55	11:55	13:55
Arrr. Andermatt	10 minutes later		

Sights in **Andermatt**: A great ski resort.

Dep. Andermatt	11:27	12:50	16:50 (4)	18:50
Arr. Goschenen	11:42	13:05	17:05	19:05
Change trains. 290				
Dep. Goschenen	12:13	13:13 (2)	17:13 (2)	19:13 (2)
Arr. Zurich	13:57	14:57	18:57	20:57

(1) Reservation advisable. Restaurant car. Change trains in Arth Goldau. (2) Light refreshments. Change trains in Arth Goldau. (3) Light refreshments. (4) Runs May 14-October 16 only.

Zurich - Arosa - Zurich

310

Dep. Zurich	06:33 (1)	07:33 (2)	08:10 (3)	09:10 (1)	10:10 (3)	11:10 (4)
Arr. Chur	08:03	08:51	09:37	10:45	11:37	12:45

Change trains. 324

The Chur–Arosa cogwheel train leaves from the front of the Chur railstation. This is a very scenic ride.

Dep. Chur	08:13	09:00	09:55	10:55	11:55	12:55
Arr. Arosa	one hour later

Sights in **Arosa**: Great Summer and Winter sports. Fantastic mountain scenery.

Dep. Arosa	10:05	11:05	12:05	13:05	14:05	15:05 (5)
Arr. Chur	11:07	12:07	13:07	14:07	15:07	16:07

Change trains. 310

Dep. Chur	11:15 (1)	12:23 (3)	13:15 (4)	14:23 (3)	15:15 (1)	16:23 (2)
Arr. Zurich	12:50	13:50	14:50	15:50	16:50	17:50

(1) Light refreshments. (2) Reservation advisable. Restaurant car. (3) Reservation advisable. Light refreshments. (4) Restaurant car. (5) Plus other departures from Arosa (parenthesis designate Chur–Arosa service) at 16:05 (1), 17:05 (3), 18:05 (1), 19:05 (4) and 20:05, arriving Zurich 18:50, 19:50, 20:50, 21:50 and 22:50.

Zurich - Basel - Zurich   300

Many of these trains have a restaurant car or light refreshments.

Dep. Zurich	Frequent times from 06:30 to 23:37
Arr. Basel (S.B.B.)	60–70 minutes later

Dep. Basel (S.B.B.)	Frequent times from 05:23 to 23:32
Arr. Zurich	60–70 minutes later

Zurich - Bern - Zurich   260

Many of these trains have a restaurant car or light refreshments.

Dep. Zurich	Frequent times from 06:00 to 00:03
Arr. Bern	90 minutes later

Dep. Bern	Frequent times from 04:51 to 23:50
Arr. Zurich	90 minutes later

Zurich - Chur - Zurich   310

Many of these trains have a restaurant car or light refreshments.

Dep. Zurich	Frequent times from 06:33 to 22:10
Arr. Chur	90 minutes later

Sights in **Chur:** This 2100-year old village is located at what has been a strategic pass in the Alps since Roman times. Walk from the station up through the small business area to a hilltop church and see the unusual cemetery there. The modern portion of it has rows of graves that are solidly decorated with living, blossoming plants.

Also see the fine stained-glass and the 12th century carved altar in the 15th century Cathedral. The Bishop's Palace. A one-hour walking tour of Chur is made easy by following red and green footprints painted on the sidewalks. The footprints are matched to a map available at the city's tourist office.

Dep. Chur	Frequent times from 06:13 to 21:13
Arr. Zurich	90 minutes later

Zurich - Landquart - Davos - Zurich

310

Dep. Zurich	07:33 (1)	08:10 (2)	09:10 (3)	10:10 (2)	11:10 (4)
Arr. Landquart	08:36	09:23	10:31	11:23	12:31
Change trains. 327					
Dep. Landquart	08:56	09:40	10:40	11:40	12:40
Arr. Klosters	09:34	10:18	11:18	12:18	13:18
Arr. Davos (Platz)	28 minutes after arriving Klosters.				

Sights in **Davos**: One of the world's most popular ski resorts. Also popular for its skating rinks, hiking trails, a sled run, horse-drawn sleigh rides, indoor swimming, hang-gliding, horseback riding and ice hockey.

Take the 22-minute ride on the Parsenn cable railway, once described by Vogue Magazine as "the Rolls Royce of mountain railways," to the ridge of **Weissfluh**. A cable car ascends from there to the summit, the start of the different ski runs to **Serneus**, **Sass** and **Klosters**.

A general-fare ticket (Sfr-280 for adults, Sfr-173 for children in 1994) allows unlimited use of the entire network of funicular railways, ski lifts and cable cars for 6 days. It also covers the buses that run every 15 minutes from one end of Davos to the other.

Dep. Davos (Platz)	12:05	13:05	14:05	15:05	16:05 (5)
Dep. Klosters	29 minutes after departing Davos				
Arr. Landquart	13:17	14:17	15:17	16:17	17:17
Change trains. 310					
Dep. Landquart	13:26 (4)	14:34 (2)	15:26 (3)	16:34 (1)	17:26 (3)
Arr. Zurich	14:50	15:50	16:50	17:50	18:50

(1) Reservation advisable. Restaurant car. (2) Reservation advisable. Light refreshments. (3) Light refreshments. (4) Restaurant car. (5) Plus other departures from Davos (parenthesis designate Landquart–Zurich service) at 17:05, 18:05, 19:05, 20:00 and 21:00, arriving Zurich 19:50, 20:50, 21:50, 22:50 and 23:50.

Zurich - Frankfurt - Zurich   77

Both of these trains charge a supplement that includes reservation fee and have a restaurant car.

Dep. Zurich	06:45	08:00 (1)	Dep. Frankfurt	16:09	16:43 (2)	17:43 (2+3)
Arr. Frankfurt	10:47	12:14	Arr. Zurich	20:15	21:00	22:00

(1) Change trains in Basel and Mannheim. (2) Change trains in Mannheim and Basel. (3) Plus another Zurich departure at 18:43 (2).

Zurich - Geneva - Zurich   260

Most of these trains have a restaurant car or light refreshments. Reservation is advisable

Dep. Zurich	Frequent times from 06:00 to 21:06
Arr. Geneva (Corn.)	3 hours later
Dep. Geneva (Corn.)	Frequent times from 04:49 to 21:57
Arr Zurich	3 hours later

Zurich - Interlaken - Zurich 280

All of these trains have light refreshments, unless designated otherwise.

Dep. Zurich	06:25	07:30 (1)	08:30	09:30 (1)	10:30	11:30 (1)
Arr. Interlaken (Ost)	09:21	10:21	11:21	12:21	13:21	14:21

Sights in **Interlaken**: See notes about sightseeing in Interlaken under "Basel–Interlaken"

Dep. Interlaken (Ost)	13:39	14:39	15:39	16:39 (2)	17:39	18:39 (4)
Arr. Zurich	16:30	17:30	18:30	19:30	20:30	21:30

(1) Change trains in Spiez. (2) Reservation advisable. Change trains in Olten. (3) Reservation advisable. Restaurant car. Change trains in Olten. (4) Plus another departure from Interlaken at 19:39 (3). Restaurant car to Olten, arriving Olten 21:30, depart Olten 21:42, arriving Zurich 22:31.

Zurich - Lugano - Zurich 290

Dep. Zurich	06:30 (1)	07:03 (2)	08:03 (2)	09:03 (2)	10:03 (3)	11:03 (2)
Arr. Lugano	09:45	10:04	11:04	12:04	13:04	14:04

Dep. Lugano	12:41 (1)	13:57 (4)	14:41 (1)	15:57 (2)	16:33 (2)	17:57 (2+6)
Arr. Zurich	15:57	16:57	17:57	18:57	19:28	20:57

(1) Light refreshments. (2) Reservation advisable. Supplement charged. Restaurant car. (3) Change trains in Arth Goldau at 10:45 (2). (4) Reservation advisable. Light refreshments. (5) Runs daily, except holidays. Light refreshments. (6) Plus other Lugano departures at 18:47 (2), 19:41 (5) arriving Zurich, 21:48 and 23:15.

Zurich - Luzern - Zurich 295

Most of these trains have light refreshments.

Dep. Zurich	Frequent times from 07:07 to 00:13
Arr. Luzern	50 minutes later

Dep. Luzern	Frequent times from 06:04 to 23:08
Arr. Zurich	50 minutes later

Zurich - Milan - Zurich   290

See the description of this very scenic trip under either "Zurich–Bellinzona–Lugano"

Reservation is advisable for all of these trains, and all of them have a restaurant car.

Dep. Zurich	07:03	08:03 (1)	Dep. Milan (Cen.)	16:25	17:20(1)
Arr. Milan (Cen.)	11:35	12:35	Arr. Zurich	20:57	21:50

(1) Supplement charged.

Zurich - Munich - Zurich   75

Reservation is advisable for all of these trains, and all of them have a restaurant car.

Dep. Zurich	07:40 (1)	09:40 (1)	Dep. Munich	14:02 (1)	18:37 (1)
Arr. Munich	11:51	13:56	Arr. Zurich	18:23	22:56

(1) Supplement payable.

Zurich - Neuchatel - Zurich   260

Dep. Zurich	07:06 (1)	08:06 (2)	09:06 (1)	10:06 (2)	11:06 (4)
Arr. Neuchatel	08:59	09:53	10:59	11:53	12:59
Dep. Neuchatel	12:06 (3)	13:01 (1)	14:06 (2)	15:01 (1)	16:06 (3+5)
Arr. Zurich	13:53	14:53	15:53	16:53	17:53

(1) Light refreshments. (2) Reservation advisable. Restaurant car. (3) Reservation advisable. Light refreshments. (4) Plus another Zurich departure at 12:06 (2), arriving Neuchatel 13:55. (5) Plus other Neuchatel departures at 17:01 (1), 18:06 (2), 19:01 (1), 20:06 (2) and 21:01 (1), arriving Zurich 18:53, 19:53, 20:53, 21:53 and 22:53.

Zurich - Rheinfelden - Zurich   300

Dep. Zurich	06:30 (1)	07:00	08:00 (2)	09:00 (2)	10:00 (3+7)
Dep. Brugg	06:57	07:25	08:25	09:25	10:31
Arr. Rheinfelden	07:26	07:56	08:56	09:58	11:08

Sights in **Rheinfelden**: A world-famed health spa since 1844. There are tours of the Cardinal and Feldschlosschen breweries. Visit the island park on the Rhine River.

Dep. Rheinfelden   13:01 (4)   13:50 (5)   15:01 (6)   16:01 (1)   17:01 (1+8)
Arr. Zurich   65 minutes later

(1) Light refreshments. (2) Restaurant car. (3) Reservation advisable. Restaurant car. Change trains in Brugg. (4) Reservation advisable. Restaurant car. (5) Change tains in Brugg. (6) Reservation advisable. Light refreshments. (7) Plus other departures from Zurich at 11:00 (1), 13:00 (1) and 14:00 (6). (8) Plus other departures from Rheinfelden at 18:00 (2), 19:01 (1), 20:01 (2), 21:01 (1), 22:02 (1), 23:05 and 23:45.

Zurich - St. Moritz - Zurich

310

Dep. Zurich	07:33 (1)	08:10 (1)
Arr. Chur	08:51	09:37

Change trains. 330

Dep. Chur	09:00 (2)	09:52 (2+6)
Arr. St. Moritz	11:18	11:58

330

Dep. St. Moritz	12:00 (2)	13:00 (5)
Arr. Chur	14:07	15:07 (6)

Change trains. 310

Dep. Chur	14:23 (3)	15:15 (2)
Arr. Zurich	15:50	16:50

(1) Reservation advisble. Restaurant car. (2) Light refreshments. (3) Reservation advisable. Light refreshments. (4) Restaurant car. (5) Plus other departures from St. Moritz at 14:00, 15:00 (2+6), 16:00 (2), 17:00 (2), 18:00 (4), 19:00 and 20:00...departing Chur 16:23 (1), 17:15 (2), 18:23 (3), 19:15 (2), 20:13 (4), 21:13 and 22:13...arriving Zurich 17:50, 18:50, 19:50, 20:50, 21:50, 22:50 and 23:50. (6) Runs Saturdays, Sundays and holidays.

Sights in **St. Moritz:** The lovely scenery of the Alps, reflected on the Lake of St. Moritz. The curative waters. Great Summer sports (swimming, sailing, fishing, golf, mountain climbing) as well as Winter sports. The creme de la creme of the international jet set is here December to April.

See the collection of porcelain stoves, furniture and carved woodwork in the Engadine Museum, open Monday–Saturday 09:30–12:00 and 14:00–17:00, also on Sunday 10:00–12:00. Many paintings of this beautiful area by Giovanni Segantini in the Segantini Museum, open Monday–Saturday 09:30–12:00 and 14:00–16:00, on Sunday 14:30–16:00.

Zurich - Schwyz - Zurich   290

Dep. Zurich	07:30	08:03(3)	09:03(3)	10:03(4)	11:03(3)	12:03(6)
Arr. Schwyz	one hour later					

Dep. Schwyz	11:01	12:01(5)	13:01	14:01(5)	15:01(6)	16:01(5)	17:01(6+7)
Arr. Zurich	one hour later						

(1) Operates early April to late October. Light refreshments. (2) Change trains in Arth Goldau. (3) Reservation advisable. Restaurant car. Change trains in Arth Goldau. Supplement charged. (4) Light refreshments. Change trains in Arth Goldau. (5) Change in Arth Goldau to a train for which reservation is advisable. (6) Light refreshments. (7) Plus other departures from Schwyz at 17:36 (6), 18:01 (5) and 19:01 (6) .

Zurich - Solothurn - Zurich   260

All of these trains have a restaurant car or light refreshments.

Dep. Zurich	Frequent times from 06:06 to 23:03
Arr. Solothurn	60 minutes later

Sights in **Solothurn**: Switzerland's oldest town. (It and Trier, in Germany, are the 2 oldest towns north of the Alps.) This is the best preserved Baroque town in Switzerland, located in the **Aare Valley**, at the foot of the **Jura Mountains**. Everything worth seeing here can be reached by walking the town's narrow streets: the town's many fine statues, 11 churches and chapels, 11 ornamental fountains...and the 11 steps leading to the entrance of the Cathedral of St. Ours which has 11 bells, 11 towers and 11 altars.

Solothurn became in 1481 the *eleventh* canton to join the Swiss Federation!

See the outstanding ancient art here. Holbein's Madonna in the Museum. Traces of the 4th century Roman wall. Farmers selling flowers, fruits and vegetables in the town center every Wednesday and Saturday. The marvelous Assumption over the high altar in the Jesuit church.

The bulb domes on the twin towers of the Town Hall. The comprehensive collection of arms and armor in the Old Arsenal Museum, said to be the second largest collection of weapons in Europe. It has 400 suits of armor among its exhibits. The Italian belltower of the Cathedral.

Dep. Solothurn	Frequent times from 05:41 to 22:56
Arr. Zurich	60 minutes later

Zurich - Stuttgart - Zurich   74

Dep. Zurich	06:30 (1)	07:13	09:13		
Arr. Stuttgart	09:13 (2)	10:22	12:22		
Dep. Stuttgart	13:42	15:42	16:52 (1+2)	17:42	19:42 (3)
Arr. Zurich	16:47	18:47	19:50	20:49	22:47

(1) Reservation advisable. Supplement charged. Restaurant car. (2) Runs Monday-Friday. (3) Runs Friday only July 1-August 26.

Zurich - Winterthur - Zurich 308

Dep. Zurich   Frequent times from 06:39 to 23:15
Arr. Winterthur   22 minutes later

Sights in **Winterthur**: More art treasures than any other place in Switzerland, at the country's National Gallery in the Am Roemerholz mansion. Great Austrian, German and Swiss paintings.

Dep. Winterthur   Frequent times from 06:27 to 23:27
Arr. Zurich   22 minutes later

Zurich - Zug - Zurich 295

Dep. Zurich   Frequent times from 07:07 to 00:13
Arr. Zug   26 minutes later

Sights in **Zug**: This village is located on the northeast shore of the 14-mile long Lake Zug. See the spires and massive towers of the 15th century Church of St. Oswald. The stained-glass for which this area is noted and also gold and silver work, embroidery and wood carvings in the Museum at the 16th century Town Hall.

See the narrow, ancient houses (most of them with overlapping second and upper floors) on Ober-Alstadt and Unter-Alstadt. The elaborately-carved choir stalls in the 15th century St. Oswald's Church.

To reach the top floor of the 3,255-foot-high **Zugerberg**, either take the 20-minute bus ride from the railstation to the **Schoenegg** suburb and then a cable railway from there, or make the 2-hour climb by foot. The splendid view at the top is of **Lake Zug** and parts of **Lake Luzern**, framed by the Alpine giants Mount Pilatus, Mount Rigi, Jungfrau, Eiger and Finsterahorn.

Visit the 7-story Glass House, facing the railstation. Its shopping center has stores that offer fine shoes, gourmet food, wine, jewelry and flowers.

There are short boat trips, to **Walchwil** and to **Arth**.

Try the local specialties: *rotel* (a tasty salmon-like fish from the lake), the local cherries that are used for producing the liqueur kirsch, and the local cake, kirsch-torte, laced with the cherry liqueur.

Dep. Zug   Frequent times from 06:28 to 23:32
Arr. Zurich   26 minutes later

SCENIC RAIL TRIPS IN SWITZERLAND

Basel - Schaffhausen - Basel   734

An easy one-day roundtrip, to see the marvelous Rhine Falls.

Dep. Basel (Bad Bf.)	08:16	10:16	12:16	14:16	16:15
Arr. Schaffhausen	09:28	11:28	13:28	15:28	17:28
Dep. Schaffhausen	10:34	12:34	14:34	16:34	18:34
Arr. Basel (Bad Bf.)	11:48	13:48	15:48	17:48	19:48

Bern - Brig - Bern   280

An easy one-day roundtrip that affords a view of **Rhone Valley** and **Lonza Valley** canyons, lakes and mountains plus the Lake Thun scenery at Spiez about which we enthuse in the "Geneva–Spiez" trip .and going through the 9-mile Lotschberg Tunnel and over the Bietschtal Bridge. This structure takes the train 255 feet above the ravine it crosses.

Dep. Bern	06:22 (1)	06:50 (3)	07:22 (1)	08:22 (3)	08:51 (4)	09:22 (1+6)
Arr. Spiez	06:52	07:20	07:52	08:52	09:21	09:52
Dep. Spiez	06:54	07:22	07:54	08:54	09:23	09:54 (7)
Arr. Brig	07:59	08:18	08:59	09:59	10:19	10:59

Sights in **Brig**: Switzerland's largest private residence, the 17th century Stockalper Castle, built by a very successful businessman.

Dep. Brig	08:01 (1)	09:01 (1)	10:01 (4)	10:42 (2)	11:01 (3)	12:01 (5+8)
Arr. Spiez	09:05	10:05	11:05	11:40	12:05	13:05
Dep. Spiez	09:07	10:07	11:07	11:42	12:07	13:07 (9)
Arr. Bern	31 minutes after departing Spiez.					

(1) Light refreshments. (2) Reservation advisable. (3) Reservation advisable. Restaurant car. (4) Reservation advisable. Light refreshments. (5) Restaurant car. (6) Plus other departures from Bern at frequent times from 10:22 to 23:28. (7) Plus other departures from Spiez at frequent times from 10:54 to 00:06. (8) Plus other departures from Brig at frequent times from 13:01 to 21:35. (9) Plus other departures from Spiez at frequent times from 13:33 to 22:01.

Bern - Brig - Domodossola - Bern

To see all of the scenery and Lotschberg Tunnel noted above under "Bern–Brig" plus having the experience of going through the 11.9-mile Simplon (Europe's longest rail tunnel), make the Bern–Domodossola portion of the Bern–Milan trip.

The Simplon is actually 2 tunnels, one southbound and a 65-foot longer bore for the separate northbound tunnel.

280

Dep. Bern	06:50 (1)	07:22 (2)	08:51 (3)	10:22 (4)	12:56 (4)
Arr. Brig	- 0 - (1)	08:59	10:21 (9)	11:59	14:27

Change trains.

365

Dep. Brig	- 0 -	09:34 (3)	10:31	12:38 (5)	14:31 (3)
Arr. Domodossola	08:50	10:02	11:00	13:07	15:00

• • •

Dep. Domodossola	09:15	10:11 (4)	10:46 (4)	12:13 (5)	14:11 (4+8)
Arr. Brig	09:45	10:40	11:14	12:43	14:40

Change trains.

280

Dep. Brig	10:01 (3)	11:01 (5)	12:01 (6)	13:01 (5)	15:01 (5)
Arr. Bern	11:38	12:38	13:38	14:38	16:38

(1) Reservation advisable. Direct train. No train change in Brig. Restaurant car or light refreshments. (2) Light refreshments. (3) Reservation advisable. Light refreshments. (4) Reservation advisable. (5) Reservation advisable. Restaurant car. (6) Restaurant car. (7) Operates late May to mid-October. Runs Saturdays, Sundays . (8) Plus other Domodossola departures at 17:13 (1), 18:13 (6) and 18:50 (7), arriving Bern 19:38, 20:38 and 21:38. (9) Runs Fridays and Saturdays July 2-August 27.

Bern - Interlaken - Brienz - Interlaken - Bern

There is fine canyon, lake and mountain scenery on this easy one-day roundtrip.

Most of the trains Bern–Interlaken and v.v. have light refreshments.

280

Dep. Bern	07:28	08:28	09:28 (1)	10:28	11:28 (2+3)
Arr. Interlaken (Ost)	08:21	09:21	10:21	11:21	12:21
Change trains. 285					
Dep. Interlaken (Ost)	08:44	09:37	10:44	11:37	12:44
Arr. Brienz	09:00	09:58	11:00	11:58	13:00
		• • •			
Dep. Brienz	09:01 (2)	10:02	11:00	12:02	13:00
Arr. Interlaken (Ost)	09:16	10:23	11:16	12:23	13:16
Change trains. 280					
Dep. Interlaken (Ost)	09:39 (1)	10:39	11:39 (1)	12:39 (2)	13:39
Arr. Bern	10:32	11:32	12:32	13:32	14:32

(1) Reservation advisable. Restaurant car. (2) Reservation advisable. (3) Plus other departures from Bern (that allow the same roundtrip) at 12:28, 13:28 (2), 14:28, 15:28, 16:28 and 17:28 (1), arriving back in Bern 15:32, 16:32, 17:32, 18:32, 19:32 and 20:32.

Bern - Interlaken - Wengen - Jungfrau - Grindelwald - Interlaken - Bern

This easy one-day trip covers the heart of the Bernese Oberland area and offers very good gorge, lake and mountain scenery. There have been popular ski resorts in this area since 1906.

The Interlaken-Jungfraujoch-Interlaken portion of this excursion is *not* covered by Eurailpass. The 1994 prices *without* a Swiss Pass were: 155.20 Swiss francs for first-class, Sfr-145.80 for second-class. *With* a Swiss Pass: Sfr-95.10.

At **Jungfraujoch,** passengers alight to look down on the great Jungfrau glacier and stroll in the "Ice Palace" carved inside the glacier. Jungfraujoch is the highest (11,333 feet) railstation in Europe. Fabulous views of the Jungfrau, Eiger and Monch peaks can be seen from the revolving restaurant, which rotates completely every 50 minutes. The highest waterfall in Europe (2,000-foot drop) is spectacular in late Spring and early Summer.

We suggest, for variety, you go from Interlaken to Jungfraujoch *via Wengen* and then return to Interlaken *via Grindelwald.*

280

| Dep. Bern | 07:28 | 08:28 (1) |
| Arr. Interlaken (Ost) | 08:21 | 09:21 |

Change trains.

287

Dep. Interlaken (Ost)	08:32	09:32
Arr. Wengen	09:14	10:24
Arr. Scheidegg	09:45	10:55

Change trains.

| Dep. Scheidegg | 10:02 | 11:02 |
| Arr. Jungfraujoch | 10:53 | 11:53 |

Sightsee in Jungfraujoch

287

| Dep. Jungfraujoch | 12:00 | 13:00 |
| Arr. Scheidegg | 12:49 | 13:49 |

Change trains. (table 288)

| Dep. Scheidegg | 13:02 | 14:02 |
| Arr. Grindelwald | 13:45 | 14:45 |

Change trains.

| Dep. Grindelwald | 13:50 | 14:50 |
| Arr. Interlaken (Ost) | 14:27 | 15:27 |

Change trains.

280

| Dep. Interlaken (Ost) | 14:39 | 15:39 (1) |
| Arr. Bern | 15:32 | 16:32 |

(1) Light refreshments.

Bern - Lausanne - Brig - Spiez - Bern

Excellent canyon, lake and mountain scenery on this easy one-day circle trip. There is time for a stopover in Lausanne and/or Spiez. You go through the 9-mile Lotschberg Tunnel after leaving Brig.

260

Dep. Bern	06:38 (1)	07:18 (2)	08:38 (3)	09:18 (2)	10:18 (2+7)
Arr. Lausanne	07:50	08:26	09:50	10:26	11:26
Change trains.	*(table 270)*				
Dep. Lausanne	07:56	08:32 (3)	09:56 (3)	10:32	11:32
Arr. Brig	09:53	10:18	11:52	12:23	13:23
Change trains.	*(table 280)*				
Dep. Brig	10:01 (4)	10:42	12:01 (3)	12:26 (3)	14:01 (2)
Arr. Spiez	11:05	11:40	13:05	13:30	15:05
Dep. Spiez	11:07	11:42	13:07	13:33	15:07
Arr. Bern	11:38	12:12	13:38	14:04	15:38

(1) Runs daily except Sundays and holidays. (2) Reservation advisable. Restaurant car. (3) Light refreshments. (4) Reservation advisable. Light refreshments. (5) Restaurant car. (6) Reservation advisable. (7) The same circle trip can be made in daylight by leaving Bern at 10:38 (3), 11:18 (2), 12:38 (3), 13:18 (2) and 14:38 (3)...depart Lausanne 11:56 (3), 12:32 (3), 13:56 (3), 14:32 (3) and 15:56 (3).depart Brig 14:01 (4), 14:42 (4), 16:01 (3), 17:01 (2) and 18:01 (6)...arriving back in Bern 15:38, 16:12, 17:38, 18:38 and 19:38.

Bern - Locarno - Bern

Complete notes on the Domodossola–Locarno portion of this easy one-day roundtrip, one of the 5 most scenic rail journeys in Europe, appear under "Brig–Domodossola–Locarno" on page 392.

280

Dep. Bern	06:50 (4)	07:56	08:51 (2)	10:22 (2)	12:56 (1)	13:22 (3)
Arr. Brig	08:18	09:29	10:19 (7)	11:59	14:27	14:59

Change trains   (table 365)

Dep. Brig	08:22 (1)	09:34 (2)	10:31 (4)	12:38 (4)	14:31 (1)	15:17 (3)
Arr. Domodossola	08:50	10:02	11:00	13:07	15:00	15:47

Change trains.

Walk from the Domodossola station and go to the underground Centovalli track. Hurry!

272

Dep. Domodossola	09:02	10:18	11:12	13:18	15:16	16:00
Arr. Locarno	10:40	11:56	12:48	14:55	16:55	17:37

Dep. Locarno	12:22	13:50	15:28	16:28	17:28	19:05
Arr. Domodossola	14:00	15:30	17:00	18:00	19:00	20:46

Change trains.

Walk from the underground Centovalli track, up to the main Domodossola station. Hurry!

365

Dep. Domodossola	14:11 (1)	15:44 (1)	17:13 (1)	18:13 (6)	19:13 (4)	21:00 (1)
Arr. Brig	14:40	16:13	17:43	18:43	19:43	21:30

Change trains   (table 280)

Dep. Brig	14:42 (2)	17:01 (4)	18:01 (1)	19:01 (3)	20:01 (2)	21:35
Arr. Bern	16:12	18:38	19:38	20:38	21:38	23:10

(1) Reservation advisable. (2) Reservation advisable. Light refreshments. (3) Light refreshments. (4) Reservation advisable. Restaurant car. (5) Operates late March to late October. (6) Restaurant car. (7) Runs Friday-Saturday July 2-August 27.

Bern - Luzern - Alpnachstad - Pilatus

Very nice canyon, lake and mountain scenery on this easy one-day roundtrip that can include a stopover in Luzern. There are good views and several restaurants at the peak of **Pilatus.**

Note in the footnotes that the Pilatus Rack Railway trip (Alpnachstad–Pilatus–Alpnachstad) operates *only* May through November. The 1994 price *without* a Swiss Pass for the one-class roundtrip was: 53 Swiss francs. *With* a Swiss Pass: Sfr-39.75.

265			*286*		
Dep. Bern	07:31 (1)	09:31 (1+2)	Dep. Pilatus Kulm	10:45	13:45 (3)
Arr. Luzern	08:46	10:46	Arr. Alpnachstad	11:25	14:25
Change trains. 285			*Change to ordinary train. 285*		
Dep. Luzern	09:09	11:09	Dep. Alpnachstad	11:30	14:30
Arr. Alpnachstad	09:26	11:26	Arr. Luzern	11:50	14:50
Change to rack railway. 286			*Change trains. 265*		
Dep. Alpnachstad	09:30	11:30	Dep. Luzern	11:56 (1)	15:13 (1)
Arr. Pilatus Kulm	10:00	12:00	Arr. Bern	13:36	16:29

(1) Light refreshments. (2) Plus other departures from Bern at 11:31 (1) and 12:48, arriving Pilatus Kulm 14:20 and 15:00. (3) Plus other departures from Pilatus Kulm at 15:45 and 16:25, arriving Bern 18:26 and 19:29.

Bern - Spiez - Bern 280

Great canyon, lake and mountain scenery on this easy one-day roundtrip. This is a portion of the "Geneva–Spiez–Geneva" trip listed earlier. Plenty of time to stroll in Spiez and enjoy the beauty of Lake Thun and the mountains above it.

Dep. Bern	Frequent times from 06:22 to 23:28
Arr. Spiez	30 minutes later
Dep. Spiez	Frequent times from 05:58 to 22:56
Arr. Bern	30 minutes later

Bern - Spiez - Brig - Lausanne - Bern

Marvelous canyon, lake, mountain and river scenery on this easy one-day circle trip. This is the reverse of the "Bern–Lausanne–Spiez–Bern" ride listed earlier. A stroll in Spiez is a nice way to break the journey. You go through the 10-mile Lotschberg Tunnel after leaving Spiez.

All of these trains have light refreshments, unless designated otherwise.

280

Dep. Bern	07:22	08:22 (1)	08:51 (2)	09:22 (3)	10:22 (3)	11:22 (3+5)
Arr. Spiez	07:52	08:52	09:21	09:52	10:52	11:52
Dep. Spiez	07:54	08:54	09:23	09:54	10:54	11:54
Arr. Brig	08:59	09:59	10:19	10:59	11:59	12:59

Change trains. 270

Dep. Brig	09:07	10:07 (3)	10:36 (3)	11:16 (2)	12:07	13:36
Arr. Lausanne	11:03	12:03	12:27	12:40	14:03	15:27

Change trains. 260

Dep. Lausanne	11:33 (1)	12:10 (3)	12:33 (1)	13:33 (1)	14:10 (3)	15:33 (1+6)
Arr. Bern	12:42	13:22	13:42	14:42	15:22	16:42

(1) Reservation advisable. Restaurant car. (2) Reservation advisable. Light refreshments. (3) Light refreshments. (4) Reservation advisable. (5) Plus others Bern departure at 12:22 (1) and 13:22 (3), arriving back in Bern 17:22 and 18:22. (6) Plus other departures from Lausanne at frequent times from 16:10 to 22:33. (7) Runs Fridays and Saturdays July 2-August 27.

Brienz - Rothorn - Brienz   283

This is a cogwheel line. It goes through forests, mountains and meadows to the magnificent view from the 7,714-foot-high peak of **Rothorn**, from which there is an excellent 4-hour walk on a good mountain path to **Brunig**. There ia a superb network of well-maintained hiking trails in this area. Extra trains run at busy times. No trains operate from late October to early June.

Not covered by Eurailpass. The 1994 price for a one-class roundtrip ticket *without* a Swiss Pass was 58 Swiss francs. *With* a SwissPass: Sfr-43.50.

Dep. Brienz	08:05 (1)	09:05 (1)	09:35 (2)	10:15 (1)	11:15 (1)
Arr. Rothorn	50-60 minutes later				

Dep. Brienz	13:05 (1)	14:15 (1)	15:15 (1)	16:15 (3)
Arr. Rothorn	50-60 minutes later			

• • •

Dep. Rothorn	09:05 (1)	10:10 (1)	11:20 (1)	13:00 (1)	13:40 (1)
Arr. Brienz	50-60 minutes later				

Dep. Rothorn	14:45 (1)	15:45 (1)	16:45 (1)	17:20 (3)
Arr. Brienz	50-60 minutes later			

(1) Operates early June 4—October 23. (2) Operates July 1 to August 31. (3) Operates early June 4-September 25.

Brig - Andermatt - Disentis - Brig   320

Fine canyon and mountain scenery on this easy one-day roundtrip. A stopover can be made (08:25 to 17:48 or 19:07) in Andermatt, a great ski resort.

This trip is a portion of the "Glacier Express" route. See details about reservations and prices under "St. Moritz–Zermatt and Zermatt–St. Moritz"

Sit on the right side for best views from Brig, on the left side from Disentis.

This trip is *not* covered by Eurailpass. The 1994 roundtrip ticket price for an ordinary train (not "Glacier Express," which charges a supplement) *without* a Swiss Pass was 115 Swiss francs for first-class, Sfr-66 for second-class. *With* a Swiss Pass: Free.

Dep. Brig	06:27 (3)	08:49	09:44 (1)	10:30 (1)	11:44 (1)
Arr. Andermatt	08:25	10:22	11:22 (2)	11:58 (2)	13:22 (2)
Arr. Disentis	09:36	11:34	12:40	13:00	14:37

Sights in **Disentis**: The stained glass in the Cathedral

Dep. Disentis	10:28 (1)	12:20 (1)	13:40 (2)	16:35	17:35 (3)
Dep. Andermatt	11:36 (2)	13:37 (2)	15:12 (1)	17:48	19:08 (3)
Arr. Brig	13:14	15:14	17:17	19:35	20:58

(1) "Glacier Express." See details about reservations and prices under "St. Moritz–Zermatt" Plus another "Glacier Express" at 13:44, arriving Disentis 16:25. (2) Operates late May to late October. (3) Change trains in Andermatt.

Brig - Arona - Brig   365

Beautiful lake and mountain scenery on this easy one-day roundtrip, which can also be seen as a portion of the Lausanne–Milan route. This ride takes you through Europe's longest (19.8km or 11.9 miles) tunnel, the Simplon.

It is the third longest tunnel in the world, after Japan's Seikan Tunnel (33.4 miles, between Tappi and Yoshioka) and Japan's Daishimizu Tunnel (13.4 miles, between Tokyo and Niigata).

Dep. Brig	08:22	09:34 (2)	10:31 (3)	14:31	15:17 (2)	
Arr. Arona	09:46 (2)	10:55	11:52	15:57 (2)	16:45	

* * *

Dep. Arona	09:53 (4)	11:16	13:16	14:43	16:16	17:16 (6)
Arr. Brig	11:14	12:43 (2)	14:40 (2)	16:13 (2)	17:43 (2)	18:43

(1) Reservation advisable. (2) Reservation advisable. Light refreshments. (3) Reservation advisable. Supplement charged. Restaurant car or light refreshments. (4) Reservation advisable. Supplement charged. (5) Light refreshments. (6) Restaurant car. (7) Plus other departures from Arona at 17:41 (8) and 18:15 (3) arriving Brig 19:20 and 19:43. (8) Runs Saturdays and Sundays June 5-September 24.

Here is the daytime schedule for the Lausanne–Milan route.

82

Dep. Lausanne	06:37 (1)	08:09 (3)	08:57 (4)	11:13 (4+5)	12:32 (6)	13:32 (3)
Arr. Brig	08:17 (1)	09:32	10:22	12:36	14:23 (1)	15:12
Dep. Brig	08:22 (2)	09:34	10:31	12:38	14:31	15:17
Dep. Arona	09:48	10:57	11:54	-0- (5)	15:43	16:47
Arr. Milan (Cen.)	10:45	11:45	12:40	14:40	16:50	17:45

(1) Change trains in Brig. (2) Reservation advisable. (3) Reservation advisable. Light refreshments. (4) Res-ervation advisable. Supplement charged. Restaurant car. (5) Train does not stop in Arona. (6) Light refreshments. Change trains in Brig.

Brig - Bern - Brig   280

An easy one-day roundtrip that affords a view of Rhone Valley and Lonza Valley farms, canyons, lakes and mountains plus the Lake Thun scenery at Spiez about which we enthuse in the "Geneva–Spiez" trip and going through the 10-mile-long Lotschberg Tunnel and over the Bietschtal Bridge. This structure takes the train 255 feet above the ravine it crosses.

We recommend a stop in Spiez and a stroll there on either the outbound or homebound leg of this trip.

For best views, sit on the right side Brig to Spiez, on the left side Spiez to Brig.

Dep. Brig	07:01 (3)	08:01 (2)	09:01 (2)	10:01 (1)	11:01 (2+4)
Arr. Spiez	08:05	09:05	10:05	11:05	12:05
Dep. Spiez	08:07	09:07	10:07	11:07	12:07
Arr. Bern	30 minutes after departing Spiez.				

• • •

Dep. Bern	09:22 (2)	10:22 (1)	11:22 (2)	12:22 (3)	13:22 (2+5)
Arr. Spiez	09:52	10:52	11:52	12:52	13:52
Dep. Spiez	09:54	10:54	11:54	12:54	13:54
Arr. Brig	66 minutes after departing Spiez.				

(1) Reservation advisable. Light refreshments. (2) Light refreshments. (3) Reservation advisable. Res-taurant car. (4) Plus other departures from Brig that allow daylight viewing in Summer months at frequent times from 12:01 to 21:35. (5) Plus other departures from Bern at frequent times from 14:22 to 19:09.

Brig - Domodossola - Locarno - Domodossola - Brig

We call the Domodossola–Locarno portion of this one-day roundtrip one of the 5 most scenic rail trips in Europe. It is a spectacular narrow-gauge local train ride offering great gorge, mountain and river scenery on the Centovalli (one hundred valleys) route.

Be sure to have your passport with you. On this trip, you go from Switzerland to Italy, then Switzerland, back to Italy, and then again to Switzerland.

This ride takes you through Europe's longest (19.8km or 11.9 miles) tunnel, the Simplon (between Brig and Domodossola). It is the third longest tunnel in the world, after Japan's Seikan (33.4 miles, between Tappi and Yoshioka) and Japan's Daishimizu Tunnel (13.4 miles, between Tokyo and Niigata).

When departing Locarno, look for the "Ferrovia Centovalli" sign that directs you to stairs descending to an underground track. Stops en route from Locarno include **Intragna**, with its many churches; **Verdasio,** which has a train connection to the mountain town of **Rasa; Palagnedra,** which has a lake; **Camedo**; and **Druogno,** the highest point on this scenic route.

See detailed notes about Locarno under "Milan–Locarno–Milan."

When changing trains in Domodossola, keep in mind that trains to and from Brig are located at street level. Trains to and from Locarno are on an underground track, connected by a walkway to the street level.

365

Dep. Brig	08:22 (1)	09:34 (2)	10:31 (3)	12:38 (3)	14:31 (4)
Arr. Domodossola	08:50	10:02	11:00	13:07	15:00
Change trains. 272					
Dep. Domodossola	09:02	10:18	11:12	13:18	15:16
Arr. Locarno	10:40	11:55	12:48	14:55	16:55

• • •

Dep. Locarno	12:22	13:50	16:28	17:28	19:05
Arr. Domodossola	14:00	15:30	18:00	19:00	20:46
Change trains. 365					
Dep. Domodossola	14:11 (4)	15:44 (3)	18:13 (6)	19:13 (3)	21:00 (2)
Arr. Brig	30 minutes later				

(1) Reservation advisable. (2) Reservation advisable. Light refreshments. (3) Reservation advisable. Supplement charged. Restaurant car or light refreshments. (4) Reservation advisable. Supplement charged. (5) Operates late March to late October. (6) Restsaurant car.

Brig - Spiez - Interlaken - Brienz - Interlaken - Brig

Very good canyon, lake and mountain scenery on this easy one-day roundtrip.

For best views, sit on the right side Brig to Spiez, on the left side Spiez to Brig. Between Brig and Spiez, the train goes through the 10-mile-long Lotschberg Tunnel and over the Bietschtal Bridge. This structure takes the train 255 feet above the ravine it crosses.

Most of the trains Brig–Spiez (and v.v.) and Spiez-Interlaken (and v.v.) below have light refreshments.

280			285		
Dep. Brig	09:01	10:01	Dep. Brienz	12:02	13:00
Arr.Spiez	10:05	11:05	Arr. Interlaken (Ost)	12:23	13:16
Change trains.			*Change trains.* 280		
Dep. Spiez	11:01	12:01	Dep. Interlaken (Ost)	12:39	13:39
Arr. Interlaken (Ost)	11:21	12:21	Arr. Spiez	12:59	13:59
Change trains. 285			*Change trains.*		
Dep. Interlaken (Ost)	11:37	12:44	Dep. Spiez	13:28	14:54
Arr. Brienz	11:58	13:00	Arr. Brig	14:29	15:59

Brig - Interlaken - Wengen - Jungfrau - Grindelwald - Brig

There is excellent canyon, lake and mountain scenery on this easy one-day roundtrip. See "Bern–Interlaken–Wengen–Jungfrau"

The Interlaken-Jungfraujoch-Interlaken portion of this trip is not covered by Eurailpass. The 1994 prices of tickets without a Swiss Pass were 155.20 Swiss francs for first-class, Sfr-145.80 for second-class. With a Swiss Pass, both the Interlaken-Wengen and Grindel-wald–Interlaken portions were free, and the one-class Wengen–Scheidegg, Scheidegg–Jungfraujoch–Scheidegg and Scheidegg–Grindelwald portions were at 25% discount, making the entire trip cost Sfr-95.10.

It is for variety that we suggest you go from Interlaken to Jungfraujoch via Wengen and then return to Interlaken via Grindelwald.

Most of the trains Brig–Spiez (and v.v.) below have light refreshments or a restaurant car.

280			287		
Dep. Brig	08:01	09:01	Dep. Jungfraujoch	14:00	15:00
Arr. Spiez	09:05	10:05	Arr. Scheidegg	14:49	15:45
Change trains.			*Change trains.*		
280			Dep. Scheidegg	15:02	16:02
Dep. Spiez	10:01	11:01	Arr. Grindelwald	15:45	16:45
Arr. Interlaken (Ost)	10:21	11:21	*Change trains.*		
Change trains.			Dep. Grindelwald	15:50	16:50
287			Arr. Interlaken(Ost)	16:27	17:27
Dep. Interlaken (Ost)	10:32	11:32	*Change trains.*		
Arr. Wengen	11:14	12:24	280		
Arr. Scheidegg	11:45	12:55	Dep. Interlaken (Ost)	16:39	17:39
Change trains.			Arr. Spiez	16:59	18:59
Dep. Scheidegg	12:02	13:02	*Change trains.*		
Arr. Jungfraujoch	12:53	13:53	280		
Sightsee in Jungfraujoch.			Dep. Spiez	17:54	18:54
			Arr. Brig	18:59	19:59

Brig - Zermatt - Gornergrat - Zermatt - Brig

Great canyon and mountain scenery on this easy one-day roundtrip that includes an outstanding 5½–mile narrow-gauge cogwheel train ride to Gornergrat (10,200 feet) for a close view of the **Gorner Glacier**, the **Matterhorn** (14,692 feet) and more than 50 other peaks.

This trip is *not* covered by Eurailpass. The 1994 prices of roundtrip tickets *without* a Swiss Pass were 141 Swiss francs for first-class, Sfr-106 for second-class. *With* a Swiss Pass, the Brig-Zermatt–Brig trip is free and the Zermatt–Gornergrat–Zermatt trip is at 25% discount, making the entire trip Sfr-39.75.

320
Dep. Brig	Frequent times from 05:10 to 20:23
Arr. Zermatt	90 minutes later
Change trains. 321	
Dep. Zermatt	Frequent times from 07:05 to 18:00
Arr. Gornergrat	45 minutes later

•   •   •

Dep. Gornergrat	Frequent times from 07:55 to 19:07
Arr. Zermatt	45 minutes later
Change trains. 320	
Dep. Zermatt	Frequent times from 06:00 to 21:10
Arr. Brig	90 minutes later

Lausanne - Zermatt - Gornergrat - Lausanne

Nice canyon, lake, mountain and river scenery on this easy one-day roundtrip. The Visp–Zermatt–Gornergrat roundtrip is *not* covered by Eurailpass.

The 1994 prices of roundtrip tickets for an *ordinary* train (not "Glacier Express," which charge a supplement) *without* a Swiss Pass were 138 Swiss francs for first-class, Sfr-105 second-class. *With* a Swiss Pass, the Visp–Zermatt–Visp trip is free and the Zermatt–Gornergrat–Zermatt trip is at 25% discount, making the entire trip cost Sfr-39:75.

270
Dep. Lausanne	06:56	07:32 (1)	08:32 (1)	09:32 (1)	10:32 (1)	11:32
Arr. Visp	08:33	09:14	10:09	11:14	12:14	13:14
Change trains. 320						
Dep. Visp	08:36	09:36	10:36	11:36	12:36	13:36 (6)
Arr. Zermatt	09:45	10:47	11:45	12:47	13:47	14:45
Change trains. 321						
Dep. Zermatt	10:00	11:12 (3)	12:00	13:12	14:00	14:48 (7)
Arr. Gornergrat	10:43	11:55	12:43	13:55	14:43	15:31

•   •   •

Dep. Gornergrat	11:07	12:19 (7)	13:07	14:19 (7)	15:07	16:19 (7)
Arr. Zermatt	11:50	13:02	13:50	15:02	15:50	17:02
Change trains. 320						
Dep. Zermatt	12:10 (2)	13:10	14:10	15:10	16:10	17:10
Arr. Visp	13:22	14:22	15:22	16:22	17:22	18:22
Change trains. 270						
Dep. Visp	13:42 (1)	14:42	15:42 (1)	16:38 (1)	17:42	19:39
Arr. Lausanne	15:27	16:27	17:27	18:27	19:27	21:27

(1) Light refreshments. (2) "Glacier Express." See details about reservations and prices under "St. Moritz–Zermatt" (3) Operates late November to late October. (4) Operates mid-December to late April and mid-June to mid-October. (5) Operates May 29-October 16. (6) Runs October 17-December 16 only. (7) Runs daily except May 29-June 10.

Chur - Brig - Zermatt - Gornergrat - Zermatt

There is fabulous Rhone Valley scenery on this ride plus crossing Oberalp Pass (6,700 feet) and going through the 8-mile long Furka Tunnel on the Chur–Brig portion. This trip crosses the highest bridges in Europe and includes the outstanding cogwheel train ride to Gornergrat (10,200 feet) for a close view of the Matterhorn (14,692 feet) and more than 50 other Alpine peaks.

This trip is *not* covered by Eurailpass. The 1994 prices for this trip on an ordinary train (not "Glacier Express," which charges a supplement) *without* a Swiss Pass were: 203 Swiss francs for first-class, Sfr-143 for second-class. *With* a Swiss Pass, the Chur–Zermatt portion was free, and the Zermatt–Gornergrat–Zermatt roundtrip was at 25% discount, making the entire trip Sfr-39.75.

320

Dep. Chur	09:03 (1+4)					
Arr. Zermatt	14:45					

Change to a narrow-gauge train. 321

Dep. Zermatt	15:12	15:36 (3)	16:00	17:12	18:00	-0-
Arr. Gornergrat	15:55	16:19	16:43	17:55	18:43	-0-
			•	•		
Dep. Gornergrat	16:19 (3)	16:43 (3)	17:07	17:55	19:07	-0-
Arr. Zermatt	45 minutes later					

(1) "Glacier Express." Restaurant car or light refreshments. See details about reservations and prices under "St. Moritz–Zermatt" (2) Operates late November to late October. (3) Runs daily except May 29-June 10. (4) Runs May 29-October 16.

Chur - St. Moritz - Chur 330

Marvelous canyon, lake and mountain scenery on this easy one-day roundtrip. It is a very scenic ride involving going through double spiral tunnels and across the amazing Landwasser Viaduct. Ask at the Chur railstation which trains have open-air cars. The views from them are even more thrilling than from the closed cars.

All of these trains have light refreshments, unless designated otherwise.

Dep. Chur	06:40	08:08	09:00	09:52 (4)	10:52	11:52 (1+2)
Arr. St. Moritz	09:00	10:18	11:18	11:58	12:58	13:58 (4)
			•	•	•	
Dep. St. Moritz	10:00 (1)	11:00 (5)	12:00	13:00 (4)	14:00	15:00 (3)
Arr. Chur	12:07	13:07	14:07	15:07	16:07	17:07 (4)

(1) Restaurant car. (2) Plus frequent other departures from Chur 12:52 to 20:57. (3) Plus other departures from St. Moritz 16:00, 17:00, 18:00 (1), 19:00 and 20:00. (4) Runs Saturdays, Sundays and holidays. (5) Runs Sundays and holidays June 18-September 24.

Geneva - Lausanne - Brig - Spiez - Bern - Lausanne - Geneva

One of the 5 most scenic rail trips in Europe.

The succession of beautiful scenes defy verbal description: 15 miles of terraced vineyards and Lake Geneva shoreline between Geneva and Lausanne. Great river scenery en route from Martigny to Brig. Upon leaving Brig, take a seat on the side of the train that faces the Brig railstation. In the 52 miles between Brig and Thun, the train goes through 37 tunnels (including the 10-mile Lotschberg) and crosses the top of 25 bridges and viaducts. The 866-foot-long **Kander Viaduct** is 92-feet high.

Upon emerging from the Lotschberg Tunnel, there is such beautiful farm and mountain scenery around tiny **Kandersteg** and **Fruitigen** that you want to get off the train and spend the rest of your life there. It is only a 15-minute downhill walk from the Spiez railstation to the castle overlooking Lake Thun, the most beautiful lake scene on this planet. If the view of Lake Thun and the mountains reflected on its surface does not thrill you, pack up and go home because you will not find any landscape more beautiful in this world. From here, you can see the peaks of Jungfrau, Eiger, Monch and Finsteraarhorn.

You can return to Geneva (via Bern) either by boarding a train in Spiez or by first taking the 45-minute boat ride (covered by Eurailpass) from Spiez to **Thun** village and then boarding the train in Thun. It is a 10-minute downhill walk from the Spiez railstation to the Spiez pier. The lake steamer ties up 100 feet from Thun's railstation.

On the way back to Geneva from Bern, you pass through the same lake and vineyard scenery you saw between Lausanne and Geneva that morning, at the start of this fabulous one-day trip.

The schedules shown below allow a stopover in Bern (see footnotes #6 and #7).

270

Dep. Geneva (Corn.)	07:48 (1)	08:20 (2)	08:48 (1)	09:48 (1)	10:34 (2+7)
Dep. Lausanne	08:32	08:57	09:32	10:32	11:13
Dep. Martigny	09:25	-0-	10:25	11:25	-0-
Arr. Brig	10:18	10:22	11:23	12:23	12:36
Change trains. 280					
Dep. Brig	10:42 (3)	11:01 (1)	12:01 (1)	-0-	13:01 (2)
Arr. Spiez	11:40	12:05	13:05	-0-	14:05
Dep. Spiez	11:42	12:07	13:07	-0-	14:07
Dep. Thun	11:53	12:18	13:18	-0-	14:18
Arr. Bern	12:12	12:38	13:38	-0-	14:38
Change trains. 260					
Dep. Bern	12:38 (1)	13:18 (5)	14:18 (5)	-0-	15:18 (5+8)
Arr. Lausanne	13:50	14:26	15:26	-0-	16:26
Arr. Geneva (Corn.)	14:34	15:02	16:02	-0-	17:02

(1) Light refreshments. (2) Reservation advisable. Supplement charged. Restaurant car. (3) Reservation advisable. (4) Restaurant car. (5) Reservation advisable. Restaurant car. (6) Reservation advisable. Supplement charged. Light refreshments. (7) Plus other Geneva departures at 10:48, 11:48 (1), 12:48

(1) and 13:48 (1)....Departing Brig at 14:01(2), 15:01 (2), 16:01 (1) and 17:01 (2)...Departing Bern at 16:18 (2), 17:18 (2), 18:18 (2) and 19:18 (2)...Arriving back in Geneva at 18:02, 19:02, 20:02 and 21:02. (8) Plus other Bern depatures at 16:18 (2), 16:38, 17:18 (2), 18:18 (2), 18:38 (1), 19:18 (2), 20:18 (2), 20:38, 21:18 (2), 22:21 (2) and 23:26.

Here are the Lake Thun (Spiez–Thun) boat schedules (covered by Eurailpass) to combine with departures from Thun village for Bern.

281 Boat

Dep. Spiez	13:17 (1)	13:49 (2)	14:58 (1)	15:14 (3)	16:03 (1)	16:43 (4+5)
Arr. Thun (Pier)	14:02	14:53	15:46	16:00	16:48	17:38

It is a 2-minute walk from the boat pier to the train.

280 Train

Dep. Thun (Stn.)	14:12	15:12	15:53	16:44 (6)	17:12 (4)	17:44 (4)
Arr. Bern	20 minutes later					

(1) Has restaurant. (2) Late May to mid-June: light refreshments. Mid-June to late September: restaurant car. (3) Paddlesteamer. Runs daily, except Monday. Supplement charged. (4) Light refreshments. (5) Plus other boat departures from Spiez at 17:04 (4), 18:03 (1), 18:59 (1) and 20:11 (2), connecting in Thun with trains that arrive Bern 18:32, 19:32, 20:32 and 21:38. (6) Runs Sunday only.

Geneva - Chamonix (Mt. Blanc) - Geneva   167

Be sure to have your passport with you on this trip filled with fantastic mountain scenery, as you will be going from Switzerland to France. From Chamonix, take the 2-mile-high cable-car ride that goes nearly to the top of the tallest mountain in Europe, the 15,771-foot Mt. Blanc, towering almost 10,000 feet above Chamonix, for a view of Alpine peaks extending 80 miles.

After descending, there is just time to also take the narrow-gauge train to see the "Sea of Ice" glacier bed (which does not operate in Winter). The tombstones in the small cemetery, a 5-minute walk from the railstation, are fascinating. Nearly one-fourth of the headstones read "died on the mountain" (climbers and their rescuers).

All of these connections are easy cross-platform train changes, each taking less than one minute.

Dep. Geneva			Dep. Chamonix	13:27	17:48
(Eaux Vives)	07:10 (1)	08:27 (4)	Arr. St. Gervais	14:18	18:27
Arr. La Roche	07:42 (4)	08:57	*Change trains.*		
Change trains.			Dep. St. Gervais	14:32 (6)	17:23 (6)
Dep. La Roche	07:50 (5)	10:00 (4)	Arr. La Roche	15:15	18:08
Arr. St. Gervais	08:52	10:43	*Change trains.*		
Change trains. 268			Dep. La Roche	15:30	-0-
Dep. St. Gervais	09:16	10:53	Arr. Geneva		
Arr. Chamonix	09:43	11:30	(Eaux Vives)	16:03	-0-

(1) Runs daily, except Sundays and holidays. (2) Runs 18 minutes later early July to early September. (3) Runs Monday-Friday, except holidays. (4) Not July 5-29. (5) July 5-29. (6) not July 4-28.

Geneva - Martigny - Chamonix - Geneva

This one-day circle trip avoids the repetition involved in the Geneva–Annemasse–Chamonix–Geneva roundtrip described in the previous listing and also allows time for the activities in Chamonix described above. The scenery Martigny–Vallorcine–Chamonix is fantastic!

All of the Chamonix–Geneva connections are easy cross-platform train changes, each taking less than one minute.

270			268		
Dep. Geneva (Corn.)	06:48 (1)	07:48 (1)	Dep. Chamonix	13:27	16:16
Arr. Martigny	08:20	09:20	Arr. St. Gervais	14:06	16:55
Change trains. 268			*Change trains.* 167		
Dep. Martigny	08:59	10:09	Dep. St. Gervais	14:32 (5)	17:23 (5)
Arr. Le Chatelard	09:48 (2)	10:45 (2)	Arr. La Roche	15:15	18:08
Dep. Le Chatelard	09:55	11:11	*Change trains.*		
Arr. Vallorcine	09:18	10:56	Dep. La Roche	15:30	-0-
Arr. Chamonix	10:03	11:50	Arr. Geneva (Eaux-Vives)	16:03	-0-

(1) Light refreshments. (2) Change trains in Le Chatelard-Frontiere. (3) Runs Chamonix-Geneva on Monday-Friday, except holidays. Must change trains in Annemasse en route La Roche to Geneva. (4) July 4-Sept. 4. (5) Not July 4-28.

Geneva - Lausanne - Geneva

Here is a short trip packed with fine scenery of 15 miles of terraced vineyards, nearly the entire route following the lovely shoreline of Lake Geneva. Complete schedules are listed under the "Geneva–Lausanne" one-day excursion on.

Geneva - Lyon - Geneva 159

The first 1½ hours from Geneva is noted for scenic canyons.

Geneva - Martigny - Geneva 270

This is a scenic trip of intermediate length, longer than the Geneva–Lausanne ride and shorter than the Geneva–Brig–Bern–Geneva circle trip. Very good canyon, lake, mountain and vineyard scenery.

Dep. Geneva (Corn.)	06:48 (1)	07:48 (1)	08:48 (1)	09:48 (1)	10:48 (2)
Arr. Martigny	08:20	09:20	10:20	11:20	12:20

• • •

Dep. Martigny	08:34	09:38 (1)	10:40 (1)	11:34	12:34 (1+3)
Arr. Geneva (Corn.)	10:12	11:12	12:12	13:12	14:12

(1) Light refreshments. (2) Plus other departures from Geneva at frequent times from 11:48 to 22:52. (3) Plus other departures from Martigny at frequent times from 13:38 to 21:34.

Geneva - Montreux - Zweisimmen - Spiez - Bern - Geneva

This narrow-gauge variation on the scenic trip described earlier (Geneva–Brig–Bern–Geneva) runs parallel and north of the Martigny–Brig route. You miss going through the Lotschberg Tunnel, but you are able to see all of the Geneva–Lausanne vineyard and Lake Geneva scenery plus Lake Thun (Spiez) and a possible stopover in Bern, en route back to Geneva.

Before traveling the normal-guage Zweisimmen–Spiez leg, there is time to take the very scenic narrow-guage 13km (9 miles) detour from Zweisimmen to Lenk (and back to Zweisimmen). Upon first arriving Zweisimmen 13:00, 15:45 or 17:00, passengers can arrive back in Zweisimmen from Lenk at 14:11, 16:55 or 18:11 before continuing on to Spiez.

There is time to leave the train in Spiez, take the lake boat from Spiez to Thun, and then take the train from Thun to Bern. See notes under the "Geneva–Brig–Bern–Geneva" scenic trip.

The narrow-guage ascent from Montreux to Zweisimmen is very scenic as the train climbs from the shore of Lac Leman to Les Avants in a series of hairpin bends. The funicular ride from **Les Avants** to **Sonloup** is worth stopping over in Les Avants and rejoining the Montreux–Zweisimmen route later in the day. **Gstaad** is a very expensive ski resort.

We recommend departing Montreux on "Panoramic Express" or "Crystal Panoramic Express." The comfortable coaches of these special narrow-gauge Observation Trains have glass domes and large side windows for viewing the marvelous scenery. Refreshments are available from vending machines in their bar car.

For "Crystal Panoramic," reservations are accepted only for groups. Individuals may ride it if there are any vacant seats.

There are seats in the front car, which has an elevated cab for the engineer. The next car is a bar car which seats 45 passengers. The third and last car is the locomotive.

Regardless which train you ride, sit on the right side Montreux-Zweisimmen for best views.

270

Dep. Geneva (Corn.)	08:48 (1)	09:48 (1)	10:48	11:48 (1)	12:48 (1)
Arr. Montreux	09:51	10:51	11:51	12:51	13:51

Change trains. 275

Dep. Montreux	10:00 (2)	11:00	12:21	13:00	14:00 (3)
Arr. Les Avants	10:22	11:22	12:42	13:22	– 0 – (8)
Dep. Gstaad	11:18	12:30	13:42	14:30	15:18
Arr. Zweisimmen	11:45	13:00	14:10	15:00	15:45

Change trains. 276

Dep. Zweisimmen	12:21	13:05	14:21	15:05	16:05
Arr. Spiez	12:57	13:51	14:57	15:51	16:51

Spiez: See notes under "Geneva-Brig-Bern-Geneva." For marvelous views of mountains and lakes, walk to the Burg Woods and Burg Hill. Spiez is an ideal base for one-day rail trips to Bern, Interlaken, Luzern, Gstaad, Montreux, Zermatt, Grindelwald, Stresa, Yungfraujoch and Solothurn.

Change trains. 280

Dep. Spiez	13:07 (4)	14:01 (1)	15:07 (6)	16:01 (1)	17:01 (5)
Dep. Thun	13:18	14:12	15:18	16:12	17:12
Arr. Bern	13:38	14:32	15:38	16:32	17:32

Change trains. 260

Dep. Bern	14:18 (6)	15:18 (6)	16:18 (6)	17:18 (6)	18:18 (6+7)
Arr. Geneva (Corn.)	16:02	17:02	18:02	19:02	20:02

(1) Light refreshments. (2) "Panoramic Express." See details in text on previous page. (3) "Crystal Panoramic." See details in text on previous page. (4) Restaurant car. (5) Reservation advisable. Light refreshments. (6) Reservation advisable. Restaurant car. (7) Plus other departures from Bern at 18:38 (1), 19:18 (6), 20:18 (6), 20:38, 21:18 (6) and 22:21 (6), arriving Geneva 20:34, 21:02, 22:02, 22:37, 23:02 and 00:09. (8) Reservation required.

Geneva - Nyon - Geneva   250

See the magnificent views of **Lac Leman** (the Lake of Geneva) and the Alps, particularly of Mont Blanc, from **Nyon**, a medieval hilltop village on the shore of Lac Leman.

Dep. Geneva (Corn.)	Frequent times from 04:49 to 00:01
Arr. Nyon	14 minutes later

Sights in **Nyon**: Sailing is popular here.

Dep. Nyon	Frequent times from 06:00 to 01:06
Arr. Geneva (Corn.)	14 minutes later

Interlaken - Mt. Pilatus - Interlaken

Great canyon and mountain scenery on this easy one-day narrow-gauge roundtrip. There are good views and several restaurants at the peak of Pilatus.

A roundtrip ticket is available in Luzern covering train or boat Luzern-Alpnachstad, rack railway Alpnachstad-Pilatus Kulm, cablecar and gondolas Pilatus-Kriens, and trolley-bus Kriens-Luzern.

The Alpnachstad–Pilatus–Alpnachstad rack railway portion operates only May through November. The 1994 price of a one-class roundtrip ticket without a Swiss Pass was 53 Swiss francs. With a Swiss Pass: Sfr-39.75.

285

Dep. Interlaken (Ost)	08:44	09:37 (2)	10:44 (1)	11:37 (2)	12:44 (2)	13:37
Arr. Giswil	09:56	10:56	11:56	12:56	13:56	14:56

Change trains.

Dep. Giswil	10:06	11:06	12:06	13:06	14:06	15:06
Arr. Alpnachstad	10:28	11:28	12:28	13:28	14:28	15:28

Change to rack railway for the ride to the top of Mt. Pilatus. table 286

Dep. Alpnachstad	10:50	11:30	13:10	13:50	14:30	15:50
Arr. Pilatus Kulm	11:20	12:00	13:40	14:20	15:00	16:20

• • •

Dep. Pilatus Kulm	12:05	13:05	14:25	15:45	16:25	
Arr. Alpnachstad	12:45	13:45	15:05	16:25	17:05	

Change to a standard train. 285

Dep. Alpnachstad	13:29	14:29	15:29	16:29	17:29	
Arr. Giswil	13:51	14:51	15:51	16:51	17:51	

Change trains

Dep. Giswil		14:00(1)	15:00 (2)	16:00(2)	17:00	18:00
Arr. Interlaken (Ost)		15:16	16:23	17:16	18:23	19:20

(1) Restaurant car. (2) Light refreshments.

Interlaken - Luzern - Interlaken

A very scenic 48-mile panorama of the Alps on this trip along Lake Brienz, an easy one-day excursion. Schedules appear under "Interlaken–Luzern."

Interlaken - Spiez - Bern - Spiez - Interlaken 280

Excellent canyon, lake and mountain scenery on this easy one-day roundtrip that includes visiting Lake Thun and a possible stopover in Bern. See earlier notes about Spiez and taking a boat on Lake Thun from Spiez to Thun village, under "Geneva–Brig–Bern–Geneva."

Dep. Interlaken (Ost)	07:39	08:11 (3)	08:39 (2)	09:39 (4)	10:39 (4)	11:39 (1)
Dep. Interlaken (West)	5 minutes later
Dep. Spiez	08:01	08:33	09:01	10:01	11:01	12:01
Dep. Thun	08:12	08:44	09:12	10:12	11:12	12:12
Arr. Bern	20 minutes later
Dep. Bern	Frequent times from 06:56 to 23:28
Arr. Interlaken (West)	45–60 minutes later
Arr. Interlaken (Ost)	5 minutes after arriving West station

(1) Light refreshments. (2) Reservation advisable. Light refreshments. (3) Reservation advisable. (4) Reservation advisable. Restaurant car.

Interlaken - Spiez - Brig - Spiez - Interlaken 280

Nice canyon, lake and mountain scenery on this easy one-day roundtrip which includes visiting Lake Thun and going through the 10-mile Lotschberg Tunnel.

The schedules below allow time to stopover in Spiez.

Most of the trains Spiez–Brig and v.v. have light refreshments.

Dep. Interlaken (Ost)	06:39 (1)	07:11 (2)	07:39	08:11 (4)	08:39 (1)	09:39 (2+5)
Dep. Interlaken (West)	5 minutes later
Arr. Spiez	07:04	07:31	07:59	08:31	08:59	09:59
Change trains.
Dep. Spiez	07:22 (1)	07:54	08:28	08:54	09:23	10:54
Arr. Brig	08:20	08:59	09:29	09:59	10:21	11:59

Dep. Brig	Frequent times from 05:38 to 21:35
Arr. Spiez	70 minutes later
Change trains.
Dep. Spiez	Frequent times from 07:29 to 23:01
Arr. Interlaken (West)	15 minutes later
Arr. Interlaken (Ost)	5 minutes after arriving West station

(1) Reservation advisable. (2) Reservation advisable. Restaurant car. (3) Light refreshments. (4) Reservation advisable. Light refreshments. (5) Plus other Interlaken departures at 10:39 (2), 11:39 (3), 12:39(3), 13:39(3), 14:39(3) and 15:39(3), arriving Brig 2½ hours later.

Interlaken - Jungfraujoch - Interlaken 287

Great canyon and mountain scenery on this easy one-day roundtrip. This spectacular route ends at Europe's highest (11,333 feet) railstation. It includes 2 stops in the tunnel through Mount Eiger, for viewing through "windows" which the railroad's builders cut in the face of the cliff.

At Jungfraujoch, passengers alight to look down on the great Jungfrau glacier and stroll in the "Ice Palace" carved inside the glacier. Fabulous views can be seen from the revolving restaurant, which rotates completely every 50 minutes. For variety, we show how to go from Interlaken to Jungfraujoch via Wengen, and then return to Interlaken via Grindelwald.

Grindelwald sits at 3400-feet altitude. The majestic peaks that rise around this village are: **Jungfrau** (13,642 feet), **Eiger** (13,026), **Wetterhorn** (12,142), **Breithorn** (12,409), **Monch** (13,449), **Schreckhorn** (13,380), **Gspaltenhorn** (11,277) and **Tschingelhorn** (11,736).

This trip is not covered by Eurailpass. The 1994 prices of a ticket without a Swiss Pass were: 170.80 Swiss francs for first-class, Sfr-161.40 for second-class.

With a Swiss Pass, both the Interlaken–Wengen and Grindelwald–Interlaken portions were free, and the one-class Wengen–Scheidegg–Jungfraujoch–Scheidegg and Scheidegg–Grindelwald portions were at 25% discount making the entire trip cost Sfr-95.10.

(Via Wengen)

Dep. Interlaken (Ost)	07:38	08:05 (1)	08:32	09:02 (1)	09:32	10:02 (1)	10:32 (2)
Arr. Scheidegg	08:55	09:20	09:45	10:10	10:55	11:20	11:45
Change trains.							
Dep. Scheidegg	09:02	09:30 (1)	10:02	10:30 (1)	11:02	11:30 (1)	12:02
Arr. Jungfraujoch	09:53	10:22	10:53	11:22	11:53	12:22	12:53
Dep. Jungfraujoch	11:00 (1)	12:00	13:00	14:00	14:30 (1)	15:00	
Arr. Scheidegg	11:49	12:49	13:49	14:49	15:19	15:45	
Change trains. (via Grindelwald) 288							
Dep. Scheidegg	12:00	13:00	14:00	15:00	15:32 (1)	16:00	
Arr. Grindelwald	12:45	13:45	14:45	15:45	16:15	16:45	
Change trains.							
Dep. Grindelwald	12:50	13:50	14:50	15:50	16:20 (1)	16:50	
Arr. Interlaken (Ost)	13:27	14:27	15:27	16:27	16:57	17:27	

(1) Does not operate May 29-June 3. (2) Plus other departures from Interlaken at 11:32, 12:32, 13:32 and 14:32, arriving back in Interlaken 16:27, 17:27, 18:27 and 19:27. (3) Plus other departures from Jungfraujoch at 14:00, 15:00, 16:00, 17:00 and 18:00 (1), arriving Interlaken 16:27, 17:27, 18:27, 19:27 and 20:27.

Lausanne - Brig - Lausanne 270

Enjoy the fine canyon, lake, mountain and river scenery on this easy one-day roundtrip.

Dep. Lausanne	Frequent times from 06:56 to 23:45
Arr. Brig	1½–2 hours later

Sight in **Brig**: Switzerland's largest private residence, the 17th century Stockalper Castle, built by a very successful businessman.

Dep. Brig	Frequent times from 05:25 to 21:36
Arr. Lausanne	1½–2 hours later

Lausanne - Brig - Spiez - Bern - Lausanne

Marvelous canyon, lake, mountain and river scenery on this easy one-day roundtrip, a portion of the "Geneva–Lausanne–Spiez–Bern–Geneva" scenic trip.

Locarno - Camedo - Locarno 272

One of the 5 most scenic rail trips in Europe. Fantastic canyon, river and mountain scenery. Hillside farms that are nearly vertical. The ride is called "Centovalli," and you will see a hundred valleys. This trip can be made either as an easy one-day roundtrip or as a portion of these routes: Milan–Locarno, Bern–Locarno, Brig–Locarno, Luzern–Locarno, and Locarno–Brig.

Please note that this trip does not start from the Locarno railstation. You catch what looks like a trolley car at the central bus stop, across from the train station.

At Camedo, a small hotel (Osteria Grutly) is only a 5-minute walk from the railstation. The granite slab roofs on the houses in this area are unique.

Dep. Locarno	08:54	10:28	12:22	13:50	15:28	16:28	17:28
Arr. Camedo	09:25	10:59	12:55	14:21	15:59	16:59	17:59

• • •

Dep. Camedo	10:05	11:22	13:20	14:23	16:22	17:02	19:24
Arr. Locarno	35 minutes later						

Locarno - Domodossola - Brig - Domodossola - Locarno

Very good canyon, mountain and river scenery on this one-day roundtrip that includes the wonderful **Centovalli** ride described in the previous trip plus going through the 12-mile

Simplon, longest main line rail tunnel in the world. Be sure to take your passport on this trip from Switzerland to Italy, Switzerland, back to Italy and then again to Switzerland.

Follow the "Ferrovia Centovalli" sign down a flight of stairs to the underground portion of Locarno's railstation. Stops en route include **Intragna**, with its many churches; **Verdasio**, which has a train connection to the mountain town of **Rasa**; **Palagnedra**, which has a lake; **Camedo** ; and **Druogno**, highest point on this scenic route.

The Domodossola–Brig (and v.v.) portion of this route takes you through Europe's longest (19.8km - 11.9 miles) tunnel, the Simplon. It is the world's second-longest tunnel, after Japan's Daishimizu Tunnel between Tokyo and Niigata (22.3km - 13.4 miles).

272		
Dep. Locarno	08:54	10:28
Arr. Domo.	10:34	12:00

Change trains. Walk from the underground Centovalli track, up to the main Domodossola station. Hurry!

365		
Dep. Domo.	10:46 (1)	12:13 (1)
Arr. Brig	11:14	12:43

365		
Dep. Brig	12:38 (2)	14:31 (1)
Arr. Domo.	13:07	15:00

Change trains. Walk outside the Domodossola station and go to the underground Centovalli track. Hurry!

272		
Dep. Domo.	13:18	15:16
Arr. Locarno	14:55	16:55

(1) Reservation advisable. Light refreshments. (2) Restaurant car. Reservation required.

Luzern - Brunnen - Fluelen - Luzern   294

Here is an excellent one-day roundtrip boat ride on Lake Luzern, that is covered by Eurailpass.

All of these boats have a restaurant, unless designated otherwise.

Dep. Luzern (Stn. Quay)	09:05 (1)	09:30 (2)	10:25	11:15 (3)	11:25 (1+7)
Arr. Brunnen	10:59	11:50	12:35	12:55	13:52
Arr. Fluelen	11:50	12:40	13:40	13:45	14:52

• • •

Dep. Fluelen	11:55 (1)	12:51 (2)	13:51	14:20 (4)	15:00 (1+8)
Dep. Brunnen	12:46	13:42	14:45	15:30	16:00
Arr. Luzern (Stn. Quay)	14:54	16:10	16:46	17:36	18:36

(1) Paddlesteamer. Runs daily. (2) Paddlesteamer in July and August, daily except Sundays and holidays. (3) Paddlesteamer. Runs Sunday only. No restaurant. (4) Runs Sunday only. (5) Runs daily all year. July and August: paddlesteamer daily. September to June: paddlesteamer only on Sunday. (6) Light refreshments. (7) Plus other departures from Luzern at 13:15, 14:20 (6) and 15:15 (6). (8) Plus other departures from Fluelen at 16:20 (5) and 17:45 (6).

Luzern - Interlaken - Luzern

Great canyon and mountain scenery on this easy one-day roundtrip. Complete schedules are listed under "Luzern–Interlaken–Luzern."

Luzern - Interlaken - Brig - Domodossola - Locarno - Luzern

This circle route includes going through the 9-mile Lotschberg Tunnel, the 12-mile Simplon and the 9-mile St. Gotthard, as well as seeing the beautiful Centovalli scenery between Domodossola and Locarno.

285		272	
Dep. Luzern	07:24 (1)	Dep. Domodossola	13:18
Arr. Interlaken (Ost)	09:16 (5)	Arr. Locarno	14:55
Change trains. 280		*Change trains*	
Dep. Interlaken (Ost)	09:39 (3)	*291*	
Arr. Spiez	09:59	Dep. Locarno	15:03 (4)
Change trains. 280		Arr. Bellinzona	15:21
Dep. Spiez	10:54 (2)	*Change trains. 290*	
Arr. Brig	11:59	Dep. Bellinzona	15:27 (3)
Change trains. 270		Arr. Luzern	17:39 (6)
Dep. Brig	12:38 (3)		
Arr. Domodossola	13:07		

(1) Light refreshments. (2) Reservation advisable. Light refreshments. (3) Reservation advisable. Restaurant car. (4) Plus other departures from Locarno at 17:03 and 18:03, arriving Luzern 19:39 and 21:39. (5) reservation advisable. (6) Supplement charged.

Luzern - Interlaken - Jungfraujoch - Interlaken - Luzern

There is marvelous canyon, lake and mountain scenery on this easy one-day roundtrip. See details about Jungfraujoch under "Interlaken–Jungfraujoch."

For variety, we suggest you go from Interlaken to Jungfraujoch via Wengen, and then return to Interlaken via Grindelwald. The Interlaken–Jungfraujoch–Interlaken portion is not covered by Eurailpass. The 1994 prices of tickets *without* a Swiss Pass were 170.80 Swiss francs for first-class, Sfr-161.40 for second-class. *With* a Swiss Pass, both the Interlaken–Wengen and Grindelwald–Interlaken portions were free, and the one-class Wengen–Scheidegg, Scheidegg–Jungfraujoch–Scheidegg and Scheidegg–Grindelwald portions were at 25% discount making the entire trip cost Sfr-95.10.

For the best views, sit on the right-hand side Luzern–Meiringen, on the left side Meiringen–Interlaken. For the return ride, sit on the right Interlaken–Meiringen and on the left Meiringen–Luzern.

285			287		
Dep. Luzern	08:24 (1)		Dep. Jungfraujoch	13:00	14:00
Arr. Meiringen	09:41		Arr. Scheidegg	13:49	14:49
Arr. Interlaken (Ost)	10:23		*Change trains. 288*		
Change trains. 287			Dep. Scheidegg		
Dep. Interlaken (Ost)			(*via Grindelwald*)	14:00	15:00
(*via Wengen*)	10:32		Arr. Interlaken (Ost)	15:27	16:27
Arr. Scheidegg	11:45		*Change trains. 285*		
Change trains. 287			Dep. Interlaken (Ost)	15:37	16:44 (1)
Dep. Scheidegg	12:02		Arr. Meiringen	16:12	17:12
Arr. Jungfraujoch	12:53		Arr. Luzern	17:36	18:36

(1) Restaurant car.

Luzern - Interlaken - Spiez - Brig - Andermatt - Goschenen - Luzern

Here is a marvelous one-day circle trip, crammed with outstanding scenery. Although this schedule allows only 50 minutes in Spiez, if you take a packed lunch from Luzern there are benches outside the Spiez railstation where you can sit while eating and have a fabulous view of the village, Lake Thun and the mountains reflected on its surface.

From Spiez to Brig, there is a good view of the Matterhorn from the right side of the train. Walk to the front of the Brig railstation to board the train to Andermatt.

En route from Brig to Andermatt, you see the beautiful Rhone Valley and go through the 8-mile long Furka Tunnel. The Brig–Andermatt–Goschenen portion of this trip is *not* covered by Eurailpass. The 1994 ticket prices for an ordinary train (not for "Glacier Express," which charges a supplement) *without* a Swiss Pass were 58 Swiss francs for first-class, Sfr-35 for second-class. *With* a Swiss Pass: Free.

285			320	
Dep. Luzern	08:24 (1)	09:24 (2)	Dep. Brig	14:17 (4+5)
Arr. Interlaken (Ost)	10:23	11:16	Arr. Andermatt	16:25
Change trains. 280				
Dep. Interlaken (Ost)	10:39	11:39	Dep. Andermatt	16:27 (5)
Arr. Spiez	10:59	11:59	Arr. Goschenen	16:42
Change trains. 280			*Change trains. 290*	
Dep. Spiez	11:54 (3)	12:54 (3)	Dep. Goschenen	17:13 (2)
Arr. Brig	12:59	13:59	Arr. Luzern	18:46
Change trains.				

(1) Restaurant car. (2) Light refreshments. (3) Restaurant car. (4) Plus another Brig departure at 16:17, arriving Luzern 20:46. (5) Runs May 14-October 16 only.

Luzern - Mt. Pilatus - Luzern   285   286

See the fine canyon and mountain scenery on this easy one-day roundtrip. The Alpnachstad–Pilatus–Alpnachstad rack railway portion operates only from May to the end of November. The 1994 price for a one-class roundtrip ticket *without* a Swiss Pass was 53 Swiss francs. *With* a Swiss Pass: Sfr-39.75. There are good views and several restaurants at the peak of Pilatus.

| Dep. Luzern | 08:09 | 09:09 | 10:09 | 11:09 | 12:09 | 13:09 | 14:09 (1) |
| Arr. Alpnachstad | 08:26 | 09:26 | 10:26 | 11:26 | 12:26 | 13:26 | 14:26 |

Change to rack railway for the ride to the top of Mt. Pilatus.

| Dep. Alpnachstad | 08:50 | 09:30 | 10:50 | 11:30 | 13:10 | 13:50 | 14:30 |
| Arr. Pilatus Kulm | 09:20 | 10:00 | 11:20 | 12:00 | 13:40 | 14:20 | 15:00 |

•   •   •

| Dep. Pilatus Kulm | 09:25 | 10:45 | 11:25 | 12:05 | 13:45 | 14:25 | 15:05 (2) |
| Arr. Alpnachstad | 10:05 | 10:25 | 12:05 | 12:45 | 14:25 | 15:05 | 15:45 |

Change to standard trains.

| Dep. Alpnachstad | 10:30 | 11:30 | 12:30 | 13:30 | 14:30 | 15:30 | 16:30 |
| Arr. Luzern | 18 minutes later | | | | | | |

(1) Plus another departure from Luzern at 15:09, arriving Pilatus Kulm 16:20. (2) Plus another departure from Pilatus Kulm at 16:25.

Luzern - Engelberg - Mt. Titlis - Luzern   293

There is very good canyon and mountain scenery on this easy one-day roundtrip. The Engelberg–Titlis–Engelberg rack railway is *not* covered by Eurailpass and does not operate late October to early December. The 1994 price of a one-class roundtrip ticket *without* a Swiss Pass was 66 Swiss francs. *With* a Swiss Pass: Sfr-49.50.

Engelberg is a popular ski resort. It also has more than 20 miles of level walking and hiking paths, toboggan runs, a gambling casino and indoor swimming pools.

There are great views from the restaurant on the top of **Mt. Titlis**. See the 11th century illuminated manuscripts in the Benedictine monastery.

| Dep. Luzern | 07:24 (3) | 08:14 | 09:14 | 10:14 | 11:14 | 12:14 | 13:14 (1) |
| Arr. Engelberg | 08:20 | 09:12 | 10:12 | 11:12 | 12:12 | 13:12 | 14:12 |

Change to the funicular.

| Dep. Engelberg | Frequent times | | | | | | |
| Arr. Mt. Titlis | 60 minutes later | | | | | | |

•   •   •

| Dep. Mt. Titlis | Frequent times | | | | | | |
| Arr. Engelberg | 60 minutes later | | | | | | |

Change to the train.

| Dep. Engelberg | 10:45 | 11:45 | 12:45 | 13:45 | 14:45 | 15:45 | 16:45 (2) |
| Arr. Luzern | 60–65 minutes later | | | | | | |

(1) Plus other departures from Luzern at frequent times from 14:14 to 19:14 for Luzern roundtrip. (2) Plus other departures from Engelberg at 17:45, 18:45, 19:45 and 20:50. (3) Change trains at Hergiswil.

Luzern - Engelberg - Mt. Titlis - Luzern - Mt. Pilatus - Luzern

From May through October, *all 3* mountains can be ascended in one day by following this schedule.

Neither the Engelberg-Titlis nor Alpnachstad-Pilatus one-class roundtrips are covered by Eurailpass. The 1994 ticket prices for them without a Swiss Pass totaled 119 Swiss francs. With a Swiss Pass: Sfr-89.25.

293		*285*	
Dep. Luzern	07:24 (5)	Dep. Luzern	13:09 (3)
Arr. Engelberg	08:20	Arr. Alpnachstad	13:27
Change to the funicular.		*Change to the rack railway.*	*286*
Dep. Engelberg	08:30 (1)	Dep. Alpnachstad	13:50
Arr. Mt. Titlis	09:30 (1)	Arr. Pilatus Kulm	14:20
• • •		• • •	
Dep. Mt. Titlis	10:00 (1)	Dep. Pilatus Kulm	14:25 (4)
Arr. Engelberg	11:00 (1)	Arr. Alpnachstad	15:05
Change to the train. 293		*Change to the train. 285*	
Dep. Engelberg	11:45 (2)	Dep. Alpnachstad	15:30
Arr. Luzern	12:45	Arr. Luzern	15:50

(1) Estimated. Thomas Cook Timetables does not publish Engleberg-Titlis schedules. (2) Plus other Engleberg departures. See above table. (3) Plus other Luzern departures at 14:09, arriving Pilatus 15:00. (4) Plus other Pilatus Kulm departures at 15:45 and 16:25, arriving Luzern 16:50 and 17:50. (5) Change trains at Hergiswill.

Luzern - Mt. Rigi (via Arth-Goldau) - Luzern

The excellent canyon and mountain scenery on this route (unlike the route via Vitznau that follows) is entirely by train. This is an easy one-day roundtrip. The rides between Arth-Goldau and Rigi are *not* covered by Eurailpass. The 1994 price for a one-class roundtrip ticket *without* a Swiss Pass was 48 Swiss francs. *With* a Swiss Pass: Sfr-36.

The Arth-Goldau to Regi Kulm (and v.v.) trains operate late May to mid-October. Times shown below are for the period early July to mid-October.

290

Dep. Luzern	09:14	10:19 (3)	12:19	14:19	15:14 (1)
Arr. Arth Goldau	09:40	10:44	12:44	14:44	15:40
Change to rack railway. 296					
Dep. Arth Goldau	10:03	11:03	13:03	15:03	16:03
Arr. Rigi Kulm	10:33	11:33	13:33	15:33	16:33

• • •

Dep Rigi Kulm	11:10	12:10	14:10	16:10	17:10 (2)
Arr Arth Goldau	11:50	12:50	14:50	16:50	17:50
Change to standard train. 290					
Dep. Arth Goldau	12:20	13:14 (4)	15:14 (4)	17:14 (4)	18:20
Arr. Luzern	25 minutes later				

(1) Plus another Luzern departure at 16:19 (4), arriving Rigi Kulm 17:30. (2) Plus another Rigi Kulm departure at 19:10, arriving Luzern 20:46. (3) Reservation recommended. (4) Reservation required. Supplement charged.

Luzern - Mt. Rigi (via Vitznau) - Luzern

There is very nice canyon, lake and mountain scenery on this easy one-day roundtrip that includes a boat ride (*covered by Eurailpass*) on Lake Luzern. From Vitznau to Mt. Rigi, the train climbs 4,000 feet in 4¼ miles. Over 450,000 passengers take this ride every year. There is good skiing at **Rigi** in the Winter. This line was constructed in 1871.

The Vitznau–Rigi ride is *not* covered by Eurailpass. The 1994 price of the (one-class) roundtrip ticket for the Vitznau–Rigi portion *without* a Swiss Pass was 48 Swiss francs. *With* a Swiss Pass: Sfr-36. *All of the boats have a restaurant or light refreshments.*

294 Boat

Dep. Luzern						
(Bahnhof.)	09:05 (1)	09:30 (2)	10:25 (3)	11:25 (1)	12:00 (3)	13:15 (4+7)
Arr. Vitznau (Pier)	09:52	10:17	11:30	12:26	12:41	14:05
Change to rack railway adjacent to the quay. 296						
Dep. Vitznau	10:10	10:45	11:45	12:40	13:30	16:10
Arr. Rigi Kulm	10:40	11:15	12:15	13:10	14:00	17:00

• • •

| Dep. Rigi Kulm | 10:45 | 11:40 | 12:40 | 14:15 | 15:00 | 16:00 |
| Arr. Vitznau | 11:25 | 12:20 | 13:20 | 14:55 | 15:45 | 17:00 |

Change to boat adjacent to the railstation. 294

Dep. Vitznau (Pier)	11:33 (5)	12:52 (6)	13:47 (1)	15:10 (2)	15:50 (6)	17:30 (1)
Arr. Luzern						
(Bahnhof.)	55–70 minutes later					

(1) Paddlesteamer. Has a restaurant. (2) Runs daily except Sundays and holidays July 1-August 31. (3) Boat has a restaurant. (4) Runs daily. July and August: this is a paddlesteamer daily. May, June and September: this is a paddlesteamer only on Sunday. (5) Light refreshments. (6) Restaurant car. (7) Plus another departure from Luzern at 14:20 (5), arriving Rigi Kulm 15:45.

St. Moritz - Tirano - St. Moritz   328

Great mountain scenery on this easy one-day narrow-gauge roundtrip into Italy. (Take your passport!) It is absolutely breathtaking. The track goes through the Bernina Pass, making this Europe's highest main rail line, reaching 7,400 feet at Bernina Hospiz. Buy a lunch in St. Moritz to eat on the train.

| Dep. St. Moritz | 07:45 | 09:05 | 09:30 | 10:00 | 11:05 |
| Arr. Tirano | 10:22 | 11:28 | 11:46 | 12:24 | 13:30 |

| | | • | • • | | |

| Dep. Tirano | 10:30 (4) | 11:30 (5) | 12:24 | 13:05 (5+6) | 14:05 (1+2++8) |
| Arr. St. Moritz | 13:02 | 13:56 | 14:56 | 15:56 | 16:22 |

(1) Special tourist train. Reservation required. Supplement charged. (2) "Summer Bernina Express." Operates mid-May to late October. (3) "Winter Bernina Express." Operates late October to late May. (4) Mid-December to mid-April: runs daily. Late May to late October: runs Saturdays, Sundays and holidays. (5) Late October to mid-May: runsdaily, except Sundays and holidays. Mid-May to late October: runs daily. (6) Change trains in Poschiavo. (7) Runs Monday–Friday, except holidays. (8) Plus other Tirano departures at 14:40 (1+2),15:05 (1+2), 15:30, 16:10 (7) and 17:30, arriving St. Moritz 16:56, 16:50, 17:39, 17:56, 18:53 and 19:56.

St. Moritz - Zermatt   and   Zermat - St. Moritz   320 + SNTO

Many ordinary trains which do not require reservation, are *not* packed, and have seats that are as comfortable as those of "Glacier Express" run every day. Their only disadvantage is that they require changing trains 4 times: in Chur, Disentis, Andermatt and Brig.

All of the schedules below are for the direct-ride, luxury, "Glacier Express," *for which a reservation is required.* During the summer, seats in its elegant 34-seat restaurant car are usually reserved several months in advance. Reservations both for assigned seats and also for lunch in the elegant 34-seat paneled restaurant car can be made as much as 2 months in advance of travel date through a travel agency — and must be made 14 or more days prior to departure from the U.S.A. Passengers may also have food served at their seats from a minibar that is rolled down the aisle.

St. Moritz–Zermatt, sit on the left for the best views, on the right Zermatt– St. Moritz. There is marvelous canyon, mountain and Rhone Valley scenery on this ride, which crosses 291 bridges (including Europe's highest ones) and goes through 91 tunnels, including the 9-mile-long Furka, as the train traverses the 6,700-foot Oberalp Pass. This "Albula Line" is one of the world's greatest feats of railroad engineering. Its **Landwasser Viaduct** towers over a rampaging Alpine stream. Some of its tunnels are spirals inside the mountains, tunnels that you exit traveling in the same direction as you entered them, but at either a higher or lower level.

On "Glacier Express," the entire route is free with Swiss Pass and Swiss Flexipass. There is no discount for Eurailpass. The 1994 charges for the Disentis–Brig or v.v. portion was $61 (U.S.) for first-class, $37 for second-class. The Brig–Zermatt–Brig portion was $90 and $54.

Dep. St. Moritz	07:05 (1)	09:00 (2)	10:00 (2)
Dep. Chur	09:03 (2)	10:55	12:16
Dep. Disentis	10:29	12:22	13:35
Dep. Andermatt	11:36	13:37	14:36
Dep. Brig	13:23	15:23	16:08
Arr. Zermatt	14:45	16:45	17:22

	•	•

Dep. Zermatt	08:54 (2)	10:10	12:10 (2)
Dep. Brig	10:30	11:44 (2)	13:44
Dep. Andermatt	12:00	13:53	15:23
Dep. Disentis	13:10	15:00	16:52
Arr.Chur	14:18	16:10	18:13 (3)
Arr. St. Moritz	16:58	17:58	19:58

(1) Change trains to "Glacier Express" in Chur. (2) Operates May 29-October 16. (3) Change to ordinary train in Chur.

Sights in **Zermatt**: Access to the Matterhorn. Great skiing in woods, pastures and hills. Displays of the challenges that mountaineers face are exhibited at the Alpine Museum. There are many hiking trails here, so easy that neither special shoes nor gear is necessary. Although each trail climbs about 2,000 feet, they are effortless because the incline is spread over many miles. Because autos have to park several miles away, the air here is pristine.

Sights in **Disentis**: The stained glass in the Cathedral.

Zermatt - Gornergrat - Zermatt 321

This is a great cogwheel train ride to the 10,200-foot high Gornergrat for a close view of the Matterhorn (14,692 feet) and more than 50 other Alpine peaks.

This ride is not covered by Eurailpass. The 1994 price of a one-class rountrip ticket without a Swiss Pass was 53 Swiss francs. With a Swiss Pass: Sfr-39.75.

Dep. Zermatt	07:05, 08:00, 08:24 (1), 08:48 (1), 09:12, 09:36 (1), 10:00, 10:24 (1), 10:48, 11:12, 11:36 (1), 12:00, 12:24 (1), 12:48 (1), 13:12, 13:36 (1), 14:00, 14:24 (1), 14:48 (1), 15:12, 15:36 (1), 16:00, 16:24 (1), 17:12, 18:00.

Arr. Gornergrat	43 minutes later

• • •

Dep. Gornergrat	07:55, 08:43 (1), 09:07, 09:31 (1), 09:55, 10:19 (1), 10:43 (1), 11:07, 11:31, 11:55, 12:19 (1), 12:43 (1), 13:07, 13:31 (1), 13:55, 14:19 (1), 14:43 (1), 15:07, 15:31 (1), 15:55, 16:19 (1), 16:43 (1), 17:07, 17:55, 19:07.

Arr. Zermatt	43 minutes later

(1) Runs daily except May 29-June 10.

Zurich - Sargans - Vaduz - Zurich   (The Trip To Liechtenstein)

There is fine scenery along the shores of **Lake Zurich** and **Lake Walen** on this easy one-day roundtrip.

It is only a 30-minute *bus ride* from Sargans to **Vaduz**, in the tiny country of Liechtenstein. Buses leave Sargans' railstation every 20 minutes for the 27-minute ride to Vaduz.

310

Dep. Zurich	07:35 (2)	08:10 (1)	09:10 (3)	09:33 (1)	10:10 (2)	11:10 (4+6)
Arr. Sargans	08:31	09:11	10:18	10:31	11:11	12:19
Change to bus. Table 311						
Dep. Sargans	08:33	09:33	10:33	10:53 (5)	11:28	12:33
Arr. Vaduz	09:02	10:02	11:02	11:32 (8)	11:57	13:02

• • •

Dep. Vaduz	13:05	14:05	15:05	16:05	17:05	18:05 (7)
Arr. Sargans	13:34	14:34	15:34	16:34	17:34	18:34
Change to train. Table 310						
Dep. Sargans	13:39 (4)	14:45 (2)	15:39 (3)	16:45 (1)	17:39 (3)	18:45 (2)
Arr. Zurich	14:50	15:50	16:50	17:50	18:50	19:50

(1) Reservation advisable. Restaurant car. (2) Reservation advisable. Light refreshments. (3) Light refreshments. (4) Restaurant car. (5) Runs daily, except Sundays and holidays. (6) Plus other departures from Zurich at 11:20 (1) and 12:10 (3), arriving Vaduz 13:02 and 13:42. (7) Plus other departures from Vaduz at 19:00, 20:00, 21:00 and 22:00, arriving Zurich 20:50, 21:50, 22:50 and 23:50. (8) Also August 1, not June 2, August 15, September 18.

Sights in **Vaduz**: Capital of the principality of Liechtenstein, a country that is 16 miles long by 4 miles wide, nestled between Switzerland and Austria. The extensive network of walking paths is very popular. Many excellent restaurants here.

See the collection of paintings by Rubens and other old masters at the National Art Gallery, open daily (April–October: 10:00–12:00 and 13:30–17:30. November–March: 10:00–12:00 and 14:00–17:30.) The exhibits of prehistoric and Roman articles: ancient weapons, coins, wood carvings, folk art and handicrafts, items from the area's medieval castles and other historical artifacts in the National Museum, open May–September daily 10:00–12:00 and 13:30–17:30. October–April: daily except Monday, 14:00–17:30.

The Postage Stamp Museum is open daily all year 10:00–12:00 and 14:00–18:00.

Zurich - Chur - Arosa - Chur - Zurich

See the good canyon, lake and mountain scenery on this easy one-day roundtrip. There is time for a stopover in Chur, as shown by the schedules below.

Most of the Zurich–Chur and Chur–Zurich trains have a restaurant car or light refreshments.

310

Dep. Zurich	07:33 (1)	08:10 (1)	09:10	10:10 (1)	11:10	12:10 (1+2)
Arr. Chur	08:51	09:37	10:45	11:37	12:45	13:37
Change trains.	324					
Dep. Chur	09:00	09:55	10:55	11:55	12:55	13:55
Arr. Arosa	60 minutes later					

Sights in **Arosa:** Great Summer and Winter Sports. Fantastic mountain scenery.

Dep. Arosa	10:05	11:05	12:05	13:05	14:05	15:05
Arr. Chur	11:07	12:07	13:07	14:07	15:07	16:07
Change trains.	310					
Dep. Chur	11:15	12:23 (1)	13:15	14:23 (1)	15:15	16:23 (1+3)
Arr. Zurich	12:50	13:50	14:50	15:50	16:50	17:50

(1) Reservation advisable. (2) Plus another Zurich departure at 13:10, arriving back in Zurich 18:50. (3) Plus other departures from Chur at 17:15, 18:23 (1), 19:15, 20:13, 21:13 and 22:13, arriving Zurich 18:50, 19:50, 20:50, 21:50, 22:50 and 23:50.

Zurich - Chur - Zermatt - Gornergrat - Zermatt

There is fabulous Rhone Valley scenery on this ride plus crossing Oberalp Pass (6,700 feet) and going through the 8-mile long Furka Tunnel on the Chur–Brig portion.

This trip includes going over the highest bridges in Europe and, by departing Zurich at 07:10 or 09:10, you can include the outstanding cogwheel train ride to Gornergrat (10,200 feet) for a close view of the Matterhorn (14,692 feet) and more than 50 other Alpine peaks.

The Chur–Zermatt, Zermatt–Gornergrat and Gornergrat–Zermatt portions of this trip are not covered by Eurailpass.

The 1994 prices of tickets for those rides without a Swiss Pass were: 203 Swiss francs for first-class, Sfr-143 for second-class. With a Swiss Pass, the Chur–Zermatt portion was free, and the Zermatt–Gornergrat–Zermatt roundtrip was at 25% discount, making the entire trip Sfr-39.75.

All of the Chur–Zermatt trains in this timetable are "Glacier Express," for which reservation is required. For services, prices and reservations, see "St. Moritz–Zermatt."

Do not let this timetable discourage you. This trip is easier to make than it was to prepare the table!

310			321		
Dep. Zurich	07:10 (1)	09:10 (1)	Dep. Zermatt	14:48 (7)	17:12
Arr. Chur	08:45	10:45	Arr. Gornergrat	15:29	17:55
Change trains. 320				• • •	
Dep. Chur	09:03 (2)	10:55 (2)	Dep. Gornergrat	15:31 (6)	17:55 (4+5)
Arr. Zermatt	14:45 (6)	16:45 (6)	Arr. Zermatt	16:15	18:37
Change trains.					

(1) Light refreshments. (2) "Glacier Express." See details about reservations and prices under "St. Moritz–Zermatt" (3) Operates mid-June to mid-October. Plus another Zermatt departure all year at 16:00. (4) Does not operates late October to late November. (5) Plus other departures from Gornergrat at 15:55, 16:19 (7), 16:43 (7), 17:07 (all year), 17:55 and 19:07, arriving Zermatt 16:39, 17:03, 17:27, 17:51, 18:38 and 19:49. (6) Runs May 29-October 16. (7) Runs daily except May 29-June 10.

Zurich - Davos - Filisur - Thusis - Zurich

In order to make a scenic *circle-trip* that avoids repeating the Landquart–Filisur route in the Zurich–Davos roundtrip, return to Zurich from Filisur via Thusis.

The Davos–Filisur portion of this trip is *not* covered by Eurailpass. The 1994 prices *without* a Swiss pass were: 14 Swiss francs for first-class, Sfr-8.40 for second-class. *With* a Swiss Pass: Free.

310

Dep. Zurich	07:10 (1)	08:10 (5)	09:10 (1)	10:10 (1)	11:10 (3+6)
Arr. Landquart	08:31	09:23	10:31	11:23	12:31

Change trains. 327

Dep. Landquart	08:56	09:40	10:47	11:40	12:47
Dep. Klosters	09:52	10:20	11:43	12:20	13:43
Arr. Davos Platz	10:24 (4)	10:46 (4)	12:13 (4)	12:46 (4)	14:13 (4)
Arr. Filisur	10:52	11:52	12:52	13:52	14:52

Change trains. 330

Dep. Filisur	11:04 (3)	12:04 (1)	13:04 (1)	14:04 (8)	15:04
Dep Thusis	11:37	12:37 (7)	13:37	14:37	15:37
Arr. Chur	12:07	13:07	14:07	15:07	16:07

Change trains. 310

Dep. Chur	12:23 (2)	13:15 (3)	14:23 (2)	15:15 (1)	16:23 (5)
Arr. Zurich	13:50	14:50	15:50	16:50	17:50

(1) Light refreshments. (2) Reservation advisable. Light refreshments. (3) Restaurant car. (4) Change trains. (5) Reservation advisable. Restaurant car. (6) Plus other departures from Zurich at 12:10 (2) and 13:10 (1), arriving back in Zurich 18:50 and 19:50. (7) Runs Sundays + holidays June 18-September 24. (8) Runs Saturdays, Sundays and holidays.

Zurich - Landquart - Davos - Landquart - Zurich

Excellent canyon, lake and mountain scenery may be viewed on this easy one-day round-trip.

Zurich - Bellinzona - Lugano   290

The Zurich – Lugano portion of the Zurich-Milan route (one of the 5 most scenic rail trips in Europe) can be seen on a one-day roundtrip from Zurich. A feast of beautiful farms, lakes, mountains, rivers and vineyards. You go through the 9.3-mile long Gotthard Tunnel.

Before the Gotthard was opened to traffic in 1882, there was no direct rail route from eastern Switzerland through the Alps to Italy. For 7 years and 5 months, 2500 men worked in 3% shifts day and night to build this engineering marvel. Immediately after exiting the third of a series of 9 tunnels, the train passes the small, white Wassen Church to your right, and about 230 feet above the track. The next time the church comes into view, after leaving Wassen Station, it is also to your right, and nearly level with the track. Later, after exiting tunnel #7, you have a third view of the church, this time to your left and 170 feet above the track.

The turns inside 3 semi-circular tunnels in this area (Pfaffensprung, Wattinger and Leggistein) are engineered so well that there is no sensation of the curves that the train is making inside those tunnels.

Try this interesting experiment: make a pendulum of any object, holding the top of a weighted string, chain or handkerchief against the inner face of a train window (a left-hand window when inside Pfaffensprung and Wattinger, a right-hand window when inside Leggistein). As the train goes around a curve, the weighted bottom will move away from the window.

Climate on the Swiss side of the tunnel is usually much cooler than the Mediterranean temperature on the Italian end. There is a beautiful descent from the Italian end of the tunnel down the Ticino Valley. The train makes 3% gradients at 45–50 miles per hour.

At Bellinzona, the line forks. One branch goes to Locarno, the other to Lugano and Milan.

Dep. Zurich	07:03 (1)	08:03 (1)	09:03 (1)	10:03 (2)	11:03 (1)
Arr. Bellinzona	09:33	10:33 (7)	11:33 (7)	12:33	13:33
Arr. Lugano	10:03	11:03	12:03	13:03	14:03

Sights in **Bellinzona**: The Museum of Costumes and Prints, located in Castello di Sasso Corbaro, 320 feet above the town. Open daily except Monday 09:00–12:00 and 14:00–17:00, there are great views from it of the Alps, the Ticino River Valley and Lago (Lake) Maggiore.

The outdoor Saturday market: peasant sausages, breads, mountain cheeses, kitchenware, clothing. The 4th century Castello Grande, sitting on a 150-foot-hight hill in the center of the town.

The Post Office on Viale della Stazione is the newest (1990) tourist attraction because of its post-modernism architecture.

One can take a passageway under the railroad tracks (starting at a point between the railstation and the Post Office) to begin walking up a hillside to the 15th century Castel Piccolo (small castle) for good views of the area.

See the views of the Ticino River Valley and the collection of medieval art, ancient coins and old weapons at the Civic Museum in the former dungeons of Castle Piccolo, open daily except Monday June–September 09:30–12:00 and 14:00–17:30: October–May 09:30–12:00 and 14:00–17:00.

The frescoed and arcaded old houses with wrought-iron balconies and marble portals, particularly Ca Rossa, called "Red House" because of the terra cotta ornaments on its facade.

The elegant clock tower on the ancient Town Hall, at Piazza Nosetto. Nearby the large rose window on the Collegiate Church and the beautiful sculptured 15th century font there. A 10-minute walk from it is the interesting frescoed wall at Santa Maria delle Grazie Church.

Dep. Lugano	10:41	11:57 (1)	12:41 (3)	13:57 (4)	14:41 (3+6)
Dep. Bellinzona	11:09	12:27	13:09	14:27	15:09
Arr. Zurich	13:57	14:57	15:57	16:57	17:57

(1) Reservation advisable. Restaurant car. (2) Light refreshments to 10:45 arrival and train change in Arth Goldau. Depart Arth Goldau 10:49 (1). (3) Light refreshments. (4) Reservation advisable. Light refreshments. (5) Reservation *required*. Restaurant car. (6) Plus other departures from Lugano at 15:57 (1), 16:33 (1), 17:57 (1), 18:47 (7), 19:41 and 20:31 (5), arriving Zurich 18:57, 19:28, 20:57, 21:48, 23:03 and 23:36. (7) Supplement payable.

Zurich - Mt. Rigi - Zurich

The Arth Goldau–Mt. Rigi-Arth Goldau roundtrip portion of this trip is not covered by Eurailpass. The 1994 price of a one-class roundtrip ticket without a Swiss Pass was 48 Swiss francs. With a Swiss Pass: Sfr-36.

The Arth Goldau–Rigi Kulm (and v.v.) schedules shown here are for the period early April to mid-October. Arth Goldau-Rigi (and v.v.) trains additional to those shown below operate early July to mid-October.

290

Dep. Zurich	09:03 (1)	10:03 (2)	12:03 (2)	14:03 (2)	15:03 (3)
Arr. Arth Goldau	09:45 (4)	10:45	12:45	14:45	15:44 (4)

Change to rack railway.

296

Dep. Arth Goldau	10:03	11:03	13:03	15:03	16:03
Arr. Rigi Kulm	10:33	11:33	13:33	15:33	16:33

• • •

296

Dep. Rigi Kulm	11:10	12:10	14:10	16:10	17:10	19:10
Arr. Arth Goldau	11:50	12:50	14:50	16:50	17:50	19:50

Change from rack railway to a standard train

290

Dep. Arth Goldau	12:15 (1)	13:15	15:15 (2)	17:15 (2)	18:15 (1)	20:15 (1)
Arr. Zurich	12:57 (4)	13:57	15:57	17:57	18:57	20:57

(1) Reservation advisable. Restaurant car. (2) Light refreshments. (3) Reservation advisable. Light refreshments. (4) Supplement payable.

Zurich - Luzern - Mt. Pilatus - Luzern - Zurich

There is fine canyon and mountain scenery on this easy one-day roundtrip.

The Alpnachstad–Pilatus–Alpnachstad rack railway portion operates only from May to the end of November. The 1994 price of a one-class roundtrip ticket without a Swiss Pass was: 53 Swiss francs. With a Swiss Pass: Sfr-39.75.

There are good views and several restaurants at the top of Pilatus.

Most of the trains Zurich-Luzern (and v.v.) have light refreshments.

295

| Dep. Zurich | 07:07 | 08:07 (3) | 09:07 (3) | 10:07 | 11:07 | 12:07 | 13:07 (1) |
| Arr. Luzern | 07:56 | 08:56 | 09:56 | 10:56 | 11:56 | 12:56 | 13:56 |

Change trains. Table 285

| Dep. Luzern | 08:09 | 09:09 | 10:09 | 11:09 | 12:09 | 13:09 | 14:09 |
| Arr. Alpnachstad | 08:27 | 09:27 | 10:27 | 11:27 | 12:27 | 13:27 | 14:27 |

Change to rack railway. Table 286

| Dep. Alpnachstad | 08:50 | 09:30 | 10:50 | 11:30 | 13:10 | 13:50 | 14:30 |
| Arr. Pilatus Kulm | 09:20 | 10:00 | 11:20 | 12:00 | 13:40 | 14:20 | 15:00 |

• • •

| Dep. Pilatus Kulm | 09:25 | 10:45 | 11:25 | 12:05 | 13:45 | 14:25 | 15:05 (2) |
| Arr. Alpnachstad | 10:05 | 11:25 | 12:05 | 12:45 | 14:25 | 15:05 | 15:45 |

Change to standard train. Table 285

| Dep. Alpnachstad | 10:30 | 11:30 | 12:30 | 13:30 | 14:30 | 15:30 | 16:30 |
| Arr. Luzern | 10:50 | 11:50 | 12:50 | 13:50 | 14:50 | 15:50 | 16:50 |

Change trains. Table 295

| Dep. Luzern | Frequent times from 06:04 to 23:08 |
| Arr. Zurich | 50 minutes later |

(1) Plus another departure from Zurich at 14:07, arriving Pilatus Kulm 16:20. (2) Plus other Pilatus departures at 15:45 and 16:25, arriving Zurich 17:53 and 18:53. (3) Runs Monday-Friday except holidays.

Zurich - Romanshorn - St. Gallen (St. Gall) - Zurich

There is excellent lake and mountain scenery on this easy one-day circle roundtrip that visits **Lake Constance** (**Konstanz** in German). One hundred miles of the lake's shore are in Germany, 16 in Austria, 43 in Switzerland. The microclimate here is so balmy taht even palm trees grow in this area.

Sights in **St. Gallen:** The history of lacemaking and embroidery from the 16th century to the present, and lacework worn by European nobility, at the Gewerbemuseum (Embroidery Museum). The paintings in the Historisches Museum. The 100,000 volumes (including illuminated manuscripts), more than 1,000 years old, in the rebuilt rococo library of the ancient abbey. The twin-towered baroque 18th century Cathedral. Near it, many old houses decorated with frescoes and oriel windows, in the city's old quarter.

305

Dep. Zurich	08:10 (1)	09:10 (2)	10:10 (2)	11:10	12:10 (4+5)
Arr. Romanshorn	09:21	10:21	11:21 (3)	12:21	13:21

Take time for a boat ride on Lake Konstanz. Table 312
(09:36–11:24, 10:36–12:24 or 11:36–13:24 — 50% discount with Eurailpass.)

Dep. Romanshorn	10:08 (1)	10:32	12:08 (1)	12:32	14:32
Arr. St. Gallen	10:40	10:55	12:40	13:00	15:00

Change trains. Table 308

Dep. St. Gallen	Frequent times from 06:03 to 23:15
Arr. Zurich	70 minutes later

(1) Light refreshments. (2) Restaurant car. (3) Reservation advisable. (4) Reservation advisable. Light refreshments. (5) Plus other departures from Zurich at 13:10, 14:10 (4) and 15:10…with departures from Romanshorn, at 15:08, 16:08 (1) and 16:32…arriving back in Zurich 16:53, 17:53 and 18:21.

Romanshorn - Friedrichshafen   314

This is the ferry service between Romanshorn and Friedrichshafen (50% discount with Eurailpass).

All of these boats have a restaurant.

Dep. Romanshorn	09:36	10:36 (1)	11:36	12:36 (1)	13:36	14:36 (1+2)
Arr. Friedrichshafen	40–45 minutes later

Sights in **Friedrichshafen**: The first rigid airship, the Zeppelin, was built here in 1900, and this town became the principal European terminal for regularly scheduled trans-Atlantic airship service to New York and Rio de Janeiro. See the models, documents, photographs and collection of engines and other parts at the Zeppelin Museum.

Many of the towns on the German shore of Lake Constance (or Konstanz) have attractions. The local wine, pleasant inns and cozy taverns along their steep, winding cobblestoned streets bring crowds of visitors to them.

At **Unteruhldingen,** the open air museum of Stone Age and Bronze Age villages features reconstructed thatch-roofed, adobe houses built on wood piles between 4,000 and 1,000 B.C.

For devotees of Baroque and roccoco decor, there are the 18th century church at **Birnau** and the banquet hall, reception rooms, library and private chambers of the palace and the interior of the 12th century abbey at **Salem**.

See **Ueberlingen**, a living page from the Middle Ages and the Renaissance: massive walls, 15th and 16th century house, a lavish Town Hall.

Konstanz is the largest city on the lake (70,000). Because it is surrounded by Switzerland, it was spared from air raids in World War II. Founded about 300 A.D., it is the best base for visiting the lake's most popular islands: **Mainau** and **Reichenau**. The sights on Mainau are its tropical orchards (bananas, lemon, orange and mandarin trees) and profusion of flowers. It also has a Baroque castle.

The Benedictine abbeys and 3 churches on Reichenau provide a view of monastic life in the Middle Ages. See the Byzantine, Baroque and Gothic art at the treasury in St. Mary's Church.

The 18th century Montfort Palace in **Tettnang** is one of the most richly decorated and lavishly furnished chateaus in southern Germany.

Dep. Friedrichshafen   10:43   11:43 (1)   12:43   13:43 (1)   14:43   15:43 (1+3)
Arr. Romanshorn   40–45 minutes later

(1) Operates March 18-May 27, 1995. (2) Plus other departures from Romanshorn at 15:36, 16:36 (1), 17:36, 18:36 (1) and 19:36 (2). (3) Plus other departures from Friedrichshafen at 16:43, 17:43 (1), 18:43(2) and 19:43 (1).

Zurich - Schaffhausen - Zurich 302

A trip to see the marvelous **Rhine Falls**.

Dep. Zurich   Frequent times from 07:13 to 23:13
Arr. Schaffhausen   38 minutes later

Sights in **Schaffhausen**: A bus takes you in 10 minutes from the railstation to the cataracts below the tumultous 7-story-high Rhine Falls (less than an hour walk from the town's waterfront). The most impressive sight is usually in early July, when the snow in the Swiss and Austrian Alps is melting. For a great view of the Rhine River, climb to the 16th century Munot Fortress.

Visit the gold and silver room in the Allerheiligen Museum. The Thursday market.

Take the uphill path, through vineyards, a 15-minute walk to the hilltop castle, for the view from there. Ride the cable car to the summit of 8,215-foot-high **Mt. Santis** for a spectacular view of many Alpine peaks, including Germany's Zugspitze.

Take the 90 minute river boat to **Stein am Rhein** to see the 11th century Hohenklingen Castle. See the depiction of 11th century life in the museum at the 11th century St. George Monastery, the ruins of Tasgetium (a Roman fort), and the stained glass, wood walls and medieval firearms on the top floor of the 16th century Town Hall.

Dep. Schaffhausen   Frequent times from 06:06 to 22:08
Arr. Zurich   38 minutes later

A GLORIOUS WEEK IN SWITZERLAND

Here is a great 7-day circle itinerary of Switzerland that gives you, in the span of one week, a visit to most of the country's major cities plus a view of much of Switzerland's great scenery. (The rides to Jungfraujoch and Mt. Rigi are *not* covered by Eurailpass.)

Day 1   Geneva, Montreux, Zweisimmen, Spiez (Lunch). Lake Thun boat to Interlaken.
Day 2   Interlaken, Jungfraujoch, Grindelwald (lunch), Interlaken.
Day 3   Interlaken, Luzern.
Day 4   Luzern, Vitznau, Mt. Rigi (lunch), Arth-Goldau, Lugano.
Day 5   Lugano, Bellinzona, Locarno.
Day 6   Locarno, Domodossola, Bern.
Day 7   Bern to Geneva or Zurich.

A MAGNIFICENT ONE-DAY TRIP

Here are several of the most scenic rail trips in Europe, combined in a single day.

All of these rides are covered by Eurailpass.

Table 280	Dep. Spiez	07:54 (1) .... Arr. Brig	08:59
365	Dep. Brig	09:34 (2) .... Arr. Domodossola	10:02
272	Dep. Domodossola	10:18 .... Arr. Locarno	11:55
291	Dep. Locarno	12:03 .... Arr. Bellinzona	12:21
290	Dep. Bellinzona	13:27 (3) .... Arr. Luzern	15:39
285	Dep. Luzern	16:24 .... Arr. Interlaken (Ost)	18:23
280	Dep. Interlaken (Ost)(1)	18:39 .... Arr. Spiez	18:59

(1) Light refreshments. (2) Reservation advisable. Light refreshments. (3) Reservation advisable. Restaurant car. Supplement charged.

THE "GOLDEN PASS" ROUTE

Luzern - Interlaken - Spiez - Zweisimmen - Montreux - Lausanne

There are snowcapped Alpine peaks, flowering meadows, and sparkling mountain streams on this marvelous one-day trip. As the timetables show, a layover in Spiez is possible.

285		
Dep. Luzern	08:24 (1)	
Arr. Interlaken (Ost)	10:23	
Change trains.		
280		
Dep. Interlaken (Ost)	10:39 (1)	
Arr. Spiez	10:59	
Change trains.		

276		
Dep. Spiez	11:08	12:03 (2)
Arr. Zweisimmen	11:55	12:39
Change trains. 275		
Dep. Zweisimmen	12:00	12:50
Arr. Montreux	14:00	14:38
Change trains. 270		
Dep. Montreux	14:07	15:07
Arr. Lausanne	14:27	15:27

(1) Restaurant car. (2) Plus other departures from Spiez at 13:08, 14:03 (transferring to "Panoramic Express" for the Zweisimmen-Montreux portion — Reservation required...see pages 398-399) and 15:08...changing trains in Zweisimmen 13:55, 14:39 and 15:55...changing trains in Montreux 16:00, 16:38 and 18:00...arriving Lausanne 16:27, 17:03 and 18:27.

INTERNATIONAL ROUTES FROM SWITZERLAND

The Swiss gateways for travel to West Germany are Basel (to Cologne), Geneva (to Frankfurt), and Zurich (to Munich). Zurich is also the starting point for the train trip to Austria (Innsbruck, and on to Vienna and East Europe) and for train travel to Italy (Milan and beyond).

Basel is also a starting point for trips to Belgium, Holland and France (Paris, and on to London or Madrid).

Geneva (via Aosta, and on to Torino) as well as Bern and Brig (via Domodossola) are also departure cities for rail rides to Italy (Milan, and beyond).

There is also rail service from Geneva to Paris, and from Geneva to southern France (Avignon) and on to Spain (Barcelona).

Basel - Amsterdam 38

Dep. Basel (S.B.B.)	13:17 (2)	14:17 (2)	23:25 (3)
Arr. Amsterdam	20:51	21:51	09:40

(1) Change trains in Maastricht at 15:22. (2) Reservation advisable. Supplement charged. Restaurant car. (3) Has couchettes.

Basel - Cologne   650 + 730

Sit on the right side of the train for best views of the marvelous Rhine River scenery.

Reservation is advisable for all of the Basel–Cologne day trains. All of them have a restaurant car.

Dep. Basel (SBB)	Every hour 07:17 to 18:17
Dep. Basel (Bad.)	7 minutes after departing S.B.B. railstation
Arr. Cologne	11:59 to 22:59

Basel - Hamburg - Copenhagen - Oslo - Stockholm   50

Dep. Basel (SBB)	07:51 (1)	11:51 (1)	-0-	17:49 (4+5)	-0-
Arr. Hamburg (Hbf.)	14:21	18:21	-0-	03:54 (5)	-0-
Change trains.					
Dep. Hamburg	15:19(2)	19:34 (4)	19:34 (4)	04:04	-0-
Arr. Copenhagen	20:20	-0-	-0-	09:25	-0-
Change trains.					
Dep. Copengagen	21:45 (3)	-0-	-0-	09:45 (6)	11:15 (6)
Arr. Oslo (Sen.)	07:37	11:46	-0-	19:42	-0- (7)
Arr. Stockholm (Cen.)	-0-	-0-	10:05	-0-	19:53

(1) Reservation advisable. Supplement charged. Restaurnt car. (2) Reservation advisable. Supplement charged. Light refreshments. (3) Reservation *required*. Carries a sleeping car. Also has couchettes. Coach is second-class. (4) Train has only sleeping cars and couchettes. No coaches. (5) Direct train to Copenhagen. No train change in Hamburg. (6) Reservation *required*. Restaurant car. (7) Runs daily to August 14.

Zurich - Munich   75

Reservation is advisable for all of these trains. All of them charge a supplement and have restaurant car.

Dep. Zurich	07:40	09:40	13:40	17:40
Arr. Munich	11:51	13:56	17:48	21:45

Zurich - Innsbruck - Salzburg - Vienna 86

About 2½ hours out of Zurich, the train passes through one of Europe's largest tunnels, the 6.3-mile long Arlberg. There is a very beautiful view of Alpine scenery as the train comes out of the tunnel.

Dep. Zurich	09:33 (1)	13:35 (1)	22:33 (3)
Arr. Innsbruck	13:16	17:16	02:46
Arr. Salzburg	15:22	19:22	04:45
Arr. Vienna (West.)	18:30	22:30	08:05

(1) Reservation advisable. Supplement charged. Restaurant car. (2) Change trains in Feldkirch [arr. 17:11/dep. 17:44 (1)]. (3) Reservaion advisable. (4) Change trains in Innsbruck, departing Innsbruck 23:29 (has couchettes). (5) Carries a sleeping car. Also has couchettes.

Bern - Brig - Milan 280

This trip takes you on the marvelous scenic route via Spiez (see "Geneva–Spiez") and through both the 10-mile long Lotschberg Tunnel Bern–Brig) and the 11.9-mile long Simplon (Brig–Milan), longest tunnel in Europe and world's third longest, after Japan's Seikan Tunnel (33.4 miles, between Tappi and Yoshioka) and Japan's Daishimizu Tunnel (13.4 miles, between Tokyo and Niigata).

Reservation is advisable for all of these trains.

Dep. Bern	06:50 (2)	08:51 (1)	12:56 (1)	15:22 (2)	17:22 (1)
Arr. Brig	08:15	10:16 (3)	14:24	16:54	18:54
Arr. Milan (Cen.)	10:45	12:40	16:50	19:15	21:10

(1) Light refreshments. (2) Restaurant car. (3)Runs Friday and Saturdays July 2-August 27.

Zurich - Milan 84

See detailed notes about the wonderful scenery on this route (one of the 5 most scenic rail trips in Europe) under "Zurich–Lugano"

Reservation is advisable for all of these trains.

Dep. Zurich	07:03 (1)	08:03 (1)	09:03 (1)	11:03	13:33 (2+3)
Arr. Milan (Cen.)	11:35	12:35 (4)	13:30 (4)	15:35	17:35

(1) Restaurant car. (2) Light refreshments. (3) Plus other Zurich departures at 15:03,17:03 (1) and 19:03, arriving Milan 19:30, 21:30 and 23:35. (4) Supplement charged.

Basel - Luxembourg - Brussels   40

Dep. Basel (S.B.B.)	08:32	13:30 (3)	16:26 (3)
Arr. Luxembourg	12:06	16:59	20:06
Arr. Brussels (Q.L.)	14:17	19:10	22:18
Arr. Brussels (Nord)	14:27	19:20	22:28
Arr. Brussels (Midi)	8 minutes after arriving Nord railstation.		

(1) Carries a sleeping car. Also has couchettes. (2) Restaurant car. (3) Reservation advisable. Supplement charged. Restaurant car.

Geneva - Milan - Venice   83

Dep. Geneva (Corn.)	08:20 (1)	10:34 (1)	11:48 (4)	23:02 (5)
Arr. Milan (Cen.)	12:40	14:40 (2)	16:50 (7+8)	-0- (6)
Dep. Milan (Cen.)	12:50	15:05 (3)	17:05 (3)	-0- (6)
Arr. Venice (S.L.)	15:52	17:57	20:02	07:00

(1) Reservation advisable. Restaurant car. (2) Change trains. (3) Reservation advisable. Supplement charged. Light refreshments. (4) Light refrehments. Change trains in Brig [arr. 14:23—dep. 14:31 (1)]. (5) Carries a sleeping car. Also has couchettes. (6) Does not call on Milan. (7) Arrives Venice Mestre. (8) Also change in Milan.

Bern - Paris   42

Dep. Bern	07:00 (1)	09:22	17:05
Arr. Frasne	08:28	10:59 (2)	18:38 (2)
Dep. Frasne	08:30	11:06 (1)	18:45 (1)
Arr. Paris (Lyon)	11:24	13:59	21:39

(1) TGV. Reservation advisable. Supplement charged. Restaurant car. (2) Change trains in Frasne.

Geneva - Paris   159

Reservtion is advisable for these trains. All are TGV, run daily and have a restaurant car, unless designated otherwise.

Dep. Geneva (Corn.)	05:40 (1)	07:45	10:00	12:37	16:50	19:10
Arr. Paris (Lyon)	09:15 (2)	11:12	13:29	16:11	20:30	22:42

(1) Runs Monday-Friday, except holidays. (2) Not July 15.

Zurich - Bern (or Basel) - Geneva - Avignon - Barcelona 81

The "Pablo Casals" (19:33 departure from Zurich) began in 1990 to carry one "Gran Clase" sleeping car, the most luxurious sleeping car in Europe. Each of its large single and double compartments has a shower and toilet. The train also has ordinary sleeping compartments and 4-berth tourist compartments. There are no coach seats. The train has a restaurant car. Travel is not covered by any rail passes. A supplement is charged. This is a direct train. No train change in Port Bou.

Dep. Zurich	-0-	-0-	-0-	19:33 (4)
Dep. Bern	-0-	-0-	-0-	20:47
Dep. Basel (S.B.B.)	-0-	-0-	18:23 (3)	-0-
Dep. Geneva (Cor.)	10:34 (1)	11:32 (2)	21:54	22:46
Dep. Avignon	15:10	15:47	01:45	-0-
Arr. Port Bou	18:23	18:51	05:25 (3)	-0-
Arr. Barcelona (Sants)	19:53	-0-	09:35	-0-
Arr. Barcelona (Franca)	-0-	20:50	-0-	09:10

(1) Operates early July to early September. Light refreshments. Geneva-Port Bou. (2) Restaurant car. (3) Has couchettes. Change trains in Port Bou at 05:25. (4) "Pablo Casals." See description above.

AOSTA-TORINO GATEWAYS TO ITALY

(1) Via San Bernardo Tunnel

Lausanne or Brig to Martigny and Martigny - Aosta - Torino

270	*(Train)*			*270*	*(Train)*		
Dep. Lausanne	06:56	15:32 (1)		Dep. Brig	06:48	15:36 (1)	
Arr. Martigny	07:45	16:21		Arr. Martigny	07:36	16:32	

• • •

269	*(Bus)*				
Dep. Martigny (Stn.)		07:55	10:55 (2)	16:30	-0-
Arr. Aosta (P. Narbonne)		10:00	17:25	18:35	-0-
Change to a train. 353					
Dep. Aosta		14:42	18:26	19:32	20:42
Arr. Torino (Porta Nuova)		16:34	20:35	21:37	22:29

(1) Light refreshments. (2) Train Martigny-Orsieres, bus Orsieres-Le Grand St. Bernard, then change buses and depart Le Grand 16:15 (operates early June to mid-September).

(2) Via Mt. Blanc Tunnel

Geneva - Chamonix - Aosta - Torino

All of the train changes Geneva–Chamonix are cross-platform, taking less than one minute.

167

Dep. Geneva (Eaux-Vives)	07:10 (1)	08:27 (3)	11:10	14:30
Arr. La Roche-sur-Foron	07:42 (3)	08:57	11:46	15:11
Change trains.				
Dep. La Roche-sur-Foron	07:50	09:56	11:53	15:35
Arr. St. Gervais	08:52	10:43	12:38	16:21
Change trains. 268				
Dep. St. Gervais	09:16	10:53	13:04	16:45
Arr. Chamonix	09:52	11:30	13:42	17:21
Change to a bus. 192				
Dep. Chamonix	10:05 (3)	15:00 (3)	16:15 (3)	17:30
Arr. Aosta	11:40	17:00	18:00	19:30

(1) Runs daily, except Sundays and holidays. (2) Runs Saturdays, Sundays and holidays. (3) Operates late June to mid-September.

Change to a train. 353

Dep. Aosta (P. Narbonne)	14:42	18:26	-0-	19:32	20:42
Arr. Torino (P. S.)	16:34	20:35	-0-	21:24	22:29

A good break in this journey is to spend the night in Aosta and continue on to Torino the next day. Here are the schedules for the other departures from Aosta:

Dep. Aosta (P. Narbonne)	07:42	09:42 (1)
Arr. Torino (P. S.)	09:32	10:35

(1) Runs daily, except Sundays and holidays.

CHAPTER 7

BRITAIN
ENGLAND, WALES AND SCOTLAND

Children under 5 travel free. Half-fare for children 5–15. Children 16 and over must pay full fare.

On British trains, first-class sleeping cars have single compartments; standard-class sleeping cars have 2-berth compartments. Sleeping-car passengers are served morning tea and biscuits free of charge. Generally, overnight passengers may remain in sleeping cars at destinations the next morning until 07:30. Pullman trains, for which reservation is advisable, offer full meals to first-class passengers at their seats.

Britain's 750 "InterCity" trains, linking more than 200 towns each weekday, average 98 to 100 miles per hour on some routes.

Reservations are required on the fast day trains. If there are vacant spaces, the conductor at the departure platform can allocate available places.

British Rail usually makes repairs to train lines on Sundays, as late as 16:00. If you plan to travel by train here on a Sunday, it is advisable to telephone the railstation and confirm the time for routes you intend to use.

BRITAIN'S TRAIN PASSES

BritRail Pass The BritRail Pass, similar to Eurailpass (which does *not* cover Britain), provides unlimited rail travel in England, Scotland and Wales. Youth-Pass (limited to ages 16 to under 25) is for standard-class space. The 1996 prices are:

	8 Days	15 Days	22 Days	One Month
First-class	$ 325.00	$ 525.00	$ 665.00	$ 765.00
Standard-class	235.00	365.00	465.00	545.00
Child 5-15				
First-class	157.50	257.50	322.50	375.00
Standard-class	115.00	177.50	222.50	260.00
Youth 16-under 25				
Standard-class	189.00	289.00	369.00	435.00
Senior Citizen 60 +				
First-class	275.00	445.00	565.00	650.00

BRITAIN

WICK

KYLE OF LOCHALSH
INVERNESS
FORT WILLIAM
AVIEMORE
ABERDEEN
DUNDEE
PERTH
OBAN
GLENEAGLES
ST. ANDREWS
STERLING
GLASGOW
EDINBURGH
BERWICK
TURNBERRY
DUMFRIES
NEWCASTLE
STRANREAR
CARLISLE
SUNDERLAND
HARTLEPOOL
DARLINGTON
SALTBURN
MIDDLESBROUGH
WINDERMERE
SCARBOROUGH
HARROGATE
BARROW
YORK
HEYSHAM
PRESTON
LEEDS
SELBY
HULL
BLACKPOOL
BRADFORD
DONCASTER
MANCHESTER
SHEFFIELD
GRIMSBY
LIVERPOOL
LINCOLN
SKEGNESS
HOLYHEAD
LLANDUDNO
RETFORD
CREWE
NEWARK
CHESTER
STOKE
DERBY
GRANTHAM
STAFFORD
NOTTINGHAM
KING'S LYNN
SHREWSBURY
PETERSBOROUGH
NORWICH
YARMOUTH
WOLVERHAMPTON
LEICESTER
ELY
ABERYSTWYTH
BURMINGHAM
COVENTRY
CAMBRIDGE
WORCESTER
RUGBY
NORTHAMPTON
IPSWICH
HARWICH
HEREFORD
STRATFORD
COLCHESTER
FISHGUARD
UPON AVON
CHELTENHAM
OXFORD
CLACTON
GLOUCESTER
READING
SWANSEA
SWINDON
LONDON
SOUTHEND
NEWPORT
WINDSOR
CANTERBURY
CARDIFF
BRISTOL
BATH
ASHFORD
DOVER
SALISBURY
BARNSTAPLE
TAUNTON
FOLKSTONE
HASTINGS
SOUTHAMPTON
EASTBOURNE
EXETER
BRIGHTON
NEWHAVEN
NEWTON ABBOT
WORTHING
TORQUAY
WEYMOUTH
PORTSMOUTH
ST. IVES
BOURNEMOUTH
PLYMOUTH
PENZANCE

These passes do not cover travel in the Republic of Ireland or in Northern Ireland (which is covered by BritIreland Railpass - see next page) and *they cannot be purchased in Britain.* They can be purchased worldwide through the offices of BritRail Travel International, its representatives, and travel agencies outside Britain. Validate these passes at the rail-station's "Travel Centre" before starting your first trip with them. The rail official will mark your pass with that day's date and also the appropriate expiration date.

It is a good idea to protect yourself from having your pass rendered partly or wholly invalid because the validity dates were entered incorrectly.

Before the rail official writes on the pass the first and last day it can be used, you should write a note with what you believe are the correct validity dates, show it to the seller, and ask if he or she agrees with those dates. Only when the official says your dates are correct, or explains why they are not, should you have the dates entered on your pass.

(Be sure to follow the European custom of showing the day of the month first, followed by the number of the month. In Europe, July 8 is 8/7. If you wanted to take a train to Edinburgh, leaving London at 2:00 PM on July 8, your note for a reservation would read: "Edinburgh 14:00 8/7.")

BritRail Flexipass   Valid for one month. (For "Youth," the 15-day pass can be used within two months.) Same conditions and purchase locations as BritRail Pass. The 1996 prices are:

	4 Days	8 Days	15 Days
First-class	$ 289.00	$ 399.00	$ 615.00
Standard-class	199.00	280.00	425.00
Child 5–15			
First-class	144.50	199.50	307.50
Standard-class	99.50	140.00	212.50
Youth 16–25			
Standard-class	160.00	225.00	340.00
Senior Citizen 60 +			
First-class	245.00	339.00	490.00

BritRail/Drive   Provides 2 options, both within one month. Either 3 days of BritRail Flexipass plus 3 days of car rental, or 6 days of BritRail Flexipass plus 7 days of car rental.

Prices vary (a) how many people travel together, (b) whether the rail portion is for first-class or standard-class, (c) whether the car is manual or automatic transmission, and (d) the size of the car. There is a very small Senior discount for those over age 60. Half-fare for children age 5-15.

UK-France Sampler   See France

BritIreland Pass Unlimited train travel in England, Scotland, Wales, Northern Ireland and the Republic of Ireland (plus roundtrip ferry between the 2 Irelands). Sold in North America by both BritRail Travel International and C.I.E. Tours International. The 1996 adult *first*-class prices are: $405 for any 5 days within one month, and $599 for any 10 days within one month. Standard-class: $299 and $429. Half-fare for children age 5–15. Children under 5 travel free.

England/Wales Pass Unlimited train travel any 4 days within one month throughout Wales and as far north in England as Berwick and Carlisle (including trips to Bath, Cambridge, Chester, Exeter, Oxford, York, the Lake District and Cotswold villages).

The 1996 prices were not available in late 1995. The 1995 adult prices were $205 for *first*-class, $155 for *standard*-class. For children age 5–15: $102.50 and $77.50.

Southeast Railpass This is a new pass for 1996. Unlimited train travel in southeast England. The 1996 *first*-class prices are: For any 3 days in 8: $90. For any 4 days in 8: $120. For any 7 days in 15: $169. *Second*-class prices: $69, $89, $119 respectively.

London Extra Flexipass *Cannot be purchased in England*. Unlimited travel on trains in Southeast England plus a London Visitor Card (see below) for same duration. Does *not* include airport transfers. The 2 passes need not be used together. The 1996 adult *first*-class prices are: $105 for any 3 of 8 days, $145 for any 4 of 8 days, and $219 for any 7 of 15 days. For children age 5–15: $35, $39 and $45. The 1995 adult *standard*-class prices are: $85, $115 and $175. For children age 5–15: $29, $30 and $35.

London Visitor Travelcard Can be purchased worldwide. Valid for unlimited travel on London's buses and subways, plus discounts on the admission prices at such attractions as London Transport Museum, London Zoo, Madame Tussaud's, Kensington Palace, Tower Bridge and the Cabinet War Rooms. (A version sold in Britain does not include discounts at historical sites.) The 1996 adult prices prices are: $25 for 3 days, $32 for 4 days, $49 for 7 days. Children age 5–15: $11, $13 and $25.

SCOTLAND'S TRAIN PASSES

Scottish Area Rover passes are sold at main railstations and Travel Centres in the area of the "ticket." All of these allow 33% discount for children 5–15. Children under 5 travel free.

The 2 passes described below are sold at main British railstations and in the U.S.A. by BritRail Travel International, 1500 Broadway, NewYork, NY 10036-4015…and by Scots-American Travel Advisors, 26 Rugen Drive, Harrington Park, NJ 07640. telephone: (201) 768-5505. They do not have discounts for children.

Freedom of Scotland Travelpass Unlimited *standard*-class train travel on British Rail lines north of Berwick and Carlisle (see "England/Wales Pass" for train travel between southeast England and those cities)…also on ferries to many scenic islands, plus discounts on ferries to Orkney and Shetland islands, and travel on some local bus services.

The 1996 prices are $159 for 8 days and $220 for 15 days.

Freedom of Scotland Flexipass Unlimited *standard*-class travel on the same train, ferry and bus services as the pass above for consecutive days. The 1996 price for any 8 days within 15 days is $185 .

NORTHERN IRELAND'S TRAIN PASSES

Both of these passes are sold in Belfast at: Tourist Information Centre, 59 North Street; NIR Travel Ltd., 28-30 Wellington Place; and Central Station.

Irish Rover Covers unlimited travel on all sceduled rail services of Northern Ireland Railways and Irish Rail. The 1996 adult prices are: £55 for any 8 days within 15 days, and £80 for any 15 days within 30 days. Children age 5-15: £27.50 and £42.50. Operates all year.

Rail Runabout Provides 7 consecutive days of unlimited train travel in Northern Ireland. The 1996 price are: £25 for adults, £12.50 for children age 5-15. Operates April-October.

COMBINING BRITAIN AND
THE CONTINENT

When planning to travel both in Britain and on the European Continent, keep in mind that the maximum value of combining a British train pass with a Eurailpass is achieved by scheduling Britain for either the start or end of a tour (see also "Eurostar" for Channel Tunnel connections). For example, to start a tour in Amsterdam and have one's itinerary then go to Paris, London, and then return to the continent for additional Eurailpass traveling would require a longer (and more expensive) Eurailpass because of consuming Eurailpass days while in Britain.

Conversely, to start a tour in London, followed by travel on the Continent, and then concluding with more travel in Britain will require a longer and more expensive British pass since the days spent on the Continent will consume British pass days.

We present in this chapter descriptions of 4 categories of rail service. First, the train connection services between London and the Continent (Paris, Brussels and Amsterdam). Next, 41 one-day rail trips that can be made comfortably out of London, with departure and arrival times, on-board-services, and what to see and do at each destination before returning to London, in most cases at dinnertime.

Third, readers will find itineraries for 4 long trips from and to London: Cork, Shannon Airport, Dublin and Edinburgh. This chapter concludes with details on 12 rail trips in Scotland from Aberdeen, Edinburgh, Glasgow and Inverness. Several of those routes are very scenic.

The extensive notes in this book about train times are intended to both help you *plan* your itinerary and are also useful after your trip begins (if you bring *Eurail Guide* along!) for making impromptu last-minute travel plans.

Before commencing any journey, always — without exception — doublecheck the

times in this book or in any published timetable, as they are subject to change without prior notice. Eurail Guide has made every effort possible to publish correct departure and arrival times, but schedules are subject to constant change.

WARNING: Many cities have 2 or more railstations. London has 8 railstations. We take pains to tell you for every trip in this book the name of the railstation from which your train departs, by noting the station in parenthesis immediately after the name of the city, such as: London (King's Cross).

All of London's railstations are interconnected by subway service, providing far easier and quicker transfers than by surface streets. For example, when entering England by rail from France, at Dover, you will come into Victoria station. To continue on to Edinburgh, it is necessary to first transfer by subway (Circle line) from Victoria (along to Thames River) to King's Cross station, on the opposite side of London from Victoria station.

A brief description of the areas served by London's 8 major railstations:

CHARING CROSS STATION This station services suburban commuters between London and Folkestone, and between London and Hastings. It connects at Dover (Priory station) with Hovercraft service to and from France.

EUSTON STATION A part of Central England and the northwestern area of Britain are reached from Euston station, starting with Coventry and Birmingham, and then running through Stafford, Chester, Liverpool, Manchester and Blackpool, on into Glasgow. Also, Holyhead, gateway to Dublin.

KING'S CROSS STATION Northeastern England (Leeds, York, Hull, Newcastle) and Edinburgh are reached by trains from King's Cross station. Newcastle is the gateway to Norway. Hull is a gateway to Denmark, Germany and Holland.

LIVERPOOL STREET STATION This station services the area immediately northeast of London: Colchester, Cambridge, Ipswich, Harwich (gateway to Holland, Germany, Austria, Yugoslavia and Norway), Norwich and King's Lynn.

PADDINGTON STATION The area in southern England, west from Weymouth (Exeter, Plymouth and Penzance), is reached out of Paddington station as is also that portion of southwestern England running north to Bristol, Swansea, Fishguard (gateway to Rosslare, at the southeastern tip of the Republic of Ireland), Gloucester, Worcester, Hereford and Oxford.

ST. PANCRAS STATION Trains going due north from London to Leicester, Derby, Nottingham and Sheffield leave from St. Pancras station.

VICTORIA STATION The London airport for charter flights is Gatwick, which is serviced from 05:30 to 23:00 by a train every 15 minutes (and hourly from 01:00 to 05:00) for the 40-minute ride to and from London's Victoria station. The transfer from airplane to train, or vice versa, is entirely indoor as the railstation at Gatwick is a part of the airport.

Victoria station services the small area of Southern England just East of but not including Portsmouth: Worthing, Brighton, Newhaven, Eastbourne, Hastings and Dover (gateway to France, Spain, Belgium, Switzerland, Italy, Austria and Yugoslavia).

WATERLOO STATION   Services South Central England: Southampton, Bournemouth and Weymouth.

HEATHROW – LONDON UNDERGROUND CONNECTION

The train service is between Heathrow airport and every subway station on Piccadilly Line between Heathrow and Kings Cross railstation. Trains depart both terminals every 4-10 minutes 05:30-23:00 daily except Sundays and holidays, and 07:30-23:30 on Sundays. Journey time is 50–58 minutes.

GATWICK – LONDON TRAIN CONNECTION

This service takes 30 minutes daytime, 45 minutes at night. Trains depart Gatwick Airport 00:10, 01:05, 02:05, 03:05, 04:05, 05:05, plus every 15 minutes 05:20-21:50, plus 22:20, 22:50, 23:20 and 23:50. Departures from Victoria railstation are 00:15, 01:00, 02:00, 03:00, 04:00, plus every 15 minutes 04:30-21:00, plus 21:30, 22:00, 22:30 and 23:00.

The transfer from airplane to train, or vice versa, is entirely indoor as the railstation at Gatwick is a part of the airport.

Gatwick Express Tickets   1996 prices: *First*-class $23, *Second*-class $17.

SUMMER TIME

Britain changes to Summer Time on the last Sunday of March and converts back to Standard Time on the last Sunday of October.

DAYS OF THE WEEK VARIANCES

For the time schedules given in this book, "daily" means Monday through Sunday. Where Sunday departure and arrival times are specified in conjunction with a list of daily schedules, this refers to *additional* service on Sunday, not to substitute service.

In other words, if a daily schedule lists departures at 10:00 and 11:12, and the Sunday schedule indicates a departure at 13:05, there are 3 departures on Sunday: at 10:00, 11:12 and 13:05.

Conversely, if Monday-Friday or Monday-Saturday schedules show departures at 10:00 and 11:12, and there is a listing of a Sunday departure at 13:05, then the only departure on Sunday for that trip is 13:05.

The same treatment applies to "Saturday only" schedules in connection with times given as "Monday–Friday" or as "daily."

SUMMER AND WINTER SCHEDULES

In most European countries, Winter schedules usually start on the Sunday following the last Saturday of September and runs through the Saturday preceding the last Sunday in May of the following year.

British timetables differ from the Continental pattern. Summer timetables for British rail service begin on the second Monday in May. There are two changes in Winter schedules, occuring on the first Monday in October and on the first Monday in January.

Unless designated otherwise, the departure and arrival times given in this chapter are for the Summer season and apply to trips that are made from early May to early October.

HOLIDAY TRAVEL

Nearly all train, bus and subway services cease on holidays. The main holidays on which to avoid travel are all "Bank" holidays (whose dates vary) and the period from December 25 through January 1. If you cannot avoid intra-city travel on a holiday, it is advisable to reserve a taxi by telephone the day prior.

London

The capital of England. See the changing of the guard at Buckingham Palace. Downing Street, official residence of the Prime Minister. The Tower of London. London Bridge. The Houses of Parliament. The Wellington Museum (Aiseley House) and Wellington Arch. Hyde Park. Tate Gallery. The London Transport Museum at 39 Wellington Street, Covent Garden, is open daily 10:00–18:00. The Kensington Gardens complex of Royal Albert Hall, the Science Museum, Geological Museum, Natural History Museum, and the Victoria and Albert Museum (closed on Fridays). Piccadilly Circus. The National Gallery and National Portrait Gallery.

The British Museum. Dickens' House (closed Sunday). St. Paul's Cathedral. Gray's Inn. The Imperial War Museum. The Royal Botanic Gardens (Kew). Regent's Park. Westminster Abbey. Nelson's Monument in Trafalgar Square. St. James's Palace. St. James's Park. The 53-acre Green Park.

Admiralty Arch.The Museum of London. The Royal Academy. The Museum of Mankind. The Sunday orators at Speaker's Corner. Marble Arch. Lambeth Palace, the residence of the Archbishop of Canterbury.

The dragon at Temple Bar Memorial. Mansion House, the residence of the Lord Mayor of London. Tower Bridge. The South Bank Arts Centre complex of National Theatre, Queen Elizabeth Hall, Royal Festival Hall, and Hayward Gallery. The Victoria Tower. Whitehall, the compound of government offices.

One of the world's greatest food stores, in Harrods Department Store, presents a spectacle of more than 500 cheeses, 120 different breads, 21 kinds of butter, produce from California, and a meat hall 90 feet long by 60 feet wide containing hams, pork, sausages, beef and lamb. There is also venison, shellfish, poultry, salmon (smoked and fresh), tinned foods from all over the world, eggs, teas from everywhere, caviars, wine, and the list goes on forever.

Don't miss London's other great food store, in Fortnum and Mason (also a complete department store), operating since 1707 on Picadilly Circus. Open 09:30–18:00, daily except Sunday. 'Fortnums', as Londoners call it, has 3 restaurants. "The Fountain," in the basement, has an American-style soda fountain. It is open 09:30–24:00, very popular for after-theater snacks. "The Patio," on a mezzanine, offers the same light menu as "The Fountain" but also has grilled meats. It is open 09:30–16:30. The elegant fourth-floor "St. James" offers more extensive and more expensive food, open 11:30–18:00.

For a different view of food, visit Smithfield Meat Market, England's largest meat and poultry market, covering over 10 acres and employing almost 3,000 people. On a busy day, it sells in 19 hours more than 4,000 tons of meat, poultry and game: grouse, ducks, partridges, rabbits, pheasant, hams, green bacon, Danish bacon, smoked bacon, Irish bacon, lamb, beef and many exotic imported meats. Open Monday-Friday 05:00–12:00.

Near Smithfield is the very interesting 12th century St. Bartholomew the Great Church. Stroll the entire area: St. John's Lane, Charterhouse Street and many narrow alleys for a look at the London of 300 years ago.

For a different view of London, explore the city on a Sunday, by foot. Walk along Whitechapel Road to see the (still working) foundry where the Liberty Bell was cast. From Whitechapel, it's an easy walk to the Tower of London and the St. Katherine marina.

CONNECTIONS WITH THE CONTINENT

Aside from the new Channel Tunnel route (see "Eurostar" for prices, conditions, schedules), the shortest route from England to the Continent is Dover to Calais or Boulogne.

The validity of one's BritRail Pass stops or starts, as the case may be, at the British shore. Similarly, the validity of one's Eurailpass stops or starts at the Continental port where your boat ride begins or ends. In all cases, the channel boat fare is *not covered* by either pass. However, the Brit France Pass *does* include a Hovercraft roundtrip Dover–Boulogne-Dover and Dover–Calais–Dover, as well as Boulogne–Dover–Boulogne and Calais–Dover–Calais.

Regular ferries run the following routes: Dover–Calais, Dover–Oostende, Folkestone–Boulogne, Harwich–Hoek van Holland and Newhaven–Dieppe.

Hovercraft service, faster and more expensive, is provided Dover–Boulogne, Dover–Calais, Dover–Oostende, Newhaven–Dieppe, Portsmouth–Cherbourg, and Ramsgate–Dunkerque.

Both regular ferries and hovercraft carry autos. *All of the regular ferries have a restaurant.*

London - Paris via Newhaven and Dieppe   and v.v. 10

Dep. London (Vic.)	08:32 (1)	20:40	Dep. Paris (St. Laz.)	10:42 (1)	22:09
Arr. Newhaven Harbour	09:55 (1)	21:55	Dep. Rouen (Rive Dr.)	12:13	23:49
Change to a ferry.			Arr. Dieppe	13:09	00:42
Dep. Newhaven Harbour	10:30	22:30	*Change to a ferry.*		
Set your watch forward one hour,			Dep. Dieppe	14:00	02:00
except late Sept. to late Oct.			*Set your watch back one hour,*		
Arr. Dieppe	15:30	03:30	*except late Sept. to late Oct.*		
Change to a train.			Arr. Newhaven Harbour	17:00	05:00
Dep. Dieppe	15:49	04:44	*Change to a train.*		
Arr. Rouen (Rive Dr.)	16:45	05:34	Dep. Newhaven Harbour	17:35	05:40
Arr. Paris (St. Laz.)	18:16	07:01	Arr. London (Vic.)	19:05	06:45

(1) Departs 7–10 minutes earlier on Sunday.

London - Paris via Portsmouth and Le Havre (regular ferry) and v.v.

Frequent trains make the 83–108 minute ride London (Waterloo) to Portsmouth and v.v.

1030 Ferry

Dep. Portsmouth	08:30 (1)	14:45 (2)	23:00 (3)
Set your watch forward one hour, except late September to late October.			
Arr. Le Havre	15:15 (8)	21:30	07:00
Change to train. 115			
Dep. Le Havre	16:44 (10)	06:43 (4)	07:57
Arr. Paris (St. Laz.)	18:52	08:57	10:01

•   •   •

Dep. Paris (St. Laz.)	12:34 (5)	17:48
Arr. Le Havre	14:40	19:57
Change to a ferry. 1030		
Dep. Le Havre	16:45 (6)	23:00 (7)
Set your watch back one hour, except late September to late October.		
Arr. Portsmouth	22:30	07:00

(1) July 1-August 31: runs daily. September 1-June 30: runs daily, except Monday. (2) Runs daily January 1- December 23. (3) Early May to mid-September: runs Friday and Saturday. (4) Runs Monday-Friday, except holidays to July 8 and from August 22. (5) Runs daily, except Sundays and holidays. (6) Runs one hour earlier September 25-October 22. Runs daily except December 24, 25, 26. (7) Runs daily except December 24, 25,26. (8) Arives one hour earlier September 25-October 22. (9) Departs one hour later September 25-October 22. (10) Runs Sunday to June 26 and from September 4.

OTHER CHANNEL-CROSSING SCHEDULES

London - Paris via Calais or Boulogne   and v.v. 10

Schedules shown here are for early June to late September.

All of the trains from French ports to Paris and v.v. have light refreshments, unless designated otherwise.

Train			
Dep. London (Vic.)	08:55	09:25	12:25 (3)
Arr. Folkestone		10:51	13:59
Arr. Dover (West.)	10:26		
Change to ferry.			
Dep. Folkestone		11:15 (1)	14:30 (1)
Dep. Dover (West.)	11:00		
Set your watch forward one hour.			
Arr. Boulogne		13:15	16:30
Arr. Calais	13:30		
Change to train.			
Dep. Boulogne		13:45	16:57
Dep. Calais	14:09		
Arr. Paris (Nord)	18:19	16:12	19:35
Train			
Dep. Paris (Nord)	07:47 (4)	10:58	14:18 (3)
Arr. Calais	10:44		
Arr. Boulogne		13:20	16:50
Change to ferry.			
Dep. Calais	11:15		
Dep. Boulogne		14:00 (1)	17:15 (1)
Set your watch back one hour.			
Arr. Dover (West.)	11:45 (2)		
Arr. Folkestone		14:05	17:20
Change to train.			
Dep. Dover (West.)	12:40		
Dep. Folkestone		14:45	18:00
Arr. London (Vic.)	14:07	16:23	19:37

(1) Hoverspeed catamaran. Reservation required. Supplement charged. (2) Arrives at Dover's Eastern Docks. A free bus transfers passengers to the railstation. (3) May 29-Sept. 4. (4) July 10-Sept. 4.

London - Brussels via Oostende (Jetfoil)   12

Reservation is required on all of the London–Dover trains. Reservation is required and supplement charged for the one-class jetfoil, which has light refreshements.

Passengers from London *must* check-in at the Jetfoil Lounge in Victoria railstation and obtain the Jetfoil boarding card at least 60 minutes before train departs.

Change to jetfoil in Dover.

Dep. London (Vict.)	08:05	11:05	13:05	16:05
Dep. Dover Docks	09:35	13:20	15:30	18:25
Set your watch forward one hour.				
Arr. Oostende	12:15	16:00	18:10	20:55
Change to train.				
Dep. Oostende	12:34	16:34	18:34	21:34
Arr. Brussels (Midi)	14:43	17:43	19:43	22:43
Arr. Brussels (Nord)	12 minutes later			

London - Brussels via Oostende (regular ferry)   12

Reservation is required for all the London–Dover trains and these ferries.
    Times shown below are for Summer service (early June to late September). Change to a ferry in Dover. All of the ferries have a restaurant.

Dep. London (Vict.)	08:05	11:05	22:05
Arr. Dover Docks	09:07	12:24	23:58
Set your watch forward one hour.			
Arr. Oostende	15:30	18:45	06:00
Change to train.			
Dep. Oostende	16:34	19:34	06:34
Arr. Brussels (Midi)	17:43	20:43	07:43
Arr. Brussels (Nord)	12 minutes later		

London - Amsterdam via Hoek van Holland (regular ferry)
and v.v. 5

Change to ferry in Harwich Parkeston Quay (en route to Amsterdam) and in Hoek van Holland (en route to London).

Dep. London (Liverpool Street)	09:25	19:00
Dep. Harwich	11:30 (2)	21:30 (1)
Set your watch forward one hour, except from late Sept. to late Oct.		
Arr. Hoek van Holland	19:00 (3)	07:00
Arr. Amsterdam (Cen.)	21:32	09:49

• • •

Dep. Amsterdam (Cen.)	09:32	19:48
Arr. Hoek van Holland	10:57	21:13
Dep. Hoek van Holland	12:00 (2)	22:00 (1)
Set your watch back one hour, except from late Sept. to late Oct.		
Arr. Harwich	18:00	07:00
Arr. London (Liverpool Street)	20:00	09:00

(1) Ferry reservation required. (2) Change trains. (3) Runs daily except Friday

ONE-DAY EXCURSIONS FROM LONDON

Here are 39 one-day rail trips that can be made comfortably, returning to London in most cases at dinnertime. Notes are provided on what to see and do at each destination.

The notation "frequent times" in these schedules means at least one departure (and usually more) every hour.

London - Bath - London   530

Dep. London (Pad.)	07:15 (1)	08:15 (1)	08:30 (3)	09:15 (1)	09:30 (3+4)
Arr. Bath	08:37	09:36	10:04	10:32	11:04

Sights in **Bath**: For interesting walking tours here, go to the Tourist Information Centre and purchase "Official Guidebook" and "Walks Around Bath." During Summer, guide 1½-hour tours on foot (at no charge) start at the churchyard of the abbey.

See the Roman baths. Buy a glass of curative mineral water in the 18th century Pump Room, above the baths. Visit antique shops around Abbey Green. The Circus, a group of 3-story, classical 18th century houses constructed of honey-colored Bath Stone, located on Gay Street. Nearby, the Museum of Costume in the Assembly Rooms. The Royal Crescent row of town houses. Queen Square. The shops on Pulteney Bridge.

The American Museum at Claverton Manor, open daily except Monday 14:00–17:00. The collection of Eltonware and Nailsea glass in the 14th century Clevedon Court manor house, open Wednesday, Thursday and Sunday 14:30–17:30. There is much elegant 18th century architecture here.

Bath is a great base for seeing many of the best sights in England. Several good, inexpensive motorcoach tours go to Gloucester, Salisbury, Stonehenge and Cheddar Gorge. These buses stop for photo-taking along the way.

Dep. Bath	12:12 (3)	12:27 (2)	13:12 (3)	13:27 (2)	14:12 (3+5)
Arr. London (Pad.)	14:05	14:00	15:05	15:00	16:05

(1) Runs Monday-Friday except holidays. (2) Runs Monday-Saturday except holidays. (3) Runs Sunday only. (4) Plus other departures from London at frequent times from 09:45 to 23:10. (5) Plus other departures from Bath at frequent times from 14:27 to 21:25.

London - Birmingham -London   540

Dep. London (Eus.)	07:15 (1)	07:45	08:05 (2)	08:35 (2)	09:05 (7)
Arr. Birmingham (New St.)	08:55	09:19 (9)	09:50 (10)	10:19 (10)	10:54 (2+10)

Sights in **Birmingham**: The Tourist Information Centre has brochures on walking tours. The Cadbury Company's "World Chocolate Experience" museum at its factory here features an exhibit on the history of chocolate. Visitors can sample a chocolate drink made from an ancient Aztec recipe, see chocolate being made, and sample chocolate at the factory's restaurant, ice cream parlor and souvenir shop.

See the restored 18th century water mill, Sarehole Mill. The 17th century house furnished as it was in its era, Blakesley Hall. The first (1734) English locomotive can be seen at the Science Museum.

Dep. Birmingham (New St.)	12:15 (2)	12:45 (2)	13:15 (6)	13:45 (6)	14:15 (6+8)
Arr. London (Eus.)	13:56	14:49	15:04	15:29	15:56

(1) Runs Monday-Friday except holidays. Restaurant car. (2) Runs daily except Sundays and holidays. Restaurant car. (3) Runs daily except holidays. Restaurant car. (4) Arrives 34 minutes later on Sunday. (5) Runs Monday-Friday, except holidays. (6) Runs daily, except Sundays and holidays. (7) Plus other departures from London at frequent times from 09:40 to 23:40. (8) Plus other Birmingham departures at frequent times from 14:48 to 22:48. (9) Runs Sunday only. (10) Departs 10 min. earlier Mon-Friday only, except holidays.

London - Bournemouth - London 502 + ABC 60

Most of these trains have buffet.

Dep. London (Wat.)	Frequent times Monday–Saturday: 05:40–23:45.
	Sunday: 07:45–22:45
Arr. Bournemouth	Monday–Saturday: 2 hours later
	Sunday: 2½ hours later

Sights in **Bournemouth**: A large seaside resort. Stroll through Pavillion Rock Garden. There are 3 gambling casinos. Many lovely parks and gardens.

Dep. Bournemouth	Frequent times Monday–Saturday: 05:15–23:02.
	Sunday: 06:14–21:45
Arr. London (Wat.)	Monday–Saturday: 2 hours later
	Sunday: 2½ hours later

London - Brighton - London ABC 31

Dep. London (Vic.)	Frequent times Monday–Saturday: 05:17–01:00.
	Sunday: 07:47–23:10
Arr. Brighton	55–70 minutes later

Sights in **Brighton**: Walk from the railstation down Queen Street to the seashore and the Aquarium at Palace Pier. See the antique shops in the many alleys, called "The Lanes." The Regency architecture prevalent here. The Royal Pavillion. The ornate chandelier in Banquet Hall.

This is one of Britain's leading antique centers. An outdoor antique market is held on Saturdays starting at 07:00, on Upper Gerdner Street, near the railstation. See the collection of Art Nouveau and Art Deco furniture and furnishings in the City Museum.

Dep. Brighton	Frequent times Monday–Saturday: 06:23–23:35.
	Sunday: 07:15–22:15
Arr. London (Vict.)	55–70 minutes later

London - Bristol - London 530

Dep. London (Paddington)	Frequent times 07:15 to 23:59 (from 08:20 on Sunday)
Arr. Bristol (Temple Meads)	90 minutes later

• • •

Dep. Bristol (Temple Meads)	Frequent times 05:45 to 21:25 (from 07:30 on Sunday)
Arr. London (Paddington)	90 minutes later

Sights in **Bristol**: A famous seaport. Everything here is either a short walk or can be reached by bus. The city operates 1½-hour guided walking tours June, July and August from the Exchange on Corn Street at 11:00 on Monday and Tuesday, at 14:30 on other days. Some of Bristol can be seen from a tour boat at the harbor. That tour operates daily at 12:00, 14:00, 15:00 and 16:00.

See the many excellent Georgian buildings on Royal York Crescent, Cornwallis Crescent, Windsor Terrace, West Mall, Caledonia Place, Queen Square and Berkeley Square. The Christmas Steps, built in 1669. The 12th century St. James' Church.

The John Wesley Chapel, world's first Methodist preaching house, with a bronze statue of Wesley in the courtyard. The 11th century St. Mary-le-Port Church. St. John's Church. The 13th century St. Mary Redcliffe, one of England's largest churches. The 12th century Cathedral.

The exhibit of period furniture in the 18th century Georgian House. The view from the top of Cabot Tower, on Brandon Hill. The collection of porcelain, models of early sailing ships and paintings of the waterfront in the Bristol Museum and Art Gallery, open every day 10:00–17:00. See the beautiful gardens and the rare animals (including the Okapi and the white tigers) at the Zoo. Brunel's Clifton Suspension Bridge, built in 1864, straddling Avon Gorge, 245 feet above the water. Tour Brunel's iron steamship, The Great Britain (the first ocean screw steamship, launched in 1843), returned to Bristol in 1970 from the Falkland Islands. It is open 10:00–18:00.

London - Cardiff - London   530

Dep. London (Paddington)   Frequent times from 07:00 to 22:00 (from 09:00 on Sunday)
Arr. Cardiff (Central)   2 hours later

Sights in **Cardiff**: Llandaff Cathedral. Cardiff Castle. The National Museum of Wales, featuring Welsh handicraft and art. It is a short train ride from Cardiff's Queen Street railstation to **Caerphilly**, whose castle is nearly as large as Windsor Castle and has many interesting exhibits.

Dep. Cardiff (Central)   Frequent times from 06:25 to 19:25 (from 08:00 on Sunday)
Arr. London (Paddington)   2 hours later

London - Bristol - Cardiff - London

As these schedules indicate, it is easy to visit both Cardiff and Bristol in one day.

These schedules are for travel daily, except Sundays and holidays.

530		*530*	
Dep. London (Pad.)	08:15	Dep. Cardiff (Cen.)	16:25 (1)
Arr. Bristol (T.M.)	09:51	Arr. London (Pad.)	18:35
Sightsee in Bristol			
532			
Dep. Bristol (T.M.)	12:25		
Arr. Cardiff (Cen.)	13:11		

(1) Plus other departures from Cardiff at 17:25, 18:25, 19:25 and 21:25.

Sights in **Bristol:** The Temple Meads railstation, completed in 1841, is one of the most beautiful in England.

   In Summer, open-top buses make a circle tour that includes Temple Meads, Clifton Bridge, the Zoo, downtown, the harbor and the 13th century Church of St. Mary Redcliffe (one of England's largest churches). Queen Elizabeth I described it as "the fairest, goodliest and most famous parish church in England."

London - Cambridge - London   581

Dep. London (King's X)	06:52(1) 07:42 (2) 08:45 (5) 09:45 (2) 10:45 (2+4)
Arr. Cambridge	70–80 minutes later
	• • •
Dep. Cambridge	Monday–Saturday: frequent times from 06:54 to 23:10
	Sundays: frequent times from 14:36 to 22:41
Arr. London (King's X)	70–80 minutes later

(1) Runs Monday–Friday, except holidays. (2) Runs daily, except Sundays and holidays. (3) Runs Sunday only. (4) Plus other departures from London Monday–Saturday at frequent times from 10:45 (2) to 21:45 (3) (5) Runs Monday-Saturday except holidays.

Sights in **Cambridge**: To see buildings that have housed great colleges for more than 700 years, take bus #101 to Market Street. See King's College Chapel and Queen's College. Visit the Wren Library at Trinity College. The medieval and renaissance armor, weapons, tapestries and manuscripts in the Fitzwilliam Museum on Trumpington Street.

   The Botanical Gardens. On Castle Street, see the Folk Museum and the modern paintings and sculpture at Kettles Yard Art Gallery. Hire a boat at Mill Bridge or Anchor Inn, and paddle along the idyllic Cam River. Four miles away is the American Cemetery

London - Canterbury - London   ABC 10 + 17

For this 2-hour ride, there are frequent departures both from London's Waterloo and Charing Cross railstations to Canterbury's West railstation. There are also frequent departures from London's Victoria station to Canterbury's East station. The walk from Canterbury's *West* station to the famous Cathedral allows you to view interesting buildings.

Canterbury's *East* railstation is nearer the Cathedral and therefore more convenient to use for returning to London after visiting the Cathedral than the West station. A departure from Canterbury's East station will take you to London's Victoria station. Or, you can depart from Canterbury's West station, arriving London's Waterloo or Charing Cross stations.

Sights in **Canterbury**: Guided tours (Monday–Friday) start at 14:15 at a kiosk in Longmarket, a pedestrian area next to Christ Church Gate.

See the great Cathedral, housing the tomb of Thomas a Becket. Medieval inns (Falstaff, Beverlie, Olive Branch). The cemetery, where Christopher Marlowe and Joseph Conrad are buried. The Old Weaver's House, built in 1500. Excavated Roman ruins. Plays, ballet, cricket.

London - Sevenoaks - Chartwell - London   ABC 15

There are many departures daily from London's Charing Cross railstation for the 45-minute ride to Sevenoaks. Take a taxi for the 7-mile trip from Sevenoaks to Chartwell.

Sights in **Chartwell:** The country house that Winston Churchill bought in 1922, where he painted and wrote his books during the years he was out of power. You will see here the best collection of Churchilliana in the world: his collection of eccentric hats, his World War II "jump suit," Knight of the Garter uniform, many of his paintings, and a model of the Invasion Day harbor at Arromanches. Also the brick wall and cottage he built with his own hands on a small part of the 79 acres there. The main house is open Wednesday, Thursday, Saturday and Sunday from April to mid-October.

London - Chester - London   555

Dep. London (Euston)	10:20 (1)	Dep. Chester	15:14 (3)	17:20 (3)
Arr. Chester	12:35	Arr. London (Euston)	18:02	20:08

(1) Runs Monday-Friday, except holidays. Restaurant car. (2) Runs daily, except Sundays and holidays. Restaurant car Monday-Friday. (3) Runs Sunday only.

Sights in **Chester**: The 2-mile-long Roman Wall. The excellent collection of Roman artifacts (glass, tools, coins, weapons, tombstones) at Grosvenor Museum. The "Rows," long covered balconies (to protect shoppers from rain) that are full-length streets above the streets of Chester. These are lined with shops. Also see St. Werburgh's Cathedral. The castle overlooking the **River Dee**. The marvelous carving of animals and historic scenes on the front of the 17th century Bishop Lloyd's House on Watergate Street. The antique shops on Lower Bridge Street and Watergate Street. The 16th century mansion, Stanley Palace. The 30-minute slide show of Chester's history, in the British Heritage Centre.

Sightseeing bus tours start in Market Square, opposite the Tourist Office at the Victorian Gothic Town Hall. Guided *walking* tours of 1 to 3 hours cost £1.95 for adults in 1992 (£1.25 for children and senior citizens). Leave from the Tourist Information Office at the Town Hall at 10:45 (May-October: daily. November–April: daily, except Sunday)…and at 14:30 (April–October: daily. November–March: daily, except Sunday).

The 130-acre open-space Zoo, just north of the city, attracts nearly 1,000,000 people a year.

London - Chichester - London   ABC 35

This service is daily. Most of these trains have light refreshments Monday–Saturday.

| Dep. London (Vic.) | Frequent times 07:50 – 22:21 |
| Arr. Chichester | About 100 minutes later |

Sights in **Chichester**: The Marc Chagall stained glass window and the John Piper Holy Trinity tapestry in the 12th century Norman Cathedral. The 2nd century Roman wall. The 16th century arcaded Market Cross. The 200-year-old "stately homes" on streets called East, West, North and South Pallant.

Go two miles westto see the museum and mosaic floors in the 3rd century Palace at Fishbourne, the largest Roman residence in Britain, open daily, March through October. See the attractive mosaic floors in the 1st century Roman villa at **Bignor**, 2 miles east, open daily except Monday, March through October.

There is extraordinary fillegree woodcarving in the 17th century Petworth House, 13 miles northeast. It is open April through October on Wednesday, Thursday, Saturday and Sunday 14:00–18:00.

A few miles west of Chichester is an 11th century Saxon church and a marvelous yacht harbor at **Bosham**, a beautiful seashore village.

| Dep. Chichester | Frequent times 07:30 to 21:16 |
| Arr. London (Vic.) | About 100 minutes later |

London - Coventry - London   540

| Dep. London (Eus.) | 07:15 (2) | 07:35 (1) | 08:05 (1) | 08:35 (1) | 09:05 (1) | 09:35 (1+9) |
| Arr. Coventry | 08:20 | 08:48 (11) | 09:18 (11) | 09:48 (11) | 10:23 (11) | 10:48 |

Sights in **Coventry**: Completely rebuilt since the Nazi air attacks, Coventry was the site of

Lady Godiva's notorious horseback ride. See the Graham Sutherland tapestry, the abstract stained-glass windows and the enormous engraved glass wall at the new (1962) Cathedral.

Dep. Coventry	12:07 (4)	12:37 (6)	13:07 (4)	13:37 (6)	14:07 (6)	14:37 (6+10)
Arr. London (Eus.)	13:26	13:56	14:29	15:04	15:29	15:56

(1) Runs daily, except Sundays and holidays. Restaurant car. (2) Runs Monday–Friday, except holidays. Restaurant car. (3) Runs daily, except holidays. (4) Runs daily, except holidays. Restaurant car Monday–Friday. (5) Runs Monday–Friday, except holidays. (6) Runs daily, except Sundays and holidays. (7) Runs daily, except holidays. Restaurant car Monday–Saturday. (8) Runs daily, except Saturdays and holidays. (9) Plus other departures from London at 10:05 (1+11), 11:05 (1+11), 11:35 (1+11), 12:05 (1+11), 12:35 (2 +11), 13:05 (2+11) and 13:35 (1+11). (10) Plus other departures from Coventry at 15:07 (4), 15:37 (1), 16:07 (6), 16:37 (1), 17:07 (4), 17:37 (6), 18:07 (4), 18:37 (6), 19:37 (5), 20:37 (6) and 21:37 (6). (11) Departs 10 minutes earlier on Monday-Friday, except holidays.

London - Dover - London   ABC 10 + 506

Dep. London (Char. Cr)	08:30 (1)	09:30 (1)	10:00 (1)
Arr. Dover (Priory)	10:17	11:17	11:41

Sights in **Dover**: It is a short walk downhill from the Priory railstation to the village. Or, you can ride a bus. See the legendary white cliffs. The mighty castle. The busy harbor. The museum in the 4th century Roman painted house.

Dep. Dover (Priory)	15:05 (1)	15:50 (1)	16:05 (3)	16:51 (1+9)
Arr. London (Char. Cr)	16:46	18:15 (1)	17:56 (1)	18:47

(1) Runs daily, except Sundays and holidays. Light refreshments. (2) Runs Sunday only. (3) Runs daily, except Sundays and holidays. (4) Runs daily, except Saturday. Light refreshments Monday–Friday. (5) Arrives 19:15 on Sunday. (6) Runs Saturday only. Light refreshments. (7) Runs daily. (8) Runs Saturday only. (9) Plus other Dover departures at 17:05 (1), 17:49 (1), 18:49 (1), 19:49 (1) and 20:49 (1).

London - Exeter - London   (main line via Reading)

(Paddington station) *510*

Dep. London (Pad.)	07:40 (1)	09:03 (2)	09:15 (4)	09:45 (1)	10:15 (4)
Arr. Exeter (St. David's)	10:16	11:12	11:57	12:40	12:47

Dep. London (Pad.)	10:35 (1)	11:35 (2)	11:45 (2)	12:35 (2)
Arr. Exeter (St. David's)	12:36	13:52	14:30	14:41 (12)

Sights in **Exeter**: The 11th century Cathedral, with its 300-foot nave and row of statutes. Rougemont Castle. The Mint. The underground water channel at Princesshay. The paintings and oak paneling in Exeter Guildhall.

The exhibit of boats from all parts of the world at the very interesting Maritime Museum.

| Dep. Exeter (St. David's) | 14:37 (1) | 15:02 (2) | 15:29 (1) | 15:42 | 16:37 (1) |
| Arr. London (Pad.) | 17:05 | 17:25 (1) | 17:45 | 18:25 (4) | 18:40 |

| Dep. Exeter (St. David's) | 16:57 (4) | 17:29 (1) | 17:38 (2) | 18:13 (2) | 18:57 (4+11) |
| Arr. London (Pad.) | 19:50 | 19:45 | 20:50 | 21:05 | 21:50 |

(1) Runs Monday-Friday, except holidays. (2) Runs Saturday only. (3) Runs daily, except holidays. (4) Runs Sunday only. (5) Runs daily, except Sundays and holidays. Restaurant car Monday-Friday. (6) Runs daily, except Sundays and holidays. (7) Runs daily, except Saturdays and holidays. (8) Arrives 17:25 on Sunday. (9) Runs Saturday and Sunday. (10) Runs daily, except Sundays and holidays. Restaurant car. (11) Plus other departures from Exeter at 19:37 (1) and 20:07 (4), arriving London 22:10 and 23:05. (12) Runs until September 17.

OR

London - Exeter - London   (via Salisbury)

Most of these trains have light refreshments.

(Waterloo Station) 511					
Dep. London (Waterloo)	07:09 (1)	07:35 (2)	08:35 (3)	08:55 (4)	10:12 (2)
Arr. Exeter (Central)	10:23	10:54	11:36	12:20	12:58
Arr. Exeter (St. David's)	5 minutes later				

•   •   •

Dep. Exeter (St. David's)	15:35 (2)	16:18 (4)	17:41 (1)	18:22 (2)	19:15 (4)
Dep. Exeter (Central)	5 minutes later				
Arr. London (Waterloo)	18:43	19:44	21:17	22:22	22:35

(1) Runs Monday–Friday, except holidays. (2) Runs Saturday only. (3) Runs daily, except Sundays and holidays. (4) Runs Sunday only. (5) Runs daily, except holidays. (6) Arrives 21:44 on Saturday.

London - Greenwich - London   suburban train

Sights in **Greenwich**: Take the Docklands Light Railway, opposite the Tower of London, for the 20-minute ride to the "Island Gardens" terminus. Walk from it through the pedestrian tunnel that goes under the Thames River, ending next to the famous 1870 clipper ship Cutty Sark. Near the Cutty Sark, see the 53-foot Gypsy Moth sailboat which Chichester sailed solo around the world in 1966–67. Both Cutty Sark and Gypsy Moth are open May-September 14:30–18:00 daily…October–April 11:00–17:00 Monday–Saturday and 14:30–17:00 Sunday.

Visit the Royal Observatory's museum of navigation, astronomy and chronometry (astrolabes, hourglasses, clockwork planetariums, quadrants, chronometers). See the Meridian Building's brass strip which marks the division of the eastern and western hemispheres. All distances and time worldwide are measured from this, the prime meridian.

See the marvelous exhibits (ship models, scientific instruments, marine paintings, chronometers, naval uniforms) in the National Maritime Museum.

Both the Royal Observatory and the Maritime Museum are open Monday–Saturday 10:00–17:00, Sunday 14:00–17:00 (October–April) and 14:00–18:00 (May–September).

See the enormous Painted Hall in the Royal Naval College, open daily except Thursday 14:30–17:00. Lunch in one of the good "pubs" at the riverside.

For the return to London, a boat ride on the Thames is an enjoyable alternative to the train.

London - Hampton Court - London   ABC 50

Dep. London (Waterloo)	Monday–Saturday: Frequent times from 06:22 to 23:24
	Sunday: Frequent times from 07:37 to 23:07
Arr. Hampton Court	35 minutes later

Sights in **Hampton Court**: This is the riverside Palace built by Cardinal Wolsey and then given to Henry VIII, after he expressed his desire to have it. Walk through the ancient maze.

Dep. Hampton Court	Monday–Saturday: Frequent times from 06:08 to 22:39
	Sunday: Frequent times from 08:06 to 23:06
Arr. London (Waterloo)	35 minutes later

London - Hastings - London   ABC 501

All of these trains have light refreshments.

Dep. London (Char. X)	08:15 (1)	09:10	10:10 (2)	11:10 (2)	12:10 (2)
Arr. Hastings	09:43	10:44	11:39	12:38	13:38

Sights in **Hastings**: This is where William became the Conqueror, of the Saxons. Take buses #5, #252, #485 or #486 to see the ancient battlefield. Visit the old fishing harbor and stroll the 3-mile promenade along the beach. Obtain a printed description of the Castle at the Tourist Information Center, 4 Robertson Terrace.

See the 243-foot-long tapestry in Town Hall, illustrating the 81 greatest events of British history since 1066: the battle of Hastings, the Boston Tea Party, the first television broadcast, etc.

Dep. Hastings	13:52 (3)	14:11 (2)	15:11 (2)	15:52 (3)	16:10 (3+6)
Arr. London (Char. X)	15:19	15:53	17:04	17:19	17:55

(1) Runs Monday-Friday, except holidays. (2) Runs daily, except holidays. (3) Runs daily, except Sundays and holidays. (4) Runs Saturday only. (5) Runs daily, except Saturdays and holidays. (6) Plus other departures from Hastings at frequent times from 17:11 to 21:11.

London - Isle of Wight (Yarmouth) - London   (via Lymington)

There are 148 miles of well-posted footpaths on Wight, including a 60-mile path along the entire coastline of this island that measures 13 miles at its widest by 23 miles at its longest. Also several bus lines. Many quiet beaches. Good fishing.

Twenty-two orchid species grow here. See the dinosaur bones in the Museum of Wight Geology over the Public Library. Carisbrooke Castle. Quarr Abbey, near Ryde. Take the boat trip that starts at Alum Bar.

ABC 60 (*Train*)		
Dep. London (Wat.)	08:32 (1)	09:32 (1)
Arr. Brockenhurst	09:55	10:53
Change trains. ABC 61		
Dep. Brockenhurst	09:58	10:57
Arr. Lym. Pier	10:07	11:06
Change to ferry.		
Dep. Lym. Pier	10:15	11:15
Arr. Yarmouth	10:45	11:45

ABC 61 (*Ferry*)		
Dep. Yarmouth	14:00 (1)	14:30 (1+2)
Arr. Lym. Pier	14:30	15:00
Change to train		
Dep. Lym. Pier	14:40	15:10
Arr. Brockenhurst	14:49	15:19
Change trains. ABC 60		
Dep. Brockenhurst	14:58	15:38
Arr. London (Wat.)	16:36	17:06

(1) Runs Monday–Saturday. (2) Plus other Yarmouth departures every 30 minutes from 15:00 to 18:30, plus 19:30, 20:30 and 21:00.

London - Kings Lynn - London   581

Dep. London (Kings X)	08:45 (1)	09:45 (1)	10:45 (1)	11:45 (1)
Arr. Kings Lynn	10:25	11:29	12:25	13:29

Sights in **Kings Lynn**: The "Town Trail" brochure, available at the City Information Center, is very helpful for touring the winding, twisting streets here in one of England's most historic towns.

See the attractive merchants' houses on Queen Street. The King John Cup and one of the oldest paper books in the world (the Red Register), at the Treasury in the 15th century Town Hall. The country market, every Tuesday near Duke's Head Hotel and every Saturday opposite Town Hall.

Dep. Kings Lynn	14:03 (1)	15:10 (5)	16:02 (1)	16:18 (3+6)
Arr. London (Kings X)	15:49	16:49	17:49	18:17

(1) Runs Monday–Saturday, except holidays. (2) Runs daily, except holidays. (3) Runs Sunday only. (4) Runs Saturday and Sunday. (5) Runs Monday-Friday, except holidays. (6) Plus other departures from Kings Lynn at 17:05 (1), 17:18 (3), 18:09 (5), 18:18 (3), 19:09 (5), 19:18 (3), 20:18 (3), 20:42 (1), 21:14 (3), 21:42 (7) and 22:14 (5). (7) Runs Saturdays only.

London - Leicester - London   560

Dep. London (St. Pan.)	07:00 (1)	07:30 (2)	08:00 (3)	08:30 (4+13)
Arr. Leicester	08:20	08:45	09:13	09:48

Sights in **Leicester**: The Jewry Wall, to see outstanding Roman ruins. The Church of St. Mary de Castro.

Dep. Leicester	12:30 (1)	13:00 (4)	13:30 (1)	14:00 (9+14)
Arr. London (St. Pan.)	13:47	14:15	14:50	15:17

(1) Runs Monday-Friday, except holidays. (2) Runs Saturday only. (3) Runs Monday–Friday, except holidays. Restaurant car. (4) Runs Monday-Saturday, except holidays. (5) Runs Sunday only. (6) Arrives 30 minutes later on Sunday. (7) Runs daily, except Saturday. Restaurant car Monday-Friday. (8) Runs Monday-Saturday, except holidays. Restaurant car Monday-Friday. (9) Runs daily, except holidays. (10) Runs daily, except Saturdays and holidays. (11) Runs daily, except holidays. (12) Runs Monday-Thursday. (13) Plus other London departures at 09:00 (3), 09:30 (3), 10:00 (3), 10:30 (3), 11:00 (1), 11:30 (4), 12:00 (1) and 12:30 (1). (14) Plus other Leicester departures at 14:30 (1), 14:45 (14), 15:00 (1), 15:30 (9), 15:57 (5), 16:30 (1),17:30 (10), 18:00 (10), 18:30 (11), 19:30 (11), 20:00 (5), 20:30 (4). (14) Runs Saturdays and Sundays only.

London - Lincoln - London

570

Dep. London (Kings X)	07:00 (3)	08:20 (3)	09:10 (3)	11:10 (3)
Arr. Newark (Northgate)	08:23	09:31	10:26	12:26
Change trains. 574				
Dep Newark	08:54 (6)	10:45 (1)	12:10 (7)	12:45 (1)
Arr. Lincoln (Cen.)	09:19	11:10	12:38	13:10

Sights in **Lincoln**: The wonderful Cathedral. Newport Arch. Roman relics in the City and County Museums. The houses on High Bridge.

Dep. Lincoln (Cen.)	13:13 (7)	15:24 (1)	16:57 (8)	17:17 (6)	19:15 (7)
Arr. Newark	13:40	15:54	17:27	17:47	19:39
Change trains. 570					
Dep Newark	14:21	16:03 (6)	17:14	18:10 (6)	20:31 (3)
Arr. London (Kings X)	15:45	17:33	18:47	19:37	21:57

(1) Runs daily, except Sundays and holidays. (2) Runs daily, except Sundays and holidays. Restaurant car Monday-Friday. (3) Runs Monday–Friday, except holidays. Restaurant car. (4) Runs daily, except Sundays and holidays. Restaurant car. (5) Runs daily, except Saturdays and holidays. (6) Runs Monday-Friday, except holidays.

London - Norwich - London   580

Dep. London (L'pool)	07:30 (1)	08:00 (2)	08:30 (4)	09:30 (4)	10:30 (5+8)
Arr. Norwich	09:26	09:42	10:23	11:23	12:23

Sights in **Norwich**: Norwich Grammar School. (Its alumni include Lord Nelson.) The Cathedral. The collection of lace, pottery, teapots, paintings and coins at the Museum in the Castle, built in 1068 by William the Conqueror.

Walk down the Elm Hill alley. See the view of Norwich from the Castle. Assembly House. The Strangers Hall. The 16th century house on the 12th century High Bridge.

Dep. Norwich	13:05 (5)	14:05 (6)	15:05 (6)	16:05 (5)	17:05 (5+9)
Arr. London (L'pool)	14:53	15:52	16:52	17:58	18:53

(1) Runs Saturday only. (2) Runs Monday–Friday, except holidays. Restaurant car. (3) Runs daily, except holidays. (4) Runs daily, except Sundays and holidays. Restaurant car. (5) Runs daily, except holidays. Restaurant car Monday-Saturday. (6) Runs daily, except holidays. (7) Runs daily, except Sundays and holidays. (8) Plus another London departure at 11:30 (7). (9) Plus other Norwich departures at 18:05 (5), 19:05 (6) and 20:40 (6).

London - Nottingham - London   560

Dep. London (St. Pan.)	07:30 (7)	08:30 (2)	09:15 (7)	10:30 (8)	12:00 (2+10)
Arr. Nottingham	09:11	10:14	11:12	12:11 (5)	13:07

Sights in **Nottingham**: The Duke of Newcastle's castle. which was a new Newcastle castle in 1679...with its art collection. The great council house. The Natural History Museum in Wollaton Hall.

Dep. Nottingham	12:33 (2)	13:39	14:24 (7)	14:38 (2)	15:33 (2+11)
Arr. London (St. Pan.)	14:15	15:17 (2)	16:02	16:29	17:17

(1) Runs daily, except Sundays and holidays. (2) Runs Monday-Friday, except holidays. (3) Runs daily, except Sundays and holidays. Restaurant car Monday–Friday. (4) Runs daily, except holidays. (5) Arrives 30–50 minutes later on Sunday. (6) Runs daily, except Saturday and holidays. (7) Runs Saturday only. (8) Runs Sunday only. (9) Runs Saturday and Sunday. (10) Plus other departures from London at 12:15 (7) and 13:30 (5), arriving Nottingham 14:14 and 15:11. (11) Plus other departures from Nottingham at 16:33 (2), 17:33 (2), 18:02 (8), 19:03 (1) and 19:30 (8), arriving London 17:50, 18:23, 19:07, 19:34, 20:01, 21:03 and 21:36.

London - Oxford - London   525

Dep. London (Pad.)	08:20 (6)	08:48 (2)	09:03 (3)	09:18 (2)	09:48 (2+5)
Arr. Oxford	60–70 minutes later				

Sights in **Oxford**: Daily guided tours by open-top, double-decker bus depart the railstation every 15 minutes 09:30–17:30 (until 18:30 in July and August). The 1994 prices were £6 for adults, £1.50 for children 5-11 years old.

This is the home of one of the greatest universities in the world, comprising 23 different colleges. Start your stroll at the center of Oxford (Carfax Tower), where the Information Center is located. There is bus service from the railstation to Carfax Tower.

Begin by walking south from Carfax Tower, down St. Aldates Street to Folly Bridge, the Cathedral and the numerous portraits (John Wesley, William Penn, Lewis Carroll, William Gladstone) at Christ Church College. Founded by Cardinal Wolsey and Henry VIII, it is the largest and most splendid of all the colleges here.

Later, see Merton College and Corpus Christi before continuing on to Oriel and then into High Street. See Bodleian Library, which has a copy of every book published in England. See the decorative bookcases in the library of Queen's College. Most popular among visitors is Magdalen College, with its beautiful main quadrangle.

At 20:55, hear "Great Tom's" 101 strokes every night as the heavy bell calls the original number of Osney Abbey's students to return to their rooms before the nightly closing of its gates.

Stroll the lane behind Holywell Street to see attractive Tudor and Elizabethan houses. There are many late 18th century houses on Beaumont Street.

Dep. Oxford	Frequent times from 07:09 to 22:38
Arr. London (Pad.)	60–70 minutes later

(1) Runs daily, except Saturdays and holidays. (2) Runs daily, except Sundays and holidays. (3) Runs Sunday only. (4) Runs daily, except holidays. (5) Plus other departures from London at 10:07 (2), 11:07 (2), 11:48 (2), 12:07 (2), 12:40, 13:07 (2), 13:40 (3) and frequent other times until 23:48. (6) Runs Monday-Friday except holidays.

Nearby: Blenheim Palace (Churchill's Birthplace)

To see lovely Blenheim Palace, take a bus in Oxford from Gloucester Green bus station for the 8-mile trip to **Woodstock**. This magnificent 18th century structure was the birthplace of Winston Churchill in 1874.

A gift from Britain to the Duke of Marlborough after this ancestor of Churchill defeated the French in 1704 at Blenheim in Bavaria, the beautiful 300-room mansion is open daily March–October, with guided tours 11:30–17:00.

Letters, documents, photos, even a lock of Churchill's hair (at the age of 5) are exhibited in the tiny room where he was born prematurely and unexpectedly on November 30, 1874, in his mother's seventh month of pregnancy.

Other rooms throughout the palace have more memorabilia: some of Churchill's paintings (see "London–Chartwell"), recordings of his speeches, his letters, etc. A visit here is worthwhile if only to see the 180-foot-long library, with its marvelous Willis pipe organ.

There is time in the same day to visit nearby Bladon Churchyard. A simple tombstone there that reads merely "Winston Leonard Spencer Churchill 1874/1965" marks the burial place (alongside his American mother Jenny Spencer) of the greatest Englishman of the last 1,000 years.

London - Penzance - London   515

Reservation is advisable for all of these trains, especially for sleeping cars and pullman service

Dep. Lon. (Pad.)	07:35 (1)	07:40 (2)	09:03 (1)	10:15 (3)	12:15 (3)	
Arr. Penzance	12:50	13:20	14:15	15:55	18:00	

Dep. Lon. (Pad.)	13:35 (2)	14:15 (3)	15:35 (2)	17:35 (9)	17:55 (1+17)	
Arr. Penzance	19:00	19:50	21:00	22:30	23:20	

• • •

Dep. Penzance	05:15 (9)	06:45 (1)	08:36 (3)	09:38 (1)	10:39 (3)	11:29 (3)
Arr. Lon. (Pad.)	10:00	11:50	13:45	14:55	16:30	17:25

Dep. Penzance	12:40 (3)	14:45 (2)	15:40 (3)	16:41 (1)	17:16 (3)	22:15 (15)
Arr. Lon. (Pad.)	18:45	19:45	21:05	22:10	23:05	06:10

(1) Runs Saturday only. (2) Runs Monday–Friday except holidays. (3) Runs Sunday only. (4) Runs daily, except Sundays and holidays. Restaurant car. (5) Runs Monday–Thursday (restaurant car) and Saturday. (6) Runs Friday (restaurant car) and Saturday. (7) Arrives 18:50 on Saturday. (8) Runs Friday and Saturday. (9) Runs Monday–Friday, except holidays. Pullman service (for which reservation is advisable) availabe in first-class. (10) Runs daily, except Sundays and holidays. (11) Runs Saturday and Sunday. (12) Arrives 30–50 minutes later on Sun. (13) Runs daily, except holidays. (14) Runs Monday–Friday, except holidays. Restaurant car. (15) Runs daily, except Saturday. Carries a sleeping car. Coach is second-class. Light refreshments. (16) Runs Monday-Friday. (17) Plus other London departures at 18:35 (18) and 23:55 (15), arriving Penzanee 00:10 and 08:19. (18) Runs Friday + Sunday.

Penzance and the rest of Cornwall deserve a stay of several days, although Penzance can be visited on a one-day train excursion from London. Sights in **Penzance**: Take the walk described in the free brochure called "A day in Chapel Street, Abbey Street and Quay Street" and visit Egyptian Shop, the Admiral Benbow Inn, the Nautical Museum and Morrab Gardens. See the view of Mount's Bay from Bolitho Gardens.

It is only a 10-mile bus trip to **Land's End**, the westernmost edge of England and a beautiful seascape of waves crashing against the granite cliffs. In another direction, it is also only a 10-mile bus ride to **St. Ives**, a quaint fishing village and the location of The Hepworth Gallery, containing the work of Britain's best-known sculptress. (Both buses leave from the terminal next to the railstation.)

Go a mere 3 miles by city bus to **Marazion** and then by small motorboat to visit **St. Michael's Mount,** a tiny island only a half-mile offshore. There has been a church at the summit since 1135. The castle has been occupied by the St. Aubyn family from 1659 to the present day. Visitors are allowed to enter most of the rooms of the castle and are provided a brochure describing its history and the many interesting contents: furniture, costumes, guns, maps, portraits, banners.

Penzance is also the gateway to the more than 100 **Isles of Scilly**. The largest island is the 3-miles-by-2-miles St. Mary's. For information, about the 2½-hour ferry-boat ride to it (600 passengers), contact Isles of Scilly Steamship Company, Quay St., Penzance, Cornwall TR18 4BD, United Kingdom.

There is 20-minute helicopter service from Penzance to both St. Mary's Island and Tresco Island. For current schedules, write to: British International Helicopters, Heliport, Eastern Green, Cornwall, England.

The northern half of **Tresco**, dominated by the ruins of the 16th century King Charles Castle and the 17th century Cromwell's Castle, is windswept and treeless. Its southern half, lush and semitropical, has wide beaches, a roofless 16th century stone fort from which there are beautiful views, and the marvelous Abbey Gardens with its collection of restored figureheads salvaged from ships that were wrecked in this area.

There is boat service from Tresco to **St. Mary's**, the commercial center of the archipelago, where the main attractions are a 16th century Star Castle and a museum open every day except rainless Sundays 09:30–12:30, 13:30–16:30 and 19:30–21:00 (old rowboats, Roman pottery, stone tools).

St. Mary's also offers sandy beaches (washed by frigid water). many beautiful gardens of sub-tropical plants, coastal walks, nature trails, and a 9-hole golf course along the seacoast. Small launches can be taken to the other inhabited islands: **Bryher, St. Agnes** and **St. Martin's**.

London - Portsmouth - London   ABC 56 + 504

See Cook's table 509 for service to Portsmouth from London's Victoria railstation and Gatwick Airport.

Dep. London (Waterloo)	07:15 (1)	07:23 (12)	08:15 (5)	08:45 (12)	09:15 (5+10)
Arr. Portsmouth (Hbr.)	08:40	08:53	09:42	10:33	10:40

Sights in **Portsmouth**: England's great naval base. See Lord Nelson's flagship H.M.S. Victory, which won the battle of Trafalgar over the combined Spanish and French fleets. The nearby Victory Museum (Nelson relics, good marine paintings, ship models) at the Naval Yard. Nearby is Henry VIII's man-of-war, "Mary Rose," raised in 1982 from the seabed where it had lain since it sank in 1545.

The Dickens Museum at the house where the author was born, 393 Commercial Road. Many fine 17th and 18th century houses on Lombard Street and High Street.

Dep. Portsmouth (Hbr.)	14:17 (6)	15:02 (5)	15:17 (7)	16:02 (8)	16:20 (4)	16:36 (12+11)
Arr. London (Waterloo)	15:59	16:30	16:59	17:33	17:59	18:29

(1) Runs Saturday only. (2) Runs daily, except Sundays and holidays. Light refreshments. Monday-Friday. (3) Arrives 40 minutes later on Saturday. (4) Runs Sunday only. (5) Runs daily, except Sundays and holidays. Light refreshments. (6) Runs daily, except Sundays and holidays. (7) Runs Saturday and Sunday. (8) Runs daily, except holidays. Light refreshments. (9) Runs daily, except holidays. (10) Plus other London departures at 10:15 (8), 10:48 (6), 11:15 (8) and 11:48 to 22:50. (11) Plus other departures from Portsmouth at frequent times 17:02 to 22:17. (12) Runs Monday-Friday only, except holidays.

London - Isle of Wight (Shanklin) - London (via Portsmouth)

As these schedules indicate, it is easy to visit both Portsmouth and the Isle of Wight in one day by stopping-over in Portsmouth at 08:53 or 09:42...until 11:30, 12:00 or 12:30.

504

Dep. London (Wat.)	07:23 (1)	08:15 (2)	08:25 (3)	08:45 (2)	09:15 (4+11)
Arr. Portsmoth (Hbr.)	08:53	09:42	10:00	10:33	10:40
Change to ferry. ABC 57					
Dep. Portsmouth (Hbr.)	09:30	10:00	10:30	11:00	11:30
Arr. Ryde Pier Head	09:48	10:18	10:48	11:18	11:48
Change to train.					
Dp. Ryde Pier Head	10:00	10:22	11:00	11:22	12:00
Arr. Shanklin	10:25	10:45	11:25	11:45	12:25

There are full-day and half-day bus tours of the island, starting from Ryde Esplanade.

Sights in **Ryde**: Six miles of pretty beaches. many nice gardens. Take the 9-mile island train from Ryde Pier to Shanklin. En route is Ryde Esplanade, a working-class resort. A 3-mile steam railway roundtrip from there offers pretty views.

Sights in **Shanklin**: One of Britain's loveliest towns. Ten minutes' walk from the railstation there are views of the sea and farms from East Cliff Promenade. On the way back to Shanklin, walk through the Chine (deep ravine) to the mile-long beach and see lovely Old Village. Buses (on Carter Avenue, 2 blocks from the railstation) go to Cowes on the north coast. Near Cowes is Osborne House, queen Victoria's summer mansion, which can be toured from the day after Easter through early October.

Dep. Shanklin	13:52	14:52	15:52	16:32	16:52 (12)
Arr. Ryde Pier Head	14:17	15:17	16:17	16:56	17:17
Change to ferry.					
Dep. Ryde Pier Head	14:30	15:30	16:30	17:00	17:30
Arr. Portsmouth (Hbr.)	14:48	15:48	16:48	17:18	17:48
Change to train. 504					
Dep. Portsmouth (Hbr.)	15:20 (4)	15:02 (5)	17:01 (2)	17:20 (3)	18:01 (2)
Arr. London (Wat.)	16:30	17:33	18:34	19:32	19:32

(1) Runs daily, except Sundays and holidays. Light refreshments Monday-Friday. (2) Runs daily, except Sundays and holidays. Light refreshments. (3) Runs Sunday only. (4) Runs daily, except holidays. Light refreshments Monday-Saturday. (5) Runs daily, except holidays. Light refreshments. (6) Runs daily. Light refreshments. (7) Runs Monday–Friday, except holidays. Light refreshments. (8) Runs daily, except holidays. Light refreshments on Saturday. (9) Runs daily, except holidays. Light refreshments. (10) Runs Sunday only. Light refreshments. (11) Plus another London departure at 10:15 (4), arriving Shanklin 13:25. (12) Plus other departures from Shanklin (Portsmouth service shown in parentheses) at 17:32 (3), 17:52 (2), 18:32 (3), 19:50 (7), 20:50 (8), 22:17 (9) and 22:32 (10).

London - Rochester - London   ABC 9

Dep. London   Frequent times from 05:22 to 00:14 (08:02 to 23:17 on Sunday)
  (Charing X)
Arr. Rochester   60 minutes later

Sights in **Rochester**: The 17th century Bull Hotel, where Charles Dickens' characters, Pickwick and his friends, spent the first night of their long and memorable trip

See the little house at 11 Ordinance Terrace, where Dickens lived from the time he was 4 until he was 9 years old, Visit the red brick mansion where he lived his last 10 years and died. The cemetery here has many markers from which Dickens took the names for the people he cast in his stories.

Visit the City Museum in Eastgate House, open daily except Friday 14:00-17:30.

Dep. Rochester   Frequent times from 05:31 to 22:29 (06:52 to 21:20 on Sunday)
Arr. London (Charing X)   60 minutes later

London - Rye - London   ABC 20

Dep. London (Charing Cross)   Frequent times from 05:35 to 21:00
                              (08:57 to 19:57 on Sunday)
Change from suburban train 90 minutes later, in Ashford.
Arr. Rye   2 hours after departing London.

Sights in **Rye**: This delightful little hilltop town was once an important seaport, but it is now 2 miles from the sea. See the 14th century city walls. The 14th century wood Monastery, now housing one of the town's 6 potteries.

It is a 10-minute walk up Conduit Hill to the 12th century Norman church and then to the oldest structure in Rye, the 13th century Ypres Tower, now the city Museum, open from Easter to the end of September, Monday-Saturday 10:30–12:30 and 14:15–17:30, Sunday 11:15–12:30.

Dep. Rye   Frequent times from 05:50 to 21:42
                                    (10:21 to 20:21 on Sunday)
Change to Suburban train 30 minutes later, in Ashford.
Arr. London (Charing Cross)   2 hours after departing Rye.

London - Salisbury - Stonehenge - London   511

Most of these trains have light refreshments.

Dep. London (Wat.)   07:35 (1)   07:54 (2)   08:35 (3)   08:55 (4)   09:35 (2)   10:12 (1+8)
Arr. Salisbury   09:04   09:21   09:51   10:37   11:00   11:31

Sights in **Salisbury**: The Cathedral, with its tombs of Crusaders and one of the 4 existing copies of the Magna Carta.

Buses operate between the Salisbury railstation and Stonehenge to view the mysterious oval of 50-ton stones there, about 4,000 years old. This is the most important prehistoric relic in Britain. How were these stupendous weights moved 20 miles from their quarry…and why?

The nearly 2-hour roundtrip departs Salisbury Monday–Friday at 10:15, 11:15, 12:15, 13:15, 14:15 and 16:15 (different but similar times on Saturday and Sunday). The 1994 prices were £3.90 for adults, £2.90 for children and senior citizens.

Dep. Salisbury   13:20 (2)   13:50 (1)   14:15 (2)   14:29 (4)   15:21 (3)   16:15 (6+9)
Arr. London (Wat.)   14:44   15:17   15:44   16:25   16:44 (5)   17:45

(1) Runs Saturday only. (2) Runs Monday-Friday, except holidays. (3) Runs daily, except Sundays and holidays. (4) Runs Sunday only. (5) Arrives 30 minutes later on Saturday. (6) Runs daily, except holidays. (7) Runs daily, except Saturdays and holidays. (8) Plus other departures from London at 10:35 (2), 10:55 (4), 11:35 (2) and 12:35 (3). (9) Plus other departures from Salisbury at 16:52 (2), 17:17 (1), 17:50 (2), 18:15 (3), 18:18 (4), 19:53 (2), 20:18 (1), 20:45 (2) and 21:06 (4).

London - Stratford on Avon - London

Although there is service between London's *Paddington* railstation and Coventry, it requires changing trains en route.

The escorted "Shakespeare Connection" service between London's *Euston* railstation, Coventry and (by bus) Stratford is preferable. Details are available from British Travel Centre, 12 Regent Street, London. The special bus that transfers passengers between Coventry and Stratford has a guide and stops near the Stratford office that books various local tours.

Dep. London (Euston)	08:55 (3)	09:45 (2)	10:25 (3)
Arr. Coventry	10:26	12:02	11:51
Change to bus.			
Dep. Coventry	10:35	12:10	12:00
Arr. Strarford	11:10	12:45	12:35

• • •

Dep. Stratford	17:15 (1)	17:55 (2)	23:15 (1)
Arr. Coventry	17:50	18:25	23:45
Change to train.			
Dep. Coventry	18:07 (4)	18:37 (3)	00:37
Arr. London (Euston)	19:29	20:17	02:37

(1) Runs Monday–Saturday. (2) Runs Sunday only (3) Runs daily except Sundays + holidays. (4) Runs daily except holidays.

Those wishing to attend a performance at the Royal Shakespeare Theater *cannot* purchase tickets for that night's performance until arriving at the theater and chance the possibility that all tickets have been sold.

The "Shakespeare Connection" combination train-and-bus ticket can be purchased only in England — at either of British Rail's central London offices (Regent Street or Oxford Street), or at London's Euston railstation.

There are many restaurants and pubs in Stratford, and visitors may picnic either by the theater or in the garden along the river.

See the house of Mary Arden, his mother. The cottage of Anne Hathaway, his wife. Shakespeare's tomb in Trinity Church. The home of John Harvard, founder of America's great university.

There are afternoon performances at the Royal Shakespeare Theater on some Thursdays and Saturdays.

London - Torquay - Paignton - London   510

Dep. London (Pad.)	07:15	08:35 (3)	09:35 (3)	10:45 (4)	11:45 (3)
Dep. Exeter (St. Davids)	10:25 (3)	-0-	12:01	12:59	14:03
Arr. Torquay	11:07	11:41	12:41	13:29	14:43
Arr. Paignton	6–10 minutes later				

Sights in **Torquay:** An 11-mile coastline that resembles a Mediterranean resort, palm trees and all. The British "Riviera." Pronounced "tor-kee." Stroll the walk along the formal gardens at the waterfront to the park, where concerts and dances are held in the Summer. Visit the Model Railroad and House Miniatures in the Victoria Arcade at the harbor.

See the collection of 17th century silver and 18th century glass at the Municipal Art Gallery and Museum in the 18th century building next to the ruins of the 12th century Torre Abbey. Nearby is the Model Village, open in Summer 09:00-22:00, in Winter 09:00 to dusk. The exhibits of archaeology, natural history and Devon folk life in the Museum of Natural History, open daily except Sunday from March through October 10:00–16:45, and Monday-Friday from November through February.

Paignton has many bed-and-breakfast inns. Sights there include the restored 14th century Great Hall of Compton Castle, open May through October on Monday, Wednesday and Thursday 10:00–17:00. The ballroom filled with silver mirrors at Oldway House, called "a miniature Versailles," open Monday-Saturday 09:00–13:00 and 14:15–17:00, Sundays 14:00–17:00.

Dep. Paignton	15:21 (3)	16:09 (6)	17:20 (3+11)
Dep. Torquay	6 minutes after departing Paignton		
Dep. Exeter (St. Davids)	15:58	16:53	18:16
Arr. London (Pad.)	19:06	19:50	20:45

(1) Runs Monday–Friday, except holidays. Restaurant car. (2) Operates early July to late August. Runs Saturday only. (3) Runs Saturday only. (4) Runs daily, except Sundays and holidays. (5) Runs Saturday and Sunday. (6) Runs Sunday only. (7) Runs Saturday only. Change trains in Exeter. (8) Runs Monday-Friday, except holidays. Light refreshments. Change trains in Exeter. (9) Runs daily, except Saturdays and holidays. Change trains in Exeter. (10) Arrives 55 minutes later on Sunday. (11) Plus another Paignton departure at 18:25 (9), arriving London 22:10 (10).

London - Winchester - London   ABC 59 + 502

All of these trains run daily.

Dep. London (Wat.)	Frequent times from 05:40 to 23:45 (07:45 to 22:45 on Sunday)
Arr. Winchester	60 minutes later (80 minutes later on Sunday)

Sights in **Winchester**: King Arthur's roundtable in the Great Hall at the Castle. The 11th century Cathedral, with the tombs of King Alfred, Jane Austen and Izaak Walton.

Dep. Winchester	Frequent times from 06:21 to 23:14 (08:02 to 23:02 on Sunday)
Arr. London (Wat.)	60 minutes later (80 minutes later on Sunday)

London - Windsor - London   ABC 67

Dep. London (Waterloo)	Monday–Saturday: Frequent times from 06:13 to 23:17
	Sunday: Frequent times from 07:50 to 22:50
Arr. Windsor (Riverside)	40–60 minutes later

Sights in **Windsor**: Windsor Castle with its collection of Da Vinci drawings and, occasionally, members of the Royal Family. See the Changing of the Guard there, at 10:25. Queen Mary's Doll House. St. George's Chapel.

In the town, stroll down the 3-mile "Long Walk." See Eton College, where once it did not matter if you won or lost, in the days when observing niceties was more important than the final score.

Dep. Windsor (Riverside)	Monday–Saturday: Frequent times from 06:08 to 22:40
	Sunday: Frequent times from 07:05 to 23:05
Arr. London (Waterloo)	40–60 minutes later

London - York - London 570

Dep. London (Kings X)	06:00 (7)	07:00 (2)	07:30 (3)	08:00 (8)	09:00 (3)
Arr. York	08:29	09:09	09:28	09:53	10:54

Dep. London (Kings X)	09:30 (3)	10:00 (3)	10:30 (3)	11:00 (3)	11:30 (3)
Arr. York	11:35	11:54	12:26	13:00	13:36 (10)

• • •

Dep. York	14:35 (7)	14:52 (3)	15:32 (3)	16:00 (2)	16:32 (7)
Arr. London (Kings X)	16:49	16:57	17:39	18:13	18:35

Dep. York	16:55 (7)	17:00 (2)	17:20 (8)	17:51 (7)	18:27 (3+9)
Arr. London (Kings X)	18:55	19:23	19:10	20:07	20:38

(1) Runs daily, except Sundays and holidays. (2) Runs Saturday only. (3) Runs Monday–Friday, except holidays. Restaurant car. (4) Runs daily, except Sundays and holidays. Pullman service available in first-class Monday–Friday. (5) Runs daily, except Sundays and holidays. Restaurant car Monday–Friday. (6) Runs daily, except Sundays and holidays. Restaurant car. (7) Runs Monday-Friday, except holidays. (8) Runs Monday-Friday, except holidays. Pullman service available in first-class. (9) Plus other York departures at 19:41 (3), 20:03 (3) and 21:39 (7). (10) Runs to June 24+ from September 5.

Sights in **York**: Free walking tours in Summer leave from the fountain across from the Information Center (Exhibition Square) daily at 10:15, 14:15 and 19:15.

Founded by Romans in A.D. 71. Very crowded with tourists in July and August. Most of the interesting places are located within the one square mile that is encircled by 3 miles of ancient walls.

York Minister, the largest Gothic cathedral in Britain (open daily 07:30 to dusk) has fantastic stained glass. Its Great East Window is the size of a tennis court. It is advisable to use binoculars to study the detail on both the windows and the plaster work on the ceilings.

See the 14th and 15th century stained glass in All Saints Church, on North Street. The brass rubbings center at St. Williams College (outside the cathedral's Great East Window). Stroll along the top of the city walls for a great view of the ancient buildings that surround the cathedral.

Walk down "The Shambles." Visit the restored Guildhall on St. Helen's Square to see its modern stained glass and timbered roof. Castle Museum, Britain's largest folk museum, off

Tower Street (open daily 09:30–18:30). The shrine commemorating the 12th century massacre of Jews at Clifford Tower, in the center of York.

Exhibits of Bronze Age, Iron Age and Roman-era remains, in the Yorkshire Museum on Museum Street (open Monday–Saturday 10:00–17:00, Sunday 13:00–17:00). The 25 old locomotives and many train cars (including Queen Victoria's ornate coach) at the National Railway Museum on Leeman Road.

There are special excursion trains from London, to the Railway Museum, for a few days in August, September, October and November each year. The all-day excursions include round-trip train service from London and 4 hours touring the Museum.

SCENIC TRAIN TRIPS

There is much fine scenery on nearly every rail route in England. The next 4 train rides offer exceptional scenic views, as do several rail trips in Scotland.

London - Pwllheli - London   ABC page 126

There is excellent coastal scenery on this ride plus a splendid view of Harlech Castle.

This trip is too long as a one-day London roundtrip.

All of these departures require changing trains at one or 2 railstations among 5 different stations—in Birmingham for most trips. The ticket office at London (Euston) will advise where to make a train change.

A layover in Birmingham should be considered.

Dep. London (Euston)	07:00 (1)	09:30	11:30 (1)	13:30	15:30 (1)
Arr. Pwllheli	14:54	16:26 (2)	18:37	20:50 (3)	22:49

Sights in **Pwllheli**: This summer seaside resort is located on the southern side of the Lleyn Peninsula. The major attraction here is boating in **Tremadog Bay**.

Dep. Pwllheli	07:11 (1)	09:27 (1)	10:25 (4)	12:39 (1)	13:16 (4+7)
Arr. London (Euston)	14:29	16:29	18:10	21:03 (5)	20:16

(1) Runs Monday–Saturday. (2) Arrives 17:35 on Sunday. (3) Arrives 21:36 on Sunday. (4) Runs Sunday only.(5) Arrives 21:48 on Saturday. (6) Arrives 23:59 on Saturday. (7) Plus other Pwllheli departures at 14:59 (1), 15:25 (4) and 17:49 (1), arriving London 23:19 (6), 22:10 and 00:48.

Leeds - Settle - Carlisle   562

The 62-mile Settle–Carlisle portion of this route is considered by many to be the most scenic train route in England. It goes through the **Pennine Hills** and the **Yorkshire Dales Na-**

tional Park, close to the Lake district. This line has 14 tunnels and 21 viaducts, including the 104-foot-high Ribblehead Viaduct.

All of these trains have light refreshments, unless designated otherwise.

Dep. Leeds	08:45 (2)	09:49 (6)	10:49 (2)	12:49 (2)	13:32 (3)	14:49 (4)
Dep. Settle	09:47	10:53	11:46	13:45	14:27	15:45
Arr. Carlisle	11:28	12:36	13:29	15:28	16:10	17:30

Sights in **Settle**: A pretty town. Since 1429, a market has been held here every Tuesday.

Dep. Carlisle	14:16 (2)	15:20 (7)	16:26 (2)	16:49 (3)	17:45 (4)	18:21 (5)
Dep. Settle	15:59	16:59	18:09	18:29	19:24	19:57
Arr. Leeds	17:01	18:07	19:09	19:30	20:22	20:59

(1) Runs daily, except holidays. (2) Runs daily, except Sundays and holidays. (3) Runs Sunday only. (4) Runs Monday–Friday, except holidays. (5) Runs Saturday only. (6) Runs daily except Sundays & holidays July 18-September 2, also July 2,9,16, September 3, 10, 17, 24. (7) Runs Saturday only.

London - Windermere - London

The breathtaking scenery of England's "Lake country."

The Oxenholme–Windermere (and v.v.) trains are second-class only.

550
Dep. London (Euston)	08:40 (1)	12:40 (2+3)
Arr. Oxenholme	12:01	16:00

Change trains.
547
Dep. Oxenholme	13:38	16:08
Arr. Windermere	13:58	16:34

Dep. Windermere	15:00	15:47	16:39	18:33
Arr. Oxenholme	15:19	16:06	17:02	18:50

Change trains.
550
Dep. Oxenholme	15:39 (1)	16:20 (2+3)	17:12	18:42 (3)
Arr. London (Euston)	19:02	20:22 (4)	21:07 (3)	22:28

(1) Runs daily, except Sundays and holidays. Restaurant car. (2) Change trains in Preston. (3) Runs Sunday only. (4) Train from Preston runs daily, except Sundays & holidays.

A DAY THROUGH WALES

There is a marvelous one-day circle train trip from London that takes you through the incredibly beautiful rural scenery in the heart of Wales, between Swansea and Shrewsbury. As shown below, this trip can be made either clockwise or counter-clockwise.

London - Swansea - Shrewsbury - London

530			*540*	
Dep. London (Pad.)	09:00 (1)		Dep. London (Euston)	07:05 (10)
Arr. Swansea	11:55 (2)		Arr Birmingham (New St.)	08:55
Change trains.			*Change trains*	
535			Dep.Birmingham (New St.)	09:25 (6)
Dep. Swansea	12:29 (9)		Arr. Shrewsbury	10:50 (11)
Arr. Shrewsbury	16:28 (8)		*Change trains.*	
Change trains.			*535*	
540			Dep. Shrewsbury	11:10 (7)
Dep. Shrewsbury	16:38 (7)		Arr. Swansea	15:22
Arr Birmingham (New St.)	17:54		*Change trains*	
Change trains			*530*	
Dep.Birmingham	18:15		Dep. Swansea	15:32 (6)
Arr. London (Euston)	20:13 (7)		Arr. London (Pad.)	18:30

(1) Runs daily, except holidays. Restaurant car Monday–Saturday. (2) Arrives 30–40 minutes later on Sunday. (3) Runs daily, except holidays. Light refreshments. (4) Runs daily, except holidays. (5) Runs daily, except Sundays and holidays. Restaurant car. (6) Runs daily, except Sundays and holidays. (7) Runs daily, except Sundays and holidays. Light refreshments. (8) Runs from July 17. (9) Runs Sunday only. (10) Runs Saturday only. (11) Change trains in Wolverhampton.

Sights in **Shrewsbury**: The 1,000-year-old castle. In **Wroxeter**, a short bus ride from here, are the reconstructed ruins of Roman baths built there 2,000 years ago.

RAIL CONNECTION WITH IRELAND VIA WALES

There is bus service between Swansea's railstation and its ferryport.

London - Swansea - Cork		Cork - Swansea - London		
530 Train		*621 Ferry*		
Dep. London (Pad.)	17:00 (1)	Dep. Cork	09:00 (2)	21:00 (2)
Arr. Swansea	19:50	Arr. Swansea	19:00	07:00
Change to ferry. 621		*Change to train. 530*		
Dep. Swansea	21:00 (2)	Dep. Swansea	20:22 (3)	08:00 (4)
Arr. Cork	07:00	Arr. London (Pad.)	23:53	11:40

(1) Runs Monday-Friday, except holidays. (2) Runs Monday, Wednesday, Thursday, Friday and Sunday June 23-September 18; Runs Tuesday, Thursday, Friday and Sunday September 20-December 23. (3) Runs Monday-Thursday only. (3) Runs Sunday only.

RAIL CONNECTIONS WITH SCOTLAND

These are the schedules for rail travel between London (*Kings Cross* railstation) and the capital of Scotland.

London - Edinburgh and Edinburgh - London 570				

Seat reservation is advisable for all of these trains, particularly for Pullman service— which is more comfortable and provides meals and refreshment service at seats.

Dep. London	06:00 (1)	07:00 (2)	08:00 (3)	09:00 (6)	10:00 (4)
Arr. Edinburgh	11:09	11:45	12:15	13:30	14:15
Dep. London	10:30 (5)	11:00 (6)	11:30 (4)	12:00 (6)	13:00 (6)
Arr. Edinburgh	14:51	15:30	16:10 (13)	16:30	17:25
Dep. London	13:30 (1)	14:00 (6)	15:00 (3)	16:00 (6)	17:00 (3)
Arr. Edinburgh	18:11	18:29	19:06	20:29	21:15
Dep. London	18:00 (6)				
Arr. Edinburgh	22:25 (8)				

• • •

| Dep. Edinburgh | 06:00 (1) | 07:00 (6) | 08:00 (6) | 08:30 (2) | 09:00 (6) |
| Arr. London | 11:07 | 11:45 | 12:44 | 13:07 | 13:39 |

| Dep. Edinburgh | 09:30 (1) | 10:00 (1) | 10:30 (6) | 11:00 (6) | 11:30 (6) |
| Arr. London | 14:08 | 14:40 (14) | 14:57 | 15:45 | 15:57 |

| Dep. Edinburgh | 12:00 (6) | 12:30 (6) | 13:00 (6) | 13:30 (2) | 14:100 (1) |
| Arr. London | 16:49 (14) | 16:57 | 17:39 | 18:13 | 18:55 |

| Dep. Edinburgh | 15:00 (11) | 15:30 (2) | 16:00 (6) | 16:30 (2) | 17:00 (6) |
| Arr. London | 19:10 | 20:21 | 20:40 | 21:25 | 21:57 |

| Dep. Edinburgh | 18:00 (11) |
| Arr. London | 23:30 |

(1) Runs Monday–Friday except holidays. (2) Runs Saturday only. (3) Runs Monday–Saturday, except holidays. Pullman service available Monday-Friday in first-class. (4) Runs Monday–Saturday, except holidays. Restaurant car Monday–Friday. (5) Runs Monday-Saturday, except holidays. Restaurant car. (6) Runs Monday-Friday, except holidays. Restaurant car. (7) Runs Monday–Saturday, except holidays. (8) Arrives 20–60 minutes later on Sunday. (9) Runs Monday-Saturday, except holidays. (10) Late June to late August: runs daily, except Sundays and holidays and has a restaurant car. Late August to late June: runs Saturday only. (11) Runs Monday-Friday, except holidays. Pullman service available in first-class. (12) Runs Sunday only. (13) RUns to June 24 & from Sept. 5. (14) Runs June 27-Sept. 2.

SCOTLAND

The 2 rail trips north from Edinburgh (to Dundee–Aberdeen and to Perth–Inverness) are very scenic. There is also train service between Aberdeen and Inverness.

From Inverness, there is a rail route to Wick in northernmost Scotland, and to Kyle of Lochalsh on the west coast of Scotland. Other train routes to the same coastal area are from Glasgow to both Oban and to Mallaig. The other principal rail service in Scotland is between Edinburgh and Glasgow.

We list 36 one-day rail excursions in Scotland.
(See "Freedom of Scotland Travelpass and Flexipass.")

Edinburgh

The capital of Scotland. Most of the 25-acre railstation is under glass. Visit Edinburgh Castle, sitting on a cliff 270 feet above the city, on a site where there have been forts since the 6th century. A cannon has been fired from there every day since 1858. The Castle is open every day in the Summer: 09:30–18:00 Monday-Saturday, 11:00–18:00 on Sundays.

The panoramic view of Edinburgh from the Castle is breathtaking.

At the Castle, see the hammer-beamed timbered ceiling in the Great Hall of James IV, the Scottish Crown Jewels, the small St. Margaret's Chapel, and the State Apartments, including the rooms once occupied by Mary Queen of Scots.

Below the Castle is the 37-acre Princess Street Gardens, with the city's main rail tracks running through it, at a lower level than the surface of the park.

Also visit the 17th century Palace of Holyrood House to see the Throne Room and also the portraits of 110 Scottish kings (painted by the same artist) in the gallery. You will notice that all 110 noses are the same ! Stroll through 648-acre Holyrood Park, which has 3 lakes.

Other interesting sights in Edinburgh: the paintings at both the National Gallery of Scotland and in the National Portrait Gallery. The National Museum of Antiquities. The collection of technology, art, archaeology, geology and natural history in the Royal Scottish Museum. The Museum of Childhood (historic books, toys and materials about child rearing), closed on Sundays. The adaptation of Athens' Temple of Theseus. The month-long International Festival of Music and Drama.

The pottery, handcrafted glass, textiles and woodwork at the Scottish Craft Center, in Acheson House, open daily except Sunday 10:00–17:00. The collection of Robert Burns, Sir Walter Scott and Robert Louis Stevenson manuscripts and memorabilia in the 17th century Lady Stair's House.

The exhibit (Picasso, Hockney, etc.) at the Scottish National Gallery of Modern Art on Belford Road, open Monday–Saturday 10:00–17:00, Sunday 14:00–17:00. Henry Moore sculptures decorate the grounds. A sign behind this museum directs you to a path that goes to Dean Village, once a grain-milling center. Nearby is St. Bernard's Well, a Doric temple built at a mineral spring in 1789.

Then stroll to Stockbridge (once an industrial village) on St. Stephen Street, where many interesting antique shops are located. Stockbridge is next to New Town, notable for its Georgian houses and elegant crescents.

Edinburgh - Dundee - Aberdeen   600

This is a very scenic rail trip.

Dep. Edinburgh	07:05 (1)	08:10 (1)	09:10 (2)	10:20 (4)	11:10 (2)
Arr. Dundee	08:27	09:26	10:26 (3)	11:35	12:26 (3)
Arr. Aberdeen	09:42	10:45	11:40	12:50	13:40

•   •   •

Dep. Aberdeen	13:10 (1)	13:10 (5)	13:35 (6)	14:20 (1)	14:55 (7+10)
Arr. Dundee	14:27	-0- (5)	15:01	15:30	16:06
Arr. Edinburgh	15:48	16:15	16:18	16:48	17:20

(1) Runs daily, except Sun. and holidays. Light refreshments. (2) Runs daily, except holidays. Departs 15 minutes earlier on Sunday. Light refreshments Monday–Saturday. (3) Arrives 15 minutes earlier on Sunday. (4) Runs daily, except Sundays and holidays. (5) Runs Sunday only. Light refreshments. Change

trains in Perth. (6) Runs Saturday and Sunday. (7) Runs daily, except Sundays & holidays. Restaurant car Monday–Friday. Light refreshments on Sunday. (8) Runs Sunday only. Light refreshments. (9) Runs Sunday only. (10) Plus other departures from Aberdeen at 15:23 (1), 16:15 (1), 17:12 (1), 18:15 (4), 19:00 (8), 20:00 (1), 20:50 (9) and 21:14 (1).

Sights in **Dundee**: A very ancient city, predating Roman occupation. Mountains of jam and preserves are processed here. Visit the Spalding Golf Museum in nearby Camperdown Park. The frigate "Unicorn," launched in 1824, now tied at Victoria Dock. The 4 castles: Dudhope, Claypotts, Broughty and Mains.

Sights in **Aberdeen:** A very popular tourist center and busy seaport. The center of Scotland's fishing industry (see the 07:00 fish market). Straddles 2 rivers. See the 15th century Cathedral of St. Machar. Streets that were laid out in the 13th and 14th centuries. The local history museum in the 17th century Provost Skene's House.

The 16th century Provost Ross's House. The 18th century St. Nicholas Church. Two very old bridges: the 14th century Brig o'Balgownie and the 16th century Old Bridge of Dee. The 19th century Music Hall. The 19th century Marischal College, considered the world's largest and finest granite building.

Edinburgh - Perth - Inverness   600

A very scenic train ride through the heart of the **Grampian Mountains**. Winter sports, including skiing, are the attraction at the **Aviemore** vacation resort.

Dep. Edinburgh	06:48 (1)	09:35 (6)	13:40	15:40 (3)
Dep. Perth	08:08 (1)	10:51	14:53 (6)	17:02
Dep. Aviemore	09:51	12:40	16:41	18:54
Arr. Inverness	10:32	13:23	17:18	19:45

* * *

Dep. Inverness	12:20 (1)	14:32 (6)	18:30 (5)
Dep. Aviemore	12:58	15:21	19:16
Dep. Perth	15:00 (1)	16:55	20:50
Arr. Edinburgh	16:15	18:12	22:10

(1) Runs daily, except Sundays and holidays. Change trains in Perth. Light refreshments Perth–Inverness (and v.v.). (2) Runs daily except holidays. Change trains in Perth. Sunday: light refreshments entire trip. Monday-Saturday: light refreshments Perth-Inverness. (3) Runs daily, except Sundays and holidays. Light refreshments. (4) Runs daily, except holidays. Change trains in Perth. Light refreshments Perth–Inverness (and v.v.). (5) Runs daily, except holidays. Light refreshments. (6) Runs Sunday only.

Sights in **Perth**: A popular tourist center. There is much whiskey distilling and weaving of tartans here. Good Winter sports. Sailing and water skiing in the Summer. See the 360-degree panoramic color slide-show and hear the stereophonic presentation at the Round House waterworks. St. John's Kirk. The Perth Art Gallery and Museum, on George Street.

A short distance from there, at North Post, visit the Fair Maid's House, an important locale in Sir Walter Scott's novel, "The Fair Maid of Perth."

Sights in **Inverness**: Located in the mountainous Highlands. Very cold Winters and cool Summers here. A popular tourist resort for hunting of grouse and deer, hiking, fishing, sailing, camping and Winter sports. Many whiskey distillers in this area. Visit the Castle. Stroll the garden paths along the River Ness. Nearby is Great Britain's highest mountain, Ben Nevis (4,406 feet).

Take a cruise on **Loch Ness,** and see if you can spot the "monster." Boats go from the lake through the **Caledonian Canal** and return to Inverness on cruises that take 2½ hours in the morning, 3½ hours in the afternoon, and 2½ hours in the evening.

Aberdeen - Inverness   595

Dep. Aberdeen	06:27 (1)	07:27 (2)	09:20 (2)	10:00 (3)	11:36 (2+6)	
Arr. Inverness	08:48	09:49	11:52	12:16	13:52	
Dep. Inverness	04:52 (2)	06:00 (2)	08:07 (2)	09:55 (3)	10:45 (2)	12:20 (4+7)
Arr. Aberdeen	07:14	08:20	10:32	12:13	12:58	14:45

(1) Runs daily, except Sundays and holidays. (2) Runs daily, except Sundays and holidays. Light refreshments. (3) Runs Sunday only. Light refreshments. (4) Runs daily, except holidays. Light refreshments. (5) Runs daily, except holidays. Light refreshments. (6) Plus other Aberdeen departures at 13:00 (2), 15:16 (2), 17:14 (2), 18:12 (2), 20:10 (4) and 21:48 (3), arriving Inverness 15:20, 17:50, 19:40, 20:35, 22:37, 23:50 and 23:58. (7) Plus other Inverness departures at 13:52 (2), 15:23 (4), 17:06 (4), 18:06 (2) and 20:45 (4), arriving Aberdeen 16:05, 17:38, 19:33, 20:33 and 23:00.

Inverness - Kyle of Lochalsh - Inverness   597

This is one of the most scenic train trips in Britain. The track climbs and descends, turns and twists through the **Wester Ross Mountains** as it often goes along the shoreline of lovely lakes through the heart of the Highlands. In the Spring, there are fields of red and orange rhododendrons. The fields of purple heather can be seen all year.

In the high **Luib Summit** area there are forests and snowcapped mountains. It is only an 8-minute ferry-boat ride from Kyle to the **Isle of Skye**.

| Dep. Inverness | 06:55 (1) | 08:00 (1) | 10:40 (2) | 12:40 (3) | 18:38 (4) |
| Arr. Kyle | 09:27 | 10:30 | 14:00 | 15:08 | 21:15 |

· · ·

| Dep. Kyle | 07:10 (1) | 10:00 (6) | 11:48 (1) | 15:10 (7) | 17:05 (1) |
| Arr. Inverness | 09:29 | 12:30 | 14:20 | 17:52 | 19:48 |

(1) Runs daily, except Sundays and holidays. Light refreshments. (2) Operates late June to early Septem-

ber. Runs Sunday only. (3) Operates early June to early September. Runs daily, except Sundays and holidays. Light refreshments. (4) Late June to early September: runs daily except holidays. Light refreshments all year. (5) Runs daily, except Sunday and holidays. (6) Runs Sunday only July 3-August 28. (7) Runs daily except Sundays & holidays July 4-Sept. 3; Sunday only July 3-Sept. 18.

Edinburgh - Dunbar - Edinburgh 570

Dep. Edinburgh   09:30 (1)   14:00 (1)   17:00 (1)
Arr. Dunbar   20-25 minutes later

Sights in **Dunbar**: A small fishing port, the birthplace of naturalist John Muir (128 High Street). See the Castle ruins at the harbor.

Take a 45-minute walk and visit the Old Harbor with its Lifeboat Museum, the roost for domesticated pigeons in Friar's Croft, and the Georgian houses (Castellau and Lauderdale). This walk is detailed in a guidebook available at the town's tourist information center in the 17th century Town House on High Street, open during Summer Monday-Saturday 09:00–19:00, Sunday 11:00–13:00.

Also visit the 1,667-acre John Muir Country Park, containing a wide variety of birds and plants. Near it are the restored 17th century Preston watermill and many old towns and villages: **Gifford, Haddington, Dirleton** and **North Berwick**. A list of hotels, guest houses and bed-and-breakfast places can be obtained by writing to the Dunbar Tourist Information Centre, if sufficient international reply coupons are enclosed.

Dep. Dunbar   07:47 (1)   09:46 (1)   13:09 (1)   16:56 (1)
Arr. Edinburgh   20-25 minutes later

(1) Runs Monday–Friday, except holidays.

Edinburgh - Glasgow - Edinburgh 590

Dep. Edinburgh   Monday–Saturday: Frequent times from 05:50 to 23:30
                                    Sunday: Frequent times from 08:30 to 23:30
Arr. Glasgow (Queen St.)   50–70 minutes later

· · ·

Dep. Glasgow (Queen St.)   Monday–Saturday: Frequent times from 06:22 to 23:30
                                    Sunday: Frequent times from 08:00 to 18:48
Arr. Edinburgh   50–70 minutes later

Sights in **Glasgow**: A major seaport. Largest city in Scotland. See the great shipyards on the River Clyde.

The dozens of antique streetcars, motorcycles and trains (including King George VI's 72-foot-long railway coach, built in 1941 with wartime armor-plated shutters) in the Museum of Transport at Kelvin Hall on Albert Drive, open Monday-Saturday 10:00–17:00, Sunday

14:00–17:00. Nearby, the fine collection of weapons, paintings (Rembrandt, Monet), Mackintosh furniture and natural history exhibits in Kelvingrove Art Galleries and Museum.

The vast collection of paintings by James Abbott McNeil Whistler—the world's best collection—in the Hunterian Art Gallery at Glasgow University, open Monday-Friday 10:30–12:30 and 13:30 17:30, Saturday 09:30–13:00. The Gallery also features a reconstruction of 3 floors of the home of the great architect Charles Mackintosh.

Many fine paintings in the Glasgow Art Gallery. The Botanic Gardens. Scottish genealogy at the Mitchell Library on North Street, Europe's largest municipal reference library. It holds over 1,250,000 books and subscribes to 40 newspapers and more than 200 periodicals. It has a helpful, knowledgeable staff and modern studying facilities.

The more than 8,000 treasures of The Burrell Collection, in Pollok House: over 700 stained glass items (one of the world's best collections). Paintings by Rembrandt, Bellini, Memling, Degas, Manet. Excellent Chou Dynasty pieces. Neolithic burial urns. The more than 8-ton marble Warwick Vase, discovered in Rome in 1771. Also on view: jade, carpets, porcelain, silver, furniture, glass and gold. Open Monday-Saturday 10:00–17:00, Sunday 14:00–17:00.

Glasgow - Oban - Glasgow   593

There is marvelous Highland scenery on this route.

Dep. Glasgow (Queen St.)	08:40 (6)	12:42 (5)	18:12 (5)
Arr. Oban	11:40	15:40	21:24

Sights in **Oban**: This has been a holiday resort for nearly a century, and a fishing port for even longer.

Dep. Oban	08:05 (6)	12:35 (7)	18:08 (5)
Arr. Glasgow (Queen St.)	11:14	15:44	21:28

(1) Operates early September to mid-June. Runs daily, except Sundays and holidays. (2) Operates mid-June to early September. Runs daily, except Sundays and holidays. (3) Late June to early September: runs Sunday only. Early September to late June: runs daily, except Sundays and holidays. (4) Operates early July to early September. Runs daily, except Sundays and holidays. (5) Runs daily, except holidays. (6) Runs daily, except Sundays & holidays. (7) Runs Sunday only.

Glasgow - Fort William - Mallaig - Glasgow   593

The Fort William–Mallaig portion, the train ride with the most beautiful scenery in Britain, offers better views than an alternative auto route does of many lochs (lakes), glens (valleys) and bens (mountains).

These trains provide a guide who tells about the sights on this route: the 4,406-foot-high Ben Nevis (highest peak in Britain), the Caledonian Canal built in 1822, Loch Long, fabled

Loch Lomond, the heather-encrusted wild Rannoch Moor, the man-made Loch Trieg, the forested Loch Eil, Bonnie Prince Charlie's monument, and the 1,000-foot-long Glenfinnan Viaduct. The highest altitude on British rail is 347 feet, at Corrour Summit, between Glasgow and Fort William.

Dep. Glasgow (Queen St.)	08:12 (11)	12:42 (11)	18:12 (11)
Arr. Crianlarich	09:53	14:25	20:11
Dep. Crianlarich	10:10	14:37	20:17
Arr. Fort William	11:55	16:22	22:08
Dep. Fort William	12:02	16:30	22:15
Arr. Mallaig	13:24	17:54	23:37

Sights in **Mallaig:** There is a 2-hour ferryboat ride from this little fishing village to Kyle of Lochalsh.

Dep. Mallaig	06:00 (11)	10:30 (11)	10:25 (7+9)
Arr. Fort William	07:22	11:47	11:47
Dep. Fort William	07:30	11:57	12:37
Arr. Crianlarich	09:15	13:46	14:21
Dep. Crianlarich	09:22	13:52	14:28
Arr. Glasgow (Queen St.)	11:14	15:44	16:28

(1) Operates early September to mid-June. Runs daily, except Sundays and holidays. (2) Operates late June to early September. Runs Sunday only. (3) Operates early September to late June. Runs daily, except holidays. (4) Operates late June to early September. Runs daily, except Sundays and holidays. (5) Train has only sleeping cars (London-Fort William and v.v.). Runs daily, except Saturdays and holidays. Departs 45-70 minutes earlier on Sunday. (6) Change trains in Crianlarich. (7) Operates late June to early September. Runs daily, except holidays. (8) Runs Sunday only. (9) Plus another Mallaig departure at 16:10 (8), arriving Glasgow 21:30. (10) Plus another Fort William departure at 17:42 (8), arriving Glasgow 21:30. (11) Runs daily except Sundays & holidays.

CHAPTER 8

CENTRAL AND EASTERN EUROPE

Overview

Everyone will tell you the same thing: travel conditions have been changing in central and eastern Europe at such a turbulent pace that guidebooks cannot possibly keep up. Travel in general has grown phenomenally in eastern Europe, and so more people need more and better information in order to experience the region in an interesting and rewarding way. With that in mind, we have investigated numerous new sources of up-to-date information and surfed through the region's offerings on the Internet. We also interviewed seasoned train travelers with recent eastern European experience and local residents in the countries represented here.

A few areas of concensus emerged. Because eastern Europe is in a state of social, economic, and political flux, it is absolutely necessary that travelers confirm and reconfirm travel information. So, remember to check information and then reconfirm newly acquired information with still other people. Then check again. A train connection time printed on a schedule at the time you purchased your ticket may very well change the morning of your trip. The 3-hour layover in Warsaw you were informed of may be reduced to an hour and half at the last minute. Track 8 may not even exist. And on and on. Jim Haynes, Paris's most famous American expatriate and author of the *People to People* guides to eastern Europe, maintains that local people "know the current situation better than any up-to-date guidebook." People who live in the countries you are about to visit are your greatest source of "real info, friendship, and security," Jim acknowledges.

Although train travel in the region is quickly coming into greater homogeny with train travel in Western Europe, train travel east of Poland remains highly exotic, often disorienting, and at times less than reassuring for western travelers. Many experienced travelers love those exciting trips through the Ukraine, Russia, and the Baltic States and are the first to advise neophyte travelers to proceed with great caution and informed intelligence. Urban train stations in the Commonwealth of Independent States and the former Yugoslavia can range from confusing and seedy to outright dangerous. Try to sort out the myth from the truth. Horror stories of theft on night trains, rowdy gangs, sleeping gas, sordid violence, and roaming pirates in the East abound, but much is lore. As the economies of the region evolve, the public relationship to money responds. In that western travelers bring cash, care must be taken in how one travels and how one handles ambiguous situations. Bring one-dollar bills and take them out sparingly and one at a time—they buy a lot and they don't require change. Jody Jenkins, an American writer who lives on a barge in Burgundy and has recently completed *The Low Lights of Winter*, a collection of stories about life in contemporary eastern Europe, contends that travelers in the East must be able to "flow with the tide." Ghengis Khan–type characters were habitually harassing Jody and his girlfriend Gwen as they trained from Moscow to Tashkent in Uzbekistan. First-class tickets cost them $5 each, but it was the on-board bribes of $10 each and a pack of chewing gum that allowed them to win over the conductor and to feel secure in an otherwise alienating environment.

Jim Haynes strongly advises western travelers to be met and dropped off at train stations in the East. And don't hang out at stations; you will invite unwelcome experiences. It's always better to hail a taxi or private car a few hundred meters from the station than to subject yourself to being ripped off by a taxi waiting at the station.

Another shared point. In the more exotic places and for the overnight and long hauls, always bring your own food. Bring an extra supply for your neighbors, conductors, and compartment mates, for whom a small act of generosity and openness will buy solidarity. Cigarettes, gum, and trinkets work wonders in gaining instant companions and bodyguards. Also think ahead in terms of your travel needs. Toilet paper, for one, is a must, as Catrinel Plescu from Bucharest reported on her recent trip from the Romanian capital to Vienna, Austria. Bottles of water, flashlights, and matches are all good ideas.

Lastly, there are now scores of general travel guides to eastern Europe. Pick up at least one or two to accompany your Eurail guide. Select editions that are as recent as possible. The travel information included here will serve as a good start, but for more detailed descriptions and commentary you'll need a more general source of data. Pick up brochures along the way and share them with other travelers. Of course, we're open to receiving your comments, suggestions, and experiences in order to better report on the region in each successive update.

TRAIN PRICES AND INFORMATION

There is one rail pass that will let you see Eastern Europe. The Central European Rail Pass was discontinued in 1995.

Eastern European Pass Unlimited first-class train travel in Austria, Czechoslovakia, Hungary and Poland. The 1996 prices are: $195 for any 5 days within 15 days, $299 for any 10 days within one month.

ALBANIA

Currently there is only one international rail connection in and out of Albania—it consists of the passenger link with Mali izi, Montenegro to the north via Lezhe and Shkoder. The longest train journey in the country runs a total of 96 miles between the capital, Tirana, and the southern port of Vlorë, and it takes approximately five hours. Otherwise, boat connections from Vlorë to Brindisi, Italy, which is only 80 miles away, and from Sarande to Corfu, just 16 miles south, exist, although travel details are difficult to confirm in advance. The train system runs east-west also between Durrës on the Adriatic Coast and Pogradec on the eastern lake frontier with Greek Macedonia. Some of the most interesting mountain villages are off the train route and must be visited by bus or car.

Train travel within the country requires tolerance and time. One seasoned traveler, John Hodgson, recently back from Albania, writes: "I have traveled by train in all the countries of Eastern Europe, and the best train journey is in Albania, from Tirana to Pogradec. The line is 147 kilometers, the journey takes seven hours, and it costs $1.50 U.S. All the railways in Albania were built by 'volunteer' young people under communism, and their technical standards are very low. Poor maintenance has also meant that speed limits are down to a crawl. Albanian railways have Czech-built diesels, and used to have Chinese carriages, but most of these were reduced to bits in the 1991 revolution and have been replaced by cast-off carriages donated by Italian railways. In 1992 I traveled from Tirana to Shkoder in an unlit train with no glass in the windows, holding an umbrella inside the compartment and 'protected' by a sinister-looking character carrying pistols under both armpits.

The Tirana-Pogradec train leaves at 5:40 A.M. and passes through most of central Albania, via Durrës, Rrogozhine, Elbasan, and Librazhd. The later part of the journey, up the Shkumbin valley, is exceptionally beautiful, with many tunnels and bridges. After a final tunnel the line emerges on lovely Lake Ohrid, which forms the border with Macedonia.

The trains are very dirty, but are companionable. Take your own food, and indeed take some to share around. Reservations are not possible. The train is normally very crowded and smoky.

Anyone who visits Albania and proposes going by train will have to fight with his Albanian host for the right to do so, because the trains are thought to be too horrible for foreigners to support. It is worth fighting for—and worth going to Albania, which is a wonderful country."

PLACES TO VISIT AND EXCURSIONS

Tirana

The predominance of indestructible and ubiquitous concrete bunkers, or "pillboxes," sprinkled throughout the countryside perpetually remind visitors of the past and this country's century-long trail of invasions. Tirana's inroads into Western Europe were best heard via its notorious attacks on capitalism on Radio Tirana broadcasts in English. Although intrigue still lurks in contemporary Tirana and tourism remains greatly undeveloped, a new atmosphere of possibility pervades daily life. There is little traffic, and at times an unsettling calm cloaks the city. Air connections to and from Rinas Airport exist with Istanbul, Athens, Sophia, Rome, Budapest, Vienna, Lubliana, and Zurich.

The Albanian capital with its 400,000 inhabitants hosts some 170 museums. The Museum of Natural History houses a worthwhile yet limited collection of prehistoric and Illyrian objects and folk art from the region as well as an imposing mosaic mural depicting examples of warriors through the ages struggling for "freedom." A large room dedicated to the communist period has been roped off but not yet removed or reorganized, a detail that indicates the conflict of the national debate on the treatment of history.

Crowning the highest hill in the city is a mammoth statue commemorating "The Heroes," which guards the cemetery below. The major buildings around the main square capture the nation's history. There is the old Byzantine church, which long ago was converted into a mosque with the addition of a tall and narrow minaret. The government buildings date from World War II, when Mussolini's troops occupied the city (1939–1944).

As the Albanian-born New York writer Fron Nazi states, contemporary Albanian life transpires in the coffee shops, where right- and left-wing politicians, corrupt intellectuals, charming criminals, ideologue artists, spies and double agents, and sleazy businesspeople all congregate and swap stories, rumors, dreams, plots, and plans for deals, articles, government reforms, and revolutionary projects.

Durrës

Albania's Adriatic port, Durrës, built on the ruins of Greek and Roman towns, offers excellent sand beaches. This city has served as the nation's resort area, offering functional hotels built for "the people." The city also has a Roman amphitheater, several interesting bazaars, and a variety of Moslem mosques, the largest located in the main square. A curiosity: a beached boat now serves as a popular coffee shop. Durrës is a good starting point for exploration to nearby villages. All train trips in Albania pass through Durrës. Each day seven trains make the 36-kilometer haul in 90 minutes between Durrës and Tirana.

Kruje

Kruje is a mountainside city north of Tirane. An interesting citadel/museum is dedicated to Skanderbeg, the national hero who led a revolt against the Turks in the middle 1400s, resulting in a brief period of independence. There is a quaint marketplace street that offers folkloric items.

Berat

Crowning the isolated steep hill is a walled citadel overlooking the broad valley below. Inside is an ancient Byzantine church which had been converted into an icon museum during the decades when religious practices were prohibited. The old part of Berat, along the riverbanks, has been preserved and restored as a museum town. The hilltop 16th-century Ardenitza Monastery has been converted into an inn.

Vlorë

This ancient seaport is surrounded by hills of olive trees which serve the local olive oil refinery. Popular lore has it that the city takes its name from the "Turk" who declared Albania's independence in 1912, Ismail Kemal Bey Vlorë. This is not so—the name dates to Roman times. The Tirana-Vlorë train makes the 155-kilometer trek in under six hours.

Sarande

Sarande is the southernmost city on the Adriatic coast, almost on the border with Greece and across a narrow body of water from the island of Corfu. The town is on a curved shoreline, making it most attractive. The walls and houses are ablaze with bougainvillea and the streets are shaded with palms. A few miles farther south are the ruins of Butrint, a city founded in pre-Greek times by Illyrians and perhaps exiled Trojans, followed by the civilizations of Greece, Rome, and Byzantium. The layers of stone ruins are clearly visible. Foundations, walls, heroic gates, colorful mosaics, fallen columns, and the citadel atop the hill all combine to make this a most interesting site.

Gjirokaster

The small mountainside city of Gjirokaster, crowned by a citadel that was used by the Italians, Nazis, and communists as a prison, is now a war museum. The monumental statue of the deceased dictator recently had been removed from this prominent spot.

Other villages worth visiting include Apollonia, Fiera, Shkodra, and Butrinti. Other train travel in Albania includes the Shkodra to Podgorica, Yugoslavia, run initiated in 1986, but this is primarily used for freight.

For information about Albanian tours, contact the Kutrubes Travel Agency, 328 Tremont Street, Boston, MA 02116; (800) 878-8566.

Tirane - Durres - Vlore   and v.v. 949

Dep. Tirane	15:25		Dep. Vlore	05:20
Dep. Durres	16:45		Dep. Durres	09:20
Arr. Vlore	20:25		Arr. Tirane	10:30

BULGARIA

BULGARIAN HOLIDAYS

January 1	New Year's Day	June 2	Memorial Day
May 1 and 2	Labor Day	Sept. 9 and 10	Liberation Day
May 24	Education Day	November 7	Revolution Day

BULGARIAN RAIL PASS

Unlimited first-class train travel in Bulgaria for 3 days in one month: $70

Bulgarians will often advise you not to take their trains—they'll tell you that they are dirty and unreliable. However, there still is no better way to see the "Jewel of the Balkans" than by rail, and the highly useful Bulgarian Flexipass is a great asset.

The most significant travel destinations in Bulgaria are the capital city of Sofia, the ancient trading center of Plovdiv, and the Black Sea resort towns of Varna and Burgas.

Train travel into Bulgaria is dominated by its routes from Bucharest, Romania; Nis, Yugoslavia; Thessaloniki, Greece; and Edirne, Turkey; with major connections to Athens, Berlin, Budapest, Warsaw, Kiev, Moscow, Vilnius, and St. Petersburg. As elsewhere in Eastern Europe, buses are often cheaper and more reliable than trains, and this is especially true when traveling between Bulgaria and Romania. The Romanian train into Bulgaria originates in Russia, and travelers often report being told they were not allowed on these trains despite their purchased tickets. A $10 "tip" in almost all cases will resolve any potential conflict. Don't get too righteous about these things—have small bills, cigarettes, and chewing gum conveniently ready. The 11-hour Bucharest-Sofia jaunt can only be taken on an overnight and unreserved basis. Be ready for horrible crowding and arrive at the station well in advance of the departure time.

The famous Orient Express from the late 1800s ran through Sofia on its way from Paris to Istanbul, and the legacy is carried forward in the form of the Istanbul Express coming from Munich and the Balkan Express coming from Warsaw. Some cost-sensitive travelers recommend buying westbound tickets up to the Turkish frontier town of Kapikule and then paying for the additional fare into Bulgaria on the train.

Traveling to Bulgaria from Greece has been reported as difficult and painful, especially at the border. The bus is preferable. However, train travel in the other direction seems less problematic. The overnight Transbalkan Express links Sofia and Athens in 18 hours. Other Greek-Bulgarian connections include the Plovdiv and Alexandroupolis run.

The Meridian Express is a daily linking Berlin and Sofia by way of Prague, Budapest, and Belgrade. The Istanbul Express runs four days a week from Munich to Istanbul via Salzburg, Belgrade, and Sofia. Since the war in former Yugoslavia, these train routes to Belgrade and beyond host all sorts of unsavory characters. Caution should be used in making this journey. No one will understand why you are heading to Belgrade and it is not certain that you'll be allowed to carry on.

The BDZ Bulgarian State Railway has an extensive system of more than 4,000 kilometers of track, and the trains come in three speeds: express, fast, or slow (putnichki). The popular Sofia-Burgas route passes by either Karlovo or Plovdiv, and travelers often opt to break up this stint with a stopover. Similarly, the Sofia-Ruse route passes by Pleven or Gorna Oryahovitsa. Book a seat and/or sleeper reservations in a Rila tourist office well in advance for the express trains to the Black Sea.

As elsewhere in Eastern Europe, train stations in Bulgaria are not always clearly marked and it is easy to miss your stop, especially when the name is written in cyrillic script! Pay attention and ask locals on the train to announce when you've arrived.

Many seasoned travelers agree that Bulgaria's most spectacular train trip is the Sofia-Mezdra climb up the Iskar Gorge on the line to Vidin and Pleven. This can be accomplished as a day trip, but two days are preferable. The Central Railway Station in Sofia is located at Maria Luiza Blvd. Call for train information or have a Bulgarian person call for you. The telephone number is 3-11-11 to 3-11-20. For international train ticket information, call 87-59-35 or stop in at 5 Gurko Street. The official train ticket offices are called Rila and are located in all Bulgarian towns served by rail.

PLACES TO VISIT AND EXCURSIONS

Sofia

Sofia's central train station has little charm and can be a bit disorienting. Platforms are called *peron* and are numbered in Roman type while the tracks or *kolovoz* are marked with Arabic numbers. Don't panic, just keep asking. There is a waiting room that is slightly more comfortable than elsewhere in the station but there is a small fee to gain access.

Ticket windows are separated by floors depending on national or international destinations. Same-day, Bulgarian train tickets are sold on the lower level. But these things change so keep asking.

Although daily life in Sofia has been transformed since the end of communist rule, the Bulgarian capital remains oppressively sedate, well behaved, and rather uneventful. The former Communist Party, under a new name, still holds the most seats in the national government, and change comes begrudgingly. The cyrillic alphabet and the Turkish mosques are clear reminders of this nation's eastern roots. Sophia hosts some of the most memorable icons in Europe, notably those found at Alexander Nevsky Memorial Church and the Byzantine 6th-century Sancta Sophia church. The Archaelogical Museum in Bouyouk, the largest mosque in Sophia, requires a visit, as do the early renaissance frescos in the brick Rotunda of the St. Georgi Church, the city's oldest standing building. Art enthusiasts should also plan to visit the medieval Boyanna Church just outside the city and the Rila Monastery, an hour and a half from the capital.

Sofia is noted for its remarkable churches. The official religion in Bulgaria is Christian Orthodox, and most of the churches in Sofia perform Orthodox services. A few key sites not to

miss include the following:
• Alexander Nevsky Cathedral. This central landmark shines from every part of the city.
• The Rotunda of St. George. This red brick rotunda church dating from the 4th century is considered the oldest structure in Sofia.
• St. Sophia Church. St. George is the oldest church, but St. Sofia is the oldest Eastern Orthodox church in Sofia.
• Banya Bashi Mosque. This Islamic shrine was built in 1576.
• Church of St. Cyril and St. Methodius and Their Five Disciples. Bearing the name Sveti Sedmochislenitsi, this church dates to 1528.

The art scene is focused on the National Art Gallery, located at 1 Alexander Batenberg Square. It's open Tuesday through Sunday 10:00 to 17:30 and is closed on Mondays. Standing exhibitions feature Bulgarian and foreign art from the Middle Ages to the present day. Extention in a crypt of the Alexander Nevsky Cathedral displays one of the largest original icon collections in Bulgaria. In addition, a surprising number of private art galleries have been appearing in downtown Sofia.

Sofia also hosts a number of restaurants, where traditional national dishes can be sampled. Try *gyuvech,* a meat and mixed vegetables dish, or *sarmi,* vine leaves filled with spicy mince meat. *Palneni chushki* (dolmas) are peppers stuffed with spicy minced meat. *Tarator* is a cold yogurt soup with chopped cucumbers and garlic, ideal in the summer. The traditional drink is what the Bulgarians consider their world famous and cheap Bulgarian wine, both red and white, and *rakiya,* a strong brandy distilled from grapes and plums. In both cases, be prepared for a headache the next morning.

The Rila Mountains

The Rila Mountains are an absolute must for travelers to Bulgaria, offering exquisite hiking possibilities. A trip across these mountainous wonders, a visit to the Complex Malyovitsa and the Rila Monastery, 74 miles from Sofia, are unforgettable. The monastery, founded in 927 as a colony of hermetic monks by Ivan Rilski, is best visited by bus. Other important sites include the 14th-century Cherepish Monastery, found in the Iskar Gorge on the way from Sofia to Vidin close to the Lakatnik rocks, approximately 35 kilometers from the capital city. Legend links the monastery with the battles of the last Bulgarian medieval tsar, Ivan Shishman, who clashed with the Turks.

Plovdiv

An ancient strategic trading hub on the Maritsa River serving early caravans that moved between Europe, Asia Minor, and Africa, Plovdiv today is Bulgaria's second largest city. The train station is an easy 10-minute walk from the Central Square and the historic old town. A visit to the Roman Forum and amphiteatre is recommended, as are visits to the Djoumaya and Imaret Mosques. The Archeological Museum houses excellent exhibits of Tracian gold utensils, although some of the most famous pieces have been moved to Sofia.

Varna

Bulgaria's largest Black Sea port dominates summer life in the country. Dating back to the days of ancient Rome and Greece, this lively seaside resort city enjoys a colorful past. When the train connecting Varna to Ruse was completed in the 1860s, a direct trade route from the Danube to the Black Sea was created. Today the city offers excellent beaches, parks, street life, and restaurants. The center of the city can be reached on foot from the train station, and a convenient luggage storage office is located across the street. The celebrated summer hydrofoil service from Varna to Nesebar, Burgas, and Sozopol was shut down in 1993 for economic reasons, although a hydrobus still runs from Varna to Balchik.

Train travel to the coast is recommended, but bus travel up and down the coast between Varna and Burgas is the most convenient form of transportation. Nesebar, which can be reached by bus or taxi, hosts the ruins of thirteen churches dating back as early as the 9th century.

Burgas

Burgas, a beach resort on the Black Sea, is less crowded than Varna. The city's connection to the national train system via Plovdiv at the turn of the century accounts greatly for its growth. A bit too industrial for many vacationers' taste, Burgas still serves as a good seaside base for Black Sea exploration. The art gallery in the former synagogue is worth a visit. The old opera house, however, has been rented out as a car showroom, an indication of the realities of post-communist Bulgaria. Thirty-six kilometers north of Burgas is Bulgaria's largest tourist resort, Sunny Beach, which offers beaches, sailing, family restaurants, and babysitting services—perhaps a relaxing destination for families.

Ruse

Ruse is Bulgaria's leading port on the Danube River and a prime stopover for Russian river traffic, despite the air pollution. A daily train from Bucharest also arrives in Ruse, bringing with it hoards of Romanians and other visitors. Ruse is only a few kilometers from the longest steel bridge in Europe, ironically named the Friendship Bridge, which carries both car and train traffic and links Bulgaria and Romania. Train-lovers should plan on a visit to the Transportation Museum near the Danube—it was here that Bulgaria inaugurated its first train station, which was built in 1866.

Gorna Oryathovitsa

This town is important as a train junction and transit point that travelers often pass through on their Bulgarian journeys. Connection times often require long waits here despite your impression that you had a through ticket. Some smart travelers opt for a bus from Gorna to save time. The Sofia-Varna and Ruse–Veliko Tarnovo routes meet at Gorna.

Pleven

Famous for its battles between Turkish pashas and Russo-Romanian armies, Pleven is located between Ruse and Sofia and offers an authentic Bulgarian experience. Osman Pasha surrendered his sword to Tsar Alexanderr II of Russia here, and you can see the sword at the National Revival Park. The greatest advantages to Pleven are that it is less visited by travelers than other towns are and that its location is on the train route that follows the stunning Iskar Gorge. From Pleven, many spirited train travelers with an open ticket jump on the unreserved 8-hour Bucharest train in the middle of the night.

ONE-DAY EXCURSIONS

Sofia - Burgas - Sofia   962

Dep. Sofia	06:30 (1)	07:00 (2)	10:15 (5)	13:35 (2)	14:15 (2)	16:00 (1)	22:45 (4)
Arr. Burgas	12:40 (1)	13:55	17:15	19:50	21:05	21:45	06:10

Sights in **Burgas**: A good beach resort.

Dep. Burgas	05:15 (3)	06:00 (1)	10:30 (2)	11:00 (5)	15:10 (2)	16:00 (1)	23:10 (4)
Arr. Sofia	11:24	11:44	16:48	18:13	21:36	22:05	06:23

(1) Reservation required. Light refreshments. (2) Light refreshments. (3) Reservation *required*. Restaurant car. (4) Carries a sleeping car. Light refreshments. (5) Restaurant car.

Sofia - Plovdiv - Sofia   962

Dep. Sofia	06:30 (1)	08:15 (4)	10:15 (7)	12:15 (4)	14:15 (4)	17:15 (1)
Arr. Plovdiv	08:26	10:40	12:39	14:42	16:34	19:20

Sights in **Plovdiv:** This city has been a commercial center for more than 2,000 years, serving the early caravans that moved between Europe, Asia and Africa. There are excellent exhibits of Thracian gold utensils in the Archaeological Museum. See the Bachkovo Monastery and, near it, the ruins of Tsar Ivan Asen II's fort. The Roman ruins. The Church of Constantine and Helena. The Turkish Imaret Djamiya.

Dep. Plovdiv	04:00 (6)	09:00 (1)	10:00 (4)	11:00 (4)	14:00 (4)
Arr. Sofia	06:30	11:10	12:25	13:35	16:23

(1) Reservation required. Light refreshments. (2) Second-class. (3) Reservation *required*. Restaurant car. (4) Light refreshments. (5) Reservation *required*. First-class only. (6) Carries a sleeping car. Light refreshments. (7) Restaurant car. (8) Plus other Sofia departures at 18:50 and 23:00 (4).

Sofia - Varna - Sofia   962

Dep. Sofia	06:30 (1)	10:30 (2)	12:15 (3)	14:15 (1)	22:00 (5+6)
Arr. Varna	14:35	18:35	20:45	21:35	06:30

Sights in **Varna:** An ancient, lively and important seaport and a very popular beach resort.

See the relics of Greek, Roman, Byzantine, Turkish and Bulgarian eras in the Museum of Art and History (41 Boulevard Dimitar Blagoev), open daily except Monday 09:00–17:00 in Summer, 10:00–17:00 in Winter. Many museums and art galleries. The oldest gold ever found (from 3,500 years B.C.) is displayed there: jewelry and decorations from a burial site.

The Roman Bath. The cells and the chapel carved into the side of a chalk cliff at the 13th century Aladzha Monastery in **Druzhba**, a few miles to the north. It is open daily except Monday 10:00–17:00.

During the Summer, a hydrofoil service goes from Varna to Nesebar, Burgas and Sozopol. In **Nesebar** (a $7-U.S. taxi ride from Burgas), there are ruins of 13 churches dating back as early as the 9th century on this small islet at the end of a causeway. See the Church of John Aliturgetus and the 16th century St. Stephen's Church.

Dep. Varna	07:10 (1)	08:10 (3)	10:30 (1)	14:00 (1)	22:15 (5)	22:40 (5)
Arr. Sofia	14:40	16:23	18:30	21:40	06:39	07:31

(1) Reservation *required*. Restaurant car. (2) Restaurant car. (3) Light refreshments. (4) Change trains in Plovdiv at 21:18. Sleeping car and light refreshments Plovdiv-Varna. (5) Carries a sleeping car. Light refreshments. (6) Plus another Sofia departure at 23:00 (5), arriving Varna 07:05.

INTERNATIONAL ROUTES
FROM BULGARIA

Sofia is the gateway for train travel to Yugoslavia (and on to Western Europe), Romania and Greece (and on to Turkey).

Sofia - Belgrade   945

There is great mountain scenery on the Dragomagoman-Crveni Krst portion of this route.

Dep. Sofia	08:20	23:10 (1)
Set your watch back one hour.		
Arr. Belgrade (Belgrade)	15:32	06:29

(1) Carries a sleeping car. Also has couchettes. Coach is second-class.

Sofia - Bucharest - Kiev or St Petersburg or Moscow   94d

All of these trains have only sleeping cars. No coaches.

Dep. Sofia	13:00 (4)	11:15 (6)	21:40 (8)
Arr. Bucharest (Nord)	23:40 (5)	23:16 (7)	09:04 (2)
Arr. Kiev	01:28 (3)	03:06 (3)	11:26 (3)
Arr. St. Petersburg	18:24	-0-	-0-
Arr. Moscow (Kievski)	-0-	21:14	-0-

(1) Runs Monday, Wednesday, Friday and Sunday. (2) Day 2. (3) Day 3. (4) Restaurant car. (5) Day 2. The section of this train that originated in Athens departs from Bucharest's Baneasa railstation. The section from Istanbul departs from Bucharest's Chitila railstation. Then, the 2 sections are combined. (6) Runs Tuesday and Friday. Restaurant car on Day 2. (7) Day 2. Departs from Bucharest's Chitila railstsation. (8) Runs Tuesday, Thursday and Saturday. Restaurant car.

Sofia - Athens or Istanbul   57 + 84 + 965 + 975

	975	965
Dep. Sofia	07:40	08:05 (3)
Arr. Athens	00:58	-0-
Arr. Istanbul	-0-	19:59

(1) Carries only sleeping cars. (2) Carries only sleeping cars and couchettes. (3) Reservation *required*. Has couchettes. Carries a sleeping car on Thursday. Coach is second-class.

COMMONWEALTH OF INDEPENDENT STATES

The CIS, the catch phrase replacing the former Soviet Union (FSU), has come to suggest many unclear notions in the minds of travelers. Few westerners can name more than a few of the fifteen states, and travel beyond Moscow and St. Petersburg is still complicated and at times even surrealist. Train travel in Russia and the Ukraine as well as the Baltic States of Estonia, Latvia, and Lituania, however, has generally become far more accessible to western travelers since 1990. For political and cultural reasons, each country in this section of this guide has been listed separately, although in many cases the rail infrastructure of one small country is connected to that of another.

Most seasoned travelers agree that Russia and its related states present some of the most exciting train trips available today. Most also agree that the sensibilities of travelers never cease to be shocked when traveling in that region, and that mental preparation for the journey is required. One highly experienced world traveler reports that he could not remember even one moment of relaxation during his month-long trek from Paris to Tashkent via Moscow. Be ready for some wonderful experiences mixed with some trying and tiring moments of international survival.

As soon as you reach the eastern border of Poland, you are confronted with a major shift in aesthetics and functionality. When the train pulls into the station at Brest in Belarussia, it is lifted into the air and its wheels are changed to adapt to the wider Russian tracks. Walking underneath the train is a strange experience. At one border crossing, passengers are intructed to disembark while the train pulls onto a siding for a wheel change. Stay close by: it is often difficult to find the train again or to find the access to that siding. A garbled announcement shouts that the train will be leaving shortly, and hoards of panicked travelers push and scramble, jump onto the tracks to get to another platform, pass battered suitcases over their heads, and so on. Then, after surviving this pandemonium on the quai, you may find yourself in an Old World dining car drinking Bulgarian champagne and downing spoonfuls of red caviar for a whopping $2! Such is the charm of Russian train travel.

Lastly, one cannot generalize about trains in the CIS. They are all different, and they depend on everything from time of year, available equipment, mood of the conductor, exchange rates, weather, destination, application of laws, and luck.

SUMMER TIME

The Commonwealth changes to Summer Time the last Sunday of March and converts back to Standard Time on the last Sunday of September.

TRAIN PRICES AND INFORMATION

Children under five travel free. Half-fare for children between the ages five and nine. Reservations are usually required for all trains. In the case you do not have reservations but need to get on a train, it's up to you to negotiate with the conductor. Don't be too passive or quick to pay a lot, but definitely be sensitive to the fact that an extra $5 or $10 may represent a month's salary to the conductor.

There are two classes of train cars in the CIS. Soft Class is the upholstered seats which convert to bunks in four-berth compartments and Hard Class are plastic or fake leather seats which sometimes convert into bunks and sometimes do not. Bedding is available at an extra charge.

Sleeping cars are also available in two-berth compartments equipped with folding tables, a closet, and a speaker over which music and announcements come. Conductors on these trains serve tea from large samovars, one of the few features you can always count on.

Because the tracks in the CIS are five feet wide, passenger cars are roomy. Of course the change of wheels at the Polish border represents a delay, but you can't have everything. One border crossing through the north of Poland on the way to the Baltic States is organized differently and instead of changing the wheels, passengers walk across the border and board an awaiting Lituanian train.

Athough the CIS has nine different time zones, all timetables indicate Moscow time only.

The topography of Uzbekistan is highly diverse. The southeast portion contains the foothills and valleys of the Tian Shan (Tien Shan) mountain range. The north central lowland portion is occupied by desert.

ARMENIA

The good news is that Armenia is a fantastically interesting country with a rich and diverse cultural heritage. The bad news is that Armenia is enduring a transportation and natural gas embargo that is causing severe food and medical shortages, frequent interruptions in electrical power, and shortages of transportation fuel. Internal travel, especially by air, may be disrupted by fuel shortages and other problems. Tourist facilities are not highly developed, and many of the goods and services taken for granted in other countries are not yet available, according to the United States State Department.

If you do go, remember that a visa is required. Without a visa, travelers cannot register at hotels and may be required to leave the country immediately via the route by which they entered.

Yerevan is the capital of Armenia. Since 1988, armed conflict has taken place in and around the enclave of Nagorno-Karabakh (located within Azerbaijan), and there is frequent shelling along many areas of the Armenian-Azerbaijani border. A ceasefire has been in effect since May 1994, though there have been some reports of minor violations.

Train transportation may be unreliable and uncomfortable. Train service to neighboring Georgia is subject to frequent disruptions and delays, and crime on board is an increasing problem.

AZERBAIJAN

Azerbaijan is located in southwestern Asia, between Armenia and Turkmenistan, bordering the Caspian Sea. With its capital in Baku, it is slightly larger than the state of Maine including the Nakhichevan Autonomous Republic and Nagorno-Karabakh, whose autonomy was abolished by the Azerbaijani Supreme Soviet in 1991. Azerbaijan borders with Armenia to the west, Georgia and Iran to the south, and Russia, Turkey, and the Caspian Sea to the east.

The country is ethnically dominated by Azeris and is predominantly Muslim. Its violent and longstanding disputes with ethnic Armenians of Nagorno-Karabakh and with the ethnic Azeri portion of Iran have not been resolved. Additionally, severe pollution problems have not helped encourage visitors to the region.

Azerbaijan is less developed industrially than either Armenia or Georgia, the other Transcaucasian states. It resembles the other Central Asian states in its majority Muslim population, high unemployment, and low standard of living. The country has more than 2,000 kilometers of railroad track, but connections with Europe are long and tiring.

BELARUS

Located east of Poland, Belarus with its 10 million people is slightly smaller than the state of Kansas. It borders with Latvia, Lithuania, Poland, Russia, and the Ukraine, with Minsk as its capital. Its people speak primarily Byelorussian and belong to the Eastern Orthodox church.

Known for its cold winters, Belarus is flat and marshy. On April 26, 1986, Belarus was severely hit by the fallout of radioactive dust from the Chernobyl nuclear power plant. In December of 1991, with Russia and the Ukraine, Belarus formed the core of the CIS.

More modernized than other CIS states, Belarus has always served as a transport link for Russian oil exports to the Baltic states and eastern and western Europe. Train travelers to Moscow undoubtedly pass through Belarus and thus get a good glimpse of the state.

GEORGIA

Located in southwestern Asia between Turkey and Russia, bordering the Black Sea, Georgia is slightly larger than the state of South Carolina. It borders Armenia, Azerbaijan, Russia, and Turkey. Georgia is a nation undergoing profound political and economic change. A newly independent nation, it is in the process of stabilizing its relations with neighboring countries.

Tourist facilities outside of the capital are not highly developed, and many of the goods and services taken for granted in other countries are not yet available. Travel, especially by air, may be disrupted by fuel shortages and other problems. The recent assasination attempt of Georgian speaker of parliament Eduard Shevardnadze hasn't helped to reassure tourists, who are eager to experience the otherwise calm Meditterranean-like Crimea.

Visitors who enter at the Tbilisi airport receive a temporary passport stamp and are instructed to obtain a visa from the Consular Division of the Ministry of Foreign Affairs.

Travelers who have a valid multiple-entry visa from Armenia or Azerbaijan are not required to obtain a Georgian visa. Those arriving from or departing to other countries, including other former Soviet states, must obtain a Georgian visa in order to leave the country. On an exceptional basis, the Georgian Ministry of Foreign Affairs can assist travelers in obtaining visas at the checkpoint at Sarpi (on the border with Turkey) and at the port of Batumi on the Black Sea. Arrangements must be made *in advance* to issue a visa at one of these entry points.

Travel in the separatist-controlled Georgian autonomous Republic of Abkhazia remains hazardous. Since March 1995, there has been increased Abkhaz terrorist activity in southern Abkhazia and attacks on United Nations personnel in the Sukhumi and Gali districts of Abkhazia. In addition, land mines pose a threat to all travelers in Abkhazia. This should tell you enough about the prospects of enjoyable travel in the region. Also, the U.S. government does not recognize an independent republic of Abkhazia separate from the Republic of Georgia. For the time being, it is recommended that you choose other countries in which to rail around.

Another warning: high crime rates in south Ossetia make unofficial and unescorted travel there risky. All train and vehicular traffic is vulnerable to robbery. Please note that terrorist incidents have occurred in the country in connection with regional conflicts. Passenger trains traveling between Georgia and Armenia have been the targets of bombings.

Georgia currently has a cash-only economy, with the use of Russian ruble being banned in July 1993.

KAZAKHSTAN

Located in Central Asia, northwest of China, Kazakhstan is immense, nearly four times the size of Texas. It borders China, Kyrgyzstan, Russia, Turkmenistan, and Uzbekistan, as well as the Aral Sea and the Caspian Sea, whose international borders are not yet determined. The country has a population of more than 17 million, of which most are ethnically Kazakh and Russian, and equally split between Muslim and Russian Orthodox religions.

The capital is Almaty. Kazakhstan is so far from Moscow by train that, other than foreign travelers on their way to Beijing, the country is seldom a selected destination.

KYRGYZSTAN

Kyrgyzstan is a newly independent nation in a state of dramatic change. Do not take anything for granted if traveling to or through this region. The capital is Bishkek (formerly Frunze). Visas from Russia and neighboring Commonwealth of Independent States, except Georgia and Tajikistan, allow for temporary stays in Kyrgyzstan for up to three days.

With the breakup of Aeroflot into many small airlines, air travel in the former Soviet Union is often unreliable. Travelers must often cope with unpredictable schedules and difficult conditions, including poor quality of service and overloading. At present, no airline provides dependable, regularly scheduled international air service into Bishkek. Most international air travelers fly to Almaty and then travel overland (approximately 3 hours) to Bishkek.

Train travel in Central Asia is irregular and arduous. About four-fifths of Kyrgyzstan is mountainous. The mountains include the Tian Shan (Tien Shan) range, extending into the Xinjiang (Sinkiang) region of northwestern China, the Kirghiz Mountains of north Kyrgyzstan, and the Alai range in the southwest. The highest elevation is Pobeda (Victory) Peak on the Chinese border (7,437 meters/24,400 feet).

Kyrgyzstan, like the other Central Asian countries, is a cash-only economy.

MOLDOVA

Moldova, according to the U.S. State Department Travelers Warning, is "a nation undergoing profound political and economic change. It is a newly independent nation still in the process of stabilizing its relations with neighboring countries. Tourist facilities are not highly developed, and many of the goods and services taken for granted in other countries are not yet available. Internal travel, especially by air, may be disrupted by fuel shortages and other problems."

Visas for travel to other former Soviet states are necessary and difficult to obtain in Moldova. The U.S. embassy in Chisinau advises that only essential travel should be undertaken into or through the Transnistria region. There are frequent checkpoints in Transnistria that are manned by armed, young, inexperienced paramilitary units who are not under the control of the Moldovan government and whose members rarely understand English. Tourists and truckers may be subject to extortion or robbery at checkpoints.

Only Air Moldova and Tarom (Romania's national airline) regularly fly to Moldova. Air Moldova service is well below Western standards. Aircraft appear to be old and cabin areas are in poor condition. Train service is also below Western standards, and an increasing number of Americans have been victimized while traveling on international trains to and from Moldova.

Mumansk

The largest city in the world north of the Arctic Circle, Mumansk was founded in 1915 as a supply post in World War I. Used in World War II as Russia's principal port for receiving supplies from Britain and the United States, the city exudes historic exoticism beneath its current commercial fishing and ship repair industries.

RUSSIA

Russia has for many years been a land of mystery and intrigue to the people of the West. For hundreds of years it has been an enigma, friend, or enemy, as the political climate has shifted time and again. Since the dissolution of the Soviet Union, Russia has bounded in diverse and often contradictory directions socially, politically, culturally, and economically, making travel hard to predict yet extremely interesting.

Traveling to Russia by train has been an experience that more and more westerners have indulged in, and most come back with fantastic stories and a will to return or venture deeper into this vast land. Most also come back with words of caution. Jody Jenkins and Gwen

Strauss tell of a horrific journey by train from Moscow to Tashkent: a band of drunken nuclear submarine captains took over one compartment while Ghengis Khan look-alikes proceeded to shake down the most vulnerable travelers. American expatriate Jim Haynes, who has traveled throughout eastern Europe and has written five books, admits that the train south through the Ukraine to Odessa and the Black Sea is the route that has peaked his imagination the most.

For first-time visitors to Russia, the train to Moscow and the Moscow–St. Petersburg route are wonderful initiations.

Due to the extraordinary political changes in Russia and changing attitudes in the United States, most sources of local information confirm loudly that it is now possible for individuals and companies to do business in Russia. Runaway inflation, however, is causing contact with local travelers to be tainted by an air of mercantilism. While there is relatively little inflation in dollar terms, inflation in ruble terms is terrifying. This situation has caused local hardship and is affecting the security of travel.

Russia is technically located in northern Asia between Europe and the North Pacific Ocean, although the area west of the Urals is sometimes considered to be Europe. Russia is the world's largest country and borders Azerbaijan, Belarus, China, Estonia, Finland, Georgia, Kazakhstan, North Korea, Latvia, Lithuania, Mongolia, Norway, Poland, and the Ukraine.

As of July 1994, the Russian population alone totaled nearly 150 million people.

Pricilla Sharp is an experienced travel writer whose comments on trains appear regularly on-line in the Train Forum on CompuServe. She has traveled extensively on trains in Russia, Belarus, and a bit of Ukraine, specifically from Moscow to St. Petersburg, St. Petersburg to Minsk, Minsk to Gomel, Gomel to Kiev, Kiev to Moscow, and St. Petersburg to Archangel. She swears that the overnight trips are the best: "You must travel first-class, and it is preferable to buy all four tickets in the compartment to ensure privacy, especially on the 'overnighters.' The trains are well-worn, creaky monstrosities. For example, on the Kiev–Moscow train, our compartment was directly over the wheels, which groaned, clanked, crunched, and made various other loud noises all night long! There is no air conditioning in summer, but the only time I was uncomfortable was on the 'local' three-hour Minsk to Gomel. There were forest fires all the way (thus, unfortunately, stirring up the radioactivity which had settled in the area from Chernobyl) and the heat was unbearable. The windows in the compartments rarely open, but the windows in the hallways do."

Pricilla also states that the bathrooms are uniformly filthy. There is nothing you can do about it except do *not* sit down. Russians will very often stand on the toilet seat and squat, thus, in her words, adding boot mud to the mixture. "Whenever I travel in Russia I always bring my own toilet paper—at least one and a half rolls per week! And, don't laugh, but I always wear long skirts when riding on trains. It's much cleaner and easier to pull something *up* around my neck than *down* toward that filthy floor!" Successful train travel in difficult places relies on the sharing of practical information like Pricilla's.

"Edible food is almost nonexistent. I always pack my own: sausages, bread, cheese, hard-boiled eggs, peanut butter, etc. We always bring our own single-pack coffee bags and just ask for hot water, which is provided by the train attendant from a huge samovar that's constantly kept boiling hot in each car. Actually, the tea is always very good, if you prefer tea. Whenever the train stops, there are usually vendors at the stations who come and offer vegetables, pirogis (little popovers of meat and bread), cookies, and the like. On the overnight trains, such as one from Moscow to St. Petersburg, you won't need any food because the train arrives at about 7:00 A.M. in St. Petersburg."

When in Moscow and in need of reliable train or other travel information, try contacting the Travelers Guest House at 50 Bolshaya Pereyaslavskaya, 10th Floor, Moscow, Russia 129401; Tel. (7095) 971-4059, 280-8562; Fax (7095) 280-7686. The Travelers Guest House is very close to the downtown area, including Red Square and the Kremlin. It would take approximately 20 minutes to get there from the closest metro station and only a few stops on the metro.

IRO Travel, an American owned and managed agency, can help in issuing train tickets, visas, and invitation letters when needed.

The Europe Library of The Travel Forum on CompuServe stores a healthy supply of relevant rail information. Here is more on the various Trans-Siberian options.

Moscow

Start at the Kremlin, the Grand Kremlin Palace, or Red Square, and satisfy the great mythic draw of this international landmark. Closed on Thursdays. Red Square, with Lenin's Mausoleum, is open daily except Monday and Friday.

The Cathedral of Saint Basil the Blessed has become a symbol of Russia to those in the West. This colorful 16th-century church sits on the north side of the Kremlin. Interestingly, Red Square is not named for the red bricks which pave it, but for the Russian word meaning beautiful, literally "Beautiful Square."

On a sunny fall afternoon Red Square is crowded with families, tourists, and vendors selling stacking dolls, shish kebab, and other small goods. The prices here, as in any area in the world frequented by tourists, will be higher than elsewhere. If you have the time, the best place to do your souvenir shopping is at Izmailovsky Park. Here there is a large flea market with hundreds of vendors selling everything under the sun. It is open on weekends only.

The south side of Red Square is bounded by Lenin's tomb (now closed to the public) and the wall of the Kremlin. The church above has beautiful bells which are rung on weekends and other times. It is well worth the time to soak in the sites and sounds of Red Square on a sunny day. Weekends are best as there are few official events. Remember that the Kremlin is the seat of government, so during the week Red Square may be closed when officials or visiting dignitaries are arriving and leaving. Try to visit at night. The buildings are caught in strong spotlights and the scene is filled with magic.

The south side of Red Square is the north side of the Kremlin, a 13th-century fortress that's surrounded by a high brick wall and many towers. Most of the towers are still crowned with illuminated red stars. It is not impossible to visit the inside of the Kremlin during some days and hours, but you should ask your Russian hosts to help set this up.

Americans and others who visit Russia for the first time will be amazed at how expensive it is. A quality hotel room will cost from $100 to $300 per night. Restaurant meals are on par with those in New York in cost, but not necessarily in quality. A taxi ride is similar in cost to those in any major city. While there are dispatched taxis, most any private car headed in your direction will give you a ride for a small fee. Hailing a taxi in Moscow rarely takes more than 30 seconds on a busy street, which is far from the reality of St. Petersburg! Agree on the fee ahead of time, and if at all possible have a Russian do the talking and negotiate the price.

Moscow has the world's busiest METRO (subway) system. It carries nearly 4 billion people each year. There are many English newspapers and maps available—most of them are free and will have a METRO map in them.

Russian cultural performances and exhibitions are truly world class. Pick up a copy of the *Moscow Times* for listings. Tickets for most events are very reasonable.

In Moscow, don't miss the Tretyakov Gallery, which just reopened after several years of renovations. Another important cultural insight is the Orthodox church. Try to stop by a functioning church. If a service is going on, don't be intimidated—services are long and most Russians don't stay for the whole thing. Orthodox church music is unbelievably beautiful.

Also see the Uspensky, Blagoveshchensky, and Archangelsky cathedrals, which date to the 15th century. The priceless jewelry, costumes, gold and and silver objects, Fabergé eggs, and weapons located in the Armory Museum will impress you. Don't miss the 16th-century 38-ton canon, Czar Pushka. The weekend bird market on Kalitnikovskaya Street is highly original. The Bolshoi Theater should be attended if possible, as well as the Lenin State Library and Lenin Museum. For public art deco, make sure you pass through the Komsololskaya, Ploshchad, Revutsi, Kropotkinskay, and Mayakovskaya metro stations.

In Moscow, there are culinary alternatives to the bland hotel food, the incredibly expensive western hotel food, and McDonald's and Pizza Hut. Georgian food comes highly recommended. Watch out the beautiful bowl of fruit on your table trick. If you want a reasonably priced meal, *don't eat the fruit*—your pocketbook will regret it.

Fun weekend things to do in Moscow include the Ismailovsky Park flea market. Russian handicrafts, souvenirs, etc., for cheap prices. Haggle. Good stuff, much cheaper than in shops. If you buy lacquered boxes, make sure they're painted, not decoupaged—a common trick.

Note that Moscow has *nine* major railroad stations:

> Byelorussia—trips to Warsaw and on to western Europe
> Kazanski—trips to Tashkent and Samarkand
> Kievski—trips to Kiev and Eastern Europe
> Kurski—trips to Sochi and the Caspian Sea
> Leningradski—trips to St. Petersburg and on to Helsinki
> Paveletski—check Thomas Cook timetables
> Riga—trips to Riga and the Baltic States
> Savelovski—check Thomas Cook timetables
> Yaroslavski—trips to Siberia, Central Asia, and Beijing

LONG-DISTANCE TRIPS
FROM MOSCOW

Here are schedules for rail trips from Moscow to 9 interesting cities, with notes on what to see at each destination.

Moscow - Kiev   and v.v. 924

The following trains are ones we recommend.

Dep. Moscow (Kiev.)	09:56 (1)	11:47 (1)	11:54 (1)	13:07 (2)	14:20 (2)	14:44 (1)
Arr. Kiev	00:01	01:57	03:16	03:30	06:00	05:53

Sights in **Kiev:** See notes about sightseeing in Kiev under "St. Petersburg–Kiev"

Dep. Kiev	04:50 (1)	10:00 (1)	11:22 (1)	12:28 (1)	16:45	17:15 (2)
Arr. Moscow (Kiev.)	21:41	04:00	05:09	06:17	09:09	10:24

(1) Restaurant car. (2) Light refreshments.

Moscow - St. Petersburg   and v.v. 901

Dep. Moscow (St. P.)	01:05	01:56	12:26	13:28	17:18	20:35
Arr. St. Petersburg (Mos.)	09:16	10:30	20:15	22:36	23:19	05:15

Moscow - Riga   and v.v. 915

Dep. Moscow (Riga)	16:55	19:53	21:08
Arr. Riga	09:20	10:55	12:25

Sights in **Riga:** An important Baltic seaport. See the great pipe organ at the 13th–15th century Cathedral. The 14th century Riga Castle.

Dep. Riga	17:40	18:30
Arr. Moscow (Riga)	10:46	12:06

Moscow - Sochi - Sukhumi and v.v. 5025 + 5080

Dep. Moscow (Kurski)	13:40 (1)	16:50 (1)	22:30 (1)	23:17 (2)	23:50 (1)
Arr. Sochi	01:12 (4)	03:14 (4)	08:24 (4)	11:16 (4)	11:51 (4)
Arr. Sukhumi	05:33	06:50	12:30	15:08	16:12
		• • •			
Dep. Sukhumi	00:57 (1)	02:16 (1)	04:10 (3)	22:45 (1)	23:00 (2+5)
Dep Sochi	04:38	06:19	08:53	02:42 (4)	05:23 (4)
Arr. Moscow (Kurski)	14:54 (4)	16:02 (4)	21:43 (4)	12:09	16:12

(1) Carries a first-class sleeping car. Coach is second-class. Restaurant car. (2) Coach is second-class. Restaurant car. (3) Coach is second-class. (4) Day 2. (5) Plus another Sukhumi departure at 23:44 (1), arriving Moscow 15:22 (4).

Sights in **Sochi:** A popular Black Sea resort. Over 800 species of trees at the Dendrarium. Scenic Lake Ritsa is a 5-hour bus trip away.

Sights in **Sukhumi**: This is the heart of Russia's subtropical area: citrus fruits, tobacco, etc. See the monkey farm used by Russian scientists in their program of studying human behavior.

Moscow - Tashkent - Samarkand and v.v.

5031

Dep. Moscow (Kaz.)	11:46 (1)	13:55 (3)	22:03 (3)		
Arr. Tashkent	04:00 (2)	04:16 (2)	08:00 (2)		
Change trains. 5133					
Dep. Tashkent	-0-	07:34 (4)	09:15 (4)	15:30 (5)	17:05 (5+7)
Arr. Samarkand	-0-	17:48	19:33	21:38	22:46
		• • •			
Dep. Samarkand	00:20 (5)	04:23 (5)	22:10	23:20 (5)	
Arr. Tashkent	06:10	09:50	03:45	05:05	
Change trains. 5031					
Dep. Tashkent	11:45	14:29	04:40 (3)	-0-	
Arr. Moscow (Kaz)	05:08 (6)	05:41 (6)	14:30 (6)	-0-	

(1) Coach is second-class. Restaurant car. (2) Day 4 from Moscow. (3) Carries a first-class sleeping car. Also has second-class couchettes. Restaurant car. (4) Second-class. (5) Has first and second-class coaches. Restaurant car. (6) Day 4 from Tashkent. (7) Plus additional Tashkent departures at 17:35 (5) and 21:25.

Sights in **Tashkent**: This has been an important center of trade and handcraft on the major caravan route (the "silk road") between Europe and China and India for nearly 2,000 years. There are many 15th and 16th century churches. Heavy Muslim cultural influence here. See:

The Academy of Sciences. The Navoi Public Library. The Navoi Theater of Opera and Ballet.

Sights in **Samarkand:** One of the oldest cities in Central Asia. Alexander the Great captured Samarkand 2300 years ago. Heavy Turkish cultural influence here since the 6th century. Uninhabited from 1720 to 1770 due to an economic decline at that time caused by constant attacks by nomad tribes. The inception of train service in 1896 revived the city. See: The enormous colored domes of the 14th century mausoleums, decorated in marble and gold. The 14th century mosque. The ruins of a 16th century aqueduct.

Moscow - Volgograd - Rostov   —   Rostov - Moscow

Here is a great combination train and boat trip: a circle, from Moscow to Volgograd by train, and from Volgograd to Rostov by ship on the Volga–Don Canal. Then, return to Moscow by train.

5030

Dep. Moscow (Pav.)	01:40 (1)	14:15 (2)	15:05 (2)
Arr. Volgograd	09:00	11:10	13:09

(1) Second-class couchettes. Restaurant car. (2) Carries a first-class sleeping car. Also has second-class couchettes. Restaurant car.

Change to a ship for the Volgograd–Rostov cruise. Check Intourist for current Volga–Don Canal cruise timetables. The complete 2,000-mile ship trip runs from Moscow to Rostov. Change to a train in Rostov.

5085

Dep. Rostov	Frequent times from 00:11 to 23:27
Arr. Moscow (Kur.)	22 hours later

(1) Operates late May to late September. (2) Carries a first-class sleeping car. Also has second-class couchettes. Restaurant car.

Sights in **Volgograd:** Renamed (from Stalingrad) after being destroyed during a 7-month battle in 1942–43. See: The enormous 63-mile canal. The huge industrial complex, particularly the Tractor Factory. But, most of all, the Soviet Union's Eternal Flame, memorial to their millions of World War II dead, in the Hall of Valor. All of those names are carved in its walls.

Sights in **Rostov:** Another post-World War II metropolis based on heavy industrial manufacturing. See the enormous theater on Teatralnaya Square. Window-shop Engels St.

Here is the reverse route for this circle trip:

5085

Dep. Moscow (Kur.)	Frequent times from 00:05 to 23:59
Arr. Rostov	22 hours later

(1) Carries a first-class sleeping car. Also has second-class couchettes. Restaurant car. (2) Operates late May to late September. (3) Plus another Moscow departure at 23:59 (1), arriving Rostov 20:25.

Change to a ship for the Rostov-Volgograd cruise. Check Intourist for current Don Canal-Volga cruise timetables. Change to a train in Volgograd.

5030

Dep. Volgograd	05:49 (1)	12:45 (1)	13:10 (1)	16:00 (3)
Arr. Moscow (Pav.)	05:15 (2)	10:10	11:00	22:42

(1) Carries a first-class sleeping car. Also has second-class couchettes. Restaurant car. (2) Arrives at Moscow's Kazanski railstation. (3) Has only second-class couchettes. Restaurant car.

Trans-Siberian Express

1. The *Trans-Mongolian* (Chinese train #4) leaves Moscow every Tuesday at 7:45 P.M. This train takes you via Ulan Bator, Mongolia, and after five and a half days and 7,885 kilometres you arrive in Beijing on Monday at 15:33 P.M.

2. The *Trans-Manchurian* (Russian train #20) leaves Moscow every Friday at 8:25 P.M. This train takes you thru Manzhouli and Harbin, and after 9,001 kilometres and six and a half days you arrive in Beijing on Friday at 6:32 A.M.

3. *To Beijing with stop in Irkutsk for 4 days and Mongolia for 4 Days (3/3 days in winter).* This highly popular trip allows you to see and enjoy both Irkutsk and Mongolia to their fullest. You will stop in Irkutsk and Lake Baikal for a total of four days and three nights.

4. *To Beijing with 1 day/1 night stop in Irkutsk and Ulan Bator.* This quick stopover option lets you get a feel for Irkutsk with maximum freedom to do it on your own. Departure from Moscow every Wednesday at 9:15 P.M.

5. *To Beijing with stop in Irkutsk for 4 days/4 nights.* You will stay in both Irkutsk and in the village of Listvyanka, right on the shores of Lake Baikal. At least one full day is spent sightseeing in Irkutsk and visiting two or three museums and churches throughout the city. Part of the tour is spent at Lake Baikal, where you will be shown the Lymnological Institute and Museum of Wooden Architecture. You'll have plenty of free time to enjoy an exciting view of Baikal Lake and its shores. This stopover includes all meals, guides, and transfers. You will stay in either a hotel or with a family (one to two people in a room) in Irkutsk. Accommodation in Listvyanka is a typical Siberian wooden house for at least one night. Departure from Moscow every Tuesday at 9:15 P.M.

6. *Stop in Mongolia for 3 days/3 nights or 5 days/5 nights.* Minimum 2 nights will be spent in a traditional Mongolian Ger (*yurt*) in a camp at Terelj (70 kilometres outside of Ulan Bator) in the beautiful Mongolian countryside, which features vast grasslands, rugged hills, and horses running free. On the remaining nights you will stay at a hotel in Ulan Bator (either

the Negdelchin or Zul).

7. *The Trans-Siberian to Vladivostok (train #2: The Russia Express)* leaves Moscow every odd day at 2:00 P.M. This train travels straight through Siberia, and after 9296 kilometres and six and half days, you arrive at Vladivostok at 9:45 A.M. local time.

Safety Tips on Traveling in Russia

One travel writer, Kathryn Coombs, offers these practical tips that all train travelers should take to heart.

If you take the train from St. Petersburg to Moscow, take a bicycle lock and one of those flexible wire "chain" things that you wind through the spokes of your bike. There have been a lot of robberies/attacks on the trains. If you loop this through the door handle of your compartment, then attach it to the luggage rack, the bad guys can't get in. When you leave the compartment for any reason during the day, chain your luggage to the luggage rack with this. And lock the luggage. Bring train munchies (all the Russians do), it's a long trip and all they offer you is endless tea. There is a big samovar (hot water boiler) on the train, so pot noodles are a good idea.

Do not drink the water in St. Petersburg. It is contaminated with an intestinal parasite that you'll have trouble getting rid of. Drink bottled water and brush your teeth in bottled water. If you take baths instead of showers, bring water purification tablets with you and drop a few in the bath and wait about 10 minutes (follow directions on package) before you get in. These parasites can enter you through either end (yuck!). This happened to a friend of mine.

Moscow water is generally safe to drink if boiled first, unlike St. Pete's, but do use water purification tablets there as well. It's all right to shower. The way to avoid getting mugged is to avoid looking obviously foreign or rich. Leave your fancy jewelry at home.

Don't wear clothes that scream out "I am an American tourist" (if you're not American, sorry for presuming). This means no plaid trousers or bright preppy greens. Do not sling your camera around your neck. Most Russians carry some kind of shoulder bag with them—as they tend to do shopping on the way home from work. Find a camera bag that doesn't look like a camera bag, and you'll blend in.

Hang around with a Russian guide whenever you can. There are good people you can hire for the whole day, or your whole stay in a city, who are cheap. They will add to your enjoyment and understanding and increase your safety, helping you blend in.

Regarding arrival at Sheremetyevo Airport, make sure your travel agent arranges your airport transport in advance. The taxi drivers that congregate in the international terminal are real sharks (will charge you as much as $100 to get to town, whereas you can book a cab in advance for about $40). Most of these sharks are safe at least, but some are not, and you never know.

Watch out for "gypsy" kids—there have been some recent problems. An elderly Canadian gentleman was mugged in front of the Moskva Hotel and beaten by 8-year-old kids. They tend to hang around the less expensive tourist hotels. Often they will pretend to be begging, or trying to sell you something (postcards, usually) with the idea that when you open your wallet, ZAP! Sadly, the best policy is to avoid giving to begging children, many of whom have been put up to it by their parents. However, the metros are full of begging grannies and disabled veterans. *Always* give to them if you can—consider it reparations for winning the cold war. These pensioners are trying to live on $9 a month and are some of the nicest people you'll meet. Grannies (babuski) are the victims of crimes, not the perpetrators, so you're safe here.

Try to keep your spending money (for ice cream, beggars, small purchases, etc.) separate from your main stash of cash, to avoid flashing large wads of bills around. Sensible advice in any big city.

You will be less conspicious if you are not in a huge group of foreigners. If you stray off the beaten track, keep to small groups of, say, four people, and have your Russian guide with you.

Watch your property when you're in restaurants—a new trick is "kidnapping" property. If they think you're a foreign businessperson, they might take your papers—worthless to anyone but you—and then send a representative to negotiate your payment to get them back. This happened when I had escorted a group to dinner at the Minsk Restaurant on Tverskaya Street, where an Azeri gang hangs out. When I had checked out the restaurant the night before, everything was OK, but I was with a group of Russians and they thought I was Russian.

Get cholera and diptheria shots before you go, just to make sure. Outbreaks in Moscow/St. Petersburg have been only a few cases, and the risk is minimal, but its best to make sure, just in case, particularly if you are older. If you have any medical problems while you are there, the place to go is the American Medical Center (takes credit cards)—all hotels know how to find number. Also, State Department travel advisory bulletins are worth getting for any country you're visiting. You can access these via CompuServe.

Trans-Siberian Express: Moscow to Vladivostok

Nothing excites the imagination more than a train ride for six days across the former Soviet Union. Six days on a train. Thoughts of Pasternak's *Doctor Zhivago* rush to mind. Heading west, the train leaves Vladivostock station at midnight. Vladivostock, rich in natural resources and labeled the Seattle of Russia, has emerged in the mid-1990s as a wild town of gangsters and street warfare. Most people get on in Moscow, but the few who manage to take the train in the other direction have a particularly pure experience, especially for the first half of the trip, when very few foreigner are on board. The problem many have with the Moscow-Vladivostock run is getting back. It's easier to continue east to Japan and fly from there. One American couple recently shared their westbound journey on CompuServe's Train Forum and some of their impressions have been incorporated here.

The Trans-Siberian Express across the nation is the longest single train ride in the world. Curiously, the entire journey is quoted in Moscow time—stops, meals, everything —even though the capital can be as much as six days away.

As is true on all long voyages in the CIS, it is advised that you bring your own food, and plenty of it. Food in varying degrees of quantity and quality is always attainable, but the negotiations and "backshish" needed to come by it is too unreliable and tiring to make the effort worth it.

The route traveled covers just under 6,000 miles: from the Pacific coast along the Amur River, across the Siberian taiga, by Lake Baikal (the biggest freshwater lake in the world), through industrial towns such as Sverdlovsk (now renamed Ekaterinberg), past enormous coal fields, over the Urals (the great Europe/Asia divide) and between huge wheat fields.

"Over the six days of the journey, we must have spent more than forty hours propped in the corridor staring out of the window. And the views? Well, interesting, but not spectacular. Or rather, we expected more. But the memories will be of the people, not the views. We had come prepared with a library of books to stave off boredom. We read Eric Newby's *Big Red Train Ride*—his account of the Trans-Siberian Railway from Moscow to the east—which was excellent read backwards. Apart from that we hardly dipped into any of the books. Time—perhaps not the train itself—certainly flew by.

Surprisingly, some of the most attractive scenery on the whole journey was on the outskirts of Moscow. As we came into the area called the Golden Triangle, we could see in the distance golden spires glowing in the sunset; we were passing through green fields and forests and then suddenly we were in Moscow. After six days, across seven time zones, in a country that seemed to be falling apart at the seams, the train pulled into Yaroslavl Station ten minutes late."

The Moscow-Khabarovsk-Yokohama route of the Trans-Siberian Express is much like the above journey, except it is advisable to stop over in Novosibirsk and Irkutsk on the 5300 mile trip.

Czar Nicholas officiated at the ceremony in Vladivostock when construction of the line began in 1891. Six separate sections were developed independently. Prisoners sent to Siberia were offered reduced sentences for working on the construction 8 months of work reduced a sentence by one year. By 1900 two unconnected sections had been completed: Moscow–Sretensk (east of Lake Baykal) and Khabarovsk–Vladivostock. Passengers traveled from Sretensk to Khabarovsk by river boat.

A line from Lake Baykal to Khabarovsk (the Chinese Eastern Railway, via Manchuria) was completed in 1903 and was much shorter than the present line. Russia lost it one year later, after the 1904 Russo-Japanese War, and had to begin building the present line from Baykal to Khabarovsk. Twelve years later the present Moscow–Vladivostock line, entirely on Russian territory, was completed and Russia began to develop Siberia.

It is necessary to check 1996 sailing dates of the Nakhodka–Yokohama (and v.v.) ships before determining dates on which to reserve Moscow or Nakhodka train departures.

929 + 5020 (Train)		
Dep. Moscow		
(Yar.)	14:00 (1)	
Arr. Novosibirsk	N/A (2)	Day 3
Arr. Irkutsk	01:38	Day 5
Arr. Khabarovsk	03:10 (3)	Day 7
Change trains.		
Dep. Khabarovsk	13:20 (4)	
Arr. Nakhodka	N/A (2)	Day 8
Change to boat.		
5050		
Dep. Nakhodka	12:00 (5)	Day 8
Arr. Yokohama	15:00	Day 10

5050 (Boat)		
Dep. Yokohama	12:00 (5)	
Arr. Nakhodka	17:00	Day 3
Change to train.		
929 + 5020		
Dep. Nakhodka	N/A (2+6)	Day 3
Arr. Khabarovsk	07:35 (3)	Day 4
Change trains.		
Dep. Khabarovsk	18:05 (1+3)	Day 4
Arr. Irkutsk	16:10	Day 6
Arr. Novosibirsk	N/A (2)	Day 7
Arr. Moscow		
(Yar.)	06:45	Day 10

(1) Carries a first-class sleeping car. Also has second-class coaches with seats that convert to berths. Restaurant car. (2) Time not available in 1993 for first time in more than 23 years. (3) Local time (7 hours later than Moscow). (4) Local time (7 hours later than Moscow). Runs only on days prior to sailings from Nakhodka to Yokohama. Carries a sleeping car. Also has second-class coaches that convert to berths. Restaurant car. (5) For specific sailing dates, check Far Eastern Shipping Co. (6) Local time (7 hours later than Moscow). Runs only on days that sailings from Yokohama arrive in Nakhodka. Carries a sleeping car. Also has second-class coaches that convert to berths. Restaurant car.

Sights in **Novosibirsk**: The Theater of Opera and Ballet, which is larger than Moscow's Bolshoi Theater. Take the 18-mile bus ride to **Akademgorodok**, the "Science Town," located along the Ob Sea, a man-made reservoir. There, top Soviet scientists and technicians live, work and shop in the USSR's most modern apartments, office buildings and stores.

Sights in **Irkutsk**: A large industrial city with no major tourist attraction. However, Irkutsk is the gateway for visiting the most unique place in the Soviet Union: **Lake Baykal**. Buses take tourists through a virgin forest to the shore of the world's deepest (6,365 feet) lake, 380 miles long and 12 to 50 miles wide, containing one-fifth of the fresh water on the earth's surface (four-fifths of the fresh water in the U.S.S.R.). Its waves sometimes measure over 15 feet.

Formed nearly 30,000,000 years ago by a rupture in the earth's crust, it is fed by 336 rivers and streams. There are 1,800 species of animals and plants in the lake. About three-quarters of them are found nowhere else in the world.

The day-trip includes a stop at the Limnological Museum, where hundreds of local flora and fauna are exhibited. The excursion to Baykal ends with a 90-minute hydrofoil ride from the Museum, up the **Angara River**, to Irkutsk.

Sights in **Khabarovsk**: Named after Yerofei Khabarov, a Slavak Daniel Boone who led a Cossack expedition to explore this area in the 17th century. Khabarovsk was first settled in 1858 by a handful of people living in tents along the banks of the **Amur River.**

When the Bolsheviks came into power in 1917, Khabarovsk was too far from Moscow for the embryonic Soviet regime to defend it, and the city was grabbed by Manchuria. Soviet rule here was re-established in 1922. By then, the old Khabarovsk had been reduced to ruins by the Manchurians. The city that exists today was started from scratch in 1922.

Its commercial air connections with Japan make Khabarovsk the Eastern gateway to the Soviet Union. Japanese tourism to Moscow and Leningrad begins and ends in Khabarovsk. The city is so geared to Japanese tourism and has so little tourism from elsewhere that several of its tourist brochures are printed only in the Japanese language.

There is a good museum here, with exhibits on the natural and political history of this area. The many 19th century wood and brick buildings are interesting. River boat excursions depart hourly from a dock that is across the park from the Intourist Hotel (one of the best hotels in Russia). **Vladivostok**, a major naval and long-range missile base, was opened to tourists in 1991 for the first time since the 1917 revolution.

Moscow - Khabarovsk - Yokohama   and v.v.

This is the eastward route of the Trans-Siberian Express.

It is advisable to stopover in Novosibirsk (population 1,500,000) and Irkutsk on the 7½-day 5,301-mile-long Moscow–Khabarovsk trip. The Hotel Novosibirsk used to have better accommodations than were available in either Irkutsk or Khabarovsk. It is always recommended to bring toilet paper and soap when traveling on Soviet trains, including the Trans-Siberian Express.

The times shown here are Moscow Time, considerably different than actual arrival and departure times as this 5,777-mile route covers 8 time zones.

For example, the real arrival time in Khabarovsk and Vladivostock is 7 hours *later* than the Moscow Time listed. Also the real departure time from Vladivostock and Khabarovsk (for the westward trip to Moscow) is 7 hours *earlier* than indicated.

The number of travel days is represented by capital letters: B = Day 2, C = Day 3 etc.

Moscow - Khabarovsk - Vladivostock   and v.v. 5020

Dep. Moscow (Yar.)	09:35 (1)	17:25 (2)	14:00 (3)	21:50 (4)
Dep. Kirov	01:22 B	07:31 B	03:56 B	20:01 B
Dep. Ekaterinberg	17:00	21:04	19:00	11:20 C
Dep. Omsk	05:10 C	08:29 C	07:03 C	02:35 D
Dep. Novosibirsk	14:51	16:42	N/A (5)	12:33
Dep. Krasnoyarsk	04:21 D	05:02 D	N/A (5) D	02:02 E
Dep. Irkutsk	23:59	23:10	01:38 E	22:13
Dep. Ulan Ude	08:14 E	07:02 E	N/A (5)	06:18 F
Dep. Chita	18:20	16:34	N/A (5)	17:03
Dep. Skovorodino	16:23 F	13:10 F	N/A (5) F	15:10
Arr. Khabarovsk	14:53	08:57 G	13:10	13:40
Arr. Vladivostock	05:35 H	22:05	02:45 H	-0-
		• • •		
Dep. Vladivostock	-0-	01:20 (4)	12:30 (6)	18:05 (3)
Dep. Khabarovsk	02:30 (1)	15:56	01:50 B	07:35 B
Dep. Belogorsk	14:35	04:25 B	12:46	18:44
Dep. Skovorodino	00:33 B	14:06	21:45	03:35 C
Dep. Chita	22:23	11:20 D	18:30 C	00:58 D
Dep. Ulan Ude	08:22 D	22:40	04:06 D	N/A (5)
Dep. Irkutsk	16:23	07:22 E	11:51	19:01 E
Dep. Krasnoyarsk	12:18 D	03:04 F	06:08 E	N/A (5)
Dep. Novosibirsk	01:50 E	17:02	18:25	N/A (5)
Dep. Omsk	11:39	03:10 G	02:28 F	13:15 F
Dep. Ekaterinberg	03:17 F	17:04	14:34	02:15 G
Dep. Kirov	20:00	08:28 H	04:33 G	N/A (5)
Arr. Moscow (Yar.)	17:12 G	23:00	18:55	06:45 H
Dep. Belogorsk	02:02 G	22:13	N/A (5) G	01:00 G

(1) Has second-class coaches with seats that convert to berths. Restaurant car. (2) Runs Wednesday and Sunday. Restaurant car. Has first and second-class coaches with seats that convert to berths. (3) "Rossia." Carries a first-class sleeping car. Also has second-class coaches with seats that convert to berths. Restaurant car. (4) Has second-class coaches with seats that convert to berths. Restaurant car. (5) Time not available for the first time in more than 23 years. (6) Runs Tuesday and Thursday. Restaurant car. Has second-class coaches with seats that convert to berths.

St. Petersburg

Many travelers consider St. Petersburg, formerly Leningrad, the most beautiful and stimulating city in the CIS. The Hermitage Museum with its 2.5 million works of art could keep you hostage for days alone. Don't miss the Summer Palace, and of course the 112 columns and gold cupolas at St. Isaac's Cathedral. The 600-ton Alexandrovskaya Column marking Russia's victory over Napoleon, the Summer Gardens of Peter the Great, and the Monument to the Heroes of the Revolution should not be overlooked. Nor should the excursion to the magnificent Yekaterinsky Palace in Pushkin be forgotten. In the summer, take a hydrofoil cruise on the River Neva.

Do not miss Tsarskoye Selo, just outside of town. A former Royal Palace turned into a school, there are entire rooms of malachite walls and columns. It is breathtaking.

The St. Petersburg metro operates from 5:30 A.M. to 12:30 A.M. Unless you really want massive intimate contact with the Russian people, try to avoid traveling during the peak commuter hours. Note that the doors in the stations weigh a ton and swing back and forth with the force of a wrecking ball.

Tickets for the two trains from Helsinki to St. Petersburg can be bought right in Helsinki. The Sibelius, whose departure is at 6:30 and arrives at 1:55, and the Repin, whose departure is at 3:32 and arrives at 11:20. The price is around $60 one way.

LONG-DISTANCE TRIPS FROM
ST. PETERSBURG

Here are schedules for rail trips from St. Petersburg to 5 other interesting cities, with notes on what to see at each destination.

St. Petersburg (Leningrad)

The Commonwealth's most interesting city. The Hermitage Museum (closed Monday) has the world's largest exhibition of fine arts, over 2,500,000 articles. Visit the Summer Palace (open daily except Tuesday, May through November). See the 112 columns, gold cupola and priceless paintings and mosaics at St. Isaac's Cathedral (closed Tuesday, Wednesday and the last Monday of each month).

The park and palace at Petrodvorets. The Winter Palace. The 600-ton, 154-foot high Alexandrovskaya Column, marking Russia's victory over Napoleon. The Peter-Paul Fortress and Cathedral. The Summer Gardens of Peter the Great. The Museum of the History of Religion and Atheism, in Kazansky Cathedral (closed Wednesday).

The Monument to the Heroes of the Revolution, in the Field of Mars. The Central Museum, at the Marble Palace. The State Museum of the History of St. Petersburg (closed Wednesday). The State Museum of Russian Art, in Mikhailovsky Palace (closed Tuesday). The Arctic and Antarctic Museum (closed Monday and Tuesday).

In the Kunstkammer, the Peter the Great Museum of Anthropology and Ethnography and the Lomonosov Museum (closed Friday and Saturday). The Botanical Garden and Museum (the museum open only Wed., Sat. and Sun.). The Railway Museum.

Take an excursion to **Pushkin** to see the magnificent Yekaterinsky Palace (closed Tuesday and the last Monday of each month). In the Summer, hydrofoils cruise the **River Neva.**

St. Petersburg - Kiev   and v.v. 907

| Dep. St. P. (Viteb.) | 12:52 (1) | 21:53 (1) | Dep. Kiev | 09:08 (1) | 22:37 (1) |
| Arr. Kiev | 19:57 (2) | 23:32 (2) | Arr. St. P. (Viteb.) | 15:56 (2) | 09:29 (3) |

(1) Restaurant car. (2) Day 2. (3) Day 3.

Sights in **Kiev:** The 11th century catacombs at the Pecherskaya Lavra Monastery. The frescos and mosaics at the 11th century St. Sophia Cathedral. The Golden Gate (Zolotiya Vorota) at the intersection of Sverlovskaya and Vladimirskaya. The Museum of Russian Art. The Museum of Western and Oriental Art.

Below are schedules for continuing on from Kiev to Odessa:

Kiev - Odessa   and v.v. 925

The coaches on all of these trains are second-class only.

| Dep. Kiev | 03:35 (1) | 11:33 (1+3) | Dep. Odessa | 11:26 | 21:40 (4) |
| Arr. Odessa | 15:05 | 22:45 | Arr.Kiev | 22:50 | 09:02 |

(1) Restaurant car. (2) Light refreshments. (3) Plus another Kiev departure at 20:41, arriving Odessa 08:09. (4) Plus another Odessa departure at 23:30 (1), arriving Kiev 11:06.

Sights in **Odessa**: A sea resort and Russia'a largest port. See the beautiful Opera and Ballet Theater. The Potemkin Stairway, descending 455 feet from Primorsky Boulevard to the waterfront.

St. Petersburg - Moscow   901

Dep. St. Petersburg (Mos.)	00:35	12:56	15:50	20:20	21:55
Arr. Moscow (Len.)	10:57	22:09	21:50	04:56	06:22

Dep. St. Petersburg (Mos.)	22:30	22:45	23:10	23:55	23:59
Arr. Moscow (Len.)	06:35	07:10	07:19	08:25	08:29

St. Petersburg - Murmansk   and v.v. 903

Murmansk is the world's northernmost passenger rail terminus.

All of these trains have a restaurant car and arrive on Day 2, unless designated otherwise.

Dep. St. Petersburg (Moskovski)	13:54	23:20
Arr. Murmansk	21:00	06:47

Sights in **Murmansk**: The largest city in the world north of the Arctic Circle. Founded in 1915 as a supply post in the First World War. Valuable in World War II as Russia's principal port for receiving war supplies from Britain and the U.S. Its ice-free harbor has made Murmansk a major ship repair center and commercial fishing base.

Dep. Murmansk	08:35	01:00
Arr. St. Petersburg (Moskovski)	14:14	08:41

St. Petersburg - Tallinn   and v.v. 910

Dep. St. Petersburg (Varshavski)	21:28 (1)	23:25 (2)
Arr. Tallinn	05:35	08:45

Sights in **Tallinn**: A fortified town for more than 2,000 years. The capital of Estonia from 1918 until that country was annexed in 1940 by the former Soviet Union, Tallinn became the capital again when Estonia left the U.S.S.R. in 1991. In the walled Lower Town, see the 13th century Toom Church. The 13th century Great Guildhall. The 14th century Town Hall. Ruins of the 13th century fort built by invading Danes on Toompea Hill. The Gothic churches, Niguliste and Oleviste. The old castle.

Dep. Tallinn	20:10 (2)	23:00 (1)
Arr. St. Petersburg (Varshavski)	07:25	09:35

(1) Reservation *required*. Carries a first-class and second-class sleeping car. Coach is second-class. Light refreshments. (2) Reservation *required*. Carries a second-class sleeping car. Coach is second-class.

INTERNATIONAL ROUTES
FROM RUSSIA

Here are the schedules for rail trips from St. Petersburg to Helsinki (and on to the rest of Scandinavia) and to Warsaw (and on to Western Europe).

Also, from Moscow to Bucharest (and on to the rest of Eastern Europe as well as to Athens and Istanbul), Khabarovsk (and on to Nakhodka, and from there to Yokohama and Hong Kong), Beijing, Tehran and Warsaw (and on to Western Europe).

St. Petersburg - Helsinki and Moscow-Helsinki   902

All of these trains have a restaurant car.

Dep. St. Petersburg (Finlandski)	-0-	08:05 (2)	15:55 (2)
Dep. Moscow (St. Petersburg)	18:17 (1)	-0-	-0-
Set your watch back one hour.			
Arr. Helsinki	09:02	14:03	21:26

(1) Carries only first and second-class sleeping cars and a restaurant car. No coaches. (2) Reservation required. Has first-class and second-class coach cars.

St. Petersburg - Warsaw   857

Dep. St. Petersburg (Varshavski)	12:10 (1)	20:25 (1)
Arr. Grodno	08:15 (2)	13:57 (2)
Set your watch back one hour.		
Arr. Warsaw (Gdanska)	15:13	21:14

(1) Carries only first and second-class sleeping cars. No coaches. (2) Day 2.

Moscow - Warsaw - Berlin   56

A 2½-hour layover in Brest is for changing train wheels to conform with Western Europe's narrower tracks.

Dep. Moscow (Smol.)	13:10 (1)	20:15 (3)
Dep. Brest	08:00 (2)	14:36 (2)
Set your watch back one hour.		
Arr. Warsaw (Cen.)	10:53	19:25
Arr. Berlin (Licht.)	17:23	-0-

(1) Carries only first-class and second-class sleeping cars. No coaches. (2) Day 2 from Moscow. (3) Carries first and second-class sleeping cars. Also has second-class couchettes. Coach is second-class.

Moscow - Beijing 5000

Both of these trains carry a first-class sleeping car. They also have first and second-class coaches that convert at night to berths and bunks, and a restaurant car.

Dep. Moscow (Yar.)	19:50 (1)	21:25 (4)
Dep. Irkutsk	03:49 (2)	05:36 (2)
Arr. Beijing	15:33 (3)	06:32 (5)

(1) Runs Tuesday only. Route is via Ulan Bator. (2) Day 5. (3) Day 7. (4) Runs Monday, Friday and Saturday. Route is via Shenyang. (5) Day 8.

Moscow - Bucharest 955

All of these trains carry only sleeping cars.

Dep. Moscow (Kievski)	14:44	16:45 (5)
Arr. Bucharest (Nord)	07:41 (2+3)	11:15 (2+4)

(1) Light refreshments. (2) Day 3. (3) Arrives at Bucharest's Baneasa Railstation. (4) Arrives at Bucharest's Chitila railstation. (5) Reservation required.

Moscow - Warsaw - Frankfurt - Berlin - Cologne - Geneva - Paris - Madrid

	94a	55	56	24	56
Dep. Moscow (Smol.)	09:01 (1)	13:10 (3)	13:10 (7)	20:15 (8)	20:15 (7)
Dep. Brest	-0-	-0-	08:00 (4)	14:36 (4)	14:36 (4)
Set your watch back one hour.					
Arr. Warsaw (Wsch.)	05:32 (2)	11:50 (4)	10:15	19:10	18:15
Arr. Warsaw (Cen.)	-0-	12:20	10:40	19:25	18:30
Arr. Frankfurt/Main	-0-	06:00 (5)	-0-	-0-	-0-
Arr. Berlin (Licht.)	-0-	-0-	18:49	-0-	-0-
Arr. Cologne	-0-	-0-	-0-	-0-	09:58 (5)
Arr. Geneva	-0-	-0-	-0-	-0-	-0-
Arr. Paris (Nord)	-0-	-0-	-0-	17:08 (5)	-0-
Arr. Madrid (Cham.)	-0-	-0-	-0-	-0- (9)	-0-

(1) Carries only second-class sleeping cars. (2) Day 2. Arrives at Warsaw's Gdanska railstation. (3) Carries only sleeping cars. Moscow-Geneva: operates all year; runs Tuesday, Thursday and Sunday. Moscow-Madrid: operates late June to late August; runs Sunday only. (4) Day 2. (5) Day 3. (6) Day 4. (7) Carries only sleeping cars. (8) Carries sleeping cars. Also has couchettes. Coach is second-class. (9) Change trains in Brussels.

Moscow - Pyongyang   5000

Dep. Moscow (Yar.)	14:00 (1)	21:25 (5)
Dep. Irutsk	01:38 (2)	05:36 (2)
Dep. Khabarovsk	13:10 (3)	-0-
Dep. Shenyang	-0-	03:46 (6)
Arr. Pyongyang	10:40 (4)	15:55 (6)

(1) Carries a first-class sleeping car. Coach is second-class. (2) Day 5. (3) Day 7. (4) Day 9. (5) Runs Saturday only. Carries a first-class sleeping car. Has first and second-class coaches. Restaurant car. (6) Day 8.

TAJIKISTAN

Tajikistan is a Central Asian country bounded on the south by Afghanistan, on the west by Uzbekistan, on the north by Uzbekistan and Kyrgyzstan, and on the east by the Xinjiang (Sinkiang) region of northwestern China. Its capital city is Dushanbe. The Russian military continues to play a major role in the region.

More than 90 percent of Tajikistan is mountainous; all of its eastern territory is in the high Pamirs, known as "the roof of the world." The highest elevation was named Communism Peak (7,495 meters).

The Tajik people, who form over half of the population, are Sunni Muslims. Unlike their Turkic neighbors, they are of Iranian origin, descended from the Persian-speaking peoples that occupied the Trans-Oxus region long before the coming of the Uzbeks and other conquerors.

Tajikistan is a poor country. Its per capita income in 1989 was the lowest of all the Soviet republics. Sheep breeding remain the leading activity, and the reality is that most westerner travelers don't spend much time in Tajikistan.

TURKMENISTAN

Turkmenistan, with its capital in Ashkabad, is a country in Central Asia bounded on the west by the Caspian Sea, on the north by Kazakhstan and Uzbekistan, on the east by Uzbekistan, and on the south by Afghanistan and Iran.

More than 80 percent of Turkmenistan consists of the Kara Kum Desert. Along the border with Iran is the Kopet Dagh, a dramatic mountain range that rises to nearly 3,000 meters.

The population is concentrated in oases in the east, along the foot of the Kopet Dagh, and along the Murgab and Tedzhen rivers. The Turkmen population, Sunnite Muslims, speak a Turkic language.

Passenger train travel is limited, although since independence, travel has increased, mostly American and European businesses negotiating agreements to develop the country's natural gas reserves, and a rail line has been started to connect Ashkhabad with the Persian Gulf via Iran. Still too exotic for the casual backpacker!

UKRAINE

Kiev

Kiev, the capital of Ukraine and the country's largest city with more than 2.5 million people, is located on the banks of the Dnepr River, at the halfway point of its 2,255 kilometers (1,400 miles) route from northwest Russia to the Black Sea. Originally founded on the river's right bank, on terrain marked by steep hills, Kiev sprawls onto both sides of the Dnepr

As the country's capital, Kiev is Ukraine's political, industrial, and cultural center and a major transportation hub and river port. Kiev is also the Ukraine's most important educational and research center. It is the seat of the Ukrainian Academy of Sciences and a number of other research institutions. The city boasts of excellent and numerous theaters and concert halls, including the Ivan Franko Ukrainian Drama Theater, the Taras Shevchenko Opera, the Ballet Theater, and the Philharmonic Concert Hall.

Most of the city's historic monuments are in Old Kiev, on the right bank of the Dnepr. The city's oldest surviving church, St. Sophia's (Holy Wisdom) Cathedral, dates from 1037 and contains the tomb of Yaroslav the Wise, the 11th-century ruler of Kiev. Other architectural monuments include the 11th-century Golden Gate, one of the city's original gates, and St. Andrew's Church (1747–53), a fine example of the Russian baroque style. Kiev's most celebrated historic site is the Pechersky Lavra, or Monastery of the Caves. Dating from 1051, the monastery covers a sprawling campus and comprises many churches, cathedrals, bell towers, and monastic cells. Two separate networks of underground caves beneath the monastery contain the mummified bodies of more than 100 monks and six subterranean churches. Of utmost importance is the Babi Yar monument (1976) marking the site where thousands of Jews and Soviet prisoners of war were massacred by the Germans during World War II, an event that the Russian poet Yevgeny Yevtuskenko immortalized in his 1961 poem "Babi Yar."

See the 11th-centruy catacombs at the Pecherskaya Lavra Monastery in Kiev. The frescos and mosaics at the 11th-century St Sophia Cathedral is definietly worth a visit. The Golden Gate at the intersection of Sverlovskaya and Vladimirskaya and the Museum of Russian Art should be included in Kiev town visits.

L'viv

L'viv, located exactly 600 kilometers from both the Baltic and the Black Sea, was founded as a fort in the mid-13th century by Prince Danylo Halitski of Galicia, a former principality of Kyivan Rus. The first mention of Lviv in early chronicles is from 1256, although archeological excavation in 1993 revealed that the first settlements appeared in the 6th century.

The city's favorable location on the crossroads of trade routes led to its rapid economic development. Galicia was taken over by Poland in the 14th century. Its nobility eventually adopted the Polish language and Roman Catholicism but the vast majority of people remained Ukrainian Orthodox and later joined the Greek Catholic Church which acknowledged the Pope's spiritual supremacy but adhered to the area's Orthodox forms of worship. Thus, you begin to understand the cultural complexity of the city.

L'viv was occupied by the Nazis from 1941 to 1944. Almost the entire Jewish population was murdered in concentration camps in and around L'viv. Under Soviet rule, L'viv became an important center of activities of Ukrainian dissidents. Since the late 1980s the city has emerged as a leading force in Ukraine's movement toward sovereignty.

On the square next to the town hall the buildings captivate visitors with their beauty. Nearby is L'viv's world reknown Great Theatre, the I. Franko Theatre. This is not to be missed.

Odessa

This major seaport of the Black Sea has inspired tourists, world travelers, and immigrants for centuries. Russia's leading sea port, maritime traffic is impressive heading through the Bosporus at Istanbul. The Opera House and Ballet Theater are particularly worth seeing, as is the famous Potemkin Stairway, which descends 455 feet from Primorsky Boulevard to the waterfront. This is where you want to send your postcards from.

UZBEKISTAN

Uzbekistan is a country in Central Asia, bordered by Kazakhstan on the north and west, Turkmenistan on the southwest, Afghanistan on the south, and Tajikistan and Kyrgyzstan on the east with its capital in Tashkent. It has the largest population of the Central Asian states; among the former Soviet republics it is exceeded in population only by Russia and Ukraine. Uzbekistan is also the main heir to the rich Islamic civilization of Central Asia, containing within its borders the historic Muslim cities of Samarkand, Bukhara, and Khiva.

Tashkent

Tashkent, the capital, with a population of more than 2 million, is the largest single city in Central Asia and has been a center of Islamic civilization in that area since medieval times. Situated in the foothills of the Tian Shan mountains in an oasis irrigated by the Chirchik River, Tashkent today is a major manufacturing and transport center and cotton-textile mill, based on its cotton-fiber production. To its credit, the urban area is served by a subway system.

An opera and ballet theater and both Uzbek and Russian drama theaters are based in Tashkent six museums including a Uzbekistan history museum and an Uzbek arts museum grace the capital.

Annexed by Russia only in 1865, Tashkent now consists of an old Asian section, with winding narrow streets, and a modern city, dating from the mid–19th century. Rail connections with Russia were completed in 1898, and industrial development followed. The city's growth was spurred in World War II, when many industries were evacuated there from the European part of the USSR. A devastating earthquake in 1966 was followed by large-scale reconstruction.

Samarkand

Samarkand, the ancient city of southern Uzbekistan, situated in the valley of the Zeravshan River about 275 kilometers southwest of Tashkent, is one of the oldest cities of central Asia. Samarkand has many noted architectural remains from the 14th to the 17th century, when it flourished as the fabled capital of the Mongol empire of Timur. The ruins of the mosque of Bibi Khanom (1399–1404), with its distinctive turquoise cupola, and the great open Registan Square, lined with the remains of three Muslim religious colleges, can be seen.

Known in antiquity as Maracanda, Samarkand is believed to date back to the 6th century B.C., when it was the capital of ancient Sogdiana. It was destroyed in 329 B.C. by Alexander the Great. After the 8th-century Arab conquest it flourished under the Samanid dynasty of the 9th and 10th centuries before it fell to Genghis Khan in 1219.

Following completion of a railroad in 1888, the city's economy developed. Samarkand served as the capital of the Uzbekistan from 1924 until 1930, when the capital was moved to Tashkent. Access is possible by train, but adventurous travelers often opt for the small plane. Recently returning Americans explained that they paid $64 to get to Samarkand from Tashkent by plane and $1 for the return portion to Tashkent! Don't try to understand.

BALTIC STATES

Estonia

Bordering the Baltic Sea, between Sweden and Russia, Estonia, with Tellinn as its capital, is slightly larger than New Hampshire and Vermont combined including its 1,500 islands in the

Baltic Sea. It borders with Latvia and Russia. Only slightly more than a million and a half people occupy this small but proud Lutheran nation, which occupies a strategic geographic position in Eastern Europe.

Bolstered by a widespread national desire to reintegrate into Western Europe, the Estonian government has pursued a program of market reforms and rough stabilization measures, which is rapidly transforming the economy. Two years after independence—and one year after the introduction of the kroon—Estonians are beginning to reap tangible benefits; inflation is low; production declines appear to have bottomed out; and living standards are rising.

The Estonian World Festival is scheduled for early August, and folk culture is at the heart of Estonian spirit.

The oldest Estonian religious beliefs probably reach back to the Stone Age. These included the belief that the spirit of a witch could leave the body and gain wisdom from the place of the dead (shamanism) and belief in the image of an animal as the emblem of tribal ancestor (totemism). The cosmogonic myths about the creation of the world from the egg of a miraculous bird, and the creation of the Milky Way from a giant tree have been preserved in folklore, and are just as old. Everything in nature (trees, stones, arable land, bodies of water, fire, wind, and so on) was believed to have a spirit (animism). The most important holiday in Estonian tradition was Christmas, which was endowed with fertility magic. The most original part of Estonian folklore, the runic folksong, originated in the 1st millennium BC, as a result of interaction between primitive Balto-Finnic singing (warbling, keening) and the songs of the Baltic tribes. Heroic legends have blended with legends about hills. Estonian proverbs have been researched in detail, and 82,000 have been published.

Major train routes include the "Balti Ekspress from Warsaw and Sestokai, the Brest-Minsk connection, the "Tallinna Ekspress" between Moscow, St. Petersburg and Tallinn, the "Admiraltejets" to and from Riga. Jim Haynes's *People to People* guide on Estonia, Lativa, and Lithuania provides valuable contacts in these towns. For train information to and from Tallinn call (+372 2) 446 756, 456 851.

Estonia, located on the Baltic Sea, is considered to be one of the most progressive of the former Soviet Republics. U.S. citizens do not need an entry visa at this time. This small country is strategically located as a transportation hub. Many of you may remember the tragic loss of life from the loss of a passenger ferry in the fall of 1994. The port of Tallinn has regular links to Helsinki Finland, it was on the way to Helsinki that the ferry was lost.

Tallinn

In Tallinn, definitely plan to walk around the Lower Walled Town. Check out the 13th-century Toom Church and the fort built by the invading Danes on Toompea Hill. Visitors to Tallinn truly feel like they have rediscovered a long lost medieval Europe.

Latvia

The Republic of Latvia, with its capital in Riga, one of the "Baltic States" of northern Europe, is bordered by the Baltic Sea on the west, Russia on the east, Lithuania and Belarus on the south, and Estonia on the north. It was independent from 1918 to 1940, when it was forcibly annexed by the USSR, an event that indelibly marked the Latvians. Independence was restored in 1991. Russian intellectuals will confirm that Riga, after Moscow, is the cultural hub of the CIS. Many small publishing houses and literary journals have emerged there since independence.

Latvia's landscape with many lakes and rivers and its seaside location have strongly effected the commercial and cultural life of the country. The river estuaries provide ice-free commercial and fishing harbors, and Latvia enjoys a moderate climate, with cool summers and mild winters.

The Latvians speak a Baltic language related to Lithuanian, use Latin script, and have a mostly Lutheran background. Ethnic Russians constitute 33 percent of the population, reduced from nearly 50 since independence when many Russians were more or less forced to leave.

Riga

Riga, the capital of Latvia with nearly a million people, is situated on the Western Dvina (Daugava) River, near the river's mouth on the Gulf of Riga, an arm of the Baltic Sea.
Riga consists of an old medieval city center, with narrow, winding streets and distinctive Gothic architecture, and a newer section with a grid street plan and modern buildings. The city has a cool, maritime climate. An attractive seacoast of sand dunes to the west of the city is the site of a popular beach resort, Jurmala.

The port of Riga carries on an active commercial cargo trade with Western Europe and serves as the base for an Atlantic deep-sea fishing fleet. As the cultural center of Latvia, the city is the seat of Latvian University (1919) and of the Latvian Academy of Sciences. Founded in 1201 by the Teutonic Knights, Riga developed as a trading center between Russia and the Baltic Sea. It was a member of the Hanseatic League. It passed to Russia in 1721 and became one of that country's major seaports; manufacturing followed during the second half of the 19th century.

Lithuania

Lithuania borders the Baltic Sea between Latvia and Russia and also borders with Belarus and Poland. Interestingly, it has a dispute with Russia in that the Nemen River border is presently located on the Lithuanian bank and not in midriver as by international standards. Its nearly 4 million inhabitants have adjusted well to a system set on distancing itself from the old Soviet ways, and many travelers will remember the tension in Vilnius, the capital, reported in the international news in 1990.

Significant outbreaks of diphtheria have occurred during the winter of 1993-94. Street crime, including purse snatchings and muggings, occur, especially at night near major tourist hotels and restaurants. Robberies have occurred on trains, in train stations, and in hotel rooms. Be careful.

Vilnius

Vilnius, the capital of Lithuania, is located on the Neris River. With a population of over a half a million, the city is an important cultural and industrial center, accounting for about one-fourth of the manufacturing output of Lithuania.

Vilnius has the ruins of a 14th-century castle and buildings in a variety of architectural styles, ranging from Gothic to baroque. It is the seat of the Lithuanian Academy of Sciences and has a university, founded in 1579.

Settled during the 10th century, Vilnius became the capital of the Grand Duchy of Lithuania in 1323 and, despite destruction by the Teutonic Knights in 1377, developed into a major trading center. It declined after Lithuania was formally united with Poland in 1569. Vilnius passed to Russia in 1795. After World War I the city was disputed between the new governments of Lithuania and Poland; the Poles won control of it in 1920. The USSR took Vilnius from Poland in 1939 and ceded it to Lithuania, only to annex all of Lithuania the following year.

Vilnius was also an important Jewish center of Eastern Europe until the Nazi extermination of the Jews in World War II.

THE CZECH REPUBLIC

As most travelers know, the country Czechoslovakia is now two countries, the Czech Republic and the Slovak Republic. And although the two republics are intimately connected—they both take the same telephone country code—the languages are diffferent, the currency is different, and ultimately the experience of traveling in the two countries is distinct. The Czech Republic is made up of two distinct regions, Bohemia and Moravia, both of which offer travelers a wealth of attractions.

After the fall of communism in Czechoslovakia, the success of the Velvet Revolution, and the election of dissident playwright Vaclav Havel, Prague opened up spiritually and materially not only to the Czechs but to the West—and at a pace that has rarely been seen before. In two years, nearly 40,000 Americans moved to Prague is search of new horizons, a Bohemian existence, and economic success. Then the prices of apartments and consumer goods shot up.

Today, among the wonders of this exquisite city, it is difficult to mill around without hearing an English twang. For Czechs, the brunt of their new ethnic jokes are Americans, their new immigrants. Upon arriving at the Prague airport or train station you are greeted by the neon sign MASTERCARD WELCOMES YOU TO THE CZECH REPUBLIC, and quickly you begin to understand who really won the cold war! Prague is particularly overrun in the summer, but don't let that dissuade you—it is still one of the most enchanting cities in Europe, where the old and the new mix and the spirit of Franz Kafka still lurks.

Travel conditions in the Czech Republic, especially in Prague, are now up to snuff with conditions in other European countries. You can buy telephone debit cards in tobacco shops for international use in telephone booths. You can reach your AT&T operator at 00-420-00101, MCI operator at 00-420-0011, and Sprint operator at 00-420-87187. There are beeper services and Internet service providers galore if you want to be accessible as you get lost in the Bohemian landscape.

Train travel within the Czech Republic is relatively easy and well developed. There is even a Prague Excursion Pass, an enhancement to holders of the Eurailpass, Germanrail pass, or Austrian Railpass. This allows you to travel from any Czech border crossing to Prague and return for as little as $49.00 for adults within a 7-day period. The Czech railways distinguish themselves between the following types of trains:
• Personal train (*osobní vlak*). Local trains that stop at all stations and have only second-class seats.
• Speed train (*spesn vlak*). Usually provide longer routes over more than one track. They stop at important stations only. The importance of a station, however, depends on the particular route. For instance, a speed train from Prague to a mountain region will stop at every village in the mountains but will skip small stations on the remainder of the route. Speed trains have first- and second-class cars. In the timetables, speed train schedules are printed in bold.
• Fast train (*rychlék*). Long-distance trains that stop at certain stations only. Some of them have dining cars, some are overnight trains and have couchettes and sleepers. You can reserve your seat in a fast train, and reservations are required for some connections. In the timetables, fast train schudules are printed bold on a gray background.

• Express train (express). Only about two connections are called express today. The difference between express trains and fast trains is too insignificant to discern.

The actual speed of the Czech trains depends on the quality of the track. For example, a personal train on the main track from Prague to Ceske Trebove may be faster than a fast train from Prague to Chomutov.

Several trains have cars or sections for smokers. In general, smoking is forbidden in all trains and stations (including platforms), but be prepared for violators. Remember, this country's president smokes three packs a day.

A word on train tickets. In addition to ticket windows, there are machines at some stations that sell tickets for rides of up to 100 kilometers. You can pay with coins or with debit cards. If you arrive late, you can buy your ticket from the conductor. If you do not have a valid ticket, report to the conductor before he approaches you and pay a surcharge of only Kc 10. Otherwise, the surcharge will be Kc 100. If there is no ticket office at your departure station (or it is not open), the conductor will sell the tickets without any surcharge. Local fares in Czech krowns are reasonable. The fares for first class are 50 percent higher than second class. There are special fares for children and dogs. No special surcharge is required for fast trains if you buy a full-fare ticket. A passenger can book a seat on a fast train for which he has got a valid ticket as long as 30 days and as little as 15 minutes before the departure. It is always advisable to reserve, and a reservation costs only Kc 10.

A note: you probably will not be traveling with a canoe, but if you are, you'll be pleased to know that in the summer months it is permissible to lug such fluvial items on the train as checked luggage.

Rail travel to and from Prague mainly revolves around two international stations: Praha Hlavni nádraze and Praha Holesovice, both accessible by subway line C. Hlavni, Prague's largest station, serves the Cheb, Karlovy Vary, Kosice, and Tabor connections. Holesovice serves the Berlin and Budapest connections. Trains to Bratislava and Brno stop in both stations, usually. To be sure, recheck connections, times, and stations before heading to catch a train.

For domestic train travel there are several other important stations: Praha Masarykovo nádraze for trains to Chomutov, Zsté nad Labem and Kolén. Train and other travel reservations and services are obtainable from the Czech national tourist agency Satur, which until 1994 was the ubiquitous CEDOK.

A visa is required to enter the Czech Republic. As of October 1995, foreigners must prove that they have a minimum of $20 U.S. cash available per day for the first ten days or a fixed amount of $270 U.S. for longer visits. (The Czech Republic has just opened a second consulate in Los Angeles to serve the demand for visas.) This measure is designed to limit the flow of drifters making Prague their beat. A fascinating update on the conditions in Prague was posted recently in the Travel Forum on CompuServe: it reported that of the thousands of Americans who are now long-term residents of the Czech Republic, many wrote for their college newspaper and hoped that the experience would land them a job at the *Prague Post* or *Prognosis,* the now defunct arts weekly. They have since learned otherwise. Be prepared to bus tables, pour beer at a sports bar, or to be a night manager of a laundromat in between English tutoring gigs. Also be aware that apartment rental rates in central parts of Prague are now comparable to those in San Francisco. Unless you have a good source of income, you'll either be living on the outskirts or sharing a one-bedroom with three or four people.

HOLIDAYS

January 1	New Year's Day	May 9	Liberation Day
	Easter	October 28	Nationalization Day
	Easter Monday	December 25	Christmas Day
May 1	Labor Day	December 26	Additional Holiday

SUMMER TIME

Czechoslovakia changes to Summer Time on the last Sunday of March and converts back to Standard Time on the last Sunday of September.

TRAIN PASSES

Czech Flexipass Unlimited *first*-class train travel any 5 days within 15 days. the 1996 price is $69. Half-fare for children age 4–12. Children under 4 travel free.

CITY-SIGHTSEEING NOTES

Prague

Despite the rapid influx of foreigners, Prague is a delight. When those who have read Kafka's *The Castle* see Prague's Hradcany Castle complex (where the government is situated), they know it is worth the visit alone. Visit the awesome medieval Jewish cemetery and nearby synagogue, the oldest in Europe, and the majestic 14th-century Charles Bridge (Karlov Most) with its thirty statues of saints and hordes of street people. The charming back streets of Mala Strana district echo Mozart and Milos Forman's film *Amadeus*.Visit the little streets beyond the Hradcany Castle and stop in at Kafka's house, number 22, on the Golden Lane (Zlata Ulicka), now a bookshop. If you have a prerevolution guidebook, references to Kafka will be glaringly absent.

There is no lack of freshly updated travel guides to Prague, though, and you'll need one. Kakfa's grave is a few tram rides from the city center; it takes a bit of an effort to find, but it's worth it. Starímestskí namesti Square is the heartbeat of the old Prague with its ancient clock tower, its 1410 Gothic horologe, the Baroque St. Nicholas Church and Tyn Church, and the medieval Carolinum, the oldest remnant of the original Prague University.

One of the great pleasures of being in Prague is simply sitting in the café of the Hotel Europa and watching people. Waiters in polyester tuxedos rush around brusquely serving sparkling water, shots of slivovitz, and portions of strudel. You will find yourself in a quirky time warp that is indicative of today's Prague.

Getting around Prague is quick and easy: aside from walking, the public transportation system is excellent. There is an underground tram system with three lines connecting all areas of the city, a dense network of trams with Lazarská as the central change point, buses serving the outskirts, and a funicular that runs from Malá Strana to the hill of Petrín.

Prague taxi drivers don't enjoy the best of reputations due to their habit of overcharging and taking circular routes. Be vigilant and never give the impression that you don't know where you are. Insist that the driver uses the meter, watch that he doesn't change the rate on the taximeter, and always ask for a receipt.

To get to the Praha Ruzyne International Airport, in the northwestern suburbs, take the 119 bus from the subway station Dejvická on the A line.

Brno

Located in the Moravian part of the Czech Republic, often overshadowed by Bohemia, Brno is noted for its craftsmanship—fine woodcarvings, lace, pottery, and costumes, as well as its excellent art galleries.

Culturally speaking, Brno is rich, and theater buffs and art enthusiasts will love it here, especially because the over-the-top commercialism that has invaded Prague has yet to reach user-friendly Brno. A visit to the Macocha and Sloup grottoes via an underground cruise is a highlight. Don't miss the Brno Castle, Moravian Museum, and the open-air market Brno makes for a perfect stop between Prague and Budapest. Highly recommended.

Ceske Budejovice

Home of the original Budweiser (Budvar) Brewery, this virtually unchanged medieval city and capital of southern Bohemia is filled with Old World wonder: it has a fascinating history. Halfway between Vienna and Plzen, Ceske Budejovice is where the Vltava meets the Malse River. Railroad buffs will want to know that it was here that the first horse-drawn railway arrived in 1832, coming from Linz, Austria. The brewery here does not have the same charm as the Urquell Brewery in Plzen, and is probably not worth the time. The best thing to do in Ceske Budejovice is to simply walk through the old streets off the large square and around Samson's Fountain and down by the river.

Cheb

Cheb is a medieval town on the Ohre River in the western part of the country. An easy day trip from either Karlovy Vary or Marianske Lazne, it is a Germanic town with scenic burgher houses in its old section. The area around the train station is reported to be particularly ugly, so don't judge Cheb by your first impressions.

Karlovy Vary

Formerly Carlsbad, Karlovy Vary is a scenic city that is world renown since the 1300s for its curative waters. Peter the Great, Bismarck, Goethe, Tolstoy, Beethoven, Mozart, Edward VII, and Karl Marx are among the people who have visited this spa for its water. The city is also famous worldwide for its Bohemian crystal.

There are express trains from Prague and Cheb to and from the Karlovy Vary station on the north side of the town. Trains to and from Marianske Lazne use the Karlovy Vary station near the bus depot.

Liberec

Noted for its 17th-centruy Reichenberg architecture, Liberec lends itself to lovely walks in the old town and in the scenic Jested Hills area on the outskirts.

Marianske Lazne

You would most likely recognize this famous spa town by its old name, Marienbad, which has been frequented by an impressive list of international celebrities. Local life revolves around the spas, walks, and the Maxim Gorky Colonnade.

Plzen

Plzen, or Pilsen, a traditional trading center halfway between Prague and Nuremberg, is the capital of West Bohemia. The 19th-century ironworks factory founded by Emile Skoda gave its name to the famous Czech car the Skoda. Beer brewing in this town is so historic that it has left its name on the process: pils. The Pilsner trademark known as Urquell internationally comes from Plzen. Go on a brewery tour and do visit the Museum of Beer Brewing, located in an original medieval malt house (but don't count on ambitious sightseeing afterwards!). Also visit the underground corridors.

Tabor

Founded in 1420 on a religious principle of communal life, contributing to the modern sense of the word *Bohemian,* Tabor is a perfect day trip from Prague. Visit the Museum of the Hussite Movement—it is all one needs to understand the history and significance of Tabor and its 14th-century reformation.

ONE-DAY EXCURSIONS

Prague - Bratislava - Prague   880

Dep. Prague (Hole.)	00:28 (1)	05:58 (2)	07:39 (3)	15:10 (2)	-0-
Dep. Prague (Hlav.)	-0- (10)	-0- (10)	-0- (10)	-0- (10)	14:41 (10)
Arr. Bratislava	05:39	11:30	12:40	19:52	20:34

Sights in **Bratislava**: An important Danube port in ancient Roman times. See the 14th–15th century castle. The Hussite House. The Old City Hall. The Cathedral. The palaces on Mirove Square, Michalska Street and Gottwald Square. Few of the museums here offer information in English language.

Dep. Bratislava	00:43 (2+10)	03:55 (2)	09:43 (3)	11:52 (10)	14:51 (10)
Arri. Prague (Hlav.)	06:29	-0-	-0- (10)	18:07	20:40
Arr. Prague (Hole.)	-0-	09:24	14:20	-0-	-0-

(1) Carries a sleeping car. Also has couchettes. (2) Carries a sleeping car. Also has couchettes. (3) Restaurant car. (6) Arrives at Prague's Holesovice railstation. (7) Operates late March to early November. (8) Plus other departures from Prague (Hlavni) at 17:36 (10) and 22:10 (10) arriving Bratislava 22:3 and 04:20. (10) Supplement charged.

Prague - Brno - Prague   880

Dep. Prague (Hole.)	05:58	07:39 (1)	09:16 (2)
Arr. Brno	09:24	10:58	12:50

Sights in **Brno**: The folk-art exhibit of woodcarving, laces, pottery and costumes in the Moravian Museum. Brno Castle. Take a cruise on one of the underground rivers to see the Macocha and Sloup grottos. The outstanding 13th century Pernstejn Castle, near Brno.

Dep. Brno	13:28 (1)	15:21 (1)	16:54 (5)	19:14 (4)	20:17
Arr. Prague (Hole.)	16:37 (5)	18:40 (3)	20:42 (3)	22:28 (5)	23:37 (5)

(1) Restaurant car. (2) Departs/Arrives Prague's Masarykovo railstation. (3) Arrives at Prague's Hlavni railstation.(4) Departs from Brno's Kralovo Pole railstation. Operates late March to early November. Restaurant car. (5) Supplement charged.

Prague - Ceske Budejovice - Prague   875

Dep. Prague (Hlavni)	06:23	07:49 (1)	Dep. Ceske Bude.	13:18	16:17 (4)
Arr. Ceske Bude.	09:05	11:10	Arr. Prague (Hlavni)	16:07	18:46

(1) Second-class. (2) Runs Sunday only. (3) Runs daily, except Saturday. (4) Plus other Ceske departures at 18:02 (2), 18:55 and 20:14 (3), arriving Prague 20:45, 21:48 and 23:01. (5) Will not run July 5-October 28, December 24,25, April 16, 30 and May 7.

Sights in **Ceske Budejovice**: This city appears the same now as it did in the Middle Ages. Visit the Budvar brewery.

Prague - Karlovy Vary - Prague   874

| Dep. Prague (Hole.) | 04:29 | 06:23 (1) 09:43 | 12:04 |
| Arr. Karlovy Vary | 08:50 | 09:47   13:40 | 16:20 |

Sights in **Karlovy Vary:** Once called Carlsbad, famous for its curative waters since 1347. Peter the Great, Beethoven, Mozart and England's Edward VII are among the celebrities that have come here to drink the elixir and use the monumental baths in their search for improved health. An international film festival is held here every July. Visit the Moser crystal glass factory. There is an interesting porcelain factory in nearby **Slakov**.

| Dep. Karlovy Vary | 05:01 (4) 09:52 | 14:10 | 17:44 | 18:37 |
| Arr. Prague (Hole.) | 08:47 (2) 14:00 | 18:07 | 21:35 (3) 22:32 |

(1) Departs from Prague's Hlavni railstation. (2) Departs/arrives Prague's Masarykovo railstation. (3) Arrives at Prague's Hlavni railstation. (4) Second-class. (5) Plus another departure from Prague (Masarykovo) at 23:46 (4), arriving Karlovy Vary 03:39.

Prague - Liberec - Prague   876

Both of these trains are second-class.

| Dep. Prague (Hlavni) | 06:51 | Dep. Liberec | 17:23 |
| Arr. Liberec | 10:03 | Arr. Prague (Hlavni) | 20:10 |

Sights in **Liberec:** This town is noted for its 17th century Reichenberg architecture. Walks in the encircling Jested Hills are recommended.

Prague - Marianske Lazne - Prague   870

Dep. Prague							
(Hlav.)	04:06	08:55	11:22	13:08 (1)	14:32	17:012 (1)	19:16 (4)
Arr. Marianske	07:34 (3)	12:03	14:23	15:49 (6)	17:52	20:13	22:23

Sights in **Marianske Lazne**: Once called Marienbad, still a famous health spa.

Dep. Marianske	05:03	05:47	06:38 (1)	12:40 (1)	14:02 (1)	15:24	17:21 (5)
Arr. Prague							
(Hlav.)	08:16	08:46	10:03	15:56	16:45 (6)	18:25	20:26

(1) Restaurant car. (2) Light refreshments. (3) Carries a sleeping car. Also has couchettes. (4) Plus other Prague departures at 20:47 and 23:52, arriving Marianske Lazne 23:49 and 03:00. (5) Plus another Marianske Lazne departure at 19:57, arriving Prague 23:04. (6) Supplement charged.

Prague - Plzen - Prague   870

| Dep. Prague (Hlavni) | 07:23 (1) | 08:55 | 11:22 |
| Arr. Plzen | 09:00 (3) | 10:30 | 13:07 |

Sights in **Plzen:** Visit the enormous Urquell brewery, where more than 200 million pints of beer are bottled annually. They have been producing beer here (hence "Pilsener") for over 800 years.

| Dep. Plzen | 14:10 (1) | 15:06 (1) | 16:40 | 18:41 | 19:03 (1+2) |
| Arr. Prague (Hlavni) | 15:56 | 16:45 (3) | 18:25 | 20:30 | 20:37 (3) |

(1) Restaurant car. (2) Plus another Plzen departure at 21:18 (1), arriving Prague 22:57. (3) Supplement charged.

Prague - Tabor - Prague   875

| Dep. Prague (Hlv.) | 07:49 (1) | 09:00 (1) | Dep. Tabor | 14:26 | 18:01 (2+5) |
| Arr. Tabor | 09:53 | 11:48 | Arr. Prague (Hlv.) | 16:07 | 19:34 |

(1) Second-class. (2) Restaurant car. (3) Runs Sunday only. (4) Runs daily, except Saturday. (5) Plus other Tabor departures at 19:05 (3), 20:02 and 21:28 (4), arriving Prague 20:45, 21:48 and 23:01.

Sights in **Tabor:** A museum town, preserved to immortalize the unusual Hussite 14th century reform movement which held that all people are brothers and equal.

SCENIC RAIL TRIPS

Bratislava - Kosice - Bratislava   885

Very good mountain scenery, through the Low and High Tatras Mountains.

All of these trains have a restaurant car.

| Dep. Bratislava | 05:45 (1) | 07:50 (1) | Dep. Kosice | 12:15 | 16:00 (1+2) |
| Arr. Kosice | 10:50 | 14:11 (2) | Arr. Bratislava | 18:28 | 21:20 |

(1) Reservation required. (2) Supplement charged.

Poprad-Tatry to Stary Smokovec and Tatranska Lomnica

This spur off the Bratislava-Kosice route is the most scenic rail trip in Czechoslovakia. Forty minutes of the spectacular Tatras Mountains. Then, you can continue on to the **Tatranska Lomnica** ski resort and take a funicular to the top of 8,645-foot **Lomnicky Stit**.

"Pleso" means "lake." It is a popular one-hour stroll to Poprodske Pleso, another of the more than 100 glacial lakes in this area. Strbske Pleso is the main ski resort in the 16-mile-long Tatra mountain range.

885		887	
Dep. Bratislava	07:50 (1)	Dep. Tatranska Lomnica	15:07 (2)
Arr. Poprad-Tatry	12:50 (4)	*Change trains.*	
Change trains.			
887			
Dep. Poprad-Tatry	14:00 (2)	Arr. Poprad-Tatry	15:45 (2)
Arr. Tatranska Lomnica	14:25 (3)	*Change trains.*	
		885	
		Dep. Poprad-Tatry	17:10 (1)
		Arr. Bratislava	21:20 (4+5)

(1) Restaurant car. (2) Change at Studeny Park. There are 25 departures each day. (3) Estimated. There are 20 departures each day. (4) Supplement charged. (5) Reservation required.

Strba - Strbske Pleso

This other spur off the Bratislava–Kosice line is a second great Tatras Mountain scenic rail trip. There are much Winter sports in the area around Strbske Pleso.

All of the Bratislava–Strba (and v.v.) trains have a restaurant car.

885			887		
Dep. Bratislava	05:50 (2)	07:50 (2)	Dep. Strbske Pleso	Frequent times	
Arr. Strba	09:42	12:34	Arr. Strba	13 minutes later	
Change trains.			*Change trains*		
887			885		
Dep. Strba	Frequent times		Dep. Strba	14:02 (2)	16:02
Arr. Strbske Pleso	13 minutes later		Arr. Bratislava	18:28	20:30 (2)

(1) Carries a sleeping car. Also has couchettes. (2) Supplement charged.

INTERNATIONAL ROUTES
FROM THE CZECH REPUBLIC

Prague is the Czech Republic's gateway to Berlin (and on to Copenhagen and all of Scandinavia), Belgrade, Budapest, Bucharest (and on to Athens), Nurnberg (and on to the rest of Western Europe), Vienna, and Warsaw (and on to Moscow).

Because the Czech Republic is not a Eurailpass country, passengers traveling from Prague to Austria, Germany (and on, to Switzerland or France) and Hungary must pay for a ticket from Prague to the border of those Eurailpass countries. None of the travel from Prague into Poland is covered by Eurailpass. Travel to Austria, Hungary and Poland is covered by European East Pass.

Prague - Berlin   680

All of these trains require reservation, unless designated otherwise. All night trains carry a sleeping car and have couchettes. All day trains have a restaurant car.

Dep. Prague (Hlavni)	-0-	-0- (1)	-0-	-0-
Dep. Prague (Holesovice)	00:35	02:05	08:47 (1)	12:47
Arr. Berlin (Licht.)	05:51	07:14	13:06 (3)	17:26 (2)

Dep. Prague (Hlavni)	-0-	-0-	-0-	-0-
Dep. Prague (Holesovice)	14:37	16:47	18:47 (4)	22:49 (1)
Arr. Berlin (Licht.)	19:26 (2)	21:26 (2)	23:15 (2)	02:51

(1) Restaurant car. (2) Arrives at Berlin's Hauptbahnhof railstation. (3) Arrives Berlins' Schonefeld. (4) Not December 24, 31.

Prague - Budapest - Belgrade or Bucharest   96b

Dep. Prague (Holesovice)	05:58 (1)	07:39 (1)	15:11 (3)	14:41 (4+5)
Arr. Budapest (Keleti)	14:42	16:28	22:42	23:50
Arr. Belgrade	-0-	-0-	-0-	07:11 (2)
Arr. Bucharest (Nord)	06:20 (2)	-0-	-0-	-0-

Dep. Prague (Holesovice)	15:10 (3)	22:22 (4+6)	23:08 (7)
Arr. Budapest (Keleti)	22:37	07:47 (2)	08:28 (2)
Arr. Belgrade	-0-	-0-	-0-
Arr. Bucharest (Nord)	-0-	23:25	-0-

(1) Carries a sleeping car. Also has couchettes. (2) Day 2. (3) Restaurant car. (4) Departs from Prague's Hlavni railstation. (5) Carries only sleeping cars. Runs Wednesday, Thursday and Friday. (6) Carries a sleeping car. Also has couchettes. (7) Carries a sleeping car. Also has couchettes. Restaurant car.

Prague - Frankfurt - Paris

	57	30	30+57
Dep. Prague (Hlavni)	13:08 (1)	16:55 (2)	20:47 (3)
Arr. Frankfurt/Main	20:43	-0-	05:35
Dep. Frankfurt/Main	-0-	-0-	-0-
Arr. Paris (Est)	-0-	09:37	-0-

(1) Reservation advisable. Supplement charged. Restaurant car. (2) Operates late May to late September. Carries a first-class sleeping car. Also has second-class couchettes and coaches. Restaurant car 17:54 to 23:40. (3) Carries a first-class sleeping car. Also has second-class couchettes. Coaches are first and second-class.

Prague - Nurnberg or Munich and Zurich   57

Dep. Prague (Hlavni)	07:23 (1)	13:08 (1+2)	16:23 (1+3)	20:50 (4+5)
Arr. Nurnberg	-0-	17:56	22:03	02:50
Arr. Munich	13:51	21:12	23:12	06:07
Arr. Zurich	18:23	-0-	-0-	-0-

(1) Supplement charged. Restaurant car. (2) For Munich, change trains in Marktredwitz at 16:36. (3) For Munich, change trains in Schwandorf at 20:54. (4)Carries a sleeping car. Also has couchettes. Light refreshments. (4) Carries a sleeping car. Also has couchettes. (5) Plus another Prague departure at 23:52 (4), terminating in Nurnberg 05:47.

Prague - Vienna   96a

Dep. Prague (Hole.)	-0-	03:24 (2)	13:11 (3)	17:11 (4)
Dep. Prague (Hlavni)	00:11 (1)	-0-	-0-	-0-
Arr. Vienna (F. J. Bf.)	06:06	-0-	-0-	-0-
Arr. Vienna (Sud.)	-0-	08:52	18:02	21:58

(1) Runs daily, except Sundays and holidays. (2) Second-class. (3) Restaurant car. (4) "Antonin Dvorak."

Prague - Warsaw   95a

Dep. Prague (Hlavni)	13:40 (1)	18:13 (2)	21:16 (2)
Arr. Warsaw (Centralna)	22:50	06:43	07:20
Arr. Warsaw (Gdanska)	23:04	06:57	07:34

(1) Reservation required. Restaurant car. (2) Carries a sleeping car. Also has couchettes.

SLOVAK REPUBLIC

The eastern half of the former Czechoslavakia, the Slovak Republic today is tucked in below Poland to the north, Hungary to the south, the Ukraine to the east, and Austria and the Czech Republic to the west.

Europe's newest country, Slovakia managed to break away from the Czechs in 1993. The country has a tremendous amount to offer nature-lovers and sport-oriented visitors. Its Tatra mountain region is ideal for hikers and skiers; its unspoiled medieval villages are priceless for their beauty and authenticity. Visitors are received in an open and friendly manner. Travelers will experience the discovery of a long-lost part of Eastern European history and tradition at reasonable prices by including Slavakia, beyond Bratislava, in their itineraries. Bratislava, of course, the country's cultural and intellectual center, necessitates a visit on its own terms.

The easiest access to Slovakia is via the Vienna-Bratislava connection. Only 64 kilometers away, 4 direct trains make this 2-hour jaunt daily. For trains from Germany and other western European countries that pass through the Czech Republic, a transit visa may be required. Other trains to Slovakia from eastern European countries that pass through the Czech Republic may also present visa problems for travelers: if travelers do not hold Czech transit visas and the train enters the Czech Republic in the middle of the night, on-board visas will not be issued and voyagers risk being put off the train. This is not like the CIS, where a huffy conductor may be tamed at the sight of Abraham Lincoln or Queen Elizabeth. Inquire. Bratislava enjoys four direct trains from Budapest (Hungaria, Balt-Orient, and Pannonia leaving from Keleti station, and the Metropol train leaving from Nyugati station), which is only three hours away. All travel via Sturovo. Many guides recommend the morning Hungaria and afternoon Metropol for getting to Bratislava; they originate in Budapest and run on time. The others connect to Budapest from Romania and are often late. Several express night trains pass through Slovakia at Trencin, but reservations are mandatory in order to board, and, again, if you don't have the Czech transit visa you may find yourself sitting in the chill of the night on the tracks at the border wondering how this happened.

The eastern Slovak city of Kosice enjoys train connections twice a day with the Hungarian towns of Miskolc and Satoraljaujhely, if that helps you. The Rakoczi express train makes the Budapest-Kosice run in under 5 hours, leaving Budapest-Keleti in the morning and Kosice in the afternoon with a partial service continuing to Poprad-Tatry. And, the Polish Cracovia express train passes through Kosice between Budapest and Kracow in the middle of the night, as does the Karpaty Express between Krakow and Warsaw.

Reservations are required and precision planning is needed to coordinate these travel options. Jumping on an express train at whistle stop in the middle of the night excites the imagination, but also requires willpower. Crawling into a sleepy compartment of strangers is not the easiest way to make friends, but at times a late-night connection may be the most practical way of joining up segments of your trip.

Kosice also serves as a stop between Prague and Moscow (the Dukla Express) and Bratislava and Moscow (the Slovakia Express). Both trains pass through Kiev in the Ukraine.

Visitors to Slovakia are required to have at least $15 U.S. or equivalent per day of their stay in Slovakia when entering the Slovak Republic.

Bratislava

Slovakia's largest city, Bratislava, aside from being the cultural and administrative capital of this young country, sits at a strategic geographic location on the Austrian border, minutes from Hungary, on the Danube River, at the foot of the Carpathians. The geography contributes to the city's historic diversity with Hungarian influence felt in the architecture and names.

The main train station is actually located slightly north of the city and is easily reached by tram. But note that there is another train station that is on the eastern side of the city, called stanica Bratislava-Nove. It is not as often used for major train connections, but things are always changing.

With its 450, 000 inhabitants, Bratislava offers a rich cultural program and ambitious economic aspirations. Start your visit with the Bratislava Castle; built on a hill it dominates the center of Bratislava, and its four towers have become a symbol of this Danube port city. Inhabited from Neolithic Hallstadt and Roman eras, the castle was first mentioned in 907. Today, after reconstruction, it shelters the historical part of the Slovak National Museum. Bratislava Castle is also the residence of the president of the Slovak Republic, with the Slovak parliament residing in the new building nearby.

The Slovak National Museum, a key point of interest, is located opposite the hydrofoil terminal on the river. Contrasting the traditional aesthetics of this museum is the very contemporary Slavak National Gallery, which holds Bratislava's most important art collection. Add to your cultural itinerary the art nouveau Reduta Palace concert hall and the turn-of-the-century National Theater, which recently celebrated its 75th anniversary.

Walking around the city is a pleasant experience. In the evening, Bratislava excels in its choice of wine cellars. Tourists are advised not to chance money on the streets—black marketeers have been known to stick gullible visitors with wads of worthless banknotes from defunct despotic republics.

Regular train connections between Bratislava and Kosice are frequent and efficient. The night train with its couchette service is a particularly good idea, and some savvy travelers who've found it difficult to land an affordable hotel room in Bratislava have even booked a couchette to Kosice as a lodging and transportation solution.

Trencin

This town of 50,000 hosts a noted castle at one of the gateways to Slovakia. Once the most northern Roman military camp, Trencin today is a textile center. The city serves aa a stopover between Bratislava and Kosice via Zilina.

Poprad-Tatry

Industrial and of little interest to travelers, Poprad requires a mention nonetheless in that it is a train hub, north and south, and the pivot point for the electric train that climbs 13 kilometers to the Tatry mountain resort of Stary Smokovec.

Kosice

The second largest city in Slovakia with nearly 250,000 inhabitants, this formerly Hungarian town is now an industrial hub specializing in metalurgy. The old town nonetheless presents much of interest to visitors, and many have used Kosice as a base for regional travel. Trains run every day to Krakow, Poland, and Budapest, Hungary. Visit the remarkable Gothic Cathedral of St. Elizabeth.

HUNGARY

Overview

Hungary has always held a special place for travels in the East. Even in the days of the communist bloc, Budapest remained the most popular holiday destination for eastern visitors. Thus, it wasn't surprising that Hungary became the first of the former communist countries to join the Eurail pass system countries, becoming the seventeenth. Just behind Prague in its massive tourist attraction to western travelers, Budapest offers cultural splendor and aesthetic pleasure, full-bodied red wine, peppery food, lively folk music, and an atmosphere of openness. Budapest represents all the positive aspects of Prague without the excess of grotesque commercialism. The prices have increased, but are still manageable. Just a jump away from Vienna, Hungary was always the first step into the East. Aside from the train, many travelers opt for the pleasant Danube river trip between the two cities via Bratislava by hydrofoil, which can be convenient (but sometimes less so). One British historian recently reported that the 5-hour river trip is almost always delayed due to insufficient water level on the Danube. The boat slows to a standstill waiting for the water level to rise. You might just prefer the train.

Ethnically unique, Hungarians are of Finno-Ugrian descent and speak Magyar, linguistically related only to Finnish and Estonian. There are slightly more than 10 million people in Hungary, of which two-thirds are Catholic. The once vibrant Jewish population of nearly 800,000 today stands at just 10 percent of that, representing nonetheless the largest Jewish community today in Eastern Europe. Hungary has one of the highest rates of suicide in the world, and also performs the highest per capita amount of abortions.

Literary and cultural life is intense with more writers in Hungary per capita than in any other European country. The president of Hungary himself is a leading contemporary writer.

Train travel to and from Hungary, aside from the Eurail passes, has gone up substantially in price over the last five years. There are direct rail links between Budapest and 25 capital cities of Europe, and 54 scheduled international trains arrive every day in Budapest. All international trains have dining and sleeping cars. Most international express trains arrive and depart from the Eastern (Keleti) Railway Station with the exception of the following trains, which use Budapest-Dáli: Adriatica, Agram, Lehár, Eurocity, Maestral, Graz.

The following trains use Budapest-Nyugati: Amicus, Aquincum, Budapest Express, Claudiopolis, Corona, Gerecse, Metropol, Partium, Varadium, Visegrád, Baia Mare, Saxonia, Miskolc, Karpaty, Pécs, Sopianae, Zagreb.

The following are railroad station information numbers:
Budapest Southern (Dáli): 175-6293
Budapest Eastern (Keleti): 113-6835
Budapest Western (Nyugati): 149-0115
For information on international fares: 122-8035

trains that run to Vienna in three hours. These trains include the Liszt Ferenc from Dortmund and Nuremberg, the Orient Express from Paris and Munich, and the Wiener Waltzer from Basel and Innsbruck. There are special Eurocity return trip fares between Vienna and Budapest as well. There are also many local trains that run between smaller cities in Austria and Hungary; reservations are not needed. The Prague-Budapest voyage is made in nine hours, a popular route among Eurailers. One traveler sharing his Prague-Budapest overnight train experience reported that he woke in the night "to find the porter had chained the car doors shut. We were on a siding somewhere around Brataslavia. He was able to make me understand he had wanted to sleep and to insure the safety of his charges had chained and padlocked the doors."

Some travelers recommend first class for its comfort; others prefer second class where it's easier to encounter local people. The Balt-Orient and Meridian express trains serve Budapest from Berlin, Prague, and Bratislava, and then continue east to Romania and Bulgaria. There are daily Budapest-Warsaw connections on the Bathory and Polonia express trains depending on which route you choose. The Bem express train from Szczecin, Poznan, and Wroclaw serves Budapest via Trencin. The Varsovia arrives from Gdansk. For Czech and Slovak connections, see those chapters in this guide. Train connections with points further east include the Ovidius Express, which runs from the Black Sea at Constanta, and the Claudiopolis train via Cluj to Budapest. The Corona from Brasov arrives in Budapest 14 hours later. For points south, Budapest is a hub. The Budapest-Belgrade express train currently is a strange shuttle for all sorts of traffic. To Croatia there is the Budapest-Zagreb express train (Adriatica, Agram, Drava, and Maestral). If you plan on departing from Budapest for a journey by train through Russia and China, see David Stanley's comments on and recommendation of Star Tours in Budapest, which is published in his excellent Lonely Planet edition on Eastern Europe. In any case, train travelers experience a rush of excitement just thinking about such journeys.

In general, connections and access in Hungary are excellent. There are eight daily

"Once you have your train ticket and reservations you can apply for a Chinese tourist visa (allow three days for processing), then a Russian transit visa ($60 U.S.), which you may be able to get in one day. If time is short, ask for the Russian train via Manchuria, which eliminates the need for a Mongolian transit visa (another three days' processing). Three-day Ukraininan transit visas are usually available at the border for $50."

There is also a car–train service operating on the Vienna-Budapest Eastern Station-Thessaloniki route during the main tourist season, July 1 to September 25. Car loading time at Budapest Keleti Station: 11:45 to 12:00 A.M. At Thessaloniki: 6:30 to 7:30 P.M. for the return voyage.

Subway service between the Keleti and Dáli railway stations exists on the M2 metro line (seven stops).

Other Intercity and express trains from Budapest to the major tourist regions in Hungary include Northern Transdanubia, Lake Balaton (north shore), Southern Transdanubia, Northern Hungary, and Great Plain.

One Budapest company called Nostalgia Trains Ltd. organizes specialized train trips in the summer months. Contact: Nostalgia Ltd., H-1055 Budapest, Teréz krt. 55. Telephone/fax: (36) 1/269-5242.

Of special interest are fifteen narrow-gauge specialized railways operating in Hungary, generally from May to September. For information contact TOURINFORM, telephone 117-9800.

Specialized information on Hungary called The Hungary Report can be obtained on-line from hungary-report-request@hungary.yak.net. For other up-to-date sources of information on Hungary consult the *Budapest Business Journal* at 100263.213@compuserve.com. You can reach the *Budapest Sun* at 100275.456@compuserve.com. You can reach *Budapest Week* at 100324.141@compuserve.com and/or Central Europe Today (free online) cet-info@eunet.cz.

The Hungary Report writes about a local train service that operates from Budapest to Csepel Island to the south of the city and to the nearby towns of Szentendre and Ráckeve. Here you can experience the majestic Danube River Bend.

Transportation buffs will be pleased to note that the first underground railway or public subway on the continent, Millenary Underground Railway (the second in the world after London's) was built in Budapest in the late 1800s and has been restored to its original state for its 100th anniversary.

Additionally, the Funicular from the Buda side of the Chain Bridge to the Buda Castle Palace has been operating since the turn of the century.

Hungarian Holidays

January 1	New Year's Day	August 20	Constitution Day
	Easter	November 7	Revolution
	Easter Monday		Remembrance Day
April 4	Liberation Day	December 25	Christmas Day
May 1	Labor Day	December 26	Additional Holiday

HUNGARY'S TRAIN PASSES

Hungarian Flexipass First-class only, unlimited train travel. The 1996 adult prices are: $55 for any 5 in 15 days, and $69 for any 10 days in a month (example June 3–July 2). Half-fare for children age 5–14. Children under 5 travel free. Sold worldwide by travel agencies and Rail Europe (U.S.A. and Canadian offices listed under "France").

CITY-SIGHTSEEING NOTES

Budapest

The city is divided into two cities, Buda and Pest, by the Danube, and locals and tourists alike will playfully disagree about which they like better and for what reasons. The great width of the river in Budapest contributes to the split personality of the city. Buda in general is the historically endowed side while Pest is the commercially vibrant side. The city's public transportation system is highly expansive and efficient, reaching far on both sides of the river with key lines converging at Deak tár.

The theater district is focused on Andrassy ut, and the offering of theatrical performances on any given night is impressive. Go see a play in Hungarian! You'll never have been more concentrated on the acting and set design than during those two hours of pure Magyar bliss.

In Buda, a visit up Castle Hill is a must. This is where the vestiges of medieval Budapest lurk. There are several possibilities for exploring the Buda Hills around the city: the Cogwheel Railway from Városmajor (2 stops from Moszkva tár on the No. 56 tram) to Széchenyi Hill and the Chairlift (Libegé) from Zugliget (at the terminus of No. 28 bus from Moszkva tár) to the look-out on János Hill (Budapest's highest point: 526 meters) are two good approaches. Plan on visiting both the National Gallery and the Historical Museum, both of which are located in the Palace of Buda Castle. From the castle you can catch the funicular down to the tunnel under Castle Hill at the foot of the famous Chain Bridge.

On Gellert Hill, above the Hotel Gellert, which, aside from being known for its unusual swimming pool that made artificial waves, was a hotbed for high-end espionage in the 1960s and 70s, you'll find the Citadella, a fort built by the Austrians, now a hotel and commemoration to the Soviet soldiers who gave their lives to liberate Hungary in 1945. In 1956, the statute on this spot was knocked down, but was later restored. From here you are afforded the finest view Budapest has to offer. On the Pest side of the world you'll want to visit the City Park, the Grand Circus, the Budapest Zoo, the Museum of Fine Arts, and St. Stephen's Basilica. For a picturesque visit of the city, try riding the newly restored Number 2 Tram on the Pest side of the river.

A fun activity for the family is a ride on the Children's Railway. This narrow-gauge railway runs a distance of 12 kilometres through the Buda forests. Don't overlook the very lovely Margaret Island and its spacious 112-acre park. Special pedal-operated vehicles for 2 to 6 persons can be hired to ride in this park.

Gyor

Well connected by express train, halfway between Budapest and Vienna, Gyor is Hungary's third-largest city. With an interesting old town, historic churches, and the striking new Kisfaludy Theater, Gyor is worth a stop.

Fertod

The Esterhazy Palace with its more than 100 rooms and grand Versailles-style baroque details merits a visit to Fertod.

Szeged

This gateway town to and from Romania and the former Yugoslavia is best known for its paprika salami and the Votive Church, which was built in the 1920s in remembrance of the devastating flood of 1879 that changed the face and history of Szeged.

Lake Balaton

This long and lively lake, the largest freshwater lake in Europe, is a popular summer swimming resort and family vacation spot. The south shore is sandier and more developed while the north shore is more scenic and historically rich. For ecological reasons motorboats are prohibited, making the lake ideal for sailing. There is constant train traffic between Balaton and Budapest and a train route around the lake as well. Kezthely, at the western end of the lake, is a large town with lots of lakefront and boating services. Siofok and Balatonszentgyorgy are also accessible by train and offer lakeside pleasures.

Heviz

This famous spa town, with its 1,500 thermal baths, is a natural wonder. Located on a thermal lake, Gyogy, the water temperature averages 30 degrees Celsius at the surface. In the winter the haze off the water renders the experience particularly strange and appealing. In addition, there are lake baths and thermal baths in Heviz.

Kecskemet

A perfect day trip from Budapest, this town in central Hungary is best known for its fruit production, more specifically its production of apricot brandy.

Pecs

In the Southern Transdanubian part of Hungary near Croatia, Pecs is Mediterranean in feel. Pecs is on the direct line to Zagreb and thus has become a departure point for Croatian travel. The first King of Hungary, Stephane I, proclaimed Pecs a bishopric in the year 1009.

ONE-DAY EXCURSIONS

Budapest - Kecskemet - Szeged - Budapest   895

As these schedules show, it is possible to visit both Kecskemet and Szeged in the same day.

Dep. Budapest (Nyugati)	07:00 (1)	10:30 (1)	11:00 (2)	14:00 (1,2 +6)
Arr. Kecskemet	08:13 (2)	11:40 (2)	12:27	15:13
Arr. Szeged	09:10	12:48	13:35	16:10

Dep. Szeged	05:20 (2)	06:20 (1)	09:50 (1)	13:20 (7)
Dep. Kecskemet	06:25	07:23 (2)	10:48	14:25 (1)
Arr. Budapest (Nyugati)	07:48	08:42	12:00	15:48 (2)

(1) Reservation required. (2) Light refreshments. (3) Second-class. (4) Runs Monday-Friday, except holidays. (5) Runs Saturdays, Sundays and holidays. (6) Plus other Budapest departures at 16:25, 18:25 (2) and 19:25 (2), arriving Szeged 18:46, 20:50 and 22:20. (7) Plus other Szeged departures at 15:30 (2), 18:10 (1), 19:35 (4) and 20:20 (5), arriving Budapest 17:48, 20:45, 22:45 and 23:07.

Budapest - Lake Balaton (Siofok and Balantonszentgyorgy) and v.v.

It is a short train and bus ride to reach Hungary's most popular resort area, the 46-mile long **Lake Balaton**, circled with spas, motels and campgrounds along its 118 miles of shoreline. Great sailboating and fishing here. Frequent ferries link the many towns on both sides of the lake.

893

Dep. Budapest (Deli)	07:00	07:15	13:15	14:25 (3)	15:45 (4)
Arr. Siofok	08:41 (2)	08:48	15:06	16:09	18:03 (5)
Arr. Balatonszentgyorgy	09:48	10:40	16:35	17:20	19:27

• • •

Dep. Balatonszentgyorgy	06:23 (2)	07:02	10:41	12:40 (2)	14:58 (2+6)
Dep. Siofok	07:26	08:39	12:08	13:52	16:08 (7)
Arr. Budapest (Deli)	09:08	10:28	14:03	15:28	17:48

(1) Restaurant car. (2) Light refreshments. (3) Departs/Arrives Budapest's Keleti railstation. (4) Plus other Budapest departures at 18:05, (2), 19:35, and 20:30 (3). (5) Plus other Siofok departures at 20:10, 21:22, and 22:42. (6) Plus other Balatonszentgyorgy departures at 16:49 (3), 18:43 and 20:18 (3). (7) Plus other Siofok departures at 18:04 (3), 20:12, 21:20 (3).

INTERNATIONAL CONNECTIONS
FROM HUNGARY

Budapest is Hungary's gateway for rail travel to Belgrade (and on to Athens and Istanbul), to Moscow, to Prague (and on to Berlin and Scandinavia), to Vienna (and on to the rest of Western Europe), and to Zagreb (and on to Italy).

Budapest - Belgrade 940

Dep. Budapest (Keleti)	06:25 (3)	11:25 (3)	15:10	17:15 (3)
Arr. Belgrade	12:18	17:12	21:38	23:30

(1) Carries a sleeping car. Also has couchettes. (2) Reservation required. Second-class. (3) Reservation required. Restaurant car. (4) Restaurant car.

Budapest - Moscow 94c

This train carries only sleeping cars.

Dep. Budapest (Keleti)	16:15
Arr. Moscow (Kievski)	11:21 Day 3

Budapest - Prague 880

Dep. Budapest (K.)	06:55 (1)	13:20 (1)	15:00 (5)	18:25 (2)	21:20 (3)
Arr. Prague (Hlav.)	-0- (4)	-0- (5)	-0-	-0-	06:29
Arr. Prague (Hole.)	14:20	22:28	23:21	02:53	-0-

(1) Restaurant car. (2) Departs from Budapest's Nyugati railstation. Carries a sleeping car. Also has couchettes. Restaurant car. (3) Carries a sleeping car. Also has couchettes. (4) Supplement payable. (5) Supplement payable in Slovakia.

Budapest - Vienna 61.

Dep. Budapest (Keleti)	05:55	08:20 (1)	09:55	12:25 (1)	13:30
Arr. Vienna (Westbf.)	09:20	11:50	12:57 (2)	15:50	19:00

Dep. Budapest (Keleti)	15:30	17:20 (3)	18:30	19:10 (4)	21:00 (3)
Arr. Vienna (Westbf.)	19:00	20:50	21:45 (2)	21:58 (2)	00:27

(1) Reservation required. Supplement charged. (2) Arrives Vienna's Subbahnhof station. (3) No restaurant car. (4) Departs from Budapest's Deli station.

POLAND

Children under 4 travel free. Half-fare for children 4–10. Children 11 and over must pay full fare.

As the *CIA World Factbook* reminds readers, Poland is slightly smaller than New Mexico and borders with Belarus, the Czech Republic, Slovakia, Germany, Lithuania, Russia, and the Ukraine. For train travelers, that comparative scale doesn't really help orient travel nor plan itineraries. The size of Poland and the placement of its national borders, however, has always been a sensitive issue in history. Poland's boundaries have responded with the elasticity of political events, and anyone with access to a chronological atlas of Europe will note that Poland, with its vulnerable flatness and lack of natural boundaries has both sprawled with expansion and retracted out of existence only to return a century later as a geographic double of its former self. In 1943, at the Teheran Conference, Churchill, Stalin, and Roosevelt decided that land east of the Oder River and Neisse River was to be returned to Poland after centuries of German control, while the eastern provinces would become part of the Soviet Union and thus postwar Poland became 20 percent of its prewar self, and yet closer to the nation it once was back in the 1200s! And this border agreement was ratified in the famous Warsaw Pact of 1955. More than a country, its the cities that have maintained a consistent cultural phenomenon, with Krakow being one of the historic intellectual capitals of Europe. An hour away by car or train, one visits Auschwitz and Birkenau, perhaps the quintessential living symbol of humanity's ability to inflict horror and cruelty. Poland is many things indeed.

Poland's Solidarnosc trade union, led by Lech Walesa, played a pioneering role in the transformation of Eastern Europe. Walesa went on to become Poland's elected president. The fact that there is a Polish Pope has not been an inconsequential factor as well in the transformation of the region. Poland, if anything, must be viewed as a vital stage on which many of the world's major issues appear and reappear. Today, despite the growing pains of converting to a market economy, Poland has a vibrant people with a fertive urge to create both art and commerce. And at this writing, Poland is by far the largest country in eastern Europe.

Poland is highly accessible by trains, and trains have played a deeply felt role in 20th-century Polish history. It is quite easy to move around the country by rail, and in general the atmosphere and openness of the Poles and their new system has removed the heaviness and oppression previously experienced when traveling in Poland.

If you have not opted for a train pass that includes Poland (the Inter-Rail pass includes Poland), you should note that train tickets purchased for Poland in the eastern countries are much cheaper than those prebought in the West. And domestic train tickets are rather reasonable. So, when planning your Polish itinerary, you can stop at the first Polish city of interest to you after crossing the border and buying the continuing tickets there.

To get to Poland from Western Europe, note that the celebrated Ost-West express train leaves Paris-Nord station everyday and arrives in Warsaw 22 hours later. This train functions like a puzzle, and cars from around northern Europe, the United Kingdom, Holland, Belgium, and so on, get coupled on along the way. Some travelers have reported that the morning train from London is a better connection than the afternoon one, which requires a change in Germany.

There are many trains between Germany and Poland, with Berlin being only an hour from the Polish border. If you're not familiar with German geography, note that Frankfurt/Oder and Frankfurt/Main are not the same place! The former is the border crossing with Poland in eastern Germany; the latter is the large city. The Eurocity Berolina makes the Berlin-Warsaw journey in under 7 hours. The Gedania Express between Berlin and Dynia by way of Szczecin takes 10 hours and has sleeping cars. There is also an overnight train between Cologne and Warsaw and Cologne and Krakow via Leipzig, Dresden, and Wroclaw.

From the other eastern countries, Poland is accessible via numerous routes. The Prague-Warsaw train, the overnight Bohemia, takes 12 hours. The Silesia Express goes between Prague and Warsaw by way of Katowice, while the Baltic Express from Prague to Gdansk via Wroclaw and Poznan takes 16 hours. From Vienna the Sobieski and Chopin express trains run both at night in the days and pass by Breclav and Katowice. Other connections may be noted in the chapters on Hungary, the Czech Republic, and Slovakia. Good deals on the Trans-Siberian Railraod can be found in Warsaw.

If you are inexperienced in international train travel in the East, the following story of an innocent traveler attempting to make two sets of reservations between Poland and Romania may be instructive: "We went to the ticket office to book our train. The woman did not speak English and there were loads of people behind us waiting (despite there being being about 15 empty windows). Using a pen and paper as our only common language we were told we didn't need a reservation on that day from Warsaw to Krakow, so we just asked for one from Krakow to Bucharest for the following day. Instead of just reservations, she issued us tickets, which we didn't want, so we had a row about that until someone helped out, and we ended up with some reservations. After we'd paid, a Polish kid came up and asked if he could help us, as he spoke English. It turned out we'd been given reservations from Warsaw to Krakow for the following day. Totally useless."

The Polish national railroad takes the ubiquitous initials PKP. Express trains with reservations assure you the fastest and most comfortable way of traveling, whereas the direct trains and local trains are slower and more crowded but afford you a greater taste of local life.

The national tourist agency Orbis serves as reservation center for all train travel, and the ease and inexpensive fees are strong reasons to use this service. The express trains heading to or coming from the capital all have dining cars and comfortable seats. And the new Intercity trains between Warsaw and Krakow in under 3 hours are state of the art. As in France or Germany, second class is perfectly comfortable. One experienced rail user adds, "First-class accommodations are inexpensive and should be used where possible. The language problem is the largest difficulty, and missing a train in a larger station a reality." Another Polish rail aficionado, Jeff Dobek, enjoys answering questions and chatting with others about Poland's railways. Contact Jeff Dobek at 76645.3660@compuserve.com. Jeff adds that travelers shouldn't leave luggage unattended in the train, even when you go to the dining car.

Others have added that travelers should be careful not to take currency that is marked in any way; only perfectly clean notes will be accepted by change bureaus or banks. Still others openly write of fearful and sleepless nights on Polish trains—one is not certain if thieves are really plotting to steal your luggage, money, passport, and travelers checks or if the ambiance of total insecurity prods the imagination into zones of paranoia.

POLISH HOLIDAYS

January 1	New Year's Day		Assumption
	Easter	November 1	All Saints' Day
	Easter Monday	November 11	Day of Independence
May 1	Labor Day	December 25	Christmas Day
	Corpus Christi	December 26	Additional Holiday

SUMMER TIME

Poland changes to Summer Time on the last Sunday of March and converts back to Standard Time on the last Sunday in September.

CITY-SIGHTSEEING NOTES

Warsaw

Warsaw has been the capital of Poland since the beginning of the 17th century. At present it has about 2 million inhabitants, which ranks it seventh in Europe both in population and area. The Main Town and Old Town are on the higher, left bank of the Vistula River, with parks and squares sloping gently down to the river. Within an easy day's travel from Berlin, Prague, Vienna, and Budapest, Warsaw is relatively accessible by train. The population of Warsaw suffered brutally under the Third Reich and the city was ultimately leveled. Some 35 percent of the Warsaw population was Jewish before the war, with the Warsaw Ghetto representing the last holdout of surviving Jews. Miraculously, the old city was reconstructed in a highly convincing way.

Most travelers arrive at the lower level of the Central Station, which has four levels. The station is well equipped with services—and pickpockets. So be warned: the thieves here are organized and efficient, working in small groups. And be wary when getting on and off trains: pairs of thieves arrange to climb on in front of and behind you, one serving to distract your attention while the other grabs the goodies.

Note that when you check your luggage at the train station, you'll be asked to assign a value to your belongings and pay a fee according to that value. This is normal. Plac Zamkowy is at the mouth of the old city (Stare Miastro) and is a good place to start your walking tour. Visit the Barbicon Wall, Blacha Palace, the Royal Way, and the ancient market here. A visit to the reconstructed Chopin Family Drawing Room in the side wing of the former Raczynski Palace should be on your list. For a bright view of the city, climb to the top of the 37th floor of the

Palace of Culture and Science. Also visit the Monument to the Heroes of the Ghetto and the Lenin Museum. For Warsaw information you can now consult the *Warsaw Voice,* Poland's only general-interest English-language weekly newspaper, now on-line on the World Wide Web.

Warsaw is also noted for its music, its art scene, and it cultural festivals.

Krakow

Undoubtedly one of Europe's most beautiful cities, Krakow was spared by the Nazis during World War II at the negotiated request of the Vatican. Krakow is the former capital of Poland, the royal residence, and a symbol of Polish culture that constantly shines with the reflection of its one-time splendor.

Krakovians see their city as the place which is said to be a mystical city: once a center of magic and astrology where Faustus began his studies; one of the seven places in the world protected by magical stones...

Start in the middle of the city at the medieval Wawel Castle. Krakow gets its name from Prince Krak, who founded a settlement on Wawel Hill. Krakow emerged as a student town in the Middle Ages, and Jagiellonian University was founded here in 1364. Spend some time walking though the Market Square or rynek Glowny and its quaint archways, and the Renaissance Cloth Hall, where crafted goods are sold. The live trumpet sounds that call out every hour from the top of the Church of Our Lady and end abruptly is a tradition dating from the 13th century, when the trumpeter was pierced in the neck by a Tatar arrow. The Kazimierz district is now silent with echos and ghosts; it was here that the Jewish community, and later, the ghetto, was situated. Spielberg filmed much of the movie *Schindler's List* on location. Nearly all the Jews of Krakow were sent to the death camps, and Oswiecim (Auschwitz in German) is only an hour from the city. The site of the Plaszow work camp can be visited outside the city.

Krakovians will suggest that a visitor buy grain for Kracow's pigeons (this is a tradition), or give a flower from the Krakow flower sellers to a passing beauty (another tradition). Rest in the "Planty" in the shade of a 100-year-old chestnut and the 600-year-old university. Walk through Kazimierz through Wolnica between Sw. Wawrzynca, Dajwor, Miodowa and Krakowska Streets. Spend some time on a street which is a really a small, elongated square, called Szeroka Street. Here you will find the Remu'h Synagogue and cemetery. In the renaissance Old Synagogue you will see a beautiful collection of Jewish art and objects.

Check the schedule for cultural events in Krakow; the city hosts a rich selection of festivals, including the Short Film Festival and Music in Old Krakow.

Auschwitz

After this day trip from Krakow, a 60-kilometer trip, you will never be the same. Be prepared to do nothing else all day. After a tour of the concentration camp, make sure you also witness the extermination camp of Birkenau, 2 kilometers away. One and a half million people, mostly Eastern European Jews from nearly 30 countries, were murdered here. One traveler reminds others not to be tempted to pay 50 zloty for an organized trip to Auschwitz from Krakow. A coach from the central bus station to Oswiecim costs just 4 zloty each way and leaves from

Stand 3. The Oswiecim rail station is 2 kilometers north of the Auschwitz camp, a 20-minute walk. There are 6 daily trains from Krakow Glowny station, 12 per day from Krakow Plaszow station, and 15 per day from Katowice.

Zakopane

Zakopane, an Alp-like mountain resort in the Tatras, has attracted visitors, hikers, skiers, and vacationers for centuries. The Tatra National Park costs 1 zloty to enter, and is highly regulated to protect the natural setting. For example, it is forbidden to pick berries, herbs, mushrooms, and so on. The guidebook *Zakopane and Its Vicinity,* by Maciej Pinkwart, available in many languages including English, is highly recommended. Should you decide to take the raft trip down the Dunajec Gorge in the Pieniny National Park, book in advance via Orbis Tourist. The queues are quite horrendous on fine days.

The train to Zakopane from Krakow took nearly 5 hours via Nowy Targ in the prewar days. Today, the Kasprowy makes the run in half that time twice a day leaving from Krakow, and the Giewont leaving from Zakopane. There is also a funicular railway up Mt. Gubalowska that offers a memorable view of the mountain valley.

The Zakopane bus trip to Morskie Oko, the largest lake in the Tatras, is available via the village of Plana Palenica; the lake is a 9-kilometer walk from there.

The seasonal Tatry Express takes 6 hours from Warsaw to Zakopane. To cover the entire north-south expanse of Poland you can ride the overnight Zakopane-Gdansk train, which stops in Wroclaw, Poznan, and Warsaw.

Wroclaw

In the heart of Lower Silesia, this tongue-twister dates back to the 13th century. On the Odra, this city boasts of more than 120 canals. Cultural life and student activity are vibrant here. The pubs fill with young people nightly. St. Dorothy's Church demands a visit.

Lublin

An ancient city with the oldest private university in the country, Lublin is worth visiting because it is authentic and deeply historic. From the castlelike architecture of the main train station slightly out of town, Lublin's old town affords visitors a taste of the decadence of times gone by. Visit the castle and the Krakoski Gate as well as the many impressive old churches.

Poznan

Between Berlin and Warsaw, Poznan is famous for its Przemyslaw Castle and sculptures at the Dzialynski Castle. Walk through the old town and then visit the unique Musical Instrument Museum. The stained glass at the Church of the Holy Virgin is of particular beauty, as is the brick Gothic cathedral at Ostorw Tumski. For train travelers, Poznan is actually easy to visit—many trains pass through the city.

Torun

This Teutonic medieval city is located on the Vistula River between Gdansk and Poznan. Visit the Gothic churches. Birthplace of Copernicus (1473), travelers can visit his house and inspect the instruments he used to determine that the earth revolves around the sun. The Church of St. John contains one of the largest bells in Poland. The honey gingerbread is a local specialty.

The Kujawiak express train serves Torun from Warsaw every day, but requires reservations.

Czestochowa

This sacred place of pilgrimage attracts Catholic worshipers from all over the country. They come to the Luminous Mountain Monastery (Jasna Gora) to worship the image of the Black Madonna, the holiest icon in Poland. There are direct train connections from Warsaw, Krakow, and Zakopane.

Gdansk, Gdynia, and Sopot

Gdansk, Gdynia, and Sopot, known as the tri-cities, are sprawled for 30 kilometers along the Gulf of Gdansk on the Baltic Sea, with Gdansk serving as Poland's leading port and shipbuilding center. Its shipyard is the birthplace of Lech Walesa's Solidarnosc labor party. Also known as Danzig, it was declared a free city in the Treaty of Versailles after World War II. There is international ferry service to and from Finland and Sweden.

Gdynia, a leading port and fishing center, is the most northern of the three cities and the only one technically on the Baltic.

Sopot is the chic seaside resort that has attracted international bathers for centuries. Connected by electric train, Sopot offers wide white beaches, but the local pollution is so intense that swimming is no longer thinkable.

Major trains stop in all three cities, while southbound trains usually originate in Gdynia. The Warsaw-Gdansk trains Neptun, Slupia, and Kaszub take 3½ hours, while the Lajkonik Express between Krakow and Gdansk takes 7 hours.

ONE-DAY EXCURSIONS

Warsaw - Czestochowa - Warsaw   864

It is only a 2½-hour drive from Warsaw by taxi on Poland's best highway.

Dep. Warsaw (Wsch.)	06:05	09:05 (2)	Dep. Czestochowa	05:37	17:47
Dep. Warsaw (Cen.)	06:25	08:15	Arr. Warsaw (Cen.)	09:25	21:40
Arr. Czestochowa	09:47	12:55	Arr. Warsaw (Wsch.)	09:39	21:54

(1) Restaurant car. (2)Change trains in Koluszki.

Warsaw - Gdansk - Gdynia - Warsaw   855

Dep. Warsaw (Cen.)	-0-	02:22 (2)	-0-	08:57 (3+6)
Dep. Warsaw (Wsch.)	01:29 (1)	02:32	07:02 (3)	09:07
Arr. Gdansk	05:36	06:35	10:31 (9)	12:30
Arr Gdynia	06:08	07:03	10:57	12:55
	• • •			
Dep. Gdynia	04:44 (3)	05:40 (3)	06:48 (3)	08:42 (5+7)
Dep. Gdansk	05:10	06:10 (9)	07:10	09:10 (8)
Arr. Warsaw (Wsch.)	08:33	09:22	10:33	13:12
Arr. Warsaw (Cen.)	10 minutes after arriving Wschodnia railstation			

(1) Carries a sleeping car. Also has couchettes. Light refreshments. (2) Carries a sleeping car. Also has couchettes. (3) Reservation required. Light refreshments. (4) Operates late June to late August. Reservations required. Light refreshments. (5) Light refreshments. (6) Plus other Warsaw (Cen.) departures 10:57 (3), 15:02 (3), 16:02 (3), 18:57 (5) and 21:02 (2),...arriving Gdansk 15:31, 18:56, 19:28, 20:17, 21:30, 23:01 and 01:30...arriving Gdynia 16:05, 19:30, 19:51, 20:48, 21:57, 23:30 and 02:07. (7) Plus other frequent Gdynia departures from 10:44 to 22:25. (8) Plus frequent other Gdansk departures from 11:10 to 22:55. (9) Runs daily except Sundays & holidays.

Warsaw - Krakow - Warsaw   865

Dep. Warsaw (Cen.)	07:00 (1)	09:00 (1)	11:00 (1)	13:00 (1)	15:00 (5)
Arr. Krakow (Glowny)	09:35	11:40	13:35	15:40	17:37 (1)
Dep. Krakow (Glowny)	01:10 (2)	02:15 (2)	06:15 (1)	07:15 (3)	08:15 (1+6)
Arr. Warsaw (Cen.)	06:00	05:25	08:45	09:45	10:45

(1) Reservation required. Restaurant car. (2) Carries a sleeping car. Also has couchettes. (3) Runs daily, except Sundays and holidays. Reservation required. Restaurant car. (4) Runs daily, except Saturday. Reservation required. Restaurant car. (5) Plus other Warsaw departures at 15:45 (4), 16:45 (4), 17:45 (4), 18:45 (1), 21:25 and 22:48, arriving Krakow 18:41, 19:35, 20:35, 22:35, 01:50 and 03:58. (6) Plus other Krakow frequent times from 10:10 to 23:00.

Warsaw - Lublin - Warsaw   869

Dep. Warsaw (Centralna)	-0-	06:47	10:47	14:47 (3)
Dep. Warsaw (Wschodnia)	02:45	06:57	10:57	14:57
Arr. Lublin	05:08	09:15	13:15	17:15

Dep. Lublin	07:00 (1)	10:30	12:30	15:00 (4)
Arr. Warsaw (Wschodnia)	09:00	12:44	14:47	17:05
Arr. Warsaw (Centralna)	10 minutes after arriving Wschodnia railstation			

(1) Reservation required. Light refreshments. (2) Light refreshments. (3) Plus other Warsaw (Cen.) departures at 16:47 (2), 18:47 (1) and 20:47 (2), arriving Lublin 19:11, 21:02 and 23:14. (4) Plus another Lublin departure at 16:30, arriving Warsaw (Cen.) 18:57.

Warsaw - Poznan - Warsaw   850

Dep. Warsaw (Wsch.)	06:15 (1)	06:30 (5)	09:10 (1)	13:25 (2)	15:15 (3)
Dep. Warsaw (Cen.)	15 minutes after departing Wschodnia station				
Arr. Poznan (Gl.)	09:37	11:00	12:45	17:00	18:38 (10)

Dep. Warsaw (Wsch.)	16:35 (11)	17:15 (1)	19:10 (3)	21:35	23:15 (5)
Dep. Warsaw (Cen.)	15 minutes after departing Wschodnia station				
Arr. Poznan (Gl.)	19:50	20:35	22:45	01:40	03:15

Dep. Poznan (Gl.)	02:05 (5)	06:30 (4)	07:08 (1)
Arr. Warsaw (Cen.)	05:55	10:15	10:20
Arr. Warsaw (Wsch.)	14 minutes after arriving Centralna station		

Dep. Poznan (Gl.)	10:07 91)	11:12 (1)	15:03 (1+9)
Arr. Warsaw (Cen.)	13:25	14:25 (12)	18:30
Arr. Warsaw (Wsch.)	14 minutes after arriving Centralna station		

(1) Reservation required. Restaurant car. (2) Light refreshments. (3) Reservation required. Second-class. (4) Reservation required. Light refreshments. (5) Carries a sleeping car. Also has couchettes. (6) Reservation required. Carries a sleeping car. Also has couchettes. (7) Runs daily, except Sundays and holidays. Reservation required. Restaurant car. (8) Runs Monday-Friday, except holidays. (9) Plus other Poznan departures at 17:17 (1), 18:18 and 19:31 (1), arriving Warsaw (Cen.) 20:20, 21:20 and 22:40. (10) Runs daily except Saturday. (11) Will not run December 24, 31. (12) Will not run December 25, Jan. 1.

Warsaw - Sopot - Warsaw   852

Dep. Warsaw (Cen.)	16:02 (2)	21:02 (1)
Dep. Warsaw (Wsch.)	10 minutes after departing Centralna station	
Arr. Sopot	19:48	01:39

Dep. Sopot	06:57 (2)	01:07
Arr. Warsaw (Wsch.)	10:42	05:47
Arr. Warsaw (Cen.)	15 minutes after arriving Wschodnia station	

(1) Carries a sleeping car. Also has couchettes. (2) Reservation required. Light refreshments. (3) Light refreshments. (4) Operates late June to late August. (5) Plus other Warsaw (Cen.) departures at 14:57 (3), 15:57 (2), 16:57 (2), 17:57 (2), 18:57 (3) and 21:07 (1), arriving Sopot 19:16, 19:41, 20:36, 21:47, 23:20 and 01:53. (6) Plus other Sopot departures at 10:54 (3), 12:50 (3), 15:55 (2), 17:55 (2), 18:36 (4) and 21:50 (1), arriving Warsaw (Wsch.) 15:12, 17:12, 19:33, 21:36, 22:22 and 02:32.

Warsaw - Torun - Warsaw   859

Dep. Warsaw (Wsch.)	06:25 (1)	16:40 (3)	22:45 (2)
Dep. Warsaw (Cen.)	06:40	17:00	23:10
Arr. Torun	09:36	19:48 (1)	02:18

Dep. Torun	06:56 (1+3)	18:24 (1)	03:55 (2)
Arr. Warsaw (Cen.)	09:45	21:15	07:10
Arr. Warsaw (Wsch.)	09:59	21:29	07:29

(1) Light refreshments. (2) Carries a sleeping car. (3) Reservation required.

INTERNATIONAL CONNECTIONS
FROM POLAND

Warsaw is Poland's gateway for rail travel to Berlin (and on to both Scandinavia and north-western Europe), Moscow, and Vienna (and on to Italy, southeastern Europe and south-western Europe).

Warsaw - Berlin 850

Dep. Warsaw (Wsch.)	06:00 (1)	16:35 (1)	22:05 (2)	23:40 (3)
Dep. Warsaw (Cen.)	06:15 (4)	16:50 (5)	-0-	23:50 (6)
Arr. Berlin (Licht.)	-0-	-0-	06:25	08:00
Arr. Berlin (Hbf.)	12:40	23:25	-0-	-0-
Arr. Berlin (Zoo)	12:25	23:01	-0-	-0-

(1) Reservation required. Restaurant car. (2) Departs from Warsaw's Gdanska railstation. Carries only sleeping cars. (3) Carries a sleeping car. Also has couchettes. (4) Will not run December 25, January 1. (5) Will not run December 24, 31. (6) Reservation required.

Warsaw - Moscow 900

Dep. Warsaw (Gdan.)	-0-	-0-	-0-	14:55 (4)
Dep. Warsaw (Cen.)	09:02 (2)	10:22 (1)	14:54 (2)	-0-

Set your watch forward one hour.

Arr. Brest	14:26	16:00	20:53	-0-

A short distance from the Brest railstation, the train is held for about 2 hours while the train's wheels are changed so as to conform to the wider Soviet track.

Dep. Brest	16:30	18:08	20:58	-0-
Arr. Moscow (Smol.)	10:00	11:49	12:15	21:54

(1) Carries only sleeping cars. (2) Carries only sleeping cars. Has restaurant car Brest–Moscow. (3) Carries a sleeping car. Also has couchettes. Coaches are second-class. (4) Light refreshments.

Warsaw - Vienna 95a

Dep. Warsaw (Wschodnia)	08:55 (1)	20:20 (2)
Dep. Warsaw (Centralna)	09:10	20:35
Arr. Vienna (Sudbf.)	17:04	06:52

(1) Reservations required. Restaurant car. (2) Carries a sleeping car. Also has couchettes.

ROMANIA

Passengers who board a train that requires reservation whithout obtaining a reservation are charged a penalty fee.

To buy a Romanian timetable, ask for "Mersul Trenurillor." The **1996 Romanian Rail are**: $60 for 3 days rail travel in any 15 days. Children 4-11: half adult fare.

ROMANIAN HOLIDAYS

January 1	New Year's Day	August 23	Liberation Day
January 2	Additional Holiday	August 24	Additional Holiday
May 1	Labor Day	December 30	Republic Day
May 2	Additional Holiday		

SUMMER TIME

Romania changes to Summer Time on the last Sunday of March and converts back to Standard Time on the last Sunday in September.

It has taken time, but the dark and perverse images of Romania that used to correspond to the reality of Ceausescu's Romania are fading quickly as the country, its people, and its institutions respond to a new world of possibilities. Romania today offers travelers more than they might have previously anticipated. Romania's history, language, and geographic beauty position it as a country worth the time one is willing spend to discover its treasures. Aside from its time-warped capital, Bucharest, Romania offers visitors the lush and romantic medieval mountain villages of Transylvania, the iconoclastic monasteries of proud Moldavia and intellectual Bukovina, and the Roman- and Turkish-influenced resort towns on the Black Sea. The infrastructure of material life in this least developed of the new Eastern European countries is still unpredictable and seemingly illogical, and many Romanians have a strangely ironic take on reality, having emerged from the horrors of one of the century's most twisted dictators. But give them a chance and show some sensitivity toward their history and you'll be touched by the local readiness to open up and share the best of the indigenous culture. If you are seeking an experience that is real, inexpensive, and filled with emotional challenge, a trip through Romania by train is highly recommended.

Romania is farther east and south than most westerners imagine, with the Ukraine and Moldova to the north and east, the Black Sea to the east, Bulgaria to the south, Yugoslavia to the southwest, and Hungary to the west. Making the journey by train from western Europe requires some time and a few long stints on the tracks. Due to the very low salaries that they receive, Romanian intellectuals and artists eager to visit other cities in Europe are almost always obliged to take the train, and thus you'll often meet fascinating folks on the Bucharest-Vienna run, for example.

Catrinel Plescu, program director at the Romanian Cultural Foundation in Bucharest, shared her recent experience on the Dacia express train to Vienna: "We left Bucharest at 4:30 and I was a bit nervous about the journey, fearing the old, worn-out carriages. Having to cross three frontiers, a nightmare in itself for an Eastern European, I am worried about the rumors we hear about train attacks in the night. Surprisingly, the carriage is brand-new and cheerfully colorful, navy blue and red, not that terrible military green that reminds one of war convoys and typified Romanians trains. The sheets and the blankets are clean; the towels are threadbare but clean too. The loo is impeccable. I am almost moved. It's the Romanian human touch of gentle corruption—I notice that the toilet paper, paper towels, and liquid soap has already been stolen. The stern schoolmarm in me wants to tell the conductor that this is not civilized, that it spoils our image, that it only confirms that Romanians have no 'klo-kultur,' as the Germans would say. But he helps us with the luggage, he has a nice face with a drooping mustache, two children, a small salary…so I let it be, the tired Romanian in me says…at least he is friendly and human. I've got my own toilet paper (ancestral wisdom) anyway."

Catrinel goes on to report of an incident at the first border crossing. "I refuse to pay the compulsory tourist tax that the custom officer tells me has just been passed in parliament. I want him to show me the law, and secondly, I tell him I'm not a tourist. My fear of people in uniforms turns to anger. This has helped me many times to be brave before 1989. I control my anger and try to sound rational, feminine, and sweet. The man in uniform threatens to put me off the train. This is Hegeshalom; I don't want to spend the night in Hegeshalom. I remember my father's advice: 'Never show them you are frightened; if they feel your fear you are finished'. At the same time I wonder if this is worth the fight. I state that I am expected at a journalists' conference and if he wants an uproar, that's OK with me. He goes off to talk to a superior, and I hear him say that that woman threatened him.They glare at me and I glare back and smile sweetly. My tummy aches. The other Romanians are staring at me because I have dared to be different. This is painfully familiar. I reaffirm what I already know; they want to make the others hate you for defending your rights. I wonder what will happen. I wait. Nothing happens. What a relief; what happiness.

"I've shown them for once, for the first time, that we are stronger than they. The conductor comes back and we drink a glass to each other's health and he tells me, 'Madame, I was so frightened for you! Why did you do that? You know people in uniforms are always right!' Well, this time they weren't. The Hungarian customs officer then asked a Japanese couple to get off the train because there was something wrong with their visas. They got off in tears, not understanding what it was all about. If I could only have explained it to them! Cultural misunderstanding!"

As for domestic travel in Romania, stories vary from western tourists, but in almost all cases a deep sense of contentment seems to pervade those who have decided to commit a part of their itineraries to this still crude land of surprises. Contact with Romanians seems to outstrip the geography or landmarks as the most rewarding aspect of Romanian travels.

One of the most moving travelogues written on Romania was penned on-line on CompuServe's Travel Forum by Melissa Harris, an assistant professor of architecture on exchange in Vienna who spent two weeks exploring the Romanian landscape and mindset by train. "When we arrived in Arad, Romania, at 5:00 A.M., we couldn't decide if it was necessary to get off the train to buy our tickets onto Bucharest. When purchased in the country of travel, tickets are significantly less expensive. We decided to get off, but failed to reboard in time and the train left without us. It would be five hours before the next train departed. It was still dark in Arad as we fumbled our way about the station, looking first for a place to purchase tickets and then for baggage storage which would free us to roam the city during our layover. At the end of the waiting room, we were instructed, there was luggage storage. When I first pushed open the swinging doors, a terrible odor confronted us. Sudden darkness blinded us temporarily. The air was thick and heavy—dank, stagnant air that stank of alcohol and caused us to choke. Perhaps it, like the people who emerged from it, had not stirred for hours. If one can conceive of space as a solid, this waiting room seemed impenetrable.

"As our eyes adjusted, we saw motionless people packed densely on the floors and benches. We moved through the room like a small wave causing ripples in a tangle of arms and legs. Coughing and moaning jostled the unconscious, though daybreak was still an hour away. Time froze as the faint light signaling the end of the room never seem to get any closer. We were moving in slow motion through invisible mud, fighting the paralysis of this violent act of contrast—the 'haves' slicing through the 'have nots.' But if one believes in fate, our ignorance of the train system blessed us with the opportunity to meet our first guardian, Imre, a 23-year-old budding businessman from Brasov. For me, Romania is best summarized by the characters of three people we met, who in each individual situation framed my perceptions and actions."

Imre went on to escort her to his colorful, rural Transylvanian village of Sacele, where, aside from slaughtering a lamb, our heroine learned the routine of daily Romanian life in the countryside.

When it came to looking for more classical means of lodging, like a hotel, Melissa writes that "this is where the myth of cheap travel in Eastern Europe is exposed. Our running joke throughout the trip was the parrotlike response we got when we asked 'How much does this cost?' The answer was always another question: 'Where are you from?' 'America' insured the highest possible rate. If you are a tourist, it is almost impossible to find a hotel room for less than $80 to $100 per night. In other Eastern European countries, accommodations in private homes cost much less, but this doesn't exist yet in Romania. If you are Romanian with proper identification, the same room costs $6."

Bucharest's Gara du Nord train station is reknown for its confusion, so take your time and keep your head. "No visitor leaves without a brush against the sticky fibers of an invisible web of complications almost too bizarre to handle," Melissa recounts. "Many innocent visitors, in fact, become stunned and temporarily paralyzed. We still have no idea if some of the people we encountered were intertwined, but as the night progressed into morning, it seemed more and more likely that we were tangled in a broader net than we could imagine." Again, just be careful, be discreet, be less than trusting, and, when possible, have local Romanians meet you and send you off. It's better to start off overprotected than find your holiday ruined by a black market scam or an unfriendly shakedown.

Melissa's description of the approach to Gara du Nord is realistic, and it should help you imagine what you may head into: "The dingy yellow light of a large bonfire in front of the station cast a spooky glow over hovering bodies and lighted our path to the entrance. A man without legs, almost indistinguishable from the color of the ground. dragged himself past as we dodged the spit of a crippled Gypsy boy retaliating against another throwing sand. My desire to flee was mounting. We were about to discover the underbelly of the infamous Gara du Nord."

If there weren't so many consistent stories about conspiring groups of thieves it would be hard to believe these horrific tales as true. Undoubtedly, things have improved since 1993 but to what degree is unclear. Melissa completed her Romanian experience in style. Her train was delayed for hours; she waited huddled on the platform with her travel companions in the station, only to discover that the track number had been changed at the last minute, and then it was a mad rush to catch it at all.

"Panic swept through our small crowd. Dave ran off to reinspect the information board and the rest of us scurried, looking for anyone in a uniform. I found the closest guy and managed to communicate that we were looking for the train to Sofia. Sympathizing with our desire, our need to get out, this man knew immediately that we were in trouble. He began to run and motioned us to follow. He wanted us to make it. We ran. Rounding the corner, passing track after track, I prayed he knew where he was going. We had pinned all of our hopes on this guy. There was maybe a minute left, maybe seconds, before departure. No more room for errors. As we raced with our packs bouncing, I was running as fast as I possibly could not for the train to Sofia but from the idea of a night in the Gara du Nord."

Of course the train was packed—other people were in their reserved seats and refused obstinately to budge—and Melissa and friends tried to obtain justice. "We remained patient as the conductor pushed his way into the controversial cabin. But when he, too, returned empty handed, irritation began to rise. We paid for these seats and we wanted them. The conductor told us to wait while he conferred with his buddies in their compartment. When he emerged, he escorted us into the business compartment as the other conductors gathered their belongings. They were giving up their seats. If things weren't complicated enough already, we then had to purchase our tickets to Sofia. We only had tickets to the border, where you must get off to buy the rest. Or you can buy them from the conductor for a slightly higher price. So before we all moved in to occupy our places for the night, this guy pulls out a price book and begins to write out the prices. Dave and I were watching closely. 'Don't trust anyone,' the man at the Romania Travel Bureau in Vienna had told us. 'No one.'

"And considering the hassle we had encountered previously with the Arad conductor who was so drunk he couldn't focus and refused to give us our return tickets back, requiring that we essentially push him aside and grab them, we were on high alert. Everything looked feasible until he slapped down a 3,200-lei figure. None of our tickets had been more than 800 lei. Now he was telling us our total would be 5,200 lei each. Though it is only ten dollars, we knew it was severely escalated. Despite our questioning, the guy remained firm. He had us and he knew it. We all forked over the money. It was worth knowing that we had our places for the rest of the night and morning. We got him to write down all the seat numbers again. Who cared about a sleeper at this point? I couldn't wait to have this seat, the protection that such a bribe would provide.

"Just as we had all settled back, leaning wearily into the vinyl seats, Ted's face dropped. He pointed to the aisle window. Briefly speechless, he then gasped, 'It's him. Oh, no. It's that fat—' It was the round man who had pushed over my shoulder while I was buying the tickets. He was now pushing his way toward our compartment. When he attempted to open the door, Ted said no, and held it closed. The guy pressed his face and hands against the glass like some horror movie. Dave quickly pulled the curtains. The man said his wife was pregnant and his family needed a place to sit. Certainly it was his crew who had already occupied our original seats. It seemed as though the entire mass of people standing outside the door wanted into our compartment. They began to pull on the door, pressing their faces to the window. Ted and Dave moved swiftly. With collected belts and luggage straps and harnessed the door and secured it. Ted sat right by the door. There would be no sleeping tonight. The frustrations, the discomfort of the weary travelers outside our door could easily turn on us. They had the numbers. Each time this nightmare seemed to end, another face appeared. We rode like this for three hours. Strangely, when we got to Ruse, just over the Romanian border, the entire train emptied."

CITY-SIGHTSEEING NOTES

Bucharest

This city needs to be walked. Have local friends or a well-recommended guide take you around. Much of prewar Bucharest remains untouched and some of the most elegant properties are now returning to their pre-Ceausescu owners. You can even visit the streets and residences that belonged to the dictator and his wife, entire portions of the city that was off-limits to citizens. One mansion is noted as having solid gold scales in the kitchen which were used to weigh the meat fed to Ceausescu's pack of doberman and German shepherds.

The gargantuan Casa Poporului, the administrative office bloc that was to be Ceausescu's legacy, rose from the ruins of churches, monasteries, and other historic buildings, now looms over the city center in front of a boulevard that dwarfs Paris's Champs-Elysées. Fountains burst in obscene spurts for kilometers in the center of this avenue while the residents of Bucharest weere deprived of drinking water in a harsh rationing scheme. The People's House was never finished and there is talk today among intellectuals of converting the monster into a Museum of Human Folly!

Near the Atheneum concert hall is Revolution Square, the site of the dramatic events of December 1989, flanked by the former royal palace, now housing the national art collection, and the former Communist Party headquarters, now housing the Romanian Senate. Visit all of these.

Brasov

Excellent Transylvania mountain scenery. Visit the 14th-century Black Church.

Bukovina

Northeast of Bucharest in the northern Moldavian region of Bukovina, priceless monasteries beckon your attention: Voronet, Humor, Sucevita, Moldovita, and Arbore. What makes these monasteries unique are the extraordinary frescoes.

Sighisoara

Sighisoara, with its lovely old citadel square, includes the birthplace of Vlad Tepes, the historical Count Dracula. Visit the museum of the walled town.

Sinaia

This lovely winter resort town, filled with mystique and lore, is noted for its late-19th-century extravaganza, Peles Castle, which Prince Carol of Hohenzollern built. Peles was designed as a residence with large halls, elaborate carving, and sumptuous decorations. Access to this and other gems of the Romanian patrimony were restricted during the long and harsh reign of Ceausescu.

ONE-DAY EXCURSIONS

Bucharest - Brasov - Bucharest   950

All of these trains require reservation, unless designated otherwise.

Dep. Bucharest (Nord)	00:50 (1)	07:45 (2)	09:08 (2)	13:25 (2+4)
Arr. Brasov	03:42	10:33	11:35	15:59

Sights in **Brasov:** Excellent Transylvania Mountain scenery in this area. See the 14th century Black Church. The Museum of History. The Art Museum. The Museum of the Romanian School. A popular Winter resort, **Poiana Brasov**, is 9 miles from here.

Dep. Brasov	02:35	03:31 (1)	04:51 (1)	05:42 (1)	06:30 (5)
Arr. Bucharest (Nord)	05:19	06:20	07:24	08:16	09:27

(1) Carries a sleeping car. Also has couchettes. (2) Restaurant car. (3) Runs Monday-Friday, except holidays. Restaurant car. (4) Plus other Bucharest departures at frequent times from 15:00 to 23:35. (5) Plus other Brasov departures at 09:33, 11:10, 12:26 (3), 15:40 (2), 17:15 (2), 17:59 (2), 19:47 (2) and 20:50 (2).

Bucharest - Constantza - Eforie - Mangalia   and v.v. 958

Dep. Bucharest (Nord)	06:05 (1)	07:05 (2)	09:15 (1)	10:05 (3)	10:30 (1+6)
Arr. Constantza	09:13	10:16 (1)	11:46 (2)	12:40	13:24
Dep. Constantza	09:41	-0-	-0-	12:52	-0-
Arr. Eforie (Nord)	10:02	-0-	-0-	13:10	-0-
Arr. Mangalia	10:55	-0-	-0-	14:05	-0-

• • •

Dep. Mangalia	05:05 (1)	-0-	-0-	13:45 (3+7)	-0-
Dep. Eforie (Nord)	05:55	-0-	-0-	14:43	-0-
Arr. Constantza	06:25	-0-	-0-	15:02	-0-
Dep. Constantza	06:44	08:50 (1)	13:15 (1)	15:15	16:10 (1)
Arr. Bucharest (Nord)	10:00	12:00	16:30	18:40 (4)	18:50

(1) Reservations required. (2) Restaurant car. (3) Operates mid-June to late September. Reservations required. (4) Arrives at Bucharest's Baneasa railstation. (5) Operates late May to late September. Reservation required. (6) Plus other Bucharest departures at 16:05 (1) and 19:00 (5), arriving Mangalia 21:08 and 23:25. (7) Plus other Mangalia departures at 15:00 (3), 15:40 (3), 17:10 (1), 18:05 (3) and 23:30 (5), arriving Bucharest 19:25, 20:48 (4), 21:55, 22:35 and 04:30.

Sights: **Constantza** is a very large resort. See the Museum of Archaeology Parvan. The Open Air Museum of Archaeology. The Roman Mosaic. The Museum of the Black Sea. **Eforie** and **Mangalia** are popular Black Sea beach resorts.

Bucharest - Galati - Bucharest   953

Dep. Bucharest (Nord)	06:10 (2)	13:35 (2)	15:10 (1)	18:10 (2)
Arr. Galati	10:05	17:07	18:50 (2)	21:55

Sights in **Galati**: The most splendid array of birdlife in all of Europe.

Dep. Galati	06:10 (2)	11:05 (1)	13:40 (2)	19:50 (2)
Arr. Bucharest (Nord)	09:45	14:50 (2)	17:29	23:21

(1) Runs daily, except Saturday. (2) Reservations required. Restaurant car.

Bucharest - Sighisoara - Bucharest   950

All of these trains require reservation.

Dep. Bucharest (Nord)	07:45	13:25 (1)
Arr. Sighisoara	11:33	17:57

Sights in **Sighisoara**: The birthplace of Count Dracula. This is an interesting medieval fortress city. See the Museum of the Walled Town. Stroll through the old section.

Dep. Sighisoara	17:49 (1)	18:55 (1)
Arr. Bucharest (Nord)	22:22	23:25

(1) Restaurant car.

Bucharest - Sinaia - Bucharest   950

All of these trains require reservation.

Dep. Bucharest (Nord)	00:55	06:38 (1)	07:45 (1)	09:08 (1)	13:25 (1)
Arr. Sinaia	02:35	08:13	09:32	10:37	15:01

Dep. Bucharest (Nord)	15:00	15:55 (2)	17:31	19:42	20:00 (3)
Arr. Sinaia	16:43	17:26	19:13	21:21	21:47

Sights in **Sinaia**: This is a major Winter resort.

Dep. Sinaia	03:36	04:34 (1)	05:55	06:10	07:32
Arr. Bucharest (Nord)	05:19	06:20	07:44	08:00	09:27

Dep. Sinaia	10:27	12:55	13:23 (2)	16:35 (1)	18:08 (1+4)
Arr. Bucharest (Nord)	11:58	14:40	15:05	18:19	19:45

(1) Restaurant car. (2) Runs Monday-Friday, except holidays. Restaurant car. (3) Plus other Bucharest departures at 21:40 and 23:15. (4) Plus other Sinaia departures at19:02 (1), 20:43 (1) and 21:45.

INTERNATIONAL ROUTES
FROM ROMANIA

Bucharest is Romania's gateway for rail travel to Belgrade (and on to Yugoslavia's Adriatic cities), Budapest (and on to Western Europe), Kiev (and on to Moscow and Leningrad), and Sofia (and on to Athens and Istanbul).

Bucharest - Belgrade   954

This train requires reservation and carries a sleeping car.

Dep. Bucharest (Nord)	23:00
Set your watch back one hour.	
Arr. Belgrade (Dunav)	10:40

Bucharest - Budapest   950

All of these trains require reservation.

Dep. Bucharest (Nord)   00:55 (1)   20:54 (1)
Set your watch back one hour.
Arr. Budapest (Nyugati)   -0-   -0-
Arr. Budapest (Keleti)   14:22   09:32

(1) Carries a sleeping car. Also has couchettes. (2) Restaurant car. (3) runs Monday-Friday except holidays. Restaurant car. Change trains in Brasov at 18:25.

Bucharest - Kiev - Moscow

All of these trains carry only sleeping cars, unless designated otherwise.

	925	94d	94d
Dep. Bucharest (Nord)	09:06	23:16	23:55 (5)
Arr. Ungeni	-0-	06:10 (3)	-0-
Arr. Vadu Siret	19:37 (2)	-0-	08:15 (3)

Ungeni and **Vadu Siret** are the Russian border stations where the wheels of the trains are changed to fit the wider Soviet rail gauge.

Dep. Ungeni	-0-	08:30 (2)	-0-
Dep. Vadu Siret	17:28	-0-	10:30 (2)
Arr. Kiev	11:26 (3)	-0-	01:13 (6)
Set your watch forward one hour.			
Arr. Moscow (Kievski)	-0-	21:14	19:33

(1) Departs from Budapest's Chitila railstation. Runs Tuesday and Friday. Restaurant car Ungeni to Moscow. (2) Estimated. (3) Day 2. (4) Runs Wednesday, Friday and Sunday. Light refreshments. (5) Restaurant car. (6) Day 3.

Bucharest - Sofia - Istanbul   98

This train runs Thursday only and carries only sleeping cars.

Dep. Bucharest (Baneasa)   08:15
Dep. Sofia   22:30
Arr. Istanbul   10:50

YUGOSLAVIA
(Serbia, Montenegro, and Kosova)

Technically, present-day Yugoslavia is the combined states of Serbia and Montenegro. Croatia, Macedonia, Slovenia, and Bosnia-Herzegovina are all independent countries and are treated separately.

Former Yugoslavia is the term referring to the whole nation prior to 1991. The war in the region has rendered daily life, let alone train travel, unpredictable. International train access to Belgrade is exclusively routed via Budapest, Subotica, and Novi Sad. The Meridian originates in Berlin and Sofia, the Skopje-Istanbul in Munich, and the Avala and Beograd in Vienna. Travel from Zagreb in Croatia to Belgrade in Serbia requires the circuitous route through Budapest, Hungary. Via Timisoara, the Bucuresti connects Bucharest and Belgrade. Other local trains connect western Romania and Yugoslavia. The Istanbul Express from Munich passes through Belgrade, as does the Meridian from Berlin to Sofia. Athens and Belgrade are linked via Skopje and Thessaloniki twice a day.

Internally, there is a very scenic route between Belgrade and the coastal town of Bar on which overnight sleeper cars are available. Interail passes are honored in Yugoslavia, but Eurail passes are not. Belgrade is gray and uninspiring, was once a popular transit city in the summer months when northern European students would migrate to the beaches of the Greek islands. Today, Belgrade, aside from being grim, is prohibitively expensive. Some travelers courageous enough to make this leg of the trip spend the day in Belgrade and book a sleeper bunk on the night train out. Most have decided not to include Yugoslavia this year.

Montenegro is seated north of Albania in the southwest corner of the country. Aside from the Adriatic city of Bar, Montenegro hosts a bucolic rail line between Podorica and Kolasin. The 100-mile Tara Canyon is located beyond Kolasin. Montenegro is highly isolated now in times of war and only the port of Bar seems like a unique contact with the outside world. Budva is the best beach in the region.

Montenegro hosts a surprising variety of natural beauty. It is difficult not to be amazed by the stunning changes that occur at frequent intervals in the landscape. Hence the fantastic and inspired descriptions of Montenegro. Nature is harsh and gentle. The region hosts some of the deepest canyons in the world.

YUGOSLAVIAN HOLIDAYS

January 1	New Year's Day	May 9	Victory Day (WWr II)
January 2	Additional Holiday	July 4	Veterans Day
May 1	Labor Day	November 29	Republic Day
May 2	Additional Holiday	November 30	Additional Holiday

SUMMER TIME

Yugoslavia changes to Summer Time on the last Sunday of March and converts back to Standard Time on the last Sunday of September.

KOSOVA

Kosova, also known as Kosovo, is the region disputed over by its Albanian majority and Serbia. The Serbian government has imposed a police state in Kosova by stripping away its autonomy, closing Albanian-language schools, dismissing Albanians from their jobs, suspending Kosova's legal parliament and government—the systematic oppression and flagrant violations of basic rights of Albanians in Kosova. The 90 percent Albanian majority of Kosova have held free elections in which they have chosen their leadership, expressed their determiniation for the independence of Kosova in the 1992 referendum, and declared the independence of Kosova, first from Serbia, then from the Yugoslav federation. The Albanian leadership has declared that it will seek a peaceful resolution of the problem of Kosova. Prishtina is the capital of Kosova.

BOSNIA-HERZEGOVINA

The Department of State warns U.S. citizens not to travel to the Republic of Bosnia-Herzegovina because of ongoing tensions. Instability around Sarajevo severely restricts the American embassy's ability to assist U.S. citizens, even in emergencies.

The Republic of Bosnia and Herzegovina, formerly one of the Yugoslav republics, continues to be in a tortured state of war. The resulting deaths, destruction, food shortages, and travel disruptions affecting roads, airports and railways, make travel to all parts of Bosnia and Herzegovina extremely hazardous. The popular religious shrine at Medjugorje is located within Bosnia and Herzegovina's borders, but tourism in the region is virtually nonexistent and the idea of travel here at this time in history is unthinkable.

Permission to enter Bosnia and Herzegovina is currently granted at the border on a case-by-case basis. Over 70 percent of Bosnia is under the control of Bosnian Serb military forces. General lawlessness and deteriorating economic conditions have brought an increase in crime, and adequate police response in the event of an emergency is doubtful. Anti-American sentiments run high in many parts of the country, particularly in Serb-dominated areas. Roadblocks manned by local militias are numerous. These militia groups frequently confiscate relief goods and trucks, and may otherwise behave unprofessionally. Sarajevo, the beautiful city of Oriental mosques which hosted the 1984 Winter Olympics, is now characterized by its main avenue, popularly called Sniper Alley.

SLOVENIA

This small country tucked in between northeastern Italy and southern Austria enjoys the geography of the Julian Alps and the north Adriatic. In 1990 Slovenia was the first to break away from communist Yugoslavia. That sense of freedom and independence is strongly felt in Slovenian cultural production—the nation offers excellent original music and a dynamic avant art scene called Neue Slowenische Kunst which not only runs an excellent Web site on the Internet but has issued its own passports to a virtual country that is wholly peaceful.

Slovenia, even today, makes for a pleasurable and surprisingly peaceful journey. Don't think of Slovenia as former Yugoslavia. Llubljana, the capital, is filled with interesting sites and activities. The most popular train routes into Slovenia are via Vienna and Salzburg to Jesenice and Llubljana. Routes from Munich and other German cities are functioning, and five trains a day run from Trieste to Llubljana. Slovenian-Croatian connections require a change of train mid-route, and via Croatia one can connect from Llubljana to Budapest.

Aside from Llubljana with its old town, Presernov Square, and triple bridge, side trips to the chic resort lake town of Bled is a must. Marshal Tito kept his summer house on a hill above this sparkling lake.

CROATIA

Before the war, the Croatian coast on the Adriatic attracted millions of tourists with its resort towns of Split and Dubrovnik. All that has changed. The islands off the coast, curiously, have not been disrupted by the war and are lovely and safe although desolate.

Zagreb, the capital and center of cultural life, remains bright and vibrant. There are overnight intercity trains from Munich to Zagreb via Salzburg and Ljubljana. Reservations southbound are required but only recommended northbound. From Vienna to Zagreb, there is the Eurocity Croatia daily. Three express trains run between Venice and Zagreb via Trieste and Ljublijana. The Simplon Express offers a connecting service from Geneva and Rome; Budapest-Zagreb connections are plentiful. Note though that there are no Serbian-Croatian train connections.

Zagreb - Ljubljana - Zargreb 935

Dep. Zagreb	05:40 (1)	06:50	08:10 (2)	10:35	
Arr. Ljubljana	08:00	09:13	10:17	12:54	
Dep. Ljubljana	12:35	15:05	19:40 (2)	20:45 (1)	21:45 (3)
Arr. Zagreb	14:50	17:30	21:50	22:55	23:59

(1) Restaurant car. (2) Reservation required. Restaurant car. (3) Second class.

Sights in **Ljubljana**: Several walking tours are described in "Ljubljana City Guide," a book with maps that is sold at the bookstore at Titov Cesta, near the corner of Subiceva Ulica in the new city. All of the walks begin at the square called Presernov Trg, where the 17th century Franciscan Church of the Anunciation is located.

See the triple bridge that crosses Ljubljana River (2 for pedestrians, one for vehicles). Ascend a hill to reach the castle for a view of the city from it.

There is free sampling of hundreds of different Yugoslav wines at the Autumn Wine Fair.

SCENIC RAIL TRIPS

Belgrade - Priboj - Bar   and v.v. 942

This is the most scenic rail route in Yugoslavia. Steep canyons, turbulent rivers and mountains. The world's highest railway span, completed in 1976, is the 495-foot-high Mala Rijeka Bridge on this route.

The 325-mile line has 254 tunnels and 234 concrete and steel bridges. The trip climbs from the Danube to heights of 4,000 feet before descending to sea level on the Adriatic coast. The line from Priboj to Bar is narrow-gauge as the train descends to the valley of the **Rzav River**.

Dep. Belgrade	05:10 (1+2)	10:30 (3)	14:20 (4)	21:30 (5)	22:40 (5+6)
Dep. Priboj	08:47	14:40	18:03	01:45	-0- (7)
Arr. Bar	12:34	18:22	21:30	05:44	06:04
Dep. Bar	09:55 (3)	14:10 (4)	15:35 (1+8)	22:00 (6)	22:20 (5)
Dep. Priboj	13:33	17:41	19:15	01:42	02:18
Arr. Belgrade	17:39	21:14	23:04	05:28	06:38

(1) Operates mid-June to mid-September. (2) Reservation required. Light refreshments. (3) Light refreshments. (4) Reservation required. First-class only. Light refreshments. (5) Carries a sleeping car. Also has couchettes. (6) Operates early June to late September. Carries a sleeping car. Also has couchettes. (7) Does not stop in Priboj. (8) Reservation required.

Ljubljana - Postojna - Ljubljana   930

The longest and most beautiful river cave of Europe is near **Postojna**, where the **Pivka River** flows through an underground passage.

Tourists, traveling through the cave on a small train, are able to see wonderful rows of stalactites and stalagmites, gigantic underground rooms, chasms and little lakes. A 16th century castle is at the entrance to the cave. Conducted tours are offered daily, every half-hour. June 1–September 1, from 08:30–16:00, plus 17:00 and 18:00. September 2 to May 31, from 09:30–13:30.

Because the cave is not deep, visitors can go a long distance through it. It extends 19 miles! A narrow-gauge railway takes passengers more than one mile into the cave. Its terminal (Postojna Station) is larger than New York's Grand Central. English-speaking guides conduct tourists from it on a 1½-mile figure-eight walk. Great Mountain Room is more than 900-feet high.

Dep. Ljubljana	Frequent times from 03:40 to 20:20
Arr. Postojna	55-65 minutes later

Dep. Postojna	Frequent times from 02:20 to 22:21
Arr. Ljubljana	55–65 minutes later

Ljubljana - Jesenice - Sezana - Ljublana

We show the long scenic route for a daylight ride to Sezana and then the shorter route for returning to Ljubljana from Sezana at the end of the day.

935

Dep. Ljubljana	10:20 (1)	15:45 (4)
Dep. Kranj	-0-	16:12
Dep. Lesce-Bled	11:00	16:34
Arr. Jesenice	11:14	16:49
Change trains. 931		
Dep. Jesenice	11:20 (2)	16:55 (4)
Arr. Nova Gorica	-0- (2)	18:40
Change trains.		
Dep. Nova Gorica	-0-	18:43 (4)
Arr. Sezana	14:15	19:35
Change trains. 930		
Dep. Sezana	19:03 (3)	21:35
Arr. Ljubljana	20:42	23:20

(1) Reservation required. Has first-class and second-class coaches. Restaurant car. (2) Direct train. No train change in Nova Gorica. (3) Restaurant car. (4) Second-class.

INTERNATIONAL ROUTES
FROM YUGOSLAVIA

There are rail connections from Belgrade to Athens (and on to Istanbul), Bucharest (and on to Kiev and Moscow), Budapest (and on to Moscow, Prague, Vienna and Warsaw), Salzburg (and on to the rest of Western Europe and to Scandinavia), Sofia (and on to Athens and Istanbul), and to Venice (and on to the rest of Italy and Southern Europe).

Belgrade - Athens   970

Dep. Belgrade	07:45 (1)	11:00 (2)	21:40 (1)
Set your watch forward one hour.			
Arr. Athens (Larissa)	06:33	08:10	20:00

(1) Carries a sleeping car. Also has couchettes. (2) Carries only sleeping cars and couchettes.

Belgrade - Bucharest 954

Dep. Belgrade (Dunav)	18:00 (1)
Set your watch forward one hour.	
Arr. Timisoara (Nord)	23:39
Arr. Bucharest (Nord)	07:35

(1) Reservation required. Carries a sleeping car.

A stopover in **Timisoara** is worthwhile, to see the opulence of the Hapsburg rulers at the Dicasterial Palace. Also the Catholic and Serbian cathedrals and the Museum of Fine Arts on Piata Unirii, a picturesque square. See a show at Puppet Theater, on Piata Furtuna.

Belgrade - Budapest - Vienna 61

Dep. Belgrade	12:35 (1)	19:30 (3)	22:05 (4)
Arr. Budapest (Keleti)	18:30 (1)	-0-	06:00
Arr. Vienna (West)	21:45 (2)	05:30	09:20

(1) Restaurant car. (2) Arrives at Vienna Sud railstation. (3) Carries a sleeping car. Also has couchettes. (4) Second class.

Belgrade - Sofia 945

Dep. Belgrade	10:15 (1)	12:50	22:00 (2)
Set your watch forward one hour.			
Arr. Sofia	19:30	22:05	07:22

(1) Light Refreshments. (2) Has couchettes.

CHAPTER 9

EURAIL GUIDE ROUTE CHART

In view of the fact that there are over 100,000 miles of railroad lines in just the 17 Eurailpass countries, it would be impossible to list every conceivable trip one could make by train in Europe. We do provide you in this chapter a list of 734 trips that most people touring Europe might make, showing the travel time and one-way first-class fare for each.

The list of ticket prices enables our readers to (a) compute the cost of ordinary tickets for an itinerary and (b) compare that total cost with one or a combination of the train passes described in Eurail Guide.

We have condensed route descriptions by listing them only in alphabetical priority. For example, the first route is Alborg to Copenhagen. If you were looking for the trip from Copenhagen to Alborg, you would refer to the name that has alphabetical priority: Alborg. Similarly, the trip Rome-Paris will be found as Paris-Rome, etc.

The rates listed are first-class fares, in U.S. dollars. To compute second-class fares, figure 66% of the first-class fare shown. While this will not always be the exact second-class fare, it will be very close to it.

Also remember that European train fares, like the prices of all other European goods and services, are subject to change relative to the exchange rates for U.S. dollars and other non-European currencies.

On the other hand, once a Eurailpass, France Railpass, German Railpass, or any other train pass has been issued to you, you are protected from the devaluation of your currency increasing the cost of your train transportation — another hidden plus to having a pass.

All the fares listed in this chapter are subject to a seat reservation fee of $3 (U.S.) per person (if you want to be sure of having a seat). This is a charge whether traveling with a ticket or with Eurailpass. However, a Eurailpass holder does not have to pay this *supplement* when riding on some EuroCity or TGV trains (savings range from $3 to $8).

Keep in mind that on trips which involve both a Eurailpass country and also a country not covered by Eurailpass such as Vienna-Athens (via non-Eurailpas Yugoslavia), the passenger holding a Eurailpass has to purchase a ticket for the non-Eurailpass portion of that trip.

Note: Because Paris has 6 different railstations, we indicate in parenthesis the name of the Paris railstation at which a train is departing or arriving.

EURAIL GUIDE ROUTE CHART

1996 first-class train fares, *not* including seat reservation fee.

	Travel Time	Fare
ALBORG		
Copenhagen	6½	66.00
ALGECIRAS		
Cordoba	4½	33.00
Granada	5	31.00
Madrid	11½	79.00
Malaga	4	27.00
Seville	6	38.00
ALICANTE		
Valencia	2	21.00
ALKMAAR		
Amsterdam	½	11.00
AMSTERDAM		
Antwerp	2½	43.00
Basel (via Roosendaal)	9½	156.00
Berlin	8½	147.00
Bremen	4	94.00
Brussels	3½	53.00
Cologne (Koln)	3	59.00
Copenhagen (Kobenhavn)	13	232.00
Dusseldorf	2½	59.00
Frankfurt	6	132.00
Hamburg	6	126.00
Hannover	5½	98.00
Heidelberg	6½	147.00
Hoek Van Holland	2	27.00

Luxembourg (via Roosendaal)	5	87.00
Milan	15½	338.00
Munich (Munchen)	8½	251.00
Paris (Nord)	5½	113.00
Rome	21	412.00
Rotterdam	1	21.00
Salzburg	10	293.00
Utrecht	½	11.00
Vienna (Wien)		
(via Passau)	15	306.00
Wiesbaden	6	124.00
Zurich	11	273.00

ANDALSNES

Oslo	7	97.00

ANDERMATT

Brig	2	50.00
Chur	2½	45.00
Luzern	2	55.00
Zurich	2	71 .00

ANTWERP

Brussels	1	11.00
Paris (Nord)	3½	72.00
Rotterdam	1½	24.00

AOSTA

Milan	3½	27.00
Turin (Torino)	1½	18.00

ARHUS

Copenhagen (Kobenhavn)	4½	48.00

AROSA
Chur	1	16.00
Zurich	3	71.00

ASSISI
Florence (Firenze)	3	24.00
Rome	2½	24.00

ATHENS
Patras	3	37.00
Thessaloniki	9	74.00

AVIGNON
Barcelona	6½	79.00
Cannes	3	66.00
Carcassonne	2½	58.00
Geneva	3½	73.00
Lourdes	7	91.00
Lyon	1½	53.00
Marseille	1	35.00
Nice	4	71.00
Paris (Lyon)	3	114.00
Port Bou	4	64.00

BADEN-BADEN
Basel	2	45.00

BARCELONA
Bilboa	9½	77.00
Carcassonne	6	58.00
Geneva	9½	134.00
Genoa	13½	148.00
Lourdes	9	98.00
Lyon	7	111.00
Madrid	7	77.00
Marseille	6½	91.00
Nice	9	121.00
Paris (Austerlitz)	11½	165.00

Rome	20	209.00
Seville	13	103.00
Toulouse (Via Port Bou)	7	73.00
Valencia	4	40.00
Vigo	18¼	118.00
Zaragoza	3½	42.00

BARI

Bologna	7½	76.00
Brindisi	1½	16.00
Messina	9	76.00
Milan	10	106.00
Naples	4	39.00
Pescara	3½	36.00
Rome	6	65.00
Taranto	1½	16.00
Turin (Torino)	13	118.00
Venice	13	94.00

BASEL

Bern	1	40.00
Brig	3	93.00
Brussels	7	107.00
Bucharest (Partly covered by Eurailpass)	29	353.00
Budapest	16	234.00
Cologne (Koln)	5	147.00
Copenhagen (Kobenhavn)	13	367.00
Florence (Firenze)	10	161.00
Frankfurt	3	113.00
Geneva	3½	100.00
Genoa	9	140.00
Hamburg	6½	266.00
Hannover	5½	220.00
Heidelberg	2½	84.00
Innsbruck	6	99.00
Interlaken	2½	64.00
Lausanne	2½	67.00
Locarno	4½	110.00
Luxembourg	4	70.00
Luzern	1½	43.00

Milan	6	121.00
Montreux	3	85.00
Paris (Est)	5	75.00
Rome	13	195.00
Rotterdam (via Brussels)	8½	137.00
Salzburg	9	152.00
Strasbourg	1	33.00
Venice	10	152.00
Vienna (Wien)	12	184.00
Wiesbaden	3½	101.00
Zurich	1	50.00

BAYONNE

Madrid	6½	81.00
Paris	4½	134.00

BAYREUTH

Nurnberg	1	26.00

BERGEN

Bodo	26½	262.00
Flam	3½	56.00
Goteborg	12	192.00
Myrdal	2½	38.00
Oslo	7	115.00
Trondheim	14½	184.00
Voss	1½	26.00

BERLIN

Bremen	5	113.00
Brussels	10	210.00
Cologne (Koln)	7	161.00
Copenhagen (Kobenhavn)	12	155.00
Dusseldorf	5½	156.00
Frankfurt/Main (via Erfurt)	6	146.00
Hamburg	3	81.00
Hannover	3½	79.00
Leipzig	2	45.00
Luxembourg	11	227.00
Malmo	9½	114.00
Munich (Munchen) (via Leipzig)	9	186.00

Nurnburg	6	131.00
Oslo	19½	253.00
Paris (Nord)	11	262.00
Rotterdam	10	171.00
Stockholm	17	214.00
Vienna (Wien) (Sudbf.) via Prague	14	143.00

BERN

Brig	2	65.00
Geneva	2	71.00
Interlaken	1	34.00
Lausanne	1	43.00
Lugano	4½	106.00
Luzern	1½	45.00
Milan	4½	89.00
Montreux	3½	78.00
Paris (Lyon) via Verrieres	5	124.00
Zurich	1½	69.00

BILBAO

Hendaye	4¼	31.00
Madrid	6	61.00
Vigo	14½	84.00
Zaragoza	4½	38.00

BODEN

Haparanda	2	41.00
Narvik	7	102.00
Stockholm	16	144.00

BODO

Goteborg	24½	275.00
Oslo	19	213.00
Trondheim	11½	154.00

BOLOGNA

Florence (Firenze)	1½	12.00

Genoa	4½	36.00
Innsbruck	6½	56.00
Milan	2½	27.00
Naples	6½	76.00
Paris (Lyon)	10	212.00
Ravenna	1½	11.00
Rimini	1½	16.00
Rome	3¼	54.00
Turin (Torino)	4½	42.00
Venice	2	21.00
Verona	1½	16.00

BONN

Cologne (Koln)	½	10.00
Frankfurt (Main)	2	52.00
Koblenz	1	16.00

BORDEAUX

Geneva	10	128.00
Hendaye	2¼	51.00
Lourdes	3½	56.00
Lyon	7½	108.00
Marseille	5½	113.00
Nice	8	140.00
Paris (Austerlitz)	3	111.00
Toulouse	2	55.00
Tours	3	70.00

BREMEN

Budapest	19½	341.00
Cologne (Koln)	3	93.00
Copenhagen (Kobenhavn)	6½	139.00
Dusseldorf	3	82.00
Essen	2½	71.00
Frankfurt/Main	3¼	166.00
Hamburg	1	33.00
Hannover	1	42.00
Heidelberg	5½	182.00
Munich (Munchen)	6	229.00
Stuttgart	5	218.00

Vienna (Wien)	9	295.00
BRIG		
Chur	4½	102.00
Interlaken	1½	54.00
Lausanne	1½	61.00
Zermatt	1½	49.00
BRUGGE		
Brussels	1½	19.00
BRUSSELS		
Budapest	20½	328.00
Calais	3	50.00
Cologne (Koln)	2½	49.00
Copenhagen (Kobenhavn)	13	279.00
Frankfurt	5½	110.00
Ghent	½	13.00
Hamburg	8	173.00
Liege	1	19.00
Luxembourg	3	41.00
Munich (Munchen)	8½	243.00
Paris (Nord)	3	103.00
Rotterdam	2	34.00
Vienna (Wien) (via Nurnberg)	15	282.00
Zurich	13	160.00
BUCHS		
Innsbruck	3	31.00
Zurich	1½	52.00
BUDAPEST		
Cologne (Koln)	18	280.00
Frankfurt/Main	15½	220.00
Hamburg	18	358.00
Milan	16½	165.00
Munich (Munchen)	11	138.00
Paris (Est)		
via Munich	18	339.00
via Basel	25	325.00
Prague	9½	89.00

Rome	25	205.00
Sofia	13	117.00
Trieste	16	132.00
Venice	13	138.00
Vienna (Wien)	4	51.00
Zurich	18	206.00

CADIZ

Madrid	8	77.00
Seville	6	17.00

CALAIS

Paris (Nord)	3	96.00
Strasbourg	9½	104.00

CANNES

Florence	11	65.00
Geneva	8	114.00
Genoa	3	38.00
Lille	7	185.00
Lyon	5	94.00
Marseille	2	43.00
Milan	7½	53.00
Paris (Lyon)	6	141.00
Rome	13	99.00
San Remo	3	20.00

CARCASSONNE

Lourdes	3	56.00
Marseille	3¼	66.00
Nice	6	97.00
Paris (Austerlitz)	6	132.00
Port Bou	2½	39.00
Toulouse	1	25.00

CHAMONIX-MONT BLANC

Geneva	2½	43.00
Grenoble	2¼	53.00
Martigny (Second-class only)	3	28.00
Paris (Lyon)	8	139.00

CHARTRES
    Paris (Montparnasse)   1   23.00

CHERBOURG
    Paris (St. Lazare)   3½   74.00

CHUR
    St. Moritz   2½   54.00
    Zurich   1½   58.00

COLOGNE (KOLN)
    Copenhagen (Kobenhavn)   10   204.00
    Dortmund   1   30.00
    Dusseldorf   ½   11.00
    Essen   1   21.00
    Frankfurt   2½   55.00
    Hamburg   5   114.00
    Hannover   3   76.00
    Koblenz   1   23.00
    Luxembourg (Via Koblenz)   4   63.00
    Luzern   7½   190.00
    Mainz   2   50.00
    Mannheim   3   71.00
    Milan   12   268.00
    Munich (Munchen)   6   173.00
    Paris (Nord)   6   101.00
    Rotterdam   3½   74.00
    Salzburg   8½   216.00
    Stuttgart   4½   109.00
    Vienna (Wien)   12   234.00
    Wiesbaden   2   50.00
    Zurich   7½   197.00

COIMBRA
    Lisbon   2½   20.00

COMO
    Lugano   ½   15.00
    Luzern   4   87.00
    Milan   1   7.00
    Venice   4   39.00
    Zurich   4   96.00

COPENHAGEN (KOBENHAVN)

Frankfurt	10½	217.00
Fredrickshavn	7	55.00
Hamburg (via Puttgarden)	5	91.00
Helsinki (Partly by Ship)	23½	163.00
Hoek Van Holland	12	207.00
Kristiansand (Ship)	15½	100.00
Luxembourg (via Koln)	13½	296.00
Malmo (Hydrofoil)	½	27.00
(Not covered by Eurailpass.)		
Milan	20	468.00
Munich (Munchen) (via Berlin)	19	327.00
Narvik	31	184.00
Odense	3	39.00
Oslo	10½	160.00
Paris (Nord)	15	331.00
Rome	25	562.00
Rotterdam	14½	237.00
Stockholm (via Hassleholm)	8	140.00
Trondheim (via Goteborg)	19	266.00
Venice	22	439.00
Vienna (Wien)	19	278.00
Wiesbaden	9½	286.00

CORDOBA

Granada	3½	21.00
Madrid	5	38.00
Malaga	2½	17.00
Seville	2	12.00

DAVOS

St. Moritz	1½	39.00
Zurich	3	77.00

DIJON

Lausanne	3	56.00
Lyon	2	44.00
Paris	2	73.00
Strasbourg (via Belfort)	4	67.00

DORTMUND

Paris (Nord)	7	129.00

DUSSELDORF

Essen	½	11.00
Frankfurt/Main	3	72.00
Hamburg	4	116.00
Hannover	3	78.00
Munich (Munchen)	6½	184.00
Paris (Nord)	6	109.00

FLAM

Myrdal (2nd class fare)	1	19.00
Oslo	6½	101.00

FLORENCE (FIRENZE)

Geneva	10	147.00
Genoa	4	30.00
Innsbruck	8	62.00
Lausanne	9	152.00
Livorno	1½	16.00
Luzern	9	132.00
Marseille	12	100.00
Milan	3	39.00
Munich (Munchen)	10	101.00
Naples	5¼	65.00
Nice	11	57.00
Paris		
(Lyon) via Iselle	15	218.00
(Lyon) via Pisa	18	179.00
(Lyon) via Turin (Torino)	18	172.00
Perugia	2½	21.00
Pisa	1½	11.00
Ravenna	3	18.00
Rome	2½	39.00

Siena	2½	12.00
Turin (Torino)	6	54.00
Venice	3	33.00
Vienna (Wien)	13	116.00

FRANKFURT/MAIN

Hamburg	3½	174.00
Hannover	2½	134.00
Heidelberg	1	39.00
Innsbruck	6	181.00
Luxembourg	4½	78.00
Mainz	½	11.00
Mannheim	1	37.00
Nurnberg	2½	66.00
Paris (Est)	6½	135.00
Rotterdam	6	135.00
Salzburg	5	178.00
Stuttgart	1¼	64.00
Vienna (Wien)	9	174.00
Wiesbaden	½	12.00
Zurich	5	163.00

FREDRICKSHAVN

Hamburg	7½	116.00
Oslo (Ship) (Not covered by Eurailpass.)	10	90.00
Stockholm (Ship) (Not covered by Eurailpass.)	7½	98.00

GARMISCH-PARTENKIRCHEN

Innsbruck	1½	15.00
Munich (Munchen)	1½	29.00

GAVLE

Stockholm	2	44.00

GENEVA
    Genoa
        via Milan   7½   103.00
        via Turin (Torino)   7   72.00
    Grenoble   2   38.00
    Grindelwald   3½   104.00
    Gstaad   2½   74.00
    Interlaken (via Bern)   3   91.00
    Lausanne   ½   34.00
    Locarno   4½   124.00
    Lourdes   10   114.00
    Luzern   3½   98.00
    Lyon   2   38.00
    Marseille (via Lyon)   5½   89.00
    Milan   6   91.00
    Montreux   1   44.00
    Nice (via Lyon)   10½   118.00
    Paris (Lyon)   3½   110.00
    Rome   9¼   176.00
    Turin (Torino)   6   64.00
    Venice   8   142.00
    Zurich   3   110.00

GENOA
    Lausanne   7   99.00
    Luzern   7½   111.00
    Marseille   6½   73.00
    Milan   2   21.00
    Monaco-Monte Carlo   3   25.00
    Munich (Munchen)   11½   112.00
    Naples   8½   88.00
    Nice   4   30.00
    Paris (Lyon) (via Torino)   12   147.00
    Pisa   2½   21.00
    Rome   7   65.00
    Salzburg   14   113.00
    San Remo   2   18.00

Turin (Torino)	2½	21.00
Venice	7	48.00

GOTEBORG

Copenhagen (Kobenhavn)	4½	78.00
Hamburg	10	171.00
Helsingborg	3	59.00
Kalmar	5	82.00
Oslo	5	94.00
Stockholm	4½	98.00
Trondheim	21	174.00

GRANADA

Madrid	6½	52.00
Malaga	3	21.00
Seville	4½	31.00
Valencia	8	73.00

GRAZ

Vienna (Wien)	3½	36.00

GRENOBLE

Lyon	1¼	35.00
Marseille	4½	53.00

GRINDELWALD

Interlaken (Not covered by Eurailpass)	1	13.00
Zurich (Only partially covered by Eurailpass)	3½	98.00

HAMBURG

Hannover	1¼	60.00
Heidelberg	5	193.00
Helsinki (Partly by Ship)	33	243.00
Luxembourg	8½	191.00
Munich (Munchen)	6	247.00
Oslo	15½	253.00
Paris (Nord)	9½	225.00

Rotterdam	6½	131.00
Salzburg	10	286.00
Stockholm	13	225.00
Stuttgart	5¼	220.00
Vienna (Wien)	10	310.00

HANNOVER

Munich (Munchen)	4½	198.00
Paris (Nord)	9½	236.00
Rotterdam	5	103.00
Wurzburg	2	129.00

HAPARANDA

Helsinki	12	92.00

HEIDELBERG

Koblenz	2	50.00
Luzern	4½	123.00
Mainz	1	26.00
Munich (Munchen)	3½	98.00
Nurnberg	4	71.00
Paris (Est)	6	122.00
Rothenburg ("Castle Road" Bus)	3	64.00
Stuttgart	1	31.00
Wiesbaden	1½	29.00

HELSINKI

Kuopio	6	64.00
Oslo (Partly by Ship)	22	164.00
Oulu	7½	86.00
Stockholm (Ship)	12½	68.00
Turku	2¼	32.00

HENDAYE

Lisbon	17	101.00
Lourdes	2½	40.00
Madrid	10	69.00

Paris (Austerlitz)	5½	139.00
Zaragoza	4¼	36.00

HOEK VAN HOLLAND
Innsbruck	13	293.00
Munich (Munchen)	12	250.00
Rotterdam	½	8.00

INNSBRUCK
Kitzbuhel	1	19.00
Luzern	6	102.00
Milan	6½	56.00
Munich (Munchen)	4	44.00
Paris (Est)	11½	204.00
Rome	12	102.00
Salzburg	4	43.00
Venice	5	50.00
Verona	5	38.00
Vienna (Wien)	8	89.00
Zurich	5	85.00

INTERLAKEN
Lausanne	2	71.00
Luzern	2	33.00
Milan	5	79.00
Montreux	3	74.00
Paris (Lyon) via Verrieres	7½	154.00
Zurich	3	85.00

KARLSTAD
Oslo	3	64.00
Stockholm	3½	76.00

KLAGENFURT
Salzburg	4	40.00
Venice	4½	41.00
Vienna (Wein)	6	54.00

KLOSTERS
Zurich	2½	71.00

KOBLENZ
Luxembourg	2½	42.00
Munich (Munchen)	5½	149.00
Paris (via Reims)	7	115.00
Vienna (Wien)	10	209.00
Wiesbaden	1	26.00

KONSTANZ
Zurich	1	36.00

KRISTIANSAND
Oslo	5	93.00
Stavanger	3½	65.00

LAUSANNE
Locarno	4	106.00
Lugano	5½	119.00
Luzern	3	78.00
Milan	4½	87.00
Montreux	½	12.00
Paris (Lyon)	4	140.00
Rome	13¼	157.00
Venice	8½	123.00
Zurich	2½	91.00

LE HAVRE
Paris (St. Lazare)	2½	48.00

LIEGE
Luxembourg	3	29.00
Paris (Nord)	4	72.00

LINZ
Salzburg	2	24.00
Vienna (Wien)	2	32.00

LISBON
Madrid (Atocha)	9	68.00
Paris (Austerlitz)	25	229.00

Porto	4	28.00
Santiago de Compostela	9	51.00
Seville	12	57.00
Vigo	9	42.00

LIVORNO

Pisa	½	3.00
Rome	3	39.00

LOCARNO

Lugano	1	23.00
Luzern	3	77.00
Milan	1	42.00
Zurich	3½	84.00

LOURDES

Madrid	12	109.00
Paris (Austerlitz)	6½	143.00
Toulouse	2	41.00

LUGANO

Luzern	3	78.00
Milan	1½	20.00
Venice	6	51.00
Zurich	3½	85.00

LUXEMBOURG

Marseille	10	138.00
Metz	1	18.00
Munich (Munchen)	7	201.00
Nurnberg	7	150.00
Paris (Est)	4	85.00
Salzburg (via Strasbourg)	10	242.00
Strasbourg	3	47.00
Stuttgart (via Strasbourg)	6	95.00
Vienna (Wien)	13	250.00
Zurich	5	120.00

LUZERN

Milan	4½	92.00
Montreux	5½	90.00

Munich (Munchen)	6½	134.00
Paris (Est)	7½	134.00
Rigi	1½	47.00
Rome	12¼	166.00
Venice	8	123.00
Vienna (Wein)	13	173.00
Zurich	1	34.00

LYON
Marseille	3	67.00
Milan	4½	79.00
Nice	5	98.00
Paris (Lyon)	2	102.00
Strasbourg	5½	84.00
Turin (Torino)	4½	62.00
Tours	7	131.00

MADRID
Malaga	7	67.00
Pamplona	8½	48.00
Paris (Austerlitz)	13	197.00
Port Bou	10	90.00
Rome	34	280.00
San Sebastian	7	67.00
Santiago de Compostela	7½	71.00
Seville	5	61.00
Toledo	1¼	8.00
Valencia	4¼	44.00
Vigo	8	71.00
Zaragoza	3	36.00

MAINZ
Munich (Munchen)	4	124.00
Paris	6½	128.00

MALAGA
Seville	3½	25.00

MALMO
Stockholm	6	115.00

MARSEILLE
Milan	9½	88.00
Nice	2½	48.00
Paris (Lyon)	5	119.00
Port Bou	4½	72.00
Rome	15	134.00
Toulouse	4	79.00
Venice	17	123.00

MILAN
Montreux	4	78.00
Munich (Munchen)	8½	95.00
Naples	6¼	100.00
Nice	5	45.00
Padua	3	30.00
Paris (Est) via Chiasso	9	212.00
Paris (Lyon) via Vallorbe	7½	182.00
Rome	5¼	76.00
Stuttgart	9	163.00
Turin (Torino)	2	21.00
Trieste	6	54.00
Venice	3	33.00
Verona	1½	18.00
Vienna	15½	116.00
Zurich	4½	101.00

MONTREUX
Paris (Lyon)	4½	115.00
Zurich	3	98.00

MOSJOEN
Oslo	14	175.00

MUNICH (MUNCHEN)
Nurnberg	2	67.00
Oberammergau	2	27.00

Paris (Est)	8½	201.00
Rome	13¼	141.00
Rotterdam	11	247.00
Salzburg	2	42.00
Stuttgart	2	78.00
Venice (via Innsbruck)	9	86.00
Vienna (Wien)	6	93.00
Wiesbaden	4	139.00
Zurich	5	112.00

MYRDAL

Oslo	5½	86.00

NANCY

Paris (Est)	3	74.00

NAPLES

Nice	14	115.00
Paris (Lyon)		
via Rome-Florence	20¼	281.00
via Rome-Pisa	23½	232.00
Reggio Calabria	5½	59.00
Rome	2	27.00
Taranto	5	39.00
Turin (Torino)	10	106.00
Venice	8½	94.00
Vienna (Wien)	18¼	180.00

NARVIK

Oslo	33	204.00
Stockholm	22	161.00

NICE

Paris (Lyon)	7	144.00
Rome (via Pisa)	10	91.00
Turin (Torino)	6	42.00
Venice	10	80.00

OSLO
Stavanger	8½	141.00
Stockholm	6½	134.00
Trondheim	7	135.00
Voss	5½	97.00

PALERMO
Paris (Lyon)	32	268.00
Rome	13	112.00

PARIS
Port Bou (Austerlitz)	10½	146.00
Rheims (Est)	2	43.00
Rome (Lyon) via Pisa	15	208.00
Rouen (St. Laz.)	1¼	38.00
Salzburg (Est) (via Munich)	10	243.00
San Sebastian (Austerlitz)	7	130.00
Stockholm (Nord)	25	451.00
Strasbourg (Est)	4	93.00
Stuttgart (Est)	6	135.00
Toulouse (Austerlitz)	7	125.00
Tours (Aust.)	2	71.00
Trieste (Lyon)	14	229.00
Turin (Torino) - (Lyon)	6½	130.00
Venice (Lyon) via Vallorbe	12¼	218.00
Vienna (Wein) - (Est)	13½	275.00
Zurich (Est)	6	141.00

PERUGIA
Rome	3	27.00

PISA
Rome	3½	42.00
Siena	2½	16.00

PRAGUE
Rome	38¼	207.00
Vienna (Wein)	8	61.00
Warsaw	13	68.00

RATTVIK
Stockholm	3	68.00

RAVENNA
Rimini	1	7.00
Venice	3	24.00

RIMINI
Venice	3½	33.00

ROME
Siena	4½	33.00
Trieste	7	88.00
Turin (Torino)	7	82.00
Venice	5¼	71.00
Vienna (Wien)	19¼	156.00
Zurich	8¼	175.00

ROTTERDAM
Vienna (Wein)	19	309.00

SALZBURG
Trieste	7½	57.00
Venice	7½	63.00
Vienna (Wien)	4	51.00
Villach	3	32.00
Zurich	8½	124.00

STOCKHOLM
Trondheim	12½	155.00
Turku (ship)	12½	37.00
Uppsala	1	15.00

STUTTGART
Vienna (Wien)	7	171.00
Zurich	4	78.00

TRIESTE
Venice	2½	21.00
Vienna (Wien)	10	83.00

TURIN (Torino)
Venice	5	54.00

VENICE
Verona	2	16.00
Vienna (Wien)	10	89.00
Zurich	7	135.00

VIENNA (WIEN)
Zurich	12	156.00

665

INDEX OF CITIES, RESORTS
AND SCENIC PLACES

Aachen, 112
Aare Valley, 458
Aarhus, 382
Aberdeen, 547
Agrigento, 356
Aix-en-Provence, 162
Akademgorodok, 579
Alborg, 381
Albufeira, 277
Alesund, 410
Alicante, 292
Alicudi, 355
Alicudi, Filicudi, Salina,
  Stromboli, 355
Alkmaar, 101
Aller River, 223
Amersfoort, 102
Amsterdam, 99, 113
Amur River, 579
Andalsnes, 410
Andermatt, 440, 448, 451
Andorra la Vella, 299
Angara River, 579
Angers, 165
Annecy, 158, 442
Antibes, 150, 162
Antwerp, 102, 113
Anzio, 343
Apeldoorn, 103
Aranjuez, 281
Arezzo, 328
Arghos, 256
Arles, 150
Arnhem, 104
Arosa, 441, 452, 492
Arth, 459
Ascona, 339
Assisi, 329, 344, 368
Athens (Athinai), 254
Augsburg, 229, 247
Aurlandsfjord, 408
Aviemore, 547
Avignon, 141
Avila, 282
Ayamonte, 277

Baarn, 102
Bad Aussee, 83
Bad Ischl, 83
Bad Schandau, 239
Baden, 75
Baden-Baden, 433

Bagheria, 355
Bamberg, 229
Barcelona, 269
Bari, 347
Barletta, 348
Basel, 118, 430
Bath, 519
Bayeux, 166
Bayonne, 152
Bayreuth, 219, 230
Beaune, 157
Belfast, 310
Bellinzona, 495
Benidorm, 292
Berat, 555
Bergen, 405
Berlin, 194
Bern, 431
Bernina Hospiz, 489
Biarritz, 152
Bignor, 525
Bilbao, 287, 300
Billund, 383
Birmingham, 520
Birnau, 498
Bjorli, 409
Blanes, 273
Blois, 167
Bobadilla, 291
Bodo, 411
Bologna, 319
Bolzano, 360
Bonn, 104, 205
Bordeaux, 142
Borromean
  Islands, 339
Bosham, 525
Bourges, 169
Bournemouth, 521
Braga, 280
Brasov, 628, 629
Bratislava, 598, 605
Bregenz, 69
Breithorn, 481
Bremen, 212
Breukelen, 107
Brig, 460, 482
Brighton, 521
Brindisi, 348
Bristol, 522
Brno, 596, 598
Bruck an der
  Mur, 79, 86
Brugge, 114

Brunig, 466
Brussels, 100
Bryher, 534
Bucharest, 628
Budapest, 610
Bukovina, 628
Burano, 328
Burgas, 560, 561
Burgos, 282

Cadiz, 288
Caen, 166
Caerphilly, 522
Caledonian
  Canal, 548
Caltanissetta, 357, 358
Cambridge, 523
Camedo, 469, 483
Campiglia
  Marittima, 325
Campione, 340
Cannes, 163
Canterbury, 524
Carcassonne, 153, 183
Cardada, 339
Cardiff, 522
Cascais, 279
Cassis, 162
Castle Road, 246
Catania, 353
Catanzaro, 348
Celle, 223
Centovalli, 482
Ceske
  Budejovice, 596, 598
Chantilly, 170
Chartres, 170
Chartwell, 524
Chausey Islands, 173
Cheb, 596
Chemnitz, 200, 211, 227
Chester, 524
Chichester, 525
Chur, 453
Cimetta, 339
Clervaux, 119
Cochem, 208
Coimbra, 278
Cologne (Koln), 195
Como, 337
Compiegne, 171
Constantza, 630
Copenhagen, 380

Cordoba, 289
Corinth, 256
Cork, 311
Coventry, 525
Cremona, 334, 338
Cuenca, 282, 292
Cuneo, 361
Czestochowa, 619

Davos, 454
Deauville, 178
Delfshaven, 111
Delft, 105
Den Haag, 106
Denia, 292
Digne, 185
Dijon, 159
Dinkelsbuhl, 247
Dirleton, 549
Disentis, 467, 490
Domokos, 259
Dortmund, 205
Dover, 526
Drammen, 404
Dresden, 195
Druogno, 469, 483
Druzhba, 562
Dublin, 309
Dunbar, 549
Dundee, 547
Durnstein, 88
Durrës, 555
Dusseldorf, 107, 206

Edinburgh, 545
Eforie, 630
Eggenberg, 76
Eiger, 481
El Chorro Gorge, 276
Elbe Canyon, 239
Elbe River, 239
En-Vau, 162
Engelberg, 486
Enns Valley, 82
Erbe River, 155
Ercolano, 322
Erfurt, 201
Escorial, 283
Eskilstuna, 420
Essen, 215
Estonia, 589
Estoril, 279

Evora, 278
Evreux, 172
Exeter, 526

Faenza, 338
Faro, 277
Fatima, 279
Fatima, 279
Feldkirch, 80
Fertod, 611
Filicudi, 355
Filisur, 441
Finse, 408
Firenze, 320
First, 509
Flam, 408
Flatmark, 410
Florence (Firenze), 320
Foggia, 348
Foligno, 368
Font-Romeu, 293
Fontainebleau, 173
Frankfurt, 196
Frederickshavn, 384
Fribourg, 437
Friedrichschafen, 498
Fruitigen, 474
Fulda River Valley, 226

Galati, 630
Galway, 312
Gandria, 340
Gata de Gorgos, 292
Gavle, 420
Gdansk, Gdynia, and
    Sopot, 619
Geneva, 431
Genoa, 320
Gent, 115
Giethoorn, 112
Gifford, 549
Gilleleje, 385
Girona, 273
Gjirokaster, 556
Glasgow, 549
Gmund, 235
Gmunden, 83
Gorna Oryathovitsa, 560
Gorner Glacier, 471
Goslar, 224
Goteborg, 418
Gouda, 108
Grampian Moun-
    tains, 547
Granada, 289
Granville, 173
Grasse, 163
Graz, 75

Greenwich, 527
Grenoble, 159
Grinzing, 68
Grossglockner, 236
Grotta Gigante, 87
Gspaltenhorn, 481
Gstaad, 444, 477
Gyor, 610

Haarlem, 108
Haddington, 549
Hallstaat, 83
Hamar, 402
Hamburg, 197
Hameenlinna, 393
Hameln, 225
Hampton Court, 528
Hanko, 394
Hannover, 197
Hastings, 528
Hattem, 112
Heidel-
    berg, 207, 231
Heilbronn, 243
Heimwehfluh, 434
Helsingborg, 384
Helsingor, 385
Helsinki, 393
Herculaneum, 322
Heviz, 611
Hildesheim, 225
Hillerod, 385
Hochschneeberg, 85
Honfleur, 177, 178
Hoorn, 109
Humlebaek, 386

Innsbruck, 66
Interlaken, 434, 455
Intragna, 469, 483
Inverness, 548
Irkutsk, 579
Isle of Skye, 548
Isles of Scilly, 534
Isola Bella, 340
Isola Madre, 339

Jerez, 290
Jungfrau, 481
Jungfraujoch, 446, 462
Jura Mountains, 458

Kahlenberg, 68
Kalamata, 256
Kalmar, 420
Kander Viaduct, 474

Kandersteg, 474
Karlovy
    Vary, 596, 599
Kassel, 216
Katerini, 259
Kavala, 259
Kecskemet, 611
Keukenhof, 109
Khabarovsk, 579
Kiev, 572, 582, 587
Kilkenny, 313
Killarney, 312
Kings Lynn, 529
Kitzbuhel, 69, 73
Klagenfurt, 86
Klosters, 454
Knokke-Heist, 114
Koblenz, 121, 208
Koflach, 76
Koln, 195
Konstanz, 497, 498
Kosice, 606
Krakow, 617
Kruje, 555

La Napoule, 163
Lac Leman, 478
Lagos, 277
Lahti, 394
Lake
    Balaton, 611, 612
Lake Baykal, 579
Lake Como, 337
Lake Constance, 497
Lake Lugano, 340
Lake Luzern, 491
Lake Maggiore, 339
Lake Mjosa, 402
Lake Trasimente, 368
Lake Walen, 491
Lake Zug, 459
Lake Zurich, 491
Land's End, 533
Landwasser
    River, 441
Landwasser
    Viaduct, 490
Langnau, 438
Laren, 102
Larvik, 405
Latvia, 590
Lausanne, 437
Leicester, 530
Leiden, 109
Leipzig, 197
Leon, 296
Lerida, 274
Lerins, 163
Les Avants, 477

Les Eyzies de
    Tayac, 158
Liberec, 597, 599
Lichtenhainer
    Waterfall, 239
Lido, 327
Liege, 115
Lillehammer, 403
Limoges, 154
Lincoln, 530
Lindau, 231
Linz, 66
Lipari, 355
Lisbon, 270
Lithuania, 591
Livorno, 330
Ljubljana, 635
Lloret de Mar, 273
Locarno, 339
Loch Ness, 548
Loenen, 107
Lomnicky Stit, 601
London, 514
Lonza Valley, 460
Lourdes, 154
Lubeck, 222
Lublin, 618
Lugano, 340
Luib Summit, 548
Luneburg, 226
Luxembourg City, 101
Luzern, 432
L'viv, 588
Lyon, 142

Maastricht, 109
Madrid, 271
Main River, 237
Mainau, 499
Mainz, 121, 208
Malaga, 276, 296
Mallaig, 551
Malmo, 386
Mangalia, 630
Mannheim, 210
Marazion, 534
Marianske
    Lazne, 597, 599
Marseilles, 144
Marstein, 410
Matterhorn, 471
Mayrhofen, 70
Medemblik, 109
Meissen, 196
Melk, 77
Messina, 353
Metz, 122
Middelheim, 103
Milan, 321

Milazzo, 355
Moesgaard, 382
Molde, 410
Monch, 481
Monreale, 354
Mont-Louis, 293
Montefalco, 368
Montreux, 443
Montserrat, 275
Mora, 422
Moscow, 570
Moselkern, 208
Mount Brunate, 337
Mt. Fagernesfjell, 412
Mt. Floien, 405
Mt. Iti, 259
Mt. Olympus., 259
Mt. Orthrys, 259
Mt. Santis, 499
Mt. Titlis, 486
Mt. Ulriken, 405
Muiden, 102
Mulhouse, 122
Mumansk, 568
Munich (Munchen), 198
Murano, 327
Murcia, 293
Murmansk, 583
Murren, 446

Naerum, 387
Namur, 116
Nancy, 174
Nantes, 155, 175
Naples, 322
Narbonne, 155, 183
Narvik, 412
Naumburg, 228
Neckar River, 207
Neckargemund, 207
Nesebar, 562
Neuchatel, 439
Neuchatel, 439, 445
Neuilly, 175
Nice, 144, 335
Nimes, 151
Nordstemmen, 225
Norrkoping, 422
North Berwick, 549
Norwich, 531
Nottingham, 531
Novosibirsk, 579
Nurnberg, 218
Nyon, 478

Oban, 550
Oberammergau, 233
Odense, 386

Odessa, 582, 588
Offenbach, 196
Ofot Fjord, 412
Olympia, 257
Orange, 152
Orselin, 339
Ortygia, 353
Oslo, 401
Oudewater, 107
Oulu, 398
Oxford, 532

Padua, 331
Paignton, 539
Palagnedra, 469, 483
Palermo, 354
Pamplona, 288
Paris, 144
Parma, 324, 331
Pecs, 611
Pennine Hills, 541
Penzance, 533
Perth, 547
Perugia, 332, 368
Pescara, 348
Pilatus, 465
Pinios River, 259
Piraeus, 258
Pisa, 325, 332, 336, 345
Pivka River, 636
Pleven, 561
Plovdiv, 559, 561
Plzen, 597, 600
Poiana Brasov, 629
Pompeii, 343, 346
Poprad-Tatry, 606
Port Miou, 162
Port Pin, 162
Porto, 279
Portsmouth, 534
Portuguese, 266
Postojna, 636
Potsdam, 203
Poznan, 618
Prague, 595
Precendenze, 323
Puchberg, 85
Puerto de
  Soller, 299
Pushkin, 582
Pwllheli, 541

Queluz, 281

Randersacker, 237
Rasa, 469, 483
Rasa;

Palagnedra, 469
Ravenna, 325
Regensburg, 233
Reggio di
  Calabria, 348
Reichenau, 499
Rheims, 176
Rheinfelden, 435, 456
Rhine Falls, 499
Rhone Valley, 460
Riga, 572, 591
Rigi, 488
Riihimaki, 395
River Dee, 525
River Neva, 582
Rochester, 536
Romantic Road, 246
Rome, 322
Roskilde, 387
Ross Mountains, 548
Rostock, 203, 228
Rostov, 574
Rothenburg, 246
Rothorn, 466
Rottach-Egern, 236
Rotterdam, 110
Rouen, 176
Roya Valley, 184
Ruse, 560
Ryde, 535
Rye, 536
Rzav River, 636

Saint Raphael, 164
Salamanca, 284
Salem, 498
Salina, 355
Salisbury, 537
Salzburg, 66
Samarkand, 574, 589
San Sebastian, 272
Sandefjord, 405
Santiago de
  Compostela, 302
Sarande, 556
Sass, 454
Savonlinna, 395
Schafberg, 74
Schaffhausen, 499
Schliersee, 235
Schoenegg, 459
Schollenen
  Canyon, 451
Schollenen
  Gorge, 451
Schreckhorn, 481
Schwerin, 228
Schwyz, 450
Segesta, 354

Selinunte, 354
Serneus, 454
Settle, 542
Setubal, 277
Seville, 272
Shanklin, 535
Shrewsbury, 543
Siegen, 210
Siena, 326
Sighisoara, 630
Sinaia, 629, 631
Sintra, 280
Sion, 447
Siracusa, 353
Sitges, 275
Skien, 405
Slakov, 599
Sochi, 573
Sofia, 558
Sognefjord, 408
Soller, 299
Solothurn, 458
Sommerhausen, 237
Sonloup, 477
Sopron, 78
Sorgenfri, 381
Spakenburg, 102
Spanish, 266
Spello, 368
Spiez, 478
Spoleto, 346
St. Agnes, 534
St. Anton, 70
St. Anton, 70
St. Claude, 158
St. Gallen, 497
St. Honorat, 163
St. Ives, 533
St. Marguerite, 163
St. Martin's, 534
St. Mary's Island, 534
St. Michael's
  Mount, 534
St. Moritz, 457
St. Petersburg
  (Leningrad), 581
Stalheim, 407
Stavange, 413
Stein am Rhein, 499
Stellendam, 111
Stockholm, 419
Stralsund, 203
Strasbourg, 148
Stromboli, 355
Stubing, 76
Stuttgart, 220
Sukhumi, 573
Sundvollen, 402

Tabor, 597, 600
Tallinn, 583, 590
Tampere, 396
Taormina, 356
Taranto, 348
Tarragona, 275
Tashkent, 573, 589
Tatranska Lomnica, 601
Tegernsee, 236
Tembi Valley, 259
Tettnang, 499
The Rila Mountains, 559
Thessaloniki, 259
Thun, 474
Timisoara, 638
Tirana, 554
Tithorea, 259
Toledo, 285
Tonsberg, 404
Torcelo, 328
Torino, 336, 341
Torquay, 538
Torquay, 538
Torremolinos, 291
Tortosa, 291
Torun, 619
Tossa de Mar, 273
Toulouse, 156
Tournai, 117
Tours, 149
Trans-Siberian
    Express, 575
Trapani, 357
Tremadog Bay, 541
Trencin, 605
Tresco, 534
Trier, 124
Trieste, 87
Troldhaugen, 405
Trondheim, 412
Trouville, 178
Troyes, 178
Tschingelhorn, 481
Turku, 396
Turku, 396

Udine, 87, 369
Ueberlingen, 498
Ulm, 236
Ungeni, 632
Unteruhldingen, 498
Uppsala, 423
Usberlingen, 498
Ustica, 355
Utrecht, 107, 112

Vadu Siret, 632
Vaduz, 491, 492

Valencia, 303
Valladolid, 285
Var Valley, 184
Varna, 560, 562
Venice, 327, 342
Verdasio, 469, 483
Verma, 410
Vernet les
    Bains, 294
Verona, 328, 342
Versailles, 179
Viaduct, 490
Viana do
    Castelo, 297
Vianden, 125
Vienna (Wien), 67
Vienne, 161
Vila Real, 277
Villefranche-de-
    Conflans, 294
Vilnius, 592
Vinstra, 403
Vladivostok, 579
Vlorë, 556
Volgograd, 574
Voss, 407
Vulcano, 355

Walchwil, 459
Wallberg, 236
Warnemunde, 204
Warsaw, 616
Waterloo, 101
Weissfluh, 454
Wengen, 446
Weser River, 225
Wester, 548
Wetterhorn, 481
Wiesbaden, 220
Wiessee,, 236
Winchester, 539
Windsor, 539
Winterthur, 459
Wolfgangsee (Lake
    Wolfgang), 74
Woodstock, 532
Worthersee, 86
Wroclaw, 618
Wroxeter, 543
Wurzburg, 237

York, 540
Yorkshire Dales
    National Park, 541

Zakopane, 618
Zaragoza, 286

Zeist, 102
Zell-am-See, 71, 72
Zermatt, 490
Zons, 206
Zug, 459
Zugerberg, 459
Zurich, 432
Zwolle, 112

ORDER FORM European Rail Passes
Prices effective Jan. 1, 1996

EURAIL PASS (17 Countries) 1st Class

15 Days	❏ $522	2 Months	❏ $1,148
21 Days	❏ $678	3 Months	❏ $1,468
1 Month	❏ $838		

EURAIL FLEXIPASS – 1st Class

10 Days in 2 Months	❏ $616
15 Days in 2 Months	❏ $812

EURAIL SAVERPASS – 1st Class

15 Days	❏ $452	1 Month	❏ $712
21 Days	❏ $578		

Price is per person / 3 people must travel together at all times. (Two people may travel between Oct. 1st and March 31st)

Children 4 - 11 half fare – Children under 4 free

EURAIL YOUTHPASS* – 2nd Class

15 Days	❏ $418	2 Months	❏ $798
1 Month	❏ $598		

EURAIL YOUTH FLEXIPASS* – 2nd

10 Days in 2 Months	❏ $438
15 Days in 2 Months	❏ $588

**Pass holder must be under age 26
on first day of use.*

EURAIL DRIVE PASS

There is an excellent Rail/Drive program that combines a Eurail Flexipass with Hertz or Avis Rent-a-Car. Call us for a brochure and prices.

EUROPASS (5 Countries)
France / Germany / Italy / Switz. / Spain

3 COUNTRIES EUROPASS – 1st Class

5 Days in 2 Months	❏ $316
6 Days in 2 Months	❏ $358
7 Days in 2 Months	❏ $400

4 COUNTRIES EUROPASS – 1st Class

8 Days in 2 Months	❏ $442
9 Days in 2 Months	❏ $484
10 Days in 2 Months	❏ $526

5 COUNTRIES EUROPASS – 1st Class

11 Days in 2 Months	❏ $568
12 Days in 2 Months	❏ $610
13 Days in 2 Months	❏ $652
14 Days in 2 Months	❏ $694
15 Days in 2 Months	❏ $736

Note: You must specify the countries when ordering and countries must border each other.

Europass Youth available for ages up to 26 in 2nd class at substantial discounts. Call us for prices.

EUROPASS ASSOCIATE COUNTRIES

These countries may be added to any EuroPass for a flat charge per country. They expand the geographic scope of the pass, not the duration.

❏ Austria $45	❏ Portugal $29
❏ Benelux $42	❏ Greece $90
(Belgium/Luxembourg/ Netherlands)	*(Includes Brendisi-Patras Ferry HML/ADN-RT)*

SPECIAL EUROPASS BONUS
*Second adult receives half fare
discount on all Europasses*

ORDER FORM European Rail Passes
Prices effective Jan. 1, 1996

AUSTRIA RAILPASS

Any 4 Days in 10 Days	❑ $165	1st Class
	❑ $111	2nd Class

BENELUX TOURPASS

Any 5 Days in 1 Month	❑ $217	*1st Class*
	❑ $155	*2nd Class*

FRANCE RAILPASS

	1st Class	2nd Class
3 Days in 1 Month	❑ $198	❑ $160
Add'l Rail Days (6 max)	❑ $30	❑ $30

Couples: Special Discounts. Call for Rates.

*France offers a comprehensive series of
Rail 'n Drive, Rail 'n Fly & Fly Rail 'n Drive
passes. Ask for our free catalog and prices.*

GERMAN RAILPASS – Adult

Validity	1st Class/Twin*	2nd Class/Twin*
5 Days in 1 Mo.	❑ $260/$390	❑ $178/$267
10 Days in 1 Mo.	❑ $410/$615	❑ $286/$429
15 Days in 1 Mo.	❑ $530/$795	❑ $386/$579

**Twin: Total price for 2 adults traveling together.
Call for German Rail youth Pass Prices.*

GREEK FLEXIPASS

	1st Class-Adult	Child
3 Days in 1 Month	❑ $86	❑ $58
5 Days in 1 Month	❑ $120	❑ $85

PRAGUE EXCURSION PASS

*From any Czech Republic border crossing to
Prague and return First Class – within 7 days.*

❑ $49 Adult	❑ $39 Youth	❑ $25 Child

SPAIN FLEXIPASS

	1st Class	2nd Class
Any 3 Days in 2 Months	❑ $180	❑ $144
Add'l Rail Days (7 Max)	❑ $40	❑ $32

(AVE & TALGO 200 require a supplement)

ITALIAN RAILPASS

*Please add a $15 admin. fee to the cost
of each Italian pass/non-refundable*

	1st Class	2nd Class
8 Days	❑ $248	❑ $168
15 Days	❑ $312	❑ $208
21 Days	❑ $362	❑ $242
1 Month	❑ $436	❑ $290

ITALIAN FLEXI RAILCARD

Any 4 Days in 1 Month	❑ $194	❑ $132
Any 8 Days in 1 Month	❑ $284	❑ $184
Any 12 Days in 1 Month	❑ $356	❑ $238

ITALIAN KILOMETRIC TICKET

3,000 Kilometers in 20 Trips.

1st Class ❑ $264	2nd Class ❑ $156	

SCANRAIL PASS

	1st Class	2nd Class
Any 5 Days in 15	❑ $222	❑ $176
Any 10 Days in 1 Month	❑ $346	❑ $278
21 Day - Continuous	❑ $400	❑ $320
1 Month - Continuous	❑ $504	❑ $404

Call for Youth and ScanRail 55+ Senior rates

SWISS PASS

*Good on Swiss National Railroads, most private
railroads, lake steamers, city transport, trams, etc.*

	Adults		Couples/each	
	1st Cl.	2nd Cl.	1st Cl.	2nd Cl.
4 Days	❑ $264	❑ $176	❑ $198	❑ $132
8 Days	❑ $316	❑ $220	❑ $237	❑ $165
15 Days	❑ $368	❑ $265	❑ $276	❑ $192
1 Month	❑ $508	❑ $350	❑ $381	❑ $262

SWISS FLEXIPASS

Any 3 Days in 15 Days	❑ $264	❑ $176	❑ $198	❑ $132

SWISS CARD

1 Month/1 Round Trip	❑ $142	❑ $116

(Couples Passes valid 5/1/96 - 10/31/96 only)

NOT SHOWN: Rail Passes for Hungary, Bulgaria, Portugal, Benelux, Holland, Norway, Finland & East Europe, Czech Republic. Call for 1996 Rates and Plans. We can also handle sleepers, ferry bookings, point-to-point tickets, groups, etc.

SHIPPING There is a $9.50 handling and priority shipping charge for all orders using 2nd Day/AIR UPS. Rush service with overnight delivery is available for $25. RAIL/DRIVE Programs are available for most countries. Call for rates and free brochures.

ORDER FORM BritRail Passes
Unlimited travel in England, Scotland & Wales
Prices effective Jan. 1, 1996

BRITRAIL PASS – Unlimited travel every day

Validity Period	Adult		Senior (60 +)	Youth (16 - 25)
	First	Standard	First	Standard
8 Days	❏ $325	❏ $235	❏ $275	❏ $189
15 Days	❏ $525	❏ $365	❏ $445	❏ $289
21 Days	❏ $665	❏ $465	❏ $565	❏ $369
1 Month	❏ $765	❏ $545	❏ $650	❏ $435

BRITRAIL FLEXIPASS – Travel any days within 1 Month

4 Days / 1 Month	❏ $289	❏ $199	❏ $245	❏ $160
8 Days / 1 Month	❏ $399	❏ $280	❏ $339	❏ $225
15 Days / 1 Month	❏ $615	❏ $425	❏ $490	❏ $340*

*Youth pass valid for 2 months

GATWICK EXPRESS

Non-stop from Gatwick Airport to Victoria Station every 15 minutes. Takes only 30 minutes. Fastest way to London! Round trip – buy two one-ways.

❏ First Class $23 OW

❏ Standard $17 OW

FREEDOM OF SCOTLAND TRAVEL PASS

8 Days	❏ $159	22 Days	❏ $269
15 Days	❏ $220	Any 8 Days in 15 Days	❏ $185

BRITIRELAND PASS
Includes round-trip ticket on Stena Line Ferry between Britain and Ireland.

Validity	First	Standard
Any 5 Days in 1 Month	❏ $405	❏ $299
Any 10 Days in 1 Month	❏ $599	❏ $429

LONDON VISITOR TRAVEL CARD
Unlimited Inner Zone
on Underground and red buses.

Duration	Adult	Child
3 Days	❏ $25	❏ $11
4 Days	❏ $32	❏ $13
7 Days	❏ $49	❏ $21

BRITRAIL SOUTHEAST PASS

Duration	Adult	Standard
3 Days in 8 Days	❏ $90	❏ $69
4 Days in 8 Days	❏ $120	❏ $89
7 Days in 15 Days	❏ $169	❏ $119

Eurostar – We are official agents for Channel Tunnel services. Trains from London operate non-stop to Paris and Brussels in 3 Hr. & 3:15 respectively. All seats require advance reservations and tickets. Various prices and advance discounts available. Call for latest rates

SLEEPERS – We can confirm overnight sleepers on Anglo-Scottish and West Country routes. Accommodation supplement is $50 per person First Class and $41 per person Second Class.
CHILDREN'S RATES (5 - 15) are half fare for most passes. **SEAT RESERVATIONS, GROUP RATES, CROSS-CHANNEL SERVICES, IRISH SEA SERVICES –** call for rates.

THOMAS COOK VISITOR'S RAIL MAP OF BRITAIN & IRELAND

Passenger rail networks and private tourist railways, shows most major tourist attractions, scenic routes, top attractions, etc. Scale 1:750,000. Folded, with protective cover.
Only $10.95 + $3 shipping

RAIL TIMETABLE OF BRITAIN, FRANCE & BENELUX
by Thomas Cook.

Schedules for thousands of trains, including complete train times, itinerary, onboard amenities – Ferry sailings within the geographic area covered – Airport to city center transport links – Sleeper services – Public holiday alerts – City center diagrams – Channel Tunnel services for both Eurostar and LeShuttle – Comprehensive index for quick reference. Published each June (for full summer) and October (for winter). 224 pages.
Only $19.95 + $4.50 Priority Shipping